Pamela Harriman died
suddenly in early Febr
1997, of a massive stroke
after a swim in the pool at
the Ritz Hotel in Paris.
How apropos!

ALSO BY SALLY BEDELL SMITH

In All His Glory: The Life of William S. Paley
Up the Tube: Prime Time TV and the Silverman Years

SALLY BEDELL SMITH

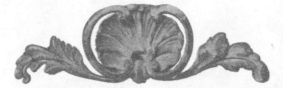

SIMON & SCHUSTER

Reflected Glory

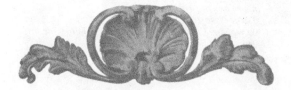

The Life of Pamela Churchill Harriman

SIMON & SCHUSTER
Rockefeller Center
1230 Avenue of the Americas
New York, NY 10020

Copyright © 1996 by Sally Bedell Smith
All rights reserved,
including the right of reproduction
in whole or in part in any form.
SIMON & SCHUSTER and colophon
are registered trademarks of Simon & Schuster Inc.
Designed by Edith Fowler
Photo research by Natalie Goldstein
Manufactured in the United States of America

10   9   8   7   6   5   4   3   2   1

Library of Congress Cataloging-in-Publication Data

Smith, Sally Bedell, date.
    Reflected glory : the life of Pamela Churchill
Harriman / Sally Bedell Smith.
        p.   cm.
    Includes bibliographical references and index.
    1. Harriman, Pamela Digby Churchill Hayward,
date.   2. Ambassadors—United States—Biography.
3. Philanthropists—United States—Biography.
I. Title.
E840.8.H27S65   1996
973.9'092—dc20   [B]   96-28681   CIP
ISBN 0-684-80950-8

Acknowledgments

Pamela Harriman's life is really the story of six lives: English debutante, wartime hostess, international femme fatale, show business wife, diplomat's consort turned Washington power broker, and American ambassador. In writing her biography, I have tried to describe each of the societies in which she lived—the privilege of the provincial aristocracy in prewar England, the excitement and danger of wartime London, the luxury and decadence of postwar Paris, the high spirits and raging neuroses of Broadway, the power and influence in political Washington, and the ceremony and prestige of diplomatic Europe. The characters are presented in some depth, especially the men who supported Pamela and helped her get ahead. Above all, I sought to explain how things worked in these very different spheres—from the intricacies of the debutante season to the financial dealings of political action committees. Besides reading histories, diaries, letters, and biographies, I interviewed many people who knew these worlds at first hand. Some preferred to remain anonymous—their perspective often included intimate knowledge of Pamela Harriman—so I cannot thank them publicly. But they know how much they helped me, and I am enormously grateful for their patience in fielding numerous inquiries, large and small, over the last five years.

Others I can acknowledge for their information and insights. Two close friends, Maureen Orth and Sally Quinn, are discerning writers and acute social observers who instructed me in the social and political customs of Washington after I moved here in 1991. Frank Rich generously shared his knowledge of Broadway history and helped me find people who crossed paths with Pamela during her show business years. Hugo Vickers, who knows every nuance of English high society, explained the complicated web of relationships in the aristocracy and pointed me toward some wonderful sources. Marie-France Pochna did the same in Paris, and once even served as my translator during an alfresco lunch at a Bois de Boulogne restaurant as a polo game thundered nearby. Two lawyers were also very helpful: Dinsmore Adams, who advised me on Averell Harriman's will, and Roger Kirby, who suggested the title for this book. Although Pamela Harriman declined my requests for interviews, in the last two years she told various friends and close associates that they were free to talk to me.

Numerous fellow journalists and biographers offered me guidance. I am particularly indebted to three who allowed me to use transcripts of interviews: Marie Brenner with William Walton, and John Pearson and Marjorie Williams with Pamela Harriman. Sandra McElwaine turned over a file of very useful newspaper and magazine clippings she had been saving on my biographical subject. I would also like to thank Jill Abramson, Rudy Abramson, Leslie Bennetts, Amy and Peter Bernstein, Michael Beschloss, Patricia Bosworth, Peter J. Boyer, Peter Braestrup, Brock Brower, Christopher Buckley, Elisabeth Bumiller, Gail Russell Chaddock, Anne Chisholm, Gerald Clarke, Shirley Clurman, Michael Davie, Fran Dinshaw, Geraldine Fabrikant, John Fairchild, Arthur Gelb, Sarah Giles, Doris Kearns Goodwin, Judith Adler Hennessee, Reinaldo Herrera, Annie Holcroft, Nancy Holmes, Margot Hornblower, David Ignatius, Peter Kaplan, Elizabeth Kastor, Louise Kerz, Khoi Nguyen, Anthony Lejeune, Janet Maslin, William McBrien, Edmund and Sylvia Morris, Alexander and Charlotte Mosley, Anne-Elisabeth Moutet, Patricia O'Brien, Maryann Ondovcsik, Joseph Persico, Ann Pincus, John Richardson, Martha Sherrill, A. M. Sperber, Annette Tapert, Evan Thomas, Susan Train, Carol Vogel, Tom Wallace, Sharon Walsh, and Susan Watters.

I conducted interviews—often at length and in some cases repeatedly—with scores of individuals who I can name, and I would like to thank as many as I can, knowing that I am bound to overlook some sources whose forgiveness I ask in advance:

Slim Aarons, Elie Abel, Peter Abeles, Morton Abramowitz, Alice Acheson, Ed Acker, Gianni Agnelli, George Albright, Alexandre, Hervé Alphand, Susan Mary Alsop, Jay P. Altmayer, Jan Cushing Amory, Walter Annenberg, Sherrell Aston, Brooke Astor, Louis Auchincloss, Rosemary Lady d'Avigdor-Goldsmid, George Axelrod, Lauren Bacall, Jean de Baglion, Sarah Norton Baring (who also shared her prewar and wartime diary with me), Felicity Barringer, Perry Bass, Elizabeth Baxter, Marion Becker, Alexandre (Sandy) Bertrand, Joan Bingham, Mervin Block, Chris Boskin, John Bowles, David Boyd, Ben Bradlee, Wendy Breck, Ann Brower, J. Carter Brown, Janet Brown, Kathleen Brown, Nicholas Brown, Evangeline Bruce, Zbigniew Brzezinski, Diana Bunting, Amanda Burden, Luke Burnap, Richard Burt, Baronne Daisy de Cabrol, Baron Frédéric de Cabrol, John J. Cafaro, Jesse Calhoon, Lady Jean Campbell, Emile Carlisi, Bill Carrick, Igor "Ghighi" Cassini, Zara Cazalet, Joan Challinor, Oatsie Charles, Winston Churchill, Countess Marina Cicogna, Clark Clifford, Alexander Cohen, Anita Colby, Clement Conger, Gary Conklin, Roderick Coupe, Consuelo Crespi, Esme the Countess of Cromer, Anna Crouse (who also gave me access to the diary of her late husband, Russel Crouse), Paul Curran, Jean Dalrymple, Frederick Davis, Peter Davis, Guy Della Cioppa, Anne-Marie d'Estainville, Piers Dixon, Jimmy Douglas, William Drozdiak, Peter Duchin, Maureen Marchioness of Dufferin and Ava, Lady Mary Dunn, Stuart Eizenstat, Dick Eton, Clay Felker, Peter Fenn, Richard Fenton, Christy Ferer, Eileen Finletter, Mary Fisk, Robert Fisk, Joe Fogg, Michael Foot, Alastair Forbes, Kalman Fox, Lady Edith Foxwell, Bill Francisco, Alfred Friendly, Jr., Pie Friendly, Clayton Fritchey.

John Galliher, Ina Ginsburg, Peter Glenville, Fred Golden, Edmund Goodman, Katharine Graham, Bettina Graziani, Judith Green, Alexis Gregory, James Grossman, Mandy Grunwald, Tom Guinzburg, Bill Hammerstein, Mark Hampton, Alan Hare, Jones Harris, Erwin Harrison, Kitty Carlisle Hart, Nicholas Haslam, Ashton Hawkins, Kitty Hawks, Bill Hayward, Brooke Hayward, Aimee de Heeren, Drue Heinz, Michael Helfer, Dorothy Hirshon, Cheray Duchin Hodges, Father Geoffrey Holt, Dennis Hopper, Leonora Hornblow, Barbara Howar, Janet Howard, Jean Howard, James Humes, Dave Hurley, Carl Icahn, Campbell James, Marshall Jamison, Morton Janklow, Philip Jessup, Ann Jordan, Mickey Kantor, Rosemarie Kanzler, Nancy "Slim" Keith, Horace Kelland, Michael Kuruc, Robert Lacey, Kenneth J. Lane, James Leasor, Robert Legvold, Helena Leigh-Hunt, Alexander Liberman, Brigitta Lieberson, James Lord, Pam Lord, Myles Lowell, Nancy Lutz, Betty Bower Macarthur, Katharine Lady Macmillan, Charles Maechling, Grant Manheim, Frank Mankiewicz, Tom Mankiewicz, Paul Manno, Lela Margiou, Anthony Marreco, Eliane Martin, Bonnie Matheson, John "Tex" McCrary, Angus McGill, Christopher Matthews, Harry McPherson, Julienne Michel, Hervé Mille, Ivan Moffatt, Harle Montgomery, Derry Moore, Alida Morgan, Edward Morgan, Henry Mortimer, Linda Mortimer, Sara Moss, Rear Admiral Daniel J. Murphy, Janet Murrow.

Mary Louise Oates, Christopher Ogden, André Ostier, Eleanor Ostrau, Violette Palewski, Tom Parr, Sandra Payson, Carolyn Peachey, Steve Pieczenik, Prince Nicolo Pignatelli, Julian Pitt-Rivers, George Plimpton, Odette Pol Roger, Princess Ghislaine de Polignac, Ernie Preg, Stuart Preston, Alan Pryce-Jones, Gerald Rafshoon, Gualberto Ranieri, P. Recanati, Baron Alexis de Redé, Lydia Redmond, Susan Remington-Hobbs, Marie Ridder, Flora Roberts, Carlo di Robilant, Margaret Robson, Aliki Lady Russell, David Rust, Cynthia Sainsbury, Mark Salzman, Henri Samuel, Marcia Meehan Schaeffer, Stuart Scheftel, Nelson Seabra, Pierre de Ségur, Irene Selznick, Mary Sethness, Bronner Shaul, William Shirer, Robert Shrum, Howard K. Smith, Robert Smith, Richard Solomon, Frank Stanton, Gordon Stewart, Liz Stevens, Burl Stiff, Ann Stock, Alexander Lord Stockton, Elaine Storey, Robert Strauss, Nona Summers, Taki Theodoracopulos, Jeanne Thayer, Michael Thomas, Jack Valenti, François Valéry, Jeanne Murray Vanderbilt, Florence Van der Kemp, Yves Vidal, Peter Viertel, Sophie de Vilmorin, Linda Wachner, Carl Wagner, Louise de Waldner, Guy Waltman, Mary Warburg, Loelia the Duchess of Westminster, Bill White, Shannon White, Sandy Whitelaw, Msgr. James Wilders, Carol Williams, Douglas Winthrop, Charles Wintour, Mary Hunter Wolfe, Jessie Wood, Perry Woolf, Peregrine Worthshorne, William Wright, Michelline Ziegler, Philip Ziegler, Z. Ziv.

For my research I had the invaluable assistance of Barbara Oliver and Jacqueline Williams, as well as Terry Lenzner and his staff. Edda Tasiemka and her archives provided me with clippings. Verne Newton, director of the Franklin D. Roosevelt Library in Hyde Park, New York, advised me on archival research, as did Kent Cooper at the Federal Election Commission. Judy Crichton at WGBH, Angela Moore at the BBC, and Tom Goodman at CBS gave me access to transcripts of televised interviews.

My editor at Simon & Schuster, Alice Mayhew, could fill a hefty volume with tributes from grateful authors. Once again I was blessed with her wide-ranging intelligence and editorial insight. Her marginal notes reflected her knowledge about so many aspects of Pamela Harriman's story—from Catholic dogma to Friday nights at Maxim's in Paris to Washington power brokers—and helped me focus my writing. Above all, her commitment to this project—her steadfast belief that it would turn out well—kept me going whenever I hit a rough patch. Her associate Elizabeth Stein assisted in countless ways as the manuscript evolved into a book, solving every problem that arose with efficiency and good humor. Elizabeth McNamara and Ann Adelman read the manuscript with sensitivity and care. Natalie Goldstein applied her usual enthusiasm and creativity to photo research. My agent and friend for three decades, Amanda Urban, offered pep talks and practical advice from start to finish.

This book would not have been possible without the support of my family. My parents, Jim and Ruth Rowbotham, gave me encouragement and love; I only wish my father had lived to see the book's publication. My mother-in-law, Nora O'Leary Smith, got the project rolling back in 1987 when she scrawled across a *W* cover story on Pamela Harriman: "Sally, your *next* book." I didn't take up her idea for four more years, but I'm indebted for her inspiration. My brother Jim provided some much-needed levity, and my dear friend Gladys Campbell managed the household so I could work with minimal interruptions.

Throughout this project, my three children, Kirk, Lisa, and David, to whom this book is dedicated, have coped with my long hours and periodic travels with remarkable good cheer and patience. Although I was often preoccupied, they knew that my life as a writer allowed me to be there for games, concerts, car pools, and bedtime reading—even if it meant a few extra hours in my attic office late at night.

No one can match the contribution of my husband, Stephen Smith, a beloved soulmate and extraordinary editor. Even while busy inventing and launching his own magazine, he was there for me every day, ready to break the logjams I encountered in my research and writing. He pored over my manuscript with a soft number-two pencil, asking questions, offering suggestions, pushing for clarity—in short, helping me be the best writer I can be.

SALLY BEDELL SMITH
Washington, D.C.
May 1996

To my children,
Kirk, Lisa, and David

Introduction

DESPITE the icy, nearly impassable roads in Williamsburg, Virginia, five hundred visitors made their way into Phi Beta Kappa Memorial Hall at the College of William and Mary on February 3, 1996. The occasion was Charter Day, the annual celebration of the school's founding in 1693. On the stage, professors in caps and gowns sat in rows as a brass ensemble played baroque music, the college choir sang *Exultate Deo* by Scarlatti, and two men in black robes carefully placed gleaming silver maces on a table covered in green velvet. But for all the pageantry on the dais, the real focus of attention was the front row, where two handsome women in colorful ceremonial robes stood facing the audience.

Superficially, they had much in common. Both were born in England in the 1920s; they had pursued careers in public life; they were known for their determination, discipline, and energy. But there the similarities ended. Pamela Digby Churchill Hayward Harriman, seventy-five years old, daughter of the eleventh Baron Digby, had vaulted from British aristocrat to fervid American Democrat when she married her third husband, railroad heir and diplomat Averell Harriman. Backed by his millions, she used a potent combination of diligence and charm to win an appointment as U.S. Ambassador to France. Margaret Hilda Thatcher, five years Pamela's junior, a middle-class shopkeeper's daughter, had muscled her way through Oxford University and the tough precincts of Conservative Party politics to become the first woman elected Prime Minister in Britain and the only person in this century to hold that office for three consecutive terms.

Just a decade earlier, these two political and social antagonists might have exchanged cool but proper greetings, but on this day they were ceremonial comrades, apparently brimming with mutual admiration. As Chancellor of William and Mary, Margaret Thatcher praised Pamela Harriman upon receiving an honorary Doctor of Laws degree. Pamela, in turn, called Thatcher "one of the great women and great leaders of this century." In a somber keynote speech on the dangers of isolationism, Pamela recalled the time she had spent during World War II with Prime Minister Winston Churchill, then her father-in-law. For those who knew her, the anecdotes were shopworn and their message familiar, but she spoke with drama and intensity, portraying herself as a witness to history.

Her voice was deep and languid, her delivery a slow, highly practiced cadence like the beat of a funeral drum, rising and falling, softening and strengthening, pausing for emphasis. Her manner was gracious, yet detached and self-contained. Her face was as meticulously composed as her words, although her flawless makeup could no longer disguise her age. Eight years after a much-admired face-lift, her skin had finally wrinkled, and her features had assumed a hawklike severity. Her eyes were hooded, her gaze opaque and frosty. Yet her smile was still sweetly radiant, like a powerful light through fog, erasing in an instant the toll of time. At such a moment, from a distance, she was strikingly pretty and remarkably youthful.

As she concluded her remarks, the audience applauded, and Timothy J. Sullivan, the president of William and Mary, called her words "powerful and penetrating." To all appearances, it was a triumphant moment, conferring the sort of respect and recognition she craved. But as with so much of Pamela's life, appearances told just part of the story. She was being honored not only because she held a prominent diplomatic post; indeed, her professional accomplishments were scant compared to previous Charter Day speakers, one of whom was Lady Thatcher. The main reason for Pamela receiving an honorary degree was her beneficence to William and Mary since 1986, when Democratic Governor Gerald L. Baliles appointed her to the school's Board of Visitors—a political payback for her help in raising money for his campaign. Since then she had donated $411,500 to the school through the W. Averell and Pamela C. Harriman Foundation.

Pamela took the accolade very seriously, and her close adviser, political consultant Robert Shrum, had talked with her frequently over the previous five months before writing the final draft of her speech. She rehearsed her delivery at least a half dozen times, first in her Paris office and then in Washington, and she brought Shrum to Williamsburg through an ice storm to help with last-minute touches.

In her own oddly disjointed tribute, Thatcher spoke of Pamela's "great influence on both sides of the Atlantic," and, somewhat elliptically, of her "great shrewdness which from an early age she always exercised." But instead of talking about the accomplishments of the day's honored guest, Thatcher retreated to Pamela's "remarkable experience of being associated with two of our greatest politicians," Averell Harriman and Winston Churchill, especially the wartime British leader whose "moral basis" for foreign policy occupied most of Thatcher's remarks. Only toward the end, almost as an afterthought, did she return to Pamela, saying: "We were so delighted that Mrs. Harriman's talents were used for themselves and for herself when she came on to the international scene" as an ambassador.

It was significant that Margaret Thatcher described Pamela Harriman through the achievements of important men, because that was how Pamela had defined herself for more than forty years: an aristocratic femme fatale who skipped from one glamorous event to the next and ordered her years by love affairs and marriages. Her life was like a movie serial, with each episode featuring its own characters and plot twists.

The eldest daughter in a noble Dorset family of exhausted fortune, Pamela

Digby first came into the public eye when she married Churchill's dissolute son Randolph, a disastrous union that produced a son named Winston and ended in divorce after five years. As a hostess in wartime London she was supported by Averell Harriman, the first in a line of wealthy and powerful men—including Jock Whitney, Prince Aly Khan, Gianni Agnelli, Elie de Rothschild, and Stavros Niarchos—who set her up for two decades in London and Paris. She found legitimacy by marrying Broadway producer Leland Hayward, and finally satisfied her yearning for great wealth by capturing Harriman, newly widowed and approaching his eightieth birthday. At the age of sixty she reinvented herself as a kingmaker in the Democratic Party, and a decade later was rewarded with her posting to Paris, where she lived in the residence built by the family of a former lover.

She was her own woman at last, independent and respectable to a degree that would have been unimaginable in her party-girl years. But true to the up-and-down pattern of her life, she frittered away the Harriman fortune, prompting her late husband's disgruntled heirs to file a series of lawsuits accusing her of being a "faithless fiduciary." Always a brass-knuckle fighter, she made headlines with a barrage of ironic countersuits—against the family whose name elevated her to Democratic doyenne, the Wall Street brokerage that provided her wealth, and the advisers who had guided her every move.

At each stage of Pamela's life, newspapers and magazines recounted her exploits and amplified her legend. But the private images were equally indelible: playing bezique late at night with Winston Churchill, enlisting Dwight Eisenhower to help in the kitchen at her officers' club during the war, exchanging confidences with Harry Hopkins in the Dorchester Hotel, sitting at Edward R. Murrow's side during his famous wartime broadcasts, feeding soup to an ailing Averell Harriman, presiding over lavish dinners at the Riviera estate of Gianni Agnelli, cruising the Mediterranean on a yacht with Stavros Niarchos, fixing chicken hash at midnight for Leland Hayward and his Broadway stars, talking one-on-one with Bill Clinton in the Oval Office.

Like a real-life Leonard Zelig, Pamela always managed to be where the action was. But unlike Woody Allen's movie creation, Pamela had no desire simply to blend in. She wanted to be noticed, and to be admired. She had neither the brilliance nor the training to be a leading player in history, but she knew how to be a subaltern to historical figures. Few people in the past fifty years dealt so intimately with so many powerful men in so many different arenas —politics, diplomacy, society, and show business. She won their confidence, learned their secrets, and saw them in unguarded moments. She achieved her own fame in their reflected glory.

For nearly twenty years she lived as a courtesan, in the precise, centuries-old definition of the word, which originated with the favorite mistress in the French king's court. Her precursors included Madame de Maintenon, Ninon de Lanclos, and Madame de Pompadour in the seventeenth and eighteenth centuries, and Cora Pearl and Léonide Leblanc in the nineteenth. Pamela was the only genuine exemplar in the twentieth, renowned like Pearl for her "golden chain of lovers." The courtesan sold her love for material rewards, but she operated at the highest levels of society and selected her patrons carefully. She used many talents, only one of which was her sexuality, to charm and hold a man of wealth for years on end.

Pamela's looks and her sexual appeal were undeniably vital in capturing the attention of important men. Friends often spoke of the ardent femininity of her "mating dance," a ballet that was both artfully flirtatious and comfortingly maternal: the forward tilt of her upper body, the cocked head, the rapt gaze, the flattering small talk and questions, the proprietary flutter of her fingers on a man's arm or lapel, the sunshine smile with its tantalizing glimpse of her tongue pressed against the back of her teeth. Yet she didn't overtly convey eroticism as much as she radiated a genuine interest in the man she was with.

"She realized that rich and powerful men could have bimbos for one-night stands," said one man who knew her well. "She knew they wanted someone with more depth and intelligence and strength of mind, and that is what she projected." Her role as a courtesan was in fact a rigorous discipline that required preparation, shrewdness, concentration, willpower, organization, taste, patience, attention to detail, and thorough knowledge of the social arts. Although she was naturally restless and energetic, she knew how to impose calm on a man. She learned how to envelop him in comfort and security, focusing on his needs and interests and making everything easy. Inspired by Pamela, Truman Capote once wrote, "There are certain women . . . who though perhaps not born rich, are born to *be* rich . . . Money in astronomical amounts is their instrument. . . . They fuse material elements . . . into fantasies that are both visible and tactile."

Aside from a small allowance and a dowry, Pamela held no hope for any part of the Digby estate, which by primogeniture was destined for her younger brother. For Pamela, the acceptable route to wealth and status was through marriage. In her generation, men controlled every realm of achievement. The women who beat the system needed extraordinary talent and usually pursued independent careers: as writers, divas, or actresses, for example. Pamela understood that her abilities had real value at a time when women were measured by how they looked on a man's arm, set a table, kept the conversation moving, managed a household, and made connections. She initially took the conventional approach by marrying early, but when most of the men she wanted were spoken for, she found money and adventure along the courtesan's path.

Her techniques mirrored those of the successful wife—the woman in the 1950s *New Yorker* cartoon wearing a negligée and holding a martini for her husband—but she elevated them to high art and used them audaciously. She was, in effect, a sophisticated social entrepreneur always willing to strike out for new territory. She could see over the horizon, recognizing, for example, that her Churchill connection had material worth. She carried it throughout her life like a brand name to enhance her standing. Fifty years after her divorce, she was still a fixture on television documentaries about the Churchills, recounting her tales in confiding, throaty tones.

Like a hard-driving tycoon, she had no compunction about trampling over others on the way to her goal. She flouted widely accepted standards of morality, and thought nothing of trying to shatter marriages, of taking money from two men simultaneously, and of leaving her young son for months at a time.

She could be a loyal and useful friend, especially to men who had supported her, but to certain women as well. Most women in her circle, however, regarded her with mistrust, exasperation, grudging admiration, or patronizing amusement. (Both Jacqueline Kennedy Onassis and Georgetown hostess Evangeline Bruce did wicked Pamela imitations.) Pamela was neither lazy nor complacent. If anything, she tended to overreach, taking some bad tumbles along the way. But she was remarkably resilient and always managed to clamber back to prominence. Contrary to common belief, she had no master plan other than wanting to live in high style and be near the center of power. She existed very much in the moment, with no regrets about the past or worries about the distant future.

Pamela had a gambler's eye for the big chance. In late middle age, she exploited the social changes in America that propelled women into the workplace and valued them for professional attainment. Pamela recast herself as a career woman, cleverly adapting many of the skills she had learned in her previous incarnations. As a political fundraiser, for instance, she made donors feel special for giving her money, much as her lovers had felt in earlier days. She seemed to occupy a time warp, at one moment a character from the nineteenth century, at the next a feminist hurtling toward the millennium. "[Women] are rooting for me, because if I fail, it is a reflection on all women," she declared in a *Washington Post* story assessing her tenure as ambassador.

Coming from someone with her history, such self-proclaimed feminism showed once again Pamela's uncommon brazenness. She was, after all, a woman who flew to the Adriatic as the American envoy to inspect an aircraft carrier but refused to wear the helmet required for landing. Her reason: She didn't want to ruin her bouffant hairstyle. "We had to be fairly creative in meeting her needs and ensuring we complied with safety requirements," said Rear Admiral Daniel J. Murphy, the battle group commander who hosted the visit aboard the U.S.S. *Eisenhower*. Not only did the crew have to shut down all aircraft engines to eliminate danger, they executed an elaborate maneuver to create complete stillness on the deck, so that when Pamela stepped out of the airplane her hair would be undisturbed; when she left the ship at the end of the day, they repeated the entire sequence. "The result justified the trouble we had to go to," said Murphy. "She charmed us all."

Over the years, Pamela took a lot of criticism, but if it bothered her, she didn't let on. "The scandal of her life she turned to ornament," wrote Maurice Druon, one of her Parisian admirers during the 1950s, in his novel *The Film of Memory*. Druon's characterization of his mysterious heroine, Lucrezia, might well have applied to Pamela: "Everyone wanted to see at close quarters whether all that was said about her was true. . . . She chose her lovers well and seldom missed a famous man within her reach without bequeathing him a memory. Her lover was glory and her bed a pantheon."

Pamela was a "bad" girl who, in the end, was applauded by world leaders and honored by esteemed institutions. She knew how to *cacher son jeu*—to hide her game. She never seemed tawdry or greedy because she was so ladylike—

except for her devouring laugh, with mouth wide open and head thrown back. Her toughness only revealed itself when her melting gaze hardened in moments of disapproval or suspicion.

Many women underestimated Pamela because she was not endowed with exceptional beauty, although her looks did improve with age. When *People* magazine proclaimed the "50 Most Beautiful People in the World" in 1993, Pamela was one of two septuagenarians on the list. (The other was Gregory Peck.) She was also a woman of limited intellect and education—Capote called her a "marvelous primitive"—whose utterances were neither witty nor memorable. She had no real sense of humor, much less irony—defects that worked to her advantage, permitting her to act without embarrassment.

Recognizing her shortcomings, Pamela cultivated a somewhat distant manner and prepared thoroughly for every public appearance, whether it was a small dinner party or a large diplomatic reception. She rewrote her life as fast as she lived it, transforming bad memories and embellishing good ones. She lived by her own rules and declared herself the winner. Soon the myth—from "riches to riches," as one of her friends irreverently described it—eclipsed reality.

"What is your secret?" Barbra Streisand asked Pamela Harriman in a stage whisper as she slid into the seat next to her at the White House Correspondents' Dinner in 1993. Pamela replied with an insouciant laugh. Countless women over the years wondered as well, and Pamela's enigmatic demeanor made the answer all the more elusive. "Don't underestimate her confidence and privileged position from the beginning: the good manners, the savoir faire, which Pamela had in spades," said theater director Peter Glenville, an old friend. The paradox of Pamela was that although her aristocratic backdrop was often overshadowed later in her life, it defined her as a young woman. Yet what lay behind her genteel debutante's exterior was a more complicated temperament. As it turned out, the English rose was made of Sheffield steel, fired by ambition, doggedness, and cunning. Stung by early disappointments, embarrassed by her provincial roots, the girl from Dorset set her sights on a most improbable goal: to become a woman of the world.

CHAPTER
One

EDWARD KENELM DIGBY was a man of simple bucolic preoccupations—
horticulture, hunting, civic duty, in no particular order. The graying remnants
of his once-bright red hair rimmed his bald head, and he sported a trim salt-and-
pepper mustache. He had a slightly goofy smile, which led some to consider
him dimwitted. A decade earlier, in his polo-playing days, he had been tall and
thin. Now he was portly. He had two conspicuous but benign affectations: the
carnation he wore in his lapel, and the box of Fortnum & Mason chocolates he
carried under his arm.

His wife, the former Constance Pamela Alice Bruce, was a handsome
woman, with prominent dark eyebrows and erect bearing. Unsentimental, almost physically aloof, she commanded respect but inspired little affection. Even
her nickname, "Pansy," failed to soften her stern aspect. Her marriage to the
eleventh Baron Digby fortified her place in the English upper class, but she had
social ambitions that reached far beyond her husband's 1,500-acre estate at
Minterne Magna in Dorset. These she invested in her eldest daughter, Pamela
Beryl Digby, seventeen years old and poised to enter Society.

"Stop, everybody," said Lady Digby to the group of friends assembled in
her drawing room at Minterne on an autumn night in 1937. "Look. Here's
Pamela. Isn't she beautiful?" The crowd murmured approvingly, and young
Pamela beamed with delight, unwilling or unable to catch the undercurrent of
skepticism among the nodding heads.

She was not beautiful, not yet. She was plump, her face as broad as the
moon, with a fleshy chin and a neck too short to suggest elegance. She had
wide eyes of deep blue, a nose with a slight aquiline curve, pouty mouth, and
milky skin scattered with freckles. Her cheeks carried a perpetual pink flush that
turned fiery when her emotions shifted. Her auburn hair swept back from her
forehead and curled down to the nape of her neck. A patch of white streaked
her hair on the left side, the result, she liked to explain, of a head injury when
she fell off a pony.

But Lady Digby was blind to Pamela's flaws. The daughter's self-
confidence rose with her mother's boasts. Pamela boldly approached her elders,
chatting about horses, hounds, and county matters. She seemed utterly agreeable, intent on pleasing her family and their friends. But even then, she knew
how to mask her real feelings. Pamela Beryl Digby was suffocating behind the

honey-colored stone facade of Minterne. She dreamed of escape—not to the next county, but to glamorous London.

IN THE HIERARCHY of English nobility, the Digby title occupies the bottom rung of the five ranks of the hereditary peerage, below duke, marquess, earl, and viscount. The Digby line began with Aelmar the Saxon in the eleventh century, and Sir Diggeby de Tilton from Lincolnshire. The family actually had two titles. The older, dating from 1620, was tied to the extensive holdings of Robert Digby in Ireland, which in the late nineteenth century amounted to 37,495 acres in King's County, Queen's County, and County Mayo. The Dorset title dated from 1765, when Henry, the seventh Baron Digby of Geashill in Ireland, became Baron Digby of Sherborne, with an estate of 1,886 acres. Until the early twentieth century, the Digbys owned two country mansions, along with a grand house in London.

Although their holdings in Ireland and England totaled some 40,000 acres at the end of the nineteenth century, the Digbys were not among the thirty top landowners of the time—a list that included the great families of Westminster, Buccleuch, Bedford, Devonshire, Rutland, and Norfolk. And while Pamela would boast in later years that her lineage included dozens of members of Parliament, this was unexceptional in aristocratic families. It was in the natural order of things for second sons, as well as firstborn heirs to titles, to sit in the House of Commons and the House of Lords. None of the Digbys who served played a prominent role in English history.

As was customary for peers, the Digby men did not work for a living. They regarded their duties in Parliament and on county councils as noblesse oblige. In the late nineteenth century their land yielded £16,000 in yearly rent, a comfortable sum but hardly remarkable. The very rich, by contrast, had unearned incomes of more than £75,000 a year. Given Pamela Digby's lifelong preoccupation with money, it is no small irony that her family's motto is *Deo non Fortuna,* which means "From God not Fortune." Those words run across the bottom of the Digby coat of arms, which provided Pamela a symbol for her writing paper and home decor: an elegant little ostrich, perched on a wreath, with a horseshoe in its beak. Beneath the ostrich, two exotic monkeys stand on their hind feet, "with collars around their loins, and chains fixed thereto."

If the Digbys did not make a mark on English history, they left a trail of engaging anecdotes. The traits that crop up most often are bravery, audacity, and beauty, along with a certain indomitableness. Stories of the unconventional paths taken by various Digbys figure prominently in the family lore, and surely served to influence Pamela.

The most heroic Digby ancestor was Admiral Henry Digby, who served with Admiral Nelson in the Battle of Trafalgar, bravely commanding HMS *Africa.* Admiral Digby was a naval adventurer known in his youth as the "Silver Captain" for all the bounty he captured on the high seas. His biggest prize was a hoard of gold coins that he seized from the Spanish treasure ship *Santa Brigada* in 1799. The Royal Navy gave him a cut of £40,000, which would be worth about $8 million today. According to Pamela's son, Winston Churchill, that sum "was to be the foundation of the Digby fortune." Admiral Digby never had a title, but he inherited Minterne in 1815 from his uncle, Robert Digby, who had bought it from the Churchill family in 1768. (The first Winston Churchill had been born at Minterne in 1620.) Admiral Digby's eldest son, Edward St. Vincent, inherited the family title from the eighth Baron Digby, an unmarried and childless cousin.

The most infamous Digby was the admiral's eldest daughter, Jane, whose colorful life was a source of fascination to her great-great-niece, Pamela. From birth, Jane was admired for the "perfect oval" of her face, her dark blue eyes, "wild rose" complexion, and golden hair that tumbled below her waist. Her temperament, according to her biographer, E. M. Oddie, was "wild, impetuous, fearless, generous, lovable, and intensely loving." She had a strong romantic streak, and a precocious talent for music and drawing as well as a great facility for languages.

When Jane made her debut in London society at age sixteen, she created a sensation, earning the nickname "Aurora" after the heroine in Byron's *Don Juan*. Shortly afterward, her parents married her off to a politically ambitious rake named Lord Ellenborough. A wealthy widower twenty years older than Jane, he was considered one of the most eligible men in London, but he was pompous and widely disliked. Jane produced a male heir three years after her marriage. After that, she and her husband no longer shared a bed. Lord Ellenborough immersed himself in his political life, and Jane plunged into the fastest crowd in London. She was captivated by Austrian diplomat Prince Felix Schwarzenberg, a womanizing playboy in military dress. Tall and handsome, with dark eyes and a luxurious black mustache, he was "the Byronesque lover of her dreams," according to Oddie.

Discreet adultery was tolerated in Georgian society, but Jane flaunted her affair. She and Schwarzenberg went to balls and parties together, and every day she arrived at his rooms on Harley Street in a green phaeton pulled by two black long-tailed ponies. Neighbors saw him wait at the window of the first-floor drawing room, and fling open the front door to greet her. Indiscretion grew into full-blown scandal when Jane became pregnant and the prince was recalled by his government. Jane obtained a divorce in 1829 and fled to Paris to join her lover, rebuffing her family and deserting her husband and her young son.

Before Jane joined Schwarzenberg in France, she gave birth to a daughter in Switzerland. Although the Prince arranged for Jane to live with him, he had no intention of marrying her. He was a Catholic, and she was the divorced mother of his illegitimate child. Moreover, he was just as politically ambitious and narcissistic as the husband she had left, and he was resentful that her impetuous behavior had disgraced him. Even before Jane had their second child, Schwarzenberg began openly pursuing other women. Jane had hoped their son, also named Felix, would bring the prince back to her, but the child only lived a few weeks. Jane was rumored to have taken several lovers before Schwarzenberg took flight to Austria and she to Munich, leaving her young daughter behind.

A yearly allowance of some £1,500 from her family gave Jane the means to act any way she pleased. In Munich she became the mistress of the "charming, kindly, slightly ridiculous but wholly lovable" King Ludwig I. Since Ludwig would never divorce Queen Theresa and marry Jane, he allowed his mistress to take another lover, Baron Carl Venningen, who had one of the oldest titles in Europe. The baron was completely enchanted by her. They were married in 1832, and six weeks later, at age twenty-seven, she gave birth to his son.

Growing restless with Venningen, Jane found a new lover in Count Spyridon Theotoky, a tall, dark Greek whom she met at a court ball. When Venningen discovered her adultery, he challenged Theotoky to a duel and wounded him. Then, in an extraordinary gesture prompted by his love for her, Venningen let Jane go. He kept and cared for her children, and remained her friend until his death.

Jane married Theotoky and lived with him for ten years in Greece, entertaining in a grand manner. They had a child named Leonidas, and for the first time, Jane showed genuine maternal devotion. Her fidelity, however, wavered again. Ludwig's son, Otto, the first king of modern Greece, was infatuated with Jane and followed his father as the second monarch to share her bed, according to Oddie. Like his father, Otto had a wife he never intended to divorce. Jane and Theotoky remained married, but their only bond was Leonidas, and that connection broke when the child fell from a balcony and died at Jane's feet.

At age forty-six, Jane sought adventure in the Middle East. In Syria, she married a Bedouin sheik. "My heart warms towards these wild Arabs," she wrote in her diary. Her husband this time, Abdul Medjuel el Mezrab, was a dark-skinned nobleman with black hair, a black beard, and dark eyes—"the magnificent, large-hearted romantic she had sought all her life," in Oddie's view. He was well read, and he knew several languages. As a measure of her devotion, Jane went native, dying her hair black and wearing it in two long braids, rimming her eyes with circles of black kohl, walking barefoot over stony terrain, and wearing the rough blue cotton garment of her husband's tribe. She milked Medjuel's camels, cooked his food, fed him with her hands, and bathed his feet. She retained her youthful looks—bright blue eyes and an unwrinkled brow—well into old age. To the end, she was a strongly sexual woman. "It is now a month and twenty days since Medjuel last slept with me! What can be the reason?" she wrote at age seventy-three after twenty-five years of marriage.

Jane Digby died a year later and was buried in a cemetery in Damascus. Her husband was so overcome that he fled the funeral carriage and galloped back to her graveside on Jane's favorite mare. The Bible found among her effects was inscribed: "Judge not, that ye be not judged."

When Jane's brother, Edward St. Vincent, the ninth Baron Digby, died in 1889 at age eighty-one, he left an estate valued at £395,753—the equivalent of $50 million today. His eldest son, Edward Henry Trafalgar, the tenth baron, could certainly afford to take drastic action when Minterne developed dry rot and an array of noxious odors. In 1903, Digby decided to tear down the house and start over. Four years later, the Digbys moved into a modern home, with central heating, hot water, and a centralized vacuum cleaning system that allowed maids to connect tubes to outlets around the house. A garage for automobiles was also included, a sure sign of the new century. When the Digbys held a garden party in 1908 to celebrate completion of the house, three hundred people came, and Lady Digby's brother "counted 58 motors."

Pamela's father, the future eleventh Baron Digby, was a classic product of late Victorian England. He was educated at Eton and Sandhurst, both of which admitted him solely on the basis of his place in society. For a country aristocrat, the military was a logical career. Kenny Digby—the name he preferred to the more formal "Ken"—was commissioned as a lieutenant in the Coldstream Guards in 1914 and fought in World War I. When he sailed to the battlefields of France at twenty-one, he took his beloved horse, Kitty, with him. The youngest officer to command a Coldstream brigade, he was wounded twice, and received the French Croix de Guerre. He returned from Cologne in 1919 so emaciated, according to his grandson Winston, that he was told "he had only months to live if he did not force himself to eat."

Major Digby rallied sufficiently to marry Pamela Bruce, the youngest daughter of Lord and Lady Aberdare, at the Guards' Chapel at Wellington Barracks in London on July 1, 1919. Pamela Bruce was of Welsh and English ancestry, with some interesting twists. Through her mother, Constance Mary Beckett, she was the great-granddaughter of the prolific American portrait painter John Singleton Copley. Born in Boston to English parents who had emigrated from Ireland, Copley returned to England on the eve of the American Revolution and settled in London with his family. His son, John Singleton Copley the younger, reached the peerage in 1826, when he became Baron Lynd-hurst.

Pamela Bruce was the youngest of three strong sisters. When she was born, her older sisters gave her the name "Pansy" because they thought her face resembled the delicate flower. Her oldest sister Margaret became a countess when she married the Earl of Bradford in 1904. Eva Isabel was the prettiest of the three sisters. After eleven years of marriage to the third Baron Belper, she got a divorce in 1922. Two years later she married Lord Dalmeny, eldest son of the fifth Earl of Rosebery, Prime Minister for one year at the end of Queen Victoria's reign, and one of the wealthiest figures in England. Not only did the Roseberys have vast holdings in Scotland, but the fifth earl's wife Hannah was the only child of Baron Meyer de Rothschild, who left her his huge fortune when he died. When their son Harry became the sixth Earl of Rosebery in 1929, he inherited £1.7 million, and Aunt Eva was set for life.

On March 20, 1920, scarcely nine months after Pamela Bruce and Major Digby married, Pamela Beryl Digby was born in Farnborough, where Major Digby was stationed in military service. Several months later, old Lord Digby died, and Major Digby inherited the family title and land—Minterne, a home on Grosvenor Place in London, and Geashill Castle in Tullamore, Ireland, plus a bequest of £50,000. Lord Digby's younger son and three daughters each received trusts in smaller amounts. The total worth of the tenth Baron Digby's estate was £146,635 before taxes—the equivalent of $4 million in 1995.

Instead of moving into Minterne, the new eleventh Baron Digby accepted a position as military secretary to Lord Forster, the recently appointed Governor-General of Australia. Lord Digby took the job for financial reasons. He had substantial inheritance taxes to pay, so he rented out Minterne and sold the house in Grosvenor Square to raise cash. Moreover, serving in a colonial backwater was a lucrative sinecure. At a time when the First Lord of the Treasury in London earned £5,000 a year, the Governor-General of Australia received £10,000, and his chief military aide somewhat less. The job came with free housing, fully staffed and maintained courtesy of His Majesty's Government. Living prudently, a man could easily double his income while living in a higher style than he could at home. He could even set some funds aside at the same time.

The Digbys, like the rest of the British aristocracy, faced unprecedented financial pressures in the first two decades of the twentieth century. The Chancellor of the Exchequer, Lloyd George, had pushed through large increases in inheritance taxes, as well as other taxes on land owned by the nobility. The expansion of agricultural production in the United States and Canada caused a plunge in English farm prices and land values. By 1921, English agriculture was in a full-blown depression.

In Ireland, land reform legislation of the late nineteenth and twentieth centuries forced the large landowners into liquidating most of their holdings, leaving them with their castles and small amounts of surrounding acreage. By the early 1920s, the great Irish estates had virtually disappeared. The Digbys sold all their cultivated land, keeping only several thousand acres of woodland that was used for shooting and some forestry. They held on to Geashill Castle, which was burned down in 1922 by agrarian nationalists following the partition of Ireland. Lady Digby haughtily made light of the loss, saying she was glad it had been burned so they would never have to live there. Still, many family treasures perished in the blaze. And without their vast tracts in Ireland, the Digbys' Dorset land—now reduced to 1,500 acres—represented a modest holding at a time when 5,000 acres was considered a "limited estate." Yet like many aristocrats with shrinking fortunes, the Digbys took retrenchment in stride. Years later, when Pamela had to sell jewels or furniture to maintain her expensive lifestyle, she did it with the same sort of aplomb.

Lord and Lady Digby set sail from England on August 21, 1920, on the SS *Ormonde*. Their infant daughter traveled separately with her nanny. In Australia, they lived in a government house surrounded by manicured lawns and traveled in the same sort of elite crowd they knew in England. Shortly after their arrival, Lord Digby won big at the Flemington Racecourse, providing his family with an unexpected infusion of cash. The following year, Pamela's sister Sheila was born.

Pamela's memories from that period were understandably scant, but in middle age she liked to recount one revealing anecdote. She claimed to have been bored one day as a three-year-old toddler. "I'll take you for a drive," Lady Digby supposedly told her. "It will cheer you up." Unfortunately, when they climbed in the car, it wouldn't start. Pamela's face crumpled into tears, she got out, shook her copper curls, stamped her foot, and said with sober prescience, "Man will come and man will fix." The arrival of a policeman shortly afterward,

Pamela liked to tell her friends, instilled her belief that men would always help when she was in need.

When Lord Digby's term ended in 1923, he and Lady Digby took the long route home by way of Japan and China. Pamela and Sheila returned on the boat with their nursemaid Nanny Hall, who later regaled the nannies of other children with stories about her two charges. Sheila was impossible, throwing the toys of other children overboard. Pamela took a different tack. After a few days at sea watching the handsome captain squire around a succession of pretty women, she marched up to him and said, "Shall we go walkies around the deck?" Every day thereafter, the captain took her "walkies." At the end of the trip, Pamela's precociousness and all-round good behavior won her the prize for best child on board.

Two

BACK AT MINTERNE, Pamela Digby settled into the rhythms of country life. It was a self-contained existence, impenetrable and mysterious to anyone outside the tightly drawn circle of the Dorset gentry. The estate at Minterne Magna unfolded behind a narrow winding road walled with greenery—hedgerows of hawthorne, privet, and honeysuckle, shaded by leafy canopies of beech trees. Next to the stone gate stood the tiny Minterne Church with its cemetery of mossy gravestones. A turn into the gravel drive yielded the first glimpse of Minterne, set on a rise overlooking a small lake and gentle downs dotted with trees. At a time when the English class system still held firm, the fifty-room mansion instilled among its occupants a comforting sense of superiority.

The main hall rose two stories to vaulted ceilings decorated with intricate stuccowork. Long corridors led to a series of airy rooms furnished with Oriental rugs, potted palms, and curtains and upholstery of silk meticulously hand-sewn by family retainers. On the ground floor were the billiard room, dining room, study, drawing room, tapestry room, and private sitting room for Lady Digby. On the second floor were seven bedrooms, each with its own dressing room, a suite of "men's bedrooms," and well beyond view, nine maids' bedrooms.

"Minterne was sensible old English," recalled Esme, Countess of Cromer, who lived nearby. "There was nothing ostentatious. There wasn't any goldleaf or things shining at you from the ceiling." Family portraits were hung prominently throughout the house—except Jane Digby's, which had been removed to a back staircase. Jane's image stirred the curiosity of the Digby sisters. In later life Pamela said that even as a little girl she was "always impressed" by the sight of Jane, "a great beauty."

Until they turned fourteen, the Digby children lived a life apart on the nursery floor at the top of the house. Each morning at eight they ate breakfast in the day nursery, a large room with a fireplace that served as a combination dining room and playroom opening onto a balcony. The adjacent night nursery had beds, a table, and fireplace. Overseeing the nursery floor was the redoubtable Nanny Hall, a homely woman with short black hair and a thin frame. She was a tough disciplinarian, but she enveloped her charges in warmth, and never played favorites.

Lessons in the Digby household started when a child reached the age of seven or eight. Like most aristocratic households, the Digbys employed a series of governesses, who tended to be well-born spinsters, only adequately educated themselves. Since Pamela and Sheila were so close in age, they were taught together. (Their brother Edward, known as Eddie, three years younger than Sheila, went off to boarding school at age eight—first to Ludgrove, then to Eton.)

The rule in prewar aristocratic households was that girls should not be "clever," the codeword for intellectually curious and well educated. Girls were raised to marry well, and a clever girl might prove too challenging for a prospective husband. Young girls could only nibble at intellectual topics, although they were encouraged to learn foreign languages, music, and art. As Pamela and Sheila grew older, they graduated to a French governess, and Pamela showed an early aptitude for languages.

For hours in the afternoons, Pamela and her sister galloped their ponies across the open country, with their dogs racing alongside. Prickly yellow gorse bushes covered the rolling downs, but the girls learned to find the narrow places that they could jump, praying that their ponies wouldn't balk and toss them in. Several miles away from Minterne, just beyond the Digby land and into the Pitt-Rivers estate, was their favorite spot—the mysterious Cerne Giant, a 180-foot-tall outline of a naked man that is cut into the chalky bedrock of a hill. Thought to represent the Roman god Hercules, the ancient figure is best known for its extraordinary phallus, fully erect and thirty feet long.

The girls loved to tear across the hillside, vaulting over the chalk trenches that marked the outline. "We all knew what the giant was," recalled Lady Edith Foxwell, who grew up in nearby Sherborne. "It was all quite innocent and fun. The penis was the deepest ditch of all. It was very funny. He certainly was something to look at." Years later, when Pamela worked briefly as a newspaper reporter, her first bylined story was about the giant, whose "indecent appearance," she wrote, was "expressive of his lust."

Until she reached her early teens, Pamela Digby saw few people outside family and retainers. Twice a week she and Sheila took ballroom dancing in Dorchester—the model for Thomas Hardy's Casterbridge—a town ten miles down the road. Since all the boys were off at boarding school, the girls glumly danced with each other. Once a week they went to a gym at Sherborne, where they struggled through gymnastic exercises such as jumping over a pommel horse and walking a tightrope.

In recalling her childhood, Pamela spun a glamorous scenario of weekend house parties and hunt balls at Minterne, when she would spy from a balcony at elegantly dressed guests singing and dancing below. Yet accounts of others close to the Digbys indicated that the family led a limited social life beyond holiday and children's parties. One or two guests, usually relatives, would come from time to time during hunting season to stay for several nights. But the Digbys rarely indulged in the sort of house-party weekend associated with early twentieth-century aristocratic England, and the only hunt ball held at Minterne was in 1939, when Pamela was nineteen years old and already launched in society. Throughout Pamela's youth, her parents' occasional dinner parties were tame affairs, invariably followed by quiet games of bridge. More often, the Digbys invited neighbors for Sunday lunch.

Twenty-two servants cared for the Digby family's every need. These workers had a self-contained fiefdom of their own: a servant's hall (where they ate all their meals), cleaning room, butler's room, butler's pantry, housekeeper's room, kitchen, two larders, scullery, and cook's room. At the top of the domestic hierarchy were the butler and head housemaid. Their staff included a cook, kitchen maids, scullery maids, two footmen, chauffeur, and of course ladies' maids for Lady Digby and her daughters. Two laundry maids worked full time washing and pressing clothes and linens. The dairy maid churned the butter and molded it into pats stamped with the ostrich of the Digby crest.

An estate manager supervised the business of farming, leaving Lord Digby more time to pursue his horticultural passions. A head gardener oversaw other gardeners who worked in the half-dozen greenhouses, including one just for peaches, another for orchids, and another for Lord Digby's prize carnations. There were carpenters as well, and a keeper who took charge of the game.

Wages were low—a head housemaid might take in £75 to £100 a year (roughly $3,700 to $5,000 today), and lesser servants might earn only around £35 pounds a year (barely $1,700 today)—all of which made a large staff possible. Serving an aristocratic family was considered a privilege, and the Digbys were not alone in regarding their servants as lesser members of an extended family. After retirement, the staff at Minterne would stay on, living in cottages on the estate.

Though the girls were never taught to cook, they did learn, by watching their mother, the logistics of a large household: how to plan menus, instruct servants, arrange flowers, and do seating charts. They also picked up the decorating style of traditional English country houses, which, Pamela later said, "always reflected what had been there for centuries." Pamela's knowledge of the inner workings of a big estate would prove a great advantage later in life.

As in most aristocratic households, the Digby children spent a carefully allotted time with their parents. Kenny Digby's study, where he worked on estate and county matters, was not off-limits, but the children needed permission to enter. For afternoon tea, Pamela and Sheila would repair to their mother's boudoir. Bundled up against the ever present chill, they would sit before a crackling fire and report on their activities.

Not until they were fourteen did the girls join their parents for dinner. Until then, Lord and Lady Digby dined alone, according to custom, she in a long "tea gown" and he in a velvet smoking jacket. They were served by their butler, dressed in a black coat, cravat, and striped trousers, and the first and second footmen, who wore livery ornamented with gold buttons engraved with the Digby ostrich. After dinner, the children would be back in the boudoir, playing patience or six-pack bezique with their mother.

Kenny and Pansy Digby sat together on the Dorchester County Council, the traditional forum for local government. They also served as Justices of the Peace, handing out verdicts on large and small matters. Lady Digby was so involved that she spent one or two days a week sitting on the bench, and she often closeted herself in her boudoir while she worked on her speeches.

While her parents were civic-minded, they abhorred politics. Both voted Conservative because that is what country aristocrats did. Lord Digby had been horrified by the deaths of so many fellow officers in the trenches of World War I. As a consequence, he was a strong pacifist. He refused even to talk about Hitler and the rise of Nazi Germany, or to discuss national politics with his family. He confined his activities in the House of Lords to local questions and ignored foreign affairs. Lady Digby also had deep mistrust for politicians of any sort, which she expressed in the bluntest possible terms.

From spring to late summer, Kenny and Pansy Digby put their county duties on hold. Like other members of the country gentry they traveled from one estate to another, turning up at the races at Newmarket, Ascot, Goodwood, Newbury, and Bibury, attending the bloodstock sales, and going grouse shooting in Scotland.

The Digbys were blissfully self-satisfied, confident that their house, their lineage, their stables, their gardens, even the food on their table, were the very best. They lived on the surface, avoiding any expression of feelings, finding refuge in the vapidities of small talk—the latest hunt, the coming shoot, the fine points of bloodstock. They were unreconstructed snobs who would never consider having anyone to dinner who was not a gentleman—and that included anyone, a lawyer or doctor for example, who had to work for a living. "The message was, 'We are the greatest,' in a low-key English way," said one neighbor in Dorset.

Women invariably called Kenny Digby "sweet" and "kind." He was an amiable sort who loved life and charmed most everyone. He could walk for miles even after he grew fat in middle age. (He never learned to drive a car, leaving that chore to the chauffeur or his wife.) Lord Digby fit the stereotype of the "hedging and ditching peer," tearing from one event to another, judging a flower show here and a horse show there, and collecting prizes for his own blooms in county contests. He never smoked and hated to drink, not out of disapproval but because he couldn't stand the taste. He was, however, a serious chocaholic. Every week, Mrs. Honey, head of the sweets department at Fortnum & Mason, sent down a standing order of chocolates from London.

Pansy Digby ruled the household with cool efficiency. She was also a teetotaler, and when she wasn't occupied with household or county affairs, she had her head in a book, usually history or a contemporary novel. She took herself extremely seriously and had little sense of humor. When she left a room, said one friend of Pamela's, "you heaved a sigh of relief." Lady Digby had no particular flair and cared little about clothes. The only magazines in the Digby household were *Country Life* and *The Field*—never anything stylish like *Vogue*. As a result, she provided no sartorial guidance for her daughters at all. "Pansy Digby was the most conventional woman you ever would meet," said Louise de Waldner, who knew the Digbys in her youth.

The Digby children knew they were loved, after a fashion. Pansy Digby seemed incapable of scooping up her children to hug and kiss them. When one of them fell ill, she never offered comfort. Lady Digby thought illness strengthened character, and Lord Digby shared his wife's tough-minded attitude. The Digby children, said one relative, "were brought up to take life as it came, to accept the good with the bad, with the knowledge that one would come up against both and cope."

Although her social position was secure, Pansy Digby aspired to even greater heights, of the sort her sisters Eva and Margaret attained by marrying wealthy earls. "It never entered Lady Digby's head that Pam would not marry someone successful," said one woman who lived near the Digbys. Success, in Lady Digby's view, was nothing less than a husband with large holdings and an old title.

Pansy Digby sensed Pamela's potential and singled her out for favored treatment, while Lord Digby preferred Sheila, who was as quiet and withdrawn as Pamela was outgoing. Although she was eighteen months younger, Sheila was three inches taller than Pamela, with dark hair, golden-brown eyes, and a genuine, down-to-earth manner. Lady Digby was irritated by Sheila's shyness, and often punished her for failing to speak to guests at tea. Whenever anything went wrong, regardless of fault, Lady Digby blamed Sheila.

Pamela, however, could do no wrong. "Pam had lovely coloring and was outgoing, but she was no beauty," observed a close Digby relative. Lady Digby "made her think she was more, and just adored her." Lord Digby was "more critical. He saw through Pam"—although he was too polite to show it. Later in life, Pamela said she had resented her father for keeping his distance. But it was her mother's indulgence that had the greatest impact, instilling a belief in Pamela that she could get away with anything, planting the seed of her uncommon boldness and sometimes self-defeating insensitivity.

During her childhood, Pamela endured only one serious crisis, which the family handled with typical upper-class detachment. In March 1928, when Pamela had just turned eight, her mother was hunting when her horse stumbled over a rabbit hole and fell, pinning her to the ground and breaking numerous bones. Pansy Digby was taken unconscious to a nearby hospital, where she lay for several days near death. She was very ill for a month, her condition complicated by pregnancy. Although her children were worried, they took comfort in the perfect continuity of the Minterne routine. Lord Digby kept to his schedule, held his emotions in check, and exhorted the children to take their mother's setback in stride. When Lady Digby returned home, she remained bedridden until she delivered her fourth child, a daughter named Jaquetta, the following October. Lady Digby treated the whole ordeal more as an inconvenience than a tragedy. Within months, she was on her horse, hunting again.

OF ALL THE ACTIVITIES that marked Pamela's childhood at Minterne, riding and hunting made the strongest impression and molded her character in important ways. Every member of the Digby family approached hunting with an almost religious fervor. Pamela was put on a pony before she could walk, and at three she hunted with a leading rein held by a groom. The Digbys had some twenty horses in their stables. Lord Digby bred horses for jumping and polo, and the children helped break them in. Both girls belonged to pony clubs and competed in jumping events at horse shows and gymkhanas, where Pamela thrived on having an audience applaud her performance. Pamela and Sheila also occupied an exalted position since their father was the pillar of the prestigious Cattistock Hunt, not only its chairman but the master of hounds from 1926 to 1930.

From an early age, Pamela was taught to look after her horse, to groom him when necessary, and to know when he should be fed. On late summer mornings she and her sister would be awakened before dawn to canter into the misty woodlands for "cubbing," when young hounds would get their first taste of blood by pursuing and killing six-month-old foxes, called "cubs." As much as they doted on their dogs and ponies, the little Digby girls learned to stifle any shred of sentiment for the young foxes.

The Digby girls toughened quickly, following the standard set by their mother. Despite her horrible fall, Lady Digby was undaunted by the highest hedges and stone walls. "It was very competitive," recalled one rider with the Cattistock Hunt. "It was every man for himself. Today, you have to follow the leader, but in those days everyone took his own line. It was a terrific challenge, to jump a big fence, and when someone couldn't follow you that was great. You took a lot of falls and you were brought up to think, 'too bad.' You couldn't be a wimp."

Pamela was a good rider, a small, determined thruster who pushed to the front of the field, testing the unknown by taking jumps before the others, and catching all the action of the hounds' pursuit. She knew the countryside, and she was well mounted on horses of the highest quality, but she also had the grace and fluidity of a natural equestrienne. At the end of a long day of hunting, when the afternoon had darkened into dusk and the riders shivered in the evening chill, she would hack homeward for several miles over the open hills and along rutted lanes.

During the season, the girls hunted every Saturday and one weekday, leaving only four days for their lessons. They broke bones so frequently that a pair of crutches and a wheelchair were always kept in the back hallway. But as with illness, Lord and Lady Digby allowed no complaints and offered no sympathy. Once when Pamela cracked her nose at age twelve, her mother only glared at her and said, "Your nose was your best feature and now that is gone." Lady Digby did send her to one of the best plastic surgeons in London, who repaired the break, but her matter-of-fact toughness registered with her daughter.

Pamela was compelled not only to suppress pain but never to speak of it. When she was well into middle age and trying to impress her new husband, Averell Harriman, she fell down at his home in Long Island. Harriman's friend Stuart Scheftel remembered Pamela waving him off when he suggested she see a doctor. That evening, she stood quietly behind Harriman, holding her arm as he played bridge for three hours. The following morning, Harriman's friends, including his doctor and next-door neighbor, Edmund Goodman, urged her to get help. Her arm was broken in two places.

CHAPTER

Three

"What I really wanted to do was to live in a big city. And I used to go up in the hills with my dogs and say, 'When I am grown up I will leave this place and I will go to a city and I will live in a city.'"

PAMELA HARRIMAN to Diane Sawyer,
CBS Morning News, 1983

PAMELA DIGBY'S YEARNINGS to reach a big city set her apart from many of her Dorset contemporaries, who wanted nothing more than peaceful lives in the country. She was motivated in large part by money—the simultaneous sense of having it and lacking it that tormented aristocratic families with small landholdings. The Digby fortune was very much tied up in the house and the land—and land that had been valued at more than £50 an acre in the late nineteenth century fetched only half that in the 1930s. At 1,500 acres, the Digby estate was worth around £40,000, equal to about $2 million today.

During the Depression, it seems unlikely that Lord Digby took in more than £5,000 a year ($245,000 today) before the expenses of running the estate. His breeding of hunters and polo ponies was one source of income. He rented out his cultivated land to tenant farmers, and derived some money from forestry on his woodland acreage in Ireland. The balance of his earnings came from the Minterne dairy farm, which was stocked with a large Guernsey herd. After World War II, with servants in short supply, Lord Digby would put on the white milkman's coat himself and drive the dark blue truck at dawn to deliver milk and butter around the county.

Far from London, the Digbys remained fiercely parochial. Their insularity made them feel secure from the social and economic forces that were eroding the influence of old, landowning families. Merchants and entrepreneurs, whose fortunes had nothing to do with land, were quickly gaining political prominence. By the early 1930s, only 10 percent of the Conservatives in the House came from the old, landed gentry. Even their titles were losing luster, as more and more peerages were awarded to self-made men like Max Aitken (Lord Beaverbrook) and F. E. Smith (Lord Birkenhead). In London, people were increasingly judged on the basis of their disposable wealth, but position and pedigree still mattered most in far-off Dorset. Even with less money than they once had, the Digbys ranked at the top of the county elite.

They lived well—in what most would consider grand style—yet the Digby girls saw little cash. If the girls used up their pocket money, no more would appear until their next allowance. Pamela invariably spent her allowance in a day, while Sheila hoarded hers. They were given a stipend for clothes, one pound a week, which they had to budget. That would come to $2,600 a year today, barely enough for one designer dress. When they were taken to London to shop for clothing, they were allowed to pick out only what they could afford. "The Digbys didn't have any money," said Lady Mary Dunn, who first knew Pamela when she was introduced to London society at age eighteen. "They had enough to keep up the house, but they hardly ever went to London."

The Digbys and other provincial aristocrats were a world apart from the flashy London social scene, where the bright young things of the 1920s shook up old society with their nightclubs and their conspicuously easy morals. But Pamela did get a taste of the glamorous life on visits to Lady Digby's exceedingly wealthy sisters, Auntie Daisy (Margaret) Bradford and Auntie Eva Rosebery. The Countess of Bradford presided over the family estate at Weston Park, an enormous house in Shropshire surrounded by vast acreage. Lady Bradford was deaf and quite fierce, so visits to her home were not entirely pleasant for the Digby children.

The Countess of Rosebery made the biggest impression on her young niece, who often visited the Rosebery estates at Dalmeny, near Edinburgh, and at Mentmore, a "great mock English Renaissance wedding cake of a house" in Buckinghamshire. Mentmore was built in 1853 by the father-in-law of the fifth Earl of Rosebery, Baron Meyer de Rothschild, who crammed it with treasures from all over Europe. It had staircases of marble, curtains of rich silk brocade, and masterpieces by Gainsborough, Rembrandt, Tiepolo, and Canaletto.

Auntie Eva's second husband, the sixth Earl of Rosebery, could be loyal and generous to his wide circle of friends, who included Winston Churchill and the newspaper magnate Lord Beaverbrook, but on the whole he was a difficult man, a charmer only when he was in the mood. Watching the strong-willed Eva Rosebery handle her challenging husband was an education for young Pamela Digby. Eva had him "under her capable thumb, but I don't think he minds," society matron Venetia Montagu once observed to Lord Beaverbrook. In Pamela, Auntie Eva recognized a kindred spirit. "Lady Rosebery said, 'The reason I don't like Pam is she reminds me of myself,' " said one Digby relative. The Countess of Cromer observed that Eva Rosebery "had very much the same sort of manner as Pam. She kicked up her heels and married very rich men." Alan Pryce-Jones, an English writer and editor who knew the Roseberys, noted, "Eva was ruthless. She was out to get what she wanted. Eva was always thinking of Eva, which sometimes caused a shock to people she talked to."

After seeing how the Roseberys lived, Pamela found the Dorset gentry boring and provincial. "Even as a girl she wanted to be top dog," said Digby neighbor Lady Edith Foxwell. "Her friend Popsy Winn once told me, 'You know what Pam said to me? She said, "When I come out, I won't date men unless they are a prince or a duke or a millionaire." ' That rather stuck, didn't it?"

Over the years, Pamela constructed a romanticized version of her girlhood, which cast her as socially and intellectually precocious as a child and headstrong and impetuous as an adolescent. Those who knew her at the time remember her quite differently. She was an obedient daughter, careful and punctual, controlled and reserved, tidy about her belongings, meticulous about her appearance. She plugged at her studies, but showed no intellectual bent.

On one point her memory squares with the perceptions of others, however: She had highly developed social skills. "Pam liked to be the center of attention," said Lady Edith Foxwell. Like her father, Pamela had a deep reservoir of charm. Her attitude was positive, her manner vivacious, especially around people she wanted to impress, and she rarely misbehaved. For all her exuberance, she didn't have much of a sense of humor. To get what she wanted, Pamela was the only Digby child who could cajole their formidable mother.

More than any other trait, her ability to manipulate set her apart from other girls. Lady Edith Foxwell said Pamela was "very determined, quite calculating and cold-blooded about what she wanted, even before the war. Pam was always up to self-promotion, which is not terribly English. Everyone got brushed aside who was not worthwhile. She had quite an old head on young shoulders." Pamela had the same take-charge manner that many observed in Lady Digby. "When you were staying with her, Pam was apt to say, 'Now we will do this or that,' not, 'Would you like to?' " said one woman who lived near Minterne as a girl.

As a small child, Pamela's face was flooded with freckles and her hair was such a bright red that other children called her "carrots." But at thirteen, she turned as plump as a pigeon, earning the new nickname "Miss Fat" to her sister Sheila's "Miss Thin." When the family traveled to Ireland for holidays, the locals would refer to her as a "fine, stout girl." Although it was intended as a compliment, Pamela understandably took it as an insult. Yet she turned aside the slight, as she so often did, thanks in part to her mother's constant stream of extravagant praise. As one childhood friend said, "She was very pleased with herself. Although she was pudgy, she was never ugly. She was very sure of herself."

IN 1935, Pamela Digby left the protected world of her parents for the first time. "I would have loved to have had a good education," Pamela told an interviewer in 1982. "You see, in my time, I had to battle to get to boarding school, and I didn't get there until I was fifteen." The notion of a "battle" is surely exaggerated. Her mother actively promoted a year away at school as a way of getting to know girls from London and furthering Pamela's skills at "housekeeping," the homely term for the art of running a large household.

A one- or two-year stint at a genteel boarding school was an integral part of the English aristocratic girl's upbringing. There were some two dozen "public" (that is, private) schools for girls in the 1930s, the most prestigious of which included Roedean, Cheltenham, and Sherborne. But even at the best schools, the focus was less on academics than on shaping character, with emphasis on neatness, good taste, and self-control. The aim was to make young girls all the more eligible for marriage.

For Pamela and Sheila, Lady Digby chose Downham in Hertfordshire, a small school catering to girls of average intelligence. Located in a drafty old manorhouse, Downham offered an even more regimented life than Minterne. The girls slept four to a room and wore a uniform of gray-green skirt and blazer, white shirt and blue tie. Life was neither spartan nor terribly comfortable. The baths were warm, but heating was minimal and the girls accustomed themselves to feeling cold all the time.

Mornings were given over to basic lessons in "maths," languages, and English, plus a small amount of science. "It was very simple," recalled a schoolmate of Pamela and Sheila. "Americans wouldn't believe how simple it was." In the afternoons the girls played tennis and other games, and took lessons in ballroom dancing, drawing and painting, and "domestic science" courses such as cooking. Girls who knew Pamela at Downham remember her as intellectually dull but outgoing. Pamela had looked forward to boarding school as an exciting change from her humdrum routine, and once there, she enjoyed all aspects of school life. "I was always the one picked out to be prefect, head girl, all that nonsense," she told an interviewer in London. "I must have been a terrible bore. But I liked the teachers and they liked me."

Her former schoolmates didn't remember her as head girl, although she was certainly a prefect—one of the half-dozen girls charged with keeping order among the rest of the students. Pamela actually enjoyed the rules and regulations at Downham, and the prefect role suited her take-charge nature.

Pamela received her certificate in domestic science from Downham in 1936. That fall, at age sixteen, she was featured in the pages of *The Tatler* as an equestrian competitor as well as a spectator at the races, dressed in a dowdy suit and looking decidedly matronly compared to such stylish contemporaries as Cynthia Hambro and Alicia Browne. In the year after Downham—from October 1936 to the summer of 1937—Pamela received her "finishing" in Paris and Munich.

Of all the educational experiences of English upper-class girls, finishing was the most enjoyable—three to six months abroad becoming fluent in one or more foreign languages and getting "a light dusting of culture . . . how to tell a Manet from a Monet," in the words of the English social historian Angela Lambert. The girls were chaperoned, but their months on the Continent allowed most of them to feel grown up for the first time.

Instead of a finishing school, which tended to be expensive—around £120 for a three-month term, roughly $6,500 today—the Digbys placed Pamela with a family of financially strapped Parisian aristocrats who took in boarders to help pay the rent. About four or five girls stayed at a time, under the supervision of three middle-aged sisters, who taught French and took their charges to visit the Louvre and other museums, Fontainebleau, and the famous châteaux beyond Paris. "On weekends my friends and I would walk down the Champs-Elysées and have the only thing we could afford, a jus de raisin. Well it's just grape juice, but to me it's still more exciting than champagne," Pamela once told *Time* magazine. Some of the girls took art courses in Paris, and Pamela said she attended classes at the Sorbonne. In later years Pamela recalled studying art, languages, and history there. But as an educational experience, it amounted to elegant dabbling.

After returning to England in February to be a bridesmaid at the wedding of her aunt Eva's daughter Lavinia, Pamela spent the spring of 1937 in Munich. Hitler had been in power for four years. Even though he had remilitarized the Rhineland, Germany during this period was hardly viewed as a dangerous place. In the years before the war, Munich was a feast of architectural beauty embodied in palaces, churches, monuments, and museums, many of them built to exacting classical standards during the early nineteenth century by none other than Jane Digby's lover, King Ludwig I. "All the girls went to Munich. It was *à la mode*," recalled Zara Cazalet, who came of age in the 1930s.

Like their French counterparts, down-at-the-heels members of the German nobility were eager to take in young Englishwomen as boarders and introduce them to art galleries and the opera, which some girls attended four or five times a week. The girls would pay around five pounds weekly for their keep, and an additional amount for a governess hired to drill the girls in German grammar. They were also escorted by sons living in the household, or by young men from London doing their Continental tour.

Pamela stayed with Countess Harrach, whose governess taught the girls German and supervised their introduction to Bavarian culture. One of Pamela's favorite moments, she later told *New York Times* columnist C. L. Sulzberger, was learning that Jane Digby was "the most wicked Englishwoman who ever came to Germany." Countess Harrach, known for only lightly supervising her charges, would see them at lunch and teatime. She went to bed each evening at nine, which allowed the girls to slip out to enjoy Munich's nightlife. Her principal advice to her boarders was to avert their eyes if they saw any anti-Semitic violence. On her one visit to Pamela, Lady Digby made a disparaging remark about the political situation, prompting a rebuke from the countess to say nothing for fear that someone might be listening.

Along with other English girls in Germany, Pamela was alarmed by the goose-stepping SS troops and the oppressive political atmosphere. According to her later reminiscences, she became determined to meet Hitler after hearing his speeches on the radio. She said she sought out Unity Mitford, a member of Oswald Mosley's English Fascist movement since 1933, whose family the Digbys knew in England. After coming to Munich several years earlier for her finishing, Unity had stayed behind, proudly wearing a black shirt and cultivating Hitler's friendship. By her oft-repeated account, Pamela coaxed Unity into taking her to tea with Hitler. "It was a frightening experience," Pamela said many years later. "I remember the sort of cardboard figure. I mean, it was—it was almost like—like the caricatures that you saw later. But he really was like a caricature. It was as if he was made out of thin metal."

Pamela said that her Munich experience raised her political awareness and gave her "an urge to get out the word that Germany was going to attack." There's no evidence that she acted on that impulse. She seemed to have kept her thoughts to herself, unlike Sarah Norton, another English schoolgirl, who was sent home from Munich for trying to remove anti-Semitic propaganda posted around the city.

Over the years, Pamela would offer increasingly inflated accounts of her education, in part because of her insecurity about lacking a university degree, in part because of her tendency to embellish her experiences. A domestic science certificate from Downham School she transformed into graduation from "Downham College." What began as a memory of some classes at the Sorbonne became, in her statement to the Senate Foreign Relations Committee considering her nomination as Ambassador to France: "My own firsthand knowledge of France goes back to 1936–1938 when I studied at the Sorbonne in Paris." Without the slightest embarrassment, several months grew to two years, with the implication that she had received a prestigious degree.

She also said she was on the Continent at a particularly dramatic moment, boasting to Averell Harriman's biographer that she was "still a student at the Sorbonne" in March 1938 when the German Army marched into Austria, and on another occasion saying she was actually in Munich that month. In fact, during February and March she was safely in England, attending the races at Somerton and Sandown (wearing a "becoming bright blue tweed suit") with Popsy Winn, Jakie Astor, and other bright young things.

Pamela Digby's "formal" education had sputtered to an end by the summer of 1937 when she was seventeen. That May she was back in London for the coronation of King George VI, who succeeded to the throne after Edward VIII abdicated so he could marry Wallis Simpson. The Duke of Norfolk was in charge of planning the coronation, and he stood beside the King during the ceremony at Westminster Abbey. As the duke's wife, Pamela's cousin Lavinia Norfolk was one of four duchesses chosen to hold a golden canopy over the King's wife Elizabeth before she mounted to her throne.

For the ceremony, Lord and Lady Digby, dressed in coronation robes, sat with the other viscounts and barons in the South Transept, while Pamela, Sheila, and Eddie took their places in the stands outside the Abbey in a special section for the families of lords. The coronation ceremony was a medieval tableau of royal red, blue, and gold. The men wore opulent robes; the women had decorated themselves with plumes and tiaras that blazed with jewels. It was one of those moments when the aristocracy could put aside the threatening social changes of the previous few decades and revel in its ancient superiority.

That autumn brought new adventures for Pamela, but very much under the watchful eye of her parents. After the usual round of shooting parties and autumn races, she accompanied Lord and Lady Digby to North America. They traveled by ocean liner and visited both New York and Toronto, where Lord Digby had been invited to judge a horse show.

In New York City, the Digbys were the guests of socialite multimillionaires William and Elsie Woodward, whom they had met on the racing circuit. Lady Digby was impressed by the Woodwards' six-story mansion on 86th Street just east of Fifth Avenue. With its capacious reception area, paneled library gleaming with silver horse-racing trophies, and staff of butlers, footmen, and maids, the Woodward establishment held its own with those of the British aristocracy. But what raised the Woodwards in Lady Digby's eyes was that their house had an elevator; years later, on other visits to New York, she was still talking about it.

Pamela and her parents attended a horse show in Madison Square Garden and dined at the '21' Club, a onetime speakeasy that had become a gathering place for society swells. But it was at several Manhattan parties that Pamela took the measure of American girls for the first time. She envied their freedom, both from parental authority and financial concerns. Pamela saw herself as the unstylish victim of Lady Digby's provincialism, and her confidence ebbed as a result. Decades later, the memory still filled her with shame: "I was allowed to bring two evening dresses. I wasn't allowed to pay more than eight pounds for them, and they were rather tacky, I suspect. Also, I was not allowed to wear black or dark clothes, and it was the middle of winter. So I was given a sort of chiffon evening dress, in a light color, and the first night I went out in New York, somebody said to me, 'Oh, in England do they really wear chiffon in winter?' And I knew it was all wrong! I knew! God, it was awful."

Four

BACK HOME IN DECEMBER 1937, Pamela Digby readied herself for the 1938 Season, the annual ritual to introduce eligible girls to London society. Through a marathon of parties, luncheons, balls, regattas, and horse races, an exclusive group of several hundred girls, most of them just eighteen years old, were displayed like fine thoroughbreds at a bloodstock sale. The aim, as simple as it was stark, was to marry off aristocratic daughters to wealthy and suitably titled young men. "Never marry for money," aristocratic mothers would slyly tell their daughters, "love where money is."

The debutante Season began in the spring, peaked in the month of June, and floated through the end of July. Certain events remained constant from year to year: the official start in April at the private showing of the Royal Academy's summer exhibition; the Oxford-Cambridge Boat Race; the Henley Rowing Regatta; the races at Ascot and Goodwood. The apex was the presentation of debutantes before the reigning monarch, usually in May, and the official close was the Royal Garden Party at Buckingham Palace at the end of July.

In 1938, more than one thousand young girls were presented at court; of those, some two-thirds turned around and returned to the country. Among the remaining third who stayed in London, about one hundred enjoyed special popularity and status. Even among that select crowd, there was a distinct hierarchy dictated by social position and wealth.

Those called Lady Mary or Lady Elizabeth had fathers who were dukes, marquesses, or earls; the daughters of viscounts and barons were "honourables" (or "hons," in the flippant vernacular of satirist Nancy Mitford). The daughter of Lord Digby was therefore the Hon. Pamela Digby (but that was just on paper, never in a face-to-face introduction). Being an "Hon" or a "Lady" was better than a "Miss," since rank still meant a great deal, especially for the daughters of peers like Lord Digby, whose status exceeded their income.

The wealthiest families gave their daughters dances in their London mansions. Others rented a ballroom at a catering establishment called 6 Stanhope Gate, or at one of London's fashionable hotels—Claridges, the Hyde Park, or the Dorchester. With an average guest list of two hundred to three hundred, the minimum cost for a debutante ball was £1,000 ($53,000 today). Despite the expense, there were four hundred dances in an average Season. During May and June, there were sometimes two or three a night. The most popular girls went out virtually every evening.

And what of their prey—the "rich young lordlings" that they hoped to snare? The English aristocracy in the interwar years still strongly believed in the importance of breeding, firmly convinced that their preeminence resulted naturally from the purity of their bloodlines. The most desirable young man was the eldest son who stood to inherit his family's title, land, and fortune. The subsequent sons were known as "supernumerary gentlemen." Historically, they had found sinecures in the military, the law, the clergy, the Civil Service, or the Foreign Service, or served as courtiers to the monarch. When times were flush, they often received yearly allowances from their families, and sometimes a second home on the family estate.

Yet by 1938 many of these young men had little more to offer than their family names. Jobs that had once been the preserve of old families were now shared with the rising middle class. Since their financial prospects were uncertain, many of the young aristocrats were looking to make matches with American heiresses.

As a consequence, the stakes were higher than ever for the debutantes. "They were very much aware that they were on show," wrote Angela Lambert. The Season, Lambert continued, "gave a girl a chance to prove herself and make her mark in a few short months, knowing that whatever impression she created might remain for the rest of her life." The prettiest girls had an edge; anyone homely or fat was almost certain to be snubbed. Poise and good manners also counted for something. But among the girls, nothing mattered as much as social position. "Family was essential," said Lady Cathleen Eliot, who came out in the late 1930s. "And to debs from good families, the rest simply didn't count. They would be ignored. You know: somebody looks at you and you just look at them expressionless and your eyes move on, like that."

Pamela approached the 1938 Season with great expectations. No matter that she was overweight; her mother had led her to believe that she would be admired and courted. Even before she had gone to America with her parents, the Digbys had been featured in a full-page publicity spread in *The Tatler*, complete with exterior and interior views of Minterne and photographs of the family. She had also participated in the "Little Season," which began late in 1937 with hunt balls in country houses.

Preparing for the Season took considerable time. In the first months of the year, there were rounds of lunches, teas, and cocktail parties for the mothers of debutantes. The purpose was for mothers to formally meet one another, to exchange invitation lists, and to plan the schedule to avoid conflicts. By early March the calendar for the Season was set, and the invitations were sent out. As May approached, the mantelpiece in a popular debutante's drawing room would be crammed with stiff white cards embossed with black letters.

Like many other mothers, Lady Digby made sure Pamela met the girls and young men with the best social and financial credentials. One essential contact, made while Pamela was visiting her aunt Eva Rosebery in West Lothian, Scotland, was Pauline (Popsy) Winn, who was also coming out in 1938. Attractive and somewhat feather-brained, Popsy was the elder daughter of Olive, Lady Baillie, a wealthy and glamorous Anglo-American who owned the most romantic country house in England, Leeds Castle in Kent, home for three centuries to kings and queens of England.

"I remember Pam came over to see my mama from the Roseberys," said Popsie's younger sister, Susan Remington-Hobbs. "She was full of charm, sort of plump. She loved hunting as we did." The visit prompted the desired acquaintanceship between Pamela and Popsy, and before long they were seen at point-to-point races together. But it was Lady Baillie with whom Pamela found instant rapport, despite their difference in age.

In March 1938, the Digbys came into a significant windfall that put the family in its best financial position in years. Lord Digby's habit of betting on horses paid off when he won the daily double on the tote in the Grand National. On a bet of ten shillings he took in £6,025—the equivalent of $318,000 today. He had just arranged to buy, at a cost of £500, a maroon Buick town car to take to London for Pamela's coming out that spring. "I have paid for the car!" he announced to Lady Digby when he arrived home from the Grand National. There was enough left over to buy a Ford station wagon for the family and a Jaguar for Pamela, to restore the church at Minterne, and to help underwrite Pamela's debut.

The Digbys rented a house for the entire Season, from May through July, on Carlos Place in the heart of London's exclusive Mayfair section. Home to the upper class for more than two hundred years, prewar Mayfair was a stylish architectural mix of Georgian brick town houses, Victorian facades of rose terracotta topped by ornate fretwork gables, and staid red-brick apartment buildings in neoclassical style. Shop windows displayed jewels, expensive hats and dresses, antiques, handmade chocolates, rare books, and paintings. "Mayfair was not Dickens' world," wrote the London historian Reginald Colby, "but it was Thackeray's, with its snobberies and vanities, its cruelties and its grandeur, its plush liveried footmen with their white padded calves taking the air outside the mansions . . . and its stone-hearted dowagers."

The Digbys took the Carlos Place house furnished, bringing only their staff and some supplies from Minterne. Across the street was the Connaught Hotel, a curving sweep of pink brick that catered to aristocrats and royalty, and around the corner was Grosvenor Square, London's most fashionable address. Aside from its central location, Carlos Place had the added virtue of placing Pamela near the residences of two of the season's most important debutantes, Popsie Winn and Sarah Norton, the daughter of Jean and Richard Norton, and goddaughter of Lady Mountbatten.

The mood in England that spring and summer was unsettled. Anthony Eden had resigned as Foreign Secretary in February in protest against Prime Minister Neville Chamberlain's appeasement of Hitler and Mussolini. On March 11, Hitler had sent his troops into Austria and installed a Nazi regime, and it was widely believed that he had designs on Czechoslovakia, now surrounded by Germany on three sides.

As if to defy these ominous currents, the bluebloods in London plunged into the Season with special abandon. Night after night, the streets of Mayfair and nearby Belgravia were clogged with cars tended by liveried drivers. On some nights there were as many as fifteen dinner parties, each with a guest list of fifty debutantes and their parents. The girls would arrive at dinner wearing their ball gowns and suitably understated jewelry—perhaps a pearl necklace and small diamond earrings. Their pale faces wore no makeup, and their feet were shod in satin slippers. The boys wore white tie and tails, and white gloves. The parents would have cocktails; the debutantes and escorts might have sherry or orange juice. Compared to American debutante parties of the same era, there was little heavy drinking, especially among the girls. At dinner each debutante, regardless of her looks or position, was guaranteed at least minimal attention from the young men on either side of her. And according to the unwritten rules, dinner escorts were expected to ask each of their dinner partners to dance.

The balls began at ten o'clock. Each girl carried a dance program with a pencil attached by a ribbon. The programs were numbered 1 to 20, and the boys scribbled their names next to the numbers, signifying which dances they would like to serve as partner. Whenever a girl faced a blank on her card, she had to sit out—an open admission of her unpopularity. More often, a girl would feign a rip in her gown and flee to the cloakroom on the pretext of having the attendant sew the tear. The boys simply congregated in the bar or at the edge of the dance floor with their friends.

Many girls slipped out and went off to nightclubs with their escorts. At the Embassy they listened to Edmundo Ros and his Latin-American band, and at Ciro's they danced on the illuminated glass floor. But the most fashionable spot was the 400 Club, where couples could entwine in almost total darkness, abetted by the obliging headwaiter, Mr. Rossi, who would warn of any approaching adults. For sheltered girls aching to be sophisticated, nightclubs were the prelude to sexual adventure. Little actually went on beyond groping and kissing in the smoky gloom, but it was a welcome diversion from the formalized routines of the debutante balls. After a few hours in the forbidden zone, the trick was to slip back into the dance before the orchestra played "God Save the King" and everyone stood at attention before going home.

The high point of the Season was the presentation at court. The ceremony started at nine-thirty in the evening. Pamela was part of the "Second Court," the second group of girls out of four to be presented that Season. It took the better part of the afternoon of May 12 to get her ready. Her white dress had a train fifty-four inches wide and no more than two yards long. Her white gloves had twenty-one buttons, and she wore the three traditional white Prince of Wales ostrich feathers in her hair, with a tulle veil—no longer than forty-five inches—hanging down behind. Several hours before the ceremony, Pamela and Lady Digby were driven in their Buick to the Mall, where they took their place in the long cortège of limousines waiting to enter the gates of Buckingham Palace as onlookers peered in the windows and shouted, "Here's to you, dearie," and, "Cheerio, Duckie."

Inside the courtyard they were greeted by Beefeaters and uniformed Gentlemen-at-Arms, and escorted to the Throne Room. Under a red canopy at the far end were the two thrones where King George and Queen Elizabeth sat. He was wearing a scarlet and gold uniform, and she was dressed in white satin. The diplomatic corps were placed in the middle of the room, and other dignitaries sat in red plush chairs along the walls. Many of the men wore dress uniforms sparkling with medals, and a military band played from the gallery. The women wore luxurious dresses of every style, from slinky silk and sequins to billowing net, and fur stoles draped their shoulders. In all, the crowd numbered some eight hundred.

Carrying large bouquets, the debutantes walked in pairs in a slow procession, taking instructions from courtiers who "would speak to you as they would to a wet dog," recalled Lady Diana Cooper. As Pamela's name was announced, she stepped forward in front of the King and executed her first full-court curtsy, an elegant variation on the deep knee bend that she had practiced numerous times under the penetrating gaze of Lady Digby. Placing one knee behind the other, Pamela dipped to the floor as low as possible with her back perfectly straight, and returned to a standing position—all in one fluid motion. She glided one and a half steps, and performed a similarly flawless curtsy to the Queen. Then she walked backward out of the room, somehow managing to avoid stepping on her long train, which she was not permitted to pick up with her hands—a maneuver nearly as well practiced as the curtsy itself.

Of all the dances that Season, a handful stood out for their sheer splendor, and Pamela was on hand for all of them. Some four hundred guests attended a party given for Sarah Norton by Lord and Lady Mountbatten in their thirty-room penthouse atop Brook House on Park Lane. Even more lavish was the dance given for Popsy Winn by her mother, Lady Baillie, at her home on the corner of Grosvenor Square and Upper Brook Street. With her American roots and vast financial resources, Olive Baillie was at the vanguard of conspicuously monied London society. Her talent for spending and ostentation was evident on the night of May 23, 1938. The guests ate in a gold and silver dining room set up in the floodlit garden just for the evening. Every room in the house glowed with candlelight, the food was abundant and expertly prepared, and the famous Austrian tenor Richard Tauber sang for his good friend Olive Baillie. One ballroom was reserved for traditional dancing, and the other for the wild gyrations of the "Big Apple," in which everyone formed a circle and ended with a "bumpsadaisy," and the Lambeth Walk, a popular dance from the West End musical Me and My Girl.

The last of that Season's elaborate parties was on June 2 at 14 Prince's Gate, the official residence of the American Ambassador to the Court of St. James, Joseph P. Kennedy. It was a dance in honor of two Kennedy daughters, Rosemary and Kathleen, who had been presented at the First Court in May. The three hundred guests entered the residence through a walkway bordered with lupins before climbing the staircase to the paneled French ballroom on the second floor, where Rose Kennedy and her daughters greeted everyone. The evening was more freewheeling than the dances given by English parents. There was swing music by Ambrose's band, and nightclub singer Harry Richmond gave a show-stopping version of "Thanks for the Memory." The star of the evening was Kathleen, nicknamed "Kick," whose effervescent and informal style had dazzled London society, earning her the title of "most exciting debutante of 1938."

Lord and Lady Digby hosted several dinner parties for Pamela at their rented house in Carlos Place, but otherwise Pamela was twice cursed. Not only were her parents unable to afford a proper dance, they stinted on her wardrobe as well. Her gowns were made by a dressmaker on Brook Street and her hats by a woman in Berkeley Square, but she was surrounded by girls who had custom-made dresses from the best English and French designers—Worth, Schiaparelli, Hartnell, Molyneux, and Victor Stiebel of Jacqmar. The most prized were by the English designer Molyneux, who created extravagant satin dresses overlaid with net and lace. A good-quality designer gown cost around £20 (the equivalent of $1,100 today). A merely decent evening dress could be found for as little as £5, which was about Pamela's range.

"My clothes were not as good or as expensive as other girls," she said many years later. "I suffered terribly from that." In her torment, she recalled, "I yearned for the things I didn't know. I had an adequate allowance but when I came out my family would not spend money on clothes or trivia. I was never allowed to spend more than eight pounds on a ball gown. . . . I had all the beautiful ponies I wanted, but what I wanted was one expensive dress. When you're young and lack confidence, clothes make a great deal of difference."

Even so, Pamela was invited everywhere, and she served on the prestigious committee for the Derby Ball, one of the most fashionable charity events of the Season. Her photograph, taken from an angle that made her look thinner, appeared on the cover of *The Tatler* magazine. She poured on the charm and tried hard to be popular. But she always kept her head, even after a glass or two of champagne.

The Digbys strove to enhance Pamela's popularity by inviting debutantes and eligible young men to Minterne for house parties, the country extension of the London Season. Nobody stayed in the city for the weekend, which began late Friday and stretched through Monday. In the shires, "coming-out balls" were held on Friday evenings in stately homes such as Mereworth Castle in Kent—the perfect start for a pleasure-filled country weekend. Although they were chaperoned, house parties offered more freedom than evenings in town. There were romantic possibilities in long rambles across the downs, riding in the woodlands, or glances across the billiard table and croquet green. With guests assigned to private bedrooms, flirtation sometimes led to midnight assignations.

House parties helped organize the upper class. "They were a way of asserting the intimacy of a group of friends, or of deciding whether to admit a new member," explained Angela Lambert. "They could be used to throw two people together for longer than just an evening. . . . They could even be used to test the social skills of a new girl. . . . Could she . . . stand up to scrutiny over a whole weekend? Were clothes, manners, even sporting prowess up to scratch?"

At Minterne, the Digbys usually invited four girls and four boys, and an equal number of adults. Sarah Norton went several times, as did Charles Manners, the Marquess of Granby and heir to the Duke of Rutland, whose good looks and prestigious title made him prime marriage material. Some of the girls brought their maids to unpack and care for their clothes, but usually the upstairs servants took care of placing everyone's clothing carefully in drawers and closets.

Dinners were formal, with arranged seating and generally six courses—soup, fish, meat, game, sweet, and savory. The women wore long gowns and the men evening clothes. Before dinner, the debutantes and their escorts played word games and "sardines," a variation on hide-and-seek. Recalled Sarah Norton, "It was terribly flirtatious. People would hide, and there was quite a lot of ooh-là-là behind the curtains. Lady Digby thought it was a lovely game. She had no idea what was going on."

Despite being invited to the best parties and being received at court, despite being on the cover of *The Tatler,* despite her mother's relentless social engineering, Pamela Digby did not have a successful Season—at least not by the hard-eyed reckoning of London's social arbiters. This was partly because of her looks, and partly because she came off as self-centered and conceited. She got high marks for her auburn hair, porcelain skin, blue eyes, and winsome smile, but otherwise, "She was way down the list of attractive girls," said a woman several years older who helped form the social consensus. Lady Mary Dunn, a close observer of the London scene, said Pamela's defects included broad shoulders, a short neck, and a "rather touchingly tubby figure." Combined with her unstylish clothes, the total effect was "dumpy and frumpy," in the words of another prominent socialite.

"English men didn't like her," said a debutante from the 1938 Season who saw Pamela frequently. "At many dances, she was often without a partner." Not only were the most desirable young men indifferent to her, some even openly ridiculed her. "I remember one dance because it has stuck in my mind," recalled the debutante. "The man I was with was Lord Derby. As Pam walked by, he said to me, 'I see the chestnut mare's in foal again.' "

Pamela was aware of her failure. "I think her London Season was not terribly happy," said a woman who came out with her. "Nobody likes to be the only one left at the table at a dance, especially Pam." Recalled an intimate from those days: "I remember when she came out, she came back from a party where she hadn't been a success. She was in tears. It had been a big dance and she was very upset."

While her confidence, once so inflated, took a battering, she kept a game face throughout the Season. "Pamela Digby smiling as happily as ever," wrote "Miss Sketch," a chronicler of London society. "She has the sweetest expression, and is so like her aunt, Lady Rosebery." Such control was natural for a girl hardened in the hunting field and trained by an unsympathetic mother to keep physical and mental pain to herself. Certainly Pamela's two friends handpicked by Lady Digby, Popsy Winn and Sarah Norton, had no sense of her unhappiness. "Popsy and Pam would talk away for hours about last night's party," said Popsy's younger sister Susan Remington-Hobbs. "I remember the two girls nattering on the telephone for hours."

Only in later years did Pamela reveal some bitterness, and even then, she shifted the blame to others. "I found it very frustrating," she once said. "All these silly dances where we had to have our parents come and sit around and watch it all. I felt very much out of it because I didn't know a lot of people. I was terribly, terribly overworried about the fact that all I knew how to do was ride a horse. I longed to be sophisticated. And my mother was very strict. They wouldn't allow us to wear makeup."

Truth be told, she did know a lot of people; her problem was fitting in. She had a forced air, an artificial jollity, that put people off. "She was a red headed bouncing little thing," Nancy Mitford wrote to a friend, "regarded as a joke by her contemporaries." At other moments she seemed pushy and opportunistic. "If she needed a partner to dance, she would grab you and your partner to talk until someone else came along," said a debutante from Pamela's year.

Pamela often spoke proudly of how close she was to "Kick" Kennedy, Kick's future husband Billy Hartington, heir to the Duke of Devonshire, and the rest of their lively crowd. But Sarah Norton had a sharply divergent memory of the time. "I can't remember what position Pam really had," she said. "She didn't seem to swim in my particular pond . . . I knew Pam but I wasn't close to her, and she wasn't close to Kick Kennedy then. If so, I didn't see it. I saw a lot of Kick, and Pam wasn't there." There's no doubt that Kick and Pamela became friendly during World War II and afterward, but during the Season of 1938, Kick thought Pamela was a "fat, stupid little butter ball," as Kick described her to her brother Jack.

Pamela's disappointment over the Season was more than just feeling self-conscious about her provincial ways, more even than having unfashionable and inexpensive clothes. Lady Digby had put Pamela on a pedestal, and the Season had knocked her off. Said one woman who knew her well at the time, "Pam found out that she wasn't what her mummy said she was. It had quite an effect."

Pamela answered disappointment with determination. She had been brought up to play the role of the aristocratic wife, to acquire power through a man. This was still her only path into the world of wealth and influence. Once she had been cut loose from the fuddy-duddy strictures of the debutante Season, she was free to proceed in her own way, as Jane Digby had done. She still had the considerable advantage of her privileged background. Now her skin was thickened against insult. She was infinitely adaptable, as she would prove repeatedly throughout her life, and she had the will to press forward to her goals, with scarcely a backward glance.

CHAPTER

Five

ONCE PAMELA WAS officially "out," she could dab powder on her nose, put on a touch of lipstick, and dine alone with men. In her embroidered recollection —summoned perhaps to help bury the setbacks of her Season—Pamela placed herself during the late summer of 1938 in Paris and the South of France, enjoying a whirl of café society parties. The more mundane truth was that in August she spent time with her family in Ireland, where she watched the Dublin Horse Show—her father was a judge—and caught the racing at Baldoyle.

Still, the Digbys' position assured her of invitations well into the autumn that year, so she joined the crowd of post-debutantes and escorts following the guns across the grouse moors and attending house-party weekends. She zipped around England and Scotland in her new Jaguar from one horse race to the next—Musselburgh, Newbury, Wincanton—cutting a sporty figure in her tweed suits and snappy felt fedoras decorated with pheasant feathers. Later in the year she caught up to the post-debutante inner circle—Sarah Norton, Billy Hartington, Charles Manners, and David Ormsby-Gore—at Loch Lomondside in Scotland for a big benefit dance at the estate of Sir Iain and Lady Colquhoun.

The frivolous young aristocrats seemed almost oblivious to the possibility of another world war—even as the rest of Britain prepared for a German invasion of Czechoslovakia's Sudetenland region. Upper-class dowagers toiled in tiny workrooms assembling gas masks, which were distributed to everyone in London, including King George VI. Men from across the social spectrum, from lords to laborers, stood shoulder to shoulder digging trenches in Hyde Park. There was talk of fifty thousand casualties from the anticipated air bombing.

On September 29 Neville Chamberlain flew to Munich and tried to appease Hitler by agreeing to Germany's annexation of the Sudentenland region. The abandonment of Czechoslovakia angered and shamed many British leaders. Duff Cooper protested by resigning as First Lord of the Admiralty, and Winston Churchill stood in Parliament on October 5 to denounce the accord as "a disaster of the first magnitude . . . we have sustained a defeat without war." In early November, Britain again heard what Churchill called "the deep repeated strokes of the alarm bell." The occasion was *Kristallnacht,* a night of savage violence by Nazi thugs against German Jews. But by the early months of 1939, the memory of that night had faded, and much of Britain had fallen into a false calm.

Preparations were under way for a new Season, even more lavish than the previous year. In the Digby household, Sheila's debut would give her a rare moment in the spotlight, although Pamela was expected to do the circuit on her own as a "Second Season." Only those girls who were already engaged or married were excused from a second year. The mating rituals intensified in the Second Season, as society girls struggled under peer and parental pressure to capture a young man.

Not that men were in short supply. London was crawling with "taxi tigers" who were eager to take advantage of husband-hunting young women. Girls were supposed to remain virgins until they married, and most debutantes did. Still, within the upper class, hypocrisy was the rule in sexual matters, especially among the role models for young debutantes: married women. A husband often had a mistress, and a wife might take a lover after dutifully producing a son and heir. While discretion was essential, the unmistakable message was that the aristocracy had its own code of conduct, quite different from the rest of society, which was expected to adhere to the standards of middle-class respectability. Pamela's attitude, expressed decades later, was strikingly blasé. "They went to bed a lot with each other," she told author William Manchester. "But they were all cousins, so it didn't really count."

If Pamela had trouble fitting the mold of a prim young debutante, she was better prepared than the other girls to take on the world. "After Pam came out, she seemed old for her age, more sophisticated than the rest of us. She was totally unshy," said Lady Baillie's daughter Susan Remington-Hobbs. Pamela set about reinventing herself as à femme fatale.

In those early days, her technique could be amusingly obvious, as it was when she met Rowley Errington, the future Lord Cromer, at a debutante dance. She called him afterward and said, "Can I come and see you? I need to ask your advice." Intrigued, he invited her over. She walked in, sat on the floor, looked up at him innocently with parted lips and wide blue eyes, and beseeched him to counsel her on how she should choose between two men who were pursuing her. As he listened, he was uncertain whether she had a genuine problem or had concocted a romantic fantasy simply to attract his attention. He was profoundly flattered by her maneuvers, but he didn't find her attractive.

"He really didn't know her very well at all," recalled Errington's wife Esme, a debutante in the 1940 Season. "They had only been introduced. And at age twenty-one he wasn't necessarily someone who could give her advice. But he was very good-looking and she had a tactic that she was trying out."

The young men and women who had been with Pamela in her first Season saw less of her in the second year. A woman who was close to Pamela in those days said, "When she remade herself, she turned people away. She was inclined to dump some of her girlfriends, Popsy Winn for one." Popsy's mother, Lady Baillie, was another matter. Next to Lady Digby and Eva Rosebery, Olive Baillie had the most influence on Pamela as she grew into womanhood. William Walton, an American journalist who met Pamela in London, called Lady Baillie

"Pam's protector." More than that, she was a mentor whose taste, behavior, and connections lit Pamela's way.

Olive Baillie issued weekend invitations with the care of a director casting a play. "She really only liked people who were very bright or decorative," said American expatriate Ho Kelland. She mingled politicians, authors, artists, and, above all, film and stage stars. Douglas Fairbanks Junior and Senior were frequent guests; Errol Flynn, Robert Taylor, Jimmy Stewart, and Gertrude Lawrence all came to stay. A contingent of continentals was always on hand. Having spent much of her early life in the South of France, Lady Baillie was an ardent Francophile. Every summer she went to the Côte d'Azur, where she was an avid gambler. "The big table in Monte Carlo would not start until she was there," said Aimee de Heeren, a frequent guest of Lady Baillie's in the thirties and forties. "She didn't want her husband to gamble, so she encouraged him to go to nightclubs with pretty girls."

Olive Baillie's husband Adrian was a member of Parliament who brought the world of politics to Leeds Castle. He was rich and good-looking, but she treated him like a child. For many years she had two lovers. One was David Margesson, the chief whip in the House of Commons, who was one of the most influential men in British politics and very pro-American. The other was Geoffrey Lloyd, a Conservative member of Parliament who had risen to second in command at the Home Office.

Pamela flattered Olive Baillie unabashedly, at least in part because she understood the value of cultivating older women who were the arbiters of society. Olive Baillie in turn saw qualities in Pamela that eluded her youthful contemporaries. "She thought Pamela was exceptional," said Esme Cromer. What potential could she have seen? Most likely she recognized Pamela's discipline and energy, her boldness and ambition. Behind the facade of the jolly debutante bounding out of the hunting field was a girl eager to learn. So Lady Baillie pulled Pamela under her wing, invited her to weekend after weekend at Leeds, giving her the chance to observe and absorb.

The turreted gray castle stood on two islands in a lake, surrounded by emerald lawns. The center of activity was the Gloriette, a thirteenth-century keep on the smaller island that was connected to the main house by a two-story corridor. Lady Baillie had transformed half of the ground floor of the Gloriette into a dramatic 75-foot-long room overlooking the water.

Guests staying in the Maidens' Tower, a square Tudor building adjacent to the main house, would straggle in between eight and ten in the morning. After breakfast they could play golf, tennis, or croquet, or go riding. The less energetic picnicked on plovers' eggs and champagne, or took walks in the 400-acre park landscaped by Capability Brown, catching glimpses of Australian black swans gliding in the moat and llamas and zebras peeking through the shrubbery.

After dinner, there might be a performance by tenor Richard Tauber or pianist Edith Baker. But most evenings a handful of guests drifted off to play cards, while others would set up a gramophone in the Gloriette and dance on the ebony floor as moonlight streamed through the tall windows. Late at night, said Susan Remington-Hobbs, "there was lots of corridor-creeping." Room assignments were often made with anticipated liaisons in mind. Once the lights went out, dark figures tiptoed down the hall and slipped into other rooms; before dawn, they would be back in their own chambers.

Pamela was enthralled by the company at Leeds. David Margesson, handsome and impeccably connected, was Pamela's particular favorite. As chief whip, he controlled the operations of the Conservative majority in Parliament and kept abreast of news and gossip in both parties, which he freely dispensed in the salons at Leeds. This was Pamela's first exposure to the sort of high-level inside information that would become her lifelong addiction. "You heard a lot of very good conversation at Leeds," said one woman who knew Pamela well. "You heard what was going on, and unless you were very dumb, you took it in."

Lady Baillie was a powerful role model. She spent vast amounts of money with style, wrote her own rules, and suffered no censure. She was unobtrusive but always in control; she made up for a lack of spontaneity with rigorous attention to detail. These were traits that Pamela would emulate when she became a prominent hostess. Pamela also picked up practical pointers about decor and entertaining, and made invaluable connections. Chief among them was Lady Baillie's Parisian interior designer, Stéphane Boudin, who would help her considerably in later years. "Leeds shaped Pam's life," said a woman who knew her intimately in her youth. "She obviously liked those people and she liked that kind of world." Said an Englishwoman who knew her then, "She could say to herself, 'With money *I* can do this and I can have my own court, too.' "

Amid the casual morality of Leeds, Pamela developed a taste for more mature men. "I never had a beau my own age, always much much older," she once remarked. Even then, Pamela was attracted to position, wealth, and power —all of which she was more likely to find in men her senior. They, in turn, fancied her unlined face and easy sexuality. "I had the feeling that among my friends my age and slightly older, the boys found her overpowering," said Sarah Norton. "She probably found them boring."

On her own in London, Pamela ran with a fast crowd. "I used to see her at the 400, at the Embassy, and the other British nightclubs," said Lady Mary Dunn. "She was usually cheek-to-cheek." During Sheila's Season in 1939, the Digbys rented a less expensive house on the north side of Hyde Park. To keep Pamela in the Mayfair mainstream, Lady Digby arranged for her to live with Sarah Norton and her parents, Richard and Jean Norton, at their home on Grosvenor Square. Unbeknownst to Lady Digby, Jean Norton was involved in a love affair with newspaper baron Max Beaverbrook, and paid little attention to Pamela's comings and goings. "Pam used to disappear off to Paris for odd weekends," recalled Sarah Norton. "We thought she was frightfully sophisticated. She didn't have money. I don't know how she managed. I don't like to think how she managed."

The seventh Earl of Warwick, with whom Pamela had a fleeting affair during this period, provided a partial explanation in a conversation with New York blueblood Edward Morgan. "If you were having an affair with Pam," he told Morgan, "she would call up and say, 'Please may I come over?' She would arrive at your house, sit down, push a pile of bills across the desk, and say, 'What am I going to do with these?' Of course they would be paid." This was the earliest evidence of her extraordinary ability to extract money from men, a trait that coexisted with her independent nature. Said one intimate from her early years: "Pam couldn't have made the life she had without being fairly self-sufficient . . . but she was not shy about asking people to help her."

Fulke Warwick was one of several older men to catch Pamela's eye during the period just before the war. Thought by some to be the most handsome man in England, the Earl of Warwick had been engaged briefly to Margaret Whigham, the ravishing "Debutante of the Year" in 1930, before marrying Rose Bingham in 1933 and divorcing five years later. The twenty-eight-year-old earl was the grandson of the beautiful Edwardian hostess Daisy Warwick, who had been a lover of the Prince of Wales and of Lord Randolph Churchill, father of the future Prime Minister. Fulke Warwick had a brief and unsuccessful movie career, and ran with the Hollywood set. Naturally, he was a great friend of Olive Baillie. It was on a weekend at Leeds that he and Pamela met and she accepted his invitation for a weekend in Paris, all expenses paid. To maintain a semblance of propriety, he would stay at the Ritz and she would register at the Plaza Athénée, a favorite of the Hollywood crowd.

Pamela recalled that her weekend with Fulke Warwick consisted only of an evening at a nightclub and a gift of jade earrings. Yet in ungentlemanly fashion, Fulke Warwick dined out on a considerably racier account of his time with the eager young Pamela. He told his friends, including his former fiancée, Margaret Whigham Sweeny (by then the wife of American stockbroker Charles Sweeny), that it was "the love affair that only lasted one night." Recalled one person who heard Warwick's account, "Pam thought she had done well enough, so she climbed back into his bed the next night, and he wouldn't have her."

Pamela was testing her limits by traveling to Paris. Before the fact, she concealed her plans from Lady Digby. On returning home, however, she defiantly arrived for lunch at Minterne wearing an expensive new hat that was unmistakably Parisian. When she announced how much fun she had in Paris, her mother was charmed rather than angered, and declined to punish her. Once again in Lady Digby's eyes, her eldest daughter could do no wrong, further reinforcing Pamela's sense that she could break the rules and suffer no consequences.

Pamela also had a fling with Philip Gordon Dunn, son of Sir James Dunn, an enormously wealthy Canadian steel manufacturer. Philip Dunn, who was handsome and intelligent and stood to inherit his father's fortune, was married to Lady Mary St. Clair-Erskine, daughter of the fifth Earl of Rosslyn. Lady Mary Dunn's father had been a notorious Edwardian wastrel who gambled away his fortune and was forced to earn a living as an actor. The marriage between Lady Mary and Philip Dunn was hardly ideal. Several years earlier, Lady Mary had fallen in love with CBS Radio mogul William Paley.

Eight years older than Pamela, Lady Mary had been impressed by the young debutante because "she was extremely considerate." But Lady Mary changed her mind in the spring of 1939, when she returned from a visit to the United States. "I was walking across Berkeley Street with a girlfriend, and I ran into Pam," recalled Lady Mary. "She kissed me and said so sweetly, 'Oh, I'm so glad you are back. Philip has been so lonely without you. I hope you don't mind, but we had dinner twice.' " Lady Mary responded with a frigid stare. Only two days earlier her husband had revealed that he had slept with Pamela while Mary was away.

"I was a very jealous person," said Lady Mary, "but what I really didn't like was the dishonesty of taking the trouble to say she had dinner two times with him when I knew there was more. She may have been very interested in Philip. He was very good-looking, and she may have thought if she married well she would get away from her conventional parents."

Pamela's worldliness was evident. One woman, slightly older, thought she had the manner of a "hot housemaid." Another considered her "blowsy." Sarah Norton was endlessly intrigued. "I thought she was so grown up when she was living with us," she said. Although Sarah never asked Pamela about her activities, she didn't really have to. "Pam had definitely known some men," said Sarah Norton. "We were amazed by that. We were complete virgins, sexually childlike. We thought if you held hands, you would get pregnant. We were never told. We were incredibly innocent, and Pam was a girl who wasn't."

Pamela observed the superficial social conventions of her post-debutante year by attending the major events and parties. In Sheila's honor, her parents held the Cattistock Hunt Ball at Minterne for the first time that January, although Pamela had to sit out because she was scheduled for an appendectomy a few weeks later. But by early April she was once again beaming for the camera at the Royal Artillery race meeting at Sandown.

The pace of the 1939 Season was frenetic. There had been hardly a ripple in the social calendar when Germany invaded Czechoslovakia in March. But then Chamberlain finally drew the line: If Poland was overrun, he told the House of Commons, Britain would go to war with Germany. Further aggression from Hitler appeared certain, and when the antiaircraft guns appeared in London's parks, war seemed inevitable.

Even so, the following weeks saw night after night of splendid parties. The Kennedys had a dance for their daughter Eunice at Prince's Gate. The Duke of Marlborough led the crowd in dancing the "Big Apple," and when the party ended at four in the morning, everyone formed a chain and ran around the house, ending in a heap on the floor. The Duchess of Sutherland gave a ball for her niece at Sutton Place, her vast country house. Jean Norton threw a ball with a New Orleans motif and convinced jazz pianist Fats Waller to play for free.

The most memorable of all the prewar balls was given in early July at Blenheim Palace by the Duke and Duchess of Marlborough for their daughter, Lady Sarah Spencer-Churchill. For the thousand guests who attended, it marked the end of a grand era. The novelist Daphne Fielding described it as an echo of the Duchess of Richmond's celebrated ball on the eve of Waterloo. The enormous house was floodlit, footmen wore powdered wigs and knee breeches, and the champagne ran in rivers. "I was loath to leave, but did so at about 4:30," wrote Chips Channon, "and took one last look at the baroque terraces with the lake below, and the golden statues and the great palace." In retrospect the gaiety of that last Season of peace seemed forced, an act of self-delusion. "It was a sort of sunset glow before the storm," wrote Channon.

Everyone left London as usual at the end of July. Overhead, airplanes on maneuvers were vivid signs of England's intense preparations for war. On August 23, Germany and the Soviet Union signed a non-aggression pact, followed within days by a formal Anglo-Polish alliance assuring that Britain would be drawn into a war to stop Hitler. On September 1, Hitler invaded Poland. Two days later, on a sunny Sunday morning, Prime Minister Neville Chamberlain announced on the radio, "This country is at war with Germany."

Along with many young men and women her age, Pamela had cut short her holiday and returned to London in August. "London was generally deserted in August, so it was very unusual," said Ivan Moffatt, a popular escort in the 1930s who became a Hollywood screenwriter. "The Ritz began to fill up." Pamela was determined to get a job in the war effort. The same idea had occurred to Sheila, but Lady Digby didn't want two daughters in London. Still favoring Pamela, she let her remain where the prospects were best for finding a husband, and she made Sheila stay in the country and join the Auxiliary Territorial Service (ATS), the women's division of the Territorial Army, where Lady Digby had been put in charge of the southern command. With the help of David Margesson, Pamela signed on at the Foreign Office as a French translator for six pounds a week.

The notion of being employed was a novelty to coddled young debutantes, as was the accompanying sense of complete freedom. The tight social structures and customs that had governed the lives of unmarried upper-class girls were falling away. The mood was romantic, almost giddy. "There was a curious pall of a nonexistent war, like a mist," recalled Ivan Moffatt. "All the boys were getting into uniform." Many girls floundered when they left the protection of their family estates, but Pamela stayed on course. The resourcefulness inculcated by Lady Digby had made Pamela more self-reliant than most girls her age. She settled into her job, and at night she could be seen in the semi-darkness of the Café de Paris, absently stirring a drink while her uniformed date stared pensively at the tablecloth. "She had an atypical existence," said Sarah Norton, "spending a lot of her time with men, not so much with the girls." Unlike the previous year, when she was widely ridiculed for being overbearing, Pamela Digby at age nineteen was already a woman of poise and maturity.

Six

AIR-RAID SIRENS WAILED at the conclusion of Chamberlain's broadcast on September 3, sending people scurrying to shelters. But nothing happened on that day or for months afterward. The "phony war" lent a surreal quality to life in London in the fall of 1939. Streetlights were cut off, and windows were hung with dark curtains. Londoners who ventured into the ink black night navigated by the pinpoint glow of cigarettes or the thin red and green crosses that passed for traffic lights.

Young men in uniform dashed into London for two-day leaves from training camps, drinking whisky and eyeing girls at the Embassy, the Café de Paris, and the 400. Thousands of children were evacuated to distant towns. Many wealthy Londoners hauled their paintings and antiques out to the country. Then they threw "house-cooling" parties, covered everything with dust sheets, and closed their London homes. They took rooms at the Dorchester, the Ritz, and the Savoy, and huddled together in the dining rooms and bars. Journalists and literary figures favored the Savoy Grill, while society and government people congregated at the Ritz.

In mid-September, Randolph Churchill entered the Ritz as Lady Mary Dunn was leaving. Then twenty-eight, Churchill had been a friend since childhood. "He made the swinging doors go round again at a vast speed so he could talk to me," said Lady Mary. "Can you have dinner?" he asked. With her bright blue eyes, turned-up nose, and lively manner, Mary Dunn was a popular dinner partner, and Churchill persisted when she declined. "I have forty-eight hours leave and no one to have dinner with on my last night," he pleaded. After a moment's hesitation, Lady Mary suggested a blind date. As she recalled years later, "I said, 'If you'd like to have dinner with a beautiful redhead' . . . actually what I really said was, 'If you want to have dinner with a red-headed whore, go round to my flat and you will find her waiting for me from two o'clock onwards.'"

The redhead was Pamela Digby, fresh off her flings with Philip Dunn and Fulke Warwick. Why would Lady Mary suggest her? "She was the first person who came into my head," said Lady Mary, who added, with a smirk, "I thought she might not have a date." Lady Mary was scheduled to meet Pamela that afternoon at the Dunns' flat near Buckingham Palace, which Pamela had arranged to rent while the Dunns moved to the country.

Instead of coming in person, Randolph telephoned the flat, and Pamela answered. "This is Randolph Churchill," he said. "Do you want to speak to Mary?" replied Pamela. "No," he said. "I want to speak to you." "But you don't know me," Pamela said. Remarkably, they had never crossed paths during the Season or at Lady Baillie's or the Roseberys'. Randolph invited her to dinner, and she agreed to meet him at seven that evening. According to Randolph's version of events, he also inquired, "What do you look like?" to which Pamela was said to reply, "Red-headed and rather fat, but Mummy says that puppy fat disappears." Afterward, Pamela asked Mary Dunn why she fixed her up. "He's great fun, he's a bit too fat, but very amusing," replied Mary. "You'll have a very good time!"

Not everyone would have agreed. With flaxen hair, pink face, and angelic blue-gray eyes, Randolph Frederick Edward Spencer Churchill had been the most promising member of a new generation of a grand English family. His father, Winston Churchill, was the famous politician; his first cousin was the tenth Duke of Marlborough, a thick-skinned bore; his paternal grandmother was the promiscuous American beauty Jennie Jerome; his maternal great-grandfather was the seventh Earl of Airlie, head of a lofty old Scottish family; his great-uncle (and, by some accounts, unacknowledged maternal grandfather) was the First Lord Redesdale, grandfather to the six famous Mitford sisters. His paternal grandfather, Lord Randolph Churchill, had been one of the most colorful politicians of the Victorian era, a fiery orator and a compelling but erratic leader. After alienating the Prime Minister, Lord Salisbury, he resigned as Chancellor of the Exchequer. Lord Randolph sank into depression and died at age forty-six of syphilis.

Winston Churchill had showered attention on his only son, spoiling young Randolph shamelessly. At the same time, Randolph's mother, Clementine, mostly ignored him. Unmaternal by nature, Clementine devoted herself completely to her husband. She was further handicapped as a mother by bouts of melancholia that several times tipped into nervous breakdowns. Both Churchills were away often, and a succession of ineffectual nannies were left to oversee Randolph. Small in size, Randolph was a naturally gregarious child, but by age seven, he had become an uncontrollable bully. "I could never brook authority or discipline," Randolph nonchalantly explained years later.

When Clementine tried to discipline the youngster, Churchill insisted that Randolph's defiant behavior showed an admirable independent spirit. "Winston never backed Clementine up. It would have been better if he had bashed Randolph, but he always let him rip," said Randolph's cousin, Lady Mosley, the former Diana Mitford. "No one seemed to notice that Randolph was becoming a young monster," wrote the British author John Pearson, who chronicled the troubles of the Churchill family.

On the plus side, Randolph was bright and confident, brilliant in speech and writing. As young as five, Randolph had been compelled by his father to stand on a stool and recite poems for weekend guests. He had his father's enviable memory for quotations—and the same showoff tendencies. He was conceited about his intelligence, yet not the least vain about his good looks.

Randolph seemed oblivious to criticism—perhaps because he never stopped talking long enough to hear any.

When Randolph was barely fifteen, his father began including him in the spirited political conversations among the high and the mighty visiting the Churchill home. When Churchill encouraged his son to express his views, the boy obligingly held forth, mirroring the opinions of his father. Randolph was more gifted at oratory than his father, who had to practice his rolling cadences and memorable lines. Churchill often goaded his son into verbal combat. "It was not training for domesticity," drily noted Randolph's friend Michael Foot, who later served as the Labour Party leader in the House of Commons. While Randolph picked up some laudable traits from his father—self-assurance, the courage of his convictions—he also absorbed a fondness for gambling, heavy drinking, and high living. "Winston drank prodigiously, but I don't think he was ever drunk. That was not the case with Randolph," said Diana Mitford Mosley. By the age of twenty-two, Randolph was known to down a large sherry, a pint of beer, and four large glasses of port—just at lunch.

Randolph was educated at Eton, and, for a time, at Oxford, where he played the part of the arrogant crown prince, strolling across the quadrangle of Christ Church in a tatty dressing gown and smoking a cigar. He spent most afternoons eating, drinking, and gambling with the campus ne'er-do-wells. When Randolph was only eighteen, he attracted worldwide attention by attacking the proposed Anglo-Egyptian treaty in a debate at the Oxford Union. He was invited to make a lecture tour of the United States, and Churchill unwisely allowed Randolph to take a leave from Oxford over the objections of Clementine, who knew her son would never return to get his degree.

Through his lively lectures and vivid journalism, Randolph became a full-blown celebrity, hailed before the age of twenty-one as "the most brilliant young man in England." For a while, Randolph seemed headed toward fulfilling his early promise, especially after he wrote a series of newspaper articles in 1932 about Hitler that were densely reported and remarkably prescient. Yet it was in politics—his father's realm—that Randolph was determined to prove himself. He was deeply conservative, but he loved to argue a contrary view simply to shock his listeners. He ran for Parliament and lost three times in the space of two years. He squabbled with Tory Party leaders and with his father.

Winston Churchill had astonishing powers of concentration, and the strength of character to muscle through his "black dog" depressions. Randolph, by contrast, had trouble applying himself, except in intense spurts. Everything came too easily to Randolph; he could always find a shortcut. Winston Churchill marched to greatness trying to vindicate his departed father. But Randolph was overwhelmed by his father's success. As Randolph later wrote, "I wanted to have a show of my own. Struggling to establish my own. individuality and personality, I often said and wrote rather reckless things."

By the late 1930s, Randolph seemed resigned to making his way as a journalist. "As a writer, he was fabulously good, but his facts were often fabulously wrong," said Stuart Scheftel, an American friend dating back to Oxford days. Randolph's earnings were never enough to support his taste for expensive hotel suites and chauffeured limousines. His gambling sunk him deeper into debt. After bitter quarrels, his father often made up the shortfall—a difficult task because he too was scraping for funds to support his own expensive lifestyle. At one point in the mid-1930s, Churchill had to raise £1,500 to bail out his dissolute son.

Randolph was notorious in the decorous drawing rooms of London society. "He was very vulgar," recalled the American journalist William Walton. "He was physically repellent. He used to pick his nose in public." He thought nothing of urinating on an open road in front of a group of women, explaining, "I am a member of Parliament." Even Lady Diana Cooper, a lifelong friend, was horrified by his behavior as a houseguest: "He staggers into my room at about 9:30 and orders his breakfast," she wrote. "His coughing is like some huge dredger that brings up dreadful sea-changed things. He spews them out into his hand. . . . As soon as I get up he takes my place in my bed with his dirt encrusted feet and cigarette ash and butts piling up around him."

He was also a bad drunk. "Going out with Randolph was like going out with a time bomb. Wherever he went, an explosion seemed to follow," wrote another American journalist, Virginia Cowles, one of his most loyal friends. He would lash out at people, for no apparent reason. "His tendency to monopolize conversations, to glory in the sound of his own voice, to argue, pick quarrels, pass judgments and talk other people down was probably his most notable and enduring characteristic," wrote Randolph's own biographer, Brian Roberts.

Because he was a Churchill, acquaintances often forgave his boorish behavior and focused on his quick wit, intellectual courage, and self-assurance. Around beautiful women, Randolph could be charming and attentive. With his grand family and handsome profile, he was more successful in love than in life. "Almost from the onset of puberty, he had been a relentless pursuer of desirable young women," wrote Brian Roberts. One of his earliest crushes was his cousin Diana Mitford Mosley, who was fond of him but kept her distance. While visiting newspaper tycoon William Randolph Hearst in California, Randolph made plays for several married women, including Dorothy Hart Hearst, the newspaper tycoon's daughter-in law, whom Randolph considered "exquisite." Randolph boasted that he lost his virginity during his stay by seducing another female guest.

In the early 1930s, he had an intense affair with Clare Brokaw, a beauty who would later become famous as the journalist and playwright Clare Boothe Luce. During their romance, she gave Randolph a photograph signed: "To the boy wonder from the girl vamp." While lecturing in America, he conducted a well-publicized romance with Kay Halle, daughter of a businessman in Cleveland. Back in England he carried on with June Inverclyde, a musical comedy star, and with Doris Castlerosse, the wife of corpulent gossip columnist Valentine Castlerosse. During a trip to Venice in 1932, Randolph flaunted his involvement with Doris—one newspaper account said that "the voice of Mr. Randolph Churchill, whom Lady Castlerosse calls 'fuzzy wuzzy,' goes booming down the canals"—and attracted headlines by starting a drunken brawl. Randolph's only lifelong love, the woman he repeatedly asked to marry him, was the dark-eyed beauty Laura Charteris. He met her in 1937, when she was estranged from her husband Lord Long but already enamored of the third Earl of Dudley.

Randolph may have desired women, but he viewed their abilities with condescension. "Randolph was a raging rampaging male chauvinist," said his friend Michael Foot. Randolph disapproved of women in politics, and he valued intelligence in a woman only up to a point. His ideal was Margot Asquith. Randolph insisted that her influence behind the scenes on behalf of her husband the Prime Minister surpassed that of the American, Nancy Astor, the first woman to serve in Parliament. "The influence of women is only successful when it's indirect," Randolph once wrote. They could exert influence, he continued, "so long as it's exercised in country houses, at the dining-room table, in the boudoir and the bedroom. . . . The better a woman speaks the more embarrassing I always find it. It makes me feel quite uncomfortable."

He was called "Randy" Churchill for good reason, pursuing many women simply for sexual release. But he had an intense romantic impulse, maintaining strong feelings for various women throughout his life. Many of those he courted most ardently were either unsuitable (the showgirl variety) or unavailable (the married variety). Yet he keenly felt the responsibility to carry on the Churchill line, and he was famous for making sudden—often drunken—marriage proposals.

At the time he encountered Pamela Digby, he had completed his first year as a subaltern in a reserve unit of his father's old cavalry regiment, the Fourth Hussars. He was in love with Laura Long and sleeping with the English actress Claire Luce (not to be confused with Clare Boothe Luce). By now he had lost his youthful beauty. His face was puffy, his waist had grown thick, and he looked older than his twenty-eight years. He was noisy, opinionated, tactless, philandering, unpredictable, rude beyond measure, alcoholic, extravagant, and unreliable—unfit for marriage in every way.

Yet he proposed to Pamela on their first night together, and she accepted. After Randolph picked her up, he took her for a drink with Lady Diana Cooper and his distant relation Edward Stanley, heir to Lord Stanley of Alderley. Edward Stanley, who considered Pamela "a pretty luscious little piece," tried to horn in and invite her to dinner himself. The next morning, Stanley told his cousin Nancy Mitford, Pamela called him at eight and asked him to come and see her. He found her in a state of agitation because she had promised to marry Randolph. When Stanley protested that she had only known her fiancé one evening, she admitted that Randolph had told her he didn't love her but thought she looked healthy and able to give him a son to carry on the Churchill name before he died on the battlefield. As Nancy Mitford explained to a friend several weeks later, "Edward then spent two hours giving the girl fatherly advice, punctuated no doubt with chaste kisses, but all, as you know, in vain. It seems that she was the 8th girl Randolph had proposed to since the war began, his best effort being 3 in one evening."

Pamela gave her son Winston a more benign version of Stanley's efforts to dissuade her: "Ed Stanley called me up to complain, 'You stood me up for dinner last night and I find you dining at a restaurant with Randolph Churchill. He's a very very bad man and you shouldn't go out with people like that.' 'But he's one of your best friends,' I protested. 'Yes, he is one of my best friends— but he shouldn't be one of yours.' "

Pamela variously ascribed her acceptance of Randolph's proposal to inno-cence ("I had had no experience of life or men," she fibbed to John Pearson) and to a yearning for independence. "You were treated as a child until you got married. The status of being married gave you your first freedom," she ex-plained to Rudy Abramson. But mostly she cited her susceptibility, in the highly charged atmosphere of wartime London, to Randolph's worldly manner. He seemed to know everyone and had an opinion on everything. Still very much the boy who performed for his father's friends, he impressed her by reciting long poems by Hilaire Belloc.

"At the time, he absolutely swept me off my feet," she told an interviewer in 1983. "It was a time when most of the men I knew, young men, were scared. They were going off to war. They were going to get killed. And here was Randolph, who was absolutely certain that the war was going to be long and bloody and terrible, but of course we were going to win. And that was very appealing. Here was somebody who had total confidence." Curiously, she was more candid about her feelings in justifying her decision to her son years after the fact: "I was getting so terribly upset by seeing all my friends going off, as they dramatically thought, to be killed, and I thought how marvelous it was to be going out with somebody about whom I didn't give a damn."

Pamela repeatedly insisted that she was never influenced by the fame of Randolph's father. "Winston's importance is something we take for granted now," she told John Pearson. "But at the time, he didn't seem a great historical figure. I certainly didn't realize his importance." Yet according to Churchill's daughter, Mary Soames, "From April onwards, calls for Churchill to be in-cluded in the Government came from all sides, and were featured almost daily in the press." By July 1939, London was filled with placards saying: "Churchill Must Come Back." And on the day war was declared, Chamberlain returned Churchill to his old post as First Lord of the Admiralty. "Winston was back in the news, he was the man of the hour, the first Lord of the Admiralty, and likely to be Prime Minister," recalled Alastair Forbes, a friend of both Winston and Randolph.

The fact was, Randolph was Pamela's best prospect at the time, and her decision wasn't as impetuous as it might seem. She certainly wasn't alone in accepting the first offer of marriage that came her way. In the weeks following the declaration of war, many girls rushed into marriage out of a sense of disori-entation when their families were dispersed and their homes were shuttered. Pamela's reasons were somewhat different. She was not exactly fresh from the nursery, and she needed some legitimacy. Her efforts to marry wealth had foundered. Her flirtations with the likes of Rowley Errington, and her brief and unhappy affairs with Philip Dunn and Fulke Warwick, had tarnished her reputation. Lady Mary Dunn, for all her dislike of Pamela, had a grudging respect for Pamela's decision. "She was not educated, but I think she was very cunning," she said. "The war had started. Randolph got her the Churchill name."

Despite the Churchills' noble lineage, they were closer in spirit to the newcomers in English society whom she had embraced to escape her dull life in Dorset. Randolph moved her into the center of power, where she could make contacts and fulfill at least some of her ambitions.

Randolph was quite open about his reasons for choosing Pamela. Even before the engagement was officially announced on September 26, he startled the American writer John Gunther by explaining—in the presence of Pamela— that he was about to marry her because "he must have a son and heir as soon as possible, since he was convinced that he would soon be killed." He told Lady Mary Dunn that "he thought Pamela was pretty smashing," although he also asked Laura Long whether he should go forward with the marriage. She declined to give him any advice and insisted that he make up his own mind.

Lord and Lady Digby made mild protests when Pamela gave them the news. "She's too young," cried Lady Digby. "They don't have any money or anywhere to live! They don't even know each other! The whole thing is absurd. They must not be allowed to do it!" The real issue, of course, was Randolph's unsuitability. But faced with Pamela's determination, they retreated quickly. "They were really very pleased with the Churchill connection," said one friend. "They were happy to get letters from Winston and to be part of the Churchill setup."

Randolph took Pamela to meet his parents at Chartwell, their ungainly brick home on a hill overlooking the Weald of Kent. Clementine had already expressed her opposition to the match, largely on the same grounds as the Digbys, but Winston and Pamela were instantly enchanted with each other. Pamela first encountered him on a grassy knoll outside his art studio some distance below the main house.

"He was a very large character, with his cigar, his black clothes, and his wonderful pink and white face," Pamela recalled. "He knew more about my family than I did. He said, 'You're no longer Catholic' [a reference to her ancestor Sir Everard Digby, who had been beheaded by King James I in the Gunpowder Plot], and he knew that the first Winston Churchill was buried at Minterne." She thought he was "a little overpowering but very very friendly."

Perhaps it was his weakness for auburn-haired women, but Winston seemed more smitten than his own son. Pamela proudly related later that he had told her she reminded him of his first love, Pamela Plowden. In a letter to his friend the Duke of Westminster, several days after meeting Pamela, Churchill pronounced her a "charming girl." Not only did Churchill bless the marriage, he urged his son and Pamela to move fast, just as he had when he met Clementine. Like his son, he almost viewed the marriage as a lark, exclaiming, "All you need to be married are champagne, a box of cigars, and a double bed!"

Both Winston and Clementine were touchingly naive about Pamela, viewing her as a fresh virgin, a welcome change from the worldly women Randolph preferred. And while her family lacked great wealth, she did bring a decent marriage settlement of about £5,000—roughly $243,000 today—some of which, according to Pamela, her father kept because of the "uncertainty of war." Even so, there was enough to help prop up the debt-ridden Randolph.

Once Pamela began to ponder the potential pitfalls of life with Randolph, she had second thoughts: "Every time Randolph disappeared, I became anxious and said to myself, 'This is absolutely idiotic. I don't know him. He doesn't know me, and there's a war on.' " She even called her mother to say she wanted to break it off, but then just as quickly changed her mind. The wedding date was set for October 4—just eight days after the engagement was announced. Using Churchill pull, Randolph circumvented the customary thirty-day waiting period for a marriage license.

Most of their friends were shocked by the suddenness of the engagement. They thought that Randolph and Pamela had little in common. In fact, they shared more traits than seemed evident at first glance. Both were tough, able to shake off setbacks and move ahead. Both projected unwavering self-confidence as a way to mask their insecurities, and they shared a somewhat arrogant sense that they deserved—indeed *were owed*—the best.

The wedding took place under cloudy skies on a Wednesday afternoon one month after the outbreak of World War II. The setting was several blocks from Parliament, at St. John's in Smith Square, a flamboyant structure of four ornate towers, oversize columns and pediments more in the spirit of Rome than London. The ceremony received wide press coverage, with Winston Churchill nearly stealing the show from the bride and groom. "Wait a minute . . . Clemmie . . . She's just coming," Churchill shouted as the clergyman was about to begin the service and Clementine hurried to take her seat. Large crowds thronged at the foot of the church steps to shout, "Good luck sir!" and to cheer repeatedly their new First Lord of the Admiralty.

Pamela wore a coat of navy blue duvetyn trimmed with fox dyed to match and a dress of the same color. She carried a cascading bouquet of pink and white orchids. Her large navy blue velvet hat came to an unbecoming point, accentuated by a tall quill standing straight up. Wearing white might have been somewhat inappropriate, given her recent history, but she said that she chose blue "to assert my independence, and it seemed very sophisticated and grown up not to appear a traditional bride in white." Randolph was dressed in his army uniform, including jodhpurs, sword, and knee-high boots with jingling spurs. As Randolph and Pamela left the church, their faces wreathed in smiles, they walked under an archway of raised swords held by the Fourth Hussars honor guard.

More than a hundred guests from government and high society turned up, including a proud Lady Baillie. "Every smart person was there," said Lady Mary Dunn. Each guest carried a gas mask in a canvas case. A number of the women used them as handbags, and Canon F. R. Barry, the Rector of St. John's, kept his in a special scarlet pouch. Most of the men wore uniforms, as did one of the women, Lady Limerick. Lady Diana Cooper was glamorously swathed in fur, and her husband Duff wore a top hat.

Afterward, the Churchills gave a reception in the state rooms at Admiralty

House, "the most romantic house in Whitehall," in the words of Diana Cooper, "looking onto the horse guards' snowy arch, the garden of 10 Downing Street and the pelicans in [St. James's] Park." The atmosphere was festive as Churchill drank champagne, ate ice cream, and exhorted his guests, "We must eat. We must eat." Lord Stanley of Alderley, wearing a long frock coat, played a frolicsome hornpipe. Pamela was in "high spirits," and "at the end Randolph expressed an unaccustomed reluctance to speak. But his brother officers compelled him to do so. Thereupon he called on his father—who blushed and retired."

The penumbra of war gave the wedding a somewhat desperate air, as if everyone knew that it might be one of the last flings before friends started dying. A year later, St. John's, Smith Square was a ruin of barbed wire and boarded windows, bombed by the Germans in the Battle of Britain. "It was a marriage done in a fortnight," said Randolph's friend Alastair Forbes. "And God struck down on the church after they were married."

CHAPTER
Seven

THE TROUBLE STARTED on their honeymoon at Belton, the home of Peregrine Cust, sixth Baron Brownlow. The setting couldn't have been more romantic: a magnificent eighteenth-century house, designed by Sir Christopher Wren, beautifully furnished and appointed. Perry Brownlow was a relatively new friend of Randolph. They had met when Brownlow was serving as lord in waiting to Edward VIII. It was Brownlow who escorted Wallis Simpson through France before the King announced his abdication. Afterward, Brownlow was such a pariah that men turned their backs on him at the bar at White's, and London socialites referred to him as "Gone with the Windsors." Randolph, however, loyally stood by him, and the grateful Brownlow was happy to lend him his Lincolnshire home for several days.

Randolph regarded Pamela as an unformed being that he could mold into the ideal wife. He thought he could instruct her about politics, sharpen her wit, and shape her character. He decided to start her off with Gibbon's *Decline and Fall of the Roman Empire,* the book that his own father had read while serving as a Hussar in India at age twenty-two as the first step in an intense education program. But Randolph misjudged both his bride's small appetite for cerebral pleasures and her inclination to absorb what she wanted, not what was imposed on her. As they lay in bed at Belton, Randolph read Gibbon aloud, pausing periodically to demand, "Are you listening?" When Pamela dutifully replied, "Yes I am," he would bark, "Well, what was the last sentence?" As annoyed as Randolph was with her, she was as deeply vexed by her new husband's presumption. "Can you imagine!" she later exclaimed to her son. "Hilaire Belloc was fine, but Gibbon was too much!"

For the first year of their marriage, Randolph and Pamela were rootless, like so many English people whose lives had been upset by the war. They alighted briefly in Tidworth, where the Fourth Hussars were stationed. Almost immediately, his regiment moved north to Beverley in East Yorkshire. Randolph and Pamela found a small semi-detached house in nearby Hull for £3 a week, which was just manageable on Randolph's £750 a year in half-pay from his job as a reporter for the *Evening Standard.* During those last months of 1939, England seemed paralyzed by the phony war. The world waited for Hitler to strike. But aside from routine German attacks on British merchant ships, the only act of aggression was Russia's invasion of Finland on November 30.

Randolph and Pamela were unhappy in Yorkshire. Randolph was upset that his regiment had not been sent abroad as he had expected. Although no soldiers had marched into battle, regiments were being deployed in Europe—except for the Fourth Hussars, which was rumored to be safe because of Randolph's presence. Priding himself on his courage, Randolph resented any such suggestion and brooded over his fate.

Christopher Sykes, a friend from Oxford days who was stationed nearby, recalled that Randolph took out his frustrations with his usual bad-boy behavior. At one country house gathering, reported Sykes, "Randolph did everything he knew, and he knew a lot, to distress, anger and exasperate and make miserable his host and every one of his fellow guests." Pamela was genuinely dismayed by Randolph's drinking. With teetotaler parents, Pamela had no experience dealing with alcoholism. There were frequent fights. "Randolph would promise to stop, but never did," said Pamela later.

Compounding Pamela's disenchantment was her unhappiness at being stuck in the middle of nowhere during one of the coldest winters on record. "There was snow and more snow," she recalled. "It was cold, there was ice everywhere. It really was ghastly." Although Randolph was momentarily challenged by "learning the ropes," as Christopher Sykes put it, he quickly grew bored. He had nothing in common with his fellow lieutenants, who were the same age as his bride. "He found little satisfaction in their conversation in the mess," recalled Pamela. But he did listen to them on one subject. According to Randolph's cousin Anita Leslie, it was only at the urging of his fellow officers that he told "a certain musical comedy actress, one of those 'sex-pots' " (most likely Claire Luce) that she could no longer visit him. "Randolph could never have worked out for himself what was circumspect behavior," wrote Leslie. "He listened however to his seniors in the mess and obeyed instructions."

The Fourth Hussars were no more taken with Randolph than he was with them. They disparaged him for being fat, and with his customary pugnacity he retorted, "Rubbish—I am tougher than the lot of you!" Appealing to his impulsive nature and weakness for gambling, they bet him £50 that he couldn't walk the 108 miles to York and back in 24 hours. On a frigid day in February 1940 Randolph accepted the challenge and set about training for a month. At the very least, the new routine would stave off his ennui, and he had the promise of £50, which he told Pamela would pay off his mounting debts. "In fact, it wouldn't have paid off a tenth of them," Pamela said later.

Randolph threw himself into his training, showing how focused and disciplined he could be when he applied himself. "I'm sure you will approve," wrote Pamela to "my dear Papa" Churchill, describing Randolph's regimen. Every day he took long brisk hikes, and he spent his Saturdays and Sundays walking and riding a bicycle to build up his endurance. He ate special food and toughened his feet by rubbing them with methylated spirits. On the appointed day, Randolph kept a fast pace during the fifty-four miles to York, where he rested for three hours at a hotel near the railroad station.

He awoke at 2:00 A.M. for the return trip. Pamela followed in her car, with strict instructions to honk the horn whenever his stride fell below four miles per hour or accelerated beyond six miles per hour. The pain in his feet became excruciating, prompting Randolph to remove his boots and walk in his socks. Still in agony, he tried to pad his socks with cotton wool, which proved useless when his feet got wet. Pride and willpower kept Randolph going, and he arrived at camp twenty minutes under the time limit. But instead of cheering, recalled Pamela, "the young officers greeted him with hoots of derisive laughter. They were furious he had succeeded and determined not to pay. . . . They never paid a single penny."

Because of Randolph's father, the couple managed to escape the confines of army life on a fairly regular basis. They visited Pamela's parents in Dorset, and Pamela showed up with her sister Sheila at the Newbury races. Sheila was dressed in her ATS uniform, and Pamela wore thick-soled shoes and an unflattering coat of black and white fur. In early January 1940, Randolph accompanied Churchill to France for an inspection of military installations and a tour of the Maginot Line. A month later Randolph and Pamela went to the coastal town of Leith in Scotland to greet the British destroyer *Cossack*. On direct orders from Churchill, the ship had overpowered a German supply vessel, the *Altmark,* freeing 299 British prisoners captured from sunken merchant ships.

It was one of the few victorious moments in those bleak months, and Pamela wrote a vivid account to her father-in-law that showed both an eye for detail and a mature sensibility. The prisoners' faces were "drawn and pinched," and she reported that some seamen had been held as long as four and a half months, subsisting only on foul-smelling black bread. She described how the British sailors had been energized by their hand-to-hand combat, and how the Germans had been so afraid they had fled by jumping through portholes. "It's comforting to know we can be ferocious," she wrote. Her words revealed that even at nineteen, she was paying close attention.

Much of her listening in those days was at the table of newspaper titan Lord Beaverbrook, who would serve as her confidant and adviser in the coming years. From the moment Randolph and Pamela were married, Beaverbrook regularly invited them to stay at his London home and at Cherkley Court, his country house near Leatherhead in Surrey. Born in Canada as William Maxwell Aitken, Beaverbrook was the son of a Presbyterian minister from a family of tenant farmers. Beaverbrook made money first in the Canadian financial markets, then emigrated to England where he won a seat in Parliament and made millions in the early years of the century out of his mass-market newspapers— the *Daily Express* and the *Evening Standard.* When he was given a peerage in 1917, Rudyard Kipling designed his coat of arms.

Beaverbrook audaciously used his newspapers as an instrument of political influence. He befriended Churchill early and became one of his closest advisers, although the two men drifted apart for periods of time. "Max was a strange and difficult man to know," wrote Churchill's daughter Sarah. Although he stood just shy of five feet nine, he seemed smaller, mostly because of his restless manner and impish face. He had what one friend called an "urchin's wink" and a wide, gloating grin. He was a man, wrote the historian A. J. P. Taylor, "of puckish illusion. He was there one moment and gone the next."

His political opinions were similarly evanescent. A member of the Conservative Party, he championed politicians on the far left and took numerous contrary positions, including support for Soviet Russia. Those who knew him best, wrote his biographers Anne Chisholm and Michael Davie, "chose not to regard his somewhat oversimplified general political views as of prime significance; they were fads, or prejudices, part of his nature, like hypochondria." But Beaverbrook took his views seriously enough to push them onto the pages of his newspapers. "Max, the old horror," said Sarah Norton, whose mother Jean had a longstanding affair with Beaverbrook. "He was an awful old ogre, threatening, bullying. If you worked for him and wrote something he didn't like and you said you believed it, he would say 'You're out.' "

Not surprisingly, he was widely mistrusted. As secretive as he was expansive, he was adept at playing both ends against the middle. His enemies thought he was an evil, behind-the-scenes manipulator who relished pulling strings just for the sake of the game, and who bought friendships with his largess. "The minister of midnight," he was called for his labyrinthine plots. Clementine Churchill considered him such a bad influence on her husband that she was once moved to write Winston, "My darling—Try ridding yourself of this microbe which some people fear is in your blood—exorcise this bottle imp and see if the air is not clearer and purer."

The source of Beaverbrook's magnetism was his intensity and high energy. He had a quick mind and formidable memory, and he was a mesmerizing storyteller. He used his insatiable curiosity to build his newspapers and insinuate himself with many powerful people. "Of course at heart I'm just an old concierge," he once told Randolph Churchill. "I like to know what's going on."

Beaverbrook rarely dined at the homes of his friends (Winston Churchill being a major exception), and avoided going to parties, banquets, and restaurants. Night after night he gathered the socially prominent and politically influential in his dining room to pick their brains, trade gossip, and instigate fierce arguments. While not an active participant, Winston Churchill's daughter-in-law was an important new member of the audience in the winter of 1939–40. From time to time she came alone to Beaverbrook's house, but more often she was in the company of Randolph. After the bleak dales of Yorkshire, the excitement of Beaverbrook's stimulating presence offered a welcome change. The regular entourage included Churchill's aide, Brendan Bracken, an indelible character with thick glasses and wild red hair; Beaverbrook's pretty blue-eyed mistress, Jean Norton; and court jester Valentine Castelrosse. There was a changing cast of Beaverbrook's reporters and editors, and visitors such as the American photographer Margaret Bourke-White.

Beaverbrook occupied a peculiar position during those months. Not only had he opposed declaring war on Germany, he continued to advocate appeasement and even urged a negotiated peace—views that put him at odds with Churchill. Always the mischief maker, Beaverbrook sought to exploit his differences with Randolph for the sake of entertaining his guests. "Randolph was defending his father, particularly against the Munichite ministers," recalled Michael Foot, then a left-wing writer for the Beaverbrook press who frequented his boss's dinners. "Quite a number of them were invited by Beaverbrook, who enjoyed seeing everyone attacking each other. It was great sport to see Randolph go after the Munichites. Beaverbrook enjoyed that. He liked to stage scenes. I had never seen such a spectacle as Randolph on the attack."

Pamela held back, avoiding involvement, assuming a decorative role while in the company of others. No longer a jolly debutante, she projected a restrained grace, a becoming contrast to her overbearing husband. Behavior that might have seemed dull in others appeared entirely laudable in Pamela. "Pamela had a very difficult time with Randolph," recalled Loelia Westminster, former wife of the Duke of Westminster. "He drank too much and was very unpopular. I remember being with them. He never stopped talking for one moment, and she never said anything. She was rather embarrassed by her new husband. I felt sorry for her." Inevitably, Pamela crossed into his line of fire. "Randolph's manners could be outrageous," said Michael Foot. "He would insult her." If Pamela even ventured a comeback, said Loelia Westminster, "he would tell her to shut up."

Michael Foot could see that underneath her demure exterior, Pamela "wasn't meek or mild. She had plenty of spirit. We used to hear that he was having rows with her, that she used to stand up for herself. Some of us thought that the marriage was not going to last." Beaverbrook noticed the strife between Randolph and his young bride. "If he saw Randolph going for Pamela, he would have got on her side," said Foot, who remembered that Beaverbrook was "critical of Randolph." But Beaverbrook had to tread carefully because, recalled Foot, "he was determined to be on good terms with Winston."

Pamela was also eager to maintain the esteem of Randolph's parents, so she couldn't go too far either. She continued to make a good show of being the compliant wife. In January 1940 she got pregnant, and several months later moved into Admiralty House. With Randolph off at training camp, Pamela found her place in the bosom of the Churchill family. She had learned some useful lessons at Mentmore and Leeds, but it was here that her real education began—her schooling in the ways of power and politics. Not only did she learn by observing the Churchills together and apart, she met every important person in London. "Nobody ever had the chance to see politics as much from the inside as I did," she said years later.

Although Winston and Clementine were preoccupied by the war, they included Pamela in everything from family meals to official dinners, treating her like an adopted daughter. Randolph's sisters, especially Diana and Sarah, were not amused by what they regarded as Pamela's "muscling in." "To Winston and Clementine, Pamela could do no wrong," recalled a friend of Diana and Sarah. "The sisters didn't like her. They used the words 'taken in.' " Quite consciously, Clementine tried to instruct Pamela in the ways of wifely devotion. "She told me in the early months of my marriage how when she married Winston she had decided to give her life totally to him," Pamela recalled. "He had a lot of bachelor dinners, and she probably stayed at home and ate on a tray three or four nights a week. She lived for Winston. And she was very good for him because she was the one person who could reprimand him and who could say to him things which other people wouldn't or shouldn't. . . . They always wrote to each other, once or twice a day, and if she thought he'd been at a dinner table she did not approve of, she would write him a little note and make him aware of it."

The same sort of thorough devotion would become one of Pamela's hallmarks—but not with Randolph. Rather, she transferred her attentions to her father-in-law. Churchill could be easily impressed by the solicitude of a fetching young woman. "Churchill was very fond of Pam, but he wasn't spontaneous in showing his emotions," said one woman who observed Winston and Pamela together. Lady Mary Dunn was convinced that "he adored Pam. When Philip and I had lunch with Winston, he would talk about her. 'Aren't I lucky to have such a pretty daughter-in-law?' he would say. I would say, 'Yes indeed, anyone would be.' But he never talked about her in depth."

Sometimes Pamela served as Churchill's hostess or played cards with him —their bezique games could run as long as two hours—but mostly she was a rapt listener, laughing at his jokes and marveling at his stories. "Winston was fascinating as a talker," said Diana Mosley. "He had so much to talk about. He knew the first half of twentieth-century politics in a way no one else did, from the inside."

With Churchill, Pamela perfected the light flirtation that she used to beguile older men. When she was given a white Pekinese puppy, she yielded to Winston's insistence that she call it Alexander, for Alexander the Great. She was intrigued by his fascination with Lady Hamilton, the disgraced mistress of Lord Nelson. Emma Hart had risen from courtesan to respectable nobility by marrying Sir William Hamilton, only to shock London society by her flagrant affair with England's greatest naval hero.

Alexander Korda gave Churchill a copy of *That Hamilton Woman*, his film about the tragic Hamilton-Nelson love story, starring Laurence Olivier and Vivien Leigh. Churchill watched it seventeen times. On three of those occasions, Pamela sat at his side for a midnight showing. The film was highly melodramatic, but laced with some discomfiting insights—such as Lady Nelson's sharp rebuke to her husband about Emma: "Find a public hero, and there you will find as sure as fate a woman parasite. Don't you realize all she wants is to flutter about in your glory, to use you for her own ambition and conceit?" But Churchill was mesmerized by the film's overt patriotism—a speech about Napoleon was said to have been written by Churchill—and the lushness of the production. "He just thought it was so beautiful," Pamela recalled. "He was very romantic. He loved beautiful things. He was a very gentle man underneath."

Pamela developed a strong emotional bond with her father-in-law. When he was depressed, he occasionally sought her comfort: "He would come in to meals and sometimes he put his head in his hands and hardly ate and then he would suddenly say, 'this is one of the hardest times.' " At such moments, Pamela was a soothing presence. "He set the tone, and you let him ruminate like that and then suddenly he would pick himself up and he would tell a story or he would hum a tune," she recalled. There's no question that Pamela idolized

Churchill. Years later, she would rhapsodize about his ability "to make you see the world through his vision, and that was larger than life."

As winter turned to spring, London was "lovely beyond even an Englishman's belief. There were bright azaleas in the window-boxes of hotel and home windows, and tulips in the court of Buckingham Palace," wrote Clare Boothe Luce, who had become a correspondent for *Life* after marrying Henry Luce, founder of *Time* and *Life*. New plays and films were opening, and the city seemed almost normal. The Rely on Us taxi service ferried young men and women through the blackout to the center of London nightlife, the Café de Paris, where Snakehips Johnson and his swing band played until 3:00 A.M. "I found something strangely comforting in the placid, unruffled atmosphere," wrote the American journalist Virginia Cowles. "You felt that no matter what happened, London would always stand."

That vaguely optimistic mood vanished overnight when Hitler's armies swept into neutral Norway and Denmark on April 9. British efforts to oust the invaders proved futile. A month later, early in the morning on May 10, Germany invaded Holland, Belgium, and France. Newspaper placards throughout London heralded the news: "Brussels Bombed" . . . "Many Killed at Lyons" . . . and most ominously, "Bombs in Kent." By evening, Chamberlain had resigned and Winston Churchill was the new Prime Minister.

Randolph hastened to London from Kettering, in Yorkshire, where his unit was stationed. The next morning, when Churchill entered 10 Downing Street, he was accompanied by Randolph and Brendan Bracken. Randolph stayed in London with Pamela at Admiralty House for the next several days as London shifted into high alert. The ten-month-old phony war had ended. Food and fuel were rationed, and each citizen was compelled to carry not only a gas mask but a tin hat, ration card, identity card, and coupons for gasoline.

The atmosphere was electric at Admiralty House and Downing Street, where Churchill and his advisers met virtually nonstop. On May 13, the family assembled in Parliament to witness Churchill's first appearance as Prime Minister and hear his stirring words: "I have nothing to offer but blood, toil, tears and sweat." Churchill had appointed Lord Beaverbrook as Minister of Aircraft Production only the day before, at which point the Prime Minister's sly old friend suddenly became vehemently pro-war. "Beaverbrook is like the town tart who has finally married the mayor!" exclaimed his *Daily Express* editor Beverley Baxter. Churchill had wisely ignored Beaverbrook's unreliable political views, concentrating instead on "his power to inspire and drive . . . to get at the heart of a problem at speed," in the words of Chisholm and Davie.

In late May, one grim bulletin followed another as German armored columns advanced toward the English Channel. Once the Belgian Army capitulated, the British government began evacuating more than 200,000 British troops from Dunkirk. By June 3, the extraordinary rescue was completed, thanks to more than eight hundred civilian and military ships that crossed the Channel, and some colossal military bungling by the Germans. Randolph and Pamela were not on hand for the tense week-long drama, but they wrote to Churchill from Nottinghamshire to offer their encouragement "at this grim moment."

Their letter contained a small reminder of the domestic strains that persisted despite the high historic drama: a thank you to Churchill for bailing out Randolph yet again with £100 for clothing and other bills.

The Churchills finally moved to Downing Street in late June, taking Pamela with them. With the fall of France on June 17, Britain braced itself for a German invasion. Iron railings were removed from homes and public buildings to be melted down for guns. All churches were ordered to stop ringing their bells so they could sound the alarm when the attack came. One of Pamela's favorite Churchill stories, recounted many times in public and private (and always in her uncannily sonorous mock-Churchill voice), concerned a stern warning the Prime Minister gave his wife and daughter-in-law about preparing themselves to battle Nazis in the streets. "What can we do without arms?" Pamela asked. "You can each take a dead German with you," said Churchill. "But papa, I don't know how to shoot a gun, I haven't got a gun," Pamela replied. With a severe look, Churchill growled, "Well you can go into the kitchen and get a carving knife."

Most weekends Pamela went either to Cherkley or to the official country home of the Prime Minister, Chequers, in Buckinghamshire. She tried to keep fit by taking long walks with Clementine and various guests. When Randolph turned up, he invariably disrupted the weekend. On one such Saturday at the end of June, Randolph abused his father during a dinner party at Chequers with a tirade against "complacency in high places." Pamela, as usual, stayed in the background. John Colville, Churchill's private secretary, viewed Randolph as "coarse and aggressive." But when Randolph asked his father to help him get on active duty, Churchill told the group that if his son died, "I wouldn't be able to carry on with my work."

In mid-August, the Battle of Britain began. The airborne combat raged for several weeks over southeastern England. By the last days of August, the Luftwaffe was sending six hundred planes a day, straining the RAF nearly to the breaking point. Yet at that moment when victory seemed within Germany's grasp, Hitler made the miscalculation that eventually would change the course of the war: He stopped attacking military targets and began bombing population centers, in hopes of demoralizing the British people.

The air-raid sirens sounded the alert at all hours, from early morning to late at night, while bombs dropped on tiny row houses in London's East End as well as the grounds of Buckingham Palace. Government buildings were fortified with heaps of sandbags and barbed-wire barricades. On Saturday, September 7, waves of German bombers struck London in earnest. It was the beginning of the Blitz, the savage bombing campaign against Britain's major cities that would continue for 57 nights, killing more than 1,000 citizens a week.

Underneath 10 Downing Street, the wine cellar was converted to a bomb shelter. It was there that the Churchill family sought safety until they could move to the No. 10 Annexe, a suite of ground-level rooms in the Board of Trade Building that were reinforced by steel girders and shutters. In the early days of the Blitz, Pamela and Clementine slept in the wine cellar, Clementine in a single bed at one end, and Pamela on the bottom bunk of a double-decker bed at the other. The top bunk was reserved for the Prime Minister.

In her reminiscences Pamela always left the impression that she and the Churchills made a cozy trio in their bunker throughout the Blitz. She often told the story about her nightly routine of falling asleep until 1:00 A.M., only to be interrupted by the arrival of Churchill. For the rest of the night she would be kept awake by his snoring and the kicking of her unborn child, nicknamed "baby dumpling." "She had a joke during the Blitz," said William Walton, "when she and Winston had to spend so much time in the shelter's bunk beds. She would laugh and say, 'I have one Churchill on top of me and one inside me.' "

But according to Churchill's official biographer, Martin Gilbert, "He is known to have gone underground to sleep on only three nights." One of Churchill's friends, Sir Archibald Sinclair, was so alarmed by the Prime Minister's carelessness about his personal safety that he wrote in mid-September, "One thing that worries me these days—that you stay at Downing Street without a proper shelter. . . . You insist on us living in basements and refuse to do it yourself!"

Each morning, Londoners picked their way through the rubble and peered at the huge craters in the streets. John Lewis's department store burned to the ground, and many other London landmarks sustained damage, among them the Tower of London, the British Museum, and the Tate Gallery. But the fortitude of Londoners was remarkable. "The shops were full, old ladies sunned themselves in the park, and soldiers and their girlfriends strolled down Piccadilly arm in arm," wrote Virginia Cowles. "I lunched at the Berkeley restaurant and found it as noisy and crowded as ever." When the United Service Club was hit by a bomb early one evening, members in dinner clothes stood transfixed as they saw through the smoke a naval captain standing at attention, a glass of port in his hand. "Thank God that did not spill!" he exclaimed.

On the day the Blitz began, Pamela went to Blenheim for the christening of the second son of the Duke of Marlborough, Winston Churchill's cousin. The child was named Winston, and Clementine Churchill stood as the proud godmother. "There was champagne and tenantry on the lawns, and nannies and cousins and healths drunk, all to the deafening accompaniment of aeroplanes skirmishing, diving, looping and spinning in the clear air," wrote Diana Cooper afterward.

While Pamela seemed coolly confident, she was distraught that the Marlboroughs had appropriated the name she planned to give to her unborn baby. On her return to Chequers she went weeping to Churchill, begging him to use his influence to have the name changed. Churchill, who fancied the idea of having a namesake grandson at a crucial moment in his nation's history, called Mary Marlborough. "But how do you know Pamela's will be a boy?" she asked. "But of course it will be," replied the Prime Minister. "And if it isn't there'll be others." "But we've already registered it as Winston," she insisted. "Then you'll have to change it." She did, to Charles Spencer-Churchill.

Winston and Clementine Churchill moved into the Annexe on September 16 and packed Pamela off to Chequers to await the birth of her baby. That same month, at age twenty-nine, Randolph unexpectedly had a chance to fulfill the political ambitions that had been denied him three times. When the Conservative member for the Preston district in Lancashire died, the party leaders there asked him to be their candidate. Because of a wartime truce, there were no elections for vacant seats, so Randolph automatically entered Parliament. It was a case of blatant nepotism, but Randolph was not the least abashed, announcing that he "hoped that at Preston he had found a political home for all time."

Randolph took his seat in the House of Commons on October 8. He wore his lieutenant's uniform, and his father and David Margesson introduced him at the Bar of the House. But as had happened at his wedding, the cheers and applause that rang throughout the chamber were not for Randolph but for his father. Sitting in the gallery were Clementine and Pamela, smiling their approval, and next to Pamela was a large box of laughing gas in the event she went into labor. Pamela had made the journey to London that day with the grudging approval of her doctor. She was a week overdue, and she was going stir crazy.

The friction between Randolph and Pamela seemed to intensify during her pregnancy. When the family was still living at 10 Downing Street, Randolph had infuriated them by staying out all night carousing at the Savoy. He had piled up even more gambling debts at his training camp, and this time Pamela pleaded with Churchill for financial help. Upon hearing that she had interceded, Randolph accused her of siding with his parents against him. But before returning to his regiment, he once again promised to reform.

Yet according to Pamela, when she went into labor after midnight on October 10, Randolph was in bed with the wife of singer Richard Tauber in London, and he arrived at Chequers only after Pamela gave birth at 4:40 A.M. As she came out of her anesthesia, the nurse said, "I've told you five times already, 'It's a boy.' " When Churchill saw his new grandson, he kissed the child and exclaimed, "What sort of a world are you being born into?" The boy was named Winston Spencer Churchill. The luck of biology—enhanced by her tearful persuasiveness after the Marlborough christening—had secured Pamela a special standing with the great Prime Minister.

The following weekend, friends, relatives, and colleagues streamed through Chequers, including Lady Digby, who came to Sunday lunch. The days were so warm and bright that it seemed like midsummer. The Prime Minister, wearing his famous siren suit, smoked an immense cigar and declaimed on the zeal of the English people to join the front lines. Little Winston lay crying in a pram by the front door, while Pamela received well-wishers in her bed upstairs. "Pam looked exceedingly pretty, with her red hair on the white linen," recalled Alastair Forbes, one of the visitors during the weekend. The glow of fatherhood did nothing to diminish Randolph's bile, however. He held forth at lunch and dinner on a variety of topics, including his admiration for the Germans' ambition to dominate the world. "Randolph is a most unattractive combination of the bombastic, the cantankerous and the unwise," noted John Colville afterward.

That month, Pamela leased a house north of London, near Hitchin in Hertfordshire, for a "peppercorn rent," an amazingly modest £52 a year. It was a Queen Anne rectory called Ickleford House, small but charming, with white-paneled walls. Her attempt to make a cozy nest there represented her most ambitious effort to salvage her marriage. "Oh! Randy," she wrote to her husband, "everything would be so nice, if only you were with us all the time. . . . Soon, so soon now, I shall be settled in a home of my own, our home— yours & mine & baby Winston's. Isn't it rather thrilling—our own family life —no more living in other people's houses."

But Randolph was hardly ready for domestic tranquility, with time out for tea with his inherited constituency on weekends. Standing at White's bar one day, he learned that Colonel Robert Laycock was forming a new commando operation for duty in the Middle East. Randolph immediately asked his Fourth Hussars commanding officer for a transfer. To Randolph's astonishment, not only did the commander agree, he told him that his fellow officers were tired of his ill-mannered behavior and would be delighted to see him leave. "Randolph, who had thought he was well regarded, burst into tears," wrote his cousin Anita Leslie.

In early November, Randolph joined the commando training camp at Largs, on the west coast of Scotland, while Pamela moved to Hitchin. To save money, she invited Randolph's sister Diana, the wife of Conservative MP Duncan Sandys, to bring her two children and share the house. Nanny Hall was summoned from Dorset to care for Winston and his cousins, freeing Pamela to volunteer for war work. She threw her energies into a communal kitchen that fed two hundred to three hundred workers from nearby factories

At first, life as a "working" mother was an adventure. Cecil Beaton, visiting Pamela shortly after she moved in, found her "radiant and triumphant . . . with Raeburnesque red curls and freckles." Beaton was there to photograph baby Winston and his mother for *Life* magazine. "For two days we photographed the brat in varying lights and moods," Beaton later wrote. "After lunch he was calm, after a bath sleepy, before lunch he would be restless and cry a lot. Pamela held him to her breast and Diana held the flashlight. . . . The weekend was a success and we laughed enormously."

Only three weeks following Winston's birth, Pamela visited the Marine Hotel in Largs, Scotland, where Randolph was staying with some officers from his commando brigade. It was a picturesque spot, a "smug, substantial modern pleasure resort," wrote Evelyn Waugh, surrounded by hills and overlooking the island of Arran. Randolph and his friends, including Waugh, were known as the "smart set," or the "dandies," as opposed to the professional soldiers under their command, who stayed elsewhere. Typically, Randolph didn't stint on his personal comfort; in his first two weeks he ran up a bill of £54 at the hotel— more than the yearly rent on Ickleford House. When presented with the charges, he picked a fight with the manager that lasted several hours.

Pamela made a good impression on Randolph's raffish cohorts during her stay. "Mrs. Randolph has freckles and a very friendly disposition," Waugh wrote to his wife Laura. He perceived a more important quality as well, which he noted in a later letter to his wife: "If you are ever in any anxiety about our welfare, do not hesitate to apply to Pamela for information, of which, in the nature of things, she has great superiority."

Randolph was in a swaggering mood during his wife's visit, according to his cousin Anita Leslie, and "perhaps to arouse Pamela's admiration," accepted another bet based on physical endurance—this time to swim through the icy water to the island off the coastline. Fortunately, Colonel Laycock prevented Randolph from accepting the challenge. Pamela was unimpressed by her husband and his wastrel friends. She felt contemptuous that they couldn't even make it through a routine nighttime landing exercise, later explaining to her son that "they gave up the water expeditions and started up the mountains. When they got to the other side of the mountains they of course didn't know what they were supposed to do next—how those poor soldiers stood for it!"

Back in Hitchin, Pamela's life had settled into a dreary routine. She spent her days at the communal kitchen, and went to bed at six-thirty so she could turn off the gas heat and conserve what little fuel she had. Randolph kept up his extravagant ways in Scotland, drinking heavily, gambling at cards, and taking excursions to Glasgow for expensive dinners. The only breaks in the pattern of Pamela and Randolph's parallel lives were various family events that drew them together that winter.

When Randolph made his maiden speech in the House of Commons in late November, Pamela perched in the gallery with Clementine and Mary, the youngest Churchill daughter. Winston was on the front bench, his back turned to his son, he later said, to avoid a display of emotion that might embarrass Randolph. A week later, baby Winston was christened at the parish church of Ellesborough in Buckinghamshire, with a reception afterward at Chequers. Max Beaverbrook, Brendan Bracken, and Perry Brownlow were the godfathers, and Virginia Cowles, a friend of Randolph's since their days covering the Spanish Civil War, was godmother. "I had always heard that the PM's emotions were easily stirred and that at times he could be as sentimental as a woman," Cowles later wrote. "On this occasion I had proof of it, for he sat throughout the ceremony with tears streaming down his cheeks."

The entire Churchill clan gathered at Chequers that Christmas. Churchill worked through the morning, then joined his family for an afternoon uninterrupted by any intrusion of wartime troubles. Following lunch, and again after dinner, Sarah Churchill's husband, the comedian Vic Oliver, played the piano while Sarah and her father sang. For one day, the fractious Churchills put their differences aside and savored a moment that would never be repeated: all four children, with spouses and grandchildren, together as a family, taking pleasure from each other's company. Eighteen-year-old Mary Churchill described the day in her diary as "one of the happiest Christmases I can remember . . . I have never seen the family look so happy or so united."

Randolph had been in the final stages of his training on the Scottish island of Arran. No sooner had he returned after Christmas than he was sent home on a two-week leave before the Eighth Commandos were to ship out for the Middle East. His wife, in the meantime, had become something of a celebrity on her own. The January 27, 1941, issue of *Life* magazine featured on its cover an eye-catching photograph of Pamela and baby Winston, shot by Cecil Beaton. Following the birth of her son she had lost weight, and she had become a beauty. Her hair slightly tousled, the gray streak near her part a gleaming wisp, her eyes heavy-lidded, her mouth pouty, her image seemed come-hither instead of beatifically maternal. An even more suggestive pose, with a plunging V-neckline exposing part of her right breast, had appeared several weeks earlier in *The Sketch*.

Inside *Life* magazine, there was another full-page photograph of her, facing a portrait of Clementine, while the other Churchill children were relegated to a gallery on the following pages. "Pretty Pamela is Randolph's Wife," said the caption on Pamela's picture, in which she was posed leaning against a yellow marble column in the main reception room at No. 10 Downing Street. She wore a striped dress with a white lace collar, and although her figure was newly svelte, she still had an ample bosom. Her skirt brushed the middle of her kneecaps, displaying slender legs. Winston Churchill, for one, was captivated by the pictures. President Roosevelt's personal representative, Harry Hopkins, writing his first impressions after meeting Churchill in London that month, noted that the Prime Minister "showed me with obvious pride the photographs of his beautiful daughter-in-law and grandchild."

Before Randolph left England on February 1, he pledged to be on his best behavior. "It's going to be terrible, being parted like this," Pamela recalled him saying. "With you living very economically and I living off my Army pay we will at least be able to pay off some of the bills, and that will be glorious." But from the moment Randolph boarded the *Glenroy* for its journey to Cairo by way of South Africa, he lapsed into a nightly orgy of gambling—poker, chemin-de-fer, roulette—for high stakes. Evelyn Waugh watched in horror from his "little poker game with the poor" as Randolph went down as much as £400 a night. By the time they reached Egypt, Randolph's accumulated loss was £3,000— about $125,000 today. "Poor Pamela will have to go to work," Waugh lamented to his wife.

Randolph immediately sent a telegram and letter to Pamela asking her to make good on his debts "in the best way possible," setting up a payment schedule of "perhaps 10 pounds a month" to each of his creditors on an attached list. He insisted that she not tell his father his predicament, a step she couldn't have brought herself to take again. Nor could she go to her parents, who lacked the ready cash to help in any case. She wrote back what Randolph's biographer Brian Roberts described as "a very tart letter . . . deploring his gambling extravagances."

Weeping and desperate, she turned to the one man she could trust, who was already deeply involved in Churchill finances: Max Beaverbrook. She asked for an advance on Randolph's *Evening Standard* salary of £1,500 a year, which Beaverbrook had earlier resumed paying in full. Beaverbrook insisted on giving her the sum instead, a gesture that Pamela later said she rebuffed. Her stated reason was not wanting Beaverbrook to own her, which seemed odd, given the degree to which she would allow him to insinuate himself into her life in the coming months. Other authoritative sources said that Pamela did indeed take Beaverbrook's check—the first of many substantial gifts she would accept from protective men, none of which she would admit to receiving. Even Beaverbrook's gift wasn't sufficient to cover everything, so Pamela took the painful steps of selling some wedding presents, among them diamond earrings and several bracelets. "It was a lesson," she said years later. "I suddenly realized that if there was to be any security for baby Winston and me, it was going to be on our own."

The marriage was over at that moment, Pamela later told her son Winston, who called his father's letter "the bombshell which was to shatter their marriage." Yet the relationship never really had a chance. Had Randolph and Pamela genuinely fallen in love, their marriage might have succeeded. But their decision to marry was as cold and premeditated as a business deal: He wanted an heir, and she wanted a name and position.

"I'd have liked to have been able to help Randolph," Pamela said years later. "He needed help, but I just couldn't give it. Had I been more mature, I might have managed more, but I was always up against the drinking, and just couldn't take it. . . . There was really no future in the marriage. It was far too insecure and difficult, and I simply couldn't cope."

The marriage may have been unhappy, but it was a tremendously valuable experience for Pamela. "She met a lot of people she wouldn't have met, especially Americans," said Alan Hare, a friend of Randolph and former editor of the *Financial Times*. "Randolph relished the American attitude toward life: the quickness, the willingness to discuss issues and the general exuberance. She also learned to cope with the most difficult of men. But he was very intelligent, and he had a wide-ranging curiosity and knowledge so he broadened her. He brought her out in the best possible way."

Eight

AS SHE WOULD DO throughout her life, Pamela turned adversity into opportunity. Eager to abandon her tiresome existence in Hitchin, she rented out the Ickleford rectory for three times what she had been paying, accepted an invitation from Beaverbrook to have baby Winston stay at Cherkley, secured a twelve-pound-a-week job at the Ministry of Supply, and headed for London, in part, her son later said, "so that my Churchill grandparents would not know what had happened."

By early March 1941 she was living in a room at the Dorchester Hotel overlooking Hyde Park. A new round of air attacks was unsettling London. Londoners were shocked by the devastation, which included a huge area around St. Paul's Cathedral, and the growing number of deaths, among them band-leader Snakehips Johnson and more than eighty revelers at the Café de Paris—victims of a direct hit late one night in the middle of the song "Oh Johnny." The young girls who survived tore apart their slips and evening dresses to make bandages for the wounded. "The capital looks like a battered old war horse," Chips Channon wrote. "All the big houses overlooking the park . . . all badly battered . . . . the rubble and debris are heaped high in the streets."

At the Ritz, the sister of King Zog of Albania camped out near the door to the hotel restaurant. At Claridges, residents dragged mattresses and pillows into the lobby each night to make their beds in every available space. Dowagers unable to sleep could be seen sitting in their robes and knitting while dance bands played in the nearby ballroom. "From the general merriment you might have thought an enjoyable (if somewhat odd) costume party was going on," wrote Virginia Cowles.

The Dorchester was thought to be the safest haven in the city because it was made of modern steel and concrete. "That gilded refuge of the rich," in the words of London hostess Ann Fleming, had become home to such fashionable figures as Lady Diana Cooper and Somerset Maugham, along with dozens of government officials and diplomats. "What a mixed brew we were," noted Cecil Beaton after a night in the Dorchester lobby among "cabinet ministers and their self-consciously respectable wives; hatchet jawed, iron grey brigadiers, calf-like airmen off duty, tarts on duty, actresses, déclassé society people, cheap musicians, and motor car agents. It could not be more ugly and vile." In the packed dining room, patrons consumed magnums of champagne and unseemly amounts of food, prompting Chips Channon to call it a "modern wartime Babylon." But even the wailing saxophones of the band couldn't drown out the din of bombs and antiaircraft fire.

For someone as financially strapped as Pamela, the Dorchester might have seemed extravagant, but she made do with the rent money from the rectory and with Beaverbrook's help. The room cost six pounds a week, and because of wartime restrictions, restaurants were permitted to charge only five shillings for a three-course dinner (oysters and other rare tidbits cost extra). While ordinary citizens struggled with ration coupons to fill their larders, the kitchens at the Dorchester, the Ritz, and fashionable restaurants such as Mirabelle on Mayfair's Curzon Street were well stocked with strawberries and smoked salmon.

In her post-debutante year, Pamela had tasted a liberty that ended with her marriage and pregnancy. Now, in the uninhibited atmosphere of wartime London, she threw herself into the social whirl. At the Dorchester, there were almost nightly dinner parties in private suites, presided over by such legendary hostesses as Sibyl Colefax, who charged her guests ten shillings apiece for the pleasure of her company. On weekends Pamela continued to alternate between Cherkley and Chequers, where she presided over tea in the great hall and hobnobbed with General de Gaulle and the Australian Prime Minister, Sir Robert Gordon Menzies, listening intently to war plans and analyses of the German character.

For a woman longing for experience and adventure, Pamela had the best of all possible circumstances: the great door opener of the Churchill name without the encumbrances of her argumentative husband or infant son. "It was the most exciting time in my entire life," she once said. "You never knew from one day to the next what was going to happen." She recalled the time she took a train into London one morning and was bombed twice during the trip. "I was shoved under the seat . . . and then somebody else fell on me. All the glass fell in and we were delayed four hours. Then I went straight to the office where I found a message that Baby Winston had very bad bronchitis, and I should come home immediately. There was no sort of differentiation between a child having an asthmatic attack and you being attacked by the Germans."

Even by the upper-class standards of the time, Pamela's attitude toward her infant bordered on indifference. Baby Winston was certainly safer in the care of the ever devoted Nanny Hall at Cherkley, but Pamela was only too willing to park him there. "My sister has never been maternal," Sheila Digby once said. Pamela's chill manner couldn't be justified by her own mother's aloofness. After all, Lady Digby had invested much of herself in Pamela, and Sheila was warm and down-to-earth. But Pamela was mainly concerned with furthering her social ambitions.

It seemed fitting that the man who walked into Pamela's life in the spring of 1941 was every bit as self-absorbed as she—and as fascinated by political power. William Averell Harriman lacked her aristocratic lineage, but his family was enormously rich, and he could meet any British peer on equal ground.

His father was the famous nineteenth-century financier Edward Henry (E.H.) Harriman, a self-made man who was branded one of the "malefactors of great wealth" and an "enemy of the republic" by President Theodore Roosevelt. Forced by his father's pinched circumstances to drop out of Manhattan's Trinity School at age fourteen, E.H. supported his family with a succession of jobs on Wall Street. As a trader he proved as bold as he was brilliant. His preternatural financial cunning brought him a small fortune, earning the respect of influential Wall Street wizards. Bernard Baruch called him "one of the best speculators I ever dealt with."

After his firstborn son Harry died in a diphtheria epidemic, E.H. gave up finance and took control of the bankrupt Union Pacific Railroad. In less than a decade, he turned it into one of the nation's best transportation systems, amassing a fortune in the tens of millions. Known as the "little giant" of Wall Street, E.H. stood less than five feet six inches, had a long and bushy mustache, and soft brown eyes that belied his hard-driving and competitive nature. "He was secretive, ruthless, manipulative, relentless," wrote Averell Harriman's biographer Rudy Abramson. In his book about the Robber Barons, Matthew Josephson concluded that E.H. "lacked the pangs of scruple and conscience."

E.H.'s wife, Mary Averell, was, by contrast, the very proper daughter of a New York banker. She was taller than her husband, stern and rigid in her manner. Except among those closest to her, she always called her husband "Mr. Harriman." With grim determination, she devoted herself to her husband and five remaining children. Averell, born in November 1891, was the second youngest, squeezed between three older sisters and a younger brother, Roland.

Averell grew up in an atmosphere of enormous privilege and oppressive solemnity. The Harrimans shuttled between a large house on Fifth Avenue and a 20,000-acre estate in the Ramapo Mountains north of New York City. Their "cottage" was a forbidding hundred-room stone castle called Arden. Although E.H. was often away on business, he kept his son under tight control. "In everything he did, he took command," Averell said years later. "Even if we went for a walk, he'd tell us where he wanted to go. He knew what he wanted to do." His relationship with Averell was a "never-ending lesson in discipline, striving and self improvement . . . sermonizing on the responsibilities of wealth . . . pressure . . . to ride properly, speak properly, achieve, do better," wrote Abramson. To that end, E.H. spared no expense. He even hired the legendary Syracuse University crew coach, Jim Ten Eyck, to come to Arden and teach Averell and Roland how to row.

"Averell's tougher than most of us. He was brought up to live such a Spartan life," Pamela once said. "It was work, then play—which meant strenuous sport—then back to work again." A diary he kept at age twelve was achingly spare: "meeting with papa at 12; ice skating; meeting with mama." "He had the dreariest life," said Nancy Whitney Lutz, the daughter of Averell's second wife, Marie. "He had no fun. He was a child who never learned to express himself. He had very Victorian parents. There was little love and laughter and warmth in that house. It was rather dour."

Both E.H. and Mary professed disdain for the frivolity of society, opting to keep to themselves rather than make the circuit of balls and formal dinner parties. Yet to some extent, their gravity was a reaction to their secondary social position. The Harrimans were never accepted by America's "old" families, who looked down on E.H. for his swashbuckling style and new money.

The couple clearly harbored grand ambitions for their children. When Averell was born, E.H. registered him at Groton, the select Massachusetts boarding school where wealthy young bluebloods were encouraged to go into government in order to serve the less advantaged. Between the rigid code of Groton's headmaster, the Reverend Endicott Peabody, and the constant exhortations of E.H., young Averell was relentlessly driven to "be something and somebody." While eager to please, Averell never distinguished himself in his studies, and he developed a persistent stammer that one of his masters attributed to E.H.'s domineering ways. Averell also endured the public spectacle of his father being investigated for stock manipulation and charged with financial improprieties by no less than the President of the United States and the Interstate Commerce Commission.

Just before Averell entered Yale University in 1909, E.H. died of cancer. He was sixty-one, and left an estate of $70 million (equal to $1 billion today). The old man entrusted his business to experienced lieutenants, but it was clear that Averell was expected to expand the family fortune—and, most important, to remove the blot on the family name left by the securities investigations. Groton and Yale were bridges to the Protestant power elite. By the time Averell graduated from Yale, he had acquired a mid-Atlantic patrician accent along with the arrogant confidence of old money.

In later years, Harriman said that his father repeatedly told him that "men should use their capital for the development of the country, for the good of the country, or they'll take it away from you." Yet as a young man, Harriman set out to make his mark as a financial entrepreneur in the E.H. mold. But his effort to build a steamship empire failed, losing millions invested by his mother as well as by classmates from Groton and Yale. A subsequent venture in Soviet manganese mines was another spectacular flop, as was his attempt to found an airline with money from such gold-plated names as Rockefeller, Lehman, Vanderbilt, and Whitney.

After bailing out of aviation, he became chairman of the Union Pacific, by then in decline. Harriman ordered a top-to-bottom modernization, including sleek new passenger cars—"streamliners"—that caught the public imagination. Improving Union Pacific service became a "consuming personal mission," wrote Abramson. In contrast to his superficial approach to mining, shipping, and aviation, Harriman "fussed . . . like a professional housekeeper." Immersing himself in the nuts and bolts of the business paid off in higher revenues and led to his biggest success. Eager to exploit tourism as a source of income for the railroad, he developed the Sun Valley ski resort in Idaho, which brought Alpine skiing to the United States and became a mecca for socialites and Hollywood celebrities.

By the time he returned to the Union Pacific, Harriman had systematically mastered the games that conferred prestige in his social circle—rowing, bridge, bezique, backgammon, bowling, croquet, skiing (with lessons at Saks Fifth Avenue, no less), sulky driving, riding to hounds, and polo, which became his passion. For a time he was the fourth-ranked American player. Even with such legends as Tommy Hitchcock, Harriman held his own. In polo, as in his other endeavors, it was more earnest diligence than innate talent that got results.

With his rather somber manner and emotional inhibitions, Harriman seemed an unlikely Casanova. But by the age of thirty-seven he was in his second marriage, and he had been embroiled in at least one scandalous love affair. His first wife was Kitty Lanier Lawrance, dark and pretty and a favorite of Averell's mother. During Harriman's dutiful courtship, the pair were riding one day on Manhattan's West Side when a passing train frightened Kitty's horse, which fell on her and broke her pelvis. Stricken with guilt, Averell proposed soon afterward, and they were married quietly in September 1915. He was twenty-three.

Although they came from the same social milieu, they were otherwise incompatible. Kitty Lawrance had a fragile physique, made more so after the birth of two daughters eleven months apart in 1917. The following year, when she contracted tuberculosis, the couple began spending long stretches of time apart. While she rested in the country, Harriman found his pleasures in the city with an array of women that included a "notoriously promiscuous" Russian émigré named Katia Krassin. Harriman's most famous lover was nightclub singer Teddy Gerard. He indiscreetly took her along on trips to Europe and set her up in an apartment in Greenwich Village. There were suggestions as well that he was involved with the actress Lillian Gish after he invested $400,000 in her film studio. By 1929, Harriman and Kitty were divorced.

In 1928 Harriman had fallen for Marie Norton Whitney, wife of Cornelius Vanderbilt "Sonny" Whitney, one of New York society's incorrigible playboys. She was a great beauty, with a stunning figure, dark wavy hair, a shapely mouth, and cornflower blue eyes. Marie was unpretentious—she cut her hair with a nail scissors—irreverent, fun-loving, profane, and much beloved by a wide circle of friends. Although she studied at the proper Miss Spence's School, she loved to lapse into mock-Brooklynese as she made caustic asides in a husky voice. An incessant gum chewer and chain smoker who could reel off baseball statistics, she had a discerning eye for modern art and a flair for design that she turned into an interior decorating business. Yet behind her evident versatility and tough-dame demeanor, she was shy and unsure of herself. "It came from her upbringing," said her daughter Nancy. "Her family never had much money, and her mother was a terrible snob who sent her children to the best schools although they couldn't afford it."

Her life with Whitney had already unraveled by the time she caught Harriman's eye. Sonny Whitney was the great love of her life, but he was irresponsible and rampantly unfaithful. With two young children to care for—Nancy and a son named Harry—"she felt she ought to get out before he threw her out," recalled Nancy. "To Mummy, Ave represented stability. She was attracted to him and admired him. I'm not sure she was mad about him. But in her mind he would be successful and dependable. He was very attractive, and he brought security and money. She wasn't the least bit acquisitive, but she liked the idea of money for safety."

Precious little in Harriman's personality inspired endearment. He was all business, even in his closest relationships, and he had an extraordinarily abrupt way of speaking. He was impatient, often irascible, frequently changing the subject when it displeased him, or numbing his interlocutor with endless questions until he got to the bottom of a problem. Small talk irritated him, and he had no sense of humor, especially about himself.

Notoriously tightfisted, he rarely carried cash in his pocket and usually let others pick up the tab. Yet he was neither snobbish nor prejudiced. His father "always went to the best authorities," and Averell had the same instinct for gravitating to people of the highest ability, regardless of their origins. Harriman admired Marie with that same sort of impartiality, overlooking a background— her mother was Jewish—that raised eyebrows among the old-WASP crowd.

Harriman and Marie Norton Whitney were married in February 1930. She was twenty-six, and he was thirty-eight. Almost immediately, she brightened his image of aloof formality. She drew him into the world of her literary and artistic friends, including George S. Kaufman, Robert Sherwood, Alexander Woollcott, and Heywood Broun. The Harrimans hosted legendary Thanksgiving weekend parties, filling the gloom of Arden with boisterous laughter and marathon games of croquet, bowling, and indoor badminton. In an atmosphere where quips flew faster than shuttlecocks, Marie's frequent japes kept Harriman's self-importance in check—and made her husband much more likable as a result. Harriman enjoyed her smart set but never entirely fit in. "Mummy told me he never understood a word they said," recalled Nancy Lutz. "He would laugh and have a good time, but he didn't get the jokes."

Marie Harriman further broadened her husband by introducing him to Impressionist and Postimpressionist art. On their honeymoon, she guided his purchase of a number of paintings in Paris, including van Gogh's superb still life of white roses—which Pamela would donate to the National Gallery of Art many decades later, winning praise and publicity for her generosity. With his backing, Marie Harriman opened an art gallery on East 57th Street in Manhattan, where she gained a reputation over a decade and a half as a serious dealer with an instinct for new talent. She also helped Harriman decorate his new streamliner railroad cars and the Sun Valley Lodge. Her style, especially her original use of color, was widely admired. It was partly at her urging that Harriman pulled away from the frivolous polo set. "She didn't like that world," said Nancy Lutz. "She pushed Ave in her own funny way. She never seemed ambitious, but she wanted him to live up to his potential, and she was going to help him."

By the early 1930s, Harriman had turned his attention to politics. His mentor was his older sister, Mary Rumsey, a strong woman with the bluestocking's passion for the downtrodden. After founding the Junior League, an organization for young debutantes who wanted to perform social service, she bolted from the family's traditional Republicanism to the Democratic Party. When she backed Al Smith for President in 1928, she persuaded Harriman to join her, and in 1932 brother and sister again broke ranks to support Franklin D. Roosevelt, the famous "traitor to his class." Harriman's reasons, as always, were practical

rather than philosophical. The Hoover administration's trade barriers and Pro-
hibition had hampered Harriman business ventures. Even more important were
the Harriman banking interests. Since the late 1920s, Harriman and his brother
Roland had been partners in the Wall Street investment house Brown Brothers
Harriman. The Roosevelt administration had pledged to tighten regulation of
the securities industry, and Harriman wanted a voice in the new order.

Harriman could see that the power center was moving from Wall Street to
Washington, and so he expediently joined the party in control. As a Republican
he was one of many, but in the Democratic Party, always eager for rich new
patrons, he could be a significant force, even though he was known as "FDR's
tame capitalist." There was also an element of revenge in his defection, of
turning on the old-money New Yorkers who never quite accepted E.H. and
Mary Harriman. It was Republican Teddy Roosevelt, after all, who had savaged
old E.H. for his financial misdeeds.

Although FDR and Harriman both grew up in the Hudson Valley, they
hardly knew each other. Harriman thought Roosevelt was an overrated patrician
who misunderstood economic issues, and Roosevelt regarded Harriman as a
nouveau riche playboy, earnest but not very bright. Nor was Averell a dependable Democrat. In 1940 he secretly contributed a hefty $25,000 to the campaign
of Republican Wendell Willkie and offered his services to a prospective Willkie
administration. By then Harriman had already pushed his way into several pe-
ripheral jobs in the Roosevelt administration, but the President still wouldn't
consider him for anything of consequence.

Determined to find a niche at the top, he befriended Roosevelt's closest
adviser, Harry Hopkins, a former social worker from Sioux City, Iowa, with a
striver's fondness for wealthy men. Hopkins was as impressed with Harriman's
tireless dedication to hard work as he was with his ample bank book. In 1941,
after Congress passed the Lend-Lease bill to send armaments and supplies to
the Allies, Roosevelt named Hopkins the program's administrator. At Hopkins's
urging, FDR appointed Harriman the top "expediter" (his official title) for the
program in London.

Not only would Harriman evaluate Britain's defense needs, he would help
persuade American military leaders back home to forgo materiel for their own
buildup. Harriman would sit in on meetings of Churchill's War Cabinet and
have access to top secret British military intelligence. "He was responsible for
all war matters between the White House and 10 Downing Street at a moment
when Britain's very survival was questionable," wrote Abramson. Hopkins saw
Harriman as the perfect go-between, a dogged problem solver whose social
prestige and numerous business contacts in England would carry considerable
weight.

When Averell Harriman arrived in England on Saturday, March 15, 1941, to
take up the first important government post of his career, he was forty-nine years
old. Lieutenant-Commander C. R. "Tommy" Thompson, Winston Churchill's
naval aide, was on hand to greet the new envoy, and immediately whisked
Harriman off to Chequers for a meeting with the Prime Minister. Pamela, only
days away from her twenty-first birthday, was spending that weekend at Cherk-

ley with her protector Max Beaverbrook, and a crowd that included Michael Foot and Valentine Castelrosse as well as the American journalist Tex McCrary.

By Pamela's account, she and Harriman met on Wednesday, March 19, when they were seated next to each other at a dinner given by London hostess Emerald Cunard at the Dorchester Hotel, where Harriman had taken a small suite of rooms. Pamela vividly described the ambiance of Cunard's dining room, with its antiques and crystal chandelier, as well as the delicious food and stimulating conversation. As she recalled her tête-à-tête with Harriman, it was hardly the stuff of romance: She supposedly briefed him on Lord Beaverbrook, whom Harriman was eager to meet. After leaving the Cunard party, according to Pamela, Harriman invited her to his room, where she called Beaverbrook and secured an invitation to dinner for both of them at Cherkley the following Saturday. By Pamela's recounting, Harriman found her completely captivating, and she thought he was "the most beautiful man I had ever met." When that night's bombing raid began, Pamela gladly spent the night in Harriman's arms after she helped him "peel off her dinner dress," according to Christopher Ogden, who wrote a biography of Pamela based on a series of tape-recorded interviews with her.

The facts indicate that Pamela's recollection is faulty. In March 1941 Emerald Cunard was in the United States, where she had gone to be with her great love, the conductor Sir Thomas Beecham, and where she would remain for another eighteen months. On the Wednesday evening in question, Harriman attended a stag dinner at 10 Downing Street with the Prime Minister. During the air raid, Churchill took his guests on the roof of the Air Ministry to "watch the fun," in the words of Martin Gilbert, Churchill's official biographer. And Pamela's briefing on Beaverbrook would have been a bit tardy. Harriman had already dined with Churchill's Minister of Aircraft Production the previous Monday night, March 17—just two days after arriving in England.

Harriman's calendar during his first month in London was packed with long workdays and official dinners, many of them with Churchill or Beaverbrook. "I am with the PM at least one day a week and usually the weekend as well," Harriman wrote to Marie several weeks after his arrival. The one weekend he spent in London—indeed the Saturday night when Pamela claimed to have joined him for the dinner she supposedly arranged with Beaverbrook—Harriman dined with his old friend Rodman Wanamaker, and the following night with Alice Astor, the sister of New York tycoon Vincent Astor. Otherwise, he was a guest at Chequers for seven of his first eight weekends; during that same period, Pamela spent most of her weekends at Cherkley.

It was at Chequers, in all likelihood, that Harriman and Pamela had their first encounter, during a luncheon on March 29, where Churchill dominated the conversation with an account of past invasions of Russia. "I first met Pam at Chequers," Harriman told an interviewer in 1982. "I saw a lot of the Churchills, and she was there one weekend." A longtime friend heard the same story from Pamela: "She sat across the table from him, and she was bowled over by him."

Does it matter where and how they met? Only as a matter of pride to

Pamela: she needed more time and effort to capture Harriman than she wanted to admit. The supposed Emerald Cunard dinner created a romantic setting; the purported conversation about Beaverbrook cast her as a woman in the know; the instant attraction between the two made her out to be the femme fatale she wanted to be.

Though their first meeting was more circumscribed than her own version, it set the stage for future encounters. The most important, indeed the moment when they probably became lovers, was on the night of Wednesday, April 16, when Harriman attended a dinner at the Dorchester in honor of Fred Astaire's sister Adele, the dancer from Omaha who married Lord Charles Cavendish, brother of the tenth Duke of Devonshire. That night, 450 bombers descended on London in the heaviest raid of the war; the din of exploding bombs and antiaircraft fire lasted from nine at night until five in the morning. Writing to Marie the next day, Harriman described the "extraordinary sight" of magnesium flares lighting London "like Broadway and 42nd Street." For a while the guests at the Cavendish dinner watched the spectacle from a room on the eighth floor. Then a bomb exploded nearby and almost blew everyone to the back of the room. They descended to the relative safety of Harriman's room on the third floor before the party broke up.

Pamela was in the Dorchester that night, and according to one of her friends from those days, she ended up in Harriman's bed. "A big bombing raid is a very good way to get into bed with somebody," said Pamela's friend. "It is a known fact, and that is how it started." In his letter to "darling" Marie, Harriman noted, "Needless to say, my sleep was intermittent. Guns were going all the time and airplanes overhead." The following morning, Pamela and Harriman were up early. Their arms linked, they walked through the Horse Guards Parade, inspecting the extensive damage. They were spotted by John Colville, Churchill's private secretary, who kept his suspicions to himself.

Throughout his life Harriman was reticent about his early fling with Pamela. Clearly he was drawn to glamorous women, and choosing someone thirty years younger was unsurprising. Just before leaving for England, he had a fleeting affair with Vera Zorina, the beautiful young dancer married to choreographer George Balanchine.

What did Pamela see in Harriman? Her memory of him as "absolutely marvelous, with his raven black hair . . . very athletic, very tan, very healthy" is somewhat at odds with the recollection of others. Clearly middle-aged, he was a tall man with a slight stoop that lent a touch of patrician dignity. He had been keeping a punishing pace from the moment he arrived at the embassy in London. He had the gaunt aspect of an undertaker, with his thin face, jutting jaw, and dark circles under his eyes. "When he's working," diplomat George Kennan observed, "he behaves as though his body was just something that trails around with him." His rumpled suits hung loosely on his lean frame, a reflection of what Kennan also called "that curious contempt for elegance that only the wealthy can normally afford." Harriman's natural expression had the somber set of perpetual dyspepsia. Yet his wide smile had a little boy's dazzle made doubly ingratiating because it was so unexpected.

Harriman's multi-million-dollar fortune obviously added to his allure, but women also were drawn to his Old World courtliness. "He was well mannered," recalled Vera Zorina. "He was debonair, and he was very rich. He was very attentive and sweet, sending flowers and all that." There was also a hint of vulnerability. "He seemed a little shy and out of it, as if he needed someone to help him. You felt that maybe if you drew him out, Ave would be fine," said Marie's daughter, Nancy. Perhaps it was the stammer, or as Abramson noted, "his sad, brown eyes—'sheep dog eyes' one woman called them." "All his life, Averell needed reinforcement of his self-esteem," the economist John Kenneth Galbraith once observed about his longtime friend.

Pamela later professed not to have known about his wealth or family background when they met—despite the front-page headlines in *The Times* announcing the arrival of "the New York financier." What she did know—and what attracted her most—was that Averell Harriman "was the most important American in London."

CHAPTER
Nine

AT FIRST, HARRIMAN AND PAMELA took pains to keep their affair secret. They maintained separate residences at the Dorchester, confining themselves to late-night rendezvous. They saw each other at Chequers, at Cherkley, and at Beaverbrook's London home, Stornoway House, which had been transformed into the Ministry of Aircraft Production.

It was inevitable that they would see a lot of each other socially. Harriman was always in Churchill's company, and Beaverbrook sought to have Harriman as his guest as often as possible. Usually Harriman and Pamela were two faces in a large, high-powered crowd, and there was little reason that their arriving or leaving together might cause suspicion. Only the most attentive might have noted that on April 22 they dined with Beaverbrook alone. A week later Harriman gave a small farewell dinner for Robert Menzies, the Australian Prime Minister, attended by Brendan Bracken, American journalist Quentin Reynolds —and Pamela.

One well-born woman who was a confidante of Beaverbrook's was "intrigued" by Pamela and Harriman when they dined with the press lord in the early days of their affair. "She was extremely interested in Averell," said Beaverbrook's confidante, "and he basked in the attention she gave him." Still, aside from Beaverbrook and John Colville, only Duncan Sandys, the husband of Winston's daughter Diana, sensed the affair. He "intercepted glances and felt vibrations" during several weekends at Chequers. Sandys didn't share his intuition with anyone else.

THE ARRIVAL of Harriman's daughter Kathleen on May 16, 1941, gave the lovers convenient camouflage. At twenty-three, Kathleen was just two years older than Pamela, who shrewdly embraced her as a friend. A graduate of the exclusive Foxcroft School and Bennington College, Kathleen was a stylishly pretty brunette, with her father's strong jaw and direct manner. She was outgoing and athletic—like Pamela, she grew up on horseback—and she brimmed with confidence. Since her college graduation in 1940, she had been working for Harriman's public relations specialist, Steve Hannagan, the man who coined the name "Sun Valley" for Harriman's Idaho resort. Kathleen was "desperate" to see action in London, so with Hannagan's help she got a job with Hearst's International News Service (INS). Laden with scarce items such as nylon stockings, Guerlain green-top lipsticks, and a dozen packs of Stimudents that Averell had requested for a "friend," Kathleen headed for England by way of Lisbon.

Less than a week earlier, London had been devastated by an assault even worse than the mid-April Blitz. Thousands of fires had burned for three days after the raids on the night of May 10, when 1,400 civilians died and 5,000 houses were destroyed. Incendiary bombs gutted the House of Commons, and Big Ben was silenced by a direct hit, although the hands on the scarred clock face eerily continued to move. "A spring sun bathed the city with its warmth," wrote Quentin Reynolds, "but there was a pall of smoke over the city, and through it the sun shone blood red."

Two days after her arrival, Kathleen was the guest of honor at a party organized by Pamela in one of the hotel dining rooms. It was a lively crowd of young aristocrats, including Sarah Norton and Michael Tree. Afterward, everyone scrambled through the darkness to dance at the 400. At a time in her life when Pamela had few women friends, she and Kathleen developed an easy camaraderie. They were young women of different character, but they were of the same class and background—and to an extent unimagined by Kathleen, they had Averell Harriman very much in common.

Kathleen was genuinely taken with Pamela, whose photograph on the cover of *Life* magazine she had seen months earlier. In a letter to her sister Mary, she called Pamela "one of the wisest young girls I've ever met." Kathleen was impressed with Pamela's savvy and understanding of British politics. Pamela had plenty of ideas and contacts that she was ready to share with Kathleen, a cub reporter eager for sources and stories.

In Kathleen, Pamela found the appreciation that eluded her among her English contemporaries. Kathleen opened the door to a crowd of clever American journalists, including Charles Collingwood and Edward R. Murrow of CBS, William Walton of Time-Life, and Bill Nichols of the *Chicago Tribune*. All were dazzled by the Prime Minister's daughter-in-law. "Pamela was ravishing . . . with skin so pure you could see right through it," Walton recalled fifty years later. "And the red hair was real."

More than anything, Pamela's friendship with Kathleen pulled her into Harriman's life on a more intimate basis. Since Pamela and Kathleen were such friends, it seemed only natural that Pamela should join the Harrimans that June when they moved to a spacious new Dorchester suite overlooking Hyde Park, with two sitting rooms, and a bedroom each for Kathleen, Pamela, and Harriman. And when Harriman offered to rent the two girls a country house for the weekends, how could Pamela have refused?

At about that time, the peculiar nature of their three-way friendship became clear to Kathleen, who had been fully aware of her father's history of extramarital affairs. If Kathleen was surprised that her friend and contemporary was sleeping with her father, she never showed it. Nor did she discuss the matter with either of them. It was an instance, Pamela later told Harriman's biographer, of "She knows and I know that she knows, and I know that she knows that I know."

When Pamela and Harriman became lovers, her husband had been away for less than three months, and her child was only six months old. Yet Pamela had fulfilled her obligation by providing a male heir, and according to high society's self-indulgent code, she was free to take her pleasure where she could find it. She was expected only to be circumspect and to keep up appearances, particularly since she was the daughter-in-law of the Prime Minister.

Kathleen's detached view of her father's amorous pursuits was true to their relationship. Both before and after his divorce from Kathleen's mother, Harriman had been a distant figure. She and her sister Mary had lived with Kitty while Harriman and his new wife Marie traveled the world. When their mother died in 1936, Kathleen and Mary were already in boarding school. As a consequence, Kathleen seemed more companion than daughter; she even called her father Ave.

By 1941, Marie and Averell Harriman were no longer intimate. "I don't think she pictured that Ave would have other women," Marie's daughter Nancy Lutz explained. "But the problem was that their sex life wasn't successful. She said it wasn't very good. It was unpleasant for her. Therefore, she didn't blame him for having affairs, although everything should be kept quiet and decent." Marie had been riled only once, by Harriman's romance with Vera Zorina. "I'm not sure whether that was too underneath Mummy's nose, or whether he became too fond of her," said Nancy. "To Mummy, it was all right if he just slept with someone, but if he got involved and threatened her, it was not something she wanted."

While Harriman had other women, his wife also carried on with other men. In 1939, she was seen at parties with a literary agent named Mark Hanna. And as the war broke out, she was often in the company of Eddy Duchin, the society musician whose late wife Marjorie had been Marie's best friend. Since Marjorie's death in 1937, Averell and Marie had been surrogate parents to Duchin's son Peter, taking the young boy into the Harriman household at Arden while the bandleader was on the road. Eddy Duchin was a frequent visitor at Arden, and he escorted Marie to her favorite New York haunts. She was so fiercely loyal to him that when the Jupiter Island Club at Hobe Sound, the Harrimans' favorite Florida resort, refused to admit him for being Jewish, Marie never walked through the door again. "She loved Eddy," said Nancy Lutz. "They had a helluva lot of fun together." According to William Paley's first wife Dorothy, a close friend of the Harrimans, Averell "knew about Marie and Eddy, and it gave him a license that he liberally used. I think he decided they would make do with their marriage, and they went about their business."

Many American friends felt that Marie had stayed in New York because of Eddy Duchin. That may have been the case, but she also had medical reasons. Her vision had been failing for more than a decade due to glaucoma, and she had eye surgery shortly before Harriman took off for England. Not only did her doctors want her nearby for further treatment, but flying in unpressurized aircraft might have caused her great harm. She also suffered from heart trouble, though this was unknown to all but her doctors.

Although their marriage had its difficulties, the letters across the Atlantic between Harriman and his wife reflected a mutual devotion based on habit and admiration. Marie kept up a newsy patter spiced with humor. "We're all dying to know who the peeress with the decayed teeth is who's in such a lather about her toothpicks. . . . After your third cable about them we decided the situation must be critical," Marie replied to her husband's repeated requests for Stimudents. Harriman wrote lengthy descriptions of people and places, confiding frustrations as well as satisfactions. Even after his romance with Pamela began, he expressed a longing for Marie's company. "Thinking . . . of you constantly," he wrote in early June 1941, as he was about to leave for an extended trip to the Middle East. Some months later, after a visit to New York, he confessed, "I miss being with you terribly. Life is lonely."

Yet given his level of self-involvement, it was easy to see how he could compartmentalize his life—with Marie in one box, and Pamela in another. In letters to Marie, his references to Pamela were notably breezy, and always in connection with his daughter. "Kathleen has teamed up with Pamela Churchill, the red-headed wife of your friend!! Randolph," he wrote in early June, describing their plans to share quarters in the country and the city. "They are both so excited about it that my departure was quite unimportant." In the event of a Blitz, he wrote, "Pamela has promised to take her to the safest spot in the hotel." At one point he even took a mild swipe at Pamela, noting his "relief" that she had gone to Chequers, leaving him alone with Kathleen for a "quiet weekend."

With Harriman, work always came before romance, and events in the spring of 1941 brought new urgency to his governmental duties. German armies rolled over Yugoslavia, Greece, and Crete, while the incessant bombardment of English cities and ports dangerously diminished food supplies. It wasn't until the end of May that the first Lend-Lease shipments arrived, including canned goods, cheese, dried milk, powdered eggs, and flour. Throughout this period, Harriman worked prodigiously long days.

Each morning he plowed through papers while eating breakfast in bed. At nine his aides came to brief him. At eleven he arrived at the office. He usually stayed at his desk until eight in the evening, and afterward had a working dinner and sometimes more late-night meetings. "Ave never knows what he's going to be doing in the evenings, so I go ahead and make plans and then cancel them at the last minute," Kathleen told her sister.

Kathleen was busy herself, turning out stories for INS. Pamela continued to put in time at the Ministry of Supply as well as the feeding center near Hitchin. She also periodically visited Randolph's constituency, listening to complaints and making speeches. But her work on her husband's behalf was more dutiful than zealous; local politics paled compared to the action in London. "She wasn't very interested," recalled one of her wartime friends. "I don't recall her going there [to Preston] except when she had to."

Days often went by when Pamela and Harriman didn't catch a glimpse of each other. Harriman was away from England for long stretches of time, traveling to the United States, the Middle East, and the Soviet Union, negotiating details of Lend-Lease shipments with political and military leaders. From June

1941 through January 1942, he was traveling for about six months and in England for just under two months.

Harriman and Pamela showed little intensity when they were together. His manner was serious in her presence; his glance carried no special sparkle. "Certainly Averell was not the demonstrative type, and Pamela was discreet," said one woman who observed them frequently during the war. "You couldn't say when you saw them, 'Oh my goodness, they are madly in love with each other.' They acted like friends. It was an affair, not a great love affair. There were too many other things going on in his life." Pamela certainly didn't give away much. "I saw them together once at Leeds," recalled Lady Mary Dunn. "One of her gifts was flirtatiousness with everyone, so she didn't show at all with anyone she was involved with. It was clever protective coloration."

The conduct of the affair was very much according to Harriman's requirements. In matters of sex, if Marie's experience was any guide, Harriman was more concerned with self-gratification than with giving pleasure to his partner. "Ave liked women as a kind of Bam! and it was over with," said Peter Duchin. "I can't see Ave involved in trying to make anyone else happy." On many occasions, Pamela would prepare for an evening or a weekend and he would fail to arrive if he got too busy.

But Pamela knew that Harriman hated angry scenes, so she never complained. She had learned from her experience with Randolph to be flexible with temperamental men. "She put herself at Averell's disposal and helped him a great deal," said a longtime friend of Pamela's. "She would find out things for him, get him what he wanted." She was also perfecting her talent for the sort of solace she gave her father-in-law. "Averell did want to be able to talk about what interested him," said one friend from those days. "She was very good company, and she was interested in everything."

By Pamela's own account, she frequently passed along reports of their conversations to Beaverbrook and her father-in-law. After Beaverbrook resigned as Minister of Aircraft Production in April, Churchill appointed him Minister of Supply, in charge of most of Britain's war production. Now Beaverbrook's work was directly linked to Harriman's, and he needed the American's help. With Lend-Lease, Roosevelt was providing Britain as much as he could, given the isolationist opposition in Congress. But Beaverbrook wanted more materiel, and he wanted direct American involvement. "Beaverbrook was using Pam," said the wartime journalist Tex McCrary. "That was how Harriman got lured to Cherkley at the weekends."

Quite apart from Pamela, Harriman was in frequent contact with Beaverbrook and Churchill—to a degree no other American could claim—virtually from the moment he arrived in Britain. Not only did Harriman have a natural instinct to push himself toward power, he was fundamentally on the British side as an ardent advocate for American intervention. Yet through her relationship with Harriman, Pamela in effect became a back-channel of information to the British leaders. Harriman, Beaverbrook, and Churchill would discuss issues in official meetings, and later Pamela would report back what her lover had said in private, filling in details and nuances.

ON THE ONE HAND, Pamela cared very much for Harriman. Yet according to Christopher Ogden, she "never believed [their affair] was anything more than a wartime romance with important strategic overtones." The bottom line was that both Pamela and Harriman knew how to use each other quite effectively.

They were uncannily well suited in personality as well as intelligence. Because of their innate reserve, they tended to be underestimated by others. The same adjectives—cool, controlling, self-serious, driven, focused, determined—applied to both. They took their time, studied their options, and seldom tipped their hands. They each had an insatiable hunger for information, not for its own sake but because they understood how to use it. Both collected people they thought were valuable. And both longed to be at the center of political activity.

Petersfield Farm, Harriman's gift to his daughter and Pamela, was a four-hundred-year-old cottage with beamed ceilings. Located just six miles from Beaverbrook's country house in Surrey, it had five bedrooms, two bathrooms, servants' quarters, a summer house, a kitchen garden lined with vegetables and fruit trees, a rose garden, rock garden, a pool stocked with goldfish, and a lawn level enough for Harriman's croquet. The house came with two servants as well as twelve chickens and a goat. There was even enough room for Pamela to bring Baby Winston and Nanny Hall over from Cherkley and install them in one of the bedrooms.

Pamela readily took command at Petersfield Farm. She had Lord Digby send two of his prize ponies from Dorset and kept them in a nearby field. She interceded with servants bristling over American customs such as iced tea and prevented them from quitting, to Kathleen's great relief. As the daughter-in-law of the Prime Minister, Pamela was able to obtain extra rations of eggs, butter, cheese, and meat.

A stream of guests passed through on weekends, mostly journalists like Quentin Reynolds, and young fighter pilots from nearby airbases. Pamela and Kathleen spent their afternoons riding through fields strewn with wildflowers. In the evenings they sat in the garden, drinking from a champagne bowl that bobbed with peaches from Fortnum & Mason, listening to the evening chorus of birds and watching the airplanes returning from their bombing runs. Kathleen often assembled her journalist friends for marathon games of gin rummy. When Harriman was away, the girls sometimes dined at nearby pubs with the pilots, some of them no older than eighteen, who wore what Cecil Beaton called "the armour of carefree gaiety." Most weekends, Pamela, Kathleen, and Harriman went to Beaverbrook's place down the road.

Cherkley during wartime was even more stimulating than before the war. It was a plain, square house, "an amazing mixture of bad taste and discomfort," observed Ann Fleming. Behind the house was a large terrace overlooking the rolling hills of Surrey, a view that Robert Bruce Lockhart, a gossip writer on Beaverbrook's *Evening Standard,* called "one of the finest of the South of

England." Even though the staff had been pared down from forty to fifteen during the war, Beaverbrook offered his guests passable food, excellent wine, and new films, usually westerns or the Marx Brothers, in his private movie theater, which was draped in silver silk. For background music during dinner, Beaverbrook favored records by none other than Eddy Duchin, which must have given the press lord a private chuckle. Beaverbrook's mistress, "cool, chic and ultracharming" Jean Norton, was usually on hand as his hostess. Amicably separated from her husband, she lived in a cottage not far from the main house.

At Chequers, the war always dominated the conversation. At Cherkley, on the other hand, where Beaverbrook collected journalists, socialites, and politicians, the atmosphere was more lively. "The talk was not at all serious," said one frequent visitor. Before dinner Beaverbrook would stand on his terrace and shout, "Come and eat." He was the impresario of the seating arrangement: "Sit there, and you there. See what lovely women there are beside you." Beaverbrook loved to surround himself with pretty females—"his attitude toward women was like a gangster to his molls," Ann Fleming once observed—and he included everyone in the conversation, even declining to send away the women during port and cigars after dinner.

"The Beaver," as everyone called him, was a model host. "He has the faculty of giving everybody he meets his 'individual' attention," observed the British novelist and diplomat William Gerhardie, a close friend of Beaverbrook. Sitting in the middle of the table so he could participate in at least three conversations, "he conducted like the leader of an orchestra, seeking to show off not himself but his guests," wrote Beaverbrook's biographers Davie and Chisholm. Pamela studied his social stagecraft: how he prodded each guest, how he enlivened conversations with gossipy tidbits; how he extracted information when he needed it—usually from guests he had plied with wine. Somehow he was able to control the velocity of a conversation, pushing it to a high pitch, then climaxing it with gusts of his own appreciative laughter.

Without her domineering husband, Pamela felt free to chime in—although she was remembered neither for the originality nor the felicity of her contributions. "I don't remember her venturing a political opinion," said Beaverbrook's granddaughter Lady Jean Campbell, who as a precocious teenager observed Pamela frequently. "She was an infinitely personal person. She was learning. Pam never pontificated. She would yield and yield, maybe offer a little fun, curious little questions and comments. She had a sunniness, an optimistic attitude toward life."

Pamela's contemporaries watched her progress with ill-concealed amazement. Now that she had the ear of great men, Pamela high-hatted the old debutante crowd, who not only took offense but refused to take her seriously. The continuing antipathy of her peers was best reflected in a journal Sarah Norton kept at the time. On March 16, 1941, Norton was at her mother's cottage at Cherkley when Pamela appeared, "even more annoying than ever." Again on April 28, after lunch at Mirabelle with her mother and Pamela, Sarah could hardly contain herself: "She irritates me so much. One day I'll hit her."

Norton recovered sufficiently to go shopping with Pamela a few weeks later, only to be struck anew by her friend's selfishness. "Needless to say," wrote Norton, "I didn't get any of MY shopping done."

The young men in Pamela's set were less likely to steam in silence. After Pamela's party welcoming Kathleen Harriman to England, Norton wrote: "Michael Tree was very funny with Pam during dinner. He told her he had heard she attended all cabinet meetings." Lacking any sense of levity, Pamela took such needling badly. Several months later, Pamela attended a dinner at the Savoy given by Paul Patterson, owner of the *Baltimore Sun*. The room was filled with journalists and politicians, and the evening was a lively parade of speeches by the likes of Brendan Bracken and Sir Walter Monckton. Following the dinner, First Lord of the Admiralty A. V. Alexander played sea chanties on the piano for hours. "The result," wrote Sarah Norton, "was great cacophony." At such moments of spontaneity and genuine good cheer, Pamela's earnestness got the better of her. "Pam Churchill sat in dead silence," Norton continued. "One might think she hated the idea of notable members of the cabinet amusing themselves. However, she left early and the tension was relieved."

The deterioration of her marriage didn't seem to bother Pamela. Randolph was in faraway Cairo, working as press officer at the British Army's general headquarters, ineligible for combat because of his father's position. "Poor Randolph has had a letter from Pam about his losses at cards," Evelyn Waugh wrote to his wife in early May 1941. "She is very vexed with him." Winston continued to send checks to keep his son solvent, and he settled more money on Pamela as well. In a letter late in the summer of 1941, Churchill offered his son £500 from royalties on his book *Into Battle,* with a plea that Randolph pay his taxes and earmark £400 for his debts, "to the bottom of which we never seem to be able to get."

But Randolph seemed incapable of making amends. In Cairo, he chased women, gambled, drank prodigiously, and insulted his hosts at dinner parties in the city's grand houses and elegant hotels. At the exclusive Mohammad Ali Club and Shepheard's Hotel, he publicly fondled his Egyptian girlfriends. "They were not platonic friendships," said Gertrude Wissa, an Egyptian friend, "I sometimes saw him in bed with the girls." Randolph even had an official mistress, Maud "Momo" Marriott, the glamorous daughter of American financier Otto Kahn and wife of Colonel John Marriott of the Scots Guards. Among Momo's noteworthy traits were her vivacity, her long red fingernails, and her tendency to sleep until noon. Momo was Cairo's leading hostess, and in the words of Randolph's biographer, was "a strong minded, intelligent well informed woman who knew everyone, entertained generously, pulled strings for her protégés and kept a merry open house for her friends . . . all the attributes that Randolph looked for in a woman." Yet she certainly knew her man, calling him "the problem child" to her friends.

In June 1941, Averell Harriman went on a fact-finding mission to assess British military needs in the Middle East. "I hope you will try to see [him] when he arrives," Winston Churchill wrote to Randolph. "I have made great friends with him, and have the greatest regard for him. He does all he can to help us." Randolph was nearly as impressed as Pamela was with Harriman. They spent ten days together touring military installations while Harriman made detailed notes on all the shortages he found. Randolph wrote to Pamela, calling Harriman "absolutely charming. . . . He spoke delightfully about you, and I fear that I have a serious rival." To his father, Randolph pronounced Harriman "my favourite American," and commented on his "extraordinary maturity of judgment . . . and sure-footedness. . . . I think he is the most objective and shrewd of all those who are around you." Harriman transmitted his own reaction in a telegram to Pamela, telling her that he found Randolph to be a delightful companion: "Beginning to understand your weakness for him."

If he intended a mildly sardonic undertone, Harriman had good reason. One evening during his visit, Randolph had organized a dinner party under the stars on a dhow that ferried them up the Nile. Randolph drank too much and did something he afterward called "unforgivable." He boasted to Harriman that he was having an affair with Momo Marriott. "I had no idea what was going on in London," Randolph told his son many years later. It was all Harriman needed to hear. If he harbored any guilt about his liaison with Pamela, Randolph's behavior put his own in a more justifiable light. With everyone straying—Marie and Duchin in New York, Randolph in Cairo, Pamela and Harriman in London—no one was in a position to judge anyone else.

CHAPTER

Ten

As the war neared the end of its second year, the mood in London eased. In June 1941, Germany turned east and attacked Russia, temporarily suspending the bombing over England. In August 1941, Churchill and Roosevelt met on shipboard off the coast of Newfoundland and issued the Atlantic Charter, a joint statement of principles that stopped short of a declaration of war by the United States. Roosevelt added Harriman to the delegation at the last minute.

Harriman was increasingly preoccupied by his newest task, which was to send supplies to Moscow. It was a tricky undertaking given American mistrust of the Soviet Union. In late September he went to Moscow with Beaverbrook to make arrangements with Stalin. "I thought I'd scream if I heard the word 'tanks' or 'Russia' mentioned again," Kathleen wrote in an account of a dinner she attended with Harriman, Pamela, Beaverbrook, and David Margesson before the Russian trip. Throughout the evening, Harriman and Beaverbrook argued, with Margesson acting as referee, while Pamela and Kathleen watched with amusement.

The Moscow mission was a success, and Harriman could only pause briefly in England before flying to Washington to brief Roosevelt and Hopkins. He and Pamela stole some time together in the country, enough for him to fill her in on the trip. Such intelligence was of more than passing interest. Her job at the Ministry of Supply had taken her into, as she put it, "doing propaganda for the States," sending dispatches to Britain's Minister of Information in America, Sir Gerald Campbell, in an effort to drum up popular support for the war effort.

Naturally restless, Pamela yearned for something more lively than a desk job, so in October she impetuously signed on with the ferry pilots who delivered airplanes from the factories to the fighting forces. "We all wanted to fly ferry planes," said Sarah Norton. "It was very glamorous, a wonderful exciting job, but the military was far too busy training pilots to train girls to be ferry pilots." Pamela kept her intentions from her family, but she did tell Kathleen, who tried to talk her out of it—telling her bluntly, among other things, that she was dangerous enough behind the wheel of a car, and that she lacked the necessary math skills. But Pamela dug in her heels and announced her intention to start flying lessons immediately.

Kathleen broke the news in a telegram to her father at Washington's May-flower Hotel. "Have exhausted my arguments," she said. "What is your reaction?" He picked up the telephone and told Pamela that the idea was silly and unrealistic. Chastened, Pamela sent him a wire thanking him for his advice: "Have taken it."

Harriman went to New York for a brief reunion with Marie—and promptly collapsed. His incessant traveling had left him a physical wreck. "Averell is a sick man," Pamela had confided to Harry Hopkins after the Moscow mission. Already worn down by a sinus infection, Harriman was in considerable abdominal pain and running a high fever. Marie summoned Edmund Goodman, a surgeon, to the Harriman home in Manhattan. Goodman discovered an abscess in Harriman's rectum that he immediately removed in a makeshift operating room. After a short recuperation, Harriman returned to London, carrying a rubber pad to cushion his sore bottom. "Eating meals off mantelpiece," he reported to Marie.

In the following weeks, Harriman tried to keep a more relaxed pace, spending tranquil weekends in the country with Kathleen. But on Saturday, December 6, he and his daughter joined Pamela at Chequers to celebrate Kathleen's birthday. Although the Prime Minister gamely offered a toast, he was clearly preoccupied by ominous reports from the Far East that Japan was readying some sort of attack, possibly on British territory.

During dinner the next evening with Harriman, Kathleen, American Ambassador John Gilbert (Gil) Winant, and Pamela, Churchill hardly said a word and seemed depressed. When the BBC's nine o'clock news came on the radio, the group was stunned to hear that Japan had bombed Pearl Harbor. At that, Churchill slapped the radio hard and bolted to his feet. He knew that America would be forced at last to declare war on the Axis powers, sealing the Grand Alliance with Britain. Harriman and Winant, Churchill later observed, showed no sign of sorrow over the news. "One might have thought they had been delivered from a long pain," he concluded. It was one of the decisive moments of the twentieth century, and Pamela was with the twentieth century's preeminent leader when it happened. Not surprisingly, she recounted the story often.

Back in Cairo, Randolph still knew nothing of Pamela and Harriman's affair. Indeed, by the fall of 1941, he was sending out conciliatory signals to his estranged wife. Evelyn Waugh reported to him from London that Pamela's "kitten eyes" were "full of innocent fun," and that she was "showing exemplary patience with the Americans," who were "ubiquitous and boisterous." In one vaguely guilty letter, Randolph enclosed a package of food unavailable in London. "It seems frightful living in this land of plenty while you are so tightly rationed at home," he wrote to Pamela. "Darling, I am so glad that you are hearing a good account of my work. I do terribly want to do something of which you can be proud."

In early January 1942, Randolph returned to London for the first time in nearly a year. When he arrived at the airport, Pamela put on an impressive performance, running to her husband, standing on tiptoe, and flinging her arms around his neck. *The Tatler* reported that Randolph's "most vociferous welcome came from his small son . . . who had heard so much of 'daddy' from his mother that he held out his arms at once to the broad-shouldered, bronzed, khaki-clad figure who suddenly appeared in his nursery." No sooner had Pamela and Randolph settled into their own room at the Dorchester than she shot off a telegram to Harriman, who had gone to New York in mid-December for a vacation with Marie. Sent in care of the State Department—Pamela never addressed a letter to Harriman at home—her wire coyly announced that she, Randolph, and Kathleen made "a happy trio."

"Randolph in good form," Robert Bruce Lockhart noted in his diary after drinks at the Dorchester. Kathleen referred to Randolph as her "half a husband," and tolerantly digested what she called his "nightly lectures." Expecting to stay in London just ten days, Randolph traded transatlantic telegrams with Harriman bemoaning their inability to connect. "Hoping I will arrive in time," Harriman wrote, and then, when it appeared he might not: "Bitterly disappointed not being London while you are there. . . . Lots of things wanted to talk over with you." But Randolph ended up staying considerably longer than anticipated.

One reason was Churchill's apparent vulnerability as Britain's leader. The British had suffered a string of setbacks in the Far East, including the siege of Singapore, which was going badly for them. From January 27 through 29, after Churchill called for a vote of confidence, the House of Commons debated the conduct of the war. On the first day, Churchill spoke masterfully for ninety minutes as Clementine, Pamela, Randolph, and his sisters looked on.

On the second day, Randolph appeared in his major's uniform to attack his father's critics. As usual, Randolph went too far and was greeted with catcalls, especially when he invoked his rather privileged military experience. As Randolph droned on, Harold Nicolson caught "his little wife squirming in the gallery, and Winston himself . . . embarrassed and shy." Kathleen later reported to Marie that Randolph had been "brilliant, spontaneous and exceeding [sic] tactless . . . but the House enjoyed it immensely." While Randolph failed to distinguish himself, he did his father no harm. On the 29th, Churchill won the confidence vote 464 to 1.

Harriman returned to London on a snowy day in early February, his bags overflowing with scarce goodies: a hat, blouse, and black skirt for Kathleen, gold "V" charms for Kathleen and Pamela, and a supply of nylon stockings, underwear, bobby pins, hairnets, and perfume. On his first night home, after various briefings and a late dinner with Beaverbrook and Kathleen where he reminisced about his "most beautiful gal" Marie, Harriman was greeted at the Dorchester by Randolph in his pajamas. They talked, Kathleen reported breezily to her sister, about "the Averell-Randolph axis."

Such jocularity could never have existed had Randolph understood the real circumstances of the "Averell-Randolph axis." For the remainder of his stay, he and Harriman continued their amicable relationship. During a weekend at Chequers, Kathleen and her father cozily joined Randolph and Pamela in their room for Sunday breakfast. Harriman and Randolph dined at Cherkley with Beaverbrook, lunched together in London, and one evening formed a threesome with Pamela for dinner—the first and only such occasion. Throughout, Pamela and Harriman carried off their charade with aplomb. "Averell could be cold-blooded about such things, and so could Pamela," said a woman who knew both of them during the war.

Near the end of his second month at home, strains began to show between Randolph and Pamela. At Beaverbrook's Sunday dinners at Cherkley, with Pamela and Harriman, Michael Foot and Labour politician Aneurin Bevan among the guests, Randolph drank heavily and made a spectacle of himself. "It was a bad evening," Robert Bruce Lockhart wrote. "The mixture of alcohol, criticism and pessimism was depressing."

Behind closed doors, Randolph and Pamela had been quarreling constantly. "We both realized we'd made a mistake," Pamela later explained. "It was difficult being married and not married." According to Randolph's biographer Brian Roberts, Randolph also "greatly resented Pamela's independence. . . . He lost no time in making his views known to his wife and family. The scenes he created greatly distressed his mother."

Pamela let Randolph know her dismay over the cavalier way he dealt with his district after her efforts to cater to his constituents during his absence. She complained bitterly that in only forty-eight hours he had nullified her good work by having a fight with the constituency chairman. At other times, Pamela and Randolph squabbled over his animosity toward his mother, whose closeness to his father he begrudged. As usual, money troubles were a recurring theme. But mostly, Randolph took exception to the way Pamela was running her life. He particularly objected that she lived in London while Little Winston remained in the country with Nanny Hall. "I want you to be with my son," he said. "He's *my* son too," replied Pamela. "No," said Randolph. "My son. I'm a Churchill."

Clementine tried to intervene, but her tendency to sympathize more with Pamela than her own son drove the wedge even deeper. She couldn't have helped matters by advising Pamela to pack up, take Little Winston with her, and "don't tell him where you're going. You can't imagine how kind and sweet he'll be when you return." Despite the evident rifts, neither side dared move toward an official separation, although Clarissa Churchill confided to a friend in early March that "Pamela had no intention of sticking to him; and that Mr. Churchill would be very sad if their marriage broke up." So they drifted through Randolph's three months in London, together in name only. "She closed up on him, if you follow me," said Lady Mary Dunn, "and he wasn't taking that." Randolph found diversion more frequently at the bar at White's, and Pamela continued to spend numerous evenings and weekends in the company of the Harrimans.

When Randolph finally left in late March, he did so with a flourish. He had volunteered for the Special Air Service, a parachute commando group being organized by an old friend, David Stirling—much to the distress of his parents, although not evidently to Pamela. "Throughout Randolph's brief training," according to Brian Roberts, "husband and wife bombarded each other with angry, unforgiving letters."

The Harrimans moved out of the Dorchester into an apartment in early April 1942, taking Pamela with them. Their new lodgings were located at 3

Grosvenor Square, one of three brick town houses adjacent to the American Embassy on the south side of the square. The first two floors of the town houses contained embassy offices, and the upper floors were divided into apartments for embassy staff, including the American ambassador, Gil Winant, who lived next door to Averell, Kathleen, and Pamela. The Harrimans had a spacious and sunny layout on the third floor, with a living room, small dining room, kitchen, two large bedrooms and one smaller one. (As in the Dorchester, Harriman, Pamela, and Kathleen kept separate bedrooms.) It was known as a "service flat" because its occupants could order food from the embassy, delivered to their door.

While on a trip to Northern Ireland with Harry Hopkins and General George Marshall to review the first contingent of American troops to arrive in Europe, Harriman contracted paratyphoid from drinking contaminated water. Delirious with fever and chills, he required constant care, which Pamela and Kathleen provided. Whatever he needed, they obtained, including Little Winston's baby food, oranges and lemons secured by the army and navy, as well as special soup prepared by Beaverbrook's cook and beef bouillon made by the chef at Claridges. Beaverbrook's personal physician, Dr. Daniel Davis, took charge, and when the crisis passed, Kathleen brought in three American Red Cross nurses. Harriman was bedridden for three weeks, most of it sleeping in a darkened room until he moved out to the country, to a new house he rented for the girls called Ruckman's Cottage. It was better appointed than Petersfield Farm, and more intimate, with barely room for one houseguest. Throughout his recuperation, Pamela stayed by his side. His gratitude was evident a year later, when he was still referring to Pamela as "the other nurse."

Pamela did her best to maintain an illusion of innocence when she moved to Grosvenor Square with the Harrimans. Yet in making an apparently temporary arrangement permanent, Pamela and Harriman blew their cover. Harriman was never directly called to account for his womanizing. Along with so many upper-class men of his generation, he was expected to have high standards in public life, but his personal affairs were his business. The blame fell on Pamela —notwithstanding Marie's own well-known romance with Eddy Duchin. Harriman benefited from the prevailing double standard, and Marie was too well liked to be judged harshly by society. That left Pamela, an unpopular figure to begin with, whose attentiveness to Harriman was perceived as gold-digging.

"They were caught out and people were a bit upset because he had a wife," said Sarah Norton. "So it wasn't considered a good thing. Living with him took it over the line. It wasn't discreet. No one had the time for a scandal, but amongst conversation it was considered that she was being a silly girl, living with a man who had a wife in America, who had no intention of divorcing his wife. We thought she was being very stupid and naughty. And we thought, 'Poor Mrs. Harriman.' "

One person who braced Harriman about the affair was Adele Astaire Cavendish, a "marvelous" friend, in Harriman's view, whose bright eyes always sparkled with amusement. At her best, he once said, she was "funny, lewd, and had everyone laughing all the time." She used so many four-letter words that her brother Fred called her "Lady Foulmouth."

One weekend, Lady Cavendish invited Harriman for a visit to her home, Lismore Castle in Ireland. "I'd like to bring a girl, Pamela Churchill," Harriman said. Well aware of Pamela's history, Adele Cavendish retorted, "Marie is my friend, and I am not going to have goddamn Pamela Churchill to my house. If you want to come, you can come. But don't bring her." Harriman retreated, but Adele Cavendish never forgot the affront.

AMERICA'S ENTRY into the war changed the character and tempo of London life. By the summer of 1942, the city was flooded with American soldiers, and the atmosphere was electric. It seemed like Christmas in July as enthusiastic young GIs passed out nylon stockings, cigarettes, candy, and cosmetics. "Life is such fun and so pleasant," Kathleen wrote to Marie. "Suddenly I feel almost ashamed. Here I am sitting over here, in the whirl of excitement, while you all stay at home with the harder end to keep up." In their apartment on Grosvenor Square—the part of London fast becoming known as "Little America"—Kathleen and Pamela entertained a parade of generals.

On one occasion, Pamela, Beaverbrook, and Kathleen had dinner with Franklin D. Roosevelt Jr., who was visiting London for forty-eight hours. Afterward, they went to a nightclub, and when Max headed home, Pamela and Kathleen took young Roosevelt on what Kathleen described as an "all night binge" that ended with breakfast at the Dorchester consisting of numerous milk punches. They all staggered to the airport, where the milk punches continued until they put Roosevelt on an airplane.

Pamela had left her job at the Ministry of Supply to join Britain's organization of several million housewives, the Women's Voluntary Services (WVS). Wearing a green WVS uniform, her curly red hair slightly disheveled, Pamela bustled about London, clutching her crocodile briefcase monogrammed with the initials of her maiden name. She served as a guide for visiting American dignitaries, making herself indispensable to the men who mattered. She spent so much time in their company that some of her friends thought they heard American inflections in her voice. Naturally energetic and resourceful, she discovered her talent for planning and organizing. "She was the girl you called if you wanted anything," said William Walton. "A flat, theater tickets, cars, restaurants. She always had that extraordinary command for detail."

During the summer of 1942, Pamela injected herself into what Kathleen called a "helluva harouche" between the WVS and the American Red Cross. The two groups were fighting over who would run the canteens and hostels for American troops. The Red Cross started opening service clubs for enlisted men that July. In addition to lodging and meals, they sponsored dances, rounded up tickets to concerts, plays, and films, organized parties and bridge games, and offered companionship to lonely GIs. Under orders from the U.S. Army, only the Red Cross was permitted to care for American troops, and William Stevenson, head of the Red Cross in Britain, decreed that all British women who wanted to help entertain the soldiers in the Red Cross facilities had to wear American uniforms.

At first, British women complied with the edict, but they strongly resisted the American uniforms. The Dowager Marchioness of Reading, formidable head of the WVS, lodged a protest with Stevenson. They had reached an impasse, and Pamela decided to appeal directly to Harry Hopkins. She wrote him a long and heated letter protesting that the American policy was "very wrong." The WVS, she argued, were the "ideal women to give hospitality . . . a comfy armchair and a cup of coffee and a home to relax in." She accused the American Red Cross of devising its policy "for publicity reasons," and insisting that Ambassador Winant agreed with her, she pleaded with Hopkins to intervene directly with the Red Cross organization in Washington. She had already appealed to Stevenson and concluded that he was "very short sighted" and would cause "a great deal of friction" between the Allies. "I am agitating as much as I can," she wrote, "but I feel our hands are tied until the American Red Cross policy is altered in Washington."

Pamela failed to win the battle over uniforms in Red Cross facilities. But her countrywomen prevailed when General Dwight Eisenhower brokered an agreement between the American Red Cross and the British Ministry of Information allowing British agencies to run their own hospitality facilities along with the Red Cross. Pamela's letter to Hopkins provided a revealing glimpse of the way she operated. With characteristic determination, she went straight to the top, pointedly criticizing her adversaries along the way. She showed ruthlessness by maneuvering behind Stevenson's back to cajole Winant and General Mark Clark—and probably Eisenhower as well. The resulting policy cleared the way for Pamela to be even more involved in hospitality for American forces.

Pamela could lodge her protest only because she had such good rapport with Harry Hopkins. She had met him when he first came to London in January 1941. "He was a dear," she later said, "the first light from the Western world." Hopkins continued shuttling in and out of London as Roosevelt's personal emissary. With his lantern jaw, hollow eyes, wispy hair, rumpled suits, and dead cigarette dangling from his lips, Harry Hopkins was not, in Pamela's words, "a pinup." But he was a man of pure power and intelligence, regarded by many as a combination of Rasputin and Svengali, who not only worked by Roosevelt's side but lived in the White House. It was generally believed in Washington that no power was dispensed or significant issue resolved without the imprimatur of Hopkins. Just as important for Pamela was Hopkins's role as Harriman's mentor and champion in Washington.

Pamela considered Hopkins a "man of steel," with a "marvelous capacity to explain president to prime minister as well as the reverse . . . he had a sensitive and clever understanding of the two." He spoke slowly, almost diffidently, with what one observer called a "nobility of expression" that impressed his British listeners. His inner strength was all the more compelling for the death sentence that shadowed him. After stomach cancer surgery in 1939, he had been told he had a month to live. Experimental transfusions of plasma had saved him, but he ignored his doctors' admonitions and continued to drink and smoke. Hopkins's habit of working virtually day and night earned him the nickname "Hurry Up Hopkins" in London.

Hopkins had a keen appetite for intrigue. His manner, Ann Fleming once noted, was one of "detached, cynical charm." Pamela was "aware that Harry Hopkins and Franklin Roosevelt quickly learned of the affair" with Harriman, wrote Christopher Ogden. "She and Hopkins talked openly about it. . . . The President, Hopkins said, got a big kick out of it." In his relationship with Pamela, Hopkins was certainly playing a double game, as he remained a close friend of Marie. Whenever he came to London, he spent evenings and weekends with Pamela and Harriman, and in the summer of 1941, Hopkins and Pamela began a correspondence that lasted three years. She sent him fourteen letters, and he sent her seven; hers were signed variously "love," "much love," "best love," "much devoted love," and "lots of love." He alternated between "ever so cordially yours" and "much love."

Compared to other prominent Englishwomen of her day, such as Diana Cooper and Ann Fleming, Pamela was not naturally inclined to put pen to paper. Once, Henry Luce told her during the war that he and his wife Clare always wrote for forty minutes each night before they went to sleep. "I remember thinking," Pamela recalled, " 'Oh, what a Goddamn bore! Imagine! If something exciting has happened during the day, the last thing you want to do is write it down.' "

Pamela was a doer, not a thinker or recorder. What she did write has the feel of dictation rather than organized thought. Her letters are valuable primarily for capturing her upbeat conversational style—"wonderful" was her favorite adjective—and her manipulative skills, already highly evolved at twenty-one. Mostly, she offered tidbits of political gossip that Hopkins could use.

Her tone was flattering and coquettish. "You'd better come soon and give the Dorchester girls someone to pursue," she wrote in 1941. "If I remember right, they did pursue you, didn't they?" Hopkins volleyed back compliments and coy rejoinders, and sent her gifts such as maple candy and oranges. He was evidently delighted to be courted assiduously by a young woman so lovely and so well connected. Pamela didn't overtly mention her relationship with Harriman, but she usually referred to him in passing. Sometimes she made light of him ("Averell is getting out of hand having all the girls to himself"), but mostly she gently boosted him ("He made a great speech last week, which was carried in full on the front pages of all the newspapers").

When Hopkins announced his engagement to Louise Macy, an elegant fashion editor and Manhattan hostess to whom he was introduced by Marie Harriman in mid-1942, Pamela was at her flirtatious best: "What is all this I hear about you and women, or rather one woman. Anyway my spies tell me she's wonderful." She congratulated him effusively, but after his marriage, the tone of their letters turned more matter-of-fact. Still, Hopkins remained an important ally, and she rarely missed an opportunity to ingratiate, praising his speeches and even using some of his lines in a talk she gave to Randolph's constituents.

While Pamela was busy establishing her place in Anglo-American relations,

Randolph was failing to find a heroic role for himself in the Middle East. In late May 1942, he joined David Stirling for his first raid several hundred miles behind German lines. During a mission to blow up enemy ships in Benghazi harbor, "everything went wrong and the mission proved hilarious in a hideous way," wrote Randolph's cousin Anita Leslie. After wandering around in the dark, the commandos couldn't inflate the rubber boats they needed to get into the harbor, so they scuttled the mission. On their way home from Alexandria to Cairo, their car collided with an army truck and overturned, killing one man and injuring three others. Randolph crushed a vertebra, "from which he would suffer through the years," wrote Leslie. In considerable pain, he was placed in a body cast and hospitalized for a month. Pamela, writing to Hopkins, minimized Randolph's injuries as "severe bruises."

Friends who visited Randolph remarked on his stoicism and positive outlook. When he was released from the hospital in early July, he sent a soothing message to his wife: "Bless you darling. . . . I love you so much. Kiss Baby Winston from me. And be nice to Alexander!" Perhaps Pamela was sending her own message when shortly afterward she banished the white Pekinese after he playfully nipped Little Winston. Alexander's replacement was a gray Persian cat that Pamela named Eisenhower.

It was during his convalescence that Randolph learned the truth about Pamela and Harriman. At first, it came in snippets of gossip from the bar at White's. But when his brother-in-law Duncan Sandys confirmed the stories, Randolph was furious. "He was not jealous," explained the Churchill family chronicler John Pearson. "But he was angry that Harriman had taken advantage of his friendship after being recommended by his father."

Randolph was due to go to England in late July to get further treatment for his back. He went first to New York, where he gave a press conference. His mood was ebullient as he fielded questions about the Middle East. At 3 Grosvenor Square, the occupants underwent what Kathleen called "a rapid shift around," as Sarah Churchill temporarily moved into Pamela's room in the Harriman apartment and loaned Pamela her apartment in another building to share with Randolph. But when he arrived in London late in July, he was no longer the "bronzed, broad-shouldered, khaki-clad figure" who had greeted his wife the previous January. Pamela, wrote Robert Bruce Lockhart, "can no longer bear the sight of Randolph, who . . . repelled her with his spotted face and gross figure." Nor did it help that Randolph was mocked by American soldiers as "Mr. Pam." Profoundly irritated by Pamela's celebrity, hating his role as cuckolded husband, Randolph went on the warpath. His fights with Pamela burst into the open. "It became obvious that the marriage was over," said one friend of the couple. "He and Pam would be together, and he would go off and stay out all night."

"She hates him so much she can't be in a room with him," Waugh wrote in his diary that August. Shortly after Randolph came home, Lord Digby tried to mediate, "I suppose urging her to bear her burden bravely," Waugh concluded. Waugh and Cecil Beaton happened to arrive at the couple's apartment as the older man tried to negotiate a rapprochement. "Panto," Waugh wrote to his wife, "paced up and down the minute hall outside the door after her father had gone. When we obliged her to come in, she could not look at [Randolph] and simply said over her shoulder in acid tones, 'Ought you not to be resting?' whenever he became particularly jolly. She was looking very pretty and full of mischief."

Pamela and Randolph still occasionally appeared in public together in the closing weeks of the summer of 1942. The bombing raids had resumed every other night but didn't crimp London's social life. There were dinners at the Ritz and weekends at Beaverbrook's country house. When CBS chairman Bill Paley flew to London that August, Pamela and Randolph met him at the airport and took him to dinner and a nightclub. On another weekend, Randolph and Pamela visited Lord and Lady Rosebery at Dalmeny in Scotland. In what might have been a perverse effort to recreate their unsuccessful honeymoon, Randolph spent most of the night reading aloud from Winston Churchill's biography of his father, Lord Randolph Churchill.

Harriman was away for several extended trips during Randolph's home leave. Even so, the two men found the time to have lunch together twice—the first time on the day after Randolph's arrival in London on July 30. That they could meet at all may indicate the emotional detachment in each man. Whatever their personal feelings, they were capable of confining their discussion to war-time matters.

Although many people eagerly assigned Pamela the blame for her relationship with Harriman, she earned considerable sympathy in her breakup with Randolph. Randolph was furious that no one seemed to recognize his side. He had bruising quarrels with his parents, who saw Pamela as the aggrieved party and had even begun supporting her with a tax-free income of £500 a year. Churchill continued to regard Pamela as "a great treasure and blessing to us all." The problem, according to John Pearson, was that Winston and Clemmie "accused Randolph of mistreating the mother of his son and heir. In fact they were mistreating each other. He was sleeping with everyone in Cairo, and she was sleeping around in London."

Did the Churchills simply avert their eyes to Pamela's affair with Harriman? As the son of the notoriously promiscuous Jennie Jerome, Churchill was hardly an innocent in such matters. Yet he was capable of self-delusion. Churchill "was impressed by the efforts Pamela was making to improve Anglo-American relations," observed Pearson. The Prime Minister also needed Harriman as a strong advocate for Britain—he even gave him the rank of minister in the British government—and Harriman went out of his way to curry Churchill's favor, showering him with gifts after each trip to the United States. Sir Archibald Clark Kerr, Britain's Ambassador to the Soviet Union, was appalled by Harriman's fawning manner, dismissing him as "no more than a kindly ass . . . a champion bum sucker."

"I don't think Winston and Clemmie thought it possible that Pam would be adulterous with Averell, even though their daughters Sarah and Diana knew," said a close friend of Randolph's. Another friend of both Pamela and Randolph contended that Winston and Clemmie were too enclosed in their own little world to notice. "Winston was involved in himself and she was involved in looking after him," said the friend. "Clemmie was a lousy mother and not particularly sensitive to her own children. She certainly wouldn't be sensitive about her daughter-in-law. You could say both of them were oblivious."

Yet Pamela detected that Churchill fully understood, and according to Christopher Ogden, she "never had a sense that Winston and Clemmie disapproved." A man who knew Pamela intimately after the war also maintained that Churchill had his eyes open. "I know Churchill put Harriman in her way so they would go to bed, so she could find things out and tell him. I am as convinced of that as of anything," said the man. "It was done in the seventeenth and eighteenth centuries by kings. Why not Winston Churchill? He was ruthless. She gave him information. She was living openly in the flat with Harriman. Of course Winston knew, even though his own son was away at war. Pam was useful to him."

Randolph had the same view, and charged his parents as co-conspirators. He told Churchill's private secretary, John Colville, that they "had condoned adultery beneath their own roof" and had submerged their concerns only because of Harriman's importance to Britain. Under those circumstances, Randolph told his parents they were hypocrites for siding with Pamela against him. "He used terrible language and created a rift that never healed," said Randolph's friend Alastair Forbes. "He said they must have known, and they said they didn't know." At one point when Churchill spoke harshly to Randolph about his fault in the marital breakup, Randolph burst into tears and vowed never to speak again to his father. Only once did Churchill give a hint of any displeasure with Pamela. "Why," Winston said to his old friend the Countess of Rosslyn, "I cannot understand it. I went out of my way to be kind to her." But Churchill never turned on Pamela, who had been kind and loyal and extremely helpful to him. He was willing to protect her, even at the expense of going against his own son.

With all the public squabbling and gossip, it was inevitable that Marie would hear about her husband and Pamela. When Harriman was home for two weeks in September 1942, she confronted him at last, telling him, among other things, that he was a fool to get involved with Churchill's daughter-in-law. "She hated Pam Churchill," said her daughter Nancy Lutz. "She was furious about Pam. I don't know how she found out. But she told me she said to Averell, 'If you want a divorce, I will give you one so you can marry Pam.' He said he didn't want to marry her, and he promised to stop seeing her. She was annoyed by Pamela because it was public. She thought it had no dignity. She was of course having a big affair with Eddy Duchin. I remember one day when she was carrying on about Pam: 'How dare she, it's so public,' I said, 'What about you and Eddy?' She said, 'That's entirely different.'"

Harriman backed off because the last thing he wanted was another divorce. His failed marriage to Kitty had embarrassed the family. An affair with the Prime Minister's daughter-in-law thirty years his junior would spark banner headlines on both sides of the Atlantic. Marie certainly had no intention of marrying

Duchin, either. "She was very fond of Ave," explained Nancy. "She would never hurt him." When Harriman promised to discontinue the affair, Marie took him at his word. "It will be fun when this business is over to start fresh and do what we want without being tied to anything enormous," Harriman wrote to Marie on his return to London. Marie in turn resumed her jocular tone: "Have a lovely Christmas hurling gadgets around," she wrote.

At age fifty-one, Harriman had a bond with his thirty-eight-year-old wife that he found difficult to break. They had shared so much, and he admired her wit and talent. While he was away, she had lent Arden to the military and closed her beloved gallery. Despite her severely impaired sight, she worked long hours —from early morning to late afternoon, and then from eight to midnight—for the Ships Service Committee, which organized entertainment for the Navy and raised money for shipboard amenities. Typically, she was pleased to be doing her bit for the enlisted men: "I don't care a rap about the officers," she said. But Harriman knew she hated the job, and he was "terribly proud" that she persevered for the sake of duty.

A number of his letters to her, even before she found out about Pamela, betrayed not only guilt but his urge to set things right. Early in 1942 he had pleaded with Marie to tell him what she wished to do now that she was out of the art business. "I will gladly finance anything you feel worthwhile," he wrote. Perhaps to show his renewed commitment after their showdown, he urged Marie to fly to London that October with Harry and Louise Hopkins. But Marie's doctor, Alvan Barach, was afraid that high altitudes would impair the drainage from one of her eyes. It would be, he said, "a risk to disturb this delicate balance."

One consequence of the confrontation between Marie and Averell Harriman was a dent in the relationship between Marie and Kathleen. "There was always coolness between Kathy and Mummy," Nancy Lutz explained. "I suspect there was a kind of jealousy." Marie rose above her resentment to show a remarkable magnanimity. When Harriman went to New York for a visit later that fall, she sent a big cache of treasures—Kathleen called it "the loot suitcase" —back to London with him. There were jeweled victory Vs, hats with green and black ostrich features, linen handkerchiefs, lipsticks, nightgowns, bathrobes, sweaters, and even baby gifts for Little Winston. Pamela's thank-you note to "Mrs. Harriman" was a classic in saccharine artifice, noting that she and Sarah Churchill had been the "envy of all" when they wore their feathered hats the previous evening.

Despite his promise to Marie, Harriman continued to spend evenings with Pamela in London. Most of the time, they were with Beaverbrook, who entwined himself in the marital and extramarital maneuvering of the Churchills and Harrimans. Beaverbrook maintained a friendship with both Pamela and Marie, but his primary loyalty was to Pamela. And he would do anything to please the Prime Minister, who had reluctantly nudged him out of office in February 1942 over Beaverbrook's misguided efforts to shape Britain's Soviet policy toward accepting Stalin's proposed expansion of his nation's borders to embrace the Baltic States. Beaverbrook, who relished knowing and keeping secrets, was especially fascinated by tangled sexual relationships. "In his view divorce was merely the termination of a contract and there were no 'guilty' or 'innocent' parties," wrote Beaverbrook biographer A. J. P. Taylor.

With Pamela's marriage to Randolph beyond repair, Beaverbrook consulted with Harriman on his financial obligations—since Randolph had nothing to offer and his parents were already giving Pamela £500 a year. "If Randolph cared, Max would have been more upset," said a close friend of Beaverbrook's. "But Max felt that if Pamela could find a rich man to keep her, Randolph would be the first person to cheer." At the end of October, Randolph moved out for good. Pamela's well-orchestrated explanation, setting the grounds of abandonment for later divorce, was that "he had been rude to her in public; had once walked out in the middle of the night; had spent evenings at the officers' mess; had told her he was 'fed up'; had 'seemed to prefer a bachelor's existence.' "

Pamela went to see her father-in-law in the Cabinet Room to tell him that she and Randolph planned to divorce. "He was very upset," she recalled years later, "but he just said, 'Now I know it is not any good for you both, so I don't want that for you, and you have my permission to go forward with the divorce.' He would have liked it otherwise but he knew it couldn't be and he was tremendously understanding."

By early November 1942, Randolph had returned to his commando unit, Harriman was visiting Marie in New York, and Pamela was installed in a luxurious new apartment at 49 Grosvenor Square, just around the corner from Harriman and Kathleen's lodgings, and a stone's throw from the house rented by Lord and Lady Digby for her debutante season. On a weekend at Cherkley, Pamela signed Beaverbrook's guest book with an extra flourish: "The Attic," she called her new home.

The entire tab for Pamela's apartment—£652 a year, $25,000 at today's values—was secretly picked up by Harriman; the middleman was Beaverbrook. Under terms worked out between Harriman and Beaverbrook, Harriman's bankers would deposit funds into Beaverbrook's account with the Royal Bank of Canada, which would then transfer the money to another Beaverbrook account at the Westminster Bank in London. From there, Beaverbrook's financial secretary, George Millar, would pay the quarterly rental for the apartment. It was a fairly straightforward plan except for Harriman's negligence in replenishing the account. For years, Beaverbrook hectored poor Millar for amounts past due. Vexed at Harriman's constant tardiness, Beaverbrook scrawled at one point that the American diplomat "should keep us in funds." Time after time, Millar had to send polite dunning notes to the American multimillionaire.

Pamela was quite pleased with her new life. Randolph was gone for good; she continued her friendship with Kathleen; she remained involved with Harriman—more discreetly—and she was financially secure. "Eventually she wanted to marry someone of wealth and importance, but for that time, she was happy with Ave," said one of her wartime friends. In addition to her apartment, Harriman gave her a substantial yearly allowance. "Ave couldn't marry her but he didn't want to give her up," said a confidante of Beaverbrook's. "So Max organized the settlement—the flat on Grosvenor Square plus three thousand pounds a year. Averell paid this. Max told me about it, and I was intrigued with it. I said to Max, 'Three thousand is not enough.' Max said, 'It is quite enough. She doesn't deserve it.' " Despite Harriman's parsimonious habits, he had always been generous to his mistresses, and in Pamela's case he felt extra pressure to do well by her. "Averell was a very nice stupid fellow," Beaverbrook's confidante continued. "He was conscience-stricken that he had given in to Marie."

At age twenty-two, only four years after being dismissed by the debutante crowd as a silly "butter ball," Pamela was set up in style, with an income from combined sources of more than $16,000 tax-free ($156,000 today) and a grand apartment on Grosvenor Square. She had vowed to find security for herself and Little Winston "on our own," and if it meant becoming a courtesan, so be it. She had flouted social convention and still had entree into the best homes in England. She had finally broken free of provincial Dorset.

CHAPTER
Eleven

PAMELA'S NEW AERIE was located at the top of a wide staircase that wound through the six floors of 49 Grosvenor Square. The building, constructed in 1927, had an elegant foyer, with a marble floor, fireplace, fluted columns, and elaborate moldings on the ceilings and walls. Although flat 11—which could also be reached by elevator—had 2,500 square feet of space, Pamela was not far off when she nicknamed it "The Attic." Most of the rooms had dormer windows and slanting walls, which provided a homey charm. There was a central hallway fifty feet long, with a study on the right and formal dining room on the left, overlooking the rear of the headquarters of MI-5, British military intelligence. The drawing room, further down the hall on the right, had a fireplace and three windows with a view of the Connaught Hotel and London skyline. There was a master bedroom and dressing room, and a second bedroom for Little Winston, who moved in with Nanny Hall a few weeks after his second birthday.

It was an inauspicious time to return a child to the city, which was still being bombed, although Little Winston's presence did lend a sense of propriety to Pamela's domestic arrangement. When Chips Channon visited Pamela shortly after the move, she talked on the phone to Harriman and Beaverbrook while Channon played with young Winston. "He is the most bumptious little boy I have ever seen; he rushes about, talks and makes a noise, a real Churchill," Channon said. The youngster's precociousness was understandable, given the company at 49 Grosvenor Square. One day when Pamela pointed to a picture of the American President and asked little Winston his name, the two-year-old cried, "Grandpa!" Even Beaverbrook objected, perhaps half in jest, to the atmosphere in which Pamela was raising her son. "It shocked me a bit when Winston ran down the hall on Thursday to ask me to have a cocktail with him," he wrote after dining at Pamela's apartment, enclosing a one-hundred-pound check for the "benefit of Winston . . . and I hope you will spend the money on his religious instruction."

In later life young Winston wrote that he had been terrified by the "piercing, spine-chilling wail of the air raid sirens," but he liked to sit by his dormer window and watch the "nightly fireworks display" of the antiaircraft guns in Hyde Park. It was Nanny Hall's job to take him down the staircase and into the air-raid shelter each night, a task that the sixty-year-old servant came to resent.

One night she wouldn't go, and Pamela "raced me downstairs herself," her son later said. Furious over the insubordination, Pamela fired the nanny who had raised her from infancy. Nanny Hall was replaced by a governess, Mrs. Raiker, known as "Bobbie."

The apartment was "very nicely furnished," recalled a woman who visited several times. "There was one minor Impressionist painting." A bookshelf contained a row of photographs of prominent Americans, including Harriman, Roosevelt (who Pamela had never actually met), Hopkins, and Eisenhower. She brought furniture from the house at Ickleford, leaving the less desirable pieces behind. She decorated the apartment with the help of Harriman. Tom Parr, chairman of the London decorators Colefax & Fowler, recalled the time he visited her London flat some years later and admired a Louis XV chaise longue. "It's nice, isn't it?" she murmured. "Averell Harriman had it sent to me from America during the war in 1942."

England's wartime deprivations hardly touched Pamela. Few private citizens had automobiles, but Pamela had an 8-horsepower Ford, courtesy of Harriman. Although gasoline was tightly rationed, she managed an adequate supply, thanks to her friendship with Lady Baillie's longtime beau, Geoffrey Lloyd, who was Minister for Petroleum. Nor did she have to cope with the complicated coupons and forms used to obtain such staples as eggs, milk, and poultry. Those duties fell to Pamela's Scottish housekeeper, Marion Martin, who kept a hoard of black market food.

Clothes had been rationed since the middle of 1941, and government edicts prohibited lace trimming on underwear and other frivolities. A new dress might account for nearly half of the sixty-six coupons allotted an individual each year, and choices were limited to the government's standardized line of "utility clothing." Although society favorite Norman Hartnell did some of the designs, the dresses were dowdy, the fabrics rough. Pamela, however, had a continuing supply of dresses, hats with feathers and veils, nylon stockings, nightgowns, bathrobes, and other luxury items, all provided by her American friends. Averell couldn't bear to see either Kathleen or Pamela in "old clothes" and prided himself on helping them to look attractive.

Like Lady Baillie, Pamela surrounded herself with influential men. Most were American, although she included top British military officers and public figures like Beaverbrook, who was always eager for nuggets of gossip. They came in the evening for what John Colville called "marvellously organized dinners," served by her butler, Sam Hudson. "We were really sort of puritanical in England about rationing," Colville recalled. "Unlike Paris, where there was a great black market, everybody took pride in sticking pretty closely to rationing. But if you dined with Pamela, you would have a five- or six-course dinner, eight or ten guests, and foods you didn't ordinarily see. My guess is that all of us around the table were sort of smirking and saying that Averell was taking good care of his girlfriend."

Generals George Marshall and Dwight Eisenhower came, along with government officials such as Assistant Secretary of War Robert Lovett and prominent writers such as Irwin Shaw, then a private in the Army. Women were made to feel unwelcome. Edward R. Murrow's wife Janet was invited once and never returned. "Pamela ignored me, more or less," she recalled. "The other women and I were sort of off by ourselves. We were there with our husbands, and there were other men. I just felt she wasn't interested in women."

Despite the big names who attended, Pamela's salon lacked the glamour of the legendary gatherings of Emerald Cunard, Ann Fleming, and Sibyl Colefax. Their salons in the thirties and forties were celebrated in the diaries and letters of Evelyn Waugh, Cecil Beaton, and Harold Acton. Pamela's salon attracted only glancing references, largely because she was a bland hostess by English standards. She was not clever like Emerald Cunard, the American heiress who returned to London late in 1942 and entertained in a suite on the seventh floor of the Dorchester Hotel. Nor did she possess the wicked wit of Ann Fleming, or the café society cachet of Colefax.

The leading London hostesses were strong personalities who stimulated their guests with provocative questions and memorable interjections. Pamela, by contrast, created an atmosphere of intimacy and ease. "She pressed my hand in her affectionate, conspiratorial way," Chips Channon wrote. She had learned to beguile through attentiveness, by responding with geniality and care, by being an "eloquent listener," as the Washington columnist Joseph Kraft put it.

It was during these evenings that one of the more provocative aspects of Pamela's personality began to emerge, her mixture of masculinity and femininity that prompted a prominent Washingtonian to call her "a wonderful robust, apple-cheeked, not exactly ribald but gutsy girl, which is very appealing to men." If someone told a dirty joke, she would laugh heartily, a reaction that was more a measure of her social dexterity than a sense of humor. "She was between earthy and refined," said a friend from those days. Pamela's saltiness —unusual in a woman of her generation—helped men relax.

Pamela could also turn a difficult conversation to her advantage. "If a discussion turned to a book that she had not read and someone tried to pin her down," said one Englishman, "she would laugh gaily, turn to the nearest man, and say, 'George has asked me such and such. What do you think?' " She had "immense half-knowledge," said Alastair Forbes. "She could mop up a bit of something. She was like one of those birds that takes food in its beak for the next meal. She would take from her neighbor at lunch, hold it until dinner, and release it. She was in well-informed circles, and her neighbor was impressed."

Though she felt restrained on political matters at Cherkley and Chequers, Pamela had freedom to maneuver at her own table. She may have lacked the authority to advance or destroy careers, but she knew how to help forge alliances and fashion introductions, and she could swap information in the way that Beaverbrook did. She had become adept at teasing out a little knowledge of her own to impress her listeners into revealing even more. "Her politics were conventional," said William Shirer, who was a CBS correspondent in wartime London. "She was not an intellectual. Pam was bright and lighthearted. Like many people in that set, she knew a lot of gossip." As one historian of the period noted, "With a big war going on, everything, even gossip, was of strategic importance. But she was not much of a figure in that time."

According to Pamela's longtime friend William Walton, hard calculation often lay behind her evenings of easy sociability. "These relationships were solid politics," said Walton. "The Americans believed in precision bombing and the British believed in area bombing. Winston used Pamela to plant these ideas on the American generals. She had crucial access at the pinnacle of strategic command. Churchill would question her on what she believed General Fred Anderson's position on certain key bombing strategies was [Anderson was one of the commanders of the American strategic bombing force]. I was reporting on the top command for Time-Life, so I knew exactly what all of these generals were thinking. During the war, the generals would take the correspondents into their confidence because they felt they could trust us, so Pam and I would trade information constantly."

What is most revealing is how well she played double agent in the gossip game—and how she would later boast about being an indispensable intermediary between wartime leaders. Pamela's assistance to Churchill in these matters ensured that he would continue to smile on her even as she turned out his son. "We would be sitting around after dinner," Walton said, "and the phone would ring and Pamela would come and say, 'I have to go. He's calling me now.'" No one had to ask who "he" was, as she proudly trotted off to the Annexe for several hours of bezique.

One of Pamela's favorite—and oft-recounted—stories from this period concerned the Saturday night in July 1943 when she was summoned to Churchill's side during the Anglo-American landing in Sicily to play bezique with him throughout the night: "Every now and again he would put down the cards and he would say . . . [her voice shifting to her resonant Churchill imitation] 'So many brave young men going to their death tonight. It is a grave responsibility.' At four in the morning they came in to say that the winds had dropped and the landings were taking place. I felt utterly exhausted but I felt at least the one thing I could do for my country was to play bezique with him until four in the morning."

While Harriman was still the leading man in her life, Pamela had a series of affairs with men who frequented her salon. "She was close to everyone," said Walton. "She knew who I was sleeping with and I knew who she was with." Unlike many of her male British contemporaries, who saw what she was up to, the Americans seemed helpless when she turned on the charm. "Her horizons were widening," noted Alastair Forbes. "It must have been about this time I overheard her say, 'My dear, a million pounds doesn't go very far nowadays.'"

In the summer of 1942, John Hay "Jock" Whitney arrived in London as a captain in the U.S. Army. With an allowance of £1,000 pounds a month ($38,000 today), he and his polo-playing friend Tommy Hitchcock moved into a large apartment on Grosvenor Square. Nearly every weekend they threw lively parties for American officers, titled Englishwomen, and show business personalities. Pamela was introduced to Whitney by Harriman and Kathleen. She soon became a regular at his parties, and he frequently turned up at her dinners. That winter Whitney took Pamela to a New Year's Eve party given by his cousin, Lady Daphne Straight. Afterward she often was seen around town with the diffident but glamorous millionaire.

Whitney had an even bigger bank account than Harriman, at least $200 million by some estimates. Tall, athletic, and handsome, with a straight nose, dark hair, and a cleft chin, he was a man of "elegant shyness," who suffered from a slight stutter. Whitney had been married twice, the second time in March 1942 to Betsey Cushing Roosevelt, a former daughter-in-law of the President. Like Harriman, Whitney had lost his father at an early age, inherited an enormous fortune, and spent his years after graduating from Yale chasing women and playing polo. As an investor in Broadway plays and films such as *Gone With the Wind*, he was prominent in New York's café society. His enthusiasm for horse racing and polo had taken him on extended trips to England before the war, including a stint at Oxford, where he intermittently studied history and literature. Among those he visited was Pamela's mentor Lady Baillie, another Whitney cousin. Before marrying Betsey, he had a long and highly publicized romance with Louise Macy, who would later marry Harry Hopkins. He had also been romantically linked with Tallulah Bankhead, Joan Crawford, and Paulette Goddard.

"Jock did sleep with Pam," said Tex McCrary, who worked and socialized with Whitney during the war. Pamela, according to Christopher Ogden, "would have loved" to marry Whitney if he had asked her. But Whitney never intended to marry Pamela, although they did become confidantes. "Jock and Pam were never serious," said one of Whitney's longtime friends. "When he mentioned her later it was with amusement, not regret or wistfulness."

It was obvious to the society crowd in London that Pamela's affairs with Harriman and Whitney were simultaneous. The two men had known each other in New York, dined together several times in London, and even shared Christmas in 1942 at a big cocktail party for Americans at the Harriman flat. (Pamela did not attend, however; she was with the Churchills at Chequers.) The Whitney-Harriman relationship was cordial enough that in a letter to Marie, Harriman praised Jock for being hardworking and serious. "Jock knew he shared Pam," said McCrary, "but he knew that all he needed to do was call her and she would be there." Their affair continued until early 1944 when Whitney left London for North Africa and Europe, where he spent the rest of the war on the staff of General Ira Eaker.

Although Pamela already was being nicely supported by Harriman, she began receiving a stipend from Whitney as well, according to a source in the Whitney family. "Jock was very taken with Pam," said a Whitney family member. "He set up a trust fund for her." In all likelihood, neither man knew what the other was doing, since talking about such financial arrangements was taboo. Harriman, after all, had gone to great lengths to conceal his subsidy for Pamela by using Beaverbrook as a go-between. Whitney's friends weren't surprised by his generosity. He was a soft touch who thought nothing of paying school tuitions for the children of his friends. "One marvelous characteristic of Jock," William Paley once remarked, "is his utter lack of suspicion of other people." As for Pamela, one wartime friend observed, "Pam was capable of getting two handouts at the same time, and she did. She would live at a certain level, and usually someone would come along who would pay for it."

Having announced his intention to stay married to Marie, Harriman had no grounds for possessiveness. Back home he went his own way—to an extent that Pamela could not have imagined. On trips to Washington during the war, he two-timed her with none other than Kay Halle, one of the women Randolph Churchill had tried to marry before he met Pamela. "When Ave came back to London, Pam was going around with other people, and there wasn't much he could do about it," explained one close observer in London. "He wasn't there all the time, and it didn't bother him that she was seeing other men. After all, he had a life in the United States. Those were the rules of the game."

The Americans in London regarded Pamela's behavior with a combination of tolerance and amusement. Kick Kennedy, who had left London in 1940 when Roosevelt removed her father as ambassador for his pro-German statements, returned from the United States in mid-1943 to work for the Red Cross and to be reunited with her beau Billy Hartington, the heir to the Duke of Devonshire. Although she had disliked Pamela during their debutante season, Kick now enjoyed her company. Kick told her brother that Pamela had surprisingly become "London's glamour girl," and observed to her parents that Pamela's friends had changed a lot from the days when she came out.

"Pam liked to go around with men, and she liked sex and she was attractive, and they liked her," explained one American journalist who knew her in London. "She said no to some and yes to some. The whole life in London was reasonably casual. It was the mood of the time. It was carefree. Most American men who came were married but had girlfriends, and nobody cared. It was a fact of life." The American men gave Pamela the nicknames "Porcupine" and "Spam," but her lovers were "reasonably discreet. Averell was discreet and Jock was too," said a friend of Pamela's.

The English, particularly the women, took a harsher view. The deep-throated laugh, the concentrated gaze of sincerity, the suggestive remarks delivered in a whisper—all grated on London's social arbiters. They were also put off by the way she looked and presented herself. "In that society of England, it was a little more of a rarity to be glamorous," explained the English stage director Peter Glenville, a friend of Pamela's for many years.

But Pamela had the same disregard for public opinion that characterized her ancestor Jane Digby whom she admired. "I don't think her reputation was something she thought about," said one American who knew her during the war. "It didn't bother her. She had her own friends and didn't give a damn what the stuffy people in London thought. She never said that, but it was in her manner." Pamela subscribed to the view that rules are made for fools to obey. "She decided she would do what she wanted and have the displeasure of some, rather than adhere to an artificial standard and be in a cage," explained another man who knew her for many years.

Pamela's parents were consumed by their war work, and far removed from the scene of her amorous adventures. But Lord Digby knew more than most people assumed. He had tried to help mend Pamela's relations with Randolph, and he was aware that Pamela had lived with Harriman in Grosvenor Square. (She brought Harriman to visit the Digbys once, at their wartime home in Cerne Abbas, near Minterne, which had been turned into a naval hospital.) Lord Digby took the practical view, according to a relation, that "unless what someone did affected the family, it was up to the individual. People were living their own lives." Lady Digby, said one intimate of the Digby family, "didn't want to believe it and didn't. She always said she didn't know about Averell. Had she known, she would have disapproved."

The Digbys also owed Harriman a debt of gratitude. In 1943, Sheila Digby began suffering muscular weakness and pain that British doctors diagnosed as incurable and progressively debilitating. Harriman had her sent to New York, where he paid for her living and medical expenses. Sheila was cured by American doctors who found that she was suffering from fibrositis mysteriously complicated by arsenic and lead poisoning. "Although her family are well to do, they cannot send money out of this country," Harriman wrote to his doctor, explaining the financial arrangements. In deference to Marie, Harriman delegated his daughter Mary to handle Sheila's care.

Throughout 1942 and 1943, Harriman continued to travel frequently, although he spent considerably more time in London than he had his first year abroad. He had moved into a position even more important than that of Gil Winant, the popular American ambassador. Winant was too much the gentleman to object when Harriman usurped his duties one by one—joining Churchill's War Cabinet meetings, flying off to Moscow to negotiate with Stalin, taking a front-row seat at all the Big Power conferences—and supplanted him in the affections of the Churchill family. The relationship with the Churchills was further complicated when Winant, who was married, had a surreptitious love affair with the Prime Minister's daughter, Sarah, who had left her husband Vic Oliver in 1941. Churchill's private secretary John Colville learned of the romance, and Sarah suspected her father knew as well. Tormented by the futility of the affair, Winant suffered from bouts of depression and flew into rages that alarmed his embassy colleagues.

Harriman thoroughly enjoyed his channel to power in Whitehall and Washington. Yet while the Roosevelt administration was pleased with his work, the President and Hopkins had tried on several occasions to move him elsewhere since the fall of 1941, when he first went to Moscow for Lend-Lease discussions with Stalin. At that time Hopkins and Roosevelt had sought to capitalize on his expertise and contacts by urging him to become Ambassador to the Soviet Union. Harriman declined, partly because he understood how bleak and isolated the Moscow post could be, but also because he relished his position as a big-time player in Britain. Only six months later, Hopkins twice suggested to Harriman that he consider returning to Washington and accepting an unspecified job with the administration. Again Harriman resisted, arguing that he had to "see through" his job in London.

The matter assumed an urgency in May 1943, when Roosevelt and Hopkins needed a new envoy in Moscow and again suggested that Harriman take the post. Roosevelt appealed to Harriman's vanity over dinner at the White House, contending that he understood Stalin better than anyone. Still Harriman balked at being sent so far from the action and becoming a "glorified communications officer." Harriman suggested that he sign on for a few months with the understanding that he could return to London if Moscow proved unproductive. Roosevelt didn't bite and dispatched Hopkins to try a new argument: The United States needed Harriman to help persuade Stalin to enter the war against Japan. Finally, in late August, Harriman accepted the job.

To Pamela's dismay, Harriman did not tell her about his impending transfer. When she wrote to him at last in Washington on September 24, her tone wavered. At first she tried to stir his jealousy by praising the American generals and bragging that "there isn't one that I'm not on the most intimate terms with!" She painted a seductive image of herself lying in the sunshine on the ledge of a window at 49 Grosvenor Square. "I have put a rug to lie on, and it is heavenly," she wrote. "In fact any moment I'll fall asleep." But she turned insistent in a note written later that evening, when she recounted the "appalling" speculation about his future and begged to know the truth. While she wished him the best if he chose Moscow, she wanted to know if he might keep his staff in London as well and visit from time to time. In a hastily scribbled postscript to "darling," she expressed her longing and love for him. "See you some day soon," she concluded. "Much love, P."

Roosevelt announced the appointment on October 1, and three days later Harriman arrived in London for his final preparations. Although Kathleen had heard rumors of the appointment weeks earlier, it was only then that her father told her she had to take a leave from the job she loved—she had advanced from cub reporter at the International News Service to correspondent for *Newsweek,* which Harriman partly owned—and accompany him to Moscow. Pamela threw herself into gathering such scarce items as coat hangers and warm clothing, including woolen underwear from Jock Whitney, for Harriman and Kathleen to take with them. Pamela and Harriman dined together with Beaverbrook on October 10, and three days later, the Harrimans were off.

By December, Pamela had taken up with thirty-five-year-old CBS Radio broadcaster Edward R. Murrow. He was married, but this time his wife wasn't across the ocean. Janet Murrow lived with her husband in London, sipped tea with Clementine Churchill, and knew very well the reputation of her new adversary. These circumstances would pose a fresh challenge for twenty-three-year-old Pamela Digby Churchill.

CHAPTER

Twelve

AVERELL HARRIMAN may have been the most important American in London, but Edward R. Murrow was surely the most glamorous. During the Blitz, his dramatic nightly broadcasts on CBS Radio helped stir pro-British sentiment and counteract isolationists in the United States. He was handsome, if somewhat careworn, with jet black hair brushed back from a strikingly high forehead, and penetrating dark eyes deepset under heavy brows. He dressed in Savile Row suits, wore his hat at a jaunty angle, and invariably had a cigarette hanging from his mouth—a habit so irritating to Dwight Eisenhower that he once remarked that it made Murrow look like a "gangster." To the British, especially the London hostesses who jockeyed to entertain him, Murrow "seemed to come from the center of America," said writer Robert Landry, who profiled him in *Scribner's* magazine.

Murrow was born in 1908 in Polecat Creek, North Carolina. He grew up poor in Washington State, the youngest child of hardworking Quakers. His father was a farmer turned locomotive engineer. His mother was a dedicated homemaker who answered the telephone with "Hey-o" for fear of using the word "Hell." In lean times, Ethel Murrow went without food to ensure that her children had enough to eat. Both parents were emotionally withdrawn, and Ethel Murrow wouldn't let her sons play cards or dance, never mind smoke or drink.

Somber, moody, studious, young Egbert Roscoe—he had changed his first name to Ed when he worked as a lumberjack as a teenager—was deeply influenced by several women who taught him public speaking in school. He first tapped the power of his unusually resonant voice as a high school debater, but it was some years after graduating from Washington State College that he finally moved into broadcasting at CBS. Transmitting from the rooftops at the height of London's bombing raids, Murrow's reports were filled with drama and what his biographer A. M. Sperber called "subtle, guarded advocacy."

In London, the onetime backwoodsman reinvented himself as a man-about-town with a passion for liberal politics. He befriended Socialist Harold Laski and the Marquess of Salisbury. He was a manic worker, often taking what his bosses considered unnecessary physical risks to report his stories. He chain-smoked and drank enormous amounts of coffee. His boss, CBS chairman William Paley, sometimes wondered if Murrow had a death wish. "Even at the peak of fame and fortune, Ed couldn't sleep," one colleague said. "He was exhausted but the will was driving him on."

Murrow was married to the former Janet Huntington Brewster, a delicate beauty with a Mayflower pedigree. Three years younger than her husband, she had pale blue eyes, coppery brown hair, and a reticent demeanor. She had grown accustomed to Murrow's absorption in his work, as well as his habit of opening their flat at 84 Hallam Street to his cronies for all-night poker games. Janet reacted by pursuing her own interests—broadcasting "women's stories" on the war for CBS and working with Clementine Churchill to organize "Bundles for Britain." Frustrated by her husband's thoughtlessness—he stood her up for movie dates to keep company with his friends—she sought companionship with a thirty-nine-year-old British reporter named Philip Jordan, who was also married. Jordan was sympathetic and considerate, and in late spring 1941 Janet had a brief affair with him that ended when his newspaper transferred him to Moscow that June.

Although Ed Murrow was often pursued by other women, he seemed awkward and shy around them. "He was indifferent to women, polite but that's all," recalled CBS correspondent Howard K. Smith. The wife of another CBS correspondent put it less delicately: "I don't think he had very strong sexual drives." His friendship with Pamela Churchill had begun in an atmosphere of camaraderie rather than romance when he joined the crowd of American journalists who often dined with her and Kathleen. Returning from a trip to the United States for medical tests back in July 1941, he had thoughtfully brought canned orange juice for Little Winston.

Janet Murrow only grew suspicious when Churchill's close confidant and Minister of Information, Brendan Bracken, offered her husband a job as editor-in-chief of the BBC in the summer of 1943. "Ed said if he took the position it would make a great difference to me," recalled Janet. "I didn't know what he meant. I was very stupid. Later I suspected that Pam might have had something to do with it because of her connection with Bracken. I do think it was her effort with Bracken to get him to the BBC. I believe she was engineering that." During a trip to New York that summer, Murrow decided against the offer.

If Murrow and Pamela were having an affair at that time, they managed to keep it quiet. But by December 1943 there was no doubt about their relationship. Late that month, Pamela and Murrow showed up for a weekend at Cherkley and signed Beaverbrook's guest book together; he gave an address on Halkin Street, not the apartment he shared with Janet. "It was when Averell went off to Moscow," said Janet. "Ed had been with Pamela a good deal in her apartment, and I think she decided when Averell disappeared that Ed was the person she wanted. He was at her apartment much more often. I had an instinct about it. I knew they were seeing a lot of each other."

Before long, Janet had more than instinct to go on. "I know they used to go out into the country for walks, and they would read poetry on some of those occasions. She always left something from these trips—once it was a book of poems which had her name in it. It was an American poet, maybe one that Ed used to read with his favorite professor at college. Another time it was a pair of Pamela's gloves in one of Ed's pockets. I thought she was sending me a message."

But Janet wouldn't rise to Pamela's provocations. "Ed never talked to me about it, and I never asked," Janet recalled. Instead, she retreated by taking a job with Ambassador Gil Winant, traveling around England to hear complaints about American servicemen and reporting to the British-American Liaison Board. As winter ended in 1944, the Germans launched a new round of London bombing raids that inflicted widespread damage. At the suggestion of the Prime Minister, Little Winston was shipped out to Chequers with Bobbie, his governess, so by April Pamela was once again on her own.

Murrow began spending nights with Pamela, who modified her life to suit his needs. "She liked being out and around," said one wartime friend. "Ed was quieter and didn't go out as much at night as a lot of the other press did. He was more solitary, so she spent time with him alone." Pamela "seemed rather happy with Ed," recalled William Shirer, although one woman who knew them couldn't help observing, "She certainly had more fun with Ave and his friends."

Pamela and Murrow stayed together at 49 Halkin Street, an apartment that CBS used for traveling correspondents. "She would be there with him for the night," said Shirer. "I thought of her as Ed's girl. He seemed proud to be going with her, the way he acted. Ed took a dim view of life; more than a cynic. He was almost a misanthrope. He had lots of friends devoted to him and he to them. But he didn't have girlfriends. He wasn't interested in that. I often wondered what drew him to Pam. He knew all the important people in London, including Randolph Churchill. Pam was in the swirl of the insiders in London."

Pamela's status may have been one reason for the attraction. "Having a romance with the fascinating daughter-in-law of the Prime Minister must have been heady wine," said Murrow's friend, Mary Warburg. "Ed was knocked off his feet by this absolutely glorious and desirable young woman," said fellow CBS correspondent Charles Collingwood. "Her connections impressed him. It was part of a journalist's job to cultivate such people. But it wasn't for any of these self-seeking reasons that he was attracted. She just bowled him over."

Pamela soothed Murrow during his dark moods; understanding his social discomfort, she made an effort to put him at ease. "She didn't have that condescension of British upper-class women, particularly to Americans," said Shirer. "She didn't put on airs with Ed, and that appealed to him. In some ways Pam enlivened Ed. He was sort of a lugubrious guy." Yet Shirer was taken aback by a change in Murrow's manner when he was in Pamela's company, a kind of forced lightheartedness of the sort practiced by the English upper class. At those moments, Shirer found Murrow disconcertingly out of character.

Unlike Harriman and Whitney, Murrow was not wealthy. He appealed to Pamela, said one of her wartime friends, because "Ed Murrow was more powerful than rich." To Pamela, Murrow was "a romantic figure," said her friend, Clay Felker, the former editor of *New York* magazine. "He was in journalism, which she understood through Beaverbrook, Winston, and Randolph. It was a world closely allied to politics."

Throughout 1944, Janet Murrow tried not to think about her husband and

Pamela, and she avoided confiding in anyone. Under the circumstances, Janet's friends found her serenity remarkable. "I did feel a strain," she recalled, "but I felt there wasn't anything I could do about it. It was difficult not to feel jealous, but I felt that was a waste of time and strength." Janet knew not only that Murrow was "both in love and infatuated," but that "Pamela was doing her best to make him so. She wanted to have a husband who was strong in some way—a person who had strong ideas or money. Of course Averell Harriman had ideas and money, and Ed just had the ideas. She really was a manipulator. Like so many English girls of that generation, she was brought up to go after men." Although Janet didn't say so at the time, she believed that "Pamela wouldn't have been happy with Ed for long because he didn't have enough money."

Even as she was going with Murrow, Pamela was having affairs with several other men—at least in part to throw Murrow off balance. Around the time of Jock Whitney's departure from London early in 1944, Pamela began sleeping with Major General Fred Anderson, the top American bombing commander whose views she had been diligently transmitting to her father-in-law. A handsome man in his late thirties with what diarist Robert Lockhart termed a "quiet impressive manner," Anderson came often to Pamela's apartment. Beaverbrook invited them to spend weekends together at Cherkley, where he pumped the general for information to use in his newspapers. (Beaverbrook by then occupied a marginal government role, negotiating postwar civil aviation routes.) During one July weekend in 1944, Pamela noted in Beaverbrook's guest book: "the bomb fell at 4:30 AM," under which Anderson wrote: "ditto."

Pamela was also linked with William Paley, Murrow's boss and friend, which posed complications for her romance with Murrow. Years afterward Paley admitted that he and Pamela had an affair for a brief period early in 1944, and his wife Dorothy said, "I have no doubt that she had an affair with Bill, as she certainly did with Jock. She was more than capable of doing two things at once." But in later years Pamela publicly rebuffed suggestions that she and the American broadcasting mogul had been intimate. "Her position is simple," said one of her close friends. "She says it couldn't have happened with Bill because of Ed." Still, some of Pamela's friends knew better. "Half the time Pamela didn't remember she went to bed with Bill Paley," said one.

Paley had the all the qualities that Pamela sought in a man: wealth, a magnetic personality, a powerful position, virile good looks. From the moment he arrived in London in March 1944 as an army intelligence officer, he was a frequent guest at 49 Grosvenor Square. Lady Mary Dunn encountered them once in Paley's suite at Claridges and noted Pamela's "very proprietary" manner toward Paley, with whom Lady Mary had once been in love. "I was filled with jealousy," recalled Lady Mary, who left the couple feeling "sour as a bit of old rhubarb."

Murrow was very much in the forefront of Pamela's life during the summer of 1944. The openness of their relationship, Murrow's biographer Sperber wrote, was "a radical departure for a man who formerly wouldn't so much as be photographed without his wedding ring." Pamela sometimes went with

Murrow while he broadcast his reports to American listeners late at night from a cramped studio. On June 6, however, Pamela stayed in her apartment while Murrow anchored CBS's D-Day coverage in London, working in the studio for fifty-six hours. "I didn't dare ring up my friends for news," she wrote to Kathleen Harriman in Moscow. "I felt the only thing was to keep quiet."

A week later the Germans unleashed their newest weapon of destruction, the V-1, a pilotless plane nicknamed the "doodlebug," which carried a ton of explosives. The V-1s were launched by the thousands from the Pas de Calais in northern France. They approached with a loud buzzing sound, then fell silent before they dove to the earth, a nerve-wracking sequence that terrified Londoners more than the bombing raids they had experienced. By the end of the first week there were nearly ten thousand casualties. Pamela maintained her calm, writing to Harriman: "I had just gotten to sleep when I was awakened by the siren and gunfire. I ran to the window just in time to see a black monster with a flaming tail roar past at the height of my window. Well anyway, it went on all day; warnings, gunfire, the buzz, the all-clear. It really is very bloody, not frightening, just uncanny and sadistic."

For nearly a year Pamela had been applying herself with characteristic energy to her most visible volunteer job in the war effort. It was the brainchild of Brendan Bracken, who felt that university-educated American officers and enlisted men needed a club where they could "escape from the noisy bonhomie of army life," in the words of the art historian Kenneth Clark, to learn about English cultural life. England was filled with clubs for GIs run by the Red Cross —service centers, dance halls, and canteens—and there were exclusive officers clubs such as the one run by the American hostess Laura Corrigan for Allied air force officers. But there was nothing that catered specifically to doctors, scientists, architects, lawyers, and other men who pursued high-profile professional careers in peacetime.

To set up such a club, Bracken had approached Pamela Churchill and Barbie Wallace, daughter of the celebrated architect Edwin Lutyens and wife of Euan Wallace, Churchill's Minister of Transport. It would be called the Churchill Club, in honor of the Prime Minister. Although Pamela was often portrayed as the sole impresario of the operation, her co-hostess played a crucial role, as did another well-born woman, Kenneth Clark's wife Jane, who oversaw the club library and arranged "cultural" programs.

The Churchill Club was located in Ashburnham House, a lovely sixteenth-century mansion near the Houses of Parliament that had served as the library of Westminster School. When the club opened in August 1943, so many servicemen appeared that the kitchen couldn't keep up, prompting a gallant Dwight Eisenhower to help with the cooking. But thanks to Pamela's efficiency, the food was plentiful and well prepared.

In the evenings, the Churchill Club offered concerts and lectures. As secretary of the club, Pamela helped organize many events, issuing invitations to guest lecturers on official Churchill Club stationery. Kenneth Clark lectured frequently on art, Vaughan Williams on music, and Walter Monckton on the law. Actors such as Peggy Ashcroft and Cecil Day Lewis gave dramatic readings, and T. S. Eliot and Edith Sitwell recited their poems. On one memorable occasion, Sitwell calmly read "Still Falls the Rain" as a buzz-bomb cut its engine and exploded nearby.

The club "was jammed all day long," recalled William Walton, and the members mingling around the fine oak staircase of Ashburnham House regarded one another as clubmen first, without regard to rank. Pamela was nearly always on the premises, delighting in the effect she had on her many admirers, smiling at them and touching each one gently on the shoulder or arm. But it was the top brass and the occasional celebrities (Clark Gable, James Stewart) whose accolades gave her the greatest satisfaction. She kept the club going for more than two years, finally shutting it down in November 1945.

During the latter years of the war, Randolph Churchill periodically appeared in London for brief but tempestuous visits. The rows with his family continued, most of them over his broken marriage. The most explosive encounter occurred in the summer of 1944 when during dinner with his family he struck his sister Sarah in the face in a drunken fury, prompting his father to call an officer to eject him. Randolph was drinking more heavily than ever—two bottles of gin a day, by Diana Cooper's account—and no one seemed capable of controlling him. Before he and Pamela had parted company in the fall of 1942, he had renewed his pursuit of his old flame Laura Charteris, who was finally divorcing her estranged husband Lord Long to marry the third Earl of Dudley. Laura had given Randolph moral support while he and Pamela were separating, and after he returned to the Middle East he wrote her passionate letters pleading with her to marry him.

In January 1944, Randolph had been posted to Yugoslavia, along with Evelyn Waugh and Freddie Birkenhead, an old Etonian classmate whose father, the first Lord Birkenhead, had been a close friend and political ally of Winston Churchill. Their mission was helping Tito and his Communist partisans fight the Nazis. After Randolph's trip home that July, his plane crashed as it approached an airstrip in Croatia. Eleven men died and nine others were injured. Randolph's legs were hurt and his back further damaged.

By then the war had begun turning in the Allies' favor. Following the landings of 850,000 American, British, and other Allied troops in Normandy on D-Day, their forces had moved steadily across France as other Allied divisions drove northward in Italy and up the Rhône River valley while the Soviet Union pushed its offensive across Eastern Europe toward Germany. After strong initial resistance to the Allied advance, German armies retreated across the Seine, and French Resistance forces staged an uprising in Paris. On August 25, 1944, the Americans and General Charles de Gaulle's Free French and Resistance forces liberated Paris.

Early that September, as British and American armies fanned north and east across the Seine, Ed Murrow flew to Paris. He was put off by the French, whose surrender early in the war seemed to him spineless compared to the grit of the British. In his broadcasts he noted with a tinge of derision that Paris had hardly been touched by the war: "those familiar, well fed but still empty-looking faces around the fashionable bars and restaurants—the last four years seem to have changed them very little." After forty-eight hours, Murrow had a bellyfull and returned to London.

Not so Pamela, who had followed him to Paris and decided to linger. A war correspondent groupie, she frequented the bar of the Ritz Hotel with Charles Collingwood and William Walton. They introduced her to Ernest Hemingway and other celebrities. "I can see her there that September," recalled Walton. "Perhaps the world looked open to her then. Paris was free. She might be able to leave London, the filth, the soot, the hunger, and leave this foolish and ambitious and terribly unlucky marriage to Randolph Churchill. I remember her standing at the Ritz bar. . . . When she turned those eyes on you, the attention was incredible. . . . It was like a beam of light that would fall on you."

Janet Murrow was crumbling under the pressure of her husband's continuing romance with Pamela. Suffering what she later termed "mental and physical exhaustion," she flew back to New York in late September and checked into a hotel. Murrow was alarmed and urged her to get medical help. Her doctors prescribed bed rest. During her absence, Pamela pressed Murrow to ask for a divorce and marry her.

William Paley sensed his star correspondent was making a major mistake. Polecat Creek was a world apart from Minterne Magna, and Pamela and Murrow had starkly different sensibilities, as their reactions to a liberated Paris had shown. Paley knew Murrow could never provide for Pamela on a level that would satisfy her, but he did nothing until Murrow told him he wanted to ask Janet for a divorce.

"At that point, Bill sat down and told Ed not to do it," said CBS president Frank Stanton, to whom Paley recounted the incident. "Bill first appealed to Ed as a friend. He knew the woman and he knew she wouldn't be good for Ed. Bill told Ed that after destroying his marriage, she would destroy him. Ed still resisted, and finally Bill pulled rank. 'Ed, you will not do it,' Bill said. Paley spoke as Ed's boss, not as his friend. 'I saved that marriage,' Bill told me at the end of 1945, and he said it to me a number of times over the years, even six months before he died. Bill admired Pamela. 'She's the greatest courtesan of the century,' he told me. He admired her for her skill, as a professional, how she operated with men. But he knew she would be bad for Ed."

Murrow continued to see Pamela nevertheless, leading her to believe that marriage was still a possibility. But he heard little from Janet back in New York, and he began writing his wife letters filled with longing, love, and self-recrimination. "Wonder what you are making of America," he wrote at the end of September. "You are the only thing over there that I want to see." He brooded that as a couple they had "missed too much. . . . If we have any sense the best years of our lives should be ahead of us. . . . My mind is weary and people sicken me. . . . Maybe we can't get away from this life and this way of making a living but it seems to me we ought to try." He rebuked himself for taking "your love and kindness and tolerance too much for granted," and the day before their tenth anniversary on October 27, 1944, he proclaimed, "Let's renew the contract . . . and I should like an indefinite option."

Murrow had previously mentioned an offer from "brother Paley" to take an executive job back in New York. Most significant was his account in the October 26 letter of a dinner at Pamela's (referred to disparagingly as "little P"). He and "the lion of the evening," Sir Charles Portal, chief of the British air staff, had spent much of the evening praising Janet. Portal's enthusiasm, Murrow reported, "didn't go down so well with the hostess. . . . I think probably the saturnine flyer is marked down as the next victim." In fact, Portal, who was also married, had been a longtime admirer of Pamela's; after stringing Portal along, she eventually spurned him. Although he was powerful and widely respected, Portal was very homely, and he lacked a great fortune.

By mid-December, Murrow was on his way with Janet to Texas for an extended vacation at a dude ranch. They remained incommunicado from CBS, loafing, riding, fishing, and repairing their relationship, blissfully removed from the pressures of London and the war. "We didn't talk about Pamela at all," Janet recalled. "We were very happy to be together."

When the Murrows returned to England the following spring, Janet was pregnant at age thirty-five. "We had always tried to have children," Janet recalled. "I just never could get pregnant, so I was thrilled, and I think he was too." Murrow declared that whatever the gender, the baby would be called Casey, although he openly yearned for a boy. As Murrow's affection for his wife rekindled, he decided against divorce. Some years later, when Mary Warburg asked Murrow why he didn't marry Pamela, he said, "I've never been so in love with anyone in my life as I was with Pam, but it wasn't meant to be." Yet even after reconciling with Janet, Murrow could not bring himself to cut loose from Pamela. "I think Ed was seeing Pamela still," Janet recalled. "He probably was, even when I was pregnant."

On May 8 Churchill announced Germany's unconditional surrender to the Allies, and London erupted in a spontaneous celebration of VE-Day. Pamela watched for a while from her Grosvenor Square window as crowds gathered in the streets. "Then, like everybody else in London, I wandered around," Pamela recalled in a television interview fifty years later. "I went into Downing Street, and Winston Churchill was already very much involved in the future." Murrow spent the day broadcasting from Piccadilly Circus, and after finishing at 2:00 A.M., he marched down Regent street with a group of his colleagues.

The birth of Charles Casey Murrow in London on November 6, 1945, marked the end of Pamela's chances to capture the American broadcaster. "Ed had always wanted a child and he wasn't going to let this one down," said Janet. A month after Casey's arrival, Murrow went to New York to negotiate his new job at CBS Headquarters.

Pamela's divorce from Randolph was filed on December 18, 1945, an uncontested action on the grounds that Randolph had deserted her for three years. (The divorce would not become official for another six months.) Neither party raised the issue of adultery, although at one point Randolph said to Stuart Scheftel, "I want to sue Averell for $1 million as a co-respondent." Scheftel recalled, "I think Randolph was thinking more of the $1 million than of Pam."

Pamela took custody of five-year-old Winston and immediately dispatched him to his Digby grandparents, who, Winston later wrote, "I scarcely knew but with whom I was to spend much of my childhood in the years to come."

Only days later, Pamela was en route to New York, on a flight with her friend Barbie Wallace and Barbie's new husband Herbert Agar, who had served as Ambassador Winant's assistant at the American Embassy. Igor "Ghighi" Cassini, who wrote the Cholly Knickerbocker "Smart Set" gossip column on international society in the *New York Journal-American*, recorded her arrival: "The Hon. Mrs. Pamela Churchill has put the broad Atlantic between her and London's Buzz-Buzz set . . . successfully escaping the behind-the-hands whispering that she was going to be Winston Churchill's ex-daughter-in-law."

"Ed was in America," recalled Janet Murrow, "and I read in the paper one day that Pamela had flown to New York. I remember thinking, 'Oh my, there she goes.' I thought it might be a last-ditch effort." It was, and it failed. "God knows what she was doing in New York then," recalled one man who saw her at the time. "Murrow was the guy she was after. She was staying at the Ambassador, feeling her oats. But Murrow turned her down." After spending Christmas in New York, Pamela was off again, this time to Palm Beach to stay with Kick Kennedy and her family.

In later years, Pamela idealized her liaison with Murrow. She described their relationship as the root of her involvement in the Democratic Party—even more important, it seemed, than Democratic Party convert Averell Harriman—since her background, outlook, and social circle would have made her a natural Republican. "Everyone is influenced when they are young," she said in the early 1980s, "and women are easier to influence than men, and are mostly influenced by men. The philosophy of several men I admired was liberal. Ed Murrow had a big influence, and he was extremely liberal."

Pamela's recollection of her last days with Murrow in late 1945 was noteworthy for the high drama she often attached to turning points in her relationships with men. She reached New York on Christmas Eve and by her account was Murrow's constant companion for the next ten days. During that period, she and Murrow supposedly dined with Lillian Hellman, John Steinbeck, Mary Warburg and her husband Eddie, and had Christmas dinner with Bill Paley.

According to Pamela, Murrow had signed his new CBS contract the day she arrived. Christopher Ogden wrote that shortly afterward, she accepted his proposal to marry her, "throwing her arms around his neck and squeezing him with all her might." By Pamela's account, they even looked at a town house they planned to buy together. When Pamela went to Florida, Murrow supposedly left for London to confront Janet; he was to return to New York in three weeks after having agreed on the terms of a divorce. Instead, Pamela said Murrow sent her a telegram saying, "Casey Wins," while she was with the Kennedys. On her return to Manhattan, she encountered Murrow, who was "full of apologies about his behavior," wrote Ogden, and "resumed his pursuit." She located Beaverbrook in the Bahamas, who offered her a hotel room for as long as she needed to escape Murrow. Even then, Murrow continued to call her in Nassau until one night he assumed she was out socializing, and he finally gave up.

Some sort of romantic pursuit occurred during that time, but the evidence strongly suggests that Pamela, not Murrow, was the pursuer. "I never saw Pam and Ed together," said Mary Warburg, when asked whether she had dined with the couple in December 1945. At the time, her husband Eddie was also still overseas. After Murrow's arrival in New York on December 8, he wrote to Janet nearly every day, "pouring out his love for her, his longing to be with the baby," according to his biographer Joseph Persico, who read all the letters. Murrow also agonized to his wife about whether to accept Paley's offer to leave the airwaves and head CBS's news operation. He took the job on December 21— four days before Pamela's arrival—and wrote Janet a long letter the next day explaining his decision. That night, according to Persico, Murrow called Janet in London in tears. "He missed her and Casey terribly, he said," wrote Persico. "Christmas came, and he spent it alone in the hotel, turning down all invitations."

Pamela's version is that she left for Palm Beach around January 3, 1946, following her ten idyllic days with Murrow, and that they reunited in Manhattan upon Murrow's return from London three weeks later. But Murrow didn't go to London then—although he probably did send the "Casey Wins" telegram to Pamela in Florida. William Walton, for one, remembered hearing about the cable at the time. Murrow spent the month of January in New York working on the logistics of his impending move home. He instructed his financial manager Jim Seward to find a town house and wrote to Janet, "Brother Seward is beating the bushes."

Every few days in January, Murrow sent a letter to his wife reporting his progress. At the end of the month, he bought a house, and in early February— just about the time Pamela had him resuming his pursuit and pestering her with phone calls—Murrow was back in London. When Pamela supposedly was visiting Beaverbrook in Nassau, he too was in London—entertaining, among others, Averell Harriman. Murrow returned to New York in mid-March with Janet and Casey in tow. After he got them settled in their new home, he left on a two-month tour of the country for CBS.

Pamela always cited her love for Murrow as proof that she wasn't motivated by money. "The only poor one," her friends would say, with a shake of the head. Broadway and film actress Lauren Bacall remembered visiting Pamela more than a decade after the breakup and encountering what she called "the myth of Murrow. The past always seems rosier. In 1959 she told me about Murrow, that they were in love, that she thought he would leave his wife, and that she had had her disappointments. Some years had passed since Murrow, and I would say it had become a drama. She didn't talk about the others, only about Murrow. That was the only personal thing she told me, and it was dramatic." But another friend of Pamela's for many years understood the reality behind the fairy tale. "She knew with Ave she would have had the kind of life she wanted," said her friend. "Although she is adaptable and she was in love with Ed, what kind of life would she have had with him?"

CHAPTER
Thirteen

AFTER MURROW, Pamela resumed her search for a man of means. "She obviously wanted to get married again," said a woman who knew her at the time. "Coming to the United States was a way to expand her horizons." Her vacation at the Kennedy compound in January 1946 was a logical first step. Pamela and Kick Kennedy had grown closer in the latter part of the war. As Pamela joked in a letter to Kathleen Harriman, "There is a great shortage of men in London now. I think I shall have to cultivate my girlfriends which will be a change won't it?"

Following a courtship of six years, Kick had finally married Billy Hartington in May 1944, but four months later he had been killed in action by a sniper's bullet. A widow at age twenty-four, Kick had remained in London as Lady Hartington and had bought a white Georgian town house on Smith Square in Westminster, across from the bombed-out church where Pamela and Randolph were married. Kick's lively circle—old pals from debutante days as well as a more worldly group of married couples in their thirties, members of Parliament, and Catholic intellectuals like Evelyn Waugh—congregated at Smith Square, drawn by the generosity, irrepressible vitality, and good humor of their hostess.

In the evenings and at teatime, Kick's friends met in her small drawing room to debate the politics of the day and trade gossip. Recognizing that Kick's house was a popular gathering place, Pamela joined the group whenever she could and in turn invited Kick to dine at 49 Grosvenor Square. Pamela went out of her way to do favors for her American friend, once offering to have Averell Harriman take Kick back home on a private plane.

When Kick reciprocated by inviting her to escape the rationing and scarcity of the grim English winter for a vacation in Palm Beach, Pamela eagerly accepted. The Kennedys had been spending the winter months in Florida for more than a decade. Like the South of France and Newport, Rhode Island, Palm Beach was a magnet for wealthy socialites from New York, Hollywood, England, South America, and the Continent. In the depths of the Depression, Joseph Kennedy bought La Guerida, a large ocean-side villa designed by the town's most prestigious architect, Addison Mizner, in a style once described as "Bastard-Spanish-Moorish-Romanesque-Renaissance-Bull Market-Damn-The-Expense."

Years later Pamela recalled the excitement of New York, but said she had been overwhelmed by the glitter and elegance of Palm Beach. Pamela made enough of an impression for Cholly Knickerbocker to list her among the "Best Sundressed Women in Palm Beach," looking "quite pale when near the other deeply tanned beauties." Rose Kennedy drew Pamela into the family, bought her the right clothes, and even introduced her to *Reader's Digest* condensed books so Pamela could quickly pick up what was current in America. On Sundays she went to the racetrack at Hialeah with the Kennedy entourage, which included houseguests, priests, politicians, and old Joe's cronies. Afterward, the Kennedy children and their friends would dine and gamble at an exclusive club called Bradley's. The intensity of the Kennedy family impressed Pamela, along with their unabashed love of politics. Night after night, Pamela sat enthralled as Joe and Rose recounted tales of Boston politicians, a world quite apart from the lofty echelon of Harriman and the Churchills.

Returning to New York in early February 1946 for a stay of several months, Pamela found a city untouched by war, thronging with thousands of servicemen on their way home. Throughout the Depression and war years, New Yorkers had been waiting and saving; at the war's end the American people had $250 billion to spend on consumer goods. The streets were filled with Buicks, Dodges, and Cadillacs, and previously scarce products such as nylon stockings could now be found in abundance.

Although her sister Sheila, by now married to an American named Charles A. Moore III, lived in a small apartment in New York City, Pamela spent her time, in the words of Cholly Knickerbocker, "luxuriating in her quarters at the Ambassador Hotel" at 52nd Street and Park Avenue, which was only slightly less fashionable than the Waldorf-Astoria and the St. Regis. Pamela immediately looked up Jock Whitney and other members of her wartime coterie. These contacts revealed one of Pamela's singular traits: her eagerness to maintain friendships with her former lovers.

"Whatever her motives, she continued to take care of her men, and none of them said anything negative about her," said the American journalist Clayton Fritchey, a longtime friend. For Jock Whitney, for example, she performed an intriguing service, according to a man who knew her well during the 1960s: "Whitney would call and say it was his wife's birthday or an anniversary or Christmas and ask for Pam's help. He was too busy to go to the jewelry store himself, so Pam would go to Van Cleef and make a selection of pieces and put them in a consignment bag and take it to his office. He would pick one to buy, and the store would give her a credit as her commission. She would build up credits to buy stuff for herself, and there was never any money to tax. Whitney asked her because she kept track of the inventory, and she could spot a good piece at a long distance. This was an extension of her real business, which was getting dough and pleasing men. It was a funny game. I know she did it for Whitney. She may have done it for the others too."

Her continuing relationships dispelled the idea that she had been rebuffed or abandoned, and even perpetuated the impression that she was irresistible to powerful men. Moreover, the friendships served as proof that among all the lovers taken by these men, Pamela was unique. Each of her former lovers had wealth and social contacts that could be useful to Pamela, who never shrank from asking favors. And there was always the possibility that an old flame might reignite and lead to marriage.

But in 1946 Pamela was looking for new conquests. "She dressed flamboyantly, in bright colors," recalled a friend who saw her in Manhattan that winter. "She wanted to be noticed." Among the men she met were Stanley Mortimer and his brother Henry, great-grandsons of Wesley Hunt Tilford, one of the founders of Standard Oil, and descendants of John Jay, first Chief Justice of the Supreme Court. Exquisitely handsome and heirs to millions, both Stanley and Henry were estranged from their wives. Stanley's wife was the celebrated society beauty, Babe Cushing, who would later marry Bill Paley, Pamela's former lover. Pamela was well aware of Babe's marital difficulties, having stayed with her at the suggestion of Babe's older sister Betsey Whitney on her way north from Palm Beach.

It didn't take long for Cholly Knickerbocker to note in his "Smart Set" column on April 1, "Pamela Churchill and Stanley Mortimer sambaing to beat the band at El Morocco." But while Pamela dated Stanley and Henry, neither was seriously interested in her. One evening Pamela and Henry went to the Maisonette in the basement of the St. Regis Hotel with a group of friends, including Harriman's daughter Kathleen, who had returned to New York in January 1946. Pamela suddenly felt sick and fainted, prompting Stanley to carry her up a steep staircase to the lobby. Then, accompanied by Kathleen, he took Pamela down the street to her room at the Ambassador, leaving Kathleen to take care of her. Stanley was more impressed with the nurse than the patient. A year and a half later, he and Kathleen were married—and Pamela claimed credit for introducing them.

In early March, Pamela had seen Averell Harriman again. They had not been together since the previous autumn when he had stopped in London for the Council of Foreign Ministers meeting and they had spent the weekend at Cherkley. She had been a faithful correspondent while he was in Moscow, sending him weekly letters filled with political news and social gossip. Harriman had been grateful for every scrap of news she sent. "Except for one," he petulantly wrote to Max Beaverbrook at one point, "my British friends in London appear to have forgotten my existence."

Pamela and Harriman reunited in New York at a dinner on March 8 with Beaverbrook and a group of British friends. Soon after, Beaverbrook whisked her to Bermuda for a week-long holiday at a cottage he had rented for the month. Beaverbrook had been a "widower" since January 1945, when Jean Norton, his longtime mistress, had died of a heart attack. Pamela obligingly served as his hostess when he entertained the Governor of Bermuda and other island luminaries.

While in Bermuda, she heard some momentous news. On March 24, 1946, Harriman was appointed by President Harry Truman as Ambassador to Britain. Harriman had left Moscow at the end of January, and had only officially resigned his post as Ambassador to the Soviet Union in mid-February. When Secretary of State James Byrnes first offered him the London job—only days after Harriman had seen Pamela in New York—he refused, in part because it seemed like a sinecure. Harriman was also eager for a fresh start back home, and ready to put the war and his entanglement with Pamela behind him. "I want to have time to get to know the U.S. again. . . . I want to relax for a bit," he told Marie shortly before he left Moscow for New York. But Truman appealed to Harriman's sense of duty, saying that a "dangerous" situation existed in Iran because the Russians were refusing to withdraw their troops as stipulated in a treaty with the British. Harriman reluctantly accepted, with the caveat that he would return to America after the emergency was over.

Smiling pleasantly and looking dapper in his pinstripe suit, he arrived in London in April, just after Pamela came home from the United States, having "bruised many a manly heart in this city," according to Cholly Knickerbocker's send-off. Harriman moved into a three-room suite on the second floor at Claridges for several months while an apartment in the embassy residence at Prince's Gate was being renovated. Harriman and Pamela resumed their affair immediately, but this time she was a divorcée and Kathleen was no longer around to provide cover. They continued to enjoy Beaverbrook's hospitality in London and at Cherkley, and spent weekends at Great Enton, a country house owned by Harriman's old friend, the American playwright Robert Sherwood.

Pamela seemed more assertive with Harriman than during the war, even though greater discretion would have been more appropriate. When Harriman hosted the annual Fourth of July party at the embassy residence, Pamela took Kick Kennedy upstairs into the private quarters and showed her how all the rooms had been redone. Pamela also kept in close touch with Kathleen Harriman in New York, sending her lists of items she needed. Kathleen obliged by sending packages of food as well as popular American novels, even as she was telling her father how glad she was that she and Marie were once again getting along. In one of the more peculiar twists of their odd friendship, Kathleen had begun her own secret subsidy of Pamela. When they met in New York earlier in the year, Pamela had told her old friend that she was broke. Not knowing the extent of her own father's support, Kathleen had signed over her weekly *Newsweek* paycheck to Pamela—a gesture of friendship and loyalty that Pamela eagerly accepted.

It appeared that Marie was the only person in London and New York society who didn't know about the continuing affair. Paul Felix "Piggy" Warburg, an old friend who served as an aide to Harriman at the embassy, worked triple time to make arrangements for Marie to join her husband in England now that the problems with her eyes had stabilized. Throughout the summer of 1946, Marie involved herself in the logistics of the move, arranging for kitchen supplies and flatware, selecting the right shade of yellow for upholstery, and sending publicity photographs to *The Tatler*. At the same time, Harriman continued to underwrite Pamela, although he remained chronically in arrears to Beaverbrook for the apartment rental; that summer he owed more than £600 (some $20,000 today).

Harriman was unhappy with his situation in London; his biographer Rudy Abramson characterized it as an "uncomfortable interlude." Not only was Harriman worried that his affair with Pamela would be publicized, he had little interest in the largely ceremonial duties of the ambassador and he had poor rapport with his embassy staff. Once the Iranian crisis abated in mid-April, he was left with little to do. At the end of July he went to Paris to help negotiate peace treaties with Germany and its satellites, an assignment that stretched into many weeks. Marie's five trunks and four cases arrived in London in early August, and she was expected at the end of September.

In April 1946, Beaverbrook had offered Pamela an opportunity to make her way in the world as an independent woman, while cushioned, of course, by unseen subsidies from her wealthy benefactors. He gave her a job on the *Daily Express,* where she worked for two months before moving to the *Evening Standard,* his up-market tabloid that had employed both Winston and Randolph Churchill. He paid her £15 a week (about $24,000 a year today), for which she would contribute items to the *Standard's* "The Londoner's Diary," a popular gossip column, and write features under her highly marketable name.

She took the position, said a friend of hers from that time, because "it was a way of getting around and seeing things." Having spent so much time with journalists during the war, she was also intrigued by the idea of playing their game. The *Standard* seemed a logical place for her. She had access to influential men in high places, she listened exceedingly well, and she understood how to use information and gossip. Her job was a natural extension of the mutually manipulative relationship she and Beaverbrook had during the war when she reported to him conversations with her highly placed lovers. Beaverbrook offered to underwrite trips abroad in pursuit of stories, and he agreed to her request for an assignment in New York that autumn when Marie Harriman arrived in London.

The offices of the *Evening Standard* in Shoe Lane near Fleet Street were raffish and noisy. There was a large newsroom, one chaotic corner of which was allocated to the "Londoner's Diary" staff of eight, supervised by editor Tudor Jenkins. A plump man with a generous white mustache, Jenkins was courtly but dictatorial. "No fine writing please," he would say, and he strictly enforced Beaverbrook's formula for the Diary: short paragraphs densely packed with information. The Diary consisted of sometimes unreliable, occasionally incomprehensible, but always lively tidbits about the social, political, artistic, literary, and theatrical worlds, many of which came straight from Beaverbrook's dinner table. "The *Evening Standard* was his house journal," wrote A. J. P. Taylor, "providing fun for himself and for those who shared his tastes." The Diary was created "on the assumption that our readers were a notch or two higher in the social scale than was actually the case," noted one contributor, Malcolm Muggeridge.

The Diary staff was handpicked by Beaverbrook as well, with such high-profile contributors over the years as Randolph Churchill, Robert Bruce Lockhart, Harold Nicolson, and John Betjeman. "He believed in having people with very good contacts," said Angus McGill, a postwar writer on the Diary. "Nearly everyone was the son or daughter of someone important. There was usually one woman with strong social connections." In 1946, Pamela was the well-connected woman, functioning largely as a high-level tipster.

Most of Pamela's "work" took place in the evenings. "I knew a lot of Americans who would come and have dinner," she once said. "Henry Luce for instance. The dinner would be over at 11:30 and Max would say, 'Write a story for tomorrow and these are the points that should be made.' " (Late in his life, Luce told his wife Clare that he and Pamela had a fleeting affair during this period.) Pamela strolled into the newsroom at around ten each morning and left in the early afternoon, spending hours on the phone in between. Because of her social position, she could get through to virtually anyone and chat on a first-name basis.

"She put in a very short day," recalled Charles Wintour, editor of the *Standard* in the late 1940s and the father of *Vogue* editor Anna Wintour. "She was quite conscientious, though. She was leading a full social life at the time, and she regarded the job as a way of keeping in touch. . . . She wrote pieces in a sense, but how far her words were used I don't know. The subeditor on the Diary would put everything into Diary style."

More important to Beaverbrook, simply for their marquee value, were Pamela's splashy bylined stories on the rich and famous in France, New York, and Britain. Her first story was a feature on the "mystery" of the Cerne Giant, whose enormous penis was a comic landmark on the Dorset countryside of her childhood. During her seven months on the job—in later years she would say her journalistic career had lasted three years—Pamela produced nine articles. "She wasn't there very long, for less than a year," said Charles Wintour. "She worked quite hard for a short time, but I didn't think her heart was in it." Like her column items, her features were polished by rewritemen. At first, her work had the wide-eyed enthusiasm of a schoolgirl; as she gained experience, she showed more confidence in tackling serious subjects.

In midsummer she spent a long weekend in Paris and in early September a week in the South of France. The stories and column items she turned out during these trips showed off her extensive social contacts—and her fixation with money. Paris, she declared in a bylined piece in early July, "is back again to pre-war standard." She carefully noted the cost of everything (32 shillings a night for a single hotel room, 5 shillings for a champagne cocktail), lovingly detailed a modestly priced six-course meal, and provided a peek into the city's "gaiety for the rich and social-minded. There is an average of three large balls a week, and many of the night clubs are open again."

From the South of France in early September, Pamela wrote a story that revealed as much about her as it did about her subject. It was an adoring profile of Peggy Hopkins Joyce, once derided by Diana Vreeland as "everyone's favorite golddigger." With six husbands to her credit—at least four of them multimillionaires—Peggy Joyce became, as one wag put it, "alimoniously rich." A former Ziegfeld girl, Joyce inspired Anita Loos's *Gentlemen Prefer Blondes* and made headlines with her romances for three decades. She was a crass self-promoter whose utterances ranged from vapid to cynical. "It is better to be mercenary than miserable," she told one interviewer.

For all that, Pamela described her as "a beautiful blonde American . . . a woman of great taste," and marveled that in her Cap d'Ail villa, "no detail, however extravagant, was overlooked." In Pamela's view, Joyce "possessed beauty, wealth and security," as well as "that careless confident walk which women acquire when they know that all eyes turn towards them when they enter a room." Perhaps seeing a reflection of herself, Pamela wrote that Peggy Joyce "had made her life for herself. She had had lucky breaks, but she had known what she wanted."

Harriman was preparing to go to New York to accompany Marie back to London when he and Pamela stole a final weekend together at Great Enton in late September. There they heard on the radio that Henry Wallace, the Secretary of Commerce, had been fired. Shortly afterward Truman called to ask Harriman to replace Wallace at Commerce. Given the chance to return to the center of power, he didn't hesitate. The "Londoner's Diary" item the following Monday had a distinctly intimate feel, with its description of Harriman's "quiet weekend in the country" and his "three minute conversation" with the President "just before midnight." The Diary noted that Harriman's salary at Commerce (£3,750 a year, about $15,000) would make "little difference," given a fortune estimated at some $50 million.

The new job effectively ended the latest chapter in Harriman's romance with Pamela, although he would pay her rent until 1950, when he closed the account at Beaverbrook's urging. Beaverbrook knew by then that Pamela was being supported in high style in Paris by Gianni Agnelli. What Harriman didn't know was that when she went off with Agnelli in 1948, she sublet the Grosvenor Square flat to various Americans, including Cary Grant, for $500 a month, or approximately £100, which she pocketed while Harriman continued his payments, which had risen to £80 monthly. George Millar, Beaverbrook's factotum, had to pester Harriman to the very end for the apartment payments and nearly blew the cover off the arrangement by trying to return an overpayment of £1 18s. to Harriman's bank account. (He finally sent cash in an envelope to the U.S. Embassy in London instead.)

Brown Brothers Harriman would keep paying Pamela's annual stipend for nearly three decades, however. "Many have put the annual figure at $20,000," one Harriman grandchild told Khoi Nguyen, writing in *The Tatler*. "The truth is, she got much more. The payments started in London and continued for thirty years." Indeed, according to members of the Harriman family, when Pamela was about to marry Harriman in 1971, someone from Brown Brothers came to him and said, "Do you still want to pay the allowance to Mrs. Hayward?" Harriman professed to have forgotten about the payments—a lapse that Pamela later laughed about with her friends.

In Harriman's final week in England, "The Londoner's Diary" offered some fresh but hardly consequential details of his situation ("Mr. Harriman plans to spend the weekend packing in London . . . he tells me he does not yet know who his successor in London will be"). Then, on October 1, he was gone. But Pamela didn't intend to give up Harriman just yet. At the end of the month she flew to New York as planned, to assume her post as correspondent for the *Standard*.

With the help of Beaverbrook, who was staying at the Plaza Hotel, she turned out an assortment of Diary items, including speculation about who would be named Ambassador to London, and Fred Astaire's plans to open a chain of dance studios in England. Her profile of Belgian diplomat Paul-Henri Spaak, president of the United Nations General Assembly, "the man who looks 'but does not act' like Churchill," was certainly her best effort to date, though its polished style owed much to the rewrite desk. Her other bylined feature was a disorganized collection of vignettes about Britons in the city. She shamelessly boosted Beaverbrook, Camrose, and Rothermere, the three "important English Press Lords" holding court at the Plaza, and reported that burglars had broken into the hotel room of her friend Barbie Agar and stolen her jewelry. Money was on her mind once more—specifically the £75 limit on what Britons could take out of the country—although she revealingly noted that in New York, "a relative or a friend is often an easy supply for money. . . . American hospitality and generosity toward friends is famous." She concluded that "in this land of light and understanding, English aristocrats are still looked on with favour and approbation."

She kept a public profile of glamour and gaiety. Cholly Knickerbocker included her in his headline "British Beauties Invade Gotham" and noted that she was "quietly seeing the town with Joseph Kennedy, ex-Ambassador to the Court of St. James's, and Franklin D. Roosevelt, Jr." Yet for all her expectations, her visit to New York went badly. Harriman was off-limits. Their closest encounter came in November 1946 when she was seated across a nightclub from a group that included Averell and Marie. One person at their table recognized Pamela, and as Rudy Abramson recounted it, the "innocent in the party started to babble about Sir Winston's famous ex-daughter-in-law as Averell sat like a cigar-store Indian, pretending not to hear; Marie defused the embarrassment of the others by standing, whipping off her dark glasses and pretending an exaggerated stare across the room." Recognizing the volatility of the situation with Harriman, Beaverbrook finally told Pamela that she could no longer work in New York, and in mid-November he packed her off, along with his paramour, the Austrian ballerina Lily Ernst, first to Miami and then to Montego Bay, Jamaica.

Pamela was unable to continue her friendship with Harriman as she had with her other lovers. For a while, they kept up a clandestine correspondence, but he declined to see her again. One reason, said one woman who knew him well, was that "Marie didn't like Pam, and I don't think Ave wanted to cause any problems." Probably more important, Harriman aspired to be Governor of New York and eventually President, ambitions that tempered his behavior. "Pam was in search of a husband, and that was not in the cards with Ave," continued Harriman's friend. His surreptitious financial support was all she could expect.

Pamela was incensed by her exile to Jamaica, but she remained for several weeks and turned out two features for the *Standard*. The second, which was published in mid-January 1947 after Pamela had returned to London, was a dramatic eyewitness report on overcrowded conditions in a government hospital in Jamaica. With the zeal of a muckraker, she described children lying in cribs "as puppies do, pushing against one another in their sleep." In one ward with twenty-two beds, fifty-three moaning men, some of them three to a single bed, looked "like corpses awaiting burial." Although the story consisted of her own impressions buttressed by minimal facts (no interviews with hospital personnel or government officials), it offered an effective snapshot of a situation that was obviously deplorable.

That was to be Pamela Churchill's last byline for the *Standard*. Because her pieces were heavily rewritten, it is difficult to judge her ability as a writer. Her personal correspondence showed scant literary merit. But she had strong powers of observation and good journalistic instincts. If she had applied herself, Pamela might have made a creditable and perhaps even lucrative career as a journalist. But her commitment to the craft was thin. In later years she said she quit when "I realised I'd never be a first-class writer, and that in journalism I'd be used—sent on interviews because of the name"—an odd concern since she so often used her Churchill connection for self-advancement. But her time in journalism was important nevertheless, for the contacts she made, the places she saw, and the experience she gained. It gave her, said Lady Jean Campbell, Lord Beaverbrook's granddaughter, "a passage into another life."

CHAPTER

Fourteen

POSTWAR LONDON was a bleak place, with bombed-out buildings and streets filled with rubble. Millions were unemployed, and many shops were shuttered. Heat and electricity were turned off for hours at a time to conserve fuel. Rationing was even more stringent than during the war. The House of Commons was reduced to serving whale and seal steaks in its dining room. "It was galling," wrote John Colville, "to watch living conditions improve month by month in France . . . while we, the victors, languished in bleak monotony. . . . London was grey. Life was grey."

Shortly after the Allied victory in Europe, Britain had held a general election in July 1945, the first such balloting in a decade. Although Churchill, by then seventy years old, had remained extremely popular for his wartime leadership, he had been unable to satisfy the country's great appetite for social change. Midway through the Potsdam Conference that he was attending with Truman and Stalin, Churchill's Conservative Party had been overwhelmingly defeated by Labour, and Clement Attlee had become the new Prime Minister.

Attlee and his Labour government had launched an ambitious social welfare program that included nationalizing industries and enacting national health insurance, all of which resulted in crippling taxes. Nevertheless, Pamela managed to live in luxury in her Grosvenor Square apartment, thanks to financial support from her American admirers and access to the black market. After an evening there in 1946, Harold Nicolson noted: "Everybody in dinner jacket and evening dress; the first time I have seen so uniformly pre-war a party." She frequently went to the country for house-party weekends, and attended Ascot and other events during the season, including her younger sister Jaquetta's debutante party.

In recalling this period, Pamela offered conflicting versions of her mood and prospects at age twenty-six. "There were so many doors open," she once told a British interviewer. "I might have been equally happy married to a wonderful man and having 10 children." But despite her social prominence during the war, beaux were hardly beating down her door. "There were periods when she had no one at all," said a woman who knew her from childhood. "She didn't have much fun in London after the war. She didn't get on with the English men."

At various times she said she considered running for Parliament "because

I'd run Randolph's constituency while he was abroad"—an exaggerated claim, since she had made only occasional visits and a few speeches. She referred to "considerations" and "complications" that stood in the way of a political career. To be sure, even the most accomplished women had trouble entering politics in those days. But Pamela had little formal education, minimal experience, and no ideological anchor. Born and raised Conservative, her political beliefs shifted along with the men in her life: Conservative with the Churchills, Eastern establishment Democrat with Harriman, left-leaning Democrat with Murrow.

Now that her wartime lovers were reunited with their wives in America, Pamela turned her attention to France. Several times she visited the British Ambassador, Sir Alfred Duff Cooper, and his wife Lady Diana. Since so many Parisian hotels had been requisitioned by Allied troops, the embassy's "airy country house bedrooms," as Diana Cooper called them, "were quickly refurbished to hold a succession of VIPS and friends." "I used to see quite a lot of Pam after the war when I saw a lot of the Coopers," recalled Loelia, the Duchess of Westminster. "She was carrying on with Harriman and staying at the embassy in Paris. There were a lot of parties, and Duff and Diana were pleased to have a pretty girl. It suited Pam too, who hadn't much money."

The British Embassy was a grand eighteenth-century palace of buff-colored stone on the rue du Faubourg St. Honoré. Once the home of Napoleon's sister, Pauline Borghese, the embassy had a rich history that included the wedding of Winston Churchill's parents, Lord Randolph and Jennie Jerome. After being shut during the war, the house had again become a glittering social center. In the green drawing room, known to all as the Salon Vert, Lady Diana presided as "an Ambassadress of international culture," in the words of Harold Acton. Every evening from six to eight, her salon opened its doors to Parisian aristocrats and assorted expatriates as well as "La Bande," her group of beauties, artists, writers, and musicians. The men dressed in black coats and striped trousers; the heavily perfumed women wore the latest fashions. Defying diplomatic protocol, Diana included collaborators as well as patriots. "One merely had to go to the Salon Vert to find out what was happening in Paris," wrote Cynthia Gladwyn, the wife of a later British ambassador. "It was also a haven of warmth in those fuel-less days with not only the bright fire and the candle light providing heat, but the animated conversation and laughter of La Bande."

Like Olive Baillie, Diana Cooper was an older woman—nearly thirty years Pamela's senior—whom she admired and sought to please. The youngest child of the Duke of Rutland, Lady Diana had defied convention to work as an actress during the 1920s. With her delicate heart-shaped face, her golden hair, and what Cecil Beaton called her "love in the mist" blue eyes, she was considered "the queen of beauty" in English society for several decades. Her mind was quick and original. She spoke in what Beaton called a "torrential flow" that could leap from "What is the most squalid thing you know?" to "What is an incubus or succubus?" Her manner was disconcertingly informal, as was her customary attire: trousers, odd hats, and vests. She was, said Beaton, "a flamboyant eccentric and a professional extrovert."

Her husband, Duff Cooper, was a respected diplomat, author, and infamous ladies' man. Harold Acton once described him as "short and stocky, with combative eyes under an intellectual forehead. He suggested a battling turkey-cock, feathers bristling." Duff Cooper had a delightfully self-mocking wit, overshadowed by a fierce temper that many found alarming. He was a man of large appetites—for wine, food, and virtually any pretty woman who crossed his path. His well-known mistresses included Pamela's friend Barbie Wallace, top model Maxime de la Falaise, Parisian aristocrat Ghislaine de Polignac, saloniste and poet Louise de Vilmorin, and Susan Mary Patten (later Mrs. Joseph Alsop), wife of an American diplomat.

The strongest connection between Pamela and Diana was their membership in Max Beaverbrook's coterie. Duff Cooper and Beaverbrook couldn't stand each other, but Diana was fascinated by Beaverbrook's power. As trustee of the £20,000 marriage settlement bequeathed by her father, Beaverbrook had insinuated himself into Diana's affairs as he had in Pamela's. Over the years, he periodically sent Diana checks (usually for no more than £100), gave her an automobile, and provided champagne for her parties. Like Pamela, she readily accepted his generosity.

While Diana was kind to Pamela, she was not overly fond of her. "I would not have listed Pam Churchill among the close friends of Diana," said Diana Cooper's biographer, Philip Ziegler. Diana was much more attached to Randolph Churchill, for all his faults, and considered him a lifelong friend. "Diana was so funny, and so clever," said a woman who was a close friend of hers. "She would have seen through Pam." Aware of Pamela's reputation, Lady Diana regarded her primarily as an ornament for her salon. "Diana Cooper viewed Pam with amusement," said Anthony Marreco, an Englishman who was in Paris at the time. "Pam was amusing in this sense: Diana knew she was bold as brass."

Pamela's presence at the embassy caused a stir. When "the notoriously promiscuous wife of a prominent politician came to stay," wrote Ziegler in his biography of Lady Diana, "Diana's only concern was lest people should think she had removed her husband to protect him from the visiting harpy. 'Indeed, indeed, I have not,' said Lady Diana. 'I would love him to have a tumble with the pretty little fool.' " Acknowledging that Pamela was in fact the "pretty little fool," Ziegler later added, "Diana's dismissal of her was ill-judged, I think, although I don't think Pamela had a fling with Duff. The fact that Diana was so dismissive meant she would not have seen Pamela as a threat."

Through the Coopers, Pamela made numerous contacts with men and women who could ease her way into Parisian society: fashionable aristocrats such as Prince Jean-Louis de Faucigny-Lucinge and Baron Frédéric de Cabrol and his wife Daisy; hostesses Marie-Laure de Noailles, Denise Bourdet, and Louise de Vilmorin; composers Georges Auric and Francis Poulenc; artists Jean Cocteau, Christian Berard, and Drian; interior designer Cora Caetani; and the wealthy and powerful industrialist Paul-Louis Weiller, an Anglophile who courted British aristocrats with lavish gifts.

By 1946, Paris once again bustled with what Balzac had called "insolent luxury." Lines formed outside shops displaying fine porcelain, fur-lined gloves, and silk scarves. Florists sold profusions of rare blossoms that hadn't been seen in nearly a decade. Couture houses showed new lines of clothes, with the least expensive dresses priced from $150 to $250—roughly $1,200 to $2,000 today. In the twelve months since VE-Day, Paris had undergone what Janet Flanner, a writer for *The New Yorker,* called "an astonishing revival . . . Paris is now like a thin, ill, handsome old woman with some natural color flushing her cheeks as she fumbles to her feet." Pamela dined at the best Parisian restaurants, attended fancy dress balls, and went to the horse races.

The more uncomfortable life became in London, the more well-connected Britons sought visas for France. "Never have the English been so popular in France as they are today," Duff Cooper reported to Harold Nicolson. Pamela exploited the magic of the Churchill name, which had assumed mythic proportions after the wartime leader visited the city in November 1944. As he drove to the Arc de Triomphe with General de Gaulle, the crowds chanted, "Churcheel, Churcheel." Diana Cooper noted: "In Paris, Winston's was a name to waken the dead. Wherever he walked . . . his way was dense with cheering enthusiasts. It made him happy to give them his V sign and to bask in their love and gratitude."

The disapproval that Pamela experienced in London vanished among her new French friends in the summer of 1946. Parisians loved to be entertained, and in Pamela they found a star: a foreigner with an aristocratic heritage, a risqué reputation, and a trail of wealthy lovers. "She was very very healthy and attractive, like a milkgirl from England," said François Valéry, son of the celebrated poet and essayist Paul Valéry. Her distinctive Anglo-Saxon coloring— the russet hair and the lightly freckled alabaster skin—was her greatest advantage. "She took the light of the evening well with that coloring," said Daisy de Cabrol.

"Nothing enchants the French so much as foreigners with a fluency in their language, especially if the speaker is a pretty girl," wrote John Colville. Pamela did not speak impeccable French, but she spoke without embarrassment, a trait Parisians admired. They warmed to her savoir faire and an avidity for Parisian life that was immensely flattering. "She had very good poise, very good bearing," said Alexandre (Sandy) Bertrand, a publisher who became a close friend. "She moved well, with assurance, but not arrogance. She was always smiling. That was one of her traits. People weren't afraid to talk to her." Her divorce carried no stigma in France. "It was easier for Pam in Paris," said Aliki Russell, the former wife of Paul-Louis Weiller. "In London you get friends for life but it takes longer. The French are quicker, more spontaneous."

Pamela decided to resettle on the Continent. In her eagerness to move, she showed no compunction about leaving behind her child and her friends. She reasoned that after the difficulties of the war, it was time to surround herself with new admirers, and to enjoy her own pleasure. "I hadn't played at all," she once said. "I'd gone straight from school into war and marriage." Her self-pity was remarkable considering that she had spent the war romancing rich Americans and playing cards with her father-in-law, the Prime Minister. "Suddenly," she remarked on another occasion, "I woke up one day and said, 'My God, you've never had any fun.' " She said she disliked British men, and found British women "insipid." A woman who knew her well had a simpler explanation: "She went to Paris because she was tired of austerity."

Her ties to London weren't completely severed, however, because of six-year-old Winston, "a boisterous boy with a head too big for his body," in the ungenerous judgment of Evelyn Waugh. Winston was now living at 49 Grosvenor Square, cared for by his mother's Scottish housekeeper, Mrs. Martin. "Of all those who looked after me during my childhood," he would later say, "it was her whom I loved most dearly." At age five, he had enrolled in his first school, Mitford Colmer, in Sloane Square. Pamela's butler, Sam Hudson, took him to and from school each day, often stopping off in Hyde Park to play soccer with his young charge. With his grandparents, retainers, and other adults to entertain him on weekends, Little Winston scarcely seemed to mind his mother's comings and goings. Yet in later life Winston did acknowledge, "If I lost something it was the opportunity to make friends with a lot of my contemporaries." As for big Winston, he wrote Lady Digby, "Everything must be centered upon the well-being and happiness of the Boy. Pamela has brought him up splendidly." Churchill had raised his own children with remarkable ineptness, so it is no wonder that he would fail to notice Pamela's inattention.

Between the war and his mother's travels, Little Winston was denied the sort of secure life Pamela had enjoyed at Minterne. Lord and Lady Digby may have been distant, but at least they were a daily force in the lives of their children. When Pamela saw her son, she tended to indulge him. For his fifth birthday, she gave him a tea party at the Churchill Club, followed by a private screening of *Bambi,* courtesy of Alexander Korda. Little Winston cried inconsolably during the forest fire in which Bambi lost his mother—an ironic emotional response under the circumstances. "She was living her own life," he said in later years. "I was a happy loner who went for walkies in Hyde Park."

Before Pamela actually moved to Paris, she often turned up on visits to France with Kick Kennedy. Kick was having an affair with Earl Fitzwilliam, a handsome rake who had an alcoholic wife and a twelve-year-old daughter. He owned one of the best stud farms in England and kept company with the international racing set. Kick had the means—an ample allowance from her father plus money from her late husband's father, the Duke of Devonshire—to come along when the crowd traveled to France for racing weekends, and she often footed the bill for Pamela as well. Kick was the perfect friend for Pamela, non-judgmental and fun-loving. As the daughter of Lord Digby, Pamela knew her way around race courses and fit in comfortably with turf society. She introduced Kick to glamorous continentals she had met at the British Embassy and on the Riviera.

Still, as Pamela passed her twenty-seventh birthday, she had yet to find a man of wealth and power. In June 1947, Kick Kennedy invited her to spend a week in Paris at the Plaza Athénée, the hotel where Pamela had stayed during her weekend with Fulke Warwick before the war. The two young women flung themselves into the Paris season. They frequented the top couture houses and bought hats from milliner Rose Descartes to wear at the Grand Prix at Longchamps. Palm Beach socialite Charlie Munn set them up in a box at the race course, where they drank champagne and smiled as Frenchmen busily kissed their hands.

That evening, they attended the annual Grand Prix Ball at the Pré Catalan Restaurant in the Bois de Boulogne, hosted by the Continent's most colorful playboy, thirty-six-year-old Prince Aly Salomone Khan, son of the Aga Khan, the billionaire leader of an estimated 15 million Ismaili Muslims in Asia and Africa. Meticulously planned by the prince—even down to the custom-designed Hermès scarves and special YLA (Aly spelled backward) perfume distributed as favors—the party was a highlight of the Paris season, attracting more than two hundred society figures, royals, politicians, industrialists, movie stars, and models, most of whom lingered until dawn. Aly Khan made a practice of seeking out new romances in such crowds, and the guest who caught his eye that night was Pamela. As they danced together under crystal chandeliers, she agreed to see him when he came to England the following week.

The Aga Khan was a popular figure in English society, familiar to the Digbys through the racing circuit. But although her sister Sheila had known his son, Aly, since before the war, Pamela had not crossed paths with him. Like everyone in international society, Pamela knew Aly Khan by sight—and by reputation. At five foot six (five foot eight by some accounts, but certainly not the six feet he claimed) he was shorter than many of the beauties he squired. He had a stocky build, a slight paunch, and sparse dark hair receding from a broad brow. He spoke with what one observer described as the "husky strangled voice of an upper class Englishman overlaid with a slight French accent." His skin, Diana Vreeland once noted, was "exactly the color of a gardenia. A gardenia isn't *quite* white. It's got a little cream in it." He had a wide, sensuous mouth, a beguilingly dimpled chin, and heavy brows that deepened the intensity of his black eyes—his most compelling feature.

Aly Khan wasn't remotely like the dark-skinned Bedouin who had captivated Jane Digby, but he had a touch of Oriental romance. His mother was an Italian dancer—he was born in Turin, the home of Gianni Agnelli—and his father a Persian descendant of the prophet Mohammad. He held his father in awe and had been extremely attached to his mother, who died of a blood clot when he was fifteen. Aly was intermittently educated by Swiss tutors and an Oxford classics scholar, and he trained briefly to be a London barrister. An avid horseman, Aly rode with the Southdown Hunt and won scores of races as a gentleman jockey. With his father, he managed a racing stable that included a dozen stud farms in France and Ireland. Few foreigners could boast such thorough assimiliation into English life. Yet though Aly had numerous friends among the English aristocracy, he felt the prejudice of upper-class provincials who dismissed him as a "wog."

Masking his feelings was a point of pride for Aly Khan, but English bigotry had a profound effect. "They called me a bloody nigger," he once said bitterly, "and I paid them out by winning all their women." His more prominent conquests included 1930s "Debutante of the Year" Margaret Whigham; Thelma Furness, who had been a favorite companion of the Prince of Wales before he met Wallis Simpson; and Joan Guinness, tall, blond, and aloof, who had divorced her husband Loel, a wealthy British banker, to marry him in 1936. Estranged in the early war years, Joan and Aly led separate lives while remaining married, giving him a convenient excuse for avoiding entanglements with blatant fortune hunters. By the time he met Pamela, Aly Khan had a legendary reputation with women. "I only think of the woman's pleasure when I'm in love," was his conspicuously repeated credo.

Compulsively on the move—always in haste, forever tardy—he flitted among more than a half-dozen houses and his corner suite at the Ritz in London. It supposedly took him only three minutes to bathe, dress, and shave with an electric razor—with the assistance of one servant for his socks, another for his trousers, and a third for his shirt. Once at the Cannes Film Festival he changed clothes in an elevator on the way from one event to the next. "I've never seen him sit still for ten consecutive minutes except at dinner and the bridge table," said party impresario Elsa Maxwell. Most nights he just skipped dinner and usually slept no more than two or three hours.

He was intelligent and cultivated, with a connoisseur's appreciation of modern paintings. He applied keen business instincts to his extensive knowledge of bloodstock, greatly improving the fortunes of the Aga's racing interests. During World War II, he served in the French Foreign Legion as well as intelligence units of the British and American armies, where he impressed his fellow officers as unpretentious and energetic. Yet his conversation often lapsed into high society prattle, and he had a reputation for puerile practical jokes such as setting off stink bombs in movie theaters.

He could overwhelm friends with generosity, inviting them to stay as houseguests indefinitely whether he was at home or not, treating them to the theater and the races. Yet he was so stunningly inconsiderate that he would make multiple dates on the same evening and leave his guests to dine without him. Easily bored, incapable of solitude, he thought nothing of summoning a friend at two in the morning. Wherever he landed, women were sure to follow. The English artist Michael Wishart once happened upon Aly at his villa in the South of France, "resplendent as a basking shark, surrounded by a claque of pretty girls wearing the lower halves of bikinis. . . . Aly wore black trunks with the would-be tantalising admonition 'not to be opened until Christmas' embroidered down the fly."

It was said that he fell in love "madly and deeply," if fleetingly, although "love" seems an inappropriate term for his almost ritualistic approach to women: the melting gaze, the suggestive touches, the stream of flattery and solicitous talk, the insistent rush of invitations that one woman said "made you feel you were on a pink cloud." "His mood and manner never vary, whether he is with an 18-year-old girl or a beauty in full bloom" wrote Elsa Maxwell. He had perfected a technique that put Pamela's evolving attentiveness to shame—the actor's gift of making the object of his affection feel she was the only woman in the room.

Most women found his vitality and magnetism irresistible. So it was with Pamela—although her decision was carefully considered. "Pam is not passionate or impulsive," said a woman who knew her for many years. "Pam definitely has chosen the men in her life." When Aly arrived in London for the races in July 1947, she became his lover. Fully aware of his unsuitability, she nonetheless understood that a liaison with him could prove worthwhile.

The centerpiece of the Aly Khan legend was his lovemaking technique, called "Imsak," which he learned from an Egyptian doctor. Imsak was a form of mental discipline that enabled a man to hold back as long as possible. Because he was so focused, imaginative, and gentle in giving women pleasure, Aly Khan had a reputation as an extraordinary lover. His technique gave him the only power he ever sought. As one English friend explained it, "He liked the effect it had on women. He liked to get them out of control while he stayed in control." Yet he could leave a woman feeling vaguely inadequate because he rarely reached a climax himself. Some of his friends suspected he was a repressed homosexual who overcompensated through his conquests. One friend said Aly had been treated for impotence.

Pamela's figure was more rounded than he customarily liked, but he favored women with fair complexions and slightly offbeat looks. She had an agreeable personality, and enough energy to keep up with his frenetic pace. While she was never very engaged in the racing world, she had enough knowledge and interest to please him. Another attraction was the opportunity to add the name Churchill to his list of conquests. All the same—perhaps out of deference to the former Prime Minister—Pamela's name failed to appear in numerous British and American newspaper accounts of Aly Khan's womanizing.

Aly was not known for giving presents or great sums of money to his lovers, but he was a ticket—literally—to places Pamela wished to go. She rode with him on *The Avenger,* his twin-engined Dove airplane, from London to Paris to his Riviera headquarters, the Château de l'Horizon, a gleaming white mock-Moorish villa with broad terraces, ten bedrooms, seven baths, a vast swimming pool, and a long staircase down to the sea. With Aly, she could live like a rich woman and have the run of his homes. It was also a badge of distinction in the international set to join Aly Khan's harem. "Every girl was entitled to a little bit of Aly," said novelist Leonora Hornblow, a close friend of Pamela's for more than three decades.

The relationship was conducted entirely on his terms. She came when he called, and when they were together, a swarm of house guests surrounded them. At l'Horizon he invited at least a dozen friends and hangers-on for lunch nearly every day. If events didn't go his way, he could be difficult, as Pamela learned once after she fell asleep on the terrace at l'Horizon. When a severe sunburn kept her in bed for several days, Aly was hardly the model of solicitude. "Furious with frustration," according to his biographer Leonard Slater, he "sulked alone."

Pamela found her own diversions when Aly was off on his own. In September 1947, she and Kick Kennedy went to Southern Ireland to stay at Lismore Castle. Owned by the Devonshire family, the eleventh-century castle was covered with moss and commanded a high bluff. Kick had organized a month-long house party, including among her guests the writer Shane Leslie, conservative politicians Hugh Fraser, Anthony Eden, and Tony Rosslyn, and Kick's brother

Jack, a newly elected member of Congress. By day, Kick and her company played golf, took long walks, and rode horses; at night, they talked politics.

Only the persistent illness of Jack Kennedy marred the idyllic holiday. On one of the few days he felt well, he set out to find the original Kennedy homestead. He asked Pamela along, and they spent most of the morning driving to the town of New Ross on the Barrow River. There Kennedy located a farmer and his wife and a half-dozen children living in a small cottage with a thatched roof. Kennedy spent an hour "in a flow of nostalgia and sentiment," as he later described it, plying the farmer with questions and ferrying the children through town in Kick's huge American station wagon. As they left, Pamela turned to him and said, "That was just like *Tobacco Road*!" Kennedy was deeply insulted by her remark. Sixteen years later on a flight to Ireland he told his aides Dave Powers and Ken O'Donnell, "I felt like kicking her out of the car. For me, the visit to that cottage was filled with magic."

Pamela tried hard to make up for her faux pas. She accompanied Kennedy back to London, and before leaving for the South of France called her doctor, Sir Daniel Davis, and had him visit Kennedy in his suite at Claridges. Davis immediately sent Kennedy to the hospital, where he was diagnosed with Addison's disease, a serious illness of the adrenal glands. Pamela had her cook prepare nourishing meals to be delivered to his bedside. Kennedy later described to a friend his amusement that the china and silver had Averell Harriman's monogram.

But despite Pamela's concern for his health, Kennedy's remark to Powers and O'Donnell showed his lingering displeasure over her insensitivity in New Ross. She managed a different interpretation of that day in the country. As she recounted it later, she emphasized that she had been "very impressed" by the dignity of the New Ross couple and suggested that Kennedy's manner toward her had sent them some flattering signals: "They never could figure out who I was. 'Wife?' They'd ask. I'd say no. And they'd say, 'Ah, soon to be, no doubt!' " In Pamela's version, it was not she but her good friend Kick who failed to understand the magic of New Ross. After returning to Lismore, Pamela said, Kick annoyed her brother by saying, " 'Well, did they have a bathroom?' "

As her relationship with Aly Khan lurched along, Pamela cast about for marriage prospects. She even sought a reunion with Harriman at the end of 1947, when she let him know she intended to visit the Kennedy estate in Palm Beach early in the new year. But Pamela scuttled her plan, Kick recounted at the time, because Harriman thought it was "bad from all viewpoints," especially his own.

Around that time Pamela found temporary accommodations in Paris, thanks to the benevolence of Paul-Louis Weiller, the prominent industrialist she had met through the Coopers. Weiller had been married twice and boasted numerous lovers. He was obsessively secretive and unattractive-looking, but he had an energetic charm, and could be extravagantly generous. To ingratiate himself with English aristocrats, he let them stay at the beautiful houses he owned all over Paris. He once gave Diana Cooper a mink coat worth £4,500, a gift she blithely called "the coat of shame."

Weiller "was impressed by the magic that made men love Pamela," said his former wife, Aliki Russell. The son of cultivated and well-connected Alsatian Jews, Weiller had made his fortune by founding several airline companies that later became Air France. As a highly decorated World War I flying ace, he had earned the title "Commandant" and his own postage stamp. There were whispers that while living in Vichy, he had sold airplane engines to the Nazis or the Japanese during World War II. Many thought that such talk was inspired by jealousy and anti-Semitism. Still, as the rumors persisted, it was advantageous for Weiller to ally himself with a woman named Churchill.

Weiller certainly thought well enough of Pamela to let her use his fully staffed house in Neuilly. It was a miniature villa of gray stone behind a garden stocked with white doves. The small rooms were appointed with Louis XIV furniture and sketches by Renoir and Cézanne. It "amused" Weiller to extend such a courtesy to Pamela Churchill, said one of his Parisian socialite friends. Pamela accepted Weiller's favors quite casually, according to the Hollywood screenwriter Peter Viertel, whom Pam invited to be an extra man when Weiller took her to a nightclub with a group of friends. "At the end of the evening I reached in my pocket to pay," said Viertel, "and Pam said, 'Let Weiller pay. He has millions.'"

Pamela was back in England in May 1948 when Kathleen Kennedy set off for a long weekend with Peter Fitzwilliam, their first holiday alone. Kick had told her parents she planned to marry Fitzwilliam once he was divorced. Furious at Kick's sacrilege, her devoutly Catholic mother said she would cut her off financially and consider her dead, while Joe Kennedy kept quiet. Now the couple were going to spend two days in Cannes and then meet Joe Kennedy for lunch in Paris to seek his blessing before they publicly announced their engagement. Pamela accompanied the couple to Croydon Airport, where Fitzwilliam had chartered a Dove eight-seat plane identical to Aly Khan's. As Pamela recounted it many times, she "put them on the plane together." Caught in a violent thunderstorm, the plane crashed into a mountain ridge north of Marseilles.

Hundreds of Kick's friends attended the high mass sung for her at the Farm Street Church in Mayfair and then boarded a special train carrying her body to the Devonshire family plot at Chatsworth. Pamela was among the mourners, and so was Randolph. Their meeting at the funeral inspired Randolph to suggest a trial reconciliation that Pamela amazingly accepted.

Randolph had grown still more unattractive. "Dear Randolph," Noël Coward observed after the war, "so unspoiled by his great failure." He had been writing for British newspapers and drunkenly crashing through drawing rooms in Paris, New York, and London in his usual obnoxious fashion. He had "a huge belly" and was "very gray," James Lees-Milne noted in his diary. Randolph lived beyond his means in a large house in Hobart Place where he periodically invited his son to join him for lunch. With Laura Charteris now married to Lord Dudley, he was lonely. "He was still looking for a nanny for himself, a nanny who looked like his mother," wrote his cousin Anita Leslie, explaining his effort to reunite with Pamela.

For their "secret trial honeymoon weekend," Randolph persuaded Laura Charteris's sister Ann, then married to Viscount Rothermere, to lend him her country house. "It was a brief and extraordinary moment," said one of Randolph's longtime friends. "But by that time Pam had considerable opportunity to compare techniques." Randolph came up wanting, as he had before. The weekend, wrote Alastair Forbes, "swiftly brought her to her senses, leastwise her cerebral ones."

By that time, Pamela's romance with Aly Khan had cooled, although she resisted letting go. As Aly Khan's son Amyn recounted to friends, Aly was eager to drop Pamela because she was getting too serious about their relationship. By her account, during the summer of 1948 she and Aly had shifted from lovers to good friends. After Aly returned from a trip to Syria that July, Pamela came to Château de l'Horizon and settled in. Within days of her arrival, Aly met the red-headed actress Rita Hayworth. She had come to the Hôtel du Cap d'Antibes hoping to reconcile with her estranged husband, film director Orson Welles, who was in Italy. Elsa Maxwell brought Aly and Hayworth together at a dinner party. Smitten with her screen persona for years, he made a more vigorous assault than usual, bombarding her with luncheon invitations and filling her hotel room with flowers. Pamela's presence at l'Horizon was awkward, so he enticed Hayworth to fly to Spain with him.

Aly Khan hated confrontations and messy breakups. When he lost interest in one woman he usually moved on to the next, assuming the rejected lover would quietly withdraw. Seldom did a woman fail to get the hint. "He didn't know how to get rid of Pam," said a woman who knew both Pamela and Aly. "That is why he left her at l'Horizon . . . and he was desperate to come back." But after her conspicuous jilting, Pamela showed no inclination to make a graceful exit. As luck would have it, humiliation soon turned to triumph. One sunny afternoon, a power launch arrived from a yacht moored off the coastline. A tan, smiling young man climbed the sea steps and saw her on the terrace. "Buon giorno," said Gianni Agnelli.

Fifteen

A<small>T TWENTY-SEVEN</small>, Gianni Agnelli was almost exactly a year younger than Pamela—a significant turnabout from her usual attraction to older men. Although he had a reputation as a boisterous Riviera bachelor, he was still a provincial. "Gianni was very young, with no experience," recalled his aunt Lydia Redmond, the sister-in-law of Agnelli's mother. "He was thrilled by Pamela Churchill. She could bring a lot of amusing people to him, and she had gone to bed with them. He was a young Italian boy brought up in a very small town. To him, Pamela was a very glamorous person."

Like the other important men Pamela had known, Agnelli was not classically handsome. He had a strong aquiline nose, heavy-lidded pale blue eyes, black wavy hair brushed back, and a trim, athletic physique. "He looked very Italian, not so handsome as he became later," said one of his lifelong Italian friends. Somewhat surprisingly, he spoke Oxford-accented English in a fluting baritone, placing rhythmic inflections every few words like small hammer blows, creating an effect that was both soothing and enticing. His allure, his wife Marella said after many years of marriage, was his ability to create "motivation, excitement, amusement, attention. . . . He knows how to make boredom disappear. . . . There is the sense of the good time ahead." The scion of the Fiat automotive empire, he was also extremely rich.

Agnelli was captivated by Pamela's provocative looks. "She was appetizing," recalled Lydia Redmond, "pink like a peach that you wanted to bite into." He invited Pamela to leave Château de l'Horizon and join him on the *Tomahawk*, his 21-meter mahogany boat rigged with red sails, for a cruise with his friend, Sicilian aristocrat Raimondo Lanza. Pamela immediately consented, but there was one hitch. Little Winston, aged "seven and three quarters," as he later described himself, was due to arrive for a stay of several days with Pamela at l'Horizon—"probably the first time I ever went abroad," he recalled. Instead of meeting her son at the airport, Pamela arranged to park him temporarily at the Riviera home of a prominent Parisian friend, Prince Jean-Louis de Faucigny-Lucinge. Little Winston was unfazed by the change of plans, because he had heard about the Lucinge family—"great friends of both my parents"—and was delighted that they had a son he could play with.

According to Pamela's account, Agnelli planned to take her for a holiday on Capri, but on the first night she was cut on the head by a drinking glass knocked over when the boat hit rough seas. Pamela recalled that Agnelli was so concerned that he took her to be stitched by a plastic surgeon in Turin, where she had to rest until the wound had healed. Agnelli settled her into a friend's apartment, after which he took her on the promised cruise to Capri. (Randolph Churchill, in the meantime, retrieved Little Winston, enraged that Pamela had left her son behind.)

Raimondo Lanza told a different story to Agnelli's sisters, who shrieked with laughter each time they repeated it. "It was a big joke. Raimondo and Gianni picked up a girl for the day and she never left," said a close friend of the Agnelli family for many decades. When Pamela had the accident, according to the family friend, "she needed a doctor, and Gianni said he had to leave for Turin. She said, 'Don't leave me alone in this condition,' so she went with him. Once she was in Turin, she decided she was staying, so she stayed. It wasn't folie d'amour, but very shrewd acting. It was very well worked out." Soon after, Pamela Churchill was installed in Agnelli's rented villa, Château de la Garoupe, just down the coastline in Antibes from Château de l'Horizon.

"For Gianni, the woman means the conquest," Marella Agnelli once remarked, "he does not fall in love." Even as a child, Agnelli made it a point to control his emotions. "I don't like people who display their feelings, who scream and squeak and make a great case" he once said. "It doesn't look nice. It is a matter of the way one disciplines oneself, how one builds oneself."

His father's family shared the austere and orderly attitudes of prominent families in his native Turin. Before his grandfather Giovanni founded Fiat in 1899, he had trained as a cavalry lieutenant at Pinerolo, a spartan military school in the foothills of the Alps. Agnelli's grandfather, known to all as "the Senator," was severe and powerful. "He was very mean," said Lydia Redmond. "He wanted to control everyone." Although Agnelli's father Edoardo received the same training, he reacted by adopting the manner of a Belle Epoque gentleman. He managed various Fiat operations creditably, but sports—skiing and sailing especially—were his life.

Edoardo made an unconventional choice for a wife. Virginia Bourbon del Monte was the daughter of a Roman nobleman, Prince Carlo di San Faustino, and a flamboyant American named Jane Allen Campbell, who came to Italy from New Jersey after her father lost his money in the Wall Street crash of 1893. Virginia was a delicate beauty, with soft brown eyes, curly chestnut-red hair, a melodic voice, and a free spirit.

She and Edoardo had seven children: four girls and three boys. Giovanni Agnelli (nicknamed "Gianni" to distinguish him from his grandfather) was the second child and firstborn son. Though judged "intelligent and gifted" by his teachers, young Gianni was a lackluster student with a strong streak of insolence. The Agnelli children grew up under a strict regimen imposed by the Senator and carried on by Edoardo. Their governess, Miss Parker, taught them perfect English, dressed them alike in sailor suits, took them on long walks through the tall colonnaded squares of Turin, forced them to eat everything on their plates, and regulated their sunbathing at the beach—ten minutes on the stomach, ten on the back.

Surrounded by servants, they lived in a thirty-room palazzo that was filled with statues, tapestries, and old master paintings. The children watched movies in a basement projection room, played basketball in their own gymnasium, spent summers at their home in Forte dei Marmi on the Mediterranean coast, and skied at Sestriere and St. Moritz in the winter. They saw their mother and father at designated times, usually in the early evening before their parents had dinner.

Edoardo Agnelli died at age forty-three when he was hit in the head by the propeller of a seaplane. Gianni Agnelli, who was fourteen, was "desperate," he later acknowledged. But he hid his feelings and retreated to his bedroom, sitting silently on the floor surrounded by newspapers. It was the sternest test of his hardening emotional discipline.

As a thirty-five-year-old widow, Virginia Agnelli liberated her children from the severity of Turin. She took them to the Riviera, where they lived a freewheeling life, speeding in cars, eating rich food, gambling at the casino, and drinking champagne and pineapple juice for breakfast. Everyone, including Virginia, paraded around nude, and, recalled his sister Suni, "Gianni and the other boys went out with tarts." Virginia took numerous lovers, prompting the Senator to seize custody of the children. He relinquished them only after a long legal battle.

Virginia Agnelli's libertine ways had a profound effect on her eldest son. According to his biographer Marie-France Pochna, Gianni renounced traditional morality, which he regarded as useless. In its place he devised an "esthetic morality," which would permit him an uninhibited lifestyle as long as he behaved with "elegance." This "cult of aesthetics" played out in Agnelli's tendency to avoid emotional involvement, to brush off personal problems, and to value appearances above all. "I like beautiful things that are well done," he said. "I even believe aesthetics are like ethics. Something that is beautiful is ethical, and unethical things aren't beautiful—from tax dodging to doing things in hiding."

The Senator provided some corrective discipline for his grandson by hiring a tutor and introducing Gianni to the automotive industry with factory tours and a trip to Detroit. He also ensured that his namesake enrolled in the Pinerolo cavalry school for training as an officer. During World War II Agnelli served with a cavalry regiment on the Russian front, "taking chances," he later said, and watching how his compatriots responded to danger. After a stint in North Africa where he was slightly wounded in an argument over a woman, he tried to join the Allied forces following Italy's surrender in September 1943. Driving south with his sister Suni, he broke his ankle in an auto accident and nearly lost his foot to infection.

In November 1945, his mother was killed in an auto accident, and his grandfather died three weeks later. At the time, the Italian authorities were pressing charges of collaboration against the Senator, who had been a staunch supporter of Mussolini. The Communists had taken over the Fiat factories, but with the assistance of the English commander of the Allied occupation forces, the Agnellis ejected the Communists. The Senator's trusted lieutenant, Vittorio Valletta, took charge and trained Agnelli to run the company.

At age twenty-four, "he had become a grown-up man," observed Suni Agnelli, "handsome and cynical," and scornful of sentiment. "Only maids are in love," he announced. "It is something for cheap magazines." His grandfather had told him, "Have a fling for a few years and get it out of your system." Agnelli enthusiastically followed his advice.

When Pamela met him in 1948, he was in full fling. His friends included decadent Italians such as Raimondo Lanza, Hollywood moguls Jack Warner and Darryl Zanuck—who provided a steady supply of girls—and playboys Aly Khan, Porfirio Rubirosa, Alfonso de Portago, and "Baby" Pignatari. Agnelli called it "rough playtime . . . the heavy game" of loose living and high-stakes gambling. "Gianni was running around in fast Ferraris, and he was not responsible," said one man who knew him then. "He was wild and charming, and his requirements for a woman were limited." Until Pamela, said Lydia Redmond, "he had known only young women and movie actresses. He hadn't seen anyone like Pamela in her spending proclivities or the way she ran a house."

Agnelli had heard about the "well-navigated" Pamela Churchill. During the war, he had met Christopher Soames, the husband of Churchill's youngest daughter Mary, and he had also encountered Sarah Churchill in Rome when she was acting in a film in 1946. "Churchill was our greatest hero," said an Italian aristocrat who knew Agnelli for decades. "Gianni knew his daughter-in-law was beautiful and rather fun, so for a provincial boy from Italy she was a great conquest." "She appealed to his sense of snobbery. He liked the idea of what she represented," said "Ghighi" Cassini, a friend of Agnelli's who first called Pamela the "international siren" in his Cholly Knickerbocker "Smart Set" column.

But Agnelli was interested in more than the Churchill name. "Aly Khan turned her over to Gianni," said Lydia Redmond. "That was amusing for Gianni." Having her as a mistress was like joining a club that grew more prestigious with the initiation of each new lover. "Averell was the first one," explained Sandy Bertrand, who was a close friend of Pamela's in the postwar period. "He created a sort of pull that brought the others along. People at that level look at each other and say, 'If Averell Harriman, such a distinguished and wealthy man, if he would have this girl, she must be quite something. Let's find out.' "

Pamela worked her way into Agnelli's life with careful calculation, according to one of his confidantes. "She didn't count on her physical attributes as much as the ways in which she could be helpful—as a superb housekeeper and a very good VIP person. She established herself as a symbol of importance, always playing one man against the other. She immediately made known to Gianni her ability to make contacts." Agnelli instantly recognized her value as a woman of the world who could give him an "éducation sentimentale."

"Gianni was not crazy in love with Pam," said another of his closest friends. "He admired her. Pam knew so much. When we all met her we said, 'That's a real lady.' She taught him how to receive, about protocol, who to invite, where to sit. She made his education." Château de la Garoupe was a large villa perched on a rocky point above the sea. On weekends and throughout the summer, Agnelli kept the house bustling with guests, much as Aly Khan did at Château de l'Horizon. Pamela made herself indispensable to Agnelli by imposing order without squelching the fun, by making his house into a home.

On short notice, she could orchestrate a dinner for forty and fill the house with flowers—organizational skills that no woman in Agnelli's experience had ever displayed. She made it her business to know and to provide exactly what he needed. "If you smoked, the cigarette was there. If you liked art, the artists were invited," said Lydia Redmond. Pamela went to extraordinary trouble, such as having the chef at Maxim's teach Agnelli's chef how to make his famous Billi-Bi soup. "The secret of her graciousness was she had a knack for making you comfortable without seeming to do too much," said the model Anita Colby, who dined with Agnelli and Pamela several times in the South of France.

Agnelli was fascinated by what he called "the Hollywood birds," most of whom were older than he. "They were fun, they were different," he said. "For us, they were real Hollywood tycoons. They lived at the Hôtel du Cap, stayed up terribly late, telephoned Hollywood, played big money, and had the stars all around them." Pamela nudged him away from purely hedonistic friendships and toward others he might find useful in the future. "She was good for Gianni in that way," said Lydia Redmond. "She made him meet men whom he wouldn't have met, who were socially connected or politically interesting."

On the social side were English aristocrats such as David Somerset, the future Duke of Beaufort. Somerset, who would become one of Agnelli's closest friends, was an international sportsman and art connoisseur. A partner in London's renowned Marlborough Gallery, Somerset helped Agnelli build a great art collection, the most conspicuous expression of Agnelli's passion for beautiful things.

As the leader of the Fiat conglomerate in later years, Agnelli was known for his political skills. "He knows his way around," noted one admirer, "how much to flatter someone, how to talk to the Prime Minister." His political education began at dinner parties organized by Pamela, whose guest lists included people of influence. Agnelli would have considered it undignified to mix business and pleasure in an overt way, but setting the stage for future favors was another matter.

Fiat needed every possible break in the unsettled postwar years when Communists seemed on the verge of taking over Italy. Pamela organized a lunch with Beaverbrook at La Capponcina, his villa in the South of France, where the newspaper tycoon carefully jotted "Mr. Annielli, [sic] his brother and friend" in his appointment diary. "Agnelli was always very quick quick quick, very intelligent and fascinating," said Beaverbrook's granddaughter Lady Jean Campbell, who met him at La Capponcina. Beaverbrook, according to Campbell, "had great respect for him and thought he would become something extraordinary."

Pamela arranged the ultimate introduction when she invited Winston

Churchill over to dine. After his party had been defeated in 1945, Churchill had dedicated himself to halting the Labour Party's costly welfare reforms. Weary of postwar economic deprivations, the voters responded to Churchill's call for "some breathing space" in October 1951 and gave the Conservatives a slim majority that brought him back as Prime Minister at age seventy-six—an office he would hold until his resignation in April 1955 because of failing health.

For Agnelli, a link to Churchill was essential to improving the business prospects of a company formerly identified with the Italian Fascists. At first, Churchill had taken a dim view of Pamela's romance with Agnelli. "What's this I hear about Pamela taking up with an Italian motor mechanic?" he had remarked. But Churchill was charmed, especially when Agnelli took a keen interest in his namesake grandson.

Little Winston stayed for weeks at a time at La Garoupe, where he water-skied and snorkeled in the Mediterranean, and took private swimming and diving lessons at the Eden Roc Hotel. Agnelli invited the boy to ski at Sestriere, always including him in the elaborate parties he gave at the resort. "Whenever Agnelli saw Winston he gave him a hundred dollars, which was a lot of money," recalled a friend from young Winston's Eton days. Agnelli's generosity did not sit well with Randolph Churchill, however. "My father took umbrage," recalled Winston. "Gianni once gave me a miniature racing car. It was fire engine red with a motorcycle engine. My father said to me, 'Here's Agnelli giving you expensive toys, and what I give you, you send into the fire.' "

Pamela was also instrumental in getting Agnelli a business foothold in the United States. She introduced him to Franklin D. Roosevelt Jr., whom Pamela had entertained in London during the war. Through Agnelli, Roosevelt landed the Fiat distributorship for North America, which proved a big financial success. According to Lydia Redmond, the Roosevelt connection "got Gianni in with the U.S. government, which gave an enormous loan to Fiat after the war that Fiat needed [in order] to recover. Young Franklin was an ass, but Gianni befriended him, and Franklin lived on the Fiat representation." At another time, in another place, Pamela might well have received a finder's fee.

The favors she performed for Agnelli brought into sharper focus the power she derived from serving men. Indeed, the more elaborate her effort, the greater the benefits she received. "She was good for any man she slept with," said Tex McCrary. "She could make a man, not just in bed. She stretched a man's horizons." Pamela's men recognized her worth and were as appreciative as they were flattered. Their gratitude took the form of money and gifts that she accepted as her due. "When I heard about Agnelli," recalled Lady Mary Dunn, "I didn't think any more than that Pam was getting on with her job." Agnelli provided her with ample cash, a beautiful apartment staffed with a butler and maid, and a Bentley with a liveried chauffeur. "He was very generous to her," said Lydia Redmond. "He kept her like a queen."

Almost overnight, Pamela's wardrobe improved. "She dressed abominably when she met Gianni," Redmond went on. "She wore little platform shoes, and everything was wrong. Gianni made her chic. He dressed her from the skin out." Agnelli set up accounts with the most fashionable couturiers—Christian

Dior, Cristóbal Balenciaga, Jacques Fath—and the bright colors gave way to more muted tones and classic lines. She was following one of the first principles of the successful courtesan: avoid ostentation and strive for subtlety and ease.

Pamela applied the same rules to the apartment Agnelli bought her in the 16th arondissement of Paris. Her new home was on the fourth floor at 4 Avenue de New York, a turn-of-the-century building of gray stone with narrow balconies bounded by wrought-iron railings. The layout was modest, with a sitting room, a small library that converted to a dining room, a master bedroom with a combination bathroom and dressing room, and a guest bedroom. But the flat's corner location, with large windows overlooking the Seine and the Eiffel Tower beyond, flooded the apartment with sunlight and created an air of grandeur.

She hired Lady Baillie's onetime decorator Stéphane Boudin and used Agnelli's money to furnish the apartment in a manner that would appeal to her patron. For Pamela, Boudin mixed eighteenth-century styles, "a great deal of beautiful Louis XVI acajou in the English taste," in the words of decorator Billy Baldwin.

The rooms were quite formal, with richly detailed silk curtains. One pair of sofas and matching chairs were covered with flowered silk that had been woven for Marie Antoinette's marriage to Louis XVI. Mahogany tables were arranged with silver-framed photographs of her Churchill relations, as well as exquisite bibelots, among them exotic miniature ostriches of bronze, vermeil, and crystal announcing her Digby heritage. Pamela added a distinctly feminine touch with embroidered pillows, a profusion of flowers (purchased at a cost of $10,000 a year, which would probably run six times that amount today), and heavily scented Rigaud candles. At night the apartment was bathed in a soft glow, an effect Pamela achieved by using pink light bulbs instead of white.

Agnelli and Pamela did not actually live together. "They were never really a couple," said one of Agnelli's close friends. "They always had two bedrooms, and they were rarely alone. There were always twenty or thirty guests." They might see one another for a weekend, and then not again for two or three more weeks. She kept Paris as her base, and he used an adjoining apartment as his pied-à-terre. Agnelli lived in Turin, working during the week for Fiat under Valletta's tutelage. Although Pamela would later refer to Turin as her "second home," Agnelli's friends and family emphasized that she came there infrequently after the early months of their affair. Winston recalled visiting Turin only once, for three or four days. "Pam couldn't stay there," said a longtime friend of the Agnellis, "because of the Catholicism and because Gianni did not want her there. Gianni in some ways is very conventional, and it was not appropriate to have her around his friends, his family and his life there. It was all right to live openly with a mistress in the South of France, but not [in] his hometown."

Pamela and Agnelli also made trips to Rome, New York, St. Moritz, and London. Agnelli helped underwrite a new London apartment after Pamela lost Harriman's subsidy for 49 Grosvenor Square in 1950. Her address at 11 Hyde Park Gardens was less fashionable, but her apartment—a duplex on the top two floors—was sufficiently comfortable, with three bedrooms and bathrooms on the fourth floor, and a drawing room, dining room, and kitchen on the fifth floor, all of which offered views of Hyde Park. "It was very simple," said Pamela's friend Leonora Hornblow, "and very English. It was mostly blue, chintzy and cozy, with big squishy chairs and tufted sofas you could take a nap in after lunch. It was adorable."

Pamela's public manner with Agnelli was quietly attentive and slightly self-effacing. She said little, only offering comments that allowed Agnelli to shine. "She didn't speak unless someone asked her something," said one of Agnelli's friends. Though Agnelli found Pamela attractive, the relationship lacked physical intensity. His demeanor toward Pamela was "more indifferent than affectionate," recalled Anita Colby. Since he regarded open displays of affection as vulgar, Pamela accepted his undemonstrative ways. After Harriman and Murrow, she was accustomed to such aloofness.

A good friend of Agnelli's explained that sexuality was not the distinguishing feature of the relationship, "because he always had other women. Pamela kept the houses, called the friends, was glamorous and amusing and useful." A woman who knew Agnelli for many years added, "Pam wanted the glamour and money, and Gianni wanted the public relations. They were a good combination, but never a love story."

The course of their affair was dictated by Agnelli, who insisted on preserving his bachelor status. Four months after they met, Agnelli took off for a visit to New York—alone. Cholly Knockerbocker, who had broken the story of Agnelli's romance with Pamela in early September 1948, called him "the leading foreign catch in town" in early December. When Agnelli returned to Europe three weeks later, Knickerbocker reported that Pamela was "waiting there anxiously for his return." Explained one of Agnelli's longtime friends, "It was very comfortable to have someone who didn't live with him. In Paris and the South of France he wanted to have an open house where he could come and go. One moment he wanted to be there, and she would have everything ready, all the guests assembled. It was her job. She waited for him, and she did it superbly."

When they were apart, "he would sometimes call her twelve times a day," said one of his close friends. " 'I must call Pam, I must call Pam,' he would say. She would share gossip with Gianni. It was his habit to call in the morning and say, 'What is the news in Paris?' " Who was the prettiest new girl, he would ask, which man was cuckolded at a party the previous evening, who had made a faux pas?

To satisfy what Agnelli's colleagues called his "monkey curiosity" and to maintain her usefulness, Pamela scoured the party circuit and mined her contacts in Paris, London, and New York for the most up-to-date morsels about international society. Pamela cultivated Beaverbrook's Paris-based gossip columnist Sam White, and Mathias Polakovitz of *Paris Match*, both of whom were brimming with information too risqué to print. "She was always phoning and running up and down," said a good friend of Agnelli's. "That is what she has done all her life." But instead of tracking military strategy and political machinations, she was now monitoring the peccadilloes of high society.

"When Pamela met a man she adored," her friend Leonora Hornblow once said, "she just unconsciously assumed his identity, as if she were putting on a glove." It was an accurate assessment, except for one thing: it was not unconscious. She worked hard to fit Agnelli's mold. Because he spoke English so beautifully, they didn't face a language barrier. Still, in Paris she answered the phone with a cheery "Pronto!," and she picked up his contagious inflections. She developed a pronounced Italian accent that provoked numerous jokes among the English aristocracy.

"Pam used to swan over from Paris in gorgeous clothes," recalled Linda Mortimer. "Mummy and her best friend Edwina d'Erlanger laughed so much once when they were playing charades and Pam said, 'How do I say this in English?' " Pamela's transformation was so complete that she even fooled the wife of *The Times* correspondent in Paris, Lady Katherine "Kitty" Giles, who told friends of meeting a "charming Italian girl with red hair."

Like an actress, Pamela changed roles with each new man in her life. The script was toughest with Agnelli because he was so unscripted. Early in their romance, Agnelli had been invited to bring Pamela to visit his friend Count Rudi Crespi in Capri. They arrived late in the evening and had already gone to bed when Crespi and his wife Consuelo returned from dinner. The next morning Crespi went to Agnelli's bedroom and found him sitting naked on the bed, drinking coffee—a perfectly natural state for a man who had grown up in a household where nudity was the dress code. Pamela's room was on the other side of an adjoining bathroom. Agnelli called her in to meet Crespi, and when she emerged from the bathroom, the girl from staid Dorset was also naked. Crespi kissed her hand, stole a glance at her white skin and red hair, and felt quite disconcerted. "Pam and Agnelli were very detached," said a woman to whom Crespi told the story. "It seemed like no situation in the world could embarrass her."

"Pamela didn't know all the women he was with," said one of Agnelli's friends from those days. "I think she knew they were not important for Gianni. She was the premiere, like the lady of the seraglio." Still, her situation was always slightly off balance. Socialite Rosemarie Kanzler and her husband could see the effects during the summer that they rented a house next to La Garoupe. "They would dine together and at midnight he would go somewhere," said Kanzler. "She wouldn't know where. She was always very dignified." Pamela knew that preserving Agnelli's freedom was essential to maintaining her hold.

Agnelli often stayed out gambling or carousing until 3:00 A.M., then got up at 7:00 to go for a sail. "It seemed like he went ten years without sleep. He looked old when he was forty," said Taki Theodoracopulos, the son of a wealthy Greek shipping tycoon, who first knew Agnelli on the Riviera. Cocaine was the temptation of choice among the international set, prompting Taki to coin a double entendre for their all-night adventures: "la grande nuit blanche." Decades later, Agnelli said that the expression only meant "a full night out" and that he had not been lured by the drug, although in the next breath he confessed, "I don't think I stopped at anything." According to Ghighi Cassini, "Gianni took cocaine, and it was difficult to have a long conversation with him.

His attention would go elsewhere." Pamela once confided to New York editor Clay Felker that cocaine had taken a toll on Agnelli.

Pamela did not take drugs, and she rarely went to the casino. In fact, she was so conscious of taking care of herself that she usually went to bed early and slept late. She was especially vigilant about her milky skin. "I have this image of Pamela walking in the garden all in white with a white umbrella," recalled one of Agnelli's friends. "She was afraid of the sun, which was so funny for us because we loved the sun at this time." Pamela's moderate habits in the company of self-destructive jet-setters even inspired a joke: Gentleman number one: "Pamela Churchill could have been an even more famous beauty if only her neck had been longer." Gentleman number two: "You could hardly expect that of a girl with her head screwed on so tight."

In the sophisticated circles of international society, Pamela was completely accepted as Agnelli's mistress. Agnelli's generosity likewise boosted her standing among Parisians, who were unfailingly impressed by money. As long as Agnelli was unattached and she was amusing and elegant, they lived within the rules. "She was so taken for granted that one didn't think about it," said Johnny Galliher, an American who saw her frequently in Paris. Another longtime friend of Agnelli's remarked that "You didn't hear mean things about her, only that she was a courtesan, and you knew that many others wanted to be and could not."

It was leading nowhere, though. By becoming a perfect extension of the men who kept her, Pamela had done her job too well: no man of wealth and rank would marry her, knowing she functioned so well as a mistress. The most dramatic evidence of Pamela's subordinate status came in the first year of her relationship with Agnelli, when she got pregnant. At his insistence, she had an abortion in Lausanne, Switzerland.

Agnelli was never nasty to her, but he made her position clear. "Being Italian," noted Taki, "he looked upon Pam as the little woman." As time went on, Pamela tired of her role. "She hated to play the mistress," said one of Agnelli's longtime friends. Increasingly, she played the grande dame, acting as if she had a right to everything Agnelli gave her. Maintaining an elevated pose was crucial; her faux pas with Count Crespi would never be repeated. She focused her efforts on enhancing her image as a prospective wife. "In that she didn't prove wise," said Agnelli's friend Carlo di Robilant. "She didn't understand him well enough, because it was very improbable that he would marry her."

In March 1950, Pamela Digby Churchill presented herself at the Church of the Immaculate Conception Farm Street, only two blocks away from 49 Grosvenor Square, where Father Joseph Christie received her into the Roman Catholic Church. Since the end of 1948 she had taken instruction at Farm Street, and she had erased her Church of England marriage to Randolph Churchill, the father of her only child, by obtaining a "decree of nullity" from the Vatican, a ruling that a marriage already ended in divorce is invalid in the eyes of the Church. Despite the presence of a child, Pamela was able to establish that her marriage had not been serious because of her immaturity and the misgivings she had experienced before the wedding. "When she was received into the Church, her marital state would have been satisfactorily resolved from the point of view of the Church and her conscience," said Father Geoffrey Holt, the Farm Street archivist who verified the date of her conversion.

By receiving an annulment, Pamela could remarry in the Catholic Church, a prerequisite for an alliance with the Catholic Agnelli family. As Leland Hayward's third wife, Slim, tartly observed, "Pam Churchill thought she would marry Agnelli, so she became a Catholic on spec." Decades later, the sting of Pamela's repudiation of her Churchill marriage was still evident in her son's reaction: "I don't know what that made me," he said ruefully. Although Winston was only nine when his mother received the annulment, he clearly recalled the circumstances: "I met Father Christie when I was eight years old. I called him Father Christmas. It was all above my head at the time. It was all specifically with a view to marrying Agnelli that she was taking instruction in the Catholic faith. . . . No doubt a contribution was made to the suitable charity in Rome by Agnelli."

No marriage plans materialized. Instead, Agnelli bought a new Riviera redoubt for Pamela to redecorate. It was a twenty-eight-room Italianate villa called La Leopolda, situated at the top of a hill overlooking the bay of Villefranche. The house had a large formal garden, and "one vast drawing room after another and one veranda after another," recalled Taki. Pamela enlisted Boudin for the decor, which became a major project, her Côte d'Azur version of Leeds Castle. "Boudin really did Leopolda for her," said his former partner in New York, Paul Manno. "She never did anything without Boudin." With Agnelli's money, Pamela and Boudin bought fine French furniture, coordinated color schemes, and installed elaborately finished paneling. "I felt that Gianni was just a visitor at Leopolda," said Anita Colby. "Pam talked as if she were the owner. 'Boudin just finished this, Gianni,' she would say. 'What do you think?' She acted as though it belonged to her, that Leopolda was her home."

She gradually assumed the posture of "maîtresse de maison." "She ran La Leopolda, and she started giving orders," said Aimee de Heeren. "That got her into trouble with Gianni's sisters." Indeed, Gianni's four sisters—Suni, Cristiana, Maria-Sole, and Clara—had been suspicious of Pamela from the outset. (His younger brother Giorgio had been committed to a mental institution several years after their mother's death in 1945, suffering from what Gianni called "nervous derangement.") At first the sisters tried to ignore Pamela, after concluding that she was both unimportant and unimpressive. But as she asserted herself, they grew concerned. They could see that she was maneuvering Agnelli toward the altar, particularly after she converted.

As they watched Agnelli "giving Pam everything under the sun," as Lydia Redmond described it, the sisters were appalled. "Pam wanted a jewel case from Bulgari," recalled Redmond. "Gianni had someone send up three from which to choose. She said, 'I'll take all three.' So Gianni gave her all three. He thought it was wonderful. This was in Rome, all the sisters were there, and I was there. The sisters were livid."

"Pam wanted to be married," said a longtime friend of Agnelli's, "and she put that position regularly to him, very much so." Suni and Cristiana "were very blunt," the friend continued. " 'You can't do this, Gianni,' they said. 'She is a kept woman.' " Agnelli found his sisters' disapproval useful. "I wasn't thinking of marrying at all," he acknowledged years later. But at the time he found it convenient to shift the blame. "His sisters helped to make a no," explained Agnelli's friend. "He could say, 'My family says no, my sisters are opposed, so let's postpone the idea.' " His position provoked a joke among his friends: "My tragedy is I can never say no," he told Consuelo Crespi, to which she replied, "If that were true, why is Mrs. Churchill not Mrs. Agnelli today?"

Pamela increased the pressure as she passed her thirtieth birthday in March 1950, the same month she converted to Catholicism. It was an important milestone in a social set where men—young and old alike—had a marked preference for women in their early and mid-twenties, who were both impressionable and at the height of their youthful beauty. Agnelli reacted by feeling "more and more cornered," said one of his close friends. "He started seeing her less and less." The tensions between them were even apparent to visitors at Leopolda. Toward the end of the affair, their relationship, said one woman who saw them several times, was afflicted by "a bit of boredom and irritation." During a dinner at Leopolda, Anita Colby felt "Gianni was ready to blow the place. He acted like a caged lion. I think she was nervous. She seemed very uneasy."

Pamela refused, as usual, to acknowledge any decline in her position. She propelled herself forward, driven by her willpower and sense of self-preservation to create new opportunities. "Pamela never doubted her ability to charm," said Lydia Redmond. "She didn't consider failure. She would just say to herself, 'I'm moving on to the next,' never, 'He's tired of me.' It was a delusion that kept her going."

If she wanted to provoke Agnelli's jealousy, she was unsuccessful. She had a brief run at Alfonso "Fon," the Marquis de Portago, heir to one of the oldest titles in Spain. As reckless as he was rich, he would die in 1957 in the famous Mille Miglia auto race. Years later, his widow, New York socialite Carroll Petrie, was still describing Pamela as "the first woman to sleep with my first husband after we got married."

In 1951, Pamela took up with André Embiricos, a Greek whose family had been building a fortune in shipping for more than a century. Embiricos owned the island of Petali off the coast of Greece, as well as a luxurious apartment in Paris and a splendid yacht. A famous ladies' man, he had been the lover of international socialite Mona Williams before he married an American fashion model named Bea Ammidown. In 1945, Cholly Knickerbocker proclaimed André and Bea Embiricos "the most soigné pair" in Manhattan. Embiricos was admired for his dark good looks and his suave manner. "He was very chic, not an unknown little Greek. He was a catch," said a Parisian friend of Pamela's. Like the others in his social circle, he was only too happy to join Pamela's honor roll of lovers.

When she began going around with Embiricos openly in the South of

France and in Paris, Agnelli registered no reaction. "He was not at all upset," said one of his friends, "because the story with Pamela was finished." Agnelli's problem was that he couldn't figure out how to extricate himself.

Pamela's affair with Agnelli drifted until the turbulent night of August 20, 1952. The occasion was a black-tie ball at La Leonina, a luxurious villa down the hill from La Leopolda that was the home of a mysterious Hungarian business-man named Arpad Plesch. Pamela was supposed to be in London, so Agnelli went to the gala alone. There he encountered a stunning twenty-one-year-old brunette named Anne-Marie d'Estainville, an acquaintance who had been on his sailboat several times. When d'Estainville started to flirt with Agnelli, he responded by offering to show her Leopolda.

As they were embracing on the terrace at 3:00 A.M., Pamela appeared and flew into an uncharacteristic rage. "She came in and threw something," recalled d'Estainville. "She started to try and hit Gianni and me. She was absolutely livid. It was so quick, it didn't last more than a minute or two. She came in yelling and screaming and then she went out. She was like a tornado. Gianni and I were staring like idiots. I didn't say anything, and neither did he. I suppose she had gone to the soirée, probably someone said he had gone, so she was probably furious before she came in."

After returning to Leonina with d'Estainville, Agnelli offered to take her home to Cap Martin. She went to retrieve her evening bag and met him fifteen minutes later in his Fiat station wagon. As they drove down the Lower Corniche to Monte Carlo, he picked up speed. "For heaven's sake, you are going too fast," d'Estainville exclaimed. Agnelli waved her off. "I knew something was wrong," she said. "He was not quite right. I think he had had something to drink. I suddenly realized it was dangerous." Agnelli later said he had "not especially been drinking," but admitted that "at four or five in the morning you surely have been drinking more than necessary." Years later, Pamela said that Agnelli also had taken cocaine.

As Agnelli pressed the accelerator, he missed a left turn at the entrance to the Cap Roux Tunnel and slammed into a small butcher's truck, pinning its three passengers against the mountainside—all of them seriously injured, but none fatally. Moments later, two of d'Estainville's friends arrived. They pulled her from the car and sped her from the scene to Monte Carlo, where they washed her cuts with gin. Agnelli had a broken jaw, and his right leg was shattered in seven places.

Pamela rushed to his bedside at the hospital in Cannes, where she kept vigil until the arrival of his sister Suni, who immediately took charge. Agnelli's leg was severely infected with septicemia, prompting Suni to transport him to the Istituto Ortopedico Toscano in Florence. When doctors there discovered gangrene, Agnelli refused their attempts to amputate. Instead, they cut out the decayed tissue and ordered him to stay in bed for nine months. By Pamela's account, she single-handedly nursed Agnelli back to health, sleeping at his bedside in Florence and then accompanying him to Forte dei Marmi and Turin.

While Pamela was undeniably with Agnelli in Cannes and in Florence, it

1

2

ABOVE Major Edward Kenelm Digby and his bride, Constance Pamela Alice Bruce, at 83 Eaton Square, London, following their wedding at the Guards' Chapel on July 1, 1919. RIGHT On inheriting his father's title, the eleventh Baron Digby and his wife embarked on August 21, 1920, for Australia, where he took a job as military secretary to the Governor-General after selling his London home and renting out his Dorset estate to pay inheritance taxes.

"Like many aristocrats with shrinking fortunes, the Digbys took retrenchment in stride."

LEFT Lady Digby with four-year-old Pamela, seated on her pony, and Sheila, age three. BELOW Minterne, with Lord and Lady Digby and Pamela in the foreground.

"At a time when the English class system still held firm, the fifty-room mansion instilled among its occupants a comforting sense of superiority."

3

5

6

ABOVE Lord and Lady Digby with Pamela and Sheila at Minterne in the "tapestry room," its walls decorated with Flemish tapestries brought to Minterne in the eighteenth century by Charles Churchill. RIGHT Jane Digby, Lady Ellenborough, whose scandalous life fascinated and inspired her great-grandniece, Pamela.

"Pamela told New York Times columnist C. L. Sulzberger that Jane Digby was 'the most wicked Englishwoman who ever came to Germany.'"

7

ABOVE LEFT Pamela *(second from left)* at the Bullingdon Club point-to-point at Somerton as the 1938 Season began, with Pauline "Popsy" Winn *(left)*, John Jacob Astor, and "Mr. Windham." ABOVE RIGHT Pamela and Sarah Norton, daughter of Richard and Jean Norton (the mistress of Lord Beaverbrook), at the Musselburgh Races in Scotland following the 1938 Season. BELOW LEFT Pamela with Charles Manners, the Marquess of Granby and heir to the Duke of Rutland, at the Cattistock Hunt Ball held at Minterne in January 1939. BELOW RIGHT Rose Kennedy, wife of Joseph P. Kennedy, United States Ambassador to the Court of St. James's, with her daughters Kathleen "Kick" *(left)* and Rosemary before their presentation at the First Court in May 1938.

"During the Season of 1938, Kick thought Pamela was a 'fat, stupid little butter ball,' as Kick described her to her brother Jack."

9

10

II

12

ABOVE LEFT Lord and Lady Digby with Jaquetta *(second from left),* Eddie, and Sheila, celebrating the Fourth of June at Eton in 1938. RIGHT Olive, Lady Baillie, with her daughters Popsy and Susan at Leeds Castle, where Pamela spent many weekends in her post–debutante year. BELOW LEFT Pamela's Aunt Eva, the Countess of Rosebery, who made a big impression on her niece during visits to the Rosebery estates at Dalmeny and Mentmore. BELOW RIGHT Sheila (wearing the uniform of the Auxiliary Territorial Service) and Pamela at the Newbury Races shortly after the outbreak of World War II.

"Leeds shaped Pam's life. She obviously liked those people, and she liked that kind of world."

3

14

15   ABOVE   The wedding of Pamela Digby and Randolph Churchill, son of Winston Churchill, First Lord of the Admiralty, at St. John's in Smith Square on October 4, 1939. BELOW   The wedding reception in the state rooms at Admiralty House *(left to right):* Lady Digby, Winston Churchill, the bride and groom, Clementine Churchill, Lord Digby, Sheila Digby; Jaquetta and Eddie are seated on the floor.

"It seems she was the 8th girl Randolph had proposed to since the war began, his best effort being 3 in one evening."

17

ABOVE Pamela standing in the main reception room at No. 10 Downing Street, a full-page photograph by Cecil Beaton in the January 27, 1941, issue of *Life* magazine. RIGHT Pamela posing with six-week-old Winston Spencer Churchill, born at Chequers on October 10, 1940.

"As she came out of her anesthesia, the nurse said, 'I've told you five times already, "It's a boy."'"

19

20

ABOVE LEFT   W. Averell Harriman *(right)*, America's "expediter" in London, with Pamela *(far left)*, his daughter Kathleen, and an unidentified man, inspecting Royal Air Force planes four months after Harriman and Pamela began their affair in April 1941. ABOVE RIGHT   Averell with Marie, his second wife, at a polo match on Long Island in 1936. BELOW LEFT   John Hay "Jock" Whitney and his wife, the former Betsey Cushing Roosevelt, shortly after their marriage in March 1942. Pamela conducted her affair with Whitney in London even as she was living with Harriman. BELOW RIGHT   William S. Paley, president of CBS, and his star broadcaster Edward R. Murrow, with whom Pamela had simultaneous affairs in 1944 after Harriman and Whitney had left London.

"Bill told Ed that after destroying his marriage she would destroy him . . . Bill admired her for her skill . . . how she operated with men. But he knew she would be bad for Ed."

21

22

"Ave couldn't marry her but he didn't want to give her up. So Max organized the settlement. . . . Averell was a very nice stupid fellow. He was conscience-stricken that he had given in to Marie."

ABOVE   Pamela with little Winston, age three, in flat II at 49 Grosvenor Square, which was secretly paid for by Averell Harriman. BELOW LEFT   Averell Harriman with Lord Beaverbrook *(left)* at a shipboard conference between Franklin D. Roosevelt and Winston Churchill. BELOW RIGHT   Pamela *(left)* arriving in New York with Princess Margarita Matchabelli in October 1946 to begin an assignment as New York correspondent for Max Beaverbrook's *Evening Standard.*

LEFT Prince Aly Khan, son of the Aga Khan, the billionaire leader of Ismaili Muslims, dancing with Princess Ghislaine de Polignac in Paris. BELOW LEFT Pamela at the Ascot Races in June 1948, one month before Aly Khan ended their romance after falling in love with Rita Hayworth. BELOW RIGHT Gianni Agnelli at the Sestriere ski resort.

"Gianni was thrilled by Pamela Churchill. She could bring a lot of amusing people to him, and she had gone to bed with them. . . . To him, Pamela was a very glamorous person."

RIGHT André and Bea Embiricos, dancing in St. Moritz. BELOW LEFT Anne-Marie d'Estainville, who was with Gianni Agnelli on August 20, 1952, when he crashed into a truck in the South of France after Pamela caught the couple embracing on Agnelli's terrace. BELOW RIGHT Marella Agnelli (*left*, wearing white-framed sunglasses), with two of her sisters-in-law, Maria-Sole (*center*) and Cristiana (*standing*), at Sestriere.

"Pam was the old mistress sticking around, and no one knew what to do. The sisters were very displeased because it was ridiculous for Pam to be kept on one side [by Agnelli] and carrying on openly with Embiricos and others. The whole story was not pleasant."

29

31

ABOVE Baron Elie de Rothschild *(right)* with *(left to right)* brother Alain and wife Mary, and their sister Cécile after the liberation of France. BELOW Pamela pointing at Stavros Niarchos during a luncheon at the Corviglia Club in St. Moritz in the 1950s. Her romance with Niarchos failed to impress Elie.

"I like a woman who is quiet in bed," Elie confided to a friend, "a woman who is lovely to wake up to. Pam was that."

34

ABOVE   Pamela (wearing mask) with Baron Alexis de Rede at a ball at the Hôtel de Coulanges in Paris in 1958. BELOW LEFT   Pamela at the 1957 opening of the theater at Groussay, the splendid château outside Paris owned by Carlos de Beistegui. BELOW RIGHT   Pamela, dressed as Titania, with her friend Sandy Bertrand, costumed as William Shakespeare, at the ball hosted by Marie-Laure de Noailles to celebrate Mardi Gras in February 1956.

"Pamela looked so ethereal in a décolleté gown of pale blue silk that Harold Acton said, 'She would have converted all the fairies to sexual orthodoxy.'"

37

Pamela dancing with twelve-year-old Winston during the Palace Hotel's Carnival in St. Moritz.

"I was very rapidly sucked into the grown-up world. If my mother didn't have a better escort, I was mobilized in my blue suit and went to dinner parties with her."

38

39

40

ABOVE RIGHT Pamela being sketched by the portrait artist Bigorie during the 1950s in Paris. ABOVE Louise de Vilmorin, a minor poet and novelist, whose friendship Pamela cultivated during her Paris years. RIGHT Pamela with the Duchess of Windsor at the memorial service for Christian Dior in 1957, when the two women were "inseparable chums," according to the *Evening Standard*.

"Once when Louise was admiring Pamela's jewelry, Pamela said, 'You poor Louise, all the presents you have are love letters.'"

41

42

TOP LEFT Leland and Nancy "Slim" Hayward on their wedding day in 1949 at the home of Bill and Babe Paley. LEFT At the wedding luncheon for Leland and Slim: *(left to right)* Bill Paley, the groom and bride, unidentified man, Leonora Hornblow, and Babe Paley. BELOW Leland Hayward kissing his new daughter-in-law Marilla as Pamela and his son Bill looked on. Pamela and Leland had married only three days earlier in a civil ceremony in Carson City, Nevada, then flew to Topeka, Kansas, for Bill's wedding.

"Pamela arrived in Leland's life with something he had never experienced, her famous talent for cocooning a man. He was taken aback and he succumbed."

43

ABOVE   The Digby and Churchill families pose in the garden of 28 Hyde Park Gate after young Winston's wedding to Minnie d'Erlanger in 1964. *Front row, left to right:* Lady d'Erlanger, Randolph Churchill, the bride, Sir Winston Churchill, the groom, his half-sister Arabella. *Back row, left to right:* Mrs. Martin (Pamela's housekeeper), Leland Hayward, Mrs. Douglas Wilson, Minnie's brother Robin, her grandmother Mrs. Sammut, Lady Digby, Pamela's brother Eddie and his wife Dione, Clementine Churchill, Pamela, Mary Soames, Douglas Wilson.

RIGHT   Leland's eldest daughter Brooke, an aspiring actress, who took an instant dislike to Pamela that turned into a lifelong estrangement.

"I would call Father at home, and a long time would go by and out of the blue I would hear her deep voice," said Brooke. *"I would think, 'My God, has she been on the phone this whole time unannounced?'"*

ABOVE LEFT Peter and Cheray Duchin arrive at the wedding reception for Pamela and Averell Harriman on September 27, 1971, just six months following the death of Leland Hayward. After Pamela and Averell were reunited on August 5, the Duchins had encouraged their renewed romance. ABOVE RIGHT With Pamela looking on anxiously, Averell Harriman scolds a photographer who caught them arriving for their private wedding ceremony at St. Thomas More Church in Manhattan. BELOW The service was conducted by Msgr. James G. Wilders, assisted by the Reverend Joseph Christie from London, with Harriman's daughter Kathleen *(left),* Pamela's sister Sheila (not pictured), and Ethel Kennedy *(right)* as witnesses.

"Pam told him she would never set foot in Washington unless she was his wife."

49

50

ABOVE LEFT   Pamela with Averell Harriman and Judge Thomas F. Croake, after her swearing-in as a U.S. citizen in December 1971. ABOVE RIGHT   Pamela on one of the four horses she kept at Willow Oaks, the Middleburg estate she coaxed her husband into buying for her in 1977. BELOW LEFT   Pamela in her bedroom suite in Harriman's Georgetown home that Billy Baldwin decorated in pastel hues. BELOW RIGHT   Pamela and Averell Harriman on the sun porch in Georgetown with Winston and Minnie Churchill.

*"A lot of people used to joke . . .
saying she couldn't care less how
much money she spent. But to me it
demonstrated what a perfectionist
she is."*

51

52

53

54

55

ABOVE LEFT Averell and Pamela Harriman with Jacqueline Onassis and Lynda Robb at a fundraising dinner for the Democratic party in 1974. ABOVE RIGHT Pamela addressing the crowd at a fundraising reception she hosted in Georgetown in 1980, with Averell *(left)*, Robert Strauss *(right)*, and congressional candidate Elizabeth Holtzman. LEFT Pamela and Averell with their friend George Stevens Jr. at Harriman's ninetieth birthday party in 1981, a fundraiser for the Harriman political action committee, Democrats for the 80's.

"When I heard she was moving into politics, I thought, 'How delicious. It is such a man's world. Now she doesn't have to have one dinner partner. She can have five hundred.'"

ABOVE   Pamela and Averell Harriman during a visit to the Soviet Union in June 1983, greeting Yuri Andropov, the former chief of the KGB, who had recently become Secretary General of the Communist Party. BELOW   Pamela through the window of her limousine as she left St. Thomas Episcopal Church in Manhattan after Averell's funeral on July 29, 1986.

"Pamela had not stinted on honoring her late husband with dignity and sweeping ceremony. When the final bill for the funeral came in, she had spent $171,082."

THE WOMEN THEY LOVED

PAMELA HARRIMAN

She has been one of the most admired women of her time. And now she is a political force to be reckoned with — one of the Democratic party's leading fundraisers. Beginning on page 18, W visits with Pamela Harriman, shown here at home in Georgetown with her Jack Russell, Marina.

58

LEFT Pamela and her many romances make the cover of *W* magazine in November 1987. BELOW Several months after Harriman's death, Pamela is photographed for *Architectural Digest* at Mango Bay, a four-bedroom home in Barbados that Averell had purchased for $1.2 million in 1984.

"By sixty-seven, Pamela was dissatisfied with her heavily lined and somewhat jowly face. . . . So early in 1988 she went to New York City for a facelift."

59

RIGHT J. Carter Brown, who is fourteen years younger than Pamela, became involved with her in 1987 and escorted her for four years. BELOW LEFT Jaquetta James, eight years younger than her sister Pamela and a widowed mother of six, pictured in 1994 at her home, Torosay Castle on the Isle of Mull in Scotland, where she built a successful tourism business (40,000 visitors a year), presiding over a tea room, gift shop, and miniature railroad. BELOW RIGHT Pamela's younger sister Sheila Moore, who married an American and as a widow moved to Ireland to breed racehorses, photographed in 1994.

"It was what the French call a marriage of convenience. Pamela needed a squire who was not threatening, and Carter liked having someone with an airplane and a house in Barbados."

60

63

64

LEFT TOP Pamela with Speaker of the House Tom Foley in June 1990 at the final fundraising party for her political action committee, an event that was criticized for cost overruns. LEFT CENTER Pamela with Washington attorney Clark Clifford during a party she gave in his honor in May 1991. LEFT BOTTOM Pamela's confidant Sandy Berger, who helped her write speeches and newspaper articles and later became deputy national security adviser in the Clinton Administration. BELOW Janet Howard, Pamela's chief aide and trouble-shooter, with Ron Brown, then chairman of the Democratic National Committee.

"Her umbilical cord was to Clifford. He got involved in lots of little things. She would ask 'Should I do this event in Cleveland? Should I deliver this speech?' Clifford made it a point to know everything."

66

65

67

ABOVE   Pamela with Albert Gore Jr. when he was a senator from Tennessee. Pamela contributed money to his campaigns, supported his presidential candidacy in 1988, and applauded
Clinton for choosing him as his running mate. BELOW   Pamela saying good-bye to presidential candidate Bill Clinton in August 1992 after he used her Georgetown home for meetings.

*"She was skeptical of Clinton because he had not abided by the Sixth Commandment. There is a
certain ironic piquancy in that."*

ABOVE Pamela greeting Republican Senator Jesse Helms of the Senate Foreign Relations Committee in May 1993 during confirmation hearings on her nomination as U.S. Ambassador to France. BELOW Ambassador Pamela Harriman in her Paris office at the embassy overlooking the Place de la Concorde.

"She was able to use her convening power well. She could have a dinner at the embassy, and they would come at the highest levels because she is Pam."

71

RIGHT TOP   Pamela in Paris with Assistant Secretary of State Richard Holbrooke *(left)*, one of her longtime advisers. RIGHT CENTER   Pamela flanked by French Foreign Minister Alain Juppé *(left)* and Secretary of State Warren Christopher *(right)* during a meeting in Washington in 1993. RIGHT BOTTOM Pamela leaving the residence of Prime Minister Edouard Balladur in February 1995 after a meeting to discuss revelations about CIA spying in France.

72

"During a visit Kitty Hart asked Pamela why she worked so compulsively. 'I don't want them to think I'm not serious,' she replied."

73

ABOVE Averell and Marie Harriman in 1954 with his two daughters, Mary and Kathleen, their husbands Shirley and Stanley, and their five children (the sixth would be born in 1957). Forty years later, Harriman's heirs sued Pamela for $40 million in a dispute over his estate.
BELOW Kathleen Mortimer at the celebration Pamela organized in 1991 to mark the 100th anniversary of Averell Harriman's birth.

"With her current financial statements in hand, Pamela told Kathleen over lunch in a Manhattan restaurant that she could not afford to help the family. Visibly distraught, Pamela said she had no money and that everything was mortgaged."

ABOVE Averell Harriman's grandson David Mortimer with his wife Shelley, the daughter of film producer Walter Wanger and actress Joan Bennett. Among the grandchildren, David and his brother Averell had been the closest to Pamela before the family filed its lawsuit. RIGHT Linda Wachner, chairman of Warnaco and Authentic Fitness Corporation, who became Pamela's informal financial and legal adviser in 1995.

"Between Pamela and Linda there is a joining of interests. Pam can offer her social legitimacy. Linda has the resources. It is really a fine merger."

78   Pamela at the U.S. Embassy residence in Paris, seated in front of Matisse's *Woman in a Blue Hat*, a painting that she sold at auction for $1,020,000 in May 1995 to raise money for a proposed settlement with the Harriman heirs. She also sold a Renoir and a Picasso.

"The Renoir was her 'laughing picture' and the Matisse her 'frowning picture.' 'When I get in one of those moods,' she told visitors to the residence, 'I come and sit in front of the right picture.'"

LEFT Pamela with actress Sharon Stone after a dinner party at the American Embassy in Paris in October 1995.
BELOW Pamela *(left)* in the front row at the Balmain couture fashion show in Paris in 1993 with *(left to right)* Annette de la Renta, Isabelle d'Ornano, and Carolyn Roehm.

BELOW Pamela with former British Prime Minister Margaret Thatcher at the College of William and Mary in February 1996 after Pamela received an honorary doctorate.

"Thatcher spoke of Pamela's 'great influence on both sides of the Atlantic,' and, somewhat elliptically, of her 'great shrewdness which from an early age she always exercised.'"

82

ABOVE Pamela at age 74 with her son Winston, 54, in the American Embassy residence in Paris. RIGHT Pamela at an embassy party in April 1996 with her grandchildren Jack, Marina, and Jennie, and her daughter-in-law Minnie, now separated from Winston, who had moved in with a Belgian jewelry designer.

"For all her glamour and energy, Pamela was an elderly woman entering a period of physical and emotional vulnerability. After she had been let down by advisers and friends and in-laws, her British family remained the place she could go and be cared for without having to give much in return."

83

was his sisters, not Pamela, who oversaw his care, according to those close to the family. "Pamela stayed in a suite at the Grand Hotel or the Excelsior," recalled one visitor to Florence during that period. "In Italy it was very difficult to sleep in a hospital if you were not Mr. and Mrs. It was a very old-fashioned country in the 1950s. Maybe she spent one night, but she came and went for visits." And she always had to contend with Agnelli's sisters, who took turns keeping him company and treated Pamela frostily.

"Pamela was considered a terrible nuisance," said a longtime friend of the sisters. "She was the old mistress sticking around, and no one knew what to do. The sisters were very displeased because it was ridiculous for her to be kept on one side and carrying on openly with Embiricos and others. The whole story was not pleasant." Eventually, according to the sisters, Pamela left Florence and made some visits to Agnelli at Forte dei Marmi.

In her version of events, Pamela omitted her pursuit of Embiricos, an inconvenient reminder that she was not as selfless and devoted to Agnelli as her legend would have it—that she had loved him ardently and faithfully. The Embiricos interlude did not fit with the romantic ending Pamela devised for her Agnelli story. According to Pamela, it was while Agnelli was convalescing in Turin that they decided together, amid tears and prayers and discussions over several days, to end the affair.

The trigger for the decision, according to Christopher Ogden, was the granting of her annulment in January 1953. But she had already received an annulment before entering the Catholic Church in March 1950. By claiming that the annulment occurred three years later, Pamela had the perfect rationalization: She "didn't fool herself," wrote Ogden. "She knew the annulment meant that if Gianni would not marry her once she was free, their affair had no future." After this epiphany, Agnelli and Pamela drove from Turin to the checkpoint at the French border, where she continued alone in her own car. Agnelli "stood in the road," wrote Ogden, "and waved sadly as Pamela drove away." A longtime friend of Agnelli commented, "It was possible Gianni waved sadly, but it was probably because he still didn't know how to get rid of her." Though Pamela by now had no hope for marriage, she still enjoyed her access to Agnelli's houses and money.

During his convalescence, Agnelli's sister Cristiana had invited a friend, Princess Marella Caracciolo di Castagneto, to stay with her in Florence. The daughter of a Neopolitan prince and an American named Margaret Clarke, Marella had been in love with Agnelli for years. They had met in Rome after the war and had engaged in what she called "a long period of flirtation." After studying art and design in Paris at the Beaux-Arts, she had worked in New York as a photographer and *Vogue* model and at one point had been engaged to another man. But she thought Agnelli was "magnificent," and when she received Cristiana's invitation, she canceled a sailing trip to be at his bedside.

To the sisters, Marella was the ideal candidate to marry their brother: well born and well bred, gracious and accomplished. "Marella was from a good family and was the prettiest girl of her generation," said Carlo di Robilant. She was tall and elegant, with a fine-boned face and long, slender neck. Her expressive brown eyes, russet hair, and musical voice gave her an uncanny resemblance to Agnelli's mother.

Agnelli was very taken with Marella, and pleased that her background was "from the Italian-American group, like my mother's family." The accident helped him recognize that it was time to find a suitable wife. "It changed my life," he said. "I stopped playing and started thinking." They were married in Strasbourg, France, on November 29, 1953, a year after their courtship began. Agnelli was thirty-two, and Marella twenty-seven. He walked to the altar leaning on two canes; Marella was three months' pregnant.

Asked years later if the marriage had been dictated by Marella's condition, Agnelli retorted, "I would have married her before or after." Sources close to the Agnelli family said an abortion was never considered and that Gianni specifically asked Marella to have his child. Agnelli knew that Marella would give him "an element of order, a sort of guideline. She has a strict approach to life, and we like a lot of the same things."

Agnelli's decision to marry Marella provided his exit from Pamela. He sold his pied-à-terre in Paris, gave Pamela her adjacent apartment and the Bentley, and made a substantial financial settlement. His generosity was motivated by a sense of responsibility that she actively encouraged. "Pam played it well, saying, 'What is going to happen to me?' The magic of Pamela is to give the guilty feeling with all the men. This is why Gianni gave her what the French call *apanage.* . . . the money to live with grandeur," said one well-connected European woman. "With Gianni and with the other men it was 'au revoir and merci.' With a great sense of guilt she made them pay afterwards and down the line."

Pamela buried her disappointment and put her own spin on the story, saying that her five years with Agnelli had run their course, and she knew it would never have worked. "I think my mother had reservations about marrying someone and having to worry about having starlets come out of the closets all the time," said Winston. In defeat, Pamela held strong. "Instead of crying, she went out and had admirers," said Aliki Russell, the former wife of Paul-Louis Weiller. "She suffered inside, but she didn't show that she was left. She had character."

Pamela traveled to Biarritz, where Ann Fleming mocked her as "international flotsam and jetsam"; to St. Moritz, where she danced with her son at the Palace Hotel's carnival ball; and to the South of France, where she rented a house near La Leopolda and called Marella periodically to ask if she could come for lunch or dinner. "She was very straightforward. She behaved very well," said one of Agnelli's friends. "She didn't try to hook Gianni again. The thing was finished, and now she was a friend, which was important to her. She was not making mischief." Her absence of rancor, said Agnelli's friend, "was part of the game." Yet her behavior toward Agnelli seemed to surpass simple practicality to a craving for approval from a man who had rejected her.

In Paris she was helped enormously by her friend Arturo Lopez-Willshaw, a multimillionaire Chilean homosexual who had married his cousin Patricia Lopez de Huici, a classic "mariage blanc." They lived in a grand home in

Neuilly, once described by Chips Channon as "a small Versailles." Lopez entertained Pamela frequently at Neuilly, took her out to lunches and dinners, treated her to excursions on his yacht, *La Gaviota,* and gave her expensive gifts. For Pamela, the fat and jolly Lopez was as amusing as he was generous. Lopez liked Pamela because she was glamorous, and for a time he even feigned that they were having an affair.

At thirty-three Pamela found herself in a paradoxical situation. Everyone knew that Lopez was merely her walker, and that her romance with Embiricos was ebbing. "Andy had never been tempted by marriage, only by being part of the club," said a woman who knew him then. Pamela disliked being regarded as a courtesan, yet she couldn't afford to be known as a woman who was only escorted by "society tame cats," those vaguely homosexual spare men known for keeping company with somewhat older women. "She was décriée," said one prominent European woman, "because she had been so openly kept and had lost it." With her cachet fading, she needed to find another man with wealth and social standing.

CHAPTER
Sixteen

*E*VERYONE KNEW it was over with Gianni when Pam stopped answering the phone by saying, 'Pronto,' " recalled Johnny Galliher. "But then she started answering, 'Ici, Pam,' and people wanted to know, 'Who has she got now?' "

Early in 1954, Pamela had added a famous new name to her pantheon of lovers: Baron Elie de Rothschild. They met one evening in a Paris bistro at a dinner organized by some American bankers. The Americans had invited Pamela specifically to meet Elie, whose wife Liliane was out of town. "We have a girl for you," said one. Elie had heard about Pamela, and as he later told a friend, he had taken a dim view of her "grand demimondaine" setup: the flat under-written by Agnelli, the Bentley, the fast crowd in the South of France, and the indiscreet affair with Andy Embiricos. Yet that evening he was enchanted by Pamela's red hair, her fair skin, and her agreeable manner. He drove her home and called her the next day. After a few more evenings together, they became lovers. "She wasn't coquettish," he confided to a friend, "just very sweet and charming and pretty. I wanted to go to bed with her and I did." He also enjoyed appending his name to Churchill, Harriman, Whitney, and Agnelli. As he later joked, "Once it is washed, it is like new!"

Pamela could not have made a more prestigious or prosperous conquest than Elie de Rothschild, a prominent member of the fifth generation of Europe's legendary banking family. The progenitor of the Rothschild fortune was Mayer Amschel Rothschild, a dealer in coins and antiquities in the Jewish ghetto of Frankfurt in the mid-eighteenth century.

When Mayer's sons came of age, he dispatched four of them to Paris, London, Vienna, and Naples, keeping the fifth with him in Frankfurt. Working together, the five brothers (whose escutcheon displays five arrows and the motto, *Concordia, industria, integritas*) became "Europe's friendly finance company," amassing several hundred million dollars by the mid-1880s. The Emperor of Austria rewarded them with the title of "Baron" in 1822, and Queen Victoria did the same in 1885.

Mayer's youngest son, James, founded the French branch, adding the aristocratic "de" to the family name. James de Rothschild was a conspicuous dandy with bohemian affectations. He became the Continent's biggest railway tycoon, but his real status derived from his place at the center of French power as banker and confidante to King Louis Philippe. "The House of Rothschild plays a much bigger role in France than any foreign government," Prince Metternich once observed. "Money is the great motive force in France."

By the twentieth century the Rothschilds had reached the top of French society without yielding an inch of their Jewish identity. Considered by many the genuine successors to the Bourbons, they acquired the regal distinction of being known simply by their first names. They owned some of the most beautiful Parisian mansions and a half-dozen castles, as well as racing stables, yachts, theaters, stud farms, resorts, and France's most prestigious vineyard, Château Lafite, which Baron James bought for $1.5 million. When James built his own extravagant palace, Ferrières, Wilhelm I of Prussia remarked, "Kings couldn't afford this. It could only belong to a Rothschild."

In the tradition of ruling families, they intermarried to keep their wealth more closely held and to maintain their bloodline. Thirty-nine out of fifty-eight Rothschild marriages from the mid-eighteenth through the early twentieth centuries were between cousins or other close relatives. The Rothschild dynasty only began to slip in the interwar years, when the fourth generation focused on managing its assets instead of expanding into new businesses. During World War II, the family fled the Continent as the Nazis seized Rothschild homes and sent 137 freight cars filled with family treasures to Germany. But the French branch managed to hide their business holdings, including millions in negotiable securities, property titles, and industrial records, which they recovered after the war to begin rebuilding their business.

Leading the revival of the French dynasty was Baron Guy de Rothschild, assisted by his cousins Elie and Alain. Together they reestablished Rothschild Frères as the largest private bank in France, and their Compagnie du Nord controlled extensive industrial interests. They developed Saharan oil, Cameroonian aluminum, and Mauritanian iron ore, and invested heavily in promising American companies such as IBM and Kodak. Estimates of Rothschild wealth in the postwar years exceeded $500 million, taking into account not only their businesses and property holdings but also their priceless collection of art, most of which was recovered from the Germans.

Known more as a sportsman than a financier, Elie de Rothschild cut an elegant figure at age thirty-six when he met Pamela, who was three years his junior. He was nearly six feet tall, slender and straight, with a thin, craggy face that conveyed an enigmatic intensity. He had a high-domed forehead and receding hair, deeply set blue-gray eyes, a falcon-beak nose, closely cropped mustache, and a broad, mischievous grin. His voice was a well-modulated baritone, surprisingly soft and light. He was by turns shockingly vulgar and boyishly charming.

His father Baron Robert de Rothschild was a quiet steward of the family fortune who raised money for Jewish refugees, and his mother Nelly was known as a great beauty and prominent Parisian hostess. By aristocratic custom Baron Robert's four children—two sons and two daughters—were raised by a British nanny, who taught them English before they learned their native French. The youngest of the four siblings, Elie grew up in the shadow of his older brother Alain, the more serious, debonair, and handsome of the two boys. When France went to war with Germany, Elie and Alain rode off to the front with their cavalry unit "like Pancho Villa," Elie said, "with a horse and saber." After German forces invaded France in May 1940, Elie and Alain, aged twenty-three and thirty, were captured at the Belgian end of the Maginot Line and sent to a military prison camp near Nienburg, Germany.

Elie tried to escape and was sent to Colditz for a year, and after that to an equally harsh camp at Lubeck where he was reunited with Alain. The two brothers were imprisoned for four years, an experience that marked Elie deeply —particularly his year at Colditz, a rigorously punitive camp for strong-willed prisoners. "We were sixteen stuffed in a room as big as my hand," he told the French author Marcel Schneider. "The only space that belonged to us was our folding bed. . . . Our cell had only Jews and priests. Each priest attached himself to a Jew whom he wanted to convert. . . . In vain I told mine he was wasting his time, that I valued my ancestors' faith above all else." Although Elie and his brother were treated by their captors as officers, they were nevertheless "despised because they were Jewish and they were rich," said a longtime friend of the Rothschilds.

During his internment, Elie wrote to Liliane Fould-Springer, whom he had known since childhood, to propose they be married by proxy "the way kings used to do," as he told Marcel Schneider. Half French, half Austrian, the Fould-Springers were rich Jewish industrialists. On the French side, the Foulds had made a fortune in ironworks; Liliane's great-uncle was Achille Fould, who had once used his connections with Napoleon III to challenge the Rothschilds' banking supremacy, only to go under himself. Despite the legacy of their bitter business rivalry with the Rothschilds, the Fould-Springers permitted Liliane to accept the proposal.

Although she was not a beauty, Liliane had a pleasant face that was illuminated by her bemused smile. She had even features, brown hair curled into a gentle pageboy, and captivating dark eyes. She was short, and in those days, recalled one of her old friends, "she had a very nice figure and legs," but she was defiantly unglamorous, refusing even to wear lipstick. What she lacked in looks she made up with a formidable intelligence leavened by a personality that was lively, down-to-earth, and rich with the sardonic humor that Elie treasured. As one friend put it, "She looks like a cook, talks like a queen, lives like an empress, and thinks like a philosopher. She is so well educated and intellectual, but she is very cozy." Elie took pride in Liliane's intellectual attainments, but the marriage had more to do with suitability than passion. "In a way it was a loveless marriage," said a longtime friend. Elie took his vows at Colditz in October 1941, and Liliane gave her pledge in Cannes, then part of the Free French Zone, in April 1942. In a photograph of the occasion, she is shown seated in a chair in front of the mayor, with Elie's chair empty beside her.

Elie de Rothschild was twenty-seven when he was released from prison in 1944 after France was liberated by the Allies. He and his brother Alain returned to the resplendent Parisian mansion in which they had grown up at 23 Avenue de Marigny, set amid several acres of gardens across the street from the Elysée Palace. Elie and Liliane had their first child, a son, in 1946, a daughter a year later, and another daughter in 1952. They went about their lives in Rothschild fashion. Meals were served by white-gloved footmen on "perfect Sèvres with a separate vintage wine to accompany each course," according to Harold Acton. Their only concession to economy—an almost comic gesture of populist solidarity by the entire clan—was to give up their Bentleys for chauffeur-driven Austin Minis.

In his approach to marriage, Elie was thoroughly a European aristocratic male, narcissistic and hedonistic. He used his wartime prison experience at least in part to justify his postwar pursuit of pleasure. "I had lost some of the best years of my life," he once explained to a friend. "I had a lot to make up. I wanted a lot of pretty women." He led a classic double life, with his wife and family on one side, his mistresses on the other.

Like Agnelli, Elie de Rothschild had inconsequential short-lived affairs until he met Pamela, whose background and abilities enabled her to command a more permanent position. She was familiar with the Rothschilds' ways, dating from her childhood memories of Mentmore, the home presided over by Aunt Eva Rosebery, who had married into the Rothschild family. It was irrelevant to Pamela that Elie de Rothschild was Jewish. He was by every other measure an aristocrat, possessing great wealth, accustomed to dynastic power, convinced of his superiority.

For all his Rothschild imperiousness, Elie's personality radiated such insecurity that his friends routinely referred to his "complexes." Although he had some traits in common with Agnelli—restlessness, biting wit, self-absorption—his needs were significantly different. He required a more soothing touch: to temper his mercurial moods, flatter his vanity, nudge his obstinacy, and muffle his childish outbursts. He could be stunningly rude, insulting women, noisily swearing at hapless waiters, and recounting crude jokes, usually about sex. "Most of us have a filter in our heads that stops us from saying certain things," said the English author Alan Pryce-Jones, who was married to Liliane de Rothschild's sister, Theresa. "It was as if Elie had just the opposite, a sluice gate through which things would pour out."

Pamela met Elie when Liliane was grieving over Theresa's death in 1953. Friends of the Rothschilds said that Liliane had always been good to Elie and that she excelled as the family's "chief executive," managing their lives with impeccable taste and attention to detail. Even through her mourning, according to those who knew Liliane, she superbly maintained her role as a Rothschild wife. She had begun to circulate in society, although she was distracted by her grief, a circumstance that Pamela exploited. Liliane had also grown stout and dowdy. "Pamela thought she looked like an old toad," noted Ogden.

According to Ogden, by taking up with Elie in her quest for money and adoration, Pamela "targeted and chose carefully." She "was not anxious to marry Elie as she had been Gianni. She liked him, but he was a colder man, and she did not love him." Why was she so open about the extent of her calculation with Elie when in other circumstances she obscured her motives? Ego is one possible explanation: her need to show her prowess over men and to downplay her unsuccessful efforts to marry Elie. Revenge might be another: unlike her other important affairs, this one left a residue of ill will that Liliane de Roth-schild helped perpetuate. In many respects, it was Pamela's least successful relationship.

She led Elie to believe that she was in love with him. Intent on making him feel at ease, she was elaborately considerate and unfailingly cheerful. "I don't know how real it always was," he said in recent years to a friend, "but of course people like to be charming, to have people see them at their best. She wanted to please, which was very appealing. She was very comfortable and agreeable." Elie didn't like to hear Pamela called a courtesan; he told friends he preferred to think of her as a European geisha.

Pamela laughed at Elie's jokes, ignored his rudeness, and deferred to him on everything. Since he spoke English better than she spoke French, he insisted they converse in English. She knew what he liked to eat and would have it on hand. She kept his sleeping pill by her bed, along with a glass of water. If he didn't like the dress she was wearing, she would change it immediately and ask which one he preferred. When he wanted to read his newspaper in peace, she would sit silently. When he wished to hear gossip, she would amuse him with tales about their mutual friends.

"I like a woman who is quiet in bed," Elie confided to a friend, "a woman who is lovely to wake up to. Pam was that." In the boudoir, Pamela catered to his wishes and never made demands. Over the years, Pamela told various friends that sex was "not very important" to her. She confided to screenwriter Peter Viertel that "the bed part is less important than all the rest," but he was skeptical: "In her case, I think it's not what she says that counts," he said. "She must have had a big physical message to hold those men. She certainly must have satisfied them in a big way."

Elie told friends that sexual intimacy was his primary interest in Pamela and that he had little in common with her beyond the bedroom. But as she had done with Harriman and Agnelli, Pamela set out to become indispensable in other ways. Unlike Agnelli, Elie didn't need Pamela's help in organizing his life or making introductions. So one of her foremost goals was to show him that she was fit to be a Rothschild. She tried to master all that was important to him, largely by imitating his wife. "All of Elie's important mistresses went about finding out how Liliane did things," said a friend of Liliane and Elie.

From her years at Minterne, Pamela knew about horses, polo, and blood sports. Now, she listened hard when the conversation turned to wine, and soon could converse knowledgeably about vintages and varietals. She quizzed gallery owners about Elie's preferences in modern art—although she never managed to match Liliane's expertise. The principal focus of Pamela's "education," how-ever, was learning about eighteenth-century French furniture and objects, a passion of the Rothschilds and other cultivated Parisians.

"My life has given me a unique opportunity to shop," Pamela once told fashion reporter Eugenia Sheppard, without the least trace of irony. In Paris during the 1950s, shopping was Pamela's main occupation. It gave her a tutorial in the decorative arts of the eighteenth century. As usual, she sought advice from experts like Gerald Van der Kemp, the chief curator of Versailles, who had worked closely with Liliane to produce a highly praised exhibition on Marie Antoinette in 1955. The socially ambitious Van der Kemp ("He only cares for blue blood," wrote Nancy Mitford) was flattered by an association with Pamela and gladly shared his expertise and his contacts, including a seamstress who embroidered Pamela's upholstery and linens.

Pamela's chief guide to eighteenth-century decor was a peculiar man named Georges Geoffroy. Known as the best interior designer in Paris, Geoffroy was famous for creating the spectacularly carved and gilded library in the British Embassy. "Georges was more than a decorator," wrote the English artist Michael Wishart, "He was a total aesthete, wit, and dandy." Geoffroy disliked the term "decorator," preferring to call himself an "antiquaire."

He was bald, with piercing brown eyes and an emphatic personality. Some regarded him as insufferably pompous; he had the preposterous habit of using seventeenth-century French expressions in his everyday conversation. Conspicuously homosexual, he surrounded himself with what Wishart called an "entourage of gigolos," and in later years expressed disdain for the "idiotic" rich women who had slavishly followed his advice. But his cachet was such that ambitious collectors overlooked his difficult temperament. Pamela dropped Boudin and attached herself to the more prestigious Geoffroy. He was, she said, her "guiding light."

"Geoffroy had a lot to do with Pamela Churchill's acceptance," said the Parisian photographer André Ostier. "In a certain group in Paris, Geoffroy was a sort of Pygmalion. He would say, 'You must have a nice flat, you must have the best table.' He would even go with women to Christian Dior for fittings." Geoffroy was enchanted by the straight lines and perfect proportions of the Louis XVI style. Pamela already had some furniture from that period, and Geoffroy intensified her interest, allowing her to distinguish herself from Liliane, who favored the grandly ornate style of Louis XIV. "I spent days and days with him, doing the antiques shops, looking and learning," Pamela said. Geoffroy knew the important dealers well enough to gain entree to the back rooms, where he taught Pamela how to determine authenticity and bargain for the best price.

Pamela collected avidly, she once said, "like a squirrel storing away nuts for a rainy day," and she traded up whenever she found something of higher quality than what she already owned. Her passion established her bona fides as a collector in the best Parisian tradition.

Friends of Elie said he was less generous with Pamela than legend would have it. After initially deriding Agnelli's financial support for Pamela, Elie came to view it as a benefit. With Agnelli having made the major investment, Elie spent little on Pamela by comparison—primarily on clothing, wine, paintings, objects, and jewelry. Among friends he boasted that "she never cost me" and laughingly called himself Pamela's "gigolo." "She had everything she needed from Gianni," he once said. "She was receiving alimony. She was like a widow." Pamela in turn convinced Elie that she valued him for who he was, not for the size of his bank account.

To dispel her image as a gold digger, she tried to create the impression that she was clever at managing her own finances. "She never had any troubles," Elie told a friend. "She never seemed to need money." She emphasized to Elie that she understood the value of money, and she shrewdly avoided asking for anything too extravagant. She even had a budget for her art purchases: no more than 50 francs for a painting and 25 francs for a drawing. "It was a time when if you had some money you could buy the most beautiful things every day, and they were not that expensive," explained Ostier. "Geoffroy knew what to buy." On a number of occasions, for example, Pamela picked out drawings by the fashionable painter Paul Helleu that Elie gladly bought because they were both reasonably priced and pretty. Her technique was straightforward. "Darling, I saw the most beautiful bracelet today," she would tell Elie. "Would you go by and take a look and see if you like it?" If Elie liked what he saw, he would buy it for her. But if he didn't admire it, or it was too expensive, he would not. She knew, he later told a friend, "if you pester a man he is gone." Above all, she made Elie feel honored to provide for her.

Because he was married to a prominent and well-liked woman, Elie had to avoid appearing with Pamela in public, which gave their relationship an air of unreality. "I didn't see her enough to know if she could be difficult," he once confided to a friend. "I never lived with her." Their assignations tended to be daytime encounters at her apartment. Arrangements were easy, however, since Elie was not exactly tied to his desk at the bank. The joke was, according to one of his friends, that "because Guy spends eleven months out of twelve at the office, Alain and Elie are able to spend one month out of twelve there."

Pamela and Elie followed no set schedule. He would usually call her late in the morning from his oak-paneled office, arrive for lunch served by her butler, followed by an afternoon in bed. From time to time they stole away for a weekend in the country or to London. Only occasionally did they stay in Pamela's apartment in Hyde Park Gardens, which Elie dismissed as a "dugout." "It was a question of when the cat's away," said Alan Pryce-Jones. "I remember when they invited me to have breakfast with them at Claridges. Elie had been very fond of my wife [Liliane's sister], so I was an odd person to invite. They were sitting eating boiled eggs and drinking large cups of coffee on a large bed. Elie was proud of Pam and wanted to show off."

Parisian society knew at once about the affair, which instantly boosted Pamela's status. Yet while her position as Elie's mistress earned Pamela whispers of praise in sophisticated circles, no one could openly acknowledge it, least of all Liliane's friends, who found the situation embarrassing. It was also remarkable that Liliane remained in the dark for many months, given Elie's inability to keep quiet. "When he gets excited, he talks a lot," said a man who knew him for decades. "He didn't talk directly about Pam, didn't give indiscreet details, but he was very much in love with her. He told me so. He told everybody. He talked about how beautiful she was. His whole attitude was highly romantic. He loved the whole notion of Pam, and he was extremely taken by her."

Despite the entrenched tradition of official mistresses in France, the wife has always had a clearly defined role to which the mistress by custom deferred.

At first Pamela seemed willing to live within the rules. But after a lull, she began urging Elie to divorce Liliane and marry her. "The women of Paris are very defensive," said Lydia Redmond. "It is perfectly all right to go to bed with their husbands but not to get into their positions." Observed Evangeline Bruce, whose husband David was American Ambassador to France in the 1950s, "It was a very very tough time in Liliane's life. She was scared to death."

Knowing that Pamela wanted to supplant her, the usually staid Liliane launched a counteroffensive. She spied on Pamela's flat and made comments about her in a loud voice at Alexandre's, the coiffeur to Parisian high society. Even worse, recalled Pryce-Jones, "Liliane used to pursue Pam and Elie in her car and write rude notes that she would leave for them." One day in a rage Liliane took the wheel of her Austin Mini and bashed into Pamela's Bentley. "Pam told me about that with great merriment," said Sandy Bertrand. "It was even funnier because the money for the repairs on the Bentley came from Liliane's bank account."

Pamela refused to take Liliane seriously. "Her view was that if others were upset, that was their problem," Bertrand went on. "Pam just laughed at Liliane and thought her quite silly." But she underestimated the strength of her opponent, who had both the standing and the energy to prevail. Although Elie hated confrontations, Pamela finally nudged him into telling Liliane that he wanted to leave her for his lover. Liliane said no, and Elie buckled. His rationale, he explained to a friend, was that "divorces only happen if the woman lets the man go."

Others viewed his actions differently. "Liliane was scared," said one aristocratic Parisienne, "but Elie was dead scared of Liliane." Pryce-Jones judged Elie a "moral coward" for not following his heart. But that view overlooked the deep ties between Elie and Liliane—their common language and heritage, their shared taste, their appreciation of each other's character. Elie genuinely felt a duty not only to his family but to the Jewish community, which would have frowned on his marriage to an Englishwoman who was also stigmatized by divorce and Catholic conversion. Elie was certainly cowardly, but only in declining to tell Pamela there was no hope. "I kept it ambiguous," he later told a friend. "What man would not?"

Once she knew that her marriage was secure and her rival could not advance beyond the role of mistress, Liliane applied herself to making Pamela's life difficult. In public gatherings she cut Pamela while Elie murmured quiet greetings. Liliane refused even to pronounce Pamela's name, and she made it clear to friends that they could never speak of "that woman" either.

To most upper-class Parisians, Liliane's approval counted for far more than Pamela's. "Quite a few people were reluctant to see Pam because of Liliane," said a man who knew both women well. "Publicly, Pam was invited to all the big parties, the dances and balls, but en privé, she wouldn't be invited by Liliane's best friends. Women like Madame Pol Roger wouldn't receive her for small dinner parties."

Ultimately it was Liliane's impudent wit that proved her most effective weapon. One evening in 1954, Liliane was seated at a dinner next to the Duke of Windsor, who turned to her and said, "Which Rothschild is the lover of Pamela Churchill?" "My husband, sir," replied Liliane. Her deadpan remark was recounted hundreds of times in the salons of France, England, and the United States. It had the desired effect of dispelling Pamela as a serious rival and turning her into what one Englishwoman called a "joke figure."

CHAPTER

Seventeen

IF PAMELA DETECTED any change in her status, she never let on. Convinced that she would triumph in the end, she played the role of a rich party girl without a care in the world. She began indulging herself as never before, adopting a high-maintenance regimen that she would follow for the rest of her life. Even by the standards of Paris, where many women spent most of their waking hours pampering themselves, Pamela set a high mark. She looked upon taking care of herself as a full-time job. One American expatriate, Jimmy Douglas, recalled, "I remember the first time I met Pamela at a luncheon. She looked marvelous, and people said that she had stayed in bed, just resting and not eating, drinking water and lemon juice for three days because she wanted to look superb."

Pamela understood the value of her looks. Had she been homely, her social standing, her famous name, and her skills as a hostess would have meant less. She knew that the beauty clock was ticking, and she felt more insecure about the way she looked than she ever let on. As she approached middle age, she worked hard to enhance her pretty face and maintain a trim figure. Whenever she began to slip, it showed first in the double chin that had plagued her as a young woman.

Pamela perfected the art of making herself up, set aside time for regular massages and manicures, and entrusted her auburn hair only to Alexandre, the celebrated coiffeur. At a time when many wealthy Parisiennes visited Alexandre's salon three times a week, he came to Pamela's apartment nearly every day, en route to his daily appointment with the Duchess of Windsor. Alexandre doted on Pamela's "Venetian" hair, cutting it in a soft wavy style and rinsing it in chamomile tea to heighten its color. Pamela was gracious to Alexandre and others who served her, although, he recalled, "Pam was not a woman of making confidences. She would mainly tell you the details of life—'My fitting was wrong,' or, 'My cook put no lemon in the apple tart.' "

At least once a week Pamela was visited by a vendeuse from one of her favorite couturiers—Dior and Balenciaga headed the list—for a fitting. Part saleswoman, part consultant, the Parisian vendeuse was an essential guide for women of leisure. Pamela would be pinned and draped in her luxurious dressing room by her longtime Dior vendeuse, Eliane Martin.

"She would offer me coffee if it was morning, or whiskey if it was afternoon," said Martin. Pamela wore a size 42 (10 American). "She had very nice legs," said Martin, "but the bad thing was her waist. She had good shoulders, and maybe I shouldn't say this, she had beautiful breasts, probably the best I ever saw in my life. She had good proportions, but she was not good in a full skirt. She was marvelous in the long straight line, and she liked décolleté because she had very nice skin and shoulders. She knew what dresses were best for her."

From Dior, Pamela generally bought twenty ensembles a year, ten each season, including evening dresses. The minimum price for a suit or day dress was 3,000 francs, which would be more than $4,000 today. An evening dress with embroidery ran three times that amount. A conservative estimate for Pamela's yearly budget at Dior alone would run close to $150,000 at today's values. "She paid the bills herself," said Martin. "She never asked lower prices. She paid when she received her dresses or at the end of the season. Payment was not a problem with this lady. However, she did not spend her money foolishly, and she knew how to wear a dress many times."

Fashion-conscious Parisiennes took a patronizing view of Pamela's deliberately understated wardrobe. "She was well dressed but she never had the great chic of those French ladies," said Johnny Galliher. Her problem, said one Parisian fashion designer, was "her couture was too detailed, and it lacked subtlety. Her taste was not very sure." Nevertheless, Englishwomen were impressed to the point of intimidation by her elegance. Years afterward, Lady Mary Dunn could vividly remember an encounter with Pamela during a house-party weekend in Wiltshire during the 1950s.

"I had on my best black 'silk' Marks & Spencer dress," recalled Mary. "When Pam arrived, she said, 'Oh Mary, do come up and talk to me while I change. I'm going to have a bath. Will you unpack for me?'" Mary complied and found "a case about twelve inches long, eight inches high, and eight inches deep. 'Should I unpack that?' I asked. She said, 'No, no, that's my country jewelry.' It was mostly semi-precious." At Pamela's direction, Mary selected a black Dior dress, Dior shoes with sparkling buckles, pearls, earrings, and some bracelets. When Pamela came out of the bath, "she wore a very expensive, obviously tight corset going down from the breast, with a strapless bra, to below the hips with suspenders [garters] extending down. It was very much like a merry widow. She said, 'I can't do this up by myself.' So I had to hook it all the way down the back while she pulled herself in. I did this dutifully. She was awfully nice, and she wasn't lording it over me." Just as Pamela was checking her reflection in the mirror, the heel on her shoe broke. "She had to be completely undressed," said Mary, "and she changed into a red satin with matching shoes."

Maintaining her prominence in Parisian society was crucial to Pamela's standing with Elie de Rothschild. A steady flow of invitations strengthened her position and provided her with gossip that she could use to entertain Elie. Her social life was "brittle but very bright," Pamela said in later years. "I guess I was a novelty to them. Being a woman alone, I wasn't regarded as a foreigner . . . so they kind of took me into their set."

"She was very seldom not doing anything," said Sandy Bertrand. For all the years she had lived alone, Pamela abhorred solitude. "Pam needs people more than a lot of people do," explained one woman who knew her for many years. If some time opened up during the day, she would call a male friend to keep her company. "She and I would walk in the Bois de Boulogne together with her little dog, and her car and driver would follow behind us," recalled Peter Viertel, then the boyfriend of Bettina Graziani, a red-headed fashion model who would later take up with Aly Khan. Many evenings Pamela would invite a small group over to play cards, and on Friday nights she usually made an appearance at Maxim's, where stylish socialites appeared in black tie and gowns. "Everyone would go to see the latest jewels or Dior dress," explained Johnny Galliher. Pamela usually dined with Arturo and Patricia Lopez in a group to one side of the front door, the prime spot in the restaurant. Afterward, there was dancing at the White Elephant or Florence's. Two orchestras played at the White Elephant, one jazz, one South American, and the international set filled the place every night. "Pam was always there," said one of her longtime friends. "I danced with Pam for hours. She loved dancing and seeing people."

Pamela was a regular at the fancy dress balls of the day. At an extravaganza hosted by the eccentric aristocrat Marie-Laure de Noailles to celebrate Mardi Gras in February 1956, each guest had to dress as an artist, writer, character in a book, or subject of a painting between the fifteenth and nineteenth centuries. Escorted by her friend Sandy Bertrand, who was costumed as Shakespeare, Pamela came as Titania, looking so ethereal in a décolleté gown of pale blue that Harold Acton said, "She would have converted all the fairies to sexual orthodoxy."

At a dinner beforehand in her apartment, she entertained an English contingent including Diana Cooper, Ann Fleming, the writer Paddy Leigh-Fermor, and *The Times* correspondent Frank Giles and his wife Lady Katherine, along with honorary Englishman Paul-Louis Weiller. In addition to food and drink, Pamela thoughtfully provided three hairdressers in her extravagant dressing room, where the men fought as fiercely over eyeshadow as the women. "It was like a rehearsal with snacks," wrote Ann Fleming. "Women and pansies were lined up to have wigs, makeup, cod pieces and ruffs adjusted." Three hundred guests made their entrees at the ball, accompanied by trumpets while mounting a grand staircase. Fresh fruit was piled in pyramids in the dining room, and everyone drank champagne and danced to three orchestras until dawn.

On weekends, Pamela was a frequent guest at grand country houses owned by friends such as Arturo Lopez and Carlos "Charlie" de Beistegui, a Spanish-Mexican multimillionaire. Beistegui lived outside Paris at Groussay, a magnificent château that he transformed into what Cecil Beaton called "an elaborate pastiche of something that no longer exists . . . inside a Russian facade . . . a long-discarded Victorian England," complete with a library three stories high, and a theater where Beistegui and his friends gave performances just as Madame de Pompadour and her courtiers had done. Beistegui surrounded himself with beautiful women whom he pampered elaborately. Pamela was one of Beistegui's favorites. "She would go to Groussay alone," recalled Anthony Marreco. "I remember her spending half the day in bed. It was that kind of life. She would be lying on her pillows and looking lovely, receiving people. There would be a dozen guests there for the weekend. It was all lavish and extraordinary."

Pamela joined the seasonal migrations of international society. Bankrolled by Agnelli's "alimony" and Elie's periodic generosity, as well as the stipends from Harriman and others, she traveled in the highest style, according to one account, bringing "her own maid, her silk Pratesi sheets . . . her perfume bottles, jar after jar of creams and bottles of nail lacquer, her hair needs—everything to maintain her well endowed beauty." It was her custom, whenever she rented a room or a house, to create a fantasy of intimacy and stability by filling her surroundings with flowers, cushions, photographs, and bibelots. Her "first move," Pamela said, was to "get rid of other people's clutter and install my own. There has to be a certain amount of clutter to enforce your ownership of a room."

After a round of polo matches, horse races, and balls in Paris during May and June, she usually alighted in London for Ascot or the Derby, followed sometimes by a visit to Deauville in July. In August she was invariably back on the Riviera, where any number of friends would invite her to stay in their homes and cruise the Mediterranean on their yachts. The late autumn usually brought her to New York, and in January and February she would go to St. Moritz, a storybook setting of chalets and horse-drawn sleighs driven by men in capes and bearskins.

Pamela usually took a suite in St. Moritz at the grandly turreted Palace Hotel, which Gianni Agnelli's wife Marella once likened to "a boat that crossed the winter." Multimillionaires like Agnelli and the Greek shipping tycoon Stavros Niarchos hosted parties in local nightclubs or the bowling alley at the Palace, and there were regular luncheons on the mountaintop terrace at the exclusive Corviglia Club, where the amenities included warmed lavatory seats, badges designed by Cartier, and a helipad to accommodate the wealthiest members. One year Noël Coward encountered Pamela in Geneva on her way to St. Moritz, finding herself "in a dreadful dilemma because there wasn't a safe in the Hotel Des Bergues big enough to hold her jewel case!"

In Paris, Pamela devoted considerable time and effort to establishing herself as a hostess, entertaining in her apartment as well as her weekend retreat in Versailles, yet another house lent to her by the admiring Paul-Louis Weiller. "A major feat for her was a successful dinner," said Alexandre. "She rehearsed her dinners as if they were plays." With the help of her staff of five, she hosted a formal dinner party every week at Avenue de New York, usually for ten people, with an eclectic guest list drawn from the worlds of international society, fashion, politics, journalism, and the arts.

The famous salonières of Pamela's day were emphatically in the French tradition, all clever in their own right. Marie-Laure de Noailles not only wrote and painted but cultivated artists and literary figures at a regular lunchtime gathering where she alternately provoked and protected her guests. The outspoken Marie-Louise Bousquet, editor of *Harper's Bazaar* in Paris, attracted designers, artists, and aristocrats at an open house each Thursday afternoon without even offering a glass of champagne as she hobbled through the crowd on a cane. And Louise de Vilmorin was a minor poet with several novels to her credit, including *Madame de,* a slender tale of aristocratic intrigue published amid great fanfare in 1951. Regarded by Diana Cooper as "the most eloquent and witty" woman in Paris, and by Evelyn Waugh as "an egocentric maniac with the eyes of a witch," Vilmorin hosted Sunday night dinners at her country house in Verrières-le-Buisson for as many as forty guests, primarily from the literary and film worlds.

An essential part of Pamela's mythology of her Paris years was that she surrounded herself with intellectuals who gave her a postgraduate education in literature, theater, art, and music, much as Geoffroy taught her about the decorative arts. Among her regular companions were the film director René Clair, the choreographer Roland Petit, and the playwright Marcel Achard. Pamela's intellectuals were not the existentialist philosophers who congregated at Left Bank cafés and shaped postwar thought. They were trendy figures who grazed in café society, earning invitations with witty conversation. Pamela encountered them mostly at Louise de Vilmorin's salon, and her contacts with them were prompted by practical considerations.

For Pamela to succeed, she had to be conversant with French culture and politics. It didn't matter if she knew subjects in depth, only that she give the impression of being well informed. "Pam Churchill was not known for her interest in literature or the arts," said one socially prominent Parisian writer, "but she was a good hostess. A good hostess often isn't interested but knows how to play the game."

Evelyn Waugh once called Pamela's Paris apartment a "gilded cage" filled with "fast and fashionable frogs." In such an atmosphere, the table talk tended to be shallow and artificial. "Boy was I glad you were not with me," wrote Pamela's friend Marina Sulzberger to her husband, *New York Times* correspondent C. L. Sulzberger, after one such evening at Pamela's apartment in 1955. "It was nothing but marquises and horsey lords, and the conversation consisted entirely about who was sleeping with whom in St. Moritz or Klosters or Davos."

As she had in London, Pamela "would spoil and attract important friends through food and extraordinary attention to detail," said former Condé Nast editorial director Alexander Liberman. "She knew how to cast a spell." She had a knack for mixing and matching. "She invited people who were interested in each other," recalled Sandy Bertrand. "Her main object was to put people in the best possible condition of comfort. Her main concern was never letting anybody get bored, so that people always had something to talk about." She tried to keep the whole table involved in the conversation. She did, however, indulge certain guests—usually men—who knew how to captivate an audience with entertaining monologues.

"Pam was surrounded by people who loved the role of being clever and she let them play it," Bertrand went on. "She showed them that she enjoyed it. She laughed at what they had to say. She was excellent for her guests, especially those not important like me. Pam paid as much attention to the little ones at the end of the table as to the Prime Minister on her right." Bertrand was being overly modest about himself and the other "little ones." He was after all publisher of *French Vogue*. "Pamela was elitist," said a man who dined often at her apartment. "She wouldn't invite an actress unless she was well known, and wouldn't invite a writer unless he was someone like [Truman] Capote."

In her Parisian incarnation, Pamela submerged the more robust aspects of her personality—those flashes of masculine swagger that she had sometimes showed in her London years—and wrapped herself in quiet femininity. "She listened carefully and injected enough to keep you telling her more," said Bertrand. "She also didn't tell you a lot and kept an air of mystery." In this way she could disguise that she was often out of her depth, and she could avoid finding herself in what Nancy Mitford called "the witness box," subjected to questions from Parisians eager to pass judgment on English inadequacies.

Still, Pamela's insecurities occasionally showed through, as when Billy Baldwin observed after a luncheon at Pamela's apartment, "She was lots of fun, but it seemed to me that she laughed almost too much." It was, of course, laughter as social emollient. Pamela was so rehearsed that spontaneous humor was impossible. She had managed to turn that deficiency to her advantage, however; lacking a sense of irony, she maneuvered through society without a trace of self-consciousness. Yet Baldwin saw that Pamela's energetic gaiety was a posture, and he detected an uneasiness behind it, along with an absence of joy.

THOUGH SHE PREFERRED to be around men, Pamela tried to make alliances with influential women, an effort that was hindered by Liliane de Rothschild. Nevertheless, three somewhat unconventional women—Louise de Vilmorin, Françoise de Langlade, and the Duchess of Windsor—played important roles in Pamela's Parisian life. More than acquaintances, but somehow less than friends, they met Pamela's needs in various ways, mainly helping to keep her socially connected.

Pamela had been acquainted with Louise de Vilmorin, who was nearly twenty years her senior, since the postwar days at the British Embassy when the aristocratic Frenchwoman doubled as Duff Cooper's mistress and Diana Cooper's intimate friend. A beautiful, slender brunette, Vilmorin walked with a limp —the result of childhood tuberculosis of the hip—but compensated for her frailty with a flamboyant personality. She was a spellbinding talker, who so craved the limelight that she once flung a butterball to the ceiling when another guest at a dinner party wouldn't allow her to tell a story.

She had been married twice, first to a wealthy Texan named Henry Leigh-Hunt, with whom she lived in Las Vegas during the 1920s, and then to a Hungarian count named Paul "Pali" Palffy, who sheltered her during the war at his splendid castle near Presbourg-Bratislava, where they entertained Hermann Goering and other Nazis. She had a string of prominent lovers, among them Aly Khan, Antoine de Saint-Exupéry, and Orson Welles. And she was notorious for having stolen two men from one woman, Etti Palffy Esterhazy Plesch, the daughter of the Countess de Wurmbrandt. The first was Palffy, who divorced his wife to marry Vilmorin; followed by Tommy Esterhazy, a lover who never made it to the altar.

Pamela and Louise de Vilmorin had in common their affinity for wealthy and powerful men, although their personalities were utterly different. "Louise had the star quality that Pam didn't have then," explained Anthony Marreco, with whom Vilmorin had an affair. When asked once why Pamela wasn't irritated when Louise tried to get all the attention, Pamela replied, "I liked it. I had my own ways." Pamela understood that she needed the approval of Vilmorin, who had great social power.

Pamela painstakingly tended her relationship with Vilmorin and invited her frequently to dinner, knowing that her witty soliloquies guaranteed a successful evening. During one such soirée at Avenue de New York in 1956, C. L. Sulzberger noted, "Louise de Vilmorin posed decoratively by the fireplace and made a long speech about how she wanted to enjoy her death." Whenever she could, Pamela went out of her way to please Vilmorin, who was highly susceptible to flattery. Once when Vilmorin asked to borrow Pamela's Bentley for a tryst with Orson Welles, Pamela agreed to let her have it for a day. Vilmorin kept it for four days, and when she returned the car without an excuse or an apology, there were burns on the upholstery from Welles's cigar. No matter. In later years, Pamela kept a framed thank-you note from Vilmorin conspicuously displayed in her house in Middleburg, Virginia.

But Vilmorin did not consider Pamela an intimate friend, according to Helena Leigh-Hunt, one of Vilmorin's daughters. "My mother loved to have pretty people around, but not as friends," said Leigh-Hunt. Pamela became part of Vilmorin's collection. "Louise occasionally disparaged Pam, made jokes, as we all did," said Anthony Marreco. "But Louise loved intrigues and affairs. She thought Pam was a woman on the make, that she was reasonably intelligent and attractive, and that she would go after men and get them. Louise didn't take a dim view of Pam. It was rather a cynical view, a realistic view. She saw her for what she was." Vilmorin was especially intrigued by the amount of money Pamela was able to extract from her lovers. "Once when Louise was admiring Pamela's jewelry," recalled the French publishing magnate Hervé Mille, "Pamela said, 'You poor Louise, all the presents you have are love letters.' " An accomplished seductress herself, Vilmorin took a great interest in Pamela's "career"—although Pamela knew, according to one friend, that "to confide in Louise would have been imprudent." Vilmorin did offer advice, however, and ensured that Verrières was one place where Pamela and Elie could appear together without seeming conspicuous.

Françoise de Langlade, an editor at *French Vogue,* fit into a different niche with Pamela—a confidante whose judgment Pamela respected. They were close in age and on a more equal footing than Pamela and Louise de Vilmorin. Twice divorced, Françoise de Langlade was a lively hostess and a leader in taste and fashion. "She and Pam mingled in the same society," said Johnny Galliher. "Françoise had no money, but she had the coziest dinners in Paris." Both women were resourceful and disciplined, and took pride in their strength. "It was almost as though they were not born of human problems like everyone else," said Sandy Bertrand. "They admired each other in many ways for how they handled themselves. They both knew when they could be tough with people and when they could get back to being soft again."

Pamela and the Duchess of Windsor had a different sort of bond. Tired of wandering, the Windsors had settled in Paris after the war and surrounded themselves with a café society crowd. Like Pamela, the duchess was on the edge of respectable society, largely shunned by the Parisian upper crust. She was obsessively devoted to her husband, and kept a perfect house, an accomplishment that Pamela greatly admired. Both women learned about art from Gerald Van der Kemp and decor from Stéphane Boudin, and both labored to achieve an ideal balance between chic and comfort in their surroundings. Perhaps seeing some reflections of herself in a woman twenty-four years her junior, Wallis Windsor embraced Pamela in the early postwar years.

Pamela marveled at the rarefied style of the duchess—the small gold pad she kept at her side during meals to record the remarks of her guests; her elegantly simple wardrobe that *Elle* magazine said "elevated sobriety to an art form"; the extravagant detail of her decor where each bibelot sat on its own custom-cut felt pad; her meticulous tidiness that included having her sheets ironed before bedtime each night; her anticipation of the duke's every need and adoption of his every interest. Many of the duchess's techniques Pamela had already learned over the years, but she did pick up some tips, most notably the famous mealtime notepad.

The attraction between the two women went beyond mere imitation and esteem, however. Each of them knew how to use her assets to the utmost. Wallis Windsor had a plain face, and she was "slim and svelte as a piece of vermicelli," in the words of Diana Cooper. But she made herself glamorous by learning, as she once said, "to dress better than anyone else." Confronted with withering scandal, first as the King of England's mistress and then as the wife who caused him to lose his throne, she held a pose of above-it-all dignity. The duchess may have been widely regarded as frivolous and crassly materialistic ("I'd rather shop than eat," she said), but to Pamela she was kind and affectionate. Once when a friend decried the duchess as "an awful woman," Pamela exclaimed, "But she was nice to me when I first came to Paris!" They frequently had lunch together, and for a period in the late 1950s they were, in the words of London's *Evening Standard*, "inseparable chums."

Pamela also tried hard to impress visitors from Britain and America, with whom she assumed a more assertive attitude than with the French. She sent her Bentley to collect influential dowagers at the airport and arranged shopping excursions for socialites such as Bill and Babe Paley. She wined and dined Evelyn Waugh and treated him to a private tour of Versailles. (He returned the favor by referring to her as a "tasty morsel.") When the famous New York hostess Kitty Miller arrived with Billy Baldwin, Pamela commandeered him, announcing to Miller, "I hated to be such a pig, but that is what I am. I just wanted to meet your Billy, Kitty, and without a lot of others, because I've heard so much about him. I hear he has the best taste in America. I'm going to listen to everything he has to say, and I know that I will adore him."

Most of the Americans came away delighted and flattered. "Pamela was looked at with a certain awe and vicarious pleasure," said Alexander Liberman. "She was part of a very grand tradition of mistresses kept on a grand scale." The stage director Peter Glenville once brought Irene Selznick, former wife of legendary Hollywood producer David O. Selznick, for dinner at Pamela's apartment. "Irene was impressed, glamorized, respectful, and mischievously thinking about the successes implied in the Marie Antoinette fabric on Pam's chairs," said Glenville. "She gave Pam full marks." One ironic exception was Averell Harriman, who during a chance encounter "rather sanctimoniously blurted out that she was ruining her life," according to his biographer Rudy Abramson.

Pamela "dispensed so much kindness and hospitality to visiting Brits that Diana Cooper dubbed her the 'universal aunt,' " recalled Alastair Forbes. Yet she found only a few allies among Britons, such as Lady Kitty Giles, who gratefully accepted Pamela's cast-off designer clothes. The link with Lady Kitty and her husband Frank helped Pamela because the Gileses were well respected and influential. Still, many of Pamela's countrymen remained skeptical—even Lady Kitty, who told friends that her husband was "safe from Pam because he wasn't rich."

Throughout much of the 1950s Pamela was persona non grata at the British Embassy, first when Oliver Harvey was ambassador and then during the tenure of Sir Gladwyn Jebb. When England's Queen Mother came to Paris in March 1956, Ambassador Jebb and his wife Cynthia excluded Pamela from embassy receptions because, Cynthia wrote, "the gratin would have been horrified to see her." Three months later the Jebbs tried to make it up to Pamela and others they had shunned by inviting them to a luncheon. Pamela "said she could not come, or perhaps would not," wrote Cynthia. The following year during a state visit by the Queen of England, the Jebbs once again kept Pamela away, despite a plea on her behalf from Kitty Giles.

Nancy Mitford, as an English expatriate in Paris, held Pamela in disdain. "I could tell you some tales" about Pamela, she wrote to a friend, demurring only because of "a certain native prudence." Among other things, she suspected Pamela of having designs on Gaston Palewski, Mitford's longtime lover, an ugly but charming diplomat who was nicknamed "l'Embrassadeur" for his lecherous ways. He had been a friend of Pamela's dating back to the war when he was with Charles de Gaulle in London. In a letter to Palewski filled with sarcasm, Mitford described his imaginary wedding to Pamela, warning him, "better very private or somebody you know might make a fuss at the altar. It's lucky she's so very Catholic."

British aristocrats never seemed to tire of making fun of Pamela. "Her lack of respectability was part of the joke. Since she had no sense of humor, she couldn't have a twinkle in her eye and giggle about it," explained one well-connected British woman. One of their oft-repeated stories had Pamela treating her father to an elegant Parisian weekend, ferrying him everywhere in her Bentley, which prompted Lord Digby to boast, "My daughter is amazing. She manages so well on only five hundred pounds a year." The Digby family believes the tale to be apocryphal. Kenny Digby "was very cagey," said one family member. "He might have made a remark as a joke but he knew exactly what was going on."

At social gatherings, "she would be pointed out. 'That is Pamela Churchill, she is the last of the great courtesans,' " said one prominent American woman who was living in Paris at the time. " 'She is with so-and-so. Look at her with that one, now she is in a conversation with another one.' Tongues wagged, and people would watch her as she made her way around the room." "She was very much the grande cocotte," said Lydia Redmond. "People referred to her that way behind her back, but they were polite to her face. She was not very respectable."

Pamela's behavior often bore out her detractors' worst suspicions. Once in the 1950s a young American woman was invited by her uncle to meet Pamela for dinner. When they arrived at Pamela's apartment, the butler took them into her drawing room. "Me and My Shadow" was playing on the phonograph, and a maid dressed in black entered the room to say that Pamela couldn't go out because there had been a misunderstanding. The uncle sent back a message saying the Pamela must see him, so she arrived shortly, wearing her dressing gown and a shower cap trimmed with lace, and carrying a pot of face cream. As he and his niece left, to their great embarrassment they encountered the butler helping to button up the pants and shirt of a man they both knew. They didn't dare give him a second look. Then, on the first floor they ran into another man in black tie headed toward the elevator to Pamela's apartment. Both the men were "very married," the young American woman said later. "They would have been in deep trouble. It made me feel strongly about her, that she had no scruples about who she tangled with. She just lived life the way she wanted to. With Pam, it was not nymphomania, which is less studied than she is. She lost face in her own eyes if she didn't have conquests."

Pamela seemed almost eager to flout public opinion and even appeared to welcome her notoriety. When one of her relatives expressed dismay about the publicity she was receiving in Cholly Knickerbocker's columns, Pamela replied, "I would rather have bad things written about me than be forgotten." At the same time, commented a woman who knew her for decades, "Pam cares about what people think of her more than she would like to admit." Whatever Pamela later said about her "years of laughter and fun," her time in Paris was neither easy nor entirely happy.

Pamela's love life had become a kind of ballet that she choreographed with precision—as the encounter with the young American woman and her uncle clearly showed. Elie de Rothshild was always in the background, while other men moved in and out of focus. "Pamela never gave the impression she was waiting for Elie," said Sandy Bertrand. "She probably arranged it so Elie could find her, but she never gave the feeling she was bound to anything. Nor did she give the feeling that she was hiding things or afraid of being discovered." As time went on, Pamela and Elie ventured out, usually to a small dinner at a restaurant or in a friend's home. Even in such settings, said a man in Pamela's circle, "they were like friends. He is a great teaser, and he behaved exactly with her as with the other ladies who were there. There was nothing showing. It was very light, and perfectly natural."

One group of Pamela's men played clearly defined roles such as teacher (Geoffroy) or walker (Lopez). Perhaps the most intriguing of these characters was Pamela's principal informant, Mathias Polakovitz, a Hungarian homosexual known simply as Mathias. He was a reporter for *Paris Match* who knew everything about everyone in society, and Pamela had been probing him for information since the Agnelli days. He was close to all the Rothschilds, especially Elie's sister Cécile. "He was the type of person certain women, even Liliane, had as a confidante," said an American expatriate who knew him in the 1950s. Irene Selznick called him Pamela's "leg man. Pamela couldn't resist him. He was grasping and conniving. He got the gossip and carried it back. What he got out of it I don't know, but he felt secure, and that a lot was due him." After some years it was clear that Mathias unnerved Pamela. The reason, according to Selznick, was that he knew too much about Pamela's life. "With Mathias she used to be disagreeable," said Alan Pryce-Jones. " 'For God's sake be quiet,' she would say. She was quite tough with him." Yet he remained a part of Pamela's coterie, "useful but a menace," according to Selznick.

Pamela seemed to prefer keeping some of her relationships with men deliberately ambiguous. "The men didn't really know where they were," said Sandy Bertrand. "It was rather amusing to her to make very important men bend to her will." Prominent figures like Gerald Van der Kemp and Belgium's Ambassador to NATO André de Staercke often had private dinners with Pamela. Van der Kemp sometimes spent the night at Avenue de New York, "on, not in," her bed, prompting one of his British friends, Linda Mortimer, to tease, "All those times at the end of the bed, but never in it. Why, Gerald?" Although the relationships with Van der Kemp and Staercke were platonic, Parisians couldn't help wondering about them, along with other men in her orbit: Were they friends or lovers? Pamela added to her mystique by keeping everyone guessing —Elie in particular.

Her liaison with Sandy Bertrand—a man five years younger than she— offered a glimpse into her subtle designs. Bertrand was a rising star who had been named publisher of *French Vogue* in 1954 at twenty-nine. When he met Pamela, he was romantically involved with Françoise de Langlade. Bertrand was exceedingly handsome, heterosexual, and impeccably connected, which made him a desirable extra man. But while he appeared frequently as Pamela's escort, they were nothing more than friends. "Maybe I was the pause that refreshes," he said long afterward with a laugh. "I was a confidant, and we would spend a lot of evenings just the two of us sitting over a little dinner and chatting away. She was very interested in what people were doing. She was interested in the press, and she laughed at the gossip. We liked each other and talked to each other about our little affairs. She confided in me, but up to what percentage of the whole truth I don't know."

It seemed natural to conclude that Pamela and Bertrand were having an affair, an assumption that neither of them discouraged. "There were no real rules," Bertrand recalled. "Elie was always wondering what was going on between Pamela and me. I didn't help him. I just looked at him laughing as if to say, 'Well, try and guess, old boy.' Elie and I were good friends, but I never let him in on what was the real nature of our relationship. If he ever asked her, Pamela would laugh it off and say, 'Don't be silly.' But she didn't mind people believing there was something going on because it would needle Elie, the one she was interested in."

The same rationale doubtless applied to a relationship Pamela had with the French writer Maurice Druon. In later years she singled him out as evidence, along with Murrow, to counter her gold-digger reputation. As one of her friends told *New York* magazine writer Michael Gross in 1993, "She also loved a poor revolutionary writer." Druon had been an adventurer with left-wing political views and a member of the Resistance during World War II. But in the years after the war he reversed course to become an ardent Gaullist, and he began to turn out popular novels. When Pamela met him he had already found celebrity with *The Film of Memory* (1955), an evocative portrait of an aging European courtesan.

Druon was stockily handsome, with blond hair, a thick neck, and a deep voice that he used to dramatic effect. A bachelor, he had a reputation as a ladies' man whose most famous romance was with Edmonde Charles-Roux, the editor of *Paris Vogue* during much of the 1950s. He could be pompous and vain, but he was a catch for an ambitious hostess like Pamela. She proudly showed him off, traveling with him several times to England and making him a star attraction at her gatherings. "He was always there at her apartment," said an Englishwoman who knew her then. "He had made his name. He was a lion. At luncheon tables in Paris, a lion would take the conversation over. At Pamela's luncheons, Druon was the lion." Her romance with him "wasn't official as it had been with Edmonde," said a Parisian friend of Pamela's. "People knew about it but it wasn't really important. It was short-lived, and they remained good friends." As with so many others, her connection with Druon proved mutually advantageous.

When Pamela was trying to nudge Gianni Agnelli toward marriage, she had taken up with a wealthy Greek to make him jealous. So it was again in the mid-fifties as she turned to an even richer Greek shipowner, Stavros Spyros Niarchos, to provoke Elie de Rothschild. At forty-six, Niarchos was a man on the rise. Born to a family of peasants, he had made millions in the years after World War II buying and selling ships and building tankers to transport oil. Niarchos and his rival, Aristotle Onassis, made shipowning the most glamorous business of the postwar era.

Having made his fortune, Niarchos was intent on ascending to the top of European society when Pamela first took up with him. He had been married since 1947 to his third wife, Eugenie, the gentle and pretty daughter of Greek shipping titan Stavros Livanos. Niarchos owned a lavish penthouse at Claridges in London, a triplex apartment on New York's Sutton Place, an eighteenth-century château in Paris, a forty-two-room Cap d'Antibes villa previously occupied by the Duke and Duchess of Windsor, and a 190-foot three-masted yacht, the *Creole,* that he filled with paintings by Renoir, Gauguin, and Cézanne. Although he cultivated an image of mystery, he knew how to capture headlines with such grand gestures as buying Eugenie a $100,000 emerald necklace when she gave birth to their first child in 1953, and celebrating New Year's Eve with the $400,000 purchase of a *Pietà* by El Greco.

Niarchos was only five feet five, but he was trim and well built, with a fine-boned face, an aquiline nose that he tended to hold aloft when he spoke, glittering brown eyes, slick black hair, smooth skin, and a thin-lipped smile that hovered between disdain and boredom. He was "as sensuous and as dangerous as a coiled snake," wrote Doris Lilly in her book *Those Fabulous Greeks.* Partially deaf from an early age, Niarchos had a nasal voice and a pronounced lisp that muffled his words as if he spoke with a mouthful of food. His rapid-fire mumble was extremely difficult to understand, a barrier that he used to enhance his power by creating unease in others.

He was, by most accounts, disagreeable, haughty, snobbish, distant, cold, and suspicious. A flagrant womanizer, he had a hot temper and drank excessively. One New York socialite called him "not very human. He doesn't seem to connect with the needs of other people." His charm, such as it was, came from his power and wealth. To win the favor of international society, he cast himself as a host legendary for his lavish generosity and perfectionism; he once had a bottle of port flown from Paris to a remote Greek island especially for the Duke of Marlborough. He lent his yachts to European aristocrats such as Lady Diana Cooper and underwrote well-publicized cruises for scores of international celebrities. Yet even as he pampered his guests, Niarchos spent as little time with them as possible. After a cruise on the *Creole,* Noël Coward remarked that Niarchos was "curiously remote. . . . He is the stuff of which dictators are made. Everyone is terrified of him."

Niarchos personified the term "tycoon," dominating those around him and acting the way he pleased without regard to consequences. This ability to play by his own rules set Niarchos apart from other powerful men Pamela had known. In later years, Niarchos's privileged position would enable him to deflect suspicions that he had a role in the mysterious death in 1970 of Eugenie. After a fierce argument with Niarchos, Eugenie swallowed twenty-five Seconals, but she died only after her husband failed to get prompt medical attention. His delay, along with extensive injuries to her body, led to charges—twice dismissed by Greek courts—that Niarchos had fatally injured her.

Pamela Churchill was naturally attracted to his wealth and power. "Niarchos was very generous then," said one of his longtime friends. "He was making money. It was pouring in. He was a big fish to catch. She saw a new star rising, and she probably wanted a crack at him before the others." In the summer of 1954 he treated her to a cruise of the Greek islands aboard the *Creole,* where she stayed in an air-conditioned cabin, attended by swarms of white-coated Italian stewards. Niarchos also included Little Winston, who boasted in a letter that he was on "the biggest private-owned sailing ship afloat." The following winter, Pamela was with Niarchos in St. Moritz, and the international set could see that their relationship was more than platonic.

Her appeal to Niarchos derived primarily from her name and the contacts she offered at a time when he was working hard to establish links with British aristocrats. "For Niarchos she knew everyone in England," said one of his longtime friends. Socialite Rosemarie Kanzler observed that "they saw each other but they were not in any way in love." He admired her, said Kanzler, because she was successful. Pamela and Niarchos went around together in London, although they behaved with discretion. "He stayed at Claridges, and she had a flat," said a man who knew them both. "They played it very very cool. He was married, so he couldn't go off with her in tête-à-tête."

Still, there were indications that the affair was not entirely pleasant for Pamela. "Niarchos embarrassed her," said the actress Anita Colby. "One heard he didn't treat her with respect." On election night in London in May 1955— called after Winston Churchill stepped down as Prime Minister the previous month—her discomfort was evident in an incident recounted to Max Beaverbrook by Ann Fleming. She said that Lord Wilton had made Pamela cry when he mistook Niarchos for a waiter and "shouted at him for cigarettes." Added Fleming, "Pamela likes rich Greeks as well as rich Americans and Frenchmen and demanded an apology but in the ensuing fracas was reduced to tears." In Sandy Bertrand's view, Niarchos "was a very rough person who didn't fit with her at all. She was intrigued at first. She wanted to find out what was behind his success. When someone mumbles, maybe he is saying very intelligent things. When she found out he wasn't, he was less appealing."

For her trouble, Pamela failed to make the hoped-for impression on Elie de Rothschild. He knew, as he told a friend, that "she went to bed with Stavros, but it wasn't much." Elie de Rothschild was unimpressed by the size of Niarchos's bank book and repelled by his manner. In Elie's eyes, Niarchos was nothing more than "a shit, really nasty."

Elie adopted a philosophical attitude toward his rivals. He never went to St. Moritz when Pamela spent two months there in the winter with Niarchos and his friends, nor did he go to the South of France where she spent her summers. Because he was married, he knew he couldn't take her out and show her off, or go on a holiday for a month alone. "You have to be ready that she would see other boys if she felt like it," he told a friend, "as long as she was nice when you were together. Maybe I was jealous, but no man, if he is married and doesn't leave his wife, has the right to lock up someone. You are taking a risk, of course, but you can't expect otherwise."

Eighteen

IN NOVEMBER 1955, Pamela checked into Columbia Presbyterian Hospital during her annual visit to New York. She later explained that she did so only because the previous summer, while cruising with Niarchos on the *Creole,* the American multimillionaire oil baron Charles Wrightsman had persuaded her to see his doctor for a complete physical examination. "In those days such things as medical check-ups were unknown among Europeans who conceived them to be typical of the hypochondriac propensities of Americans," her son Winston later wrote. But Pamela, now thirty-five, knew she needed medical attention: she was in pain.

What happened to her in the hospital is not entirely clear. By her account, a Pap smear showed she had cancer of the uterus. Only a few years earlier, Pamela's sister Sheila had been diagnosed with ovarian cancer and had undergone a successful hysterectomy while still in her twenties. After an anxious Thanksgiving with Jock and Betsey Whitney, Pamela switched to New York Hospital, which had been virtually built by the Whitney family, to have a biopsy and exploratory surgery in early December. When Max Beaverbrook came to visit, he found Pamela uncharacteristically distraught. Within days, his *Evening Standard* reported that she had had "a serious operation . . . is progressing very well, but will remain at the hospital about three weeks." Her son viewed the situation even more gravely, writing in his memoir that after falling "seriously ill," she had a "major operation" that "saved her life."

Pamela's own account was oddly contradictory. She said that the exploratory surgery confirmed the cancer diagnosis, and her new physicians recommended a hysterectomy. Pamela "felt particularly lonely sitting in New York looking at x rays and wondering how long she had to live," wrote Christopher Ogden. Nevertheless, she decided to delay the operation until the following June—an unusual display of sang-froid even for Pamela. After leaving the hospital in mid-December, she recuperated at the St. Regis Hotel under the care of an English nurse and spent Christmas on Long Island with the Whitneys, then went to their estate in Georgia for a week of quail and turkey shooting. She returned to Paris in January 1956, and in the following months she kept a full social calendar of fancy dress balls and trips to London and the South of France, where she stayed with Beaverbrook and her former father-in-law. She even paid

$1,500 to reserve a small yacht, fully stocked with whiskey and champagne, for a month's cruise along the Riviera in July.

In June, Pamela was back in New York Hospital for further surgery. During the operation to remove her uterus, Dr. Frank Glenn discovered the real cause of her distress: part of her intestine had been twisted and pushed down, probably from birth, a condition that had been gradually worsening. The operation corrected the defect, and for the first time in years, Pamela was free of pain. "I feel reborn," she wrote to Max Beaverbrook, to whom she confided the details of her condition. "I astonished all the hospital by refusing my injections against pain after the operation," she wrote. "They could not believe that with my whole stomach split open I had no pain. But it was true in comparison with the pain of the last few months, I just did not suffer at all." Lady Digby, who had trained her daughter to silently endure illness and injury, would have been proud.

Pamela failed to mention any malignancy to Beaverbrook. One of Pamela's doctors, Connie Guion, flatly told a woman who knew Pamela well, "Sheila had cancer but Pamela did not." But Pamela did not correct the misimpression: fighting off cancer added to her mythology. "My mother is very strong," her son boasted to a friend years later. "After her hysterectomy they wanted to give her cobalt and she refused. She had read up on it and decided to risk a recurrence of cancer, which never came back."

"Most of her friends checked in with her while she was ill," wrote Ogden, "including Elie and Gianni, who called constantly." Yet in her letter to Beaverbrook, Pamela asked him to convey the news of her surgery to Agnelli, who had sent her a cable that she had not yet answered. If Agnelli was more remote than Pamela liked to remember, Elie did keep in touch. He generously covered the costs for both operations, although his solicitude became "a sore subject," as he told a friend, when he felt that "she two-timed me" after hearing that Agnelli and Niarchos also paid for the operations.

The one person who stayed by Pamela's side throughout her ordeal was Betsey Whitney. Sheila Digby Moore was stunned when she entered Pamela's hospital room to find Betsey holding a basin as Pamela vomited while coming out of the anesthesia. As Sheila said at the time, "Pam does have a way of winning people over."

When Pamela was released from the hospital at the end of June, she moved with her English nurse into an exquisitely appointed bedroom at Greentree, the Whitneys' Long Island estate. Situated amid six hundred acres of fields bounded by white fences, the Whitneys' sprawling seventy-six-room home of understated gray shingle stood at the center of a self-contained world. There were riding stables, kennels, greenhouses, a nine-hole golf course, three grass tennis courts, a polo field, a swimming pool, and a sports annex containing an indoor pool with adjoining steambath, courts for squash as well as the ancient game of court tennis, a gymnasium, and a paneled screening room. The Whitneys' extraordinary collection of art caught the eye at every turn, even on the walls of the bathrooms, and Betsey filled the rooms with bountiful flower arrangements. At the touch of a mother-of-pearl button, Pamela could summon one of the Whitneys' more than one hundred servants at any time of day or night.

Pamela reported to Beaverbrook that the Whitneys took care of her as if she was "their own flesh and blood. They live a very quiet life also, which is wonderful for me. I feel like a child who has not a care in the world." As she gained strength, Pamela moved to the Whitney summer estate on Fisher's Island, where she spent a tranquil month in equally comfortable surroundings of wicker and chintz and soft sea breezes. "See no one and do nothing," Pamela told Beaverbrook.

Betsey Whitney may have been motivated more by self-defense than friendship. "She decided that the only way to deal with Pamela was to invite her to everything rather than attempt to keep her out, the theory being that Betsey would see what she was doing," said one woman who knew Pamela for many years. "Betsey always put a face on it," observed a longtime friend of Pamela's. "You would have thought being with Pam was her greatest pleasure, but you knew it was not."

Betsey's sister, Babe Paley, was not so amenable. When Pamela decided in mid-August to continue her convalescence in Bermuda with the Paleys, Babe couldn't hide her anxiety. "Bill and Babe took an enormous house with a lot of houses on the property," recalled Anita Colby, who was staying with Babe at the time. "One day at lunch Babe said, 'Pamela's coming. I've got to find a house for her. The only thing I have is a house on the property, and she wants a house near us. My God, I don't know whether I'm taking a chance.' " Although Babe had not been married to Paley when he had his brief wartime affair with Pamela, she still viewed the Englishwoman as a threat. As it turned out, the week passed without incident.

Pamela never took her planned Riviera cruise. She asked Beaverbrook to help her retrieve the $1,500 deposit, and the newspaper baron obliged by publishing a story in the *Standard* disclosing her prolonged stay in the United States and announcing, "she chartered a yacht in Cannes for a month and now wishes to sublet it." Pamela was back in London that September, her arrival announced by the *Standard,* which reported that she looked "happily completely recovered from the illnesses and operations which she has endured for nearly a year." Although she limited her activities for the next several months in Paris, before long she was out at dinner parties making light of the ordeal. As Alastair Forbes recounted it, her surgeon had given her a line that she used to brighten her "humourless table talk." She reported gaily that as she emerged from her anesthetic after her hysterectomy, the doctor had said, "Little lady, we've taken away your baby-carriage but left you your play pen."

After each of her operations, Pamela summoned her fifteen-year-old son Winston, and each time he jumped at the opportunity to spend time with the mother he rarely saw. Pamela's only child had an odd, itinerant existence. Like many English upper-class parents, she had packed him off to boarding school at age eight. He attended Le Rosey in Switzerland because, he later said, his mother felt the mountain air would be good for his asthma and eczema. Since there were tight restrictions on the export of British currency, the tuition was paid by some relatives of Pamela's who lived outside the country—a debt that Pamela eventually repaid. After his first year, Pamela reported to Clementine

Churchill that he was "wonderfully well. . . . He has already gained 4 pounds, and his appetite is enormous and his cheeks bright pink. . . . He has completely forgotten his home sickness."

While not a diligent student, young Winston learned adequate French and became an avid skier at Le Rosey. At the end of his third year he was thoroughly enjoying himself when he was visited by Field Marshal Montgomery, an old friend of his grandfather's. Montgomery reported to Churchill that his grandson was attending "a school for snobs" that had begun to damage the boy's character. At Churchill's insistence, Pamela abruptly removed Winston from Le Rosey, although Montgomery's "terrible invasion of privacy" rankled her. She installed Winston at Ludgrove, a preparatory school in Britain, where he hated the food and suffered the brutality of caning. "I always seemed to draw unlucky with those who chose to beat me and into whose power I had been delivered," he once observed.

When he reached thirteen, he was sent to Eton, where he was a favorite target of bullies. Although Eton was filled with sons of privilege, none had a name as famous as Churchill, and none had grown up in such unconventional circumstances. "He was not someone who made proper friends," said one of his Eton classmates. "He moved around too much." He spent his happiest school holidays at Chartwell and Minterne and otherwise alternated between the contrasting worlds of his mother and father. "I had a strange combination of country life with my Churchill and Digby grandparents on the one hand, and sort of a rather glitzy life in the South of France or the Palace Hotel in St. Moritz on the other hand," he said. "My experience was not a miserable childhood. It was wonderfully varied." Nevertheless, he added, "I spent more time with my grandparents than my parents."

Randolph had married June Osborne in 1948. A lovely blonde with a vivacious manner, she was the only daughter of a colonel in the British Army. A year later, Randolph and June had a daughter, Arabella. In theory, Randolph and June offered the more settled atmosphere, first at a London house given to them by his father as a wedding present, and later at a home in Suffolk that they bought when Randolph vowed to give up drinking and gambling.

But life for anyone close to Randolph Churchill was stormy, and his drinking only grew worse. Young Winston developed the constant vigilance of a child subjected to frequent verbal abuse. Most of Randolph's rages came when he was drunk, often in a public place such as a restaurant, which compounded the embarrassment for the boy. Nor was Randolph any less beastly to his second wife. He and June quarreled constantly. Unlike Pamela, June was highly strung and neurotic, as much in need of coddling as Randolph. In Randolph's presence, "her smiles faded and she became withdrawn, even morose," wrote his biographer Brian Roberts. Not long after a mortifying scene in a London restaurant in which Randolph berated her as "a paltry little middle-class bitch," June left the house in Suffolk for good, taking her daughter Arabella with her.

Pamela's world was less tempestuous, considerably more dazzling, but hardly more stable for a young boy. She flickered into view and then disappeared for months at a time. Winston had enjoyed the Agnelli years because he had the pleasure of La Garoupe and Leopolda, along with the generosity and warmth of his mother's lover. But he harbored what he later described as "ill-concealed distaste" for Elie de Rothschild, who gave the boy little time or attention. "Gianni was always open and smiling and fun and laughter," recalled Winston. "Elie was bottled up and reserved and aloof and cool."

Still, young Winston was awestruck by his mother's friends, even the unpleasant Mr. Niarchos. Winston remained a loner who was indulged with gifts and grew accustomed to great privilege—all of which was noticed and envied by his schoolmates at Eton and later at Oxford. "He lived on a different scale," explained one of his classmates. "He had an electric typewriter while I had a manual. He had a Jaguar. I had a Mini. He went by private planes. Winston never had a lot of money, but he knew people with money."

Pamela "was a focal point," this classmate said, "but she was always abroad." As Randolph's friend Alastair Forbes wrote, "Little Winston's mother, like Big Winston's before her, was to shine only as the evening star, to be loved, no doubt, but loved at a distance." Mrs. Martin, Winston's "linchpin," as he called her, tried to fill the void. "My mother couldn't come very often," Winston explained, "and Mrs. Martin would come and bring me a chocolate cake that she baked. . . . On being maternal, I wouldn't give my mother the highest rating there. If she was one who came less, it was because she was fending for herself and moving in a very glamorous world." When his mother did visit at Eton, he later wrote, "heads would turn, and there would be many a comment" about the "very beautiful redhead" that at least one boy (ironically Jacob Rothschild, a cousin of Elie's) refused to believe was Winston's mother.

The London interior designer Nicholas Haslam, who was an Eton classmate of Randolph's, had a vivid reaction when Winston asked him to have tea with his mother. "We waited in the rain at New School's yard," Haslam recalled. "Slowly a burnished cabriolet Rolls-Royce with lights on inside turned into the gate. Pam was in back, wearing a blond rough tweed suit, a blond fur coat, and very restrained gold country jewelry. The door opened and out on the running board came a perfectly shod crocodile foot and an arm with a perfect crocodile bag. It was absolutely imprinted on my memory."

Other snapshots offered a more wistful glimpse of the distance between mother and son even during their time together. When Pamela and Winston flew to Paris from New York after her surgery, for example, she sat in first class while he stayed in the rear of the Stratocruiser. "Why shouldn't she be comfortable in first class?" said Sandy Bertrand, who encountered mother and son on the plane. "It made no difference to him to ride in the back."

During the Agnelli years, Gianni was usually the instigator when Winston was included in his mother's activities. Once Pamela brought Winston aboard Agnelli's new yacht, en route to Corsica for a cruise. "I was on board for lunch," said Winston, "and was going to be dropped off at St. Tropez. I wasn't enthusiastic about being dumped and sent off with a driver. Gianni said, 'Let him come, Pamela.' My mother felt I might have been a bit surplus to their requirements, but Gianni said, 'Bring him.' "

By Winston's own account, he had to "grow up very quickly." That much seemed true to Susan Mary Alsop when she had to take care of him once in Paris. Pamela had telephoned to ask Alsop's help when bad weather postponed her return from Italy with Agnelli. "Winston was a sweet little boy aged nine or ten," recalled Alsop. "I felt so sorry for him." After she introduced herself, "He said, 'You can count on Mummy. She'll be here in no time.' This little boy was faced with a stranger in an unknown city, he was so confident of his mother, and had no qualms about going to an unknown house." After two days, Winston told Alsop he wanted to repay her kindness. "Why don't I take you for a drink at the Ritz," he said. "That is where people take Mummy."

The symbol of Winston's early maturity was a navy blue suit that he received at age eight. "I was very rapidly sucked into the grown-up world," he said. "If my mother didn't have a better escort, I was mobilized in my blue suit and went to dinner parties with her." Parisian friends sketched an image of "Le Petit Winston," as they all referred to him, sitting with her on a banquette at Maxim's or greeting the guests when she gave dinner parties. Many nights he sat up until two in the morning, listening to the adult conversation and saying nothing. Still, he was flattered to be included, he said, because "not every mother who is divorced wants the impediment of having a young son coming along to dinner parties." Nor, it should be added, did every mother have the benefit of a son named Winston Churchill.

Winston's early exposure to adult company not only bolstered his confidence, it sharpened his tendency toward arrogance. He spoke "with a lot of bombast," said one man who knew him in school, but "he never commanded a serious audience." Although reasonably bright and quick, he didn't apply himself to his studies. "The problem is not so much ability as character," said one friend of the Churchill family. "He is mentally lazy."

At Eton, Winston achieved neither academic nor athletic distinction, and at Oxford he devoted most of his time to skiing. He joined the Oxford Union but remained aloof from university life. Though he knew how to be charming, he came off as selfish and unlikable most of the time. "It was unusual that he was not elected to any club," recalled a classmate. "He was socially ostracized. He was brash and forward, which was not very British. He had a more interesting life than any of us, and people were jealous." According to Winston, his mother's unconventional love life "never struck me as strange. I hadn't ever known what used to be the stereotyped family. . . . It was perfectly normal that she had glamorous escorts who lasted three or four or five years. . . . My life was just on a different plane if not a different planet."

Pamela dismissed any suggestions that she neglected Winston when he was a boy. "She was one of the best mothers," said her friend Leonora Hornblow. "She never abandoned him. Remember that in England kids go away to school at an early age." Yet while examples of her financial generosity abound, there was little evidence of sustained emotional support in his formative years. "Even Winston says that he was alone a lot, but she doesn't face what she doesn't want to face," said a friend of Pamela's for several decades. "She pretends it is not there."

Nineteen

*B*Y THE LATE 1950S, still in Paris and still unmarried, Pamela consoled herself by focusing on her next move. "In the dreaming hours of the early morning, between sleeping and waking, I take my house and in my imagination build on it," she later wrote. "In my mind I organize all the things I'd like to have— that extra room, that extra fantasy." Sandy Bertrand, her friend and confidant, called Pamela a "practical dreamer." "She was telling herself the story of her life and making it a lovely story," he said. "When she was by herself, which was quite often because her men were busy married or otherwise absent, she had time to imagine the fairy tale would be something else."

Elie de Rothschild was living in his own timeless rhythm, following the traditions of his class and his culture. He and Liliane had moved into a home of their own, the grand Hôtel Masserano located near the Invalides, that they restored and embellished as a team. After a visit there, Susan Mary Alsop described them as "an enthusiastic warm couple who adore their children." More out of habit than mutual devotion, Elie and Pamela stayed together, but behind her back he engaged in his own flirtations. "I went to bed with other women when I was with Pam," he told a friend. "She never knew."

By continuing with Elie, Pamela was drifting toward obscurity. A friend who was staying in an adjacent room at the Palace Hotel in St. Moritz recalled hearing her weeping one night. "She was going through a difficult period," he said. Pamela was now in her late thirties, and after working hard for years to keep her figure trim, she had put on weight following her surgery, which had also left scars on her stomach. If Pamela had any doubts about her course of action, they were dispelled by the novelist Somerset Maugham, whom she saw in the South of France. "Don't you think it is time to get married?" he asked.

After the months Pamela spent convalescing in the United States, she had begun exploring ways in which she might find a husband and settle there. "We had lunch in New York," recalled the photographer Jean Howard, who had previously seen Pamela in Paris and on the Riviera. "It was clear that she wanted to live in America." Pamela paid more frequent visits to wealthy friends from her Riviera circle like Charles Wrightsman and his wife Jayne, unabashed social climbers who imported European aristocrats to impress Manhattan society. (The Whitneys had moved to London early in 1957 when President Eisenhower appointed Jock Ambassador to the Court of St. James's.)

She also made contacts who might help her. "She was hell-bent on wooing me," recalled Broadway producer Irene Selznick. "In Paris she gave a dinner party for me and I said, 'Why?' I didn't understand it. I tried to resist and she insisted. When I couldn't get into Claridges or the Connaught, she would say, 'Please use my flat. I have a wonderful cook and housekeeper.' So I would stay there. She was building me up. She had a role for me, had things in mind. I would be useful in many directions. A lot of men in which she was interested were friends of mine."

In 1957, Pamela took up with Albert "Bert" Rupp Jr., who was four years younger and married to the former Cynthia Foy, granddaughter of automotive tycoon Walter P. Chrysler and daughter of Thelma Foy, one of Manhattan's glittering hostesses. Rupp was a handsome wastrel who ran an automobile dealership on Long Island (selling Chevrolets, not Chryslers) and longed for the high life. Cynthia Foy was tall and painfully shy, only twenty years old when she and Rupp wed. With access to her fortune, Rupp became a big spender on the international society circuit, a collector of eighteenth-century furniture, an incessant partygoer, and a nightclub regular.

As Pamela was becoming involved with Rupp, she courted Cynthia just as assiduously, showering her with favors when the Rupps visited Paris, setting up appointments with hairdressers, finding things she needed. "That was her way," Cynthia later told a friend, "so the woman wouldn't notice. It was very clever, actually. She would go out of her way to be nice to the wife in the hopes the wife would think of her as a friend. In that way she could carry on as she wished."

The affair continued in New York, where Rupp paid for Pamela's room at the Plaza Hotel during her increasingly frequent visits. He gave her money and expensive jewelry, which he easily concealed from his wife because he handled their joint bank accounts. "I remember being on the street one day in New York," recalled a prominent New York socialite. "I looked into a Rolls and saw Bert Rupp. I said hello and looked further into the car. There was Pamela in a fur collar, looking like the cat who swallowed the canary. Her expression seemed to say, 'Hey, look at me.' I think she liked oneupsmanship, to top everyone else." Cynthia remained unconcerned, however. She thought Pamela was "quite buxom" and not particularly attractive. There were plenty of other pretty women who would have caused her to worry.

That December, Rupp organized a Christmas holiday at the Palace Hotel in St. Moritz. Pamela was staying in her customary suite, and she joined the Rupps at dinners and parties. Because the Rupps had a small child, Cynthia usually left before midnight while Rupp stayed behind. All the while, Pamela kept up her campaign to charm Cynthia. When Cynthia mentioned that her favorite satin shoes had been soiled, Pamela offered to have her maid clean them. On impulse after ice-skating one afternoon, Cynthia carried the shoes to Pamela's suite, knocked, and entered the sitting room. Cynthia was shocked to hear her husband and Pamela in the adjacent bedroom. Later, she confronted Rupp and demanded that he stop seeing Pamela.

Rupp nonetheless kept the affair going for some months until Pamela broke it off. Rupp was drinking heavily, and he quickly found another woman. The following year, in July 1959, he killed himself with an overdose of sleeping pills. Only after his death did Cynthia discover the extent of his generosity to Pamela in the trail of receipts from Manhattan's most exclusive stores.

By then Pamela had locked onto a more promising prospect, the legendary agent and producer Leland Hayward. Pamela said she met Hayward briefly in the late 1940s on a yacht in the Mediterranean. She and Hayward had numerous mutual friends, including Irene Selznick; playwright Moss Hart and his wife Kitty Carlisle, whom Pamela had known since the early 1950s; and socialite Kitty Miller and her portly husband Gilbert, a prestigious theatrical producer in London and New York. In Paris, Pamela knew the expatriate screenwriter Harry Kurnitz and Irwin Shaw, both of them close to Hayward and filled with tales of the multimillionaire producer's exploits in film, theater, and television. He was a romantic figure with numerous connections in Hollywood and New York. Celebrated for his charisma and his dashing style, Hayward was also a neurotic and needy man—a "notorious egomaniac," wrote Stephen Farber and Marc Green in their book *Hollywood on the Couch*.

Hayward's somewhat haggard face, *Life* magazine once observed, bore "a look of tense enthusiasm when he was with friends, and a blank washed out expression when confronting a movie executive." He had a prominent nose and riveting blue eyes that pleaded for attention. His "radiant effervescent" smile was "always ready to tell you something or sell you something," remarked Jules Stein, founder of the MCA talent agency. His crewcut of gray hair gave him "the aspect of an elderly Yale freshman," according to *Life*. He was tall and rangy, with a slight paunch, and he had a rough virility despite his delicate bone structure and strikingly small feet (size $7\frac{1}{2}$) and hands.

He spoke in a rasping voice with a rapid-fire delivery liberally peppered with profanity. "He slanted backward when he stood and had an explosive way of talking that made him sound as if he were covering up on something," wrote the screenwriter and playwright Ben Hecht. When he unleashed his charm, his third wife, Slim, once wrote, "Leland was blasphemous, direct and relentless— but always amusing and stylish." Above all, he knew how to use charm to manipulate people—a talent that served him well personally and professionally.

Leland Hayward was born on September 13, 1902, in Nebraska City, the only child of a lawyer, Will Hayward, and the grandson of Monroe Leland Hayward, a U.S. senator from Nebraska. After his parents divorced when he was nine, Hayward lived in New York with his father and stepmother, an heiress named Maisie Manwaring Plant, in her mansion on Fifth Avenue that was decorated with paintings by Fragonard. Hayward's mother remarried, traveled extensively, and moved to California. His father, Hayward later said, was a strict disciplinarian.

Hayward attended the elite St. Paul's School, graduated from the equally prestigious Hotchkiss School, and dropped out of Princeton twice without finishing. His interests were artistic, and he was strikingly unathletic. "He would have been physically what other boys called chicken," said his son Bill. Hayward rarely talked about his boyhood, although he described one dramatic boarding school memory, according to Jones Harris, the son of the actress Ruth Gordon and producer Jed Harris. "The boys picked on him," recalled Harris. "He had to take off his clothes and stand against the wall in the rain and the boys threw tennis balls at him. He survived the bullying, but he never fought back."

While still a college student in 1921, Hayward married a Texas beauty named Lola Gibbs, divorced her a year later, and remarried and divorced her yet again in 1934. He tried his hand at nearly two dozen jobs, including newspaper reporter, press agent, talent scout, and producer of B-movies, before he found his metier as a talent agent. With astonishing ease, he broke into a business where women were "girls" and the men drank heavily and talked tough.

He negotiated unprecedented fees for a list of clients that included Fred Astaire and his sister Adele (who as Lady Cavendish had declared herself Pamela Churchill's sworn enemy when they met during the war), Henry Fonda, James Stewart, Gene Kelly, Helen Hayes, and Ginger Rogers, as well as authors such as Ernest Hemingway, Edna Ferber, Lillian Hellman, and Ben Hecht. Hayward stood out among the Hollywood sharpies by packaging himself as a debonair gentleman. He wore white flannel trousers and linen underwear and was the first Hollywood executive to decorate his office with antiques. He prided himself on such offbeat touches as an overnight case monogrammed "LH 10%" and a yardstick he flourished while negotiating deals with movie moguls.

Hayward had a passion for the telephone, conducting most of his business while lying on a sofa in his office with the receivers for three separate lines resting on his chest. On an average day, he could log $200 worth of phone calls that continued through lunches at '21' and the even more fashionable Colony, where the maître d' set his table with a bottle of Wild Turkey marked with his name on a silver chain.

He dated a series of what Broadway impresario Billy Rose called "firecracker femmes," including Greta Garbo and Katharine Hepburn, both of whom were his clients. Women were captivated by his boyish attentiveness; he seemed less interested in conquest than in the pure delight of their company. He repeatedly pressed Hepburn to marry him, but she turned him down because she preferred to remain single. "How can you like him?" her mother asked. "I don't understand it. His hands are so small." Hepburn enjoyed being with Hayward, she later wrote, because "nothing was a problem. There were solutions to everything. Joy was the constant mood. Everything was like a delightful surprise."

During the thirties, Hayward crisscrossed the continent, piloting his own plane between Los Angeles, where he was living with Hepburn, and New York, where he was courting actress Margaret Sullavan. Sullavan, also a client, had previously been married to Henry Fonda and director William Wyler, with whom she fought incessantly. When Hayward got Sullavan pregnant, he quickly married her in Newport at the elegant summer home of his father and stepmother. Afraid to confront Hepburn with the news, he sent a wire instead. Hepburn was unexpectedly upset at the loss of Hayward's companionship to a rival. "I was thunderstruck," she recalled. "No—not nice—not fair! . . . I was furious. Weeping. How could he? So wicked!"

Margaret Sullavan was petite (five feet two) and delicately pretty, with wavy golden-brown hair, wide brown eyes, and a whisper of southern gentility in her breathy voice. She had come to prominence on Broadway with her performance in George S. Kaufman's *Dinner at Eight,* and found stardom in Hollywood films. She had a magnetism that came through even in bad performances. Pauline Kael praised her "elusive, gallant sexiness" in the otherwise awful *Three Comrades.* Offscreen, Sullavan was a nonconformist with an impish sense of humor; she rode motorcycles and wore bluejeans at a time when they were considered unladylike.

The three children from Hayward's marriage to Sullavan—Brooke, born in 1937; Bridget in 1939; and Bill in 1941—were photogenic enhancements to what appeared to be a sparkling Hollywood duo. But psychologically they were orphans, deriving little emotional sustenance from either of their parents. "This family was characterized by a total lack of love," said Michael Thomas, the writer who was married to Brooke for three years in the late 1950s. "Gestures were made, but I think it was impossible for Maggie or Leland to focus on any of their children for more than ten seconds without thoughts of themselves breaking in."

There was a dark side to Sullavan's elfin image. She was shy and hypersensitive at one moment, demanding and aggressive the next. She had rigid views, and insisted that her husband and children follow her lead. She had a mean streak as well, and a penchant for lying that infuriated her friends. In 1941 Sullavan had decided to "retire," and in the following years she pulled her family from one house to another in California and Connecticut as she vacillated between pursuing her idealized notions of motherhood and plunging back into her career.

Sullavan hated her husband's business, which she considered beneath him. "Flesh peddler!" she used to shout when he reached for the telephone. Largely at her insistence, he sold his agency in 1945 at a substantial profit to join the more prestigious realm of Broadway producers. In the next five years, Hayward had four celebrated hits—John Hersey's *A Bell for Adano* and the Pulitzer Prize–winning *State of the Union,* along with two money machines, *Mister Roberts* and *South Pacific.*

Hayward had, in the words of a young apprentice on one of his productions, "a highly organized mind—and the energy of a Diesel." A former colleague recalled that Hayward "bought twelve magazines at a time. He read *Vogue* when nobody read *Vogue.* He read *Popular Mechanics* and *Scientific American.* He read not as a student but as a skimmer." After spotting *Mister Roberts* in *Atlantic* magazine, Hayward bought a partial dramatization from Tom Heggen sight unseen and coaxed out a play by bringing in the wizard director Joshua Logan as Heggen's collaborator.

Dismissed in some theatrical circles as a lightweight—David Merrick called him "the chic gentile"—Hayward was undeniably a great Broadway producer in his prime. "I would put Leland way up there," said longtime Broadway producer Alexander H. Cohen. "He got in it late and died prematurely, but the years he functioned he gave us wonderful things." Most notably, Hayward cared deeply about quality. "I think you have to do things you believe in and like," he told *New York Times* reporter Sam Zolotow, "and that if you think every time of only making money, therein lies disaster."

Hayward excelled at taking the big idea and bringing it off with big talent —behind the stage as well as on it. He was the first producer, for example, to use fashion designers such as Mainbocher for costumes. "Leland was a great promoter and casting genius. His real strength was conning people into doing things," said Alexander Cohen. That skill flowed directly from his years as an agent. "When there were a lot of conflicting personalities, Leland held them together with a special kind of glue he invented—his enthusiasm and sincerity about the work," said Bill Hammerstein, the son of *South Pacific* lyricist Oscar Hammerstein II.

As Hayward enjoyed greater success, Sullavan became increasingly erratic, her moods swinging between gaiety and depression, and she left her husband alone for long stretches of time. During one such period he fell in love with Nancy "Slim" Hawks, a chic, long-legged California beauty who was unhappily married to Howard Hawks, the acclaimed director of such film classics as *Scarface, To Have and Have Not,* and *His Girl Friday.* Hawks was aloof and notoriously unfaithful, and Slim was ready to leave him.

The daughter of a prosperous cannery owner and real estate investor, Slim had grown up on the Monterey Peninsula south of San Francisco. After dropping out of convent school, she trained briefly as a singer and moved to Hollywood, although she had no intention of becoming an actress. Her sole aspiration was to penetrate the Hollywood social scene and find an eligible man. While dancing with producer Cubby Broccoli at the Clover Club in the summer of 1938, she met Hawks, who was twenty-two years older and married. "Handsome, charming and successful, he was exactly the package I wanted," she later wrote. She had to wait three years before Hawks could get a divorce and marry her.

Slim, who got her nickname from William Powell, who starred in *The Thin Man,* was "straight like a dagger, full of self possession and pizzazz," according to her lifelong friend Irene Selznick. A fixture on the "best-dressed" lists, Slim had great style, "spare and sensual," with a "boldness that nobody else could carry off," in the words of Brooke Hayward. But Leland Hayward fell as much for Slim's agile intelligence and irreverent wit as he did for her looks.

Most of Hayward's friends blamed Sullavan for the subsequent marital breakup. "It was an essential arrogance," said Millicent Osborn, wife of the playwright Paul Osborn, "of wanting things the way she wanted them without regard to what Leland wanted." "Basically I'm absolutely monogamous," Hayward later said, "basically romantic and faithful, as long, that is, as I know I'm cared about." Nevertheless, said photographer Jean Howard, "Leland broke Margaret Sullavan's heart."

Leland Hayward married Slim Hawks in the garden of Bill and Babe Paley's home in Long Island in 1949. They stood at the center of a circle of Broadway luminaries that included Mary Martin and her husband Richard Halliday; Josh Logan and his wife Nedda; Richard Rodgers and his wife Dorothy; Oscar and Dorothy Hammerstein; and producer Arthur Hornblow Jr. and his wife Leonora, along with socialites in the Paley, Whitney, and Vanderbilt crowd. Slim was a popular hostess, known for her relaxed, high-spirited gatherings where guests sat on the floor, drank too much, and laughed far into the night. The Haywards were an exuberant pair; he called her "Nan," she called him "Hay." They worked well as a social team, prompting each other's stories about fabled Hollywood characters. "He adored having somebody to make him laugh," recalled Slim's daughter, Kitty Hawks. "She wasn't competing. She was complementary. You rarely get two out of two, both on the same wavelength."

Slim also took great pride in her skills at upper-class "housekeeping." She knew how to spend her husband's money to run a lavish household, and how to anticipate his needs by hiring great chefs, decorating in a style pleasing to his eye, and providing services to pamper him. Once a week Slim's manicurist Kay Blair came to their Sutton Place apartment or their weekend home in Manhasset, Long Island, to give Slim and Leland manicures and pedicures. But even Slim later admitted that much of the emotional focus on their marriage was on her. Kitty Hawks remembered, "In Mom's household, everything was because Mom loved it—the wonderful food and scents and flowers and objects. She loved to please herself, and everyone in her wake was having a ball."

Professionally, Slim provided valuable support that went beyond accompanying Hayward to out-of-town tryouts in Boston, Philadelphia, and New Haven. She loved show business, and she had keen instincts about talent and good writing. It was Slim who coaxed her husband into buying Ernest Hemingway's novella *The Old Man and the Sea,* which he persuaded *Life* magazine to publish. Slim wanted Hayward to adapt the book for the stage as a dramatic reading by Spencer Tracy, but Hayward signed Tracy to star in a film version instead. During rehearsals for Broadway shows, Slim sat quietly and observed. Only when asked did she offer her views, which often coincided with Hayward's down-to-earth sensibilities. "Slim and Leland talked a lot about shows," said Jeanne Murray Vanderbilt. "He would say, 'Nan said this,' or, 'Nan said that.' He was not ashamed to talk about her role, and she loved that world, loved being a part of it."

After his enormous success with *South Pacific* in 1949, Hayward had three quick back-to-back flops before he regained his footing late in 1950 with the smash hit *Call Me Madam,* a star turn for Ethel Merman as Washington's "hostess with the mostest" Perle Mesta. But then came another rocky patch: four plays, two of which were modest financial successes, and two outright flops.

Hayward brooded over his failures and took surprisingly scant satisfaction in his successes. Exhausted and dispirited by Broadway, he decided in 1953 to turn his attention elsewhere. "Please forgive me," he wrote to Josh Logan that year, asking to bow out of three new projects. "I just don't feel like producing for a while." He spent the next five years trying to become a big-time Hollywood film producer.

The Haywards moved to California, where they rented a house across the street from Humphrey Bogart and Lauren Bacall. They ran with the Hollywood smart set—Jimmy and Gloria Stewart; Rosalind Russell and her husband Freddie Brisson, a movie producer; screenwriter George Axelrod and his wife Joan; film producer Bill Goetz and his wife Edie, the daughter of Louis B. Mayer. In Hollywood, both halves of the famous Hayward team felt very much at home.

Hayward never really made it as a movie producer, however. His only hit was *Mister Roberts,* which in 1955 set a record as the longest-running movie at Radio City Music Hall. Two years later, *The Spirit of St. Louis,* starring Stewart as aviation hero Charles Lindbergh, had one of the shortest runs at the same theater. His final effort in the movies was *The Old Man and the Sea,* neither a critical nor a popular success, despite a strong performance by Spencer Tracy. "Hollywood was the Waterloo for Leland," said Michael Thomas. "Slim thought of herself as Mama Hollywood. She was strictly for winners, and Leland was slipping."

Hayward achieved his greatest acclaim in the nascent medium of television. In June 1953, he produced the *Ford 50th Anniversary Show,* which ran on two networks and attracted 60 million viewers. With choreography by Jerome Robbins, a sparkling musical medley featuring superstars Mary Martin and Ethel Merman, and commentary by Edward R. Murrow, the show was television's first "spectacular." A year later, Hayward made headlines again with his vibrant TV staging of *Peter Pan,* a musical starring Mary Martin that had flopped on Broadway.

Hayward had become a multimillionaire on the strength of his Broadway productions of *Mister Roberts* and *South Pacific* back in 1948 and 1949. Each spawned feature films as well as a dozen road companies that poured hundreds of thousands of dollars into Hayward's bank account every month. (The stage productions of *South Pacific* alone earned him $3 million, the equivalent of $16 million today.)

But Hayward spent money as fast as he made it. "He would walk past a shop window and buy something if he liked it," said Leonora Hornblow. Bill Hayward regarded his father as "a strange character who lived right up to his income all his life. He was like someone who had been badly injured in the Depression, although he hadn't been. He didn't believe in real estate investments or stocks and bonds. Everything he had like that he sold to live well."

For Leland Hayward, life could only be first class—from weekends at the Ritz in Paris to vacations in Batista's Cuba where, as Slim told Mary Martin, "we go at the drop of a telegram." Hayward owned upward of fifty pairs of cufflinks, traveled with at least thirty shirts, ordered plain black silk neckties by the half dozen from Edward & Butler on the Place Vendôme in Paris, and bought hundreds of pairs of shoes at such exclusive stores as Mancuso's in Venice. His compulsive spending on photographic equipment, Hayward told the photographer Slim Aarons, was "better than giving the money to my psychiatrist."

Glib and breezy, he was a well-known gossip, with insatiable curiosity, as one of his friends put it, about "who was sleeping with whom, who knew, and who didn't know." His gossiping skills were provocatively feminine; he read *Women's Wear Daily* to pick up morsels about fashion and jet-set society. "He was cozy," said Hornblow. "He always wanted to know the woman's opinion. He could make you tell him everything." Yet, according to his daughter Brooke Hayward, "he was also capable of a certain kind of cruelty, but although he could and did say savage things, his intention never was to hurt. His cruelty was unthinking."

Hayward surrendered little about himself. He signed his letters to men as well as women "love and kisses," but many of his friends said he was difficult to know. He lived as if on a stage, playing an outsize role at all times. "Early in his life he adopted a manner to appall his parents," said Michael Thomas. "After a while it was so *in* him there was nothing else. He believed his role. He believed that was the way he had to be in order to be Leland Hayward. He gave a very engaging performance."

Superficially carefree, Hayward drove himself hard. "He seemed so sure of himself," said Lauren Bacall, "but he was a demon worker." He smoked three packs of Camels a day, and Margaret Sullavan once compared him to "a mosquito the way he hops around." "I have a complete inability to work on anything other than 24 hours a day," he told CBS executive Hubbell Robinson. Once a work binge ended, he could sleep for several days, waking up at intervals to drink milk. His frenzied pace took a terrible physical toll. Three times—in 1943, 1946, and 1954—Hayward collapsed from massive internal bleeding that seemed to come from ulcers but could not be conclusively diagnosed. Each time he was forced into many months of convalescence.

Hayward was eccentric in his eating habits. He avoided most vegetables and fruits, preferring "white food" such as scrambled eggs, custard, and chicken hash. His favorite lunch was caviar and vanilla ice cream. He suffered from allergic rashes and eczema as well as persistent insomnia. To calm himself in the middle of the night, he baked bread or printed photographs. He also used an array of sleeping pills (Seconal, Nembutol, Carbromal, Tuinal, and Phenobarbital), augmented periodically by the amphetamine Dexamyl, all of which he regularly ordered from Dr. Saul Fox, a Beverly Hills physician who provided soporifics and stimulants to Hollywood stars. Hayward's theory, according to Leonora Hornblow, was, "If you take one kind of pill one night, you should take another the next night. He tried different things to sleep." He stored his cache of pills in a leather suitcase that had its own collapsible stand where he would "perch it while he pored over its contents," according to his daughter Brooke.

"He had tremendous inner tension," said Mary Hunter Wolfe, who worked with him on several television projects. Toward the end of his marriage to Margaret Sullavan, he had begun seeing Dr. May Ginsburg Romm, a popular Hollywood analyst. According to Brooke, Romm told her father, "There's no question that you are crazy, but you also happen to function better than anyone I've ever seen"—a dubious judgment given Hayward's compulsive habits.

Throughout the 1950s, according to Slim, "Leland was having a very difficult time in his career . . . Leland was, beneath the surface enamel, a very emotional, very fragile man. . . . His failures were beginning to wear on him."

In the summer of 1955, the two younger Hayward children walked out on their mother and moved in with their father. (Brooke was on a holiday in Scotland before going off to college at Vassar.) As Hayward explained it to Arthur Hornblow, "Maggie announced to me that she wanted me to take Bill and Bridget, because she couldn't handle them." The Hayward children, though bright and creative, were very troubled. "Leland had a difficult time relating to his own children," Slim wrote. As a result, it was Slim who coped with their sullen moods, hunger strikes, and defiant behavior as she moved to a larger house in Los Angeles and got them ready for school.

Hayward, meanwhile, flew from one continent to another on various projects, wringing his hands from a safe distance. His stepdaughter Kitty Hawks, who called him "Pops" and got on well with him, said he was "cowardly" with his own children. "He didn't like the dirty stuff," she said. His daughter Brooke was more blunt: "I would be the first to say that father was not a very good father."

In 1950 Margaret Sullavan had married Kenneth Wagg, described by Brooke as a "mild-mannered, slightly stuffy Englishman." Sullavan had been under psychiatric care for a number of years, and in late 1956 she had a severe mental breakdown. When she was found curled into the fetal position under her bed, she entered the Austen Riggs Foundation, a mental hospital in western Massachusetts. At the same time, Brooke Hayward got pregnant, dropped out of Vassar after her sophomore year, married Michael Thomas, then a student at Yale, and had two children. "Our family was so fragmented they probably saw it as a problem removed; I lowered the water level slightly," said Brooke.

Both Bridget and Bill Hayward had their own mental collapses in 1956 as well. After her freshman year at Swarthmore, Bridget was sent to Austen Riggs, and Bill was removed from the Lawrenceville School before he was sent for treatment at the Menninger Clinic in Topeka, Kansas. Leonora Hornblow's son Michael, a classmate of Bill's, was there the day Hayward arrived to take away his son. "He can still see Leland standing there, his face a terrible color, with such a look of anguish," recalled Hornblow.

By his own admission, Bill Hayward was frequently depressed. "I've been in states so bad I've been paralyzed with fear," he told Brooke. "Literally couldn't get out of my bed for weeks." His father had him removed from boarding school on the recommendation of psychiatrist Dr. Lawrence Kubie, a godlike figure to his show business clientele. Still, most of Leland Hayward's friends—and Slim as well—felt that committing his sixteen-year-old son to a mental institution was an overreaction. "If his father hadn't been well off and if Billy had had to struggle a bit," Slim later wrote, "I think his difficulties would have been resolved." As it turned out, Bill Hayward was at Menninger's for nearly three years.

In the early 1950s, Slim suffered several miscarriages and delivered a still-born baby in the seventh month. Like Pamela, she was jolted by a positive Pap smear and underwent a hysterectomy, as she later said, "to be on the safe side." Disappointed by her misfortune, overwhelmed by the stress of dealing with the neurotic Hayward children, and resentful of her husband's narcissism, Slim soured on Leland.

"Slim was a restless woman," said Lauren Bacall, a close friend since 1944 when Howard Hawks modeled her screen image on Slim in the film *To Have and Have Not.* "Slim needed attention. She had a very fragile ego." At first Slim satisfied that need by flirting with other men, which, as she later acknowledged, "used to drive Leland crazy." With her natural streak of independence, fortified by an inheritance of over half a million dollars (the equivalent of about $3 million today) from her father, she indulged herself with long trips, rationalizing that her husband fully supported her "wanderlust tendencies."

She had a one-night stand with Frank Sinatra, followed by a six-month affair with Pamela's Parisian friend Peter Viertel, Leland's screenwriter on the film of *The Old Man and the Sea,* who would later marry the actress Deborah Kerr. Slim confided to Viertel that her marriage to Hayward "had become a companionate one." For whatever reason, she decided to tell Hayward about her infidelities. "I begged her not to," said Leonora Hornblow. "I paraphrased Graham Greene and said, 'Truth is for mathematicians. A kind lie the Lord forgives.' But she was so vain she wanted him to know how irresistible she was. Afterwards, she said he got very pale and walked out of the room. I told her, 'For a smart woman you're the biggest fool I know.' " Leonora knew how hurt Hayward was. "You had only to look at him," she said. "He didn't want to know what she had done."

In the view of Lauren Bacall, Slim's problem was that she took her husband for granted. "She thought he would always be there," said Bacall. But the problem ran deeper than simple complacency. "Slim was lovable and enchanting and funny," said Hornblow, "but she couldn't go the distance. Not with anybody. She wanted someone, and then when she had him, she didn't want him. She would make her nest and then tear it apart." In the presence of their friends she turned her famously lethal wit on her husband. "She was so mean about him," said Jeanne Murray Vanderbilt. "She put him down. He didn't say anything. He laughed it off and joked, and didn't fight back."

In the spring of 1958, Hayward embarked on the most furiously productive period in his life. He produced a farce on Broadway called *Who Was That Lady I Saw You With?* that drew mixed reviews and failed financially. In the following months he completed the film of *The Old Man and the Sea* for an October premiere; launched Jerome Robbins's *Ballets USA* on Broadway; and developed several television proposals including a show about the war between the sexes.

At the request of Mary Martin, Hayward also began negotiations with the Baroness von Trapp for the rights to produce *The Sound of Music* on Broadway —a task that would take him to Europe eleven times over eighteen months and that he would later describe as "one of the most difficult things I ever did in my life." He signed up his old friends Howard Lindsay and Russel Crouse to adapt the story and Rodgers and Hammerstein for the score.

Around the same time Ethel Merman asked Hayward to join David Merrick as a producer on the musical *Gypsy* because she wanted a "gentleman" on the team to protect her from Merrick. Hayward made a few key contributions to the production; he argued strongly for his friend Jerome Robbins as the choreographer and director. But for the most part his role was confined to holding Merman's hand.

After a steamy summer working in Manhattan, Hayward celebrated his fifty-sixth birthday during the autumn rounds of theater openings and parties. His mood seemed buoyant as Slim planned an October excursion to see the bullfights in Spain with Lauren Bacall. Slim would be gone for two weeks, and she would meet Hayward in Paris before they both traveled to Munich for a meeting with Baroness von Trapp. For once Slim had a persuasive reason for taking her trip: Bacall's husband, Humphrey Bogart, had died of cancer the previous year. Bacall was afraid to travel alone, so Slim offered to keep her company. She was not nearly so solicitous toward her husband. Hayward had remained faithful and uncomplaining even after Slim started having affairs and making fun of him in front of their friends. But though Hayward was emotionally fragile, he still had his pride. "Leland was a fooler," said Peter Viertel, "the kind of man who takes it and takes it and suddenly goes."

*B*EFORE SLIM LEFT for Europe on October 11, 1958, Babe Paley asked her for a favor. Betsey Whitney had called from London and wanted to know if Babe would help entertain Pamela Churchill, who was coming to New York for a week. Although Babe was unnerved by Pamela's continuing friendship with Bill Paley, she recognized her social obligation, since Pamela had entertained the Paleys generously in Paris. "May I borrow Leland one night to go to the theater as Pam Churchill's date?" Babe asked. Slim agreed. She knew all about Pamela Churchill's reputation, but didn't consider her a threat because "men supported her . . . but they just weren't available for marriage."

Hayward was also well aware of Pamela. Several nights before his planned date, he took Jeanne Murray Vanderbilt to a concert at Carnegie Hall. "We were sitting there and along came Elsa Maxwell and a woman who was dumpy and nondescript," recalled Vanderbilt. "Leland said, 'Look, there's Pam Churchill.' Leland was clearly impressed."

The name of the play taken in by the Paleys and their guests is long forgotten, and according to a close friend of Pamela's, nothing sexual happened that night between Pamela and Hayward, who sat through the show and a supper afterward, laughing and conversing with evident pleasure. Brooke Hayward, however, often said that her father and Pamela left at intermission and later that night called Bill Paley from Hayward's bedroom. "Pam said, 'Guess where I am? I'm with Leland. Isn't that divine?' and they both laughed," according to Brooke. "Pam thought it was fun to tell him where she was in a *La Ronde* kind of way."

As much as it enhances Pamela's legend, Brooke's story is implausible on several counts. Pamela's appeal to men was her ability to create an atmosphere of intimacy and trust. For all her superficial gaiety, her approach was invariably serious. A frivolous call to a former lover seems out of character, not to mention a distraction from the object of her intense interest. Even more important, the need for discretion was essential to nurturing a relationship with Hayward. Had she really made a call to Paley, the word would have been out within twenty-four hours. In fact, the affair remained a secret until late the following spring.

But clearly something clicked that night at the theater, and Pamela saw Hayward a few more times during her visit. A week or so later, Slim and Lauren Bacall arrived at the Ritz in Paris to find a stack of messages from Pamela

Churchill. Much as she had cozied up to Cynthia Foy Rupp, Pamela lent the women her Bentley and entertained them at Avenue de New York. During one "quiet supper" there, the talk turned to marriage, and Slim found herself admitting to Pamela "in carefully chosen words that although I deeply loved Leland, she might have the better set up." When Pamela's butler called the hostess away for a transatlantic telephone call, Slim had no idea that the caller was her husband, who was due to fly to Paris the next day. "I remember Pamela told Slim she'd be happy to send her car to meet Leland at the airport," said Bacall. "Slim thought, 'Great!' Neither of us knew Pam had started already."

Pamela organized a dinner party for twenty at her apartment, with French and American friends including Irwin Shaw and the French playwright Jean-Pierre Grédy. Afterward, they went to see *Lucy Crown*, a play adapted from one of Shaw's books. Pamela sat next to Hayward and translated. Slim sat two seats away from her husband. At a nightclub, Pamela and Hayward danced without arousing Slim's suspicion. "If it was anyone's fault it was mine for not paying attention," Slim said years later. "Any woman with any sense has her guard up."

What Slim did not realize, she would later write, was that "like a brilliant chess player, [Pamela] knew her moves way in advance. She knew both where to place herself and how to maneuver you into a position where you couldn't intrude on her plans. And so her mission had been completed long before I'd even begun to realize what was happening." Pamela had no guilt whatsoever about her actions. "I can't help it if somebody doesn't want their husband and then somebody else besides them decides they do," she said years later. "It's not my fault."

The Haywards and Bacall left for Munich the next day. When Leland returned to New York, he seemed preoccupied by his work and family matters. His mother came from California for Thanksgiving and landed in the hospital after breaking her kneecap and her nose in a fall. In the following weeks, Hayward devoted himself to her medical care and recovery. Pamela saw Elie and maintained her busy social schedule, making her customary trip to St. Moritz for the winter holidays.

Bacall, who had gone to London to make a film, was somewhat surprised that "Pamela became solicitous of me. When she was in London she called and we had lunch, and she called me to find out when I was coming to Paris. When I was in Paris I had lunch at her flat. She wanted to know how Slim was, how the marriage was. She asked in the course of the conversation. It was subtly done. Also at that lunch Pam told me about her feeling it was time to leave Paris, make a life for herself. She wanted to get married."

Meanwhile Hayward conducted a romance with Pamela by transatlantic phone calls and during a few trips to Europe on *Sound of Music* business. "He was planning some kind of meeting with Pam in England or France," recalled Marshall Jamison, a writer and director who worked with Hayward on many productions. "He used to go to '21' almost every day and call London or Paris from there. I was his beard. This went on for maybe a month. It was kind of a surprise to me that he did that. I had never thought of him that way."

The following February, Slim went to the Main Chance spa in Arizona with Edna Ferber to get in shape; Slim had begun to gain weight, belying her famous nickname. Pamela arrived in New York almost simultaneously and settled into an apartment in the Carlton House that belonged to William Astor, the former husband of Pamela's friend from debutante days, Sarah Norton. Before she left town, Slim told Leland to take care of Pamela. "She has been so hospitable," Slim said, "so do what you can." Pamela and Hayward had what she later described as their first real "date," when they saw Gwen Verdon in a musical comedy called *Redhead*, the hottest show in New York. That night they did leave at intermission, but only because Pamela felt ill. Although they dined publicly in subsequent days, their romance remained under wraps.

Slim returned to New York at the end of the week to be told by her husband that they were having dinner in Pamela Churchill's apartment at Carlton House. "The first thing I noticed when I walked in," Slim recalled, "was that the room was filled with a certain kind of white rose that Leland had always sent to me." Pamela told Slim only that "someone" had given her the flowers, prompting Slim to throw her husband a look that said, "You sonavabitch." While it was clear that Leland was having a fling with Pamela, Slim refused, either out of vanity or complacency, to take her rival seriously.

Pamela was playing the sort of double game she knew well. Shortly after her return to Paris at the end of February 1959, Cholly Knickerbocker headlined his column in the *New York Journal-American:* PAMELA MAY GET TO WED ROTHSCHILD. "The talk of the international set has been for some time that one of the Rothschilds is trying to win his freedom to marry beautiful Pamela Churchill," he wrote. "Pamela was here recently and rumors ran riot that the reason for her visit was a romantic interest here in New York. The truth is that the strawberry-haired social siren . . . may become Baroness Rothschild."

Pamela was in fact still giving Elie her full attention—and receiving his favors—although the notion of marriage remained as remote as ever. That spring, Lauren Bacall visited Pamela and Elie at Pamela's London flat. "It was just the three of us, and Pam and Elie were cozy," said Bacall. "We went to an antique shop after lunch because she wanted to show him a painting. He got it for her, naturally. Who knew from Leland? Not I."

By Pamela's account, Hayward asked her to marry him in March, just after her thirty-ninth birthday—only weeks after Knickerbocker had touted "Rothschild" as a serious rival. She was charmed by Hayward's ebullient personality. His career had hit a new peak with *Gypsy* and with the highly touted *Sound of Music* on the way. Like several of her previous lovers, he was an older man, by eighteen years. And Hayward had the sort of visibility that would keep her in the limelight and expose her to the kind of people she wanted to know.

Although he lived like a wealthy man, Pamela knew his bank account was significantly smaller than Agnelli's or Rothschild's. "He wasn't in great physical shape when she met him," said Leonora Hornblow. "He had financial obligations. He had three children who were problems." Still, observed Peter Viertel, "he wanted to marry her when the other guys all wanted to keep her."

Hayward was particularly vulnerable to Pamela's brand of glamour. "Leland was always star-struck," said Marshall Jamison. "He was a little in awe of Pam when he first met her. The fact that she was a Winston Churchill relation even by marriage was enough to knock him over. He was still a boy from Nebraska, and Pam was like marrying royalty." At the same time, he continued, "I think Leland felt Pam was tremendously romantic. She had affairs with guys who were rich and well known. Leland thought, 'I'll show her who is a real guy.' " Murrow in particular enhanced Pamela's appeal because Hayward greatly admired the famous newscaster, with whom he had stood proudly at the conclusion of his Ford television special several years earlier.

Pamela's physical appeal—"ripe and round, with a nice full breast," as Slim Aarons described it—went without saying. There were stories in later years that Hayward boasted about Pamela's sexual prowess to publisher Bennett Cerf. But intimates of both men said such an indiscretion was highly unlikely. While Hayward relished gossip about others, he avoided discussing sexual details about his own life. "Leland didn't talk about Pam directly," said a close associate for many years. "There was a privacy of that sort with Leland. He was a midwesterner."

It was important to Hayward that Pamela knew her way around. "She was someone Leland didn't have to worry about. He felt easy with her," said Aarons. "When you are in your fifties, you want someone to relax with." Brooke Hayward often said that her father fell for Pamela because he needed a "nanny" to provide all his creature comforts. But that isn't quite right. Slim had always looked after him, even when their marriage was strained. "Leland didn't need a nanny," said Leonora Hornblow. "He needed a wife. He needed Pamela for a kind word." Hayward had been deeply hurt by Slim. Yet "fooler" that he was, he had already been married four times, and he might have stayed with Slim had Pamela not come along. "Leland really loved Slim," said Lauren Bacall, "but finally he needed something for himself and Pamela provided it."

Hayward was also preoccupied during this period by what he described as "the eternal problems of men versus women." In a long letter in 1959 to the photographer Richard Avedon, with whom he was working on a television show, he mused about "women's continuing increase as a domineering and overpowering influence," and he wondered whether America would become a place "where women run everything and the men are slaves to the women and work for the women and perform for the women, as the women desire and wish." He seemed to be struggling with his own private torments when he asked, "What do American women want? Why are they so unhappy? Where do men fail them?" and then, perhaps with Pamela in mind, he observed that "women really aren't that terrible. What they really want is to have a strong man to be married to."

Even after Hayward's marriage proposal in March, Pamela hesitated. She confided her dilemma to several Parisian friends. "What should I do?" she asked one man over lunch. "If you think you should go, then go," he told her. "She said she didn't want to because she was very much in love with Elie. But she was worried about herself and her future. 'This thing in Paris isn't leading to anything,' she said. She was obsessed by that, about settling down." Françoise de Langlade took a harder line, urging her to go to the United States and pursue Hayward. "Françoise didn't have too much trouble persuading Pamela to leave because she was on her way anyway," said Sandy Bertrand.

Besides slipping away for three days to the Ritz in Paris, Hayward spent most of April in Philadelphia supervising rehearsals for *Gypsy*, which opened there in the middle of the month, and completing negotiations with Baroness von Trapp. Slim busied herself with the itinerary for a tenth wedding anniversary getaway to Spain, France, and Italy. Hayward seemed to look forward to the trip as well, describing it to Mary Martin's husband, producer Richard Halliday, as "two weeks rest, which I very much need."

The *Gypsy* opening in New York on May 21, 1959, was a triumph shared by nearly all of Leland and Slim Hayward's friends at a post-theater party— Hornblows, Fondas, Cerfs, Wassermans, Lindsays, Crouses, Vreelands, Harts, Vanderbilts, Selznicks, Axelrods, and scores more. "Start shopping for pearls!" an exultant Slim wired to screenwriter Harry Kurnitz in Paris. "We are rich! 'Gypsy' smash!" Slim flew to Paris to meet Kurnitz the next day. Because the *Gypsy* opening had been later than originally planned, Hayward told Slim he had to delay his departure by a week. In fact, he was waiting for Pamela to join him in New York.

Though Pamela had spread word of the romance to friends in Paris, their secret held in New York. Shortly after the opening, Hayward took the Hornblows into his confidence. "I want to leave Slim," he told them behind closed doors in his office. "I can't stand it anymore. There was a time I thought she was the most entertaining woman in the world. Now she is the most boring." He said he was in love with Pamela and hoped they would like her. When he asked what he should do about Slim, Leonora advised, "Tell her right out. She will be gallant and behave beautifully." He said he would confront Slim, but the Hornblows knew that he was "scared to death."

While Slim was being escorted around Paris by Harry Kurnitz and other friends, Pamela and Hayward were turning up together all over New York. Toward the end of May they saw *A Raisin in the Sun,* which had opened to rave reviews two months earlier. Pamela looked "ravishing" in what Leonora Hornblow described as "the most beautiful brown taffeta coat." The ever vigilant Truman Capote was there that night with Betsey Whitney and Babe Paley's sister, Minnie Fosburgh. Afterward he dashed off a mischievous telegram to Slim in Paris, a takeoff on a promotional slogan for the Clark Gable movie, *Adventure,* co-starring Greer Garson: "Pamela's here and Leland's got her!"

Capote recounted his nasty prank to the Hornblows and other friends assembled at the Cerfs for Memorial Day. The Hornblows were outraged but said nothing. The official megaphone of international society, Cholly Knicker-bocker, headlined his June 1 column: PAMELA CHURCHILL HERE SECRETLY, but all he could offer was that she had "arrived here secretly a week ago. . . . Evidently her visit had nothing to do with young and rich Leon Lambert of the powerful Lambert banking firm of Brussels (to whom she has been linked romantically by international gossip) because Leon left for Europe on Sunday and Pam is staying another week." Baron Lambert, like Elie descended from a German Jewish banking family, was not one of Pamela's serious suitors.

In early June, after a second week's delay, Hayward flew to Madrid for the dreaded showdown with Slim. Typically, he couldn't bring himself to tell the truth. He could only manage an equivocal proposal: in order for their marriage to survive they should "take a sabbatical" from each other. When he offhandedly mentioned that he had dined with Pamela Churchill several times in New York, Slim cracked, "That should have been your opening line. . . . It is not very original of you, but if you want to have a love affair with Pam Churchill, there's nothing I can do to stop you. But whatever you do, for your own protection, for your own dignity, don't marry her. You don't have to. Nobody *marries* Pam Churchill." Hayward didn't deny that he was having an affair, but he reassured Slim that marriage was not in the picture. Just to deepen the ambiguity, he sent Slim $500 worth of the famous white roses.

It was only after Hayward left for New York by way of Paris that Slim's friend Sam Spiegel told her that "everybody" knew her husband planned to marry Pamela Churchill. Contrary to Leonora Hornblow's prediction, Slim fell apart. "Slim was in such a shattered state, in tears, in bed for two days," said Lauren Bacall. Slim sailed off on Spiegel's yacht, traveled to Italy with Jerome Robbins, had an affair with a Spaniard, and collapsed in Biarritz. "She wasn't used to losing anyone, much less a man," said her daughter Kitty Hawks, who spent the summer in Biarritz. "Mom was emotionally devastated, taken by surprise, humiliated, her vanity offended."

Hayward was thrown by Slim's histrionic reaction. For a moment he seemed to waver in his resolve. When Kitty Hawks was leaving New York for Biarritz, he gave her a box from Cartier to deliver to her mother—without, of course, explaining what had happened. In the box was a necklace of lapis lazuli beads with a note saying: "These beads are blue like your eyes and my heart. I will always love you. Leland." "The note was romantic," recalled Kitty, "which made Mom even more nuts."

Unbeknownst to Hayward, Pamela had yet to play her final card with Elie. She invited him to her apartment and wasted no time getting to the point. "Leland Hayward wants to marry me," she said. "It is now or never." "Never," replied Elie, who hated confrontations. "My son wins," he added, oddly enough echoing Murrow's reply some fifteen years earlier. Elie was, he later told a friend, "very cross" that she would deliver such an ultimatum. They parted on a frosty note.

Pamela was in and out of Paris that summer, making arrangements for her departure. She had already rented a house in Cannes for the season—further evidence that she had been hedging her bet on Hayward—but she was only able to spend a short time there in July. Her lodgings met her usual standard of luxury, with "a garden . . . full of cyprus trees and hibiscus and a marvellous view and grilled lobsters and all around us her various millionaire friends at our service," said her friend Marina Sulzberger, who came for a visit.

Pamela sold the Paris apartment Agnelli had given her, for the princely sum of $500,000 (around $2.5 million at today's values). She left her dog with her maid, sold some of her belongings at auction, and offered other pieces of furniture to friends such as Alexis de Redé, who bought a fauteuil. "It was quick," said one Parisian socialite. "When people were saying Elie was not going to marry her, she was already gone."

No one was especially surprised by her hasty departure. "It was the sort of thing she would do," said one man to whom she had confided her problems with Elie. "Forget the past, start a new life." Few Parisians were impressed by Elie's replacement. "To the general amazement," sniffed Nancy Mitford, Pamela attached herself to "an infinitely dreary American with whom she seems to have settled down." Elie made certain that Parisian society—and London society for that matter—knew Pamela had forced a showdown and lost. "When Gianni left her," explained one prominent European woman, "it was important for her to have Elie. To have Leland was even more important later. With Leland it was a question of survival."

Pamela Churchill and Leland Hayward were certainly intrigued by one another, yet they seemed to fall short of a genuine love match. Both had evident doubts, and both engaged in deceptions before making a final commitment. For all of his charm and energy, Leland Hayward was "on a glide path," in the words of Peter Viertel, with his best years behind him.

CHAPTER

Twenty-one

"TOUT NEW YORK is divided into warring camps," Truman Capote wrote to Cecil Beaton in August 1959. On one side, the "Pro-Slim contingent" was led by Babe Paley (who, according to Capote, referred to Pamela as "that bitch"), her sister Minnie Fosburgh, Jerome Robbins, and Mainbocher. On the other side, Capote said, were Babe's other sister, Betsey Whitney, "Mrs. C's greatest partisan (so grateful is she that the threat to her own happy home has been removed)," and Leonora Hornblow, who had been "sent to the firing squad" because she gave a dinner for Hayward and Pamela. "I am a Slimmite to the death," Capote proclaimed.

News of the romance broke in Cholly Knickerbocker's column at the end of June. He coyly identified Pamela's new "rich and powerful admirer" as "LH, a noted figure in the theatre and movie world." Three weeks later, Knickerbocker wrote that "beautiful Pamela Churchill and her 'secret' admirer, LH, have become the talk of New York—just as they were the talk of Paris." At the end of July, show business trade papers finally named names and predicted, according to Knickerbocker, that "the elegant Slim Hayward is ready to bow out" of the marriage.

Without identifying the Paleys, Knickerbocker reported in mid-August that "the very famous social couple" who set up Pamela's first date with Hayward "are no longer speaking to her. They remain best of friends with the estranged Mrs. Hayward." A month later, in a column headlined: STORM HOVERS OVER PAM, Knickerbocker wrote, "The battle of Britain was nothing compared to the siege Long Island society ladies seem to be carefully laying down against femme fatale Pamela Churchill. . . . The bewitching glamour girl of the international set made all those smart set females furious because she charmed producer Leland Hayward. . . . Meantime, Pamela seems oblivious to the furor she's caused." As usual, Pamela's demeanor was deceptive. Her sister Sheila was so appalled by the publicity that she contacted Knickerbocker, who was a friend. She told him she disapproved, and he replied that she should call if there was anything she didn't think he should write. But Sheila never called, because Pamela made it known to anyone who asked that she rather liked the publicity.

With the eruption of even racier scandals—notably Aristotle Onassis's estrangement from his wife Christina after a highly publicized affair with opera star Maria Callas—New York society tired of the Pam–Leland–Slim triangle. It was hard to get too indignant about Pamela stealing Hayward from Slim because Slim, after all, had stolen Hayward from Margaret Sullavan years earlier. And besides, said a longtime friend of the Haywards, "People felt Slim had left her husband to the hunter." Many Hayward friends, feeling divided loyalty, maintained cordial relations with both Slim and Pamela. That was certainly the case with the Hornblows, who had the two women to dinner in alternating weeks.

Babe Paley was a special case because she "always felt responsible," according to Slim, for having set up Pamela's original date with Hayward. "Pamela will never darken my door again," Babe told Lauren Bacall. "But that didn't happen. They remained friends," said Bacall. Even Capote, the devoted "Slimmite," worked hard to cultivate Hayward (whom he called "Big Daddy") and Pamela, escorting her to events when Hayward was away, joining her for chatty lunches, writing them both fawning letters—all the while sniping gleefully behind Pamela's back to a contingent of wary wives.

In the end almost everyone accepted Pamela, largely out of loyalty to Leland Hayward. "They could see that Pamela made Leland happy," said Leonora Hornblow, "and they well remembered how mean Slim had been to him." "I thought you were wrong about Pamela," Babe Paley said to Hornblow, "but I think you are right. Leland fell into a tub of butter."

Pamela had mixed success with Hayward's family. Hayward's initial approach to Bill and Bridget, both still institutionalized, was typically to tell them nothing of their prospective new stepmother. During a visit to Menninger's, Bill recalled, Hayward explained that "he and Slim were having marital difficulties. I recall his having said that she had an affair with another man, and that she had gotten impatient and bored. My father was very distressed."

Brooke Hayward was another matter. In the summer of 1959, her three-year marriage to Michael Thomas had broken up. She was living in Greenwich, Connecticut, with her two toddler sons and trying her hand at modeling until she could get a job as an actress. Hayward had an uneasy relationship with his eldest daughter, whose pretty profile had graced the cover of *Life* when she was fifteen years old for a fashion feature on "Daughters of the Stars." In her mannerisms, expansiveness, and deliberate eccentricity she resembled her father, but by her own description she was "moody and mercurial." She "adored her father but she didn't get much from him," in the view of Michael Thomas. According to Marshall Jamison, Brooke "was critical of Leland, critical of his attitude, that he didn't give her enough attention." Hayward favored Bridget, an ethereal, flaxen-haired teenager with bright blue eyes and a shy manner, while he blew hot and cold on Bill, who spent his adolescence making desperate bids for his father's attention.

With her father's marriage a shambles and a mother struggling with depression, Brooke "had no anchor anywhere," said Thomas. Three weeks after Hayward returned from his face-off with Slim in Madrid, he took Brooke to dinner at Pavillon to celebrate her twenty-second birthday. As Brooke described the evening nearly two decades later in her memoir, *Haywire,* her father, after several glasses of champagne and a mind-numbing double Wild Turkey, shocked her by revealing his plan to marry Pamela. By Brooke's recollection, Hayward boasted about Pamela's luxurious life in Paris, her ivory and auburn coloring, her noble birth and Churchill connection, and her legions of lovers, capping his story by declaring her "one of the most accomplished courtesans of the century." "His description of her was quite thrilling," Brooke wrote. "She sounded like a mixture of Brenda Starr and Mata Hari." Not once, according to Brooke, did Hayward mention the word "love."

Leonora Hornblow was skeptical that Hayward would have called his future wife a "courtesan." "I talked to Leland nearly every day of my life. I knew his vocabulary," said Hornblow. "It's not a word he would use about anybody, much less the woman he wanted to marry." When he eventually discussed Pamela with his son Bill, Hayward was admiring and respectful. "He never referred to her as a courtesan when he talked to me," said Bill Hayward. "He never talked about her romantic past. I heard about Murrow and Harriman, but from somewhere else."

Still, Brooke repeatedly insisted on that account, along with her recollection of her first meeting with Pamela a few nights later. Pamela had moved into a suite at the Drake on Park Avenue, at the time one of Manhattan's most stylish hotels, managed by the fashionable White Russian Colonel Serge Obolensky. Pamela quickly personalized her suite with flowers, perfumed candles, and bibelots, as well as fine Impressionist paintings borrowed from Mary Lasker, a prominent art collector she had met through the Whitneys. When Brooke entered the apartment, she recalled, "Pamela's first words were, 'I have a present for you.'" Pamela held a pin of carved ebony, a Venetian blackamoor with a turban encrusted with diamonds and sapphires that she pinned to the lapel of Brooke's black suit. "Don't ever give this away or sell it," Pamela told Brooke. "It's very valuable."

Brooke knew that such pins were not only expensive, they were, as she later said, "the 'in' jewelry at the time," chic favorites of such style setters as Diana Vreeland, who had worn them "in rows and rows" since she first discovered them at Cartier in Paris. Brooke loved glamour, and in different circumstances she might have been thrilled by Pamela's gesture. But instead of feeling gratitude, she was offended. The pin, she later said, was "vulgar" and "not my taste," and she recoiled at Pamela's clumsy reference to money. To Brooke, "Pamela revealed the first aspect of her character . . . I watched her more carefully and determined she liked to have expensive things."

Over dinner with her father and Pamela that evening, Brooke found her disappointing in every way. "My father's sales pitch was a whole lot more colorful than the actual person," Brooke recalled. "Maybe she was subdued that evening, but I saw nothing. Really interesting women were crazy about my father—women who were bigger than life and dazzling—my mother, Slim, Babe Paley. I didn't get it. There was no razzle-dazzle. I couldn't figure this out. She didn't know about politics or the theater. She was a banal milkmaid, a little plump, certainly not beautiful. She wore expensive clothes but she didn't have flair."

What Brooke failed to appreciate was that her father needed a respite from the solipsistic theatricality of Slim and Maggie. "Pamela arrived in Leland's life with something he had never experienced, her famous talent for cocooning a man," said Michael Thomas. "He was taken aback and he succumbed. Pamela was also a very sexy woman, and she came into this sterile, neurasthenic, hyper-noisy atmosphere. These people were the most asexual group, never a whiff of pheromones in the air. They were glamorous but unromantic. Pam was European. She had something none of them had."

At the end of the summer, Brooke dined with Pamela again and found her intriguingly transformed: "She was no longer flat about politics and theater," she said. By reading show business newspapers and paying close attention to discussions about theatrical productions, Pamela had learned enough about Hayward's world "to keep the conversation in play." She had absorbed box-office grosses, learned the names of entertainment figures, and even studied the way other wives performed their duties. "She was fascinated by show business," said a woman in their social circle. "She was hanging on every word, Leland's or anyone's."

In her fashion, Pamela tried to win the affection of the three unruly young adults who entered her life. "I had never been exposed to problems like that, so I really didn't believe it," she later said. "I thought it was just because someone hadn't taken care of them, so I tried."

"Pamela spent a lot of time trying to charm everyone," said Bill Hayward. "She gave beautiful presents to the girls, and she was terribly nice to me. It was very important that the children approve of Leland and Pamela being together." She doted on Brooke's little boys, inviting them to tea and stuffing their pockets with candy. She helped Brooke decorate an apartment in New York and lent her a cleaning woman twice a week. "I didn't like her, but I was impressed," Brooke said. "Despite the fact that she was entering a world that was totally Slim's turf, that didn't seem to affect Pam. She was like some bizarre mutant—an insect doing what it has to do despite all the dreadful things around it."

Brooke sided with Slim, although they weren't close. While reserving her maternal love for Margaret Sullavan, Brooke had managed to incorporate Slim comfortably into her life, largely because she admired her stepmother's personality and style. It was different with Pamela. "For Brooke, Pam would have constituted a real threat to her relationship with her father," said Michael Thomas. "She behaved badly when Pam came along."

Bridget Hayward moved from Riggs to a Manhattan studio apartment in the fall of 1959 and fell in love with William Francisco, a promising young stage director at Yale for whom she did production work. Knowing that Bridget was Leland's favorite, Pamela tried her best to win her over. She frequently invited her for dinner and took her on shopping expeditions to Seventh Avenue clothing designers. Long parted from her mother, Bridget warmed to the attention from her father and his new friend. "Bridget was very devoted to Leland and to Pamela," said Leonora Hornblow. In his many conversations with Bridget, Bill Francisco never heard her criticize Pamela. "My feeling was that Bridget was so crazy about Leland, anything that made him happy was okay with her. Pamela was really marvelous to both of us, friendly and warm and open," said Francisco.

In the months after he separated from Slim, Leland Hayward was nearly overwhelmed by stress. He was racing to open *The Sound of Music* in November, and *Goodbye Charlie,* a comedy by George Axelrod starring Lauren Bacall, in December, to be followed by a live television show, *The Fabulous Fifties,* on CBS in January 1960. "It was a harrowing period," said Axelrod. *The Sound of Music* tried out in two cities, New Haven and Boston, while *Goodbye Charlie* was on the road for eight weeks in Pittsburgh, Detroit, Cleveland, Baltimore, and Philadelphia. "I remember long airplane rides between Boston and Pittsburgh, Boston and Detroit, Boston and Philadelphia, and trying to settle all the problems of both plays at the same time," Hayward wrote years later.

"It is utterly miserable here right now," he reported at the end of July 1959 to Lauren Bacall, who was resting in Biarritz before her Broadway debut. "I'm really swamped . . . I am sitting in black-dark-dirty un-airconditioned theatres looking at hundreds of people and wondering what in God's name ever made them think they had any talent in the theatre."

"I'm spinning like a top," he reported to Bacall in August, confiding that he had been faking his progress on the fifties show to the CBS sponsor, General Electric. When CBS pressed him, he became testy. "This show is the most difficult undertaking anyone has ever had in television," he crabbed to CBS executive Dick Lewine. "I beg of you please don't get on my back, because it only drives me crazy and makes me quit work for a couple of days."

Pamela, meanwhile, set about organizing her life with Hayward. While she stayed at the Drake, Hayward parked in an apartment lent to him by Harry Kurnitz. By September, Pamela had rented an apartment at the Carlyle Hotel so she and Leland could live together at last. Cholly Knickerbocker announced Pamela's two-year lease in his column, adding that she was "redecorating the apartment for all it's worth." She brought in the furniture that remained from Paris, which, Knickerbocker noted in his column, was "given to her back in the days when she was being courted by Fiat tycoon Gianni Agnelli," and she enlisted Paul Manno, the top Manhattan interior designer associated with her old friend Stéphane Boudin, to help her with the redecoration.

She took on her new role as theatrical helpmate, accompanying Hayward on the road for his out-of-town tryouts. But she stayed in the background, and Hayward seemed inclined to keep her there. At the runthrough before *The Sound of Music* hit the road, Russel Crouse and his wife Anna met Pamela for the first time as she stood with Hayward at the rear of the theater. Hayward took them aside, told them that Slim was sitting in the front with Jerome Robbins, and said, "You must not tell Slim that Pam is here." "That made us feel very peculiar," said Anna Crouse. "We were fond of Slim." Pamela remained so unobtrusive that in his diary Russel Crouse noted her presence just once, during drinks at the Ritz on the day they all arrived in Boston. "She just did not make an impression," said Anna Crouse.

The Sound of Music, starring Mary Martin, opened on November 16, 1959, with a black-tie party afterward for hundreds of friends at the St. Regis Hotel Roof. "It was a rare phenomenon," wrote Broadway columnist Dorothy Kilgallen, "to see male first nighters with tears streaming down their cheeks." The evening also served as Pamela's official debut as Hayward's fiancée. Dancing with Pamela "eclipsed the entire evening," pianist Colin Romoff wrote to Hayward afterward. In photographs of the event, Pamela looked matronly, with a slight double chin and full upper arms accentuated by her sleeveless evening dress. Needless to say, Slim did not appear.

The most influential critics, led by Brooks Atkinson at *The New York Times,* dismissed the plot of the new musical as hackneyed and sentimental. *The New Yorker*'s Kenneth Tynan called the show "Rodgers and Hammerstein's Great Leap Backwards. . . . The book is damp and dowdy, like a remaindered novelette." But audiences were enchanted by the sweet score and uplifting tale of a fresh-faced governess who captures the heart of an Austrian aristocrat and his children during the Nazi *Anschluss.* The day after the opening, hundreds of people lined up waiting for ticket returns. "Make no mistake about it," Hammerstein said after the mixed reviews, "this is a huge hit."

Hayward was not so lucky with *Goodbye Charlie,* the story of what he once described as a "kind of Frank Sinatra wolf" who dies and comes back to earth as a woman. Despite incessant tinkering by George Axelrod, who was both the author and the director, audiences and critics were repelled by the show's conceit. After a dismal opening night in Pittsburgh, Pamela shocked the company by reading the hostile reviews aloud, adding her own surprisingly vulgar characterizations of the reviewers. "She stood up on a chair," recalled one onlooker that evening. "She was improvising, and I was embarrassed for Leland, who was sort of subdued in a corner. She was livid, and she uttered words that came from left field."

On December 16, *Goodbye Charlie* limped onto Broadway, where the New York critics tore it apart. After a three-month run, the show was declared a financial flop by *Variety,* although the investors sold the screen rights and recovered all their money. *Goodbye Charlie* was a blow not only to Hayward and his company but to Pamela as well. The morning after the opening, she wrote to property developer Harold Christie in Nassau, a friend of Max Beaverbrook's, asking if he could help her locate a cottage complete with a maid or cook that she could rent for two to three weeks. "I want to come and rest," she wrote, "and be as far away from the gay crowd as possible."

Hayward, meanwhile, was encountering stiff resistance from Slim about the divorce. Throughout the summer and fall he had made numerous efforts to mollify her. "Give Nan my love," he said at the end of each of his letters to Bacall in Biarritz. Slim had made her displeasure known through the gossip columns. On August 16, Cholly Knickerbocker announced that "Slim Hayward's close pals say that producer-husband Leland will have to pay a high price for his freedom. Slim will ask for a good part of their properties as well as a hefty financial settlement."

In October, Hayward's business manager Herman Bernstein wrote to Slim offering a "rooting interest" of one quarter of 1 percent of *The Sound of Music* that Hayward had bought on her behalf for $2,000. As producer of the show, Hayward received for his services the rights to 10 percent of the profits, but he hadn't invested any of his own money. To give Slim her own small stake,

Hayward bought a sliver of the 5 percent owned by Lindsay and Crouse as investors. "I had the right to put up about fifteen cents," Hayward groused to Sam Spiegel. "What I had the right to put up, I gave to Nan, and that was as much as I wanted to."

Slim signed the agreement for her *Sound of Music* share, but she was not assuaged. When she returned to New York in mid-October from Europe, her injured feelings had turned to rage—in part because Pamela overplayed her hand. "I went to our house in Manhasset," she later wrote, "and learned from my cook that Pam had been in residence. Leland vehemently denied it—but there, on furniture and paintings, were red stickers that Pam had planted to indicate which treasures she wanted Leland to get in the divorce." Slim decided, she later said, "to get the toughest lawyer in town to fight for my fair share."

Pamela tried to allay the money worries of Hayward's daughters. "She told us this divorce was going to be crippling financially, but all was going to be well because she had all the jewelry anyone could want, all the furs, all the Louis XVI furniture," said Brooke. Concluding that Pamela was as boastful as she was materialistic, Brooke came to dislike her even more.

On New Year's Day 1960, three hours before she was due onstage in a new play trying out in New Haven, Margaret Sullavan committed suicide by taking an overdose of sleeping pills. Hayward asked Pamela to bring the bad news to Brooke, the closest of the three children to Sullavan. Brooke was preparing for her role in *Marching Song,* an Off-Broadway play, when Pamela arrived, "her face a phantasmagoria of white against a background of black sable." Her black limousine, Brooke noted ominously, was "like a sleek bird of prey, one wing outstretched to encompass me." Explaining her presence, Pamela said, perhaps too pointedly, that Hayward was "all tied up with phone calls to Bridget and Bill."

Brooke was angry at her father for failing to appear in person, but she was even more resentful of Pamela, despite the "indescribably sweet tone to her voice" and her "understanding smile." When Pamela awkwardly raised the possibility of suicide, Brooke was angry. "She had never even *met* mother," Brooke wrote in her memoir. "There was something obscene about *her* telling me that. . . . No aspect of this was any of Pamela's business. . . . The last thing I'd asked for was the insinuation of an outsider, particularly a lady who was working too hard at becoming my next stepmother."

Back in the apartment at the Carlyle, Pamela worked the phones to help make arrangements after Sullavan's distraught husband, Kenneth Wagg, proposed what Hayward called "some sort of macabre service while she's being cremated." Most of Pamela's efforts were directed at Bridget, because Hayward feared she might fall apart. "Leland and Pamela kept Bridget with them," said Bill Francisco. "She had her own apartment but they took her in and took care of her."

Brooke was galled by the efficiency with which Pamela busied herself with logistics. "Leland darling, the Logans thought it might be nice for all of us to come out to the country for lunch the day after tomorrow," Pamela interjected at one point. "It would be a lovely drive—and they do agree that there *must* be some form of memorial service, so we'll talk to Kenneth again in the morning and explain to him how everyone feels about it." Reflecting later on Pamela's performance that day, Brooke dryly observed, "Life was so easy, if one could learn how to compartmentalize it."

Hayward and Pamela seemed only momentarily diverted by Margaret Sullavan's death. Barely a week later, they popped up in the columns, with the London *Evening Standard* reporting: "Mrs. Pamela Churchill has found a firm friend in Broadway producer Leland Hayward. The couple have been dining and dancing until the early hours in New York's El Morocco Club." Hayward was once again immersed in his work as he hurtled toward the January 31 deadline for his CBS special on the fifties. Television fascinated Hayward, especially the immediacy of live broadcasts. Since his successful stagings of the Ford show and *Peter Pan* earlier in the decade, his efforts to make another splash had been repeatedly thwarted. In 1954, one of his attacks of internal bleeding had forced him to withdraw from producing a series of "spectaculars" on NBC, a retreat that filled him with regret and, as he put it, "tremendous guilt."

From September 1959 onward, Hayward had been scribbling memos every week or so to his second in command, Marshall Jamison, bursting with ideas for the program he envisioned as a "roller coaster ride through the decade's spots, high and low, great and small." As Jamison recalled, "Leland always had good ideas, but we had to forget some of them."

One scheme that preoccupied Hayward for five months was a proposal to have a camera crew film French sex symbol Brigitte Bardot—who was confined to her bed for a difficult pregnancy—reading the Declaration of Independence in broken English. The juxtaposition, Hayward believed, would "give the audience a kind of zing." Mercifully, Bardot's producer Raoul Levy wrote Hayward in January to say that he had "neither the time nor the courage to convince her" that reading the Declaration "would do her any good."

Hayward nevertheless managed to put together an all-star cast for the CBS program: Henry Fonda and newsman Eric Severeid as hosts; Rex Harrison and Julie Andrews in a scene from *My Fair Lady;* Jackie Gleason in *Take Me Along;* comedians Shelley Berman, Mike Nichols, and Elaine May; singers Frank Sinatra and Bing Crosby; and Ed Murrow, who supplied segments from his documentary series, *See It Now.* The two-hour spectacular attracted a huge audience, universal accolades, and an Emmy Award.

Two weeks after the CBS show, Hayward and Pamela moved into a rented house at 282 Camino Carmelita in Palm Springs for what he told friends was a "three or four weeks rest." After nearly two years without a day off, Hayward was thoroughly exhausted. He slept at least twelve hours a night and spent most of his days relaxing in the sunshine while Pamela tended to his every need. The Goetzes, the Stewarts, and other Hollywood luminaries came to visit, and Pamela captivated them all.

Hayward's relationship with Slim had grown increasingly bitter. "Leland had the balls to ask *me* to sit out in Nevada for six weeks so he could get a quick divorce and marry Pam pronto," said Slim years later. Slim refused. After several weeks in Palm Springs, Hayward moved to the Sands Hotel in Las Vegas to satisfy the six-week residency requirement for a Nevada divorce.

Hayward and Pamela played the slots and the blackjack tables during the week and escaped across the border to Palm Springs for the weekends. Hayward conducted business long-distance, reading scripts and keeping in touch with his colleagues on Broadway and at the television networks. With little else to do but eat, Pamela put on fifteen pounds. According to an affidavit filed with Leland Hayward's estate, Slim ultimately initiated a divorce proceeding in April 1960. Her new boyfriend, Ted Bassett, a socialite who made his living gambling on backgammon and bridge games at the Racquet & Tennis Club on Park Avenue, leapt at the chance to bring legal documents to Hayward in Las Vegas. Boyfriend and ex-husband-to-be spent several days together at the gaming tables.

The final settlement with Slim "wasn't drastic," said one of Hayward's advisers. "Slim was a wealthy lady." At the moment of his divorce, Hayward had cash to spare. The banking records for just one account in his name at Bankers Trust in 1959 show deposits totaling $947,856 (roughly $5 million today). "There was good cash flow," said his adviser. Slim got the house in Manhasset, along with a lump-sum financial settlement, furniture, and some art.

Eventually the animosity receded between Slim and Hayward. Within two years she married a wealthy English divorcé, Sir Kenneth Keith, and gained a place in the English upper-class world of shooting parties and formal dinners. A decade later she moved back to New York—alone—and lived proudly as Lady Keith. "Ten years, that was usually my run," she said. For all her bad behavior during their marriage, she never got over Hayward—and he kept his affection for her. When she was seriously ill in the late 1960s, Hayward wrote her a tender letter saying he hoped she felt better: "You have no right to ever be sick." "My number isn't up yet," she replied to "dearest Hay." Behind Pamela's back, Hayward visited Slim periodically in her apartment at the Pierre Hotel. He would announce himself by calling her from a phone booth: "Can I come up and say hello?" "He'd zip over," she wrote, "and five minutes later he'd be talking about the children or his work."

Pamela and Leland were married on May 4, 1960, only hours after his divorce was final. They flew to Carson City for a ceremony performed by Chief Justice Frank McNamee of the Nevada Supreme Court. "It happened all so quickly," said her son Winston, who was then a student at Oxford. "The first I knew was when I got a photo of them getting married in Nevada and honeymooning in Las Vegas." In Pamela's eyes, a perfunctory civil service was totally inadequate, however. As a Catholic, she wanted to be married properly. Hayward's civil marriage to Slim was invalid in the eyes of the Church, and Margaret Sullavan was dead. So was his first wife, Lola, but that union "was a problem," Pamela explained, because Leland had married her in a Catholic church and consequently needed an annulment. Lola "had died in an alcoholic home," said Pamela, "so they had to go to Cardinal Spellman to get a dispensation for

Leland." It took another year of sworn statements that the two marriages to Lola were invalid before an annulment was granted. Leland and Pamela Hayward were sanctified in a Catholic service near the home of Josh and Nedda Logan in South Brookfield, Connecticut. Afterward, the Logans blessed them socially with a reception in their quaint red saltbox house, and Pamela finally had everything in order.

After the civil ceremony in Nevada, Cholly Knickerbocker had observed, "So now Pamela has traded her famous last name to become Mrs. Hayward. It must be love." Knickerbocker assumed too much. Pamela had no intention of stripping Churchill from her I.D., even though her annulment ten years earlier gave her the means to do so. She chose to call herself Pamela Churchill Hayward. On paper she styled herself "The Honorable Mrs. Pamela Churchill Hayward," the "Honorable" deriving from her Digby days, not from her Churchill affiliation.

As if Las Vegas, Carson City, and Palm Springs weren't alien enough for a Dorset-born aristocrat, three days after her wedding Pamela found herself at a Holiday Inn in Topeka, Kansas, for the marriage of Bill Hayward, recently enlisted in the army, to Marilla Nelson, an Iowa girl who checked herself into Menninger's after her parents were killed in an auto accident.

Pamela's relations with Bill had begun shakily in the frantic days following Margaret Sullavan's suicide. After being discharged by Menninger's, Bill was living in a nearby apartment and majoring in math at the University of Kansas when his father called. Before flying home for the funeral, Bill had tried to use his father's credit card to buy a black suit, only to have his purchase vetoed by "some lady" back in New York. He called Brooke, assuming she was the culprit, and learned for the first time about Pamela. Once again, Hayward's instinct for avoidance had caused an unnecessary rift. "I knew that Father and Nan had some kind of problem; he'd told me that," said Bill. "But I had no idea there was another woman involved. And she nixed the charge . . . I was extremely pissed off."

Pamela made amends when she invited Bill to stay at the Carlyle. "She just made me feel wonderful in a weird way, with her eye contact, her sincerity, her tone of voice," he recalled. "She was not maternal and not sexual, just attentive and charming. It may have worked on me because I was eighteen and unsophisticated." When they next met in Topeka for his wedding, Pamela still held him in her spell. "In that early going I was charmed by her, yes I was," he said. Brooke and Bridget were also on hand for Bill's wedding, and Brooke was amused to watch Pamela's efforts to seem comfortable in tacky surroundings of plywood paneling and motel modern. "Father took everyone to dinner at a nearby steak house," Brooke wrote in her memoir. "All the women except Pamela, Bridget and me wore their hair in sprayed beehives."

After a brief stop in New York, Pamela and Hayward landed in London on May 18 for a three-week honeymoon, shuttling between her snug flat in Hyde Park Gardens and the Ritz in Paris. They visited friends and saw plays in London's West End.

In Parisian society, Pamela's return as a married woman sparked a new round of chatter. *Paris Match* director Hervé Mille gave a lunch with a guest list that included Stavros Niarchos and social chronicler Elsa Maxwell. "From the beginning of lunch until the end," reported Maxwell, "we discussed one subject—Pamela Churchill, now Mrs. Leland Hayward. It was so amusing for two hours to hear some of the fine minds of Paris interested only in Pam. The man that she married—what was he like? Was he attractive? Was he rich? I said that he is an attractive man, of course, an old friend of mine, I added, very much in the theater. When he is a success on Broadway, he is rich; when he has a flop or two, which happens to all producers, he is broke. I told them I received a telegram from the Haywards saying how happy they were."

That much was evident to those who saw them. They had triumphed over the difficult circumstances of their courtship—public criticism, suicide, hostile children, and an antagonistic former wife—in large measure because of the adaptability and determination Pamela displayed after committing herself to marry Hayward. "Once Pam appeared on the scene, she dug in and never let go," said Brooke Hayward. For his part, Hayward seemed grateful. "I saw happy people who wanted to get on with their lives," said Leonora Hornblow. "They couldn't believe they had found each other. There was great harmony between Pamela and Leland. There had been stormy passages in their lives and now they had a safe harbor."

Twenty-two

BARELY A MONTH after she and Hayward returned from their honeymoon, Pamela arranged the purchase of a fifteen-room apartment—three times the size of any place Leland Hayward had lived in with Slim. Located at the corner of Fifth Avenue and 83rd Street, the Haywards' new residence took up an entire floor of one of the Upper East Side's most desirable buildings and overlooked Central Park and the Metropolitan Museum of Art.

For the second time within a year, Pamela brought in Paul Manno and Stéphane Boudin to handle the redecoration. This time the work was considerably more extensive. According to Manno, the cost came to "the equivalent of $1 million today" Pamela paid $220,000 (around $1.1 million in current dollars) of the money she pocketed from the sale of her Paris residence to buy the apartment, but the bill for redecorating was taken care of by Hayward.

The effect Boudin created was formal and decidedly French, sumptuous but rather cold. At the entrance to the new apartment, a spacious gallery led down several steps to a large drawing room with high ceilings and oversize windows facing the park. The sunken drawing room, in which Pamela arranged the best Louis XVI pieces she brought from Paris, was painted and glazed a pale gray, with gilded moldings. Boudin draped the windows in fuschia silk curtains and covered all the cushions in pale silk. To create a harmonious setting for Pamela's furniture, he installed an eighteenth-century French mantelpiece to replace the handsome antique English one that had been the pride of the apartment's previous owners. Pamela had an impressive collection of antique clocks, and these were placed around the room: "clocks like lions that spout water out of their mouths, clocks with little men who run down hills, clocks that tock and rock," in the words of an awed writer for *Town & Country* magazine. The only notable paintings were a Vuillard interior and a portrait of a young man by Soutine. Both had been purchased by Hayward and Sullavan in 1944 for $4,900 and $1,600, respectively.

On one side of the foyer was a library and on the other a dining room where Boudin covered the walls with canvas painted in a design of trellises and flowers. The painting was done in Paris by the noted muralist Pierre-Marie Rudelle, who also painted the window shades with bouquets of flowers tumbling from urns. A round mahogany table seated a dozen guests. Boudin also redid the bedrooms. In the European manner, Pamela and Leland had separate rooms, with a sitting room between. Hers was silky and feminine, with a lovely small fireplace.

Hayward indulged Pamela's expensive tastes as he had Slim's. After Pamela's new chef complained about the heat in the kitchen, Hayward contacted a top executive at General Electric to find the ideal air conditioner. But while Hayward was accustomed to beautifully decorated homes, he seemed vaguely uncomfortable in his surroundings at 1020 Fifth Avenue. "It was too grand for Leland," said Anita Colby. "He liked to be in his stocking feet."

Besides decorating, Pamela spent several months attending weekly cooking classes taught by Helen Worth. Along with other prominent women in the school, including Bennett Cerf's wife Phyllis, Pamela's goal was less learning how to cook than understanding how to instruct her new chef and plan menus for dinner parties in the American style. Hayward busied himself trying to find a new Broadway show. On weekends they escaped to a cottage in Bedford, New York, that Irene Selznick had lent them for the summer. Although Hayward disliked the country, he fell into a relaxing routine by devoting virtually all his time to photographing flowers. Young Winston Churchill, by then twenty years old, spent most of the summer with his mother and new stepfather, whom he took to instantly. "I enjoyed his open manner and dry humour," he later wrote, "as well as sharing his passion for photography and later for flying."

Winston had been eager to meet Hayward as early as June the previous year, when he came to Paris and "got word that there was a new man in my mother's life." Winston went to a dance and returned home at dawn determined to greet Hayward when he arrived three hours later. Instead, Winston fell asleep in his evening clothes. On awakening that afternoon, Winston learned that Hayward had gone. "My mother didn't wake me," explained Winston, "because she thought I might react as adversely to Leland as I had to Elie, and she didn't want to get off on the wrong foot."

When Winston came back to New York after his mother's honeymoon, he needed a car to replace the Fiat 600 she had given him several years earlier. Winston had suggested a modestly priced new car, but when he showed her a brochure on the automobile, she announced, " 'I don't think much of that,' adding," Winston recalled, "almost as an afterthought, 'I would like to give you a Jaguar!' " Thanks to Hayward, she had the funds to do so. That summer Pamela seemed eager to make up for her previous inattention to her only child. "Winston seemed a nice straightforward eager-beaver kid," said Brooke Hayward. "He was very attached to his mummy, attentive to her and she to him." Winston wrote in his memoirs, "I had not seen my mother so radiant and happy in many a year."

The radiance dimmed under the shadow of another family tragedy. Bridget Hayward, who had been showing signs of a deepening depression, committed suicide on October 17, 1960—nearly ten months after her mother's death. "I am convinced Maggie's suicide set the idea in Bridget's head," said Bill Francisco, who along with Leland Hayward found Bridget dead in her small East Side apartment. "It was Maggie's death plus her own illness that drove her to suicide." The exact nature of her illness remains unclear. In her memoir, Brooke said it was epilepsy, for which Bridget was being treated with Dilantin, an anti-convulsive medication. According to Francisco, however, Bridget learned that summer that she was suffering from some sort of degenerative condition. "The doctor she saw in New Haven indicated Bridget had three or four years to live," said Francisco, who only heard about the diagnosis from Hayward and Pamela several months after Bridget's death.

Bridget took an overdose of sleeping pills, which, like her father, she relied on for severe insomnia. Leland Hayward was evidently the source of her supply. In a letter to Dr. Saul Fox on October 5, Hayward had asked, in addition to the regular order for himself, that Fox send each of his daughters a large bottle of "the only thing in the world that makes Mary Martin and Nedda Logan sleep . . . Di-Seds, the ones where half goes off now and half four hours later." Brooke recalled receiving the pills ordered by her father. "Sure, I was horrified," she said. "But I also thought it was funny and didn't realize how serious it was."

Once again Leland asked Pamela to break the news to Brooke. When she appeared at the door of Brooke's apartment on West 81st Street, "I gazed at her," Brooke wrote in her memoir, "hypnotized by the inexorable chic of her pale blue suit and the long twisted rope of pearls and turquoises banded by a row of diamonds every two inches or so that hung gracefully knotted against her silk blouse." As Pamela relayed the details of Bridget's death—the "disturbing" note she left, the need for an autopsy—Brooke considered the "brisk businesslike tone I admired for its British sense of mission." But she bristled when Pamela insisted that Brooke check her emotions when she saw her father, for fear that too much stress could set off one of his episodes of internal bleeding. "You must be strong and brave, Brooke, absolutely no tears, really, because I cannot have him made any more upset than he already is. . . . You are supposed to be an actress." Recalling that moment three decades later, Brooke was still angry. "It was a helluva burden she put on me," said Brooke.

Driving across town in her father's recently purchased limousine, Brooke watched Pamela "automatically" reach for her compact, powder her face, and apply lipstick, while taking note of her "freshly polished" fingernails and her "newly shaped . . . auburn hair, with its natural gray streak rising perfectly from her forehead." Once in the apartment with the Logans, Axelrods, and Bill Francisco, Brooke embraced her father while tears streamed down his cheeks. Again Brooke marveled at Pamela's composure. "Come Leland darling," Pamela said. "We're having your favorite—vichyssoise and chicken hash—a new recipe from the head chef at the Beverly Hills Hotel."

Pamela showed kindness to Bill Francisco. "The night of the suicide her concern was getting me food, getting me into a room and to sleep. She called a doctor who came in and gave me a sedative," he recalled. "Then she sat with me during the funeral and held my hand and took care of me." With her customary efficiency, Pamela also dealt with numerous details. She found a burial plot in Hartsdale, New York, planned a buffet luncheon to follow the funeral, and enlisted Brooke to help select a dress in which Bridget would be buried.

Brooke and Pamela went to Bridget's apartment together. After they chose the dress, according to Brooke, they retrieved some of Margaret Sullavan's jewelry that had been stored in the apartment for safekeeping: two strands of pearls that Sullavan had designated for her two daughters, along with a valuable 3.89-carat emerald ring that Hayward had bought for Sullavan. By Brooke's account, Pamela urged Brooke to entrust her with the jewelry. To reassure her stepdaughter, Pamela gave her a tour of her custom-built safe at 1020 Fifth Avenue. The safe extended from the floor to the ceiling in Pamela's dressing room and contained more than a dozen drawers. Each drawer, lined in gray moleskin, had its own combination lock and contained a specific kind of gem— diamonds in one drawer, pearls in another, emeralds in another. Brooke said both Pamela and her father told her that the pearls and emerald ring would be secure in Pamela's custody, but Brooke never saw them again. Asked by a *Washington Post* reporter in 1983 about Brooke's story, Pamela replied, "What jewels? I was never asked to hold any jewels. I never knew her mother had any jewels."

Brooke also recalled hearing from Pamela that Bridget had left her father her trust fund (set up by Margaret Sullavan two decades earlier with earnings from a hit play), along with $25,000 in her savings account (the proceeds from a Sullavan life insurance policy). According to Brooke, Pamela remarked that the money "certainly will come in handy at this particular time." "My God, I thought," Brooke wrote in her memoir. "Is this what happens whenever somebody dies?"

In the months following Bridget's suicide, Hayward was occupied with a promising new play. A French agent named André Bernheim had alerted Hayward to a new hit comedy in Paris called *"L'Idiote"* by Marcel Achard. Arthur Hornblow, who was fluent in French, read the script and urged Hayward to buy it. The day of Bridget's suicide, Hayward and Pamela had been preparing to fly to France, and they made the trip a month later. After seeing the play, Hayward bought the rights on the spot and hired Harry Kurnitz to write the English adaptation, to be called *A Shot in the Dark*. Harold Clurman signed on to direct, and he brought in Julie Harris to star. Although Pamela played no special role in the negotiations, her friendship with Achard and Bernheim smoothed Hayward's way. "In Paris, Pam and Leland worked the city well," said a former associate of Hayward's. "She knew Achard and the other Continental types. She was very much at ease with them. She also knew all the couturier people, who were always rushing into the hotel with boxes."

Kurnitz zipped through four drafts of the play in eight months, a process that took the Haywards on several transatlantic trips, with stops in Paris, London, and the Riviera, where Pamela took Hayward to dine with Max Beaverbrook at La Capponcina. *A Shot in the Dark* opened on October 18, 1961, just a year after Bridget's death. The critics loved it, the show was a certified hit, and Hayward's spirits soared.

The Sound of Music, meanwhile, was expanding and prospering. A second company starring Florence Henderson began a triumphant national tour in Detroit in February 1961. The Haywards, writers Lindsay and Crouse, and Richard Halliday journeyed out on the train, a traveling cocktail party where everyone drank for hours and traded "bum jokes," according to Crouse. After opening night, recalled Marshall Jamison, "I remember Leland and Pam were really ecstatic. They were very happy together. That was a very good night for Leland, and she looked absolutely gorgeous. I thought then it was going to be a terrific marriage."

The London opening in May was a major event. Many members of Pamela's family, including Lady Rosebery and the Duke and Duchess of Norfolk, as well as an assortment of Churchills, were invited as guests of honor. The night before the official opening, there was a benefit performance for the Duchess of Kent's favorite charity. "Tonight royalty, tomorrow night royalties," cracked Russel Crouse in a telegram to Hayward.

After a year of marriage, Pamela had defined her role as a producer's wife. She always accompanied Leland on out-of-town tryouts and laid down precise requirements for their accommodations: a two-bedroom suite with a living room and kitchen (or at the very least a refrigerator), along with an adjacent bedroom for her maid. Pamela filled the rooms with flowers, rearranged the furniture, and unpacked her special suitcase full of pillows, table covers, photos, and bibelots. Because Hayward was so finicky about his eating and drinking, she ordered that the refrigerator be stocked in advance with everything he would require, including milk, chocolate and vanilla ice cream, white bread, eggs, and cold chicken. She also packed an electric frying pan if there was no kitchen in the suite.

Late at night, as Hayward and his production team argued over scripts, "I would cook them chicken hash because after eleven at night there was no hotel service," Pamela told Diane Sawyer in 1983 on the CBS Morning News. "I was very good at that. I got into a habit. I always went out and got my chicken and diced it up and got my frying pan and got it all—all organized. There were strange smells in the corridors of the hotel but my chicken hash was very good."

In numerous interviews over the years, Pamela dispensed a stock characterization of the theatrical life: "The theater and politics are alike. They're both made up of triumphs and disasters." Beyond that observation, she had little to say publicly about Hayward's profession—and she certainly never duplicated her unseemly outburst in Pittsburgh during *Goodbye Charlie*. Still, in the early years of their marriage, she tried to exert some influence on her husband's professional life. At rehearsals she sat in the theater as Slim had done, and took notes. During discussions afterward she would make observations that Hayward took in along with everyone else's comments.

Following the success of *A Shot in the Dark*, Hayward threw himself into producing a new musical called *Mr. President* that seemed destined to succeed, primarily because of the stellar collaboration of Broadway veterans behind it: composer and lyricist Irving Berlin; director Josh Logan; producer Leland Hayward; and the writing team of Howard Lindsay and Russel Crouse, who dreamed up the show in May 1961. The two writers had previously crafted three enormous hits for Hayward: *State of the Union, Call Me Madam,* and *The Sound of Music.*

At age seventy-three, Lindsay was a Broadway mainstay with extensive experience as an actor, director, and playwright. Crouse had been a press agent and journalist before forming a partnership with Lindsay in 1934. Lindsay was somewhat pompous, while Crouse, four years his junior, was gentle and droll. Together, according to Irving Berlin's biographer Laurence Bergreen, they excelled at "devising Broadway vehicles—literate, intriguing scenarios—rather than expressing their own ideas and emotions." In *State of the Union,* Lindsay and Crouse had effectively dramatized a campaign for the presidency. Now they sought to write a musical about a President retiring from office after two successful terms, and trying, in Hayward's words, to "remain a useful citizen." When Lindsay and Crouse described the plot, seventy-three-year-old Irving Berlin was, according to Hayward, "deliriously happy," and came out of a ten-year retirement to write the first four songs within a week. The show would cost $450,000 to produce. Columbia Records invested $200,000, and the five members of the production team put up the remaining $250,000.

Having succeeded by basing *Call Me Madam* on an identifiable Washington celebrity, Hayward and his colleagues saw an opportunity to capitalize on the glamour of John Fitzgerald Kennedy's Camelot by portraying a charismatic Irish American President, Stephen Decatur Henderson, and his fashionable wife. For Leland and Pamela Hayward, the Kennedy connection reflected their social aspirations more than any political beliefs.

Leland Hayward's politics had little to do with ideology and everything to do with expediency. In the postwar years, he joined the Finance Committee of Citizens for Eisenhower-Nixon, chaired by Jock Whitney. In addition to contributing $1,000, Hayward solicited funds from many show business friends, including Irene Selznick, Richard Rodgers, Howard Lindsay, Irving Berlin, and Gilbert Miller, and recruited talent for a rally in Madison Square Garden to promote Eisenhower's candidacy. Eisenhower wrote Hayward thanking him for his "strong support."

Pamela knew Jack Kennedy through his late sister Kick, but Hayward had not met him before his election. Hayward did know the President's father and brother Bobby. Joe Kennedy had become acquainted with Hayward through his investments in Hollywood movies in the late 1920s, and he greatly admired Hayward's ability as a television producer. In November 1960, Leland had sent a congratulatory wire to the senior Kennedy, who immediately invited Hayward and Pamela to the inaugural celebration. Somewhat surprisingly, they never appeared. Pamela told a television interviewer in 1992 that Hayward's work on *The Sound of Music,* coupled with the frigid weather, had prevented them from leaving New York for the inauguration. In fact, Pamela and Leland were in Palm Beach, vacationing at the home of Loel and Gloria Guinness.

The Haywards' official allegiance in the sixties was with the Democrats. They socialized with the Kennedys, attending several dinners at the White House and celebrating New Year's with them during vacations at the Guinnesses when the Kennedys were in residence at Palm Beach. Yet the Haywards were on equally friendly terms with prominent Republicans such as New York Senator Jacob Javits. Despite Pamela's contention that she and Hayward were "politically involved," their activism was limited to occasional modest financial contributions.

As *Mr. President* began taking shape in early 1962, both Haywards were eager to pull the Kennedys into the show's promotion. "It was Leland's idea and she supported it because of her chance to brush up against the famous," said a former associate of Hayward's. The Kennedys were flattered to be the subject of an adulatory musical by Irving Berlin. Just as Hayward was eager for their help in publicizing his show, they saw an opportunity to promote themselves. They agreed to sponsor the Washington premiere in September at the National Theater as a benefit for two Kennedy family charities. After the performance, British Ambassador David Ormsby-Gore and his wife, whom Pamela had known since her debutante year of 1938, were to give an opening-night party at the British Embassy.

Robert Ryan was cast as the President, with Nanette Fabray as First Lady. The production team chose Ryan, who had no experience in musical comedy, because "they wanted someone the audience would believe had the authority of the President," said Anna Crouse. Hayward was pleased with the casting, although in retrospect his first choice was more intriguing. "Ronald Reagan is very anxious to do a Broadway show, and is willing to sign for an unlimited time," he told Lindsay, Crouse, Berlin, and Logan. "As you will recall, he used to sing in the early Warner Brothers movies." *Variety* touted *Mr. President* as the biggest event of the fall season, boosting advance ticket sales to a new record of $2.65 million.

But by the time the show began its Boston tryout in late August, it was obvious that the production had substantial problems. Ryan was miscast, the story was shaky, the characters ill-defined. Berlin's score was among his worst, with forgettable tunes and lyrics that were embarrassingly out of touch with the times. After Boston critic Elliot Norton pronounced the show "dreadful," everyone flew into a panic. Berlin refused to tamper with the score or to cut even one song, although Lindsay and Crouse agreed to revise the script. But both writers were hampered by serious illness. When the show was being cast, Crouse had been stricken with a blood clot in his intestines and had undergone emergency abdominal surgery that he barely survived. Lindsay was so ill with leukemia that he would spend most of the Washington run in bed. "I begged Leland to postpone the show but he had arranged that big benefit for the Kennedy Foundation," said Anna Crouse. "He was all hell-bent to make it."

The Washington premiere of *Mr. President* on September 25, 1962, attracted a sold-out crowd of politicians, diplomats, and socialites. Bill and Babe Paley made the trip, as did Henry and Clare Luce, for what Nanette Fabray called "the biggest party of all time." Bobby and Ethel Kennedy were in the audience, along with several Kennedy sisters. First Lady Jacqueline sat in the presidential box next to her husband's empty rocking chair. Hayward fumed as he delayed the curtain by a half hour in hopes that the President would appear. But Kennedy didn't arrive until after the intermission. His absence distracted both the audience and the actors, making a bad show even worse. Kennedy's tardiness had not even been caused by the press of business. He had been watching a heavyweight boxing match between Floyd Patterson and Sonny Liston on closed circuit television at the White House. He and Jackie left the theater before the final curtain.

After the party later that night at the British Embassy, the Haywards, Crouses, and Berlins bought the *Washington Post* and rode up in the same elevator at the Mayflower Hotel. As the Haywards got off on their floor, Russel Crouse started to follow them. "Don't you come, you're bad luck," Hayward said. "I'll always remember those words," said Anna Crouse. "Russel had never been bad luck for Leland." Two nights later, Crouse called Hayward's suite, and Pamela answered the phone. "Anyone with any sense hates the play. I wish we could close it," she snapped. "I could have killed her that night," said Anna Crouse. "When they were trying their hardest, having someone say something like that didn't help." She wrote a note to Pamela pointing out that no matter what she might have thought, it was a time for encouragement. Pamela apologized to Russel Crouse for her harsh words.

The show opened a month later in New York to tepid reviews. When the Cuban missile crisis hit the headlines shortly afterward, the sentimental *Mr. President* seemed even more irrelevant. The advance ticket sale carried the production for eight months, and when the orders ran out, the show closed. Hayward made some money from *Mr. President*, but its critical reception flattened him. "Leland never got in touch with Russel after *Mr. President*," said Anna Crouse. "I find that unforgivable. Pam made Leland feel that Russel and Howard were no longer hot properties. It hurt Russel that he never heard from Leland again."

Leland Hayward had turned sixty on September 13, 1962, a milestone that he laughed off to friends as "the day I reach majority." It also marked a turning point in his career. After *Mr. President*, Hayward never again mounted a major production on Broadway, although he continued to pursue properties that caught his eye. He tried in vain to make two film classics—the romantic comedy *Roman Holiday* and the poignant drama *How Green Was My Valley*—into musicals; to transform the novel *The Film of Memory*, by Pamela's friend Maurice Druon, into a play; and to adapt the hit French play, *Croque Monsieur*, for the New York stage. Hayward spent a lot of his money on the *Croque Monsieur* project, including $10,000 for the French author, Marcel Mithois, and struggled for nearly two years until he lost the option.

In 1965 Hayward seemed on the verge of another hit, a musical based on William Inge's acclaimed play, *Picnic*. Josh Logan, who had directed the play, signed on for the new version, called *Hot September*. The writer was Paul Osborn, who had written Hayward's first Broadway play, *A Bell for Adano*. Hayward and Pamela—accompanied as usual by her personal maid—moved into a suite at the Ritz Carlton for the Boston tryout in early September. The show ran barely a month before Hayward shut it down, canceled the Broadway opening, and plunged into depression. "Bad luck plagues me," he wrote to Harry Kurnitz.

Hayward's relentlessly inquisitive temperament was still very much attuned to the times, and the Broadway stage in the sixties was as hospitable to Hayward-style productions as ever, with the arrival of Neil Simon's *Plaza Suite* and Arthur Miller's *The Price*, as well as the smash musicals *A Funny Thing Happened on the Way to the Forum* (which Hayward originally developed and then dropped when Jerome Robbins got tired of the rewriting and left the production), *Hello Dolly, Funny Girl, Fiddler on the Roof, Mame, and Cabaret.* "The money was easy, the capital was available, the productions were inexpensive, and the ticket prices hadn't zoomed out of sight," recalled veteran Broadway producer Alexander H. Cohen. Yet Hayward seemed to have lost his nerve; in a speech to the New Dramatists he admitted to feeling "genuinely frightened" about losing large sums of money on Broadway productions.

The key to Hayward's magic had always been his close relationships with the top talent of the day. But as big names like Oscar Hammerstein, Lindsay, and Crouse fell ill or died, Hayward had fewer personal connections on Broadway. He was not known for discovering young new playwrights. In his view, too many of the new generation were flawed by "a stubbornness about changes that exceeds those of established playwrights." He preferred plays "clearly and sharply written, no excess of words, with a driving instinct to tell a story." Of the hundreds of scripts he read each year, he estimated that only half of 1 percent satisfied his standards for storytelling.

Beyond the difficulty he had finding properties he wanted to stage, and attracting backers to finance them, Hayward suffered one significant turn of bad luck that hastened his decline as a producer. In 1964, his longtime manager Herman Bernstein died. Whereas Hayward's talent lay with promoting, casting, and raising money, Bernstein knew the nuts and bolts of putting a show on the stage—from structuring a deal to lining up a theater to hiring a master electrician and a prop man. Bernstein came to the office each day at seven-thirty and devoted himself totally to his boss. When Hayward lost Herman Bernstein, he lost his right arm, and he was unable to find a replacement as knowledgeable or reliable.

Hayward had also developed a serious drinking problem, although only his close associates were aware of it. His routine began each morning at the office where, according to Marshall Jamison, "He would have a couple of belts of Wild Turkey for mouthwash." At lunch he had another tumbler of his favorite bourbon, and afterward he usually took a nap before once again reaching for the glass on his desk. "He was the most contained heavy drinker I know," said a man who had lunch with Hayward frequently in the 1960s. Only at night, after Hayward switched to scotch, would he show signs of his boozing. "He got sleepy and groggy, but not boisterous," said a former associate. "That was his way of getting drunk." For all her attentiveness, Pamela proved as incapable of dealing with Hayward's alcoholism as she had been with the excesses of Randolph Churchill. After all, Hayward's mellowness was no doubt a welcome contrast to Randolph's famous tirades. "Pam rolled with it," said Jamison.

In later years Slim Keith wrote, "After I made my exit . . . coincidentally I'm sure—Leland never had a hit again." Though she conveniently ignored his success with *A Shot in the Dark*, her assessment was essentially true. It's impossible to know if Slim might have made a difference to Hayward's career, but when she left, he lost an important sounding board. Pamela didn't have a genuine zest for show business or the good instincts of her predecessor. "Pam never had the same feel for the business that Slim did," said Jamison.

In the beginning, Hayward had been grateful for Pamela's involvement. As his fortunes faded, that gratitude crumbled into exasperation. "She would come out with an opinion about the theater, and my father had a tendency to get short with her," said Bill Hayward. At a dinner with the architect Philip Johnson and the Haywards during the run of *Mr. President,* Anita Colby recalled, "Pamela said, 'You know, Leland, the trouble with it is the music isn't good.' Leland said, 'You don't know what the hell you're talking about. You haven't a fucking idea about the stage.' " Colby was shocked, and Pamela, recalled Colby, "didn't say a word."

CHAPTER

Twenty-three

*A*FTER THE AMUSEMENT and entertainment of the Slim years, Leland Hayward's life with Pamela was considerably more restrained. "The difference is really in the two women," said Kitty Hawks. "There was a sense that Pam was an island of calm. Voices weren't raised, there was not raucous laughter. With Leland, Pam's relationship had an almost conspiratorial quality. She would whisper in his ear, laugh with him. With Mom, it was open and fun because she was like that. With Pam, in the end it was better manners and you just buckled into it."

Pamela took care of Hayward with her geishalike devotion. He was accustomed to lunching at the Colony, but Pamela enticed him home for lunches followed by his customary manicure and pedicure, to which she added a new indulgence, a professional massage. Friends who called the Haywards on the telephone found themselves in three-way conversations, with Hayward on one extension and Pamela on another, listening and commenting. Visitors to their Fifth Avenue apartment were amazed to see her kneel down on the floor by his chair, remove his shoes, and gently put on his slippers. Lady Mary Dunn recalled a time in the early sixties when she arrived just as Hayward came home from work: "He was looking rather gray. Pam said, 'Darling, you haven't got a lot of time to change.' He said, 'Oh Christ, are we going out?' She said, 'To dinner with Jack and Jackie.' My eyes were on sticks. 'Do we have to?' he said. 'Of course not,' she said, 'I'll ring them up.' She came back carrying carpet slippers like a faithful dog. 'It's all right. I have ordered supper on two trays. We will eat quietly alone.' She put the 'alone' part quite firmly."

As was her habit, Pamela absorbed her husband's interests as her own, in the process integrating herself into her adopted country. She started watching television with Hayward, baseball games and other programs that interested him. "In her conversation, her interests, her approach to life she had become American, completely different from the way she was in Paris," said London decorator Tom Parr. After observing Pamela closely, Jeanne Thayer, the wife of Jock Whitney's business associate Walter Thayer, concluded, "She paid total attention to Leland but she didn't hover in an unattractive way. In a roomful of people, many of whom were very attractive men, she had her eyes for what Leland might want. She had books by her bedside table, and she would mark them up and give them to him, focusing on what he would be interested in that would widen his horizon. The interesting thing is that her attentiveness should be easy to imitate. But American women don't want to bother. They want to be competitive."

Pamela's elaborate attentions had a price, however. "I had the feeling Leland was very connected to her and dependent on her," said Clay Felker. Hayward allowed Pamela to structure their life just as she wished—to set the rules without ever seeming the least bit selfish. At her urging, they bought a country house forty miles north of Manhattan in Yorktown Heights in June 1962. Hayward paid the $90,000 purchase price (about $500,000 in current dollars) and placed the property in his wife's name. Pamela was able to overcome her husband's aversion to country living by convincing him that he needed a restful place to escape the hard-driving pace of the city and by promising to build him a room of his own, including a darkroom where he could develop his photographs.

She chose low-key Westchester County instead of Long Island, the intensely social domain of Slim Hayward and Babe Paley. "It was a whole different playing field," said a woman who socialized frequently with the Haywards. "They were new to the neighborhood, and no one had to take sides." The house Pamela selected looked like a box, with a peculiar arrangement of identical floor plans on two stories, each complete with a kitchen—"a hideous modern house," in the view of decorator Billy Baldwin. But the house sat on a hilltop, surrounded by fifty-seven acres of fields and woods, with a splendid view of Croton Lake in the distance. "One had a sense that she bought it for the land, and that it was the English in her," said a Westchester County neighbor. In the English tradition, she wanted the house to have a name. Pamela and Hayward settled on "Haywire House," named after his cable address. Once again Pamela brought in Boudin and Manno to do the decor.

At formal dinners in New York and Sunday lunches in the country, Pamela reveled in her position as the married hostess. Like the Duchess of Windsor, she kept a list of reminders for the cook on a small silver-framed pad, noting when the spinach soufflé was too dry, recording the name of a particular guest's favorite brandy or cigar. After she bought one of the first microwave ovens, she threw a luncheon around the pool at Haywire and gave each of her guests a hot dog with instructions on how to use the new gadget. "She was always looking for a treat of some kind to give us," said a regular at Haywire. Even in a crowd of thirty, Pamela fussed over everyone.

She continued her practice, honed in Europe, of encouraging general conversation, listening intently, guiding the attention toward Hayward, responding agreeably to everything she heard. "She never stopped laughing at Josh Logan's amusing stories even though she had heard them a hundred times," said the jewelry designer Kenneth Jay Lane. Her aim, as always, was to make people feel comfortable. "Slim had a sharp tongue," said a woman who dined frequently at Pamela's table, "but Pamela had a genuine interest in everyone. It might last half a minute, but she seemed to have interest for a moment of fixed time."

"Leland was more subdued with Pam," recalled George Plimpton, another periodic luncheon guest. "She was always saying, 'We will now go in for lunch, we will do this or that.' There was always a walk after lunch, a constitutional. People wore tweed coats. There was good conversation and elegant food. Leland was doing photo portraits of flowers, and we would look at the latest of these. She seemed very much a controlling force, but pleasant. She wasn't bossy but she was clearly master of the house."

Pamela's gatherings were as well cast as they had been in Paris and London. "Weekends at Haywire were riveting," said Nicholas Haslam, the London designer, "with a mix of show business and society—Margaret Case [*Vogue's* society editor], Gary Cooper, Yul Brynner, Arlene Francis, the Cerfs, Truman Capote, a mishmash of fun famous people." While the Haywards continued to see some of Leland's old friends—the Hornblows, playwright Paul Osborn, the Logans—Pamela drew him away from the old Hollywood and Broadway group and toward international socialites such as Gloria and Loel Guinness, whose former wife Joan had been married to Aly Khan. "The current people useful to Leland would get the full treatment," explained a friend of Hayward's. "The A team got the Haywire weekend, with fine food, and she would hire extra staff. The B team were taken out to dinner."

After the first year of their marriage, Pamela's eagerness to please her stepchildren subsided, and she made it difficult for Brooke and Bill to deal with Hayward directly. Whenever they wanted to have dinner with their father, they had to schedule the date with Pamela. Nor could they speak to him on the telephone alone unless they called the office. "I would call Father at home, and a long time would go by and out of the blue I would hear her deep voice," said Brooke. "I would think, 'My God, has she been on the phone this whole time unannounced?'" No matter that three-way conversations were the rule with everyone; Brooke and Bill felt unnerved. Kitty Hawks sensed the shift as well. "There was no question whose access was strongest," said Kitty. "Pam had a relationship with this person that you were not part of. You weren't included, and you were reminded of that."

Her effort to control eventually provoked confrontations with Bill and Brooke that ruptured their relationships with their father. In both cases the disputes concerned the suitability of prospective spouses. Even if she was acting out of legitimate concern, Pamela showed insensitivity in the way she tried to manage the behavior of her husband's adult children. Hayward, for his part, was a willing co-conspirator. Pamela secured her husband's complicity by playing on his conflicted feelings about each child—guilt and disappointment with Bill, guilt and irritation with Brooke. "Pam told me that Leland was fed up and didn't want to deal with Brooke, who was nothing but a problem to him," said Cheray Duchin, a friend of the Haywards along with her husband Peter, the surrogate son of Averell and Marie Harriman who had become a society bandleader like his father Eddy.

In 1961, Brooke met twenty-five-year-old actor Dennis Hopper when both were appearing on the New York stage in a play called *Mandingo*. She was twenty-four and had been on her own for two years, trying to make a name as an actress. Hopper had come to prominence six years earlier playing a teenage thug in the film classic about youthful alienation, *Rebel Without a Cause,* a role that helped shape his image as a symbol of the emerging counterculture. Admired for what one critic called his "intuitive, improvisatory" acting style, Hopper also had a reputation for being difficult. He had long hair (by the standards of the day) and never wore a suit—two breaches of propriety that profoundly annoyed the fastidiously dressed Leland Hayward, who had his crewcut trimmed every two weeks.

Pamela had been trying to steer Brooke toward several men she considered suitable, including the up-and-coming film director John Frankenheimer, who would later establish himself with *The Manchurian Candidate* and *Seven Days in May*. Brooke took offense at Pamela's attempts at matchmaking. "I didn't like the idea that my love life was up for discussion, and that she disapproved of the people I liked," said Brooke. Hopper may have been alluring to Brooke, but she was clearly rebelling when she decided to marry him and move to California with her two sons. "Pamela was trying to set her up with all these Eastern establishment types, and Brooke ends up with an actor who was black-balled by the major studios," said Bill Hayward.

Brooke and Hopper met with Hayward and Pamela several times to try to get their blessing. Pamela's attitude, recalled Hopper, was, "I was way below her class. She was a class-conscious person, and I was riffraff. She never made an effort to be nice to me." Hayward's criticisms were more professional than personal. "Don't marry him," Hayward told Brooke. "He is an actor and it will end badly. If you are successful, he will resent you. If he is successful, you will be left behind."

At the insistence of Pamela and Hayward, Hopper and Brooke planned a small wedding at the United Methodist Church on Park Avenue, with a luncheon reception at Jane Fonda's apartment afterward. On the eve of the wedding, Hayward told his daughter, "It's not too late to stop." Hayward and Pamela attended the service but contributed nothing to the event. "The wedding bouquet I brought with me was the only single festive note. . . . No music, not another flower, NOTHING," wrote matron of honor Josie Mankiewicz Davis to her mother Sara, the wife of Hollywood screenwriter Herman Mankiewicz.

Bill Hayward, meanwhile, was serving in the Army in North Carolina and spending periodic weekends with his father in New York. "I would stay at the apartment, and after a while I thought that was where I lived," said Bill. "Pamela was terribly nice to me. When they had dinner parties, I would be included. I was very much a part of the family." Bill's marriage to Marilla broke up in 1961, and in early 1962 he was transferred to Germany. That spring his father called to suggest they meet in Switzerland for a vacation to celebrate Bill's twenty-first birthday. Bill asked if he could bring along his new girlfriend, a young German woman named Gerda who worked as a barmaid, and Hayward agreed. A few weeks later, Hayward called back to say that the vacation would be in London because Pamela's father was ailing, and that Bill should come alone.

According to Bill, he then learned from his commanding officer, a major named Forbes, that his relationship with Gerda was being investigated at the request of Leland Hayward. Horrified, Bill called his father, who professed to know nothing. Shortly afterward, by Bill's account, Hayward apologized and told him Pamela had requested the probe to determine if Gerda was a prostitute trying to use Bill to obtain an American visa. Pamela had supposedly contacted the Army through Kay Summersby, a former aide to Dwight Eisenhower who had been romantically linked to her boss during their service together in World War II. By the 1960s, Summersby was living in New York and working in the costume department of CBS Television. "Apparently Kay Summersby knew everyone in the Army who counted, and she had done Pamela a favor," recalled Bill.

When Bill flew to London, he brought Gerda against his father's wishes. Pamela and her son met them at the airport, arriving in two cars. Pamela, according to Winston, was ready for "fireworks." "I have a vague recollection of my mother saying, 'Leland Hayward, I'm not going to sit down with a hooker,' " said Winston. For the drive into London, Gerda went with Winston, and Pamela asked Bill to come with her. In the car, by Bill's account, Pamela lectured him on "traveling across an international border with a woman when I wasn't engaged." Bill accused her of hypocrisy, countering that she and his father had traveled under the same circumstances. When he asked Pamela about the investigation, she told him it was in his best interest, and that she had sent along the report to a psychiatrist in London who had originally treated him at Menninger's.

"Everything changed from that moment on," said Bill. "Launching that investigation was a total overreaction by Pamela. I was very rude, too. I'm sure she got angry. I was stupid and young and misjudged her importance in my father's life. It wasn't an enormous fight, but I knew a lot about Pam and threw back at her what I knew. It breached whatever relationship we had." Afterward, Bill was no longer invited to stay at the Fifth Avenue apartment. "I was seriously put out by that," he said, "because I thought that was where I belonged."

When Brooke was in New York after her father returned from England, the dispute with Bill over his German girlfriend came up during a dinner Brooke and Dennis Hopper had with Hayward and Pamela at a popular Broadway steakhouse called Frankie and Johnnie's. According to Brooke, Pamela "worked herself into a rage. She said Bill shouldn't have left Menninger's, that he clearly had animus against my father that was pathological. Pam was really shrill. She said Bill wanted to destroy Father by humiliating him publicly, bringing an unspeakable girl around." After standing up for her brother, Brooke had to withstand Pamela's criticisms of her husband as well.

Dennis Hopper's film acting career had stalled, and he was experimenting with illegal drugs. "I smoked a joint once in a while," recalled Hopper. "I was drinking, but there was no cocaine in my life yet." Nevertheless, Hopper's personal habits understandably made Hayward and Pamela apprehensive about his fitness as a husband and stepfather. In an effort to appear respectable, Hopper, who customarily dressed only in bluejeans, had purchased a suit at Brooks Brothers to wear to dinner. Both Brooke and Hopper recalled that Pamela had openly disparaged Hopper when explaining why she had chosen a Broadway restaurant instead of the Colony. Hopper recalled, "Pamela said to Leland,

'Think how embarrassed we would be if we had gone to a really good restaurant. Look at that raincoat he's wearing.' There was no humor in her voice. She showed no humor in my presence, ever. She was a nasty piece of work. She really insulted me."

Brooke recalled that "the rest of the conversation that night was incredibly uncomfortable, but Pam never stopped smiling sweetly." During an exchange about Hayward's small collection of paintings, according to Brooke, "Pam said, 'Leland, I am convinced you must leave your paintings to a museum, and the sooner the better. If you give your paintings now you can keep them on your walls until you die.' " Afterward, said Brooke, "Dennis told me, 'That woman is out to get you. Do you realize she brought that up because she didn't want the paintings to pass on to you or your brother's hands?' Dennis planted the idea we would be disinherited—and the barmaid and Dennis would be the reason, along with the notion that we, those crazy Hayward children, were trying to destroy our father."

Hopper was amazed, he later said, that "Pamela did everything right in front of us. It was like Leland and she were having a private conversation in front of the bad children, talking about how bad we were." Hayward, recalled Hopper, "didn't seem to pay any attention. It was her show. It wasn't as if he said, 'Oh Pamela, come on.' He just went along with it." After several disagreeable encounters, Hopper singled out Pamela as "one of the few people in the world I truly hate. She was one of the most despicable people I have ever met. I'm in a pretty tough business, the movie business, which doesn't breed angels, and I have never seen anything like her. She was mean-spirited." Her antagonism, Hopper later figured, was "like a power thing. She was so confident about her relationship with Leland that she could be openly nasty in front of me."

Hopper, Brooke, and Bill were now united in their antagonism toward Pamela. When Bill was discharged from the service on New Year's Eve 1962, his father brushed him off by giving him an airplane ticket to California so he could spend the holidays with Brooke. Instead of coming back to New York, Bill cashed in the return ticket and settled in California, where he drifted through a series of jobs before landing at Universal Studios as a film editor. Brooke and Dennis Hopper also remained on the West Coast, but their marriage fell apart in the years following the birth of their only child, a daughter named Marin, in 1962. "Brooke had the ability to get under his skin, and Dennis behaved in an appalling way most of the time," said Bill Hayward.

Leland and Pamela Hayward made periodic trips to California on business or to visit his mother, but they rarely went out of their way to see either Brooke or Bill. Writing to Mary Martin and Richard Halliday at the end of 1962, Hayward indicated his ambivalence in a description of a forthcoming trip to San Francisco. He mentioned that he might fly to Los Angeles to see his new granddaughter, "to say nothing of her Mother and my other two grandchildren. Why can't I get more excited about them?" Hayward didn't make the visit then —or later. According to Hopper, "Leland never saw Marin until she was five. They just stopped seeing us. Leland stopped seeing his two grandsons, Jeff and Willie Thomas, too."

Many years later, when Pamela was asked to explain her relationship with Brooke, she said, "I hardly knew her and she hardly knew me. She was married when I married Leland, and she was not living anywhere near." Pamela's treatment of Bill was more disturbing. According to a friend of Hayward's, "Pam was very hard on young Bill. He was a troubled boy, and Pam was lofty about it. Pam was hard on Bill more in the sense of ignoring him than anything else. Both Brooke and Bill saw her as another wall to climb over to get to their father. They were afraid of her."

Estranged from Leland's children and frustrated in her efforts to have a say in his Broadway career, Pamela decided in 1963 to find a new role for herself as the owner of an exclusive boutique, the ideal outlet for her well-known talent as a "dedicated shopper." She approached Paul Manno about opening a New York branch of the successful Jansen boutique in Paris. Although Stéphane Boudin was the guiding light of Jansen, Pamela chose as her model Cora Caetani, the widely admired exemplar of taste who ran his Parisian shop. She also knew where Caetani bought her goods at little cost. With some startup capital and her network of connections, Pamela thought she could duplicate Caetani's success in Manhattan. She formed a partnership with Manno and Jansen-Paris, and Hayward put up the funds, not only for his wife's share but for Manno's as well. "When we make money," Pamela grandly told Manno, "you can pay me back."

On October 1, 1963, the Jansen Boutique opened at 42 East 57th Street, a prime location on the south side of the block between Madison and Park Avenues. Although she had no experience in retailing, Pamela knew how to create the right atmosphere and had a flair for salesmanship. In some respects, her shop was a variation on her successes with the Churchill Club (selling British hospitality), as the mistress of La Leopolda (selling Gianni Agnelli to a new crowd of influential friends), and as a self-styled Parisian salonière (selling herself).

"Opening a shop was gutsy of her," said one prominent Manhattan socialite. "I was amazed at how she pulled it together, using her contacts." She got free legal advice from Whitney adviser Walter Thayer and hired a socially prestigious sales staff that included Colette Harrison, the wife of actor Rex Harrison, as well as Marcia Meehan, daughter of the prominent Wall Street financier Joseph Meehan. "These women," said Manno, "were not the type you would find in Bloomingdale's."

Pamela stocked her shop with antiques as well as tasteful and practical reproductions that looked expensive but were reasonably priced: bamboo plant stands and telephone tables, tiny glass salt and pepper shakers for use on breakfast trays, *lampes bergère* burning Floris perfume, fur throw pillows, casels of steel and gilt to hold small paintings, black lacquer folding tables—the sort of merchandise that Roger Horchow would popularize two decades later in his mail-order catalogues. Some of the items Pamela designed herself, such as an oversize ottoman that revolved on casters. To emphasize the shop's chic European provenance, Pamela used Caetani's wrapping paper, which had become a status symbol in Paris. Pamela even subtly promoted her husband's hobby by framing his photographs of flowers in lucite (before lucite became common-place) and displaying them around the shop.

"In a very very short time, it became known as 'Pam's Shop,' " said Manno, who left the boutique's operation to her while he oversaw the Jansen decorating and top-of-the-line antique business in separate quarters above the shop. Pamela hired a manager, Philip Austin, to handle the accounts, and she designated Marcia and Colette to wait on walk-in customers. Pamela came to the shop every day, operating out of a small office in the rear and catering to the high society clientele who specifically asked for her. "She was a real working girl who would go back to the stockroom and carry something out," said Anita Colby.

Pamela demonstrated her famous persuasive powers by regularly calling New York socialites to alert them to new items they would like. "I hated to see her in there," Anita Colby added, "because she could sell me anything." Pamela's hardest sell was Babe Paley, recalled Colby, because "Babe never liked to have anything that anyone else had." Pamela was more than a glorified sales-woman. According to Paul Manno, "She had tremendous business sense. Pam knew what things cost and what they should sell for. She is a detail person. She knew exactly what was going on. She was the major domo." Even when she paid a premium for an object she coveted, she managed to sell it for twice what she paid.

Several times a year Pamela took Manno or Marcia Meehan on two-week buying trips. In San Francisco, she barreled through a wholesale antique and specialty market the size of an airport hangar. In Spain and Portugal, she visited Caetani's source for making reproductions of eighteenth-century furniture, as well as the place where Mallet's of London obtained centerpieces fashioned in the shape of silver swans. In London, she prowled antique shops so relentlessly that she left her companions breathless. Notebook in hand, Pamela recorded the price for every item she purchased.

"At first she gave you a sense she was vulnerable or helpless when she wanted something," said Manno. "Her femininity came out so strongly, and she got everyone to do what she wanted. Yet she had to be very tough. When she thought something was too expensive, the femininity disappeared and she became a businesswoman and discussed prices. Any man would say that she could charm you out of your wits, but she was also no nonsense."

She supervised her staff of five well, with thoughtful touches that earned their loyalty. She hosted an annual staff picnic and arranged tickets to Broadway shows. Once when her manager was ill with the flu, she had chicken soup sent to him at home.

The shop made a modest profit, but its importance to Pamela transcended the balance sheet. Both the *New York Times* and the *New York Herald Tribune* ran glowing feature stories about her accomplishments. She had the opportunity to travel on her own, to cultivate her own identity, and to enjoy a measure of freedom—which she was careful not to abuse. Leland Hayward was intrigued by Pamela's project and proud of her evident acumen. At the end of the day he often walked the three blocks from his office to her shop so he and his wife could stroll home together.

Pamela's career as a shopkeeper didn't diminish her penchant for spending her husband's money, however. The new levels of luxury that she introduced to their life created growing pressures on Hayward to bring in more income at a time when his career was faltering. Pamela may have been savvy in her business, but there was a difference between knowing how to price a piece of furniture and being unable to resist buying what she fancied. Recalled Anita Colby, "There was a woman who worked for Pam who said to me 'Miss Colby, you don't know. The way she picks over a couple of cents and then goes off and spends a fortune.' "

Leland Hayward, a spendthrift himself, made no effort to rein in Pamela's extravagance. "His attitude was that he was always going to be on a roll," said Leonora Hornblow. When he bought Pamela her country house, Hayward made a feeble attempt to apply the brakes by asking her to limit her decorating budget, but that proved impossible. Haywire House became one costly project after another: first the addition for Hayward designed in the shape of an octagon (an eye-catching variation on the elegant drawing room in Syria built by Pamela's infamous ancestor Jane Digby), followed by what Billy Baldwin called "the most luxurious swimming pool and swimming pool house that I have ever seen anywhere."

In his previous marriages, Hayward had routinely employed a cook and a butler. To this, Pamela added a full-time chauffeur and limousine, a service to which she had become accustomed in Paris, along with the personal maid who accompanied her on the road. With Pamela's encouragement, Hayward also purchased a three-seater Bell helicopter to ease their travel to the country. To help run Haywire, Pamela brought her longtime retainer, Mrs. Martin, from England. Between the apartment and the country house, with the various maids and gardeners and helpers, the Hayward household staff numbered around eight—all employed to maintain a style of living on a par with the Paleys and Whitneys and Guinnesses. "They spent $20,000 a month on the household easily" (the equivalent of $100,000 today), said a man who knew Hayward well. "They gave a couple of parties a week, big dinner parties."

For a time, Hayward's royalties—principally from *The Sound of Music*— kept him flush. *The Sound of Music* proved even more lucrative than Hayward could have imagined. In addition to the 10 percent stake he was given for producing the show, he later bought Mary Martin's 12.5 percent share at the insistence of Richard Halliday, who wanted to take advantage of a tax break on her capital gains. "Halliday got a fair price," recalled Mary Martin's friend, Burl Stiff. "But it turns out *The Sound of Music* was an unequaled annuity." Hayward's royalties doubled, and one former associate estimated that he earned $1 million annually in the early 1960s (about $5 million at current values). Martin never expressed regret about selling her share to Hayward, although as Slim's close friend she did begrudge in later years watching royalties go to Pamela after Hayward's death. "You don't know how painful it is for me to sign checks to her," Martin told Stiff.

By the mid-1960s, Hayward's royalties were tailing off, and he had nothing on Broadway to bring in fresh cash. He had signed a $50,000-a-year consulting contract with Bill Paley in 1960, but that turned into an embarrassment as the network rejected one idea after another—including such farsighted proposals as a weekly newsmagazine that prefigured *60 Minutes*. In 1965, CBS finally canceled the contract.

The pressure Hayward felt to find new sources of income showed in the way he mishandled his only television series, *That Was the Week That Was*, which was broadcast on NBC in 1964 and 1965. In late 1963, he produced a special based on a weekly British show featuring sketches and satire on current events that caught the public's attention with its clever writing and inventive format. NBC picked up *That Was the Week That Was*, known as *TW3*, as a series the following January. Hosted first by Elliot Reed and then by David Frost, *TW3* was an instant hit with the critics and the audience. Hayward was taking a $5,000 weekly fee even before the show turned a profit, but he needed to make more.

Hayward threw himself into *TW3*, inundating his producer and director, Marshall Jamison, with long memos filled with criticisms and ideas for sketches drawn from his voracious magazine and newspaper skimming. In the past Hayward had been revered for stimulating his staff and bringing out their best, but now his exhortations took on a harsh, demoralizing edge as he consistently second-guessed his writers. "The writing is mushy, soft and old hat," Hayward wrote to Jamison after the show had been on the air two months, adding his dismay over the "hideous unattractive middle aged people who were on the show this week" and the production style, which he said was in "desperate need" of a new approach. "I have over a quarter of a million dollars invested in television, and so far have not drawn a nickel [in profits]," Hayward complained. "If the show were what it should be, we would be besieged with advertisers. The opposite is quite true."

TW3 did move into the black, more than doubling Hayward's weekly income. But because of the show's sharp political commentary during the Johnson-Goldwater presidential campaign, NBC began hearing from sponsors as well as the targets of its barbs. In June 1964, Robert Kintner, the president of NBC, called a meeting with Hayward and Jamison. Recalled Jamison, "Kintner said, 'No more Lyndon Johnson.' I said, 'We can't do this unless we have equal rights to hit them both.' But Bob Kintner was a big money-raiser for Johnson and these were the orders from the White House. After the word came from Kintner, we didn't do anything on the Democrats at all. I don't think Leland cared too much about LBJ. He wasn't crazy about Goldwater either. And he didn't like the fact that Kintner made an ultimatum. But Leland caved to Kintner because the money was too alluring."

Jamison quit the show that July, never to work with Hayward again, although they did remain friends. The following fall the Republicans exacted their revenge by buying the *TW3* time period for political messages six out of the nine weeks preceding the election. "The show attacked crazy warmongering Goldwater while Johnson was escaping," said a man who worked on the show. "It was a smart thing for the Republicans to do. The show continued after the election but it was dead. The audience had gone."

The demise of *TW3* was followed closely by the disastrous closing of *Hot September* in Boston. Both failures seriously demoralized Hayward, and his drinking intensified. "The problem of TW3 haunts me day and night," Hayward wrote to Kintner several months before its cancelation. "Leland was not making enough money," said Marshall Jamison. "Here was a guy with everything in the world. He had been lionized and loved by people, and all of a sudden he wasn't. The dust showed on his suit. I felt Pam was putting pressure on him. She spent all kinds of money on that house, the swimming pool, the rows of cabanas. It was very expensive. That is wonderful if you have all the money in the world, but if you don't it hurts. For a while, she made him quite happy. Then I don't know. I think he felt pressure. You don't spend money like water when it isn't coming in. Maybe he didn't resent it, but it worried him."

Occasionally Hayward let slip a comment that revealed his concern. One evening magazine editor Clay Felker was having dinner with Hayward at "21" when Jimmy Stewart came up to the table. "At least we all put enough money away so we could be comfortable in our old age," Stewart said at one point. "Maybe *he* did," muttered Hayward as he sat down.

At the end of 1966, Hayward suffered "an excruciating attack of pancreatitis," as Brooke described it, that landed him in the hospital and ended his drinking days (he switched from Wild Turkey to Diet Rite Cola). Not long afterward, Pamela decided to close the Jansen shop, which after three years was still only marginally profitable. "She didn't have the time to devote to it," said Manno, "so we sold it to Bonwit Teller."

Pamela had no significant financial resources to draw from beyond her tangible assets and some money from former lovers. Lord Digby had died in January 1964 at the age of sixty-nine, leaving an estate of £141,854 before inheritance taxes ($2 million at current values). According to custom he left nearly everything to his son Eddie, who became the twelfth Lord Digby. Pamela's mother received £3,000 tax-free, her choice of two horses (plus saddles), two cars, two cows, and four pieces of jewelry, as well as the use of the Cerne Abbas house for her lifetime. Pamela and her sisters received nothing.

The Haywards' troubles were temporarily relieved in 1968 when Leland received approximately $300,000 from a $1 million judgment settling a dispute he and Richard Halliday had with Richard Rodgers over music royalties from the film version of the *The Sound of Music*. By then the Haywards were selling off possessions to stay afloat. They unloaded their grand Fifth Avenue apartment in 1969, and Pamela sold quite a few antiques—including a treasured clock powered by rolling ball bearings. For his part, Hayward sold a prize Giacometti bronze that he had kept on the mahogany desk in his office.

The Haywards said they were moving to the country "for Leland's health," but their Manhattan friends understood the real reason. "To have two establishments like that was very expensive," said Clay Felker. "He was at the end of his career, and selling the apartment and much of its contents was an enormous cutback. Pam never said anything bitter to me. She once said, 'Sometimes it is inevitable, you have to change your lifestyle.' She accepted it and dealt with it."

Instead of a full-time chauffeur, the Haywards used moonlighting off-duty

New York City firemen and policemen. Hayward moved his luncheons from the Colony to the less expensive Carlton House. And while in the old days Pamela would buy weekend provisions at the upscale Lobel's meat market on Madison Avenue and have them driven to the country, she settled for a less expensive butcher near their Yorktown Heights home.

Even so, Pamela and Leland Hayward continued to live beyond their means, burning through the proceeds from the sale of their possessions. They cruised the Mediterranean and took extended vacations in Europe. They kept a cook, maid, and butler in the country, where Pamela planned further projects including construction of a gardener's cottage. For their nights in Manhattan they bought a tiny apartment at the Beekman on the corner of Park Avenue and 62nd Street. Pamela couldn't resist hiring Billy Baldwin to decorate the place. "This was a real pied-à-terre in every sense of the word," Baldwin wrote, "and it was also the real height of luxury. The whole thing consisted of a sitting room, bedroom and terrace. We hung the walls of both rooms with a lovely fabric, and we were lucky enough to be able to take most of the museum quality furniture from the big apartment she was leaving and use it in the little one."

After a four-year drought, Hayward brought a play to Broadway in February 1969, with backing from Joseph E. Levine and Avco Embassy Pictures. He had spent a year developing the production, which was a peculiar choice for a man defined by a classy image. Written by Jerome Weidman, it was called *The Mother Lover*. The so-called comedy concerned a man's hatred for his mother, and the plot included vicious verbal sparring, a sleazy nude scene, and a suicide. Hayward called his old friend Marshall Jamison the day before the show was due to open and asked if he could fix it. Jamison declined and suggested Hayward shut it down. "He had a lot of enthusiasm for that miserable play," said Jamison. "I didn't understand why he did it. He was definitely desperate." The play opened on February 1 and was uniformly panned. *The New Yorker*'s critic Brendan Gill called it "cruel, disgusting, and wholly synthetic . . . a repellent exercise in dramatic carpentry." It closed before another performance.

That summer at age sixty-six Leland Hayward had a stroke that partly paralyzed one side of his body. He underwent intense physical therapy—in style, of course, with therapists bringing a portable table to his office three times a week. But although he regained most of his strength and mobility, Brooke recalled that the stroke "left him irritable, something of a curmudgeon." His target was usually Pamela, though as a couple they were not known to be quarrelsome. Explained one woman who knew Pamela for many decades, "Leland was not easy. It wasn't that he snapped at Pam. He was just moody, and he put a lot of demands on her."

Peter Duchin and his wife Cheray visited Haywire a number of times and were struck by Pamela's steely forbearance, which she had displayed earlier with Randolph Churchill and Gianni Agnelli. "Leland would get very aggravated over something she said and freeze her out and not speak to her," said Cheray. "In front of other people he would just ignore her. I remember she would take me aside and say, 'Oh well, he's in a bad mood.' She would toss it off."

On one level Hayward appreciated what Pamela did for him, but his feelings seemed oddly impersonal. One of his lunch companions in the sixties recalled, "He said to me, 'Pamela is a very good girl because she is getting me in my later years and taking care of me. She is living up to a bargain.' To live up to a contract is one of the greatest compliments in the theater, and he said it unsentimentally about her, almost like an agent." Other friends detected an undercurrent of resentment toward Pamela, who now controlled the relationship. But in Marshall Jamison's view, Hayward lashed out at his wife mostly out of guilt: "One of the big things that hurt him so bad in the end was that he hadn't measured up to what she thought of him," said Jamison. "She didn't give that off, but I could see it in him."

As Hayward became more crotchety, Pamela's attentiveness grew more exaggerated. She kept up the pace of entertaining, inviting friends to Haywire for lunches and dinners. During a vacation in Lyford Cay, she called his friend Stuart Scheftel with a plaintive request. "Leland is not well," she said. "Would you cancel your golf game and come and play bridge with him?" Scheftel recalled, "She treated him like Dresden china. She did all the fetching for him."

After maintaining a facade of insouciance for so long, Pamela and Leland Hayward revealed their concerns about finances to Bill and Brooke in the summer of 1970 after both children had reconciled with their father. Hayward had welcomed Brooke back in 1967 once she decided to divorce Hopper. " 'Congratulations,' he announced to me in Los Angeles from his office in New York City," Brooke recounted in her memoir, " 'on the first smart move you've made in six years.' " Bill had restored himself briefly after he remarried in 1964 and produced two grandchildren, only to fall from his father's favor again several years later by leaving his second wife. Finally, in 1969, Bill earned Leland Hayward's respect and approval with his first major professional and financial success as co-producer, with Peter Fonda, Jack Nicholson, and—ironically enough—Dennis Hopper, of the hit film *Easy Rider*. (When Pamela and Hayward came to a screening of the film, Hayward greeted his former son-in-law cordially, while Pamela ignored him.)

"In the end, when he had been ill, I talked to my father a good deal about finances," said Bill Hayward. "For Pam, it was a disaster. She made it very clear that she was desperately worried. She didn't understand how it could happen. But she had developed this style, and it was very difficult to live another way altogether. I seem to recall her saying she had gone through her assets and contributed whatever she felt she could." Brooke Hayward remembered hearing the same lament during a month-long visit to Haywire with her children: "One day Pam stopped the car and broke into tears. 'Your father is having terrible money problems and he won't do anything about it,' she said. This was extraordinary behavior. I had never seen her cry before. I couldn't figure out why she was telling me this; maybe to get my help."

Brooke couldn't help, and neither, for that matter, could anyone else. Even as they fretted, both Haywards kept spending money at a rapid clip. Walter Thayer tried to give Pamela advice, but to no avail. "Leland had debts," recalled Jeanne Thayer. "Walter had worried over the years about Leland and money. He was worried that he hadn't left a substantial estate and was worried that

Pamela hadn't been handling what he did have well and wouldn't handle it well." As always, Leland Hayward felt if he could find another hit, he could solve his problems.

Despite his infirmity, Hayward managed to pull together one last theatrical production, his twenty-first play in a career spanning a quarter century. *The Trial of the Catonsville Nine* was an anti-war drama by the Jesuit Father Daniel Berrigan based on his trial, along with his brother Philip, also a priest, and seven others, for burning draft records to protest the Vietnam War. It was the dramatic potential of the piece, not its politics, that attracted Hayward, who wept when he read it. "I want to buy it immediately," he said to agent Flora Roberts. "I see Hank Fonda as Dan. I see Greg Peck as Philip and then we go to Broadway." Roberts persuaded him to avoid big-name stars and go Off-Broadway, but to start first at the Mark Taper Forum in Los Angeles. Once educated to the possibilities of Off-Broadway, Hayward's enthusiasm surged. He even got his son Bill to invest in the show. "It was an interesting piece of theater, it had a lot of innovative stuff, mixed media and slides. I think he felt this was him getting on the cutting edge," said Bill.

When Daniel Berrigan disappeared before he was scheduled to begin his federal prison sentence, Pamela panicked. Hayward told Flora Roberts that Pamela wanted him to drop the play because the author was a fugitive. But Hayward insisted on going ahead, and Pamela acquiesced. In August 1970, Hayward traveled to Los Angeles with Roberts, where the play was introduced by a recording of Berrigan's voice "speaking from the underground." "This is the most fun of any play I have ever had," Hayward told Roberts. But although the play "made a lot of noise," as one participant put it, Hayward had reservations about whether it was compelling enough to be commercially successful.

Back in New York, he secured financing from a wealthy backer named T. Edward Hambleton. They hired a new writer to rework the play and shorten it into one act, with a cast including Ed Flanders and Sam Waterston. Hayward decided to stage the production in the Good Shepherd Faith Church, on Manhattan's West Side, which was certain to bring added attention to the production. Daniel Berrigan was in prison, and new federal indictments against him and twelve others for allegedly plotting to kidnap Henry Kissinger had spurred fresh publicity. In a *Women's Wear Daily* feature in January 1971, Hayward was upbeat: "I hate to talk about a play as 'interesting,' because that's sure death, but this play has more than usual."

Barely a week later, talking on the telephone, Hayward suddenly stopped in midsentence. He had suffered a second stroke. Pamela had him taken to New York Hospital, where surgeons repaired his blocked right carotid artery. "An unqualified success," Pamela reported by telephone to Brooke and Bill. Coming out of his anesthesia, Hayward began lobbying to return home so he could make opening night of his new play four days later. But on February 7, Hayward was still hospitalized, so Pamela went to the opening with a small group of friends, including Dr. William Cahan, a prominent cancer specialist, and a lawyer, Ashton Hawkins. After the performance, the group returned to Hayward's room to report that the play was a great success. Hayward was out of bed, in his robe and slippers, as Pamela poured champagne for everyone. "Leland and I talked for ten minutes about the Berrigan brothers and the play," recalled Hawkins. "It was a remarkably spirited and excited dialogue." The celebration was premature. Although praised by the critics, *Catonsville* would close Off-Broadway after a three-month run, reopen on Broadway, but shut down shortly afterward.

Hayward left the hospital two days after the *Catonsville* opening, against his doctor's recommendation and Pamela's futile objections, and was driven in his limousine to Haywire. There he suffered another stroke and was rushed back to the hospital in an ambulance. Doctors removed a blood clot from an artery on his left side, but by then he had already suffered brain damage. He was hospitalized for nearly a month, with Pamela overseeing every aspect of his care. She hired private nurses, and organized friends and relatives into shifts so someone would be with Hayward at all times. Sheila Digby Moore, by then living in Connecticut, was a great help to her sister during this period, according to friends. Brooke and Bill joined the vigil at the beginning and end of their father's hospital confinement, but it was Pamela who sat by his side for many hours each day. During one visit, Bill asked his father to name the ten most beautiful women he knew, and the list as Brooke recounted it in her memoir included his first three wives, Lola, Maggie, and Slim—but pointedly not Pamela. Bill's request had been suggested by Slim, and Bill admitted to being pleased by Pamela's exclusion.

Although Hayward could still speak and recognize faces, his moments of lucidity were diminishing. Knowing that he was failing, and mindful of how much he hated hospitals, Pamela took him home to Haywire in early March so he could die in privacy. Her gesture had deep meaning for Hayward, who had broken with his stepmother Maisie in 1946 over her treatment of his own father when he was dying. "He didn't want to go back to the hospital when he did," Leland Hayward had written Maisie in a bitter letter, "but back he went because you wanted him there and not in the house because it made you nervous to have a sick person around you." Hayward made certain Pamela knew how he felt. One of her longtime friends recalled, "Leland said, 'Pam, I hope you have a pill to give me. Never put me in the hospital. Don't do this to me.' He said it many times."

At Haywire, Pamela hired Franciscan monks who were also nurses and placed Hayward in a hospital bed in the octagon room. She summoned friends to make their last visits. "Leland is dying," she told Katharine Hepburn. "He loved you more than he loved any of us. Will you go see him?" When Pamela called Marshall Jamison, she warned him that her husband might not know him. During the visit, Jamison recalled, "He woke up and said, 'I love Marsh,' and Pam said, 'I do too.' "

The next day, March 18, 1971, Leland Hayward died at age sixty-eight. Pamela held a wake at Haywire with a luncheon for some seventy-five guests. A line of limousines formed as the mourners from show business and society came to call—Rosalind Russell, Jacqueline Onassis, Diana Vreeland, the Hornblows, Gregory Peck, Frank Sinatra. There were flowers everywhere and a blanket of carnations on the open casket in the octagon room. Pamela was the consummate hostess, gracious as always, cool and dry-eyed. A small group including the Logans, Hornblows, Marshall Jamison, and Hayward's lawyer Thomas Ryan accompanied Pamela and the family to the burial the next day. The memorial service, with hundreds in attendance, was held several weeks later at St. James's Church on Madison Avenue in Manhattan. "It was almost like a wedding where the sides fell into place," recalled Anna Crouse. "Pam and the Paleys and the socialites were on one side, and Jerry Robbins, the Mermans, and I were on the other. Ethel leaned over and said, 'The help's on this side.' "

Pamela Digby Churchill Hayward was still a controversial figure, but she had impressed everyone with her behavior in sickness and in health. In her world, where so many wealthy people were removed from everyday cares, her actions were viewed as extraordinary. Pamela had fulfilled her bargain to Hayward. As Leonora Hornblow often said, "With Pamela, a deal is a deal." Pamela's New York years were far more difficult than she could have envisioned, but her performance as a Broadway wife added to the legend. She had put on a great show, keeping up appearances, shielding her worries. As her friend Brooke Astor put it, Pamela was "cheerful and nice right up to the end."

Twenty-four

PAMELA EMERGED from her eleven-year marriage to Leland Hayward in a precarious position. She still had her reputation as a man's woman, but she had no money to speak of. Again she was at a crossroads, as she had been when her marriage to Randolph fell apart, and when she was rejected in turn by Ed Murrow, Aly Khan, Gianni Agnelli, and Elie de Rothschild. Each time she had bounced back, using her cleverness, seductive wiles, and talent for self-invention to propel herself into a new life. But now time was working against her: She was fifty-one years old, still pretty but decidedly plump, and strapped for cash.

Almost immediately she faced a challenge from Brooke and Bill Hayward over the disposition of the Hayward estate. The bad feelings created by the dispute would plague her for the rest of her life.

The bitter feud began shortly before the memorial service when Pamela told them the lesson would be read by Winston, not by either of them. "Pamela was trying to tell us, you do not exist," Brooke said in 1988. The more serious grievances, however, revolved around money and possessions.

During the reading of the will before the guests arrived for Hayward's wake, Brooke and Bill were surprised to learn that they would receive half of their father's estate, and Pamela the other half. Both children—Brooke was then thirty-three years old and Bill was twenty-nine—had assumed they would be disinherited. Brooke frequently said that Pamela was equally surprised by the will's provisions and had "an enormous temper tantrum" in her bedroom at Haywire the evening after the wake. "She wheeled around," recounted Brooke, "and said, 'I can't understand how I could have been so stupid as to have been married to a man for eleven years and have nothing to show.'" For a year before Hayward's death, according to Brooke, Pamela had been "obsessed about finding out where his will was."

Brooke's account is at odds with the facts. "Before Leland married me he told me under the terms of his divorce from Maggie Sullavan that he had to leave half of his estate to his children," Pamela said, describing an arrangement that was widely known in Hayward's circle. According to Leonora Hornblow, "Leland told everyone he had made a deal with Margaret," and "everyone" included Pamela, both Hornblows, and Slim, who had complained about the split during her marriage to Hayward.

Hayward's attorney, Thomas H. Ryan, drew up a four-page will on August

28, 1962, incorporating a key section of the April 1, 1948, property settlement between Hayward and Margaret Sullavan that obligated him to leave half of his estate plus half the value of his insurance policies to the children from that marriage. The will also required Hayward's executor to buy an annuity policy to pay his mother, Sarah Tappin, $300 a month for life, and bequeathed $5,000 to his longtime secretary Kathleen Malley. Hayward signed the document in his room at the Ritz Carlton Hotel in Boston during the tryouts for the ill-fated *Mr. President.* The witnesses were Irving Berlin, Marshall Jamison, and Russel Crouse—none of them sworn to secrecy. On February 17, 1971, when Hayward was dying, Kathleen Malley turned over the document and several photocopies to his lawyers.

As executor, Hayward had appointed Charles Miller, the son-in-law of MCA president Jules Stein. Pamela immediately moved to assume the position herself. She needed the approval of Brooke and Bill Hayward, which they gave, in signed documents, only five days after their father's death. "Pamela was terribly concerned about money. She was very worried about how she was going to live," said Bill. "She could get a fee for being executrix. It was important that she got it and someone else didn't." By Bill and Brooke's recollection, their approval was based on a quid pro quo agreement with Pamela. In the subsequent fight over the specifics of the deal, relations between Pamela and her stepchildren unraveled.

The total value of Hayward's estate was $400,000 (roughly $1.5 million in current dollars). It included the Hayward apartment on Park Avenue and Sarah Tappin's house in Van Nuys, California. (Haywire House had been in Pamela's name since 1962.) According to Bill Hayward, he and Brooke agreed to give Pamela their $55,000 half interest in the Park Avenue property. "Pamela had spent too much money with Billy Baldwin redoing it," Bill recalled. "I thought we couldn't recover it, so it was worth more to her than anyone." In exchange, the children assumed ownership of their grandmother's house in Van Nuys.

The rest of the agreement between Pamela and the Hayward children concerned personal effects. Bill was to get all his father's camera equipment, along with clothing and some personal items from Haywire House, as well as the contents of Hayward's office, some of which he would buy from Pamela at the appraised value. Bill went to Haywire to collect his father's belongings, only to find that Hayward's large cufflink collection was missing, along with most of his watches and some cameras. "Probably thirty to forty cameras came to me," said Bill. "Some were worthless, some quite valuable. Most of them were collector's items, valuable but not useful." But "the more immediate practical useful modern stuff, maybe three or four cameras and the lenses that went with them," had disappeared. Bill assumed Pamela had given them to Winston, who like Bill was a camera buff, although he also heard that Pamela had sold them to Fox & Sutherland, a general store in nearby Mount Kisco, New York. (Neither Kalman Fox, the owner, nor his manager at the time, Emile Carlisi, could recall buying any equipment from the Hayward estate. "Our policy has always been not to purchase used equipment," said Fox. "We only take it on trade.")

Already irritated about the missing items at Haywire House, Bill became incensed over the distribution of his father's office property. After Bill had bought the desk and piano, Pamela gave him a price for his father's books that seemed reasonable. Then, said Bill, Pamela "changed the ground rules" and had the books reappraised for "an outrageous amount of money"—in the thousands instead of the hundreds. When Bill couldn't afford the inflated price, Pamela donated the books for a tax credit to the New York Public Library, along with Hayward's collection of photographs that Bill had also wanted.

Brooke clashed with Pamela over the two pearl necklaces and the emerald ring that she said she had given Pamela for safekeeping after Bridget's death. By Brooke's account, she had asked about the jewelry after the sale of the Fifth Avenue apartment in 1969, and Pamela had assured her the pieces had been removed to her bank safe-deposit box with other valuables. When Pamela became executrix, according to Brooke, an agreement to return the jewelry to Brooke was part of the deal. (Bill said the matter of the jewelry actually arose after the agreement was struck.)

On the day of Hayward's memorial service, according to Brooke, she had met with Pamela in her father's office. "What about the pearls?" Brooke recalled asking. "Pamela was evasive," said Brooke. "She said she couldn't find them. She said she had given my father a Cartier watch and she couldn't find that either, nor could she find a lot of his cufflinks. She totally defused it." The implication, Brooke said, was that her father had sold Brooke's possessions. Brooke recalled asking Kathleen Malley if she had any record of his having sold the jewelry. She had none. Malley told Brooke, "He never lost anything either."

Her exchange about the jewelry was witnessed, Brooke said, by Leonora Hornblow and Irene Selznick. Selznick died in 1990, and though Hornblow clearly remembered, as did Brooke, a discussion about Brooke's refusal to wear a black mantilla to the service, she recalled nothing about the jewelry. "I don't remember a thing about the pearls, nor a discussion about the cufflinks, but that doesn't mean it didn't happen," said Hornblow. "I was very very upset myself to be in his office again. . . . Maybe my recollection is not as sharp because of that."

Brooke was convinced that Pamela either kept or sold her jewelry and was trying to shift the blame onto Hayward. Pamela's friends, and even her detractors, dismissed Brooke's accusations as groundless. "Pamela had an awful lot of jewelry," said one woman who had long felt ambivalent about her. "She didn't have to steal a string of pearls from anyone." Pamela, of course, denied receiving the jewelry in the first place. Could Pamela have earned Brooke's allegiance by graciously giving her some good pieces from her own collection? Perhaps, although Brooke was nursing so many other grievances that she might not have been easily mollified.

In *Haywire*, her best-selling memoir published six years later, and in interviews about Pamela, Brooke depicted her stepmother as a calculating opportunist, self-obsessed, greedy, and predatory. According to Bill Hayward, Pamela tried to make light of Brooke's enmity, dismissing her as "this absolute mad dog out there." But in fact Brooke's vendetta, which continued for decades, became a serious problem for Pamela. The story of "the pearls" was its totemic centerpiece. "The pearls!" said Washington lawyer Edward Bennett Williams when Pamela hired him to block her portrayal in a CBS movie based on *Haywire*. "The pe-e-e-e-a-rls!"

As THE FIGHT with Pamela intensified in the weeks after Hayward's death, Bill Hayward settled on a new strategy. A recent graduate of the University of West Los Angeles College of Law, he decided to file suit against her. "I was pissed about the cameras . . . pissed off about a number of different things," he recalled. "Brooke was nuts about the jewelry. We had worked ourselves into a snit about Pamela and her greed. I remember very clearly thinking, 'I'll probably never win the lawsuit, but while this is going on she won't get the money.' I wanted to make her miserable. It was just a revenge trip. Frankly, I think Brooke talked me into it."

Pamela kept mostly to herself during this period, dealing with the estate, fending off the stepchildren, assessing her finances, pondering her future. "She didn't go out for a month," said Kenneth Jay Lane. "Our first 'date' was dinner and a movie. We had dinner with Oscar and Françoise. [Pamela's old Parisian friend, Françoise de Langlade, was by then married to clothing designer Oscar de la Renta.] She had come out of deep mourning." Pamela's share of the Hayward estate—more than half of which was tied up in the Manhattan pied-à-terre—was insufficient to sustain a country house and apartment for very long. Her informal financial adviser, Walter Thayer, advised her to sell the Yorktown Heights property immediately. "He was irritated with her for wanting to spend money that she didn't have," said Jeanne Thayer. But Pamela resisted. Instead, she got a supply of cash by taking out a $30,000 mortgage ($113,000 in current dollars) on the Yorktown property.

In April she went to Palm Springs to stay with Hayward's old friend, Frank Sinatra. At Hayward's wake, recalled Leonora Hornblow, "I was standing with Frank and Freddie Brisson . . . Pamela passed by and she looked so sad and worn. Frank said to her very kindly, 'When you catch your breath and things are settled, why don't you come out to the desert and stay for a while.' " After making a courtesy call to Hayward's mother, Pamela did just that, arriving in time to join Sinatra's regular crew of springtime visitors.

Then fifty-six, Sinatra had reached a turning point in his life as well. After thirty years as one of America's top entertainers, with more than a hundred albums and fifty-five feature films to his credit, Sinatra had announced in March that he would retire after a farewell concert the following June. Sinatra had alienated many people with his hot temper, rude behavior, and vulgar language, but he was also capable of great loyalty and magnanimous gestures.

He was always on his best behavior with "the older crowd that he cultivated to be more respectable," according to Brad Dexter, an actor who was a close friend of Sinatra's. "I called them 'The Late Show' ": the Goetzes, Brissons, Hornblows, Cerfs; Claudette Colbert and her husband Dr. Joel Pressman; Sears, Roebuck heir Armand Deutsch and his wife Harriet; Harry Kurnitz, Ruth Gordon, and Garson Kanin; and the Haywards. On weekends and over the holidays at Christmas and Easter, Sinatra would invite them all to Palm Springs and overwhelm them with his hospitality.

Sinatra's Palm Springs compound was a collection of cottages, each a bedroom suite with his and hers bathrooms, pullman kitchens brimming with food and liquor, and large closets furnished with new bathrobes and slippers. A kitchen in the main house was open day and night, offering room service to every guest. Sinatra even designated certain cottages for his favorite friends and had their names inscribed on the doors: "Cerf Cottage," "Hornblow Cottage," and so forth. The grounds of his estate boasted several pools, a tennis court, a health spa in a converted railroad box car, and a helipad.

When "The Late Show" crowd came to visit, they sat around the pool for hours, reading and talking, occasionally playing tennis. The ladies took excursions to the beauty shop; the "boys" watched ball games on television. Sometimes the group went to a restaurant in Palm Springs for dinner. Afterward, Sinatra might show a new film, or he would sing while one of the group played the piano. Their wildest moments came when they pushed each other into the pool with their clothes on.

Hayward had entered the Sinatra group during his brief career as a Hollywood movie producer. Sinatra, according to Slim, "hung around our house in California a lot. It was no big deal—he'd walk in at six o'clock and say, 'I've come for a drink,' and I'd look up from my reading or letter writing or whatever and say, 'Okay, you know where the bar is.' " Even after Slim confessed her brief affair with Sinatra to Hayward, the singer remained a friend. Hayward featured him on his television spectaculars and enjoyed his swaggering company. After the *Hot September* debacle in 1965, Sinatra flew Leland and Pamela Hayward out to Palm Springs in his private jet and organized a two-week vacation to lift them from the doldrums. Two months later they were back for a New Year's house party. The Haywards, in turn, often entertained Sinatra at Haywire when he was staying with the Cerfs as their "summer boarder."

In the legend of Pamela and her men, her relationship with Sinatra holds a prominent although exaggerated position. Kitty Kelley, Sinatra's biographer, noted almost parenthetically that he "would have married" Pamela Churchill Hayward, "but the British beauty had declined the offer shortly after the death of her husband, producer Leland Hayward." Christopher Ogden, on the other hand, insisted that the opposite happened, that Pamela pursued Sinatra after Hayward's death, that she overstayed in Palm Springs to the point that the singer had to throw her out, and that he had even consulted his neighbor, Walter Annenberg, for advice on how to get rid of her. (Annenberg, who was serving as Ambassador to the Court of St. James at the time, denied having been asked for such advice.) "The singer found her boring, arrogant, pompous, pretentious and generally phony," wrote Ogden.

In fact, neither version is true. Close friends of Sinatra who observed him with Pamela described an easy rapport that was an extension of the singer's great admiration for Hayward. "If there was a sexual chemistry between Pamela and Frank, no one was ever aware of it," said a longtime friend of Sinatra's.

"Frank's demeanor toward Pamela was no different from what it was toward anyone else." According to Leonora Hornblow, "Pamela was a guest in his house, and a friend. He was lovely to Pamela, as he was good to all of us."

Still, no one who knew them both ruled out the possibility of a brief fling. "I wouldn't bet against romance between Pamela and Frank," said Hornblow. "He was not married and she was a widow. They liked each other, but Pamela certainly didn't want to marry Frank." Indeed, Sinatra may have had money and celebrity, but he was trouble when it came to women.

During Pamela's visit to Palm Springs in the spring of 1971, English gossip columnists began speculating about a possible romance. A longtime confidante of Sinatra's who was in Palm Springs at the time recalled the reaction when the rumors surfaced: "It sent Frank into an absolute fit of rage. We were all around the famous pool. Frank was very upset and Pamela was upset too. Bennett [Cerf] was asked to call and say it was not true, but it put a pall on everything. We were all really mad." Pamela left shortly afterward with the group, according to Sinatra's confidante, who said, "we moved in a caravan."

Pamela had to contend with additional stories back in New York about her relationship with William Cahan. He and his wife Sisi had been frequent visitors in Yorktown Heights during Hayward's last years, and Pamela's attentiveness to the handsome cancer surgeon had caused comment. "I remember going with Fulco [de Verdura] for lunch at Haywire," recalled Tom Parr, "and I remember Dr. Bill Cahan was there. After we left, Fulco said to me, 'Do you think what I think was going on?' Something was said, or some look, or something." The gossip intensified after he escorted Pamela to the opening of *Catonsville*, even though Hayward had asked him to do so. The Cahans' marriage was already shaky, and, as Cahan wrote in his 1992 memoir, the Catonsville evening "became another bone of contention" with his wife. As so often happened, the reality— whether Pamela did or did not have an affair with Cahan—mattered less than the perception that her flirtatious behavior created. "There was a lot of buzz about her," said a friend from those days. The married women of New York society were once again on the alert.

Pamela retreated to Europe. Faced with flying tourist class for the first time, she called friends in England to find out how she could get upgraded to first class without paying for it. She couldn't, so she squeezed herself into the back of the plane and flew to England. Instead of staying in a suite at Claridges —she had given up her Hyde Park Gardens flat in the late sixties—she bunked in a tiny bedroom in her son Winston's apartment near Parliament that she compared to a "closet." "That was the only time in my life I was totally desolate," she later said. She sought out old acquaintances and spent weekends at Winston's home in Sussex. Her stay in London, according to a woman who was in touch with her then, "was not a success. Things had changed since the war. Most of her friends were not around, and life wasn't very social."

Her brother Eddie was married and living at Minterne, having converted half of their ancestral home into apartments; her widowed mother was in the house at Cerne Abbas; and her youngest sister Jaquetta had moved to Scotland.

Young Winston was a recently elected Conservative member of the House of Commons, and in 1964 he had married Minnie d'Erlanger, the daughter of the founder of British Airways, who came from a well-known French banking family. Their wedding was a hurry-up civil ceremony, and seven months later their first child, a son named Randolph, was born. "Pamela didn't get on with Winston," said a friend. Her favorite Churchill, old Winston, had died in 1965, followed by her former husband Randolph three years later.

After several unhappy weeks in England, Pamela realized, according to Brooke Astor, that "she was more American than English." She traveled to the South of France, where she joined Loel and Gloria Guinness on a cruise. She returned to Haywire House in early August 1971. "I'd headed home in a panic," she recalled years later. "You know those sort of awful August days when there's no sun, everything is sort of dark and raining, and it's not summer?" she mused to a *Washington Post* reporter in 1983. "I came home to an empty house—and the *depression* of coming back."

Shortly after her arrival she had a call from *Washington Post* publisher Katharine Graham, an acquaintance since the early 1960s. Graham's divorced daughter, Lally Weymouth, lived near Haywire House and had become friendly with Pamela. Weymouth had called her mother with a suggestion. Graham was having a dinner the next day, August 5, in honor of Arthur Schlesinger, Jr., and his wife, to which Weymouth had a longstanding invitation. "Do you mind if I fink out?" Weymouth said to her mother. "I would like to do something else. If you need to fill in for me, Pam Hayward is just back and said she is feeling very low. I know she'd love to be asked." Graham extended the invitation, and Pamela accepted instantly. On the official guest list, "Weymouth, Mrs. Elizabeth," is crossed out, and underneath is written in hasty script: "Pam Hayward."

Pamela flew to Washington, and as she entered the Graham garden, the first person she spotted in the crowd of forty-six Washington VIPs was Averell Harriman, seventy-nine years old and widowed a year earlier. According to Rudy Abramson, Harriman "had no inkling that Pamela was to be at Kay Graham's." She and Harriman spoke at length during the cocktail hour. "It was just as if those years had never been," she said later.

They were seated at different tables—she between *Washington Post* executive editor Benjamin Bradlee and columnist Tom Braden, he between Bradlee's wife Toni and the wife of journalist Hal Bruno. There was a story that Pamela arranged the seating chart to place herself back to back with Harriman so she could dramatically turn around and exclaim, "Oh Averell," and Harriman would have to exert himself to talk to her by twisting in his seat. "The idea that she could have planned that or I could have planned it is nonsense," said Katharine Graham. "I have no idea who is back to back at my parties."

After dinner, Pamela and Harriman huddled in the garden until nearly everyone had left. "I didn't know who he was sitting with," recalled Liz Stevens, a close friend of Averell and Marie's who brought Harriman to the party. "I came out to find out if he was all right. He said yes." Harriman mentioned nothing about Pamela either to Liz or her husband George when they went home with him. "I don't remember any conversation about her before or after," said Liz Stevens.

After leaving Pamela in London in 1946 to become Commerce Secretary in Truman's cabinet, Harriman had led the sort of busy, big-league life he thrived on, edging as close as he could to the men in power. Though he had little use for the Commerce Department, Harriman had worked long days because he savored the prestige of a cabinet post and wanted to acquit himself well. Truman rewarded him in 1948 by sending him to Paris as administrator of the Marshall Plan to rebuild Europe. With his customary tenacity and blunt manner, he coaxed the Europeans to work together and effectively supervised sixteen Marshall Plan offices throughout Europe. After Truman's surprise re-election that November, Harriman hoped to be named Secretary of State—despite the fact that he had thought Truman a sure loser and had contributed only $500 to his campaign. Harriman was deeply disappointed when Truman appointed his old schoolmate Dean Acheson instead.

Harriman's next assignment, as Truman's national security adviser, brought him back to Washington in the summer of 1950. Harriman realistically considered himself "more a fixer than a strategist," and he enjoyed some success as a troubleshooter in the latter part of the Truman administration. He spent much of the summer of 1951 trying to broker peace negotiations between Britain and Iran after Iranian Prime Minister Mohammad Mossaddeq nationalized a major British oil refinery. He failed to bring the two sides to the negotiating table, but helped stabilize the crisis.

Back home, Harriman began maneuvering toward an ambition he had quietly held for nearly a decade—the Democratic presidential nomination. Truman wanted Illinois Governor Adlai Stevenson to succeed him, but Harriman launched his own campaign. He was a painfully dull orator who lacked the politician's knack for spontaneity and affability. He also was hindered by his old Groton stammer. "It was an emotional problem," recalled one veteran of the campaign. "He could talk in the comfort of his living room and never have the stammer. He only stammered in public. It was agony to listen to him." Stevenson easily won the 1952 nomination, but Harriman had caught the political bug.

Two years later he was elected Governor of New York by only 11,000 votes out of 5 million cast—the smallest margin in the state's history. Primed by two savvy advance men who stood in the crowd and yelled, "Attaboy, Ave. Give 'em hell, Ave"—an echo of Truman's 1948 "Give 'em hell, Harry" campaign—Harriman overcame his stammer and learned how to campaign more enthusiastically. He secured the support of the dubious bosses of the New York City machine, and he crusaded for progressive new social programs. Harriman loved, as he later said, "being elected instead of selected," and proudly called himself "Governor" for the rest of his life.

But instead of the "bold adventurous administration" he promised, his tenure as governor was, as the *New York Times* editorialized, "a pedestrian performance, disappointing in achievement." He had neither a clearcut agenda nor the leadership skills to work with the Republican legislature, and he was determined to rein in the state budget. "He talked a good liberal line," said his political adviser, George Backer, "until somebody showed him a deficit. At that point he became a conservative."

Midway through his term he made another ill-considered bid for the presidency, once more losing the nomination to Stevenson. As he prepared to run again for governor in 1958, Harriman became embroiled in a nasty struggle over the Democratic nominee for Senate. He vacillated among several choices (including, fleetingly, Edward R. Murrow) and alienated the eventual candidate, Manhattan District Attorney Frank Hogan. In the end, Tammany Hall boss Carmine de Sapio, who was Harriman's political patron, humiliated the governor by secretly backing Hogan while Harriman dithered between two other candidates.

At a time when Democrats easily won the off-year elections, Harriman lost in a landslide to Republican Nelson Rockefeller, an exuberant multimillionaire who kept Harriman on the defensive by portraying him as a "tool of the machine." Harriman's final indignity occurred on election eve when Dorothy Schiff, publisher of the liberal *New York Post* and George Backer's former wife, endorsed Rockefeller. Schiff later confided to *New York* magazine editor Clay Felker that she had evened an old score: Years earlier in Paris during Harriman's playboy period, he had stood up Schiff for dinner and sent her a bouquet of wilted flowers.

Resilient as ever, Harriman plotted his comeback at age sixty-seven, aiming again at Secretary of State. He promoted himself by traveling the globe to meet with foreign leaders, including Soviet Premier Nikita Khrushchev, and belatedly joined John F. Kennedy's presidential campaign in 1960. He contributed $30,000 and supplied the young candidate with advice on Africa after one of his private missions there. At the urging of Arthur Schlesinger, Jr., and John Kenneth Galbraith, Kennedy first appointed Harriman ambassador at large and then to a lesser position as State Department specialist in Far Eastern Affairs. Harriman hid his chagrin and slipped into his old role of troubleshooter.

When Communist forces backed by the Soviet Union threatened to take over Laos in 1962, Kennedy sent Harriman to the Geneva Conference convened to settle the conflict. Harriman helped negotiate a cease-fire and broker a neutrality agreement that set up a coalition government. Shortly afterward, Kennedy made him the third-ranking official at State, Undersecretary for Political Affairs. In that role, Harriman negotiated the Nuclear Test Ban Treaty with the Soviet Union, one of his proudest accomplishments. But his time at State was otherwise unsatisfying. Secretary of State Dean Rusk and his number two, George Ball, kept him on the sidelines, prompting Harriman to force himself into meetings, once even traveling to Vienna in an unsuccessful attempt to join the summit with Khrushchev.

Harriman tried to curry favor with the President's brother Bobby. "Averell artfully set himself up to bypass Dean Rusk and go directly to the Kennedys," said Charles Maechling, one of his deputies at State. "That damaged Averell. Ball and Rusk rigged it so that neither was out of the country at the same time, which meant Averell could never be acting Secretary of State." In 1963, Harriman stumbled badly when he co-authored a compromising cable to Ambassador Henry Cabot Lodge that led to the overthrow and assassination of South Vietnamese President Ngo Dinh Diem. Although Kennedy never rebuked him, noted Abramson, "Averell knew Kennedy's confidence in him was shaken."

When Lyndon Johnson became President after Kennedy was assassinated in November 1963, Harriman launched what Abramson termed "a largely unsuccessful campaign of flattery and self-promotion," including lavish parties for Johnson's two daughters before their weddings. Johnson eventually named him ambassador at large. But Johnson didn't trust him, largely because of his close friendship with Bobby Kennedy. Still, Harriman labored hard to support the President and the war in Vietnam.

Johnson acknowledged Harriman's loyal service by making him his representative to the talks in Paris to end the Vietnam conflict. After a stalemate of five months, North and South Vietnamese delegates finally agreed in the fall of 1968 to negotiate when the talks broke down over the shape of the table. At issue was the status of the Viet Cong, the Communist guerrilla force in South Vietnam. Ten weeks later the participants settled on a large round table for everyone, flanked by two rectangular tables for Communist and non-Communist staff members.

Harriman felt he had created the conditions for talks to proceed, but the election of Richard Nixon in November 1968 had put an end to his involvement. Typically, Harriman couldn't resist pressing his own case, even if it meant joining the Republicans. Much as he had secretly supported Republican Wendell Willkie while serving Roosevelt, Harriman vainly put out feelers to Nixon before leaving Paris and reluctantly returning to private life.

His marriage to Marie had evolved into a contented partnership, "a tribute to sticking it out," said Katharine Graham. "In the end they were very close and very supportive." They never overcame the sexual incompatibility that had developed early in their marriage. They simply adjusted and didn't let their lack of physical intimacy impinge on their mutual devotion.

When he was Secretary of Commerce, Harriman had resumed his wartime affair with Kay Halle, who had become a Washington journalist and resident expert on the Churchill family through her continuing friendship with Randolph. Halle pursued Harriman, telling friends that he wanted to marry her. Marie was even more vexed by Halle than by Pamela because of Halle's "high visibility and earnest intentions," according to Abramson. Harriman dropped her, and from then on he found more discreet and transitory companions. "Ol' Averell likes women," Lyndon Johnson once explained to Washington lawyer Joseph Califano, then a top aide to the President. "Tell him we'll put a couple of pretty nurses on the plane and they'll start working on him as soon as the wheels are up and by the time he gets to Santiago, he'll have it up!"

Marie became a successful political hostess, first in Washington where she amused her guests by turning her famously sardonic wit on the city's self-important strivers—Harriman included. "Oh Ave, come off it," she would croak in her whiskey voice whenever he got too pompous. They were a capable duo in Paris as well, where Marie entertained diplomats and journalists nonstop in the Left Bank apartment that she filled with her choice Impressionist paintings. Marie even managed to liven up Albany, importing writers, artists, and Broadway celebrities from Manhattan.

Over the years, Harriman relied heavily on Marie's political instincts. According to her daughter Nancy Lutz, their political partnership began during the trip to Iran in 1951, the first time Marie accompanied Harriman on a diplomatic mission. She gave him good advice, and, said Lutz, "he decided to use her politically. She said to me it was the first time she felt useful." It was Marie who pushed him to support Jack Kennedy in 1960 and then sent messages through an intermediary that her husband wanted to help. "She had an instinctive thing for phonies and Ave had none," said Lutz. "He consulted her a lot about people in government." She read and commented on his speeches, taking special aim at his clumsy attempts at humor. "Ugh, Ave, that's the worst," she would say, and he would obediently make revisions.

He never seemed to mind her somewhat eccentric habits. He usually went to bed at eleven and rose early, while she stayed up until two or three in the morning and rarely awoke before noon. "Marie was a wonderful character," said Edward Morgan, the former husband of Nancy Lutz. "She had this incredible business of staying up all night and playing cards and just talking. She was never dull." Nor was she the least bit vain. She grew stout as she aged, wore thick glasses, smoked heavily, laughed raucously, drank moderately, and made herself up haphazardly. She still dressed well, but she didn't like to spend much money on clothes.

Since she wasn't the acquisitive type, Marie didn't mind Harriman's famous frugality. Whether it was changing the linoleum in the kitchen at their vacation home in Hobe Sound or repainting the peeling walls in their Georgetown house, Harriman invariably protested the cost. "Cheap old bastard," Marie used to mutter to friends—but with a sense of irreverence rather than spite. "Marie and Averell lived as if they didn't have much money. He drove himself in a nondescript car," said one Georgetown matron. "You didn't have the feeling of someone running a wealthy household."

Harriman paid little attention to creature comforts. What he craved was company, so Marie kept him busy with guests who always felt welcome in the informal, relaxed atmosphere she fostered. He nearly deaf, she nearly blind, they clung together, surrounded by their Washington friends. "Marie was a Washington hostess, and Ave liked a dinner party every night," said Dean Acheson's widow Alice.

In the last several years of her life, Marie suffered declining health, although she didn't complain about it. The only sign, except for her diminished activity, was the locket she wore containing nitroglycerine tablets that she took for angina. "Marie was very gallant," said a woman who knew her for many years. "Nobody thought she was dying." Her references to death were predictably jocular. Walking through the graveyard at Arden, she announced, "I don't want to be beside Mr. and Mrs. Harriman. They were such bores. I would rather be beside Bill Kitchen [the late Harriman caretaker] and the other staff."

In September 1970, the Harrimans were at their home in Sands Point with her daughter Nancy. Late one night, Marie mentioned that her chest hurt as she rubbed her left arm. Harriman woke up at 2:00 A.M., stalked in, and took away her cigarettes. As he left, Marie began talking about dying. She even mentioned that she had her successor already selected: Mary Russell, her close friend and Georgetown neighbor, a Russian aristocrat who was the widow of newspaper correspondent Ned Russell. According to Nancy, however, "Mary Russell wasn't the least bit serious. Mummy was always joking, 'If I die, Ave, you'll have to get married right away because you're so helpless.' "

Marie came down with a cold and traveled back to Washington with her friend and secretary Ann Sardi Gina. There her chest pains worsened, and she went to George Washington University Hospital at Harriman's urging. The next morning she died after a massive heart attack. When Harriman arrived at the hospital, he was dismayed to discover that Marie was wearing the wedding band given her by Sonny Whitney. "Ave took it off. He was furious," said Nancy. "Ann Sardi found Ave's ring and put it on Mummy's finger." (In an even more peculiar twist, Harriman took Peter and Cheray Duchin with him to visit Marie's body at the Gawler Funeral Home. They opened the casket, and at Harriman's direction, Cheray Duchin removed Harriman's wedding ring from Marie's finger. Harriman later gave it to Bobby Kennedy's widow Ethel as a token of friendship.) Marie's funeral was held at Arden. Her grave in the family cemetery was alongside the space reserved for her husband—and near his dour parents.

Harriman was crushed by his loss. Back in his Georgetown house, Nancy Lutz found him "walking from room to room, going into my mother's room and staying there. He used to sit in her room and cry." He scarcely left the house and rebuffed attempts to console him. Knowing that Harriman hated to be alone, Nancy's daughter Alida Morgan, then a freshman at Georgetown University, visited him every day. She stopped by at breakfast to discuss the day's meals with his cook and secretary, and usually returned for lunch or dinner, often serving as his hostess. But, noted Rudy Abramson, "in that melancholy autumn, he looked and acted like an old man who had come to the end of the road."

He spent the winter in Hobe Sound, where he was joined by Peter and Cheray Duchin and their young children. As Alida Morgan had done in Washington, the Duchins organized dinners as well as croquet and bridge games. What really rejuvenated him, however, was a trip to the Soviet Union with Maine Senator Edmund Muskie.

In the spring of 1971, Harriman began to come out of his mourning. He testified before the Senate Foreign Relations Committee on the Vietnam War, reopened his office, and started entertaining again. He dined with Georgetown hostesses Mary Russell, Kay Halle, and Luvie Pearson, the widow of columnist Drew Pearson, each of whom would have been pleased to be the next Mrs. Harriman. It was only natural that he would accept Katharine Graham's invitation to honor his old friend Arthur Schlesinger at a dinner in her garden.

Pamela had been keeping track of Harriman since January 1965, when she had encountered him at Winston Churchill's funeral. They traveled home together in President Johnson's plane. "It had been a memorable moment in Harriman's life," wrote Abramson, "saying goodbye to the leader he idolized, and seeing the woman who still possessed him and talking with her for hours as they crossed the Atlantic." In the following years, Harriman had encouraged young Winston in his political ambitions. When Winston came to Washington in 1968, Harriman invited him to dinner. They discussed how Pamela was doing, and afterward, Winston made a report to his mother at Haywire House.

"I would see Marie and Averell in their town house in New York," recalled Washington journalist Clayton Fritchey, "and I would be going out and Averell would ask me, 'Who are you going to see?' I would say, 'An old friend of yours.' And I would tell him, Pamela, and I could tell he was still in love with her. It was nothing he would say. He would never say anything like that, but I could just tell."

Pamela had encouraged his attentions. The morning after Hayward's death, she had called Peter and Cheray Duchin at Harriman's home in Hobe Sound. "I had no idea Leland had died," Cheray recalled. "Pamela told me to make sure Averell read the *New York Times* that morning. I felt it was rather peculiar. I wasn't that close to Leland and Pam. I didn't tell Averell at the time. I didn't know how to do it. I felt very awkward. I felt I was being used. I didn't tell him to read the paper, but I kind of think it was discussed, although I don't remember if Peter brought it up. It was awkward."

It took a while for Harriman to make the next move, although he "had been thinking about Pamela since hearing of Leland Hayward's death in March," wrote Abramson. In June 1971 he called William Walton, Harriman and Pamela's mutual friend since the war, and asked where he could find her. Walton told him she had gone to Europe. In an interview with Marie Brenner, Walton recalled: "Averell said, 'Do you think Pamela would want to see me?' I said, 'Of course.' "

Harriman's reunion with Pamela at Katharine Graham's dinner party had an air of inevitability. Thirty years after their first meeting across the luncheon table at Chequers, they were even more well matched, not only by temperament but in their goals and values. Pamela may have been derided in the jet set as the "widow of opportunity," but Harriman was every bit as opportunistic.

Nearly eighty, Harriman also longed for companionship. "It didn't show in his external self, but Ave was a very physical man," said Alida Morgan. "Even though he and Grandmère hadn't had a physical relationship in years, in his grieving, when he would hug me it was a real hug. When he was mourning, he would hold my hand half the time. When he was crying in Grandmère's room, he would clutch a pillow, smelling it or holding it close. It was more than loneliness. It was a tactile loss. He needed to be held. One of the things Pamela could do was give him sex and that kind of contact."

Moreover, with the loss of Marie, said Nancy Lutz, "his whole world had turned upside down. There was nobody to direct it, to make his life easy. His way had been greased for years." Judged by the size of his bank account, Harriman was a great catch, but he was an irascible skinflint. With Pamela, the two sides of Harriman were easily reconciled. He had supported her financially, so he knew her price, and he also knew that she was worth it: She would work hard, take good care of him, and not simply grab his money. She knew that he was prickly and self-absorbed, but she also knew that he was utterly dependable —and vulnerable enough to yield to her coaxing ways. Both of them had their eyes open.

CHAPTER

Twenty-five

WHEN PAMELA'S FRIEND Gerald Van der Kemp heard that she had been reunited with Harriman, he exclaimed to his wife Florence, "Mais on ne peut pas rechauffer le chauffage central!" To the skeptical Parisian, once a love affair had ended, it was nearly impossible to start up again. But Van der Kemp underestimated Pamela's ability to rekindle old passions.

Harriman was spending weekends at Sands Point in the modest single-story house he had lent to Peter and Cheray Duchin for the summer. After the Graham dinner party, Pamela called Peter on Long Island: Would he mind asking Harriman if she could come for the weekend? "I don't know if Ave was being the diplomat," Cheray recalled, "but he said, 'Let me think about it,'" before he ultimately agreed. As a buffer, the Duchins also suggested inviting Mike Forrestal, who like Peter had been a surrogate son of Harriman's since his father James Forrestal, the former Secretary of Defense, committed suicide in 1949.

Pamela drove down from Haywire the following Friday. "She leapt out of her beige Cadillac wearing summer tweeds, looking competent, efficient, and beautifully groomed," recalled Peter Duchin. "She arrived with an effusion of gushiness, love, and twinkling eyes." On Saturday night, after dinner out with neighbors George Backer and Edmund and Marion Goodman, Pamela and Harriman were alone in the house together before Cheray and Peter Duchin returned home. Although their precise memories of the evening differed, each had a strong recollection of flipping on the lights and discovering fifty-one-year-old Pamela and seventy-nine-year-old Harriman in a passionate embrace on the sofa.

"Averell's top was open and his pants were undone. He had lipstick on his face and chest. Her blouse was unbuttoned," said Peter. "Averell yelled, 'What!' and sat up. I said, 'Oh God, I'm so sorry,' turned off the light, and fled." "It was like catching two teenagers. No one knew what to do," Cheray recalled.

Later that night, Peter Duchin heard a crash and rushed to Pamela's bedroom to ask if she was all right. "Fine," she said. "Something fell over. Go to bed." The next morning, according to the Duchins, Pamela was only too eager to recount her amorous adventure. Peter remembered her bursting into their bedroom with a "beatific expression," while Cheray recalled encountering her in the breakfast room. Both said Pamela reported that frisky old Averell had crept outside the house, tapped on her window, and fallen through the screen while climbing into her bedroom. "She told me how romantic Averell was," said Cheray. "How he had been wearing silk pajamas. I remember thinking, 'I can't believe Averell would do this.' She was overcome by the romance of Averell, how sweet, kind, gentle, and wonderful he was."

For Harriman's first visit to Haywire in early September, she invited the Duchins along as well. "Pam was very cheerful, girlish and full of energy, not in the sense of waiting on him but showing full attention in an upbeat, flirtatious sort of way," recalled Cheray. Pamela plied Harriman with nostalgia. "She would spark Averell's mind, bring him back to that era of World War II which must have been very important to him," said Cheray. "They had this past together, and she was able to recreate it. It would be 'remember when,' and she would tell stories and elicit from him. None of it was personal. It was about incidents in the war. She had good detailed recall about it, and she would have him laughing about incidents. It was wonderful to see, amazing to see."

Harriman was overjoyed to be in her company again, marveling in the ways she made everything so easy. After his somewhat spartan life at Sands Point, recalled Cheray Duchin, "he went into her house, and there were flowers everywhere, wonderful food, beautiful linens on the beds, ice water brought in morning and night. I think Averell had never seen anything like this. He was fascinated and he was in awe. I do remember him saying, 'Isn't she wonderful? Look at this wonderful house, how comfortable it is. Look at this woman alone, and how she does things and manages.' She was shooting the moon and determined to give him the perfect weekend. Not everyone has that kind of confidence."

As the weekend drew to a close, Harriman asked her to visit him in Georgetown, since he was shutting down the Sands Point house at the end of the summer season. "She told him she would never set foot in Washington unless she was his wife," said Cheray. Two weeks later, Averell Harriman and Pamela Hayward announced their engagement. She explained to the *New York Times* that she and Harriman were "very firm friends," and he said they expected to marry in the first week in October. Sensitive to their twenty-nine-year age difference, they were both eager to set a date before Harriman's birthday in November. "He was determined that he not be eighty when they married," said Winston, who was nevertheless "surprised at the speed of it all."

They married even sooner than expected, on Monday, September 27— barely eight weeks after their reunion in Washington and six months after Leland Hayward's death—in Our Lady's Chapel at St. Thomas More Roman Catholic Church on East 89th Street in Manhattan. Pamela arranged for the Reverend Joseph Christie, the Farm Street Jesuit who had converted her to Catholicism, to be flown over to assist in the service. It was a private ceremony that Harriman and Pamela tried to keep secret by inviting only three guests, all of whom served as witnesses: Pamela's sister Sheila Moore; Harriman's daughter Kathleen Mortimer; and Ethel Kennedy—wearing Marie Harriman's wedding ring that Harriman had given her a year earlier—who was chosen because one witness had to be Catholic. Pamela's son Winston wasn't included, nor was

Harriman's daughter Mary Fisk, although both were invited to a cocktail reception afterward. When a photographer for *Women's Wear Daily* caught the bridal party arriving at the church, Harriman gestured at the camera and growled, "Don't publish that picture," while Pamela watched anxiously. The picture appeared in the newspaper anyway.

Afterward, they went to Harriman's East 81st Street town house, where 150 of their friends had been invited for a five-thirty cocktail party, with no purpose specified. Harriman wore a navy pinstripe suit, and Pamela an off-white wool crepe Halston dress set off by a necklace of rubies, emeralds, and pearls. "We did it! We did it!" Pamela exulted to her friend Kitty Carlisle Hart as she walked in the door. "He never looked happier and younger, and she never looked more beautiful," Cheray Duchin said.

The guest list was a select group of socialites, politicians, and theatrical figures—as well as former lovers Bill Paley and Jock Whitney, and former beau and Kathleen's husband Stanley Mortimer. "This reminds me of the movie 'La Ronde,' " quipped one guest. "It was either the beginning or the end of an era, whichever way you want to take it," announced Truman Capote. "I was delighted to see Pamela married again."

Pamela decorated Harriman's dreary old house with big bouquets of country flowers—iris, daisies, cornflowers, anemones—and she had on hand a supply of calling cards reading: "Mrs. Averell Harriman." There was no wedding cake, however (too "corny," said Pamela), and only one toast, given by Shirley Fisk, the husband of Harriman's daughter Mary.

For a wedding present, Harriman gave his new bride the painting *Lady Hamilton as the Vestal Virgin* by George Romney, which Marie had bought years earlier. Perhaps recalling those wartime evenings watching *That Hamilton Woman* with the British Prime Minister, Pamela had expressed an interest in the portrait. Harriman ignored the irony of giving his wife the likeness of a notorious courtesan. Pamela's gift to Harriman was a pledge to become an American citizen, which she would fulfill two months later before a federal judge.

The festivities continued in Washington with a second reception thrown by Harriman. Five hundred friends and acquaintances thronged his Georgetown home on a rainy night in early October to meet Pamela, who wore her wedding dress and stood with her husband, Winston and Minnie Churchill, and Kathleen Mortimer. "There were columnists, TV celebrities, Senators, Beautiful People, Supreme Court justices, ambassadors, authors, New Frontiersmen, Old Frontiersmen, and Perle Mesta," wrote Kandy Stroud in *Women's Wear Daily*.

Pamela's role as Averell Harriman's wife was her top priority—an essential first stage in her bold effort to create a new identity. She continued to woo her new husband in ways large and small, and to take control of his life. One of her early maneuvers was to scuttle a biography of Marie that Harriman had arranged with Viking Press president Thomas Guinzburg.

It was a vanity deal under which Harriman would pay Viking $20,000 to underwrite a $25,000 advance to the author, William Wright. "Harriman was wildly enthusiastic," recalled Wright, who spent a day at Sands Point in the summer of 1971 to discuss the project. "He was telling me wonderful stories, what a terrific character Marie was, giving me names of sources." Once all the details were worked out, Wright signed the contract, which then went to Harriman's office for his signature. "Just at that moment, he married Pamela," said Wright. "Two months went by. Then Tom Guinzburg called me on a Saturday morning and said, 'He seems to have lost interest. I feel terrible about it.' When Pamela came into Harriman's life there never was a Marie Harriman. The last thing Pamela wanted was for her husband to build a Taj Mahal for his previous wife at Viking Press."

An even more dramatic example of Pamela's success in solidifying her marriage was the breathtaking speed with which she convinced Harriman to give a generous bequest and an extravagant gift to Winston for his thirty-first birthday. Alarmed by her tales of her son flying his single-engine Piper Arrow back and forth between London and his Manchester constituency on "dark nights and foggy days," as Winston described it, Harriman gave him an $85,000 twin-engine Piper Seneca.

At the same time, Harriman set up a $1 million trust fund to benefit Winston, his wife and children. In later years, Winston insisted that the $1 million came from Pamela. "She had some money of her own," he said, "and some pieces of furniture were sold." Yet in an effusive letter written on October 15, 1971—less than a month after his mother's marriage to Harriman—Winston thanked his new stepfather for "what you plan to do for us and the children" that "will certainly make a big difference in our lives."

Even with an inheritance from his grandfather (the foreign rights to his book *A History of the English-Speaking Peoples*) augmented by journalism and lecture fees, Winston told Harriman he had been concerned about the cost of raising his growing family. (Although his wife Minnie's family had been wealthy, she was not.) His parliamentary salary, he disclosed to Harriman, had left him the previous year with only $1,000 after paying his secretary and other parliamentary expenses. As an expression of their gratitude, Winston and Minnie Churchill named their fourth child, born several years later, John Averell.

With Winston's financial security assured, Pamela's next project was Harriman's Georgetown home. Within days of the wedding, she and Billy Baldwin flew to Washington for the initial decorating consultation at 3038 N Street. Baldwin urged restraint after he had sized up Harriman's house, a three-story red-brick Federal built in 1805, with a white front door topped by a fan light. "This is not a beautiful London house," he cautioned her. "Georgetown never was famous for its fine houses, but it's full of charm, and you must behave. . . . You have to respect his life there and his age. . . . You just play it low."

Pamela did not share his respect for Georgetown architecture. "I must say, I don't think too much of those doorways," she exclaimed as they arrived. She made an even more sweeping judgment on entering the first of two sitting rooms. "We'll just rip that mantel out," she said. Baldwin retorted, "Pamela, we will do nothing of the kind. That mantel is harmless. It's a good American copy of a French mantel. . . . *You will not* make people think that you feel that

Averell has been living in a dump, because he hasn't." Disregarding Baldwin, Pamela went through the entire house declaring that changes had to be made.

She replaced Marie's furniture with her own Louis XVI pieces reupholstered in soft flowered chintzes and fattened with new down filling. She selected restful earth tones that she accented with what her friend William Walton described as "fresh garden hues: here dark green, next a soft rose, there tawny gold playing with lettuce green, and everywhere, notes of blue." For the dining room she imported eighteenth-century Chinese handpainted wallpaper from England. She hired architect Hugh Newell Jacobson to enclose the sun porch with removable glass panels. In contrast to Marie Harriman's simple backdrop for her collection of paintings, Pamela's interiors were, as usual, highly decorated, with heavy curtains and elaborate furniture.

Determined not to sleep in Marie Harriman's bedroom, Pamela chose new quarters: as Baldwin described them, "quite a big bedroom, another single room, a sitting room and two baths, and she just made that into a suite for herself. It was high up and had a beautiful view and it was really charming." She had Baldwin decorate her suite in pastel hues and install a four-poster double bed with a fabric canopy. Harriman had his own bedroom, dressing room, and bath; Pamela made sure he had an an extra-long mattress so his feet would no longer dangle beyond the end of his bed.

In 1970, Harriman had talked to the National Gallery of Art about donating Marie's art collection as well as his Georgetown home in which to exhibit the masterpieces. But when the gallery questioned the wisdom of maintaining the N Street property as an annex, negotiations had broken down. The talks resumed after Harriman's marriage to Pamela. Recalled Baldwin, "Every space in the house had been covered with a fine impressionist painting, none of which meant anything to [Pamela] and which she didn't even like. Pamela urged Averell to give them as a memorial to Marie, and let her have some money to spend on the house, which is exactly what he did." After conferring with Pamela, Harriman kept a choice group of Marie's paintings, including van Gogh's prized *White Roses,* Picasso's *Mother and Child,* Matisse's *Woman in a Blue Hat,* and Renoir's *Portrait of Mademoiselle Demarsy,* along with a Degas bronze of a ballerina.

Under the revised plan, the National Gallery received twenty-one of the paintings and one drawing—a trove including five Cézannes, two Gauguins, a Rousseau, Picasso's exceptional *Lady with a Fan,* and a Seurat worth $825,000, the highest price tag of the group. The paintings were valued at $6,020,000 when they were donated in January 1972, and Harriman received a tax deduction for his charity.

Shortly after their wedding, Pamela persuaded Harriman to sell the Manhattan town house he had shared with Marie. The rest of Harriman's properties Pamela incorporated into her life in varying degrees. For much of their first decade together, Pamela tolerated Harriman's longstanding attachments to these places even as she worked to change some houses and discard others.

They took their winter and Easter vacations at his home in Hobe Sound, where Harriman amused himself playing croquet and swimming in the pool. But Pamela never liked the sedate old-WASP atmosphere and the reminders of Harriman's former life. The house had been Marie's, given to her by Harriman as penance for his wartime adulteries, and the Hobe Sound crowd were Marie's friends. Pamela replaced Marie's old retainers, a black gardener and his wife, and began renovations. "Under Pamela, Hobe Sound was totally different, down to the formal English gardens she put in," said Alida Morgan. "The house had been a bungalow and it got very formal and elaborate." It wasn't until 1979 that Harriman sold the place for $500,000 to Douglas and K. K. Auchincloss after Pamela convinced him that the weather in a Caribbean resort would be more reliable.

They spent even less time at the summer house in Sands Point. Harriman rented it to friends, and in 1973 sought permission to build a thirty-five-home development on the eighty-eight wooded and waterfront acres around the house—a plan that would not be approved for fourteen years.

During the early years of their marriage, Pamela and Harriman used Haywire House—which Pamela renamed "Birchgrove" after Brooke Hayward titled her caustic 1977 memoir *Haywire*—as their principal country retreat, spending occasional weekends and a portion of the summer months there. But Pamela wanted an estate near their Georgetown home, so in 1977 Harriman bought her a gray fieldstone house on sixty acres in the horse country in Middleburg, Virginia, for $740,000. It was called "Journey's End," which Pamela thought struck the wrong note. She changed the name to "Willow Oaks," inspired by the grove of elegant trees near the house.

Willow Oaks became Pamela's most ambitious project, surpassing her expenditures on Haywire House during the 1960s. The house at Willow Oaks was unprepossessing: a traditional but by no means grand colonial with several bedrooms, a library, drawing room, dining room, and sun porch. But Pamela was captivated by its setting, which she often said reminded her of Dorset. The house was situated at the crest of a hill, its rear balustraded terrace overlooking a woodland sloping down to the broad waters of Goose Creek, and in the distance the foothills of the Blue Ridge Mountains.

In addition to redecorating the house, Pamela hired a Dutch landscape gardener, Bill Hoogeveen, and four assistants to transform the grounds and gardens. They dug a large pond, replanted the rose garden and the native dogwoods, converted a paddock into a wildflower meadow, regraded the lawns, made over the formal Gray and White Garden, installed terraced herb, vegetable, and cutting gardens, and had water pumped from Goose Creek to create a maze of tiny streams and waterfalls bordered by rocks, hosta, and fern. In an effort to evoke Minterne—which Hoogeveen visited for inspiration—they turned the rear slope into a woodland garden with winding paths, and they planted banks of rhododendrons on an adjacent hillside. To create the perfect view from her bedroom window, Pamela had Hoogeveen reshape the hillside with bulldozers so she could gaze at horses grazing beyond the rhododendrons.

Pamela put in a croquet lawn for Harriman and refurbished the stable, where wooden plaques marked the names of the four horses Harriman bought for his wife. She renovated the guest cottage and poolhouse, which had separate bathrooms and changing rooms for men and women. A new satellite dish, camouflaged in a grove of pine trees, was installed near the tennis court. When the placement of the swimming pool displeased Pamela, she had it filled in and built a new pool in a different location. "A lot of people used to joke about that, saying she couldn't care less about how much money she spent," said Guy Waltman, Harriman's financial adviser during the late 1970s. "But to me it demonstrated what a perfectionist she is."

As she had done with Hayward, Pamela expanded Harriman's household staff, signing on a full-time butler, Michael Kuruc, and hiring a chauffeur to drive their new maroon Cadillac, which had a customized hood ornament in the shape of an ostrich holding a horseshoe from the Digby family crest. She brought in a new chef and an assistant chef, and a parlormaid and chambermaid in addition to the personal maid and housekeeper Marie had been permitted. "When I first started to work for them, I told her my salary and she said the Governor wouldn't pay that," recalled one former employee. "I said, 'I'm sorry I can't work for you.' " Pamela's response was to increase the amount and pay the difference out of petty cash.

To coax Harriman into spending money, Pamela would try to convince him that what she wanted was in his best interests. Failing that, William Walton recalled, she would "pout and stick out her lower lip and make him dissolve and feel bad." Above all, she was patient. "She wouldn't walk in and say, 'Ave, I think you should do X. I know you don't agree, but you should,' " said Waltman. "Her approach was more subtle and sophisticated. It might take days, or weeks, or months. She would persuade rather than ask or demand. 'Ave, don't you think it would be a good idea to do whatever?' she would say. I never saw her throw temper tantrums. She brought him around to her point of view. She didn't always succeed, but her batting average was very high. If she were a baseball player, she would be Hall of Fame material."

Pamela's most tireless campaign, begun in 1973, was for a private jet. "She would start working on him, citing the ladies she admired like Mrs. [Paul] Mellon," recalled a friend who witnessed one of their discussions that year. When Harriman balked, Pamela would retreat, wait a while, and then return with a modified proposal. Finally, in March 1983, Harriman approved the purchase of a used Westwind jet for $2.8 million. It was less elaborate than Bunny Mellon's Gulfstream, with its artwork by Braque, Klee, and Dufy, and less elegant than Jock and Betsey Whitney's mahogany-paneled Fairchild, but it wasn't bad for a woman who had been nearly broke twelve years before. It had ten seats, a bathroom, and a small galley. Pamela assured Harriman that the Westwind would make his life easier; he would no longer have to go to crowded airports, change planes, or worry about his luggage. "Averell benefited from her spending, and he never denied it," said a Washington friend. "He came to appreciate what she did because she made a great difference in his life."

Eventually Pamela took full authority over everyday expenses. "Pamela's energies were focused on running the households," said Guy Waltman. "She was not on an allowance, and Averell was, in terms of Pamela, very generous."

One visitor to the Harrimans in Hobe Sound was surprised by Pamela's recreational spending. "Pam's idea of an outing was driving into Palm Beach and spending thousands of dollars," the visitor recalled. "My wife wasn't interested in that. She didn't want to go and watch Pam shop. Pam was not at all pleased by that." Pamela still had to secure Harriman's approval for large outlays such as the $50,000 driveway she had built at Willow Oaks in 1978. "We had to discuss how to break the news to the Governor," said Waltman. "He would flinch, but I don't recall him ever saying no."

From time to time, Harriman conducted a light audit of her expenditures. When she proposed renting in Barbados after Hobe Sound was sold, Harriman asked, "How much is this house going to cost?" "One thousand dollars," replied Pamela. Harriman paused to digest the amount. "Is that for a week or a month?" "Ave," replied Pamela, "it's for a month." Recalled a man who heard the exchange, "She knew she had to end the conversation, so she made it up at a level she thought he would find reasonable. The place probably cost a thousand dollars a day." "I know Pamela spends a lot of money, but you aren't to worry about it," Harriman told Guy Waltman.

Over time, Pamela succeeded in removing all traces of Marie Harriman from their surroundings—from the cottages at Arden and Sun Valley as well as from the Georgetown house. She assumed Marie's place on the various Harriman philanthropies. After the Marie Harriman Collection was given to the National Gallery, even the remaining artwork became identified with Pamela. One painting, actually a copy by William Walton of Walt Kuhn's *Green Apples and Scoop*, which had gone to the National Gallery, was inscribed: "Hommage à Marie." At Pamela's request, Walton painted over his inscription.

Pamela also set about distancing members of Marie's family who had strong ties to Harriman: Marie's children Nancy Lutz and Harry Whitney; her grandchildren; and her surrogate son, Peter Duchin. Harriman kept up a friendly correspondence with all of them, and from time to time invited them for lunch or dinner. But in formalizing Harriman's routines the way she had Hayward's, Pamela was able to curtail contact with Marie's relatives. As she had done with Leland's children Brooke and Bill, Pamela needlessly alienated those who might otherwise have been allies. "Perhaps this is a profound sense of possessiveness that borders on an affliction," Clayton Fritchey told the journalist Marie Brenner. "Pamela might have felt threatened and wanted to hold all the power." Averell Harriman was every bit as complicitous as Leland Hayward had been. "If you are a decent man, you don't let a woman separate you from your children or grandchildren or stepchildren," said Nancy Lutz. "But I think Averell was thrilled out of his mind and wasn't about to jeopardize that for a bunch of kids."

Marie's granddaughter Alida Morgan was the first to feel the chill. She and her sister Pam had long enjoyed a close relationship with their step-grandfather. Throughout their childhood they had visited Hobe Sound every Easter and had spent half of each summer at Sands Point. At Marie's urging, Harriman had paid their tuition at Foxcroft, and for some years he had given each of them the maximum yearly nontaxable gift of $3,000. "Ave knew them better than his own grandchildren and treated them well," said their father, Edward Morgan. And it was Alida who had helped Harriman through his mourning.

In the fall of 1971 Alida had transferred to Yale, and one weekend while staying with a friend in Washington she decided to visit Harriman. "A butler I didn't know answered the door and asked me to wait on the stairs," she recalled. "He came back and said they were busy and I should make an appointment. He asked for my visiting card." Nonplussed, Alida walked around to the kitchen entrance where she found Marie's housekeeper Gina and her personal maid Lucinda. "Both of them burst into tears," said Alida. "They said they had stayed because Ave had asked them to. But it was obviously a very different regime."

Neither Alida nor Pam Morgan was able to speak privately with Harriman again. "If you got him on the phone, Pamela would get on the line and join in," said Alida, echoing the lament of Brooke and Bill Hayward. "I gave up other than to send an occasional note to Ave." Except for a few luncheon parties at Birchgrove, Alida was no longer welcome, not even when she returned to Washington to run a shop in Georgetown, although her wealthy business partner, Sophie Englehard, was invited to numerous fund-raising dinners at the Harriman home.

Nancy Lutz had her own reckoning when she visited Hobe Sound with her youngest daughter Vicky, who was then about eleven years old. Pamela had recently redone the house, removing in the process all photos of Marie and her children. "How do you like it?" Pamela asked Lutz. "Don't you think it looks a lot better?" Lutz was speechless.

It was Peter Duchin who bore the deepest grudge. Orphaned at fourteen when Eddy Duchin died in 1951, Peter always regarded Marie and Averell Harriman as "Ma and Ave." "Peter is a member of our family," Harriman once wrote in a letter of introduction to the American Ambassador to Greece in the early 1960s. The Harrimans had overseen Peter's education at Hotchkiss and Yale, and they had encouraged his career as a pianist and bandleader. He shared with Harriman a lively interest in Democratic politics, as well as a passion for croquet and bridge. "Peter fit in very well," said Cheray Duchin. "He could hold a conversation with Ave, who would sound off to Peter. Ave respected him."

Peter had always deferred to Harriman and trusted him completely. Marie had planned to bequeath her exquisite Degas bronze of a dancer to Duchin. But when Harriman pointed out that the statue was an integral part of Marie's collection designated for the National Gallery, he persuaded her to leave Duchin a Daumier bronze and cash bequest instead. On Marie's death, Duchin learned from her lawyer, Sol Rosenblatt, that he was not named in Harriman's will. Duchin accepted the news without protest; Harriman had been otherwise generous to him, offering, from time to time, gifts of Union Pacific stock to him and his children. Still, when the Marie Harriman artwork was given away, Duchin noted that the Degas statue was not included. Two decades later he would understand the magnitude of his loss when Pamela sold the statue for $7 million to help fulfill an $11.5 million gift Harriman had pledged to Columbia University.

Peter and Cheray Duchin had been proud of their role in Harriman's courtship of Pamela and had rejoiced at the marriage. Peter was stung when Harriman excluded him from the ceremony, and he was even more wounded when he received a package from Pamela containing "every single picture that we had given to Ave and Marie—every single photo of Peter and Averell and our children," recalled Cheray Duchin. "I guess it was cleaning house, but I remember everything changing after that." No longer could Duchin come and go at N Street, letting himself in with his own key. If he wanted to visit, he had to arrange it with Pamela.

Nevertheless, Duchin held his tongue and adapted to Pamela's terms. But when the Hobe Sound house was sold, Duchin turned on Pamela. Years earlier, according to Duchin, Harriman had told him that he could have "a little acre on the ocean" next to the Hobe Sound house. In the same spirit, Harriman had deeded land in Sands Point to his next-door neighbor and personal physician Edmund Goodman. The Duchins had hired an architect, who developed a plan, and they made inquiries about membership in the Jupiter Island Club. They put off building because they couldn't afford it, but they kept the house as their dream.

In 1979, when Duchin happened to sit next to Pamela at the Al Smith political dinner in New York City, he told her he had heard Hobe Sound was on the market. "What about the acre of land?" he asked. "Aren't you giving that to me?" "She looked right at me," he recalled, "and said, 'Why should I? It's not in writing.' "

The decision may well have been Harriman's—as it had been when he kept the Degas statue. Harriman had a habit of taking back items of value that he considered rightfully his. In her will, Marie Harriman had specified that her daughter Nancy Lutz have the contents of the Sands Point house. But when she went to retrieve a valuable set of plates, she discovered that Harriman had removed them. "I wrote him a note and asked if I could have them," she recalled. "He said, 'I've given them to Pamela.' "

Whenever Harriman decided to provide for relatives and friends financially, he did so in his own exacting way. "I am not aware of any case, other than the possibility of paintings someday going to the National Gallery, that Ave said at a future time he would make a gift," said Guy Waltman. "When he made gifts he made them." Evidently Harriman had no such intent with the Hobe Sound property, but Duchin was unwilling to press him. Duchin explained, "Pam knew I wouldn't say, 'Hey, Ave, what about that piece of land?' I was in awe of Ave and never talked money with him."

Duchin's reaction was complicated by his anger over never being adopted officially by Harriman and Marie. "Peter was so hurt about that," said Nancy Lutz. "He didn't belong to anyone, and he talked about it with a good deal of bitterness. He thought Ave loved him, but I don't think Ave loved anyone." Intimidated by Harriman, Duchin could more readily blame Pamela, since it was she who had callously dismissed his claim to the Hobe Sound land and tried to cut him out.

Like Brooke Hayward, the socially well connected and outspoken Peter Duchin turned out to be a formidable adversary. But Pamela could not have anticipated the explosive possibilities when Duchin divorced Cheray and in 1985 married Brooke. Bill Hayward, meanwhile, softened toward Pamela. Shortly after her marriage to Harriman, Bill dropped his lawsuit because he knew he could never prevail against her new financial resources. At the same time, Pamela persuaded Harriman to set up two trust funds of about $50,000 apiece for Bill's children. Bill decided, he later said, that there was "a nice side to her."

For all her cavalier treatment of Marie's family, Pamela was correct and cordial with Harriman's children and grandchildren, which was consistent with her husband's remote relationship with them. Both his daughters approved of Harriman's marriage to Pamela. Though Kathleen and Pamela had lost touch since the postwar years, they shared the strong bond of their wartime experience, and Pamela credited herself with making the match between Kathleen and her husband, Stanley Mortimer. Kathleen was well aware of Pamela's drawbacks, but she genuinely liked the new stepmother who was two years her junior. Pamela's arrival, Kathleen and Mary knew, meant that their father would be well cared for. According to an old friend of Kathleen's, "She thought Pam was a gold digger but that she was probably the right person for her father. She thought it was better for her father to marry someone they knew and grew up with than fall in the hands of another lady."

Neither daughter had reason to feel threatened by Pamela. They felt secure in their inherited wealth and were comfortable in the traditional roles of upper-class women. Although educated at intellectually self-conscious Bennington College, neither was expected to have a career. Rather, in the manner of Harriman's sister, Mary Rumsey, who founded the Junior League, they were supposed to devote themselves to good works, and to live quiet, proper lives as wives and mothers. Averell Harriman would have been dismayed had they spent their time indulging themselves or becoming publicity-seeking socialites who organized parties for chic charities.

Mary Fisk hewed to her father's expectations most faithfully. A tall, shy woman, she was married at twenty-three to a respected Manhattan internist named Shirley Fisk. Seven years her senior, Fisk had graduated from Yale like Harriman and received his medical training at Columbia University. In the first eight years of their marriage, Mary Fisk had three children. Having servants allowed her to work as a volunteer with the Public Education Association. As one of a dozen founders of the New York City School Volunteer Program in the late 1950s, she taught remedial reading at a school in Spanish Harlem. She also attended luncheons and lectures at the Cosmopolitan Club, a gathering place for upper-class matrons with intellectual aspirations. Generous and unassuming, described by her relatives as a "saint," Mary kept the lowest profile of anyone in her family.

At first, Kathleen led a more visible and colorful life, primarily because of her years as her father's hostess in London and Moscow, and her work in journalism during World War II and the immediate postwar years. But after marrying Stanley Mortimer in 1947, Kathleen quit her job at *Newsweek*. They had three children (his children from his first marriage, Amanda and Tony, lived with their mother, Babe Paley), and Kathleen's daily routines virtually mirrored those of her sister. Thin and erect in her bearing, Kathleen also found great pleasure in vigorous athletics—riding, hiking, and skiing. She had her father's unsentimental and abrupt manner, but unlike Harriman, she was attentive to her children, the second of whom was born with impaired sight and went deaf from medications given him after his premature birth. "Kath was more of a mother to me, did more of the things a mother should do, than my own mother," said her stepdaughter Amanda Mortimer Burden. "Kath was steady and devoted and dependable."

The Mortimers and Fisks lived in spacious apartments on New York's Upper East Side and spent their weekends and summers at the family compound at Arden, the vast estate in upstate New York that had been built by E. H. Harriman. Although Averell Harriman had given his father's hundred-room house to Columbia University after it had served as a Navy hospital and lookout post during World War II, family members continued to live in an assortment of modest cottages that had once belonged to naval officers and servants. With its stables, its stream stocked yearly with trout by Harriman's brother Roland, its two lakes, and its thousands of acres of woodlands, Arden was an idyllic retreat that reinforced the family's sense of privilege and solidarity. The men played golf at the nearby Tuxedo Club, where the Mortimer family had been prominent since the turn of the century, and parents and children enjoyed long morning trail rides, followed by spirited tennis matches, fishing in the summertime or bird shooting in the winter. This was the Harriman world, along with skiing vacations at the other family retreat in Sun Valley and winter forays to Florida.

Their storybook lives were marred, however, by the illnesses of Stanley Mortimer and Shirley Fisk. Mortimer worked for several years on Madison Avenue before settling into the New York clubman's life of racquet sports, leisurely lunches, backgammon games, and snoozes in deep leather chairs. His business stationery was even engraved "Stanley G. Mortimer, Jr., 370 Park Avenue," a sly signal to those in the know who recognized the address as that of the exclusive Racquet & Tennis Club. For all his courtliness and fine-boned features, however, Mortimer was tormented by manic depression. He controlled the condition with medication much of the time, but he was periodically debilitated, sometimes spending long stretches in the hospital. Shirley Fisk endured the physical pain of muscular dystrophy. He was diagnosed late in the 1960s after his retirement from medicine, and for the next ten years he experienced a steady deterioration of his muscles as the disease progressed. He died on Christmas day 1979 at age sixty-nine.

The families bore these burdens discreetly and suffered no financial distress. Shirley Fisk had made a good living as a doctor, and Stanley Mortimer had an inheritance from his parents. The Mortimer fortune—from Manhattan real estate on his father's side and from Standard Oil on his mother's side—was shared by Stanley, his three brothers, and two sisters. It provided a six-figure income for Stanley and his family. Both Kathleen and Mary were already wealthy in their own right, having received their first inheritance in 1936 when their mother died. The previous year their father had also established four trust funds in their names that by the 1970s were worth more than $1 million each—at a time when Harriman himself was worth well in excess of $100 million. In 1960, Harriman established similar trusts for each of his six grandchildren. During the sixties he also began to give his heirs annual tax-free gifts of Union Pacific stock —$3,000 apiece initially and then $10,000. He presented the stock at Christmas, with a letter directing that it be treated as "capital, not income."

In this manner, Averell Harriman yoked his heirs to the values and expectations of an upper-class entitlement system. E. H. Harriman, who had built the family fortune, had instilled in his son Averell the ambition and drive to acquire what had eluded him: social position and respectability. As Averell Harriman's six grandchildren came of age in the 1970s, he exhorted them to pursue public service with the knowledge that they would always be provided for. He didn't expect them to build a fortune anew, but he did try to imbue them with the work ethic, a quaint notion in a world cushioned by unearned income.

Harriman even provided an automatic philanthropic outlet that would guarantee his heirs prominent positions in their communities whatever line of work they chose: A fund originally established by his mother in 1925, the Mary W. Harriman Foundation had an endowment valued at more than $10 million by the early 1980s. Its income, which exceeded $700,000 annually, allowed Kathleen and Mary and all their children to designate their favorite beneficiaries —from private schools and community ambulance corps to research funds set up by their family physicians—for yearly donations, some of them in the tens of thousands. When the fundraisers called, the Harriman heirs played the patrons, with a seemingly inexhaustible source of funds.

The heirs took pride in their Harriman legacy, and most proved worthy of the Harriman name. After Yale and George Washington University Law School, Robert Fisk served as an Army captain in Vietnam, worked in poverty law at Neighborhood Legal Services, and set up a solo practice in Washington, D.C., specializing in family law, with the aim, he once said, to provide "objective legal services at reduced rates to lower-income people." His sister Kitty, equally earnest, followed her mother's route through Bennington into school volunteer work in Brookline, Massachusetts. She also served as a trustee of Concord Academy, her alma mater, which received annual donations anywhere from $15,000 to $35,000 from the Mary Harriman Foundation. Kitty's husband Charles Ames was the managing partner of Hill & Barlow, a Boston blueblood law firm where, it was said, studying the classics at Harvard was an entrance requirement. As the scion of an old Yankee family, Ames blended easily with the Harrimans. Ames's uncle was longtime Harvard law professor Archibald Cox, a former U.S. Solicitor General who served as Watergate Special Prosecutor. Averell, the baby of the Fisk branch, strayed farthest from his grandfather's expectations. After graduating from the University of Denver, at the time a favorite fallback school for East Coast preppies who didn't make it into the Ivy League, he turned into a full-fledged playboy, with a string of girlfriends and two failed marriages. His intermittent working life wobbled from manufacturing T-shirts emblazoned with clouds to playing the high-risk commodities market to dabbling in real estate. Harriman could barely conceal his disapproval of Averell Fisk's penchant for polo—his own history as a polo player in his youth notwithstanding—and for what he characterized as the young man's weakness for "quick money."

The oldest of the three Mortimer sons, David, also studied at the University of Denver before joining the American Assembly, a think tank at Columbia University established by Dwight Eisenhower and subsidized by $50,000 in yearly grants from the Mary Harriman Foundation. Because of his deafness, Jay Mortimer attended special secondary schools and tried a series of colleges until he graduated from the University of Bridgeport. He found his niche as a physical therapist at the Burke Rehabilitation Hospital in White Plains, New York. Averell Mortimer graduated from the University of Colorado at Boulder, received an MBA from Columbia University, and went to work on Wall Street as an investment banker specializing in new businesses.

When Pamela reentered their grandfather's life, most of Harriman's grandchildren were still in school. They were intrigued by her, a bit apprehensive, but certainly not resentful. Harriman treated his heirs the same as he always had, with the air of a Victorian paterfamilias. "Averell was not a Norman Rockwell grandfather type," said Robert Fisk. "He loved his grandchildren but he had other things to do." Harriman made no particular effort to see his heirs, and rarely mentioned them in conversation. "His grandsons didn't interest him much, and he wasn't close to them," recalled a man who knew Harriman well for several decades. He did, however, readily do favors for his grandchildren when asked, such as the note he wrote to the dean of Columbia University's Graduate School of Business on behalf of Averell Mortimer.

In letters to Harriman over the years, his heirs offered thanks for his various financial gifts, as well as reports on their educational and professional progress. Always addressed to "Ave," never "Grandpa" or even "Grandfather," their tone was stiff and occasionally apologetic if the Harriman standard wasn't being met. After receiving a promotion one year at the American Assembly, David Mortimer expressed a yearning to leave the security of his position and "try to advance myself so that, perhaps, I can gain the stature and someday rejoin the American Assembly as a trustee." On another occasion David confessed his embarrassment about using that year's annual gift to ski in the Canadian Bugaboos; he tried to mitigate his extravagance by stressing the spartan conditions of the trip—"sleeping on bunks in a dorm and all the meals are buffet." In one lengthy thank-you letter, Averell Mortimer invoked E.H's dictum that "if you are given money and don't put it to good use, then it should be taken away from you." Harriman's reply corrected his grandson, noting that his father's words were "it *would* be taken away from you," and cautioning that E.H. had said it before the arrival of income and inheritance taxes. Even Averell Fisk tried to reassure Harriman about his lifestyle, once writing that no unearned income was financing his polo expenses and emphasizing that through the game he was meeting such luminaries as Prince Charles.

Harriman saw his daughters and grandchildren mostly in semi-official family gatherings—meetings at Brown Brothers Harriman to discuss Harriman Foundation grants, and Harriman's annual birthday celebration, a command performance requiring everyone to dress up and prepare a toast, or in Jay Mortimer's case, a celebratory poem that Harriman eagerly anticipated. The day began with meetings about family business. Then came lunch, hiking and riding, and dinner in Harriman's honor. The family came to know Pamela primarily through these gatherings, as well as occasional visits to Hobe Sound, Sun Valley, and later Barbados. "Access to Ave was not circumscribed," said one family member.

Such protectiveness was unnecessary with the Mortimers and the Fisks. Pamela understood the formality of their relationship with Harriman, especially compared to his closeness to Marie's grandchildren. "Don't you get it?" Alida Morgan once heard David Mortimer say to Averell Fisk. "*They* were the real grandchildren." In her dealings with her husband's family, Pamela drew on her instinctive ability to size up human strengths and weaknesses. "After a while she will understand what your soft spots are," said Brooke Hayward, "and she will file it away and she will use it against you. It is her way of getting the upper hand." The soft spots of the Mortimers and Fisks were as evident as their cultivated speech. They were a tame bunch, secure in their patrimony. Measured against Pamela's ambition and brazenness, they seemed incapable not only of making a scene but even murmuring a protest.

Twenty-six

PAMELA DIGBY CHURCHILL HAYWARD HARRIMAN swept into Washington with great expectations, and she was honored at one party after another, including a dinner for 20 at the British Embassy given by Ambassador Rowley Cromer and his wife Esme, who had known Pamela since her girlhood, and a buffet for 140 at the Georgetown home of David Bruce, former U.S. Ambassador to England and France. "I have a vision of the older ladies looking Pam up and down," recalled Esme Cromer. "There was a lot of interest in her, and people were very skeptical—an Englishwoman coming here with her reputation and marrying Averell, who was very much the elder statesman. I remember a certain coolness to start with, but she charmed them all."

Perhaps not quite all. The journalist Barbara Howar, a prominent Washington socialite at the time, recalled: "She cut a quick swath. It wasn't like Pamela was the scullery maid marrying the boss. She floated right in. She was never left out of anything. But Pamela engendered a great deal of overt politeness and a lot of snideness behind her back." Washington in 1971 was a stodgy and conservative city where Pamela's famous relationships with men were considered vaguely threatening by the social leaders of Georgetown.

Susan Mary Alsop, who had known her since Paris, dined out, sotto voce, on the details of Pamela's history as a courtesan. Alsop's husband Joseph, the influential journalist and host, "accepted Pam with harrumphing and nasty asides," said Howar. Marie Harriman's close friends Luvie Pearson and Mary Russell, according to Alida Morgan, "adored my grandmother, felt things were different and they were shut out. Even when I came back to Washington in 1981, things were still so partisan." Kay Halle, who had lost two men to Pamela —Randolph Churchill and Averell Harriman—"publicly bore no resentment," recalled Piers Dixon, an Englishman who had been married to Randolph Churchill's niece Edwina. "Kay said to me, 'There are women men adore and others men don't.'" Privately, however, Halle disparaged Pamela, mainly because she eclipsed Halle as the capital's primary source for Churchill lore.

With her aristocratic background, links to the Churchill family, and her connections in London, Paris, and New York, Pamela felt she was entitled to a warmer reception in Washington. Not long after her wedding, she unburdened herself to Cheray Duchin. "She was lonely and she thought the women were tough," recalled Cheray. "I remember tears running down her face, and I remember her saying how cold everyone was and how difficult it was." At that point Pamela hadn't yet figured out a way to conquer Washington.

To a newcomer, the nation's capital is a place of mystifying contradictions. In cities like Philadelphia and Boston, bloodlines supported by wealth keep outsiders from penetrating the highest social echelons. In Manhattan, the worlds of society, art, literature, commerce, and politics intersect, and big money and lavish entertaining can transform nobodies into eminences overnight. Washington's social structure is open yet unforgiving, meritocratic yet exclusive, ruthless yet idealistic. Its official pecking order is codified in the *Green Book,* a publication that doubles as a social register and a protocol guide. It contains a "precedence list" ranking congressmen, ambassadors, and political appointees by their importance. At the same time, some of the most prestigious people in Washington have no official rank.

If Washington were a mathematical formula, power would be the constant, and people with access to it would be the variables. The power radiates outward from the President, the Cabinet, the leaders of Congress and the judiciary to the top-tier journalists who cover them, along with the lawyers, lobbyists, and advisers who work behind the scenes. Washington is a place where a White House chief of staff with scant financial resources and a state university diploma has greater standing than a multimillionaire with an Ivy League degree and a Mayflower pedigree. As social arbiter Carolyn Hagner Shaw once said, "The desirable guests are the ones in key political or government posts even if they sometimes are sprinkled with hayseed."

When Pamela arrived in 1971, the Washington elite was predominantly Democratic in its politics, and its epicenter was Georgetown, a neighborhood of eighteenth- and nineteenth-century brick town houses with gardens shaded by magnolia trees. The "Georgetown Set" included such prominent names as Acheson, Kennedy, Graham, Alsop, and Harriman. Once a person was accepted by Georgetown, Ambassador David Bruce observed, "It seems an insult to have to go out to dinner anywhere else." The postwar Georgetown social core had its origins in the 1930s, when prominent Jewish members of Franklin Roosevelt's administration were prevented from living in many Washington neighborhoods by restrictive covenants. Georgetown had no such limitations, so it became a magnet for liberals. Fresh Democratic recruits arrived during the Kennedy and Johnson years, and many of them never left. Democrats, *Washington Post* writer Henry Allen once observed, "always act as if they'd been born owning Washington, as if power were something akin to the family silver. . . . When Democrats are out, they act like resentful nobility."

There were, of course, other socially self-important groups operating in Washington—the "cave dweller" bluebloods boasting several generations of residency in the affluent Kalorama neighborhood, the suburban country club aristocracy in Chevy Chase, the African-American elite with its 16th Street mansions, the fox hunters and equestrians of outlying Middleburg, Virginia. Members of these groups were considered part of the Washington establishment if they had political or journalistic connections, but the groups themselves hovered on the periphery.

Because of the shifting nature of political power, Washington society is "all come and go," as Theodore Roosevelt's daughter Alice Roosevelt Longworth, a social fixture for most of her ninety-six years, put it. For anyone with a powerful government post, admission is automatic. In that sense, Washington is a simple meritocracy. The tricky part is how to keep one's standing in the elite after losing a high-ranking job. Many people simply drop from sight, happy to return home and resume ordinary lives. But others, addicted to the aroma of power, can't bear to leave the capital. At first they seem vaguely poignant as they mutter about the dinner parties to which they are no longer invited, but the most adroit repackage themselves as lobbyists, consultants, or journalists. "You stick around this town long enough," said one veteran Senate staffer, "and you acquire the aura of respectability."

Averell Harriman was a perfect specimen of the breed, a man who labored doggedly to maintain ties with powerful figures in each succeeding administration. He had tenure in the Washington establishment as one of the "wise men" who shaped American foreign policy after World War II. But as he moved into his eighties, he was a man with an illustrious past but no future. During the Nixon administration, he had virtually no political entree.

At first, Pamela sought to create a place for herself by becoming a model political wife, serving the needs of her prestigious husband in her usual fashion. "Right now I'm interested in doing what the governor is doing," she told a reporter in late 1971. "He's just been giving ten lectures at George Washington University, and I go along with him. I like to share in his life as much as possible." Attentive to his ego, she made certain to assure him of his success. After a speech at American University, Harriman proudly reported to Pam Morgan that Pamela thought he had done well, "or at least I had them laughing and applauding."

In the 1972 Democratic primaries, Harriman backed his friend, Senator Edmund Muskie of Maine. He gave $6,000 to Muskie's primary campaign, his most generous donation in years. He had given nothing to Hubert Humphrey four years earlier, and less than $3,000 to the Democratic National Committee during Richard Nixon's first term. Harriman's brother Roland had donated more than $75,000 to the Republicans in the same period, and in 1972 gave $43,500 to the GOP, half of it earmarked for Richard Nixon. Unlike his brother, Roland Harriman sought no public role for his political activities.

When Muskie faltered in the early primaries, Averell Harriman decided at age eighty to seek a place in the New York State delegation to the Democratic Convention. He ran as an independent opposed to the liberal, anti–Vietnam War candidate, Senator George McGovern of South Dakota. Pamela enthusiastically drove her husband around upstate New York in their station wagon as he canvassed for votes much as he had nearly two decades earlier. His effort ended in humiliation when he was beaten handily by a nineteen-year-old college student. Harriman and Pamela nevertheless attended the convention in Miami. By the time McGovern made his acceptance speech, the Harrimans had left for Hobe Sound.

Pamela embraced her husband's other principal interest as well, listening to him expound on U.S.–Soviet relations and accompanying him on a series of trips to Moscow and Eastern Europe. Pamela prepared for these journeys by reading briefing papers, but Harriman did not permit her to talk policy with the Soviet leaders. Consigned to a traditional First Lady role, she was sometimes allowed to take notes on her husband's discussions. More often, she would be dispatched on expeditions—to visit horse farms, for example—that were deemed compatible with her interests. In Harriman's presence, Pamela offered no independent opinions on the Soviet Union. Young Winston Churchill often disagreed with Harriman's views on the Soviets, and his mother, Winston recalled, "would take Averell's side. She believed what he believed."

During the early years of their marriage, Pamela seemed content to mold herself as a Harriman woman of wealth and standing. Harriman didn't seem to mind her questionable past, but now that she was his wife, he didn't want her to be considered frivolous. Though she tried to conform publicly to the Harriman way, she clung to some of her old socialite habits. When she was named one year to the best-dressed list, Harriman was not impressed. Yet when his secretary, Pie Friendly, made light of the award, Pamela shot back, "I've waited all my life for this." On another occasion, Pamela eagerly provided details to *Women's Wear Daily* about how she organized her three closets ("walk-in for coats and afternoon dresses, with shelves and a double mirror . . . fabric-lined for evening dresses . . . two tiered for separates").

Yet she also knew she had to appear serious, so she got involved in the worthy causes supported by her husband's own fund for charitable contributions, the W. Averell Harriman Foundation. One woman who tried to enlist Pamela's help for a family counseling center in the early 1970s recalled her deliberate approach. "We did our presentation, and afterwards she was on the phone at the crack of dawn with very specific financial questions from Averell," said the fundraiser. "He formulated them, and she asked them. She did that maybe five times, and then she invested some money."

Harriman knew that Pamela had little familiarity with the world of finance, so he sought help from his well-connected friend Robert Strauss, the Washington lawyer and Democratic power broker. In 1972, Harriman had sent a telegram to every Democratic governor promoting Strauss's candidacy for chairman of the Democratic National Committee, and now it was time for Strauss to return the favor. "Bob, I can do many things for Pamela, but I can't ask any of my friends to put her on their boards," Harriman told Strauss. "You have great relations with the American business community. Pamela needs to know something about business. She is going to have to handle money for a long time after I'm gone. Can you help me?" Strauss mentioned that he was leaving the board of Braniff International Corporation and would urge the company's chairman, Harding Lawrence, to name her as his replacement.

Pamela was delighted with the appointment, which she held from 1977 to 1981. Since she had no qualifications for the position, it was more a tutorial for her benefit than a service for the Braniff shareholders. But she was determined to overcome the stigma of being picked merely because she was the wife of a wealthy and prominent man. "She used to do her homework before board meetings," recalled Guy Waltman, Harriman's financial adviser at the time. "She took it seriously." More to the point, Pamela used the position to ensure that *she* would be taken seriously.

She was most effective doing what came naturally, serving as a glamorous representative of the airline at receptions and dinners thrown by Lawrence. "She was a real star at those occasions," said Texas oilman Perry Bass, who served with her on the Braniff board. "It gave her an opportunity to practice her charm on people who could be very helpful to the company."

In the boardroom Pamela naturally enough exhibited little knowledge or insight about the airline business, which was in a state of overheated expansion following government deregulation. Lawrence bought numerous new airplanes and rapidly added new routes beginning in 1978. When the price of fuel rose, he didn't have enough passengers to meet his new costs and pay the debts he took on to finance the expansion. In 1980 alone, the airline lost $128.5 million. Lawrence's style was to tell the directors what he had done rather than solicit their advice. "There was no way Pam could improve her business skills," said Bass. "Analyzing and making suggestions wasn't possible." Eventually, the board designated Bass to fire Lawrence, but by that time, said Bass, "Pam had left. As soon as things began to get pretty tough, she resigned."

In Washington, Pamela's most visible role was as a traditional hostess, the position ambitious women had long held in a city where power historically belonged almost exclusively to men. From Dolley Madison and Peggy Eaton in the nineteenth century to Evalyn Walsh McLean and Perle Mesta a hundred years later, these women achieved a prominence unknown to their counterparts in New York, Chicago, and Los Angeles. "As every close student of Washington knows," wrote Arthur Schlesinger, Jr., "half the essential business of government is still transacted in the evening. . . . The sternest purpose lurks under the highest frivolity." For a hostess, this meant arranging introductions and providing places for influential men to exchange views in a relaxed, neutral setting. The hostess could take satisfaction in what John Kenneth Galbraith called "that glow that comes from a sense of being 'in' "—a condition also known as "Potomac Fever."

Drawing on skills she had been perfecting for most of her life, Pamela developed a regular routine of lunches and dinners in what Lucy Moorhead, the wife of Congressman William Moorhead, referred to as "the ideal British tradition of continuing hospitality." Pamela still kept an Asprey silver-framed notepad at her place while she entertained, but now, instead of comments on the quality of the soufflé, she jotted down remarks made by her guests and took notes on political issues she needed to pursue.

A man who arrived in Washington in the early 1970s as a bright young correspondent for one of the television networks remembered the way Pamela often invited him and his wife because "we fit a place at her table. The first night we went the guest list was perfectly orchestrated and balanced. There was the bright young politician, Joe Biden [senator from Delaware]; the old pol, Gaylord Nelson [senator from Wisconsin]; there were Clayton and Polly Fritchey, Clark Clifford, Winston and Betty Bao Lord. It was one of those places where the men went into the study for cigars and conversation after dinner, and the women went upstairs. My wife said Pamela did it in such a way that she wasn't the least offended."

Her technique as a hostess, according to one guest, was tightly choreographed: "now circulating among her guests, now posing a question to move a lagging conversation, now quieting the table and launching a discussion by noting that the Senator or Cabinet officer on her right 'just said something I'd like him to share.' " "She isn't the number one hostess," gushed Robert Strauss, "She's also number two, three and four. . . . She's a natural at this sort of thing. . . . Pamela loves power, and politics is power. This is where it all is, honey. A lot goes on at dinner parties here. You never know what they're talking about over there by the fireplace, but it's probably not the weather."

These were low-key affairs, designed primarily to keep Averell Harriman engaged in public affairs and to enlarge Pamela's network of acquaintances. The capital was rocked by the Watergate scandals and Nixon's resignation, then relaxed during Gerald Ford's easygoing presidency. Pamela's socializing was conducted out of the limelight. "Pamela spent those early years wisely," said Barbara Howar. "She played the dutiful role, cared for Averell, read up and listened up."

The only time a Harriman dinner party attracted attention was in 1975, when the *Washington Post*'s executive editor Ben Bradlee came with journalist Sally Quinn, who happened to be writing a profile for the newspaper on Senator Frank Church, then a Democratic presidential candidate. At the end of dinner, Pamela tapped a glass with a spoon and announced, as was her custom, "Now the ladies will join me upstairs and the gentlemen will join Averell in the sitting room where Senator Church will discuss his plans." Quinn was outraged that she had been ordered to retire with "the ladies" when she wanted to hear Church. She started to follow Bradlee to tell him that she had decided to leave when Harriman confronted her. "This is my house," he boomed, "and in my house the ladies retire upstairs." Quinn replied, "I am not going upstairs, Governor, I am leaving." She bolted outside and found shelter in a limousine until Bradlee came out to join her.

"There was not a word from Pam," recalled Quinn, "although she was solicitous afterwards. I think she was horrified." Not horrified enough, evidently. Four years later, the Harrimans were still subjecting their guests to postprandial separation of the sexes. British Ambassador Nicholas Henderson noted in his diary after a dinner at N Street in the summer of 1979 that "when the ladies had withdrawn Harriman said that if Kay Graham had been there she would have insisted on staying behind with the men."

As the years passed, Pamela seemed less satisfied by the vicarious pleasures of the hostess. Entertaining may have been regarded as significant and highly useful in the Washington elite, but it was "women's work," lacking any genuine power. The city's most powerful woman was Katharine Graham, whose position as chair of the Washington Post Company gave her equal billing with men even as she served as the city's most prestigious hostess. "I wish the phrase 'dinner party' had never been invented," Pamela told Lucy Moorhead in the mid-1970s.

"To me a dinner is about something serious. You get substance from a dinner. You learn something. A party is a celebration, like someone's birthday. . . . Averell and I far more often have dinners. A dinner has a purpose."

During the Carter–Ford election campaign of 1976, Pamela tried to move into the political process and work directly on behalf of candidates. Her first foray resulted in a major misstep, a result of tactlessness and political naivete. The Democrats were set on capturing the Senate seat held by New York Conservative-Republican James Buckley, and the outspoken Democratic Congresswoman Bella Abzug was the leading candidate in a crowded primary field and the choice of limousine liberals. Pamela decided to campaign for Abzug in New York, even after Daniel Patrick Moynihan, formerly an aide to Harriman when he was governor, belatedly entered the race.

In her public comments, Pamela was ungracious about Moynihan. At a chic fundraiser she sponsored in Manhattan, she produced a letter from Harriman urging Democrats to "give Bella the chance she so richly deserves," and announced that Abzug was a "true Democrat serving only with her party," a rebuke to Moynihan, who had served in the Nixon administration. Several weeks before the primary, Pamela deepened the insult by declaring, during a campaign appearance for Abzug, that it was unwise to try talking to Moynihan after lunch. Both Moynihan and his wife Liz—who had also worked for Harriman—were furious that the wife of the "Governor" would publicly imply Moynihan had a drinking problem. After beating Abzug and then Buckley, Moynihan put aside the affront, but Liz Moynihan never forgave Pamela, adding another name to the long list of Pamela's enemies.

Pamela often told journalists that she was, as the *New York Times* reported, an "early and fervent supporter of Jimmy Carter." But in fact, she and Harriman came late to the Carter bandwagon. "Jimmy Carter? How can that be?" Harriman asked when he and Pamela heard that the former Georgia Democratic governor had won the New Hampshire primary in February 1976. "I don't even know Jimmy Carter, and as far as I know none of my friends know him either." By the end of March, Carter seemed the likely nominee. On April 1, Pamela Harriman gave the candidate $1,000, followed by another $1,000 from Averell Harriman on May 20 after Carter had all but sewn up the nomination.

Barely two weeks before the election, Pamela held her first major fundraiser, a reception so hastily assembled that the invitations were photocopied rather than printed, and she only raised several thousand dollars. Although it was a modest beginning financially, the party kicked off a wave of effusive publicity for Pamela. THE AMERICANIZATION OF PAMELA HARRIMAN, read one headline in the *Washington Star*. PAMELA HARRIMAN'S ROLE: HOSTESS TO THE POWERFUL, announced the *New York Times*. The *Baltimore Sun* called her WASHINGTON'S OTHER FIRST LADY.

She relished the attention, granting interviews and opening her fundraising parties to the press. She offered selective glimpses of her background, along with recollections of Churchill, Roosevelt, and Hopkins. In the *Washington Star,* she explained her easy transition from English Tory to American Democrat by citing the early influence of Harriman and Murrow, along with all the "socialists . . . I knew and admired" during the war. (She didn't specify which "socialists" she meant, nor did she mention that Winston Churchill was emphatically anti-socialist.)

With the exception of intermittent notes about her wardrobe, Pamela had been virtually ignored by the media during her first five years in Washington. Accounts of a party in Harriman's honor in 1974 barely acknowledged Pamela, except to mention her "low necked flowered chiffon" dress. With her customary chutzpah, Pamela managed to make a plus out of her own insignificance. "She shuns interviews and other publicity, just as she shuns ostentation and anything that hints of frivolity or shallowness, but invitations to her dinner parties have long been prized in Washington," the *New York Times* noted in early 1977.

In interviews, Pamela repeatedly emphasized how much she enjoyed being a "backroom" or "backstage" figure in the political world. "Backstage people," she told the *New York Times*, "are the ones who get the show on the road." Since her wartime days, Pamela savored the satisfaction that came from knowing secrets and exerting her influence quietly. She also found security in the shadows. There was danger in exposure, a lesson she had first learned when London society found her to be a drab debutante. Her determination to avoid the mocking laughter she had suffered as a teenager seemed to motivate her constant drive for self-improvement. At the same time, Pamela found publicity irresistible. Her ego was simply too large for her to stay confined to the backrooms of Washington.

On the eve of the election, the Harrimans gave a buffet for sixty Carter supporters, followed by a considerably larger party on inauguration night, attended by actors Jack Nicholson and Warren Beatty as well as several members of the Carter cabinet. Within days of the inauguration, Pamela was on the phone to Zbigniew Brzezinski, Carter's national security adviser, offering a rent-free apartment in a house Harriman owned at 3032 N Street next to their home. Pamela explained that Brzezinski would need time to find a place to live, so he was welcome to stay as long as necessary—five months, as it turned out. He arrived in January 1977, followed a few months later by Marshall Shulman, an adviser on the Soviet Union to Secretary of State Cyrus Vance. Shulman tried several times to move out, but Harriman enticed him to stay by giving him more space. "Harriman was anxious not to lose a tenant who was in the thick of the action at Foggy Bottom," wrote Abramson.

The relationship between Brzezinski and Harriman had begun badly some years earlier when Harriman criticized Brzezinski's views of the Soviet Union for being too hard-line, adding, "What would you expect of someone who is Polish?" Brzezinski had written an indignant letter, prompting Harriman to apologize and invite him for lunch in Yorktown Heights, where they made peace. According to Abramson, Harriman met with Carter days after the election, and one of his objectives was "to put in strong reservations about Zbigniew Brzezinski as . . . national security adviser." Harriman, wrote Abramson, "disliked Brzezinski personally." Nevertheless, Harriman and Pamela gave Brzezinski the royal treatment when he moved in. He was invited to meals whenever he wished, and they included him in numerous dinner parties. When Brzezinski came down with the flu, he recalled, Pamela "was very protective. She got all sorts of pills and was very concerned about my well-being." Pamela meanwhile sent his wife Muska various gifts, one of which, a cover for the swimming pool at their new house, she declined as too extravagant.

Neither of his hosts asked for anything specific in return. "I was never pressed to provide entertainment at social events," said Brzezinski. "The dinners I was invited to I was happy to attend, because there were interesting people, and it was useful to talk to them." At such occasions, Harriman usually held forth on the Soviet Union. "He fancied himself as an expert," said Brzezinski. During informal meals, however, Harriman's reasons for cultivating the younger man were clear. "I assume this was of interest to him because he wanted to be involved in shaping policy, and through me he thought this was possible," said Brzezinski. "He would talk about American-Soviet relations, and he would have comments and criticisms. He would want to see the President, which I arranged maybe two or three times."

After Brzezinski moved out of the N Street house, his relations with the Harrimans cooled, largely because his tough views on the Soviets were at odds with the accommodating approach of Harriman and his longtime protégé, Secretary of State Cyrus Vance. The dinner-party invitations ceased, along with the largesse—neither of which bothered Brzezinski, who had never fallen under Pamela's spell.

Harriman continued to seek a position with the Carter administration through Vance. A New York lawyer and former deputy to Johnson's Secretary of Defense Robert McNamara, Vance had worked closely with Harriman on the Paris peace talks. Vance and his wife Gay had also become social friends of the Harrimans, and on many weekends they came to stay in the guest cottage at Willow Oaks. Although Vance got Harriman inside the Oval Office on several occasions, he failed to secure an ambassador at large title for the eighty-five-year-old diplomat.

Instead, Harriman contented himself with lobbying for the Panama Canal Treaty and the SALT II nuclear weapons limitation treaty. Harriman and Pamela gathered groups of politicians, business leaders, and journalists to discuss the treaties over dinner—the sort of "dinners with a purpose" that Pamela so enjoyed. In the end, the Panama Canal Treaty was ratified, although the SALT II effort collapsed after the Soviet Union invaded Afghanistan.

During these years, Harriman's favorite man in the administration was Richard Holbrooke, who was serving as Assistant Secretary of State for East Asian and Pacific Affairs—the same job Harriman had held in the Kennedy administration. Holbrooke had been in Vietnam as a foreign service officer and had worked for Harriman during the Paris peace talks in the late 1960s. Back in Washington, Holbrooke edited *Foreign Policy* magazine before he joined the Carter camp. After Brzezinski moved out, the Harrimans invited Holbrooke to take his apartment. Holbrooke's second marriage had just ended, he was broke, and he welcomed the opportunity. When Holbrooke needed a loan for the

down payment on a house, Harriman handed over $57,000 at 10 percent inter-
est, which Holbrooke repaid, as promised, six years later.

Bright, energetic, and shrewd, the thirty-five-year-old Holbrooke under-
stood the dynamics of Washington power better than most of his elders. "He's a
Washington fanatic," said his friend Sally Quinn. "He's an obsessive, a junkie."
Holbrooke was an unabashed admirer of Harriman and eagerly tried to help him
gain entree with the Carter administration. He periodically briefed Harriman on
China and filled him in on State Department news.

Along the way, Holbrooke and Pamela grew close. She recognized Holbrooke as an invaluable resource, an insider who could teach her the ropes and
whose loyalty to the Governor—and by extension to her—could be counted
on. "Holbrooke was a great mentor," said Barbara Howar. "He took care of
Pamela, and there was a quid pro quo. She had houses and she was connected.
Nothing pleases Dick Holbrooke more than when you say, 'Dick, why did that
happen?' He loved telling her things and she would be star-struck, particularly
about things involving international relations."

Pamela tackled American politics with the same enthusiasm she had applied
to decorative arts and the American theater. She had neither the time nor the
temperament for probing inquiries. "She asks a thousand questions to the point
that you say, 'My God, stop!' But she asks only what she needs to know," said
a former aide to the Harrimans. Her very directness carried a certain power that
was simultaneously impressive and flattering. "She gets to the heart of the
matter immediately and doesn't beat around the bush," said a prominent Washingtonian.

From time to time Pamela couldn't resist showing off her new knowledge,
using her old trick of dispensing morsels of information at luncheon or dinner
parties to impress her companions. But in the company of experts, her lack of
depth could be embarrassing. "When she started in politics, I thought she was
going to make a horse's ass of herself," said William Walton. "She would
begin to tell smart, politically sophisticated tables all about the details of the
Democratic Party she was learning until someone told her not to talk about it
so much in front of women like Katharine Graham . . . who had known about
it forever."

In 1979, Pamela served as chairperson of the Democratic House and Senate
Council dinner. The position was honorary; she merely had to identify wealthy
donors, though the Harrimans' own generosity was limited. In 1979 and 1980
they gave $3,000 to the House and Senate Council, and $2,750 to Jimmy
Carter, along with a scattering of contributions to senators and congressmen:
$1,500 to Gary Hart, $1,000 each to Russell Long, Senate Democratic whip
Alan Cranston, and House majority leader Jim Wright, and $500 apiece to
Christopher Dodd, Warren Magnuson, Pete Flaherty, and James Corman.

So it came as something of a surprise in May 1980 when the National
Women's Democratic Club cited Pamela as its Woman of the Year, an honor
previously bestowed on such established Democratic stars as Representative
Barbara Jordan and Muriel Humphrey, the wife of former Vice President Hu-

bert Humphrey. The award had been expected to go to the wife of the Vice President, Joan Mondale, and many members grumbled that Pamela really hadn't done enough to deserve it. She had not actually sought the honor; Carol Williams, the club's president, had chosen her largely for marquee value. "Quite frankly it was a way of giving the club some visibility," said Williams, "to help raise money and to pull Pamela in and get her involved."

A crowd of 250, including the Vances, First Lady Rosalynn Carter, and Senators Henry Jackson and Claiborne Pell, showed up for the ceremony, where Robert Strauss made what *Washington Star* reporter Jurate Kazickas termed a "curious, rambling introduction" of the guest of honor: "Pamela—formerly Mrs. Averell Harriman, but now it's Pamela in her own right. The hell with Averell," drawled Strauss. "She's a unique woman. . . . I said to Averell, 'When you found Pamela, you discovered an oil well. I want 10 percent overriding interest.' " Williams recalled, "Pamela was so delighted to receive the award. She loved the adulation she got."

For all their efforts, the Harrimans never really connected with the Carters. Jimmy Carter, Pamela observed years later, "wasn't a people's person. Though he was a very bright clever man, it was sort of technical cleverness." Carter showed the Harrimans respect, but, according to a top Carter official, "I don't think he thought about Averell and Pamela Harriman much." Nevertheless, once they committed to the Carters, the Harrimans remained loyal, and in 1983 their foundation donated $35,000 to Carter's Presidential Library.

Late in the summer of 1980, in an effort to bring a measure of professionalism to her political activities, Pamela hired a Texan named Janet Howard, a woman who would become one of the most influential—and controversial—forces in Pamela's life. While serving as chairperson of the Democratic House and Senate Council dinner the previous year, Pamela had worked with Howard for the first time and had been impressed by her skills as a fundraiser. At age thirty-four, Howard was a political pro who was well versed in the intricacies of Capitol Hill.

She had been intrigued by politics since childhood, an interest that deepened at thirteen when she was hospitalized for a year in a body cast following a spinal fusion to correct scoliosis. During that difficult time she occupied herself by closely following the 1960 Kennedy-Nixon presidential campaign on television. She studied government and public administration at American University in Washington, graduated from the University of Texas in 1968, and joined the staff of Texas Senator Ralph Yarborough.

She moved through a series of political jobs—researcher, fund-raising consultant, and staff positions with Senator John Glenn and Congressman Peter Rodino, where she worked on his committee in charge of impeachment proceedings against Richard Nixon. Along the way she acquired a reputation for getting jobs done regardless of the difficulties or time pressures, a trait that pleased her bosses and antagonized her subordinates and co-workers. "Janet was an aggressive individual," said one Glenn staffer who worked with her. "If she had an assignment, she wouldn't let anyone stand in her way."

Howard caught the eye of multimillionaire San Francisco real estate developer Walter Shorenstein, a major Democratic fundraiser, when she directed the House and Senate Council. Shorenstein had just been made chairman of the White House Preservation Fund, which had been set up in the offices of the White House Historical Association on Lafayette Square. The fund's mandate was to raise money to buy and restore furnishings for the executive mansion, and Pamela had agreed to serve as one of Shorenstein's board members. With Pamela's concurrence, Shorenstein gave Janet Howard the plum position of executive director of the fund. "She was such a strong personality that a lot of people in the office including me found it difficult to cope with her," recalled Clement Conger, the curator for the White House at the time.

Howard spent much of the summer of 1980 working on Shorenstein's personal staff, arranging a dinner to raise $600,000 for Jimmy Carter at the Shorenstein home outside San Francisco. Within weeks of the event, a prominent midwestern executive complained to Democratic officials that his $10,000 contribution had been solicited with the promise of a ride to the dinner on Air Force One. Shortly afterward, Shorenstein asked Pamela if she could take Howard on. "Pamela called me on a Sunday," recalled John Bowles, a Wall Street executive and Democratic activist. "She had been talking to Walter Shorenstein, and it was clear that Janet was going to have to leave the fund. She said, 'What about taking on Janet as my personal assistant?' I said, 'It sounds like you would be a safe harbor until she can sail out in a year or two.'" Averell Harriman expressed reservations about Howard's reputation for extravagance, but he permitted Pamela to hire her for $40,000 a year. As one former Harriman staffer explained it, "Janet owed her a big favor, because Pamela saved her."

In Janet Howard, Pamela had the sort of tough-minded backroom operator—a demon worker enraptured with logistical details—who could free her boss to move to the forefront. Howard made a good appearance, which was important to Pamela. She wore expensive clothes, mostly from Rizik's, a stylish Washington specialty shop. She was big-boned but not overweight, with pretty brown eyes and a bouffant of black hair that inspired staffers on Capitol Hill to compare her with the lead singer in the retro rock group, the B-52s. Her personality was vibrant, her mind was quick and astute, and she had a strong network of contacts and the sort of can-do fervor that could be extremely useful to Pamela. With the prominent figures in Pamela's world, she could be charming and confident, but behind the smiling blandishments was a streak of ruthlessness. In many ways, Janet Howard was an exaggerated version of a classic Washington type. "She loves to do things and think that people don't know what she has done," said a former co-worker. "She is not that well educated but she is really cunning. She catches things and can see around corners."

Howard quickly established herself as an indispensable asset to Pamela Harriman, not only by ordering her political activities but by assuming responsibility for the household. Howard retrieved Pamela's jewelry from the safe, supervised the servants, cleared Pamela's clothing through Customs, bought the Harrimans' Christmas gifts, oversaw Pamela's correspondence, and even mastered her signature, which she frequently applied to Pamela's green-bordered cards and letters with a green felt-tip pen. Within months, Howard moved into an apartment at the rear of 3032 N Street behind her office, where she enjoyed free rent, free food, and free transportation. In return, Janet Howard was on call for the Harrimans twenty-four hours a day, seven days a week.

On election night 1980, the Harrimans hosted a large party to follow the returns on television. Clutching tally sheets for each race assembled by Janet Howard, the Georgetown Set watched with long faces as Ronald Reagan trounced Jimmy Carter. Most leading Democrats, the Harrimans included, had underestimated the personal and political appeal of the former California governor. Only months earlier, Pamela had dismissed him by saying, "I loved him in the movies." The Republicans also captured the Senate for the first time since 1954, and gained thirty-three seats in the House. Although the House remained in Democratic hands, the Republicans often fashioned majorities by persuading conservative Democrats to vote with them.

"Outraged" by what he called the "dismal event," Harriman convened a dinner shortly after the election, with a guest list including Robert Strauss, Democratic political counselor Clark Clifford, House Speaker Tip O'Neill, majority leader Jim Wright, and Senators Alan Cranston, John Glenn, Dale Bumpers, and Gary Hart. Their task was to explore ways to revive the Democratic Party, which badly needed more money, better organization, and a new image. The Democrats had drifted leftward on a tide of liberal positions such as legalization of abortion, affirmative action, homosexual rights, and increased expenses for welfare and other social programs, all to be paid for with higher federal taxes.

"The Democratic Party was in a deepseated depression," said Stuart Eizenstat, Carter's domestic policy chief and a participant at the dinner. "We had not just lost the election. We had lost our way. We knew the New Deal was over, but we didn't know what to supplant it with." With Pamela in the background, Harriman addressed the group and gave "a tremendous performance," according to Richard Holbrooke. Pamela "didn't take the lead because no one would have taken her seriously," said one participant. "She was not in a position to say what the Democrats should do."

That evening the Harrimans were encouraged to set up their own political action committee (PAC) to raise money and distribute it to candidates. Such committees had been around for nearly forty years, used principally by labor unions to collect political donations from their members. Campaign finance laws passed in 1974 following the Watergate scandal had limited the amount of money wealthy individuals could donate to politicians and parties but affirmed the right of corporations, interest groups, professionals, and trade associations to establish their own PACs. By 1980, PACs had proliferated, and among the newer entries were committees devoted to issues such as women's rights, protection of the environment, and welfare reform.

Pamela often claimed that the PAC was her idea. When asked directly about her husband's role by his biographer, Rudy Abramson, Pamela snapped, "Ave didn't have anything to do with setting up the PAC." Harriman himself told a reporter in 1982 that "Pam was the first to say, when we had that choking defeat in 1980, that something had to be done." Others had different recollections, however. The PAC was an idea, said Pamela's friend Kitty Hart, that Harriman "put into her head." At eighty-nine, Harriman knew he lacked the stamina to lead such an effort on his own, so he urged Pamela to do it for him. Harriman was bullish from the start, Pamela less so. She had no doubts about her ability as a fundraiser. She had spent her life raising money, as her husband knew. But she worried about taking on a public role in politics.

During a holiday in Barbados after the election, Harriman stubbornly pressed the case. Said one witness to the discussions: "It was his way of keeping young, of staying in the center of things. 'Sure you can do it,' he said. 'You ran the Churchill Club. You can do this well.' But Pam was terribly nervous about it. She had never been on TV. She wasn't very good at making speeches." Harriman countered that he would hire writers and media coaches to help her with public speaking and television appearances.

She consulted an array of advisers and experts on federal election law. Robert Strauss, with whom Averell Harriman often talked about raising Pamela's political profile, was surprisingly negative. It was an idea, he said, that "might work but it will be very limited in its effectiveness." Strauss "didn't think she could put something together," said Eizenstat. "She didn't have the network or the nuances, in his view. A lot of people didn't take her seriously. They saw her as an ornament to Governor Harriman, and a foreign ornament at that." Other skeptics questioned whether Pamela could persuade people to hand over their money when they could easily donate to candidates in their own names. "Pamela kept saying, 'Why should I do this? Aren't we going to have problems with other things like the House and Senate dinner? Won't my doing this take away from other activities I am involved in?' " recalled Democratic fundraiser John Bowles.

Even when the party leadership gave a green light, Pamela wavered. "After she did a lot of investigating and thinking, she called me and told me she had decided not to go ahead," said Jesse Calhoon, president of the Marine Engineers Beneficial Association (MEBA). "I said, 'If you want that to be your decision, go ahead, but I think you're chicken.' 'Chicken!' she said in a high voice, like she was in shock. Then she called me later and said she was going ahead, and that if it hadn't been for me calling her chicken, she wouldn't have done it."

The Harrimans provided the Democrats with a variation on what advertising people called the unique selling proposition—a distinctive attribute that could be used to push a product. What made the committee singular was the mystique of the Harriman name. Called "Democrats for the 80's," it was instantly nicknamed "PamPAC." Its stated goals were to help Democrats regain the Senate and increase control of the House, as well as to develop new ideas for the party. But the PAC was also designed to boost the confidence of Democratic candidates and officials, and to strengthen their relationships with wealthy donors, who had to be reassured that the party was exciting and worthy of their support. "The idea of the PAC was not to change the direction of policy in any area of government," said John Bowles. "It was about networking and fund-raising."

To that end, Averell and Pamela Harriman would market themselves: their familiar name, their wealth and background, and their reputation as consummate insiders. Harriman was a patrician diplomat associated with every Democratic president since Roosevelt. Pamela had her British pedigree, her wartime experience and impeccable Churchill connections, not to mention the glamour she derived from her links with European aristocrats, show business luminaries, and famous playboys. Their base of operations was the Harriman house on N Street, with its antiques, photographs of world leaders, and paintings by van Gogh, Picasso, Renoir, and Matisse. It was an unbeatable combination. "We said, 'We will raise money on all that,' which had never been done," said Bowles.

From Franklin D. Roosevelt to John F. Kennedy, the Democratic Party had a fascination with "enlightened" aristocrats; certainly Averell Harriman found a more congenial home in the party than he ever knew with the GOP. "I know how it feels to be a Republican," Harriman once said. "I was one before 1928. I have had a hell of a lot more fun out of life being a Democrat." As the party most closely associated with business and wealth, Republicans were accustomed to the likes of the Harrimans. If anything, Republicans traditionally spent a lot of time downplaying their upper-class connections: indeed, the Harrimans' wealth and social standing might have been a liability in the GOP. For the Democrats, the Harrimans represented glamour—as well as the party's appeal to people of all stations.

In December 1980 the Harrimans proudly kicked in the first donations to PamPAC—$5,000 from Pamela and $1,750 from Averell, followed by $1,000 from Bowles, $5,000 from Calhoon's MEBA political action committee, $5,000 from the United Auto Workers Good Government Fund. To John Bowles, "it was like buying a stock as a venture capitalist. You knew Pamela had the right ingredients. The fundamentals were superb." For Jesse Calhoon, the motivation was slightly different: "I had great respect for Averell Harriman. It was like sitting down with history. . . . A conversation with him was very dear to me."

To spread the word, the Harrimans hosted a reception for eighty-five labor leaders and put on two dinners, one for Democratic leaders on the Hill, the other for up-and-coming senators and congressmen. At the second gathering, Thomas Foley, the House majority whip, likened an evening with the Harrimans to an invitation to the White House. "Normally to have fifteen people at a Democratic gathering, you have to invite forty," said Foley. "Tonight we invited fifteen and there are forty." As Pamela listened, John Bowles was watching: "When she heard what Tom Foley said," recalled Bowles, "it struck a gold mine. Pamela just glowed."

By the time the group announced its formation in February 1981, Pamela was given full credit for the idea in an admiring *Washington Post* story headlined: PAMELA HARRIMAN'S PLAN TO SAVE THE DEMOCRATIC PARTY. But Pamela had no ideological goals; her politics had always been situational, fitting those of the man in her life. Like her husband, she knew that Democrats had more fun than Republicans. "She doesn't seem to have great political theories," said her friend

Clay Felker. "It is very personal. The Democrats are her friends, so she will help them, and the Republicans are not her friends. It is not ideological."

Pamela's initial reason for launching a political action committee may have been to please her husband, but the real point of PamPAC was Pamela. "She had no agenda other than her own political respectability," said one prominent political consultant. She had, in a sense, been preparing for the role her whole life, and she had been studying the ways of Washington for ten years. "If ever there was a place for a polished courtesan," said Barbara Howar, "it was Washington." The skills she had used on her lovers—the energy, the focus, the followthrough—would now be applied to the Democratic Party. She would fuse her capabilities as a hostess with her aptitude for extracting money from wealthy patrons to support the only philanthropic work that mattered in Washington: advancing the careers of political candidates. "When I heard she was moving into politics, I thought, 'How delicious. It is such a man's world. Now she doesn't have to have one dinner partner. She can have five hundred,' " said the wife of a prominent Democratic contributor.

The PAC gave Pamela her own court. Now she had to establish herself as a woman of substance, because that was the way the Washington game was played. Harriman's wealth and prestige provided a base, but to be taken seriously she needed to sell ideas, to dispense information, to be seen as someone who could influence political events. By tying the Harriman riches to a political agenda, she could enjoy both influence and visibility, and she could transcend the hostess stereotype to become a peer of the Washington establishment. After years on the margins of power, she would be back at the center as she had been during World War II, but this time as a participant, admired and respected for her own accomplishments. To achieve that status she had to build up her credentials. Even if she didn't develop genuine expertise, she had to create the appearance of mastery and success. Aware of her inferior formal education, she knew she had to work that much harder, but application had never been a problem for Pamela, and now she had vast resources to help her toward her goal.

CHAPTER

Twenty-seven

PAMELA HARRIMAN had turned sixty on March 20, 1980. Unlike her husband, who expected a big fuss for his birthday, Pamela preferred to ignore hers. She had maintained a preternatural youthfulness through her fifties, but was now beginning to show her years. Her thick auburn hair, swept high off her forehead, had been enhanced by coloring, although she kept the distinctive white streak rising from her left temple. Her pale skin retained its translucent glow, but lines creased her forehead, puffy pouches defined her deep blue eyes, and her double chin was very much in evidence. Custom-made suits by Halston, with long jackets and trailing scarves, could not entirely disguise her matronly figure.

But the men of Washington seemed oblivious to her imperfections. With her unwavering, somewhat theatrical gaze, low, chesty voice, and tactile manner, she knew how to beguile them, young and old. Like her adventurous forbear Jane Digby, she radiated a dewy femininity as an older woman, even as she commanded attention with a somewhat masculine mixture of charm, authority, and vigor. "She has a strength in her personality," said Stuart Eizenstat. "She is striking physically and she speaks with a great deal of conviction and energy. She simply has that aura of commitment and intelligence and personality that makes you want to follow." When many women of her generation were slowing down and settling into a life of leisure, Pamela was accelerating. As she approached her sixty-first birthday, she felt the thrill of public attention and desperately wanted more.

As promised, Harriman gave her all the help she required, principally a blue-chip board of directors for PamPAC. Robert Strauss, Stuart Eizenstat, and Samuel R. "Sandy" Berger, a lawyer and former speechwriter for Cyrus Vance, formed the core of the first advisory group. "The three of us selected the board," said Eizenstat. "We wanted a balance within the party, and labor and business leaders." The board was heavily weighted toward figures from the Democratic establishment such as former senators Edmund Muskie and Frank Church; Lyndon Johnson's former counsel, Harry McPherson; and McPherson's law partner, Berl Bernhard. John Bowles and Jesse Calhoon got spots, as did the Women's National Democratic Club president Carol Williams. The only outsider was the man who had just been turned out as Governor of Arkansas, thirty-four-year-old Bill Clinton.

Pamela would later take credit for discovering Clinton. "He was the first person I invited [on the PamPAC board]," she told *Vogue* magazine in 1992, after he captured the Democratic presidential nomination. "He had just lost, and he was thinking of running for the head of the Democratic National Committee. He paced and paced trying to decide what to do." Clinton was actually brought in by Sandy Berger, who had first known him when they worked together on the presidential campaign of George McGovern in 1972. Clinton attended several board meetings at which he impressed Pamela and the Washington veterans with his intelligence and earnestness. "It was clear someone had told her Bill Clinton had a future," said John Bowles. "She really liked him." Nevertheless, according to a PamPAC official, "his contribution was minimal. He was getting ready to run for reelection and we didn't want candidates on the board." By early 1982, when he started running for governor again, Clinton left the board, although he did return periodically to attend Pamela's fund-raising events.

Berger, a protégé of Averell Harriman, served as Pamela's de facto chairman. "She had enormous faith in him," said a former PamPAC staffer. "The genesis was the Governor's faith. Berger had stature because Ave found him on Vance's staff. Pamela latched onto Sandy through that relationship because he had passed the test. If Ave thought the guy was great, then so did she." With Berger, as with the other important men in her life, Pamela's judgments were purely visceral: If someone responded earnestly to her and made her comfortable, she would accept him.

Some board members like Calhoon, Williams, and Muskie supplied connections to various groups; others played more active roles. Berger supplied her with policy ideas and served as a political confidant. McPherson and Bernhard drew up lists of candidates to support and periodically canvassed their clients for money. Eizenstat devised what became the signature of PamPAC: the "issues evening," a dinner party at the Harriman home for guests who ponied up $1,000 each. The group would discuss a specific topic in what was billed as a modern "political salon."

Robert Strauss was Pamela's entree to the major donors in the Democratic Party. The smooth-talking Texan was one of the party's most effective operatives, as persuasive and pragmatic a guide as she could find to twisting arms and flattering big-money egos. Strauss may have been skeptical about PamPAC, but not about Pamela. "Bob was awed by her and worshipped this grand British beauty," said one woman who observed them together frequently. "And she needed him, too, to get her some credibility." Strauss's instincts for putting people together were superb, and Pamela followed his advice on who to cultivate and who to avoid.

Flirtatious and outrageously outspoken, Strauss was also the sort of man Pamela thoroughly enjoyed. They had obvious chemistry, so obvious that stories of a possible affair began to circulate around Georgetown. At first, Strauss seemed to wink at the speculation. "We used to say that if Bob Strauss had the choice between having an affair with the most beautiful woman in the world secretly or not having an affair and having people think he was, he would go for the latter," said a former high-ranking Carter administration official. "To be seen with Pamela and to have people think an affair was possible was much better for him, so he fostered that illusion." When a *Washington Post* reporter started making inquiries, however, Strauss grew nervous and ended the game, issuing a flat denial and declaring his undying devotion to Helen, his wife of more than forty years.

Ever the diligent student, Pamela quizzed her directors closely, often asking each the same question before she would feel confident about a candidate. "At the beginning she was willing to be guided by guys who had made politics their life's vocation, who knew from whom to get money and to whom to give it," said Harry McPherson. "She had a wish to raise money for Democrats and to be a figure. She wanted to be a big player in the Democratic world, but she didn't seem to have any firm convictions or standards about what she was willing to do financially and what she wasn't. She accepted the board's help with appreciation and charm, but as time went on you had the feeling that this charming English naif had become something different. She was quite tough, very tough, had sized up with some kind of mental caliper the dimensions she was going after and those who she was going to give to. It didn't happen at once, like a little girl who suddenly develops a figure. But she was developing a political figure. She was becoming as smart and as practical as she needed to be."

Democrats for the 80's set up shop in the second Harriman house at 3032 N Street, where Pamela replaced the guest-room beds with desks and file cabinets. For her first executive director, Pamela chose Peter Fenn, who had been chief of staff for recently defeated Idaho Senator Frank Church. Janet Howard was on hand, of course, ever the devoted factotum. If she was offended that Pamela didn't tap her for executive director, she kept it to herself. Besides supervising the Harriman households, Howard organized the fund-raising activities because, Fenn admitted, "I hated shaking down people."

In the early months, Georgetown doyennes tittered about "Pammy's PAC" and some political professionals pegged Pamela as a dilettante. She had the dazzle, but did she have the dedication to see her task through? A turning point came in May 1981, when PamPAC took on the National Conservative Political Action Committee (NCPAC), which had been running a negative advertising campaign against Senator Paul S. Sarbanes, a Democrat from Maryland. Fenn had firsthand experience with such attacks, which had helped bring down Frank Church. He proposed that PamPAC spend $20,000 to help Sarbanes by funding a radio advertisement attacking the conservative group as an "extremist right-wing organization" that used "lies and distortions" against its opponents. Pamela, recalled Fenn, "liked the idea. She said, 'Go for it.' She didn't like the NCPAC people. . . . It was easy to tell I had hit a hot button. She was nervous, but she wanted to do it."

Not only did Pamela like the idea, she saw it as a clever political tactic that could generate publicity for her fledgling organization. In considerable pain after breaking a vertebra in a fall from her horse, Pamela nevertheless held her first press conference. Although she had a statement prepared by a PamPAC consultant, and Fenn rehearsed her with sample questions, "she was concerned about whether she could handle it," he recalled. She was obviously nervous, and her delivery was stiff, but she got the message across.

The CBS Evening News ran the story, along with the *New York Times,* the *Baltimore Sun,* and *Newsweek,* which quoted John T. Dolan, chairman of NCPAC, calling the PamPAC accusations "the most vitriolic, vicious, mean untrue stuff I've seen," and Fenn countering that somebody had to "get down in the gutter with NCPAC" to fight back. Fenn was terrified that Pamela would rebuke him for his words. Instead, he said, "She thought it was a kick."

As Pamela knew from her own experience, even negative publicity meant that people were paying attention. Because the ad ran on local radio, all the Washington politicos knew about it, including Sarbanes, who heard it in a taxi on the way to his office. At a subsequent Democratic Senate retreat, Sarbanes singled Pamela out for praise. "That made her feel really good," said Fenn. So did the turnabout in the nay-saying Bob Strauss, who could barely contain his excitement. "Before that, Strauss didn't think we were going anywhere," said Fenn. "He was on the board, but it was as if he were patting her on the head and humoring her. But when we went after the right wing and there were stories about it, Strauss thought it was great. 'Hey,' he said, 'let's have the board meeting at my office!' "

Pamela's most important job was to persuade wealthy Democrats, as well as unions and business lobbyists, to donate generously and regularly to her committee. Her highest level of donations came in the committee's early years. During PamPAC's initial six months—and mostly before the committee kicked up any dust in the press—she raised $165,719 from seventy-eight individual donors and $31,700 from eleven labor unions and other political committees, a tribute to her technique and her celebrity.

In the first two years of PamPAC's existence, the 1981–82 "election cycle," as it is known in campaign financing parlance, she raised $1,049,100. During each of the subsequent two cycles she pulled in around $900,000, and in the latter part of the eighties she attracted some $500,000 for each cycle. Her total raised during the decade was $3.9 million—an amount that was respectable but by no means extraordinary. In the same period Independent Action, a political action committee created by a group of liberal Democrats in the House, raised $4.5 million, and the National Committee for an Effective Congress, a group founded by Eleanor Roosevelt in 1948 to help liberal candidates, raised $11.8 million.

A significant number of contributors gave PamPAC as much as $5,000 apiece each year—the maximum permitted by federal law—and many more consistently handed over at least $1,000. Pamela's list included such predictable Democratic establishment stalwarts as Blanchette Rockefeller ($14,800 in contributions over seven years) and her son, West Virginia's Democratic Senator John D. Rockefeller IV ($34,000 over ten years), Thomas Watson, former chairman of IBM ($54,000, along with his wife Olive, over ten years), and tobacco heir Smith Bagley ($44,000 with his wife Elizabeth in ten years), as well as more far flung fat cats such as Mark Dayton of Minneapolis ($19,000 in ten years). Among Pamela's regular union supporters were communications workers, machinists, steelworkers, seafarers, garment workers, and Jesse Calhoon's merchant mariners. She also gathered support from business interests, including Wall Street firms Morgan Stanley and Drexel Burnham, as well as auto dealers, airline executives, and trial lawyers. Pamela even tapped obscure sources from her past such as the shipping tycoon George Livanos, whom she had known through Stavros Niarchos.

During the 1980s Pamela held nearly one hundred "issues evenings" (seven of them in the first six months alone), each with a guest list of thirty to forty wealthy individuals, union and party leaders, and up-and-coming politicians, drawn together ostensibly to formulate new ideas for the party in the Harrimans' living room. Stuart Eizenstat developed the themes, helped select the "experts" who would address the group, and provided Pamela with "talking points," usually in verbal briefings. The "issues" were usually topics in the news, and the experts were familiar figures such as Congressman Les Aspin on strategic defense, or Congressman Dan Rostenkowski on tax policy.

The format was tightly structured and unvarying. After a round of drinks and canapes starting at 7:00 P.M., the guests would assemble in the living room, which was set up with rows of small gilt bamboo chairs. Facing the group would be Averell Harriman, dapper in his pinstripe suit, sitting in a large comfortable chair, with the evening's moderator and speaker on a sofa, and Pamela seated nearby. Pamela would make a brief greeting before yielding to the moderator, usually Clark Clifford or Robert Strauss, who would introduce the speaker and the issue. The speaker would talk for a half hour and take some questions. Then everyone would move to the glassed-in porch where four or five tables would be set for dinner. Afterward, the group would reconvene in the living room for another round of questions, and everyone would be out the door by ten-thirty.

Pamela monitored every detail of her evenings, from the menus to the flowers to the table setting. She spent hours on the seating arrangements, making sure that a bright young senator would be seated next to a potential contributor who had flown in from out of town, or that a union chief and a Wall Street financier might make contact and trade information. "She knew more about the people than most hostesses, and she wanted them to have great conversations, not just that so-and-so would get along, but that these two would fit together," said a former PamPAC employee. Joan Challinor, a regular contributor to the committee, said, "She often told me why I was sitting next to whomever, that I should talk to this person about the environment, or that this person was from a certain state and I should focus on that."

During the living-room discussions, Pamela asked occasional questions to clarify points or to move the conversation along. "She tried to make sure that everybody had an opportunity to say what they wanted," said Peter Fenn. She neither pressed particular ideas nor engaged in arguments; she merely wanted to keep the "juices flowing." Well aware of her celebrity, Pamela captivated her guests with her plummy English accent, her repertoire of Churchill anecdotes, and her evident interest in political issues. "I was dazzled by the way she moved those bozos around," said Barbara Howar. "They were like huge cats she brought into the house."

The evenings had their desired effect, giving contributors the sense that they had received good value for their hefty contributions. They had rubbed elbows with the great and near great, they had picked up some useful information, and they had gawked at the legendary Harrimans and their historic house. "Psychologically, it made being a Democrat not only respectable but gave it cachet," observed Joan Challinor. The only jarring notes came when Harriman's hearing aid would go on the fritz, beeping and whining and making it seem as if he was communicating with someone in outer space.

Pamela publicized her "issues evenings" with press releases announcing topics and featured guests, although reporters were excluded and the discussions were off the record—with one infamous exception. In the autumn of 1981, when Pamela was recuperating from another riding accident and couldn't attend a session on the economy, it was presided over by New York investment banker Felix Rohatyn. Pamela customarily taped the evenings, with a view, she later explained, to editing portions for newspaper opinion pieces or position papers. This time, however, a full transcript of the Rohatyn evening was given by a PamPAC staffer to James Perry, a *Wall Street Journal* reporter. In a sardonic front-page story, Perry described figures of "affluence and influence" engaging in "constant stroking," and "the oft-stated proposition that these are important people running the fast track." But the article's skeptical tone got lost in the controversy over a remark by Clark Clifford: Ronald Reagan, he said, was an "amiable dunce." The comment was picked up and repeated in another wave of complimentary magazine and newspaper articles about PamPAC—the *New York Times* called the "issues evenings" "gems of the genre"—proving once again that a moment of notoriety could translate into positive publicity for Pamela and her organization. As she told a reporter from *Newsweek,* "It's better to be talked about than not talked about."

In a world where even the wealthiest donors were often herded en masse into huge hotel ballrooms, Pamela's fund-raising techniques were a refreshing novelty. People who knew her could see that she had successfully adapted the approach she used so well on men: First, create a mood of intimacy, then follow up with favors and thoughtful gestures. "She has thousands of friends," said Mary Sethness, a Chicago heiress to a manufacturing fortune who contributed $19,000 to PamPAC. "She remembers little things about them. . . . She personally kept in touch."

When she wanted to bring in important new contributors, Pamela would invite one or two of them to lunch at N Street. John Bowles attended one such session with a top Wall Street financier and the chairman of a large corporation. "You go in there and you feel it is the most exclusive club you have ever been in," said Bowles. "She knew the way these men operated. . . . She was well briefed. . . . I don't recall Pam asking directly for money. It was more indirect. Obviously there was a purpose to the luncheon. These two guys had worked both sides of the street, Republican and Democrat. It was the ambiance of the room, the charming woman who had done her homework, who was very attractive and a couple of years younger, the whole setup. These two guys left the lunch in love with her. They each gave a thousand dollars, which gave an umbrella blessing to a lot of other people."

John J. Cafaro, a manufacturer of Avanti automobiles in Youngstown, Ohio, had first appeared on Pamela's radar during the House–Senate dinners in the late 1970s. Until 1981, he had never supported a political action committee, but in the first four years of PamPAC's life, she coaxed $15,000 from Cafaro. With Pamela, Cafaro said, "It was nice and quiet and small and social. If you are five hundred miles away you don't want to go to dinner with a thousand people. . . . You felt you were going to a friend's home for dinner. . . . Even those who didn't know her well felt that they did."

Illinois attorney Kenneth Montgomery and his wife Harle were longtime Democratic patrons who gave Pamela $52,000 over a decade. Pamela had courted them through a mutual friend. Many fund-raising appeals to the Montgomerys "would end in the wastebasket," Harle Montgomery recalled, "but Pamela's always had a personal feel to them. They seemed more compelling, and after she got going I admired her so much for what she was doing that I wanted to funnel my contributions through her." When they saw Pamela, "she was always so cordial and friendly. My husband always felt very flattered by her attentions."

In interviews Pamela sometimes protested that she found fund-raising "frightening," and even distasteful. "It's terrible to be so concerned about money, isn't it!" she once exclaimed—without a flicker of irony—to a *New York Times* reporter. Those who worked with her saw no evidence of such feelings, marveling instead at how easily she handled an inherently awkward task. Pamela knew how to pace her requests, and she sensibly avoided spreading herself too thin. She delegated much of the phone solicitation to Janet Howard and to professional fundraisers she would hire.

"Janet and Pamela were the greatest one-two female punch in political fund-raising," said John Bowles. "Janet had a sense of who people were, she knew when to call someone in to get help, and obviously she had a list that was very strong. She had an essential factor in fund-raising. You get ten people in a room, find three or four to give money, and then get them to form their own circle. She wouldn't stop with raising a thousand from you. She would say, who do you know, who can you bring into the mix of the next dinner? She went right up to the limit before people got angry." Howard was equally effective with union leaders. "Talking to the president of the machinist union, she could speak man to man," said a former PamPAC staffer. "She could be chatty. She was not frightened of anyone. She had power by association."

As a rule, Pamela confined herself to contacting people she knew fairly well, but she wouldn't hesitate to pick up the phone if someone was on the fence. When Pamela called, people knew it was important. Her approach was direct, serious but pleasant, neither threatening nor desperate. She was careful not to ask anyone to support her personally, always emphasizing that a donation to PamPAC would help the party. She talked of the "exciting event," and if she was helping a specific politician, she might say, "It is very important to my friend if you could be here, and I would love to see you."

When the donors were men, Pamela's fund-raising technique had an added psychological dimension. "I'm a man. She's a lady, a good-looking, attractive woman. She's had a lot of men in her life," said Jay P. Altmayer, a self-proclaimed "yellow dog Democrat" and Alabama investor five years her senior, who gave PamPAC $12,475. At various times, a half-dozen male contributors asked one former PamPAC fundraiser if Pamela would go out to dinner with them, and one prominent contributor even wondered if she might sleep with him. "Here was a guy who was tough in business," recalled the fundraiser. "You couldn't bullshit him, but his eyes would glaze when he was around her."

Just as important as raising money was Pamela's scheme for disbursing it. Under federal law, political action committees were permitted to donate as much as $5,000 to a candidate for national office in a primary election, and $5,000 for a general election—a total of $10,000 for each candidate. (Individuals, by contrast, were only allowed to give a candidate for federal office a maximum of $2,000 for both elections.) In the 1981–82 election cycle, the committee spent $234,150 on 392 Democratic candidates for the House, and $91,400 on 30 Senate candidates. Three Senate candidates—Robert Byrd of West Virginia, George Mitchell of Maine, and Ted Wilson of Utah—received the $10,000 maximum, and the remainder were given anywhere from $100 to $9,900. In the House, the maximum donation was $5,100, which went to nine candidates, including Thomas Foley of Washington, Philip Burton of California, and Dante Fascell of Florida.

Pamela's first round of choices was a largely conventional group, following the list of potential recipients supplied by McPherson and Bernhard, with some additional guidance from California Congressman Tony Coelho, the chairman of the Democratic Congressional Campaign Committee. She also drew from an extensive analysis conducted by Peter Fenn, a state-by-state breakdown of every race that included voting statistics, media resources, fund-raising goals and results, important issues and perceptions of the candidates.

At Fenn's urging, PamPAC supported some unknowns running for open seats and challenging Republican incumbents. In the beginning, Pamela rarely met with candidates, but she could be won over by handsome, aggressive young challengers who actively sought her support. One of them was Robert Mrazek, who was running for a seat in the third congressional district in New York. Although he was not expected to win, Pamela not only gave him $3,600, she paid for a poll that helped focus his campaign. When he won, Pamela had secured his eternal loyalty.

As she grew more self-assured, Pamela clearly enjoyed appraising candidates on her own and identifying the most promising. "She is not interested in a grid of positions on issues when she is figuring out who to support," said Peter Fenn. With her PamPAC war chest, she had enough resources to spread her bets so that she would invariably pick winners. "She learned early in life about politics and the relationships of people to power," said one longtime friend. "She has a good instinct for successful people. . . . All she had to learn was who the players were."

Pamela also loved being courted for money, and her donations began showing her personal preferences. According to a former member of the Pam-PAC staff, candidates like Robert Byrd, who didn't really need the committee's support, received the maximum because he had conspicuously boosted Pamela, calling her, among other things, the "soul of the Democratic party." "You would make a kind of well-meant suggestion, like, 'Let's support Senator So-and-so. He's a nice man who did his best to get the homeless bill,' " recalled one of her advisers. "But if it was someone who had not been responsive to Pam, or if she thought he was a jerk, or that he didn't have a chance to win, she would write him off. A line was drawn right through his name."

Beginning in 1983, Pamela's focus shifted away from congressmen to senators. In 1983–84, PamPAC gave $201,000 to twenty-seven Senate candidates, and only $127,250 to sixty-eight House candidates. The following election cycle, $241,000 went to twenty-nine Senate candidates, and $63,250 to fifty-four House candidates. By 1987–88, $211,000 went to senators, and a mere $13,150 to congressmen. The stated reason for the change was a need to concentrate on recapturing the Senate, which the Democrats did in 1986. But while Pamela kept her alliances with the House leadership and certain congressional stars, she preferred the company of big-time players in the Senate. "Senators are more prestigious," explained John Bowles. "There are too many congressmen, too many risks. By staying with the Senate, it was a question of impact."

In addition to her PamPAC activities, Pamela organized private fund-raising events for her most favored few, including Senators Edward Kennedy, Alan Cranston, Thomas Daschle, Gary Hart, George Mitchell, Al Gore, and John Kerry. These dinners and receptions, she boasted, were "never less than $100,000 an evening." Other sources confirmed that some events pulled in as much as $130,000 or $140,000, but many evenings yielded more in the range of $50,000 or $60,000.

Though candidates appreciated their PamPAC contributions, the private fundraisers were the real payoff for associating with the Harriman operation. The $50,000 or $100,000 she would raise in a night was a drop in the bucket in most senatorial campaigns—Alan Cranston, for instance, spent $11 million in his 1986 campaign—yet Pamela's benefactors were grateful for her blessing because it often attracted the attention of other fundraisers.

An important adjunct to her direct support of candidates was the money spent on PamPAC's *Democratic Fact Book*. A nearly 400-page primer on economic, social, and foreign policy issues, the fact book offered thumbnail summaries of Reagan administration initiatives spiced with embarrassing quotes as well as easy descriptions of Democratic positions. PamPAC distributed three editions of the book—in 1982, 1984, and 1986—to every Democratic candidate for the House and Senate, as well as state and local hopefuls and officeholders, at a total cost to the committee of around $270,000. Although the books offered no new ideas or visions, they were probably the most useful legacy of PamPAC.

Like the issues evenings, the fact book was the brainchild of Stuart Eizenstat, who modeled it on a similar compendium put together by the Democratic National Committee in the early 1970s. To research the book, Pamela resourcefully tapped into the pool of out-of-work Democratic policy specialists. She invited forty of them to N Street and enticed them to work for little or no pay. "For Pam it was a ten-strike," said John Bowles. "She got these bright young people involved, and they loved Pam because she got them into print." She took great pleasure from her collection of hired brains, from whom she gleaned information as well as loyalty, and whose work she held in the highest regard. "She read the galleys but she didn't make substantive contributions," said one of her contributors. "She knew and trusted the experts."

Pamela was a master at gathering and spending other people's money, but she also encouraged the idea that she was a magnanimous benefactor in her own right. How generous were Pamela and Averell Harriman? He was downright cheap, and she rarely approached the $25,000 yearly cap on contributions by individuals to candidates for national office, party committees, and PACs. In various news accounts, Pamela claimed that she and her husband routinely hit the annual legal maximum of $50,000 for a couple. In fact, aside from his yearly $5,000 donation to PamPAC, Averell Harriman gave a mere $6,000 to candidates during the 1980s. He contributed no money whatsoever to the Democratic Party or other political action committees.

As for Pamela, she gave $500 and $1,000 donations to an array of candidates, mostly for the Senate, totaling anywhere from $3,000 to $10,000 annually. Every year she gave at least $1,000 to the House and Senate Council dinner; for each of three years in the early 1980s she gave $5,000 to the DNC's "travel escrow account"; and she gave $1,000 donations to assorted Democratic presidential candidates (Mo Udall in 1982; John Glenn, Ernest Hollings, and George McGovern in 1984; and Richard Gephardt, Al Gore, and Paul Simon in 1987). Her biggest annual contributions were in 1986, when her combined federal political donations amounted to $22,500, and in 1987, when she gave a total of $21,000. Otherwise, her yearly totals during the eighties fluctuated from $11,000 to $17,000.

Curiously, Pamela didn't always give her own committee the maximum donation of $5,000 each year. In 1985 and 1987, in fact, she didn't contribute a cent to PamPAC, while supporters like the Montgomerys and the Bagleys never missed a year. Because the PamPAC offices were located on their property, and so many events were held in their home, the Harrimans received sizable reimbursements from Democrats for the 80's in order to comply with election law. In 1983, for example, they donated $10,000 to the committee, but they received $21,179, which included rent, office equipment, labor during fundraisers, and $3,618 for the use of the Harriman jet—in effect making a profit of $11,179 on their political activities.

Pamela fell short of the legal ceiling in donations monitored by the Federal Election Commission, yet there are indications that she was generous with what is called "soft money," for which there were neither reporting requirements nor monetary limits during the 1980s. Soft money—also known as "non-federal" money—was given either directly to state and local political parties or to the Democratic or Republican National Committee, and supposedly earmarked for use by state party organizations. In theory, these funds were to be used for such activities as voter registration and distribution of campaign materials at the state and local level. In practice, most of the soft money found its way back into the campaigns of national candidates in the name of "party building." The sole purpose of soft money was to buy and sell influence.

One of the most ingenious purveyors of soft money was Congressman Tony Coelho, a Pamela favorite. A small, hyperkinetic man, Coelho, according to a former Capitol Hill staffer, "goes to bed and thinks from twelve to six A.M., who is out to get him, who he can get. He is all strategy. Tony is always thinking. The problem is that he can't turn it off." In 1982, Coelho hatched a plan to help the Democrats build a modern television studio where candidates could tape campaign commercials at minimal cost. Facing capital and operating startup costs of $1 million, he asked Pamela for a $400,000 interest-free loan to buy and refurbish a Capitol Hill town house. "She was initially very excited," recalled Peter Fenn. "She was real excited but concerned and wary." Her husband gave her the go-ahead to make the loan after consulting with Clark Clifford. "Clifford thought it was a very good idea," said Fenn. In exchange for Pamela's support, Coelho did everything he could to help her operation. "He gave legitimacy to the political side of her PAC," said Peter Fenn. "He included her in meetings on the Hill."

When the Democratic National Committee built its new headquarters several years later, Coelho moved the television studio to larger quarters in the basement. The new facility was filled with $2.5 million in equipment bought by soft-money donations of up to $100,000 from unions and business PACs. Pamela publicly associated herself with the media center in November 1985 by serving as master of ceremonies at a benefit dinner that raised $250,000. The new studio opened in April 1986, renamed the Harriman Communications Center in honor of Pamela and Averell. By then much of Pamela's loan had presumably been repaid, but she converted part of the sum into an outright soft-money gift of $150,000—the kind of substantial contribution that was necessary to join the prestigious club of powerful top supporters of the Democratic Party. It was also an amount that would have made Pamela's tightfisted husband blanch; a loan was one matter, but a six-figure contribution—not even tax-deductible—quite another. By then, however, Harriman was in no position to object. Ninety-four years old, ailing, almost totally deaf and blind, his mental capacity was significantly diminished. The Governor was now in the background, leaving Pamela center stage.

Twenty-eight

IN THE EARLIEST DAYS of Democrats for the 80's, Averell Harriman had assumed a visible if not very active role, and Pamela had taken care to commend his efforts. "If anybody can bring Democrats together, it's Averell Harriman," she told the *New York Times* in October 1981. At the issues evenings Harriman liked to make a few remarks, usually in praise of Pamela. Those evenings, said Stuart Eizenstat, "helped keep Ave alive. They gave him a sense of purpose and involvement and enriched his years."

Harriman had enjoyed keeping track of PamPAC's activities, even down to walking through the offices and turning out the lights to save money. "It was clearly her deal from the beginning, although she would ask his advice," said Peter Fenn. From time to time, Harriman injected himself into as much of the substance of PamPAC as he could muster. Before launching the attack on NCPAC, Pamela asked Harriman to review the press release. "He couldn't see well or hear at all," said Fenn. "I read him a two-page press release and he said, 'In paragraph two do this,' and, 'In paragraph eight do this.' "

For the most part, Harriman had happily served as the figurehead for Pamela's fund-raising machine. "I never saw anybody [being] used who enjoyed it so much," noted Clark Clifford. Pamela employed her husband's symbolic value to the utmost, no more so than during the ninetieth birthday party she threw to raise money for PamPAC and the Democratic National Committee in November 1981. The guest list of 1,500 was a Who's Who of Washington politicos and New York socialites. With contributions ranging from $500 to $5,000, they pumped $200,832 into PamPAC.

Every table had a miniature Union Pacific Railroad centerpiece, and Kitty Carlisle Hart sang "Always" to the birthday boy. "My wife and I have been married for ten years," Harriman told the crowd, "and in that period of time I have been able to see more of the things I care about than at any time." From across the room, at the table where Peter Duchin and various Harriman family members sat, "there was an audible boo," recalled Marie Ridder, a longtime friend of Marie Harriman, who was sitting with them.

The years with Marie, it seemed, had utterly vanished. In almost every respect, Pamela was Marie's opposite, and Harriman both benefited and suffered from the differences. Harriman lived in greater luxury than he had with Marie. Instead of Marie's offhand and capricious manner, Harriman enjoyed

Pamela's unique brand of assiduous care. When he went for walks in George-town, Pamela would ask their butler, Michael Kuruc, to follow him in case he slipped and fell. To amuse him during dinner with friends, she would show a movietone newsreel of the Yalta Conference, or a video of her horse, the Governor, winning a show-jumping championship at Madison Square Garden. Pamela often returned from shopping excursions with a necktie or sweater wrapped in a package that Harriman would gleefully open.

When they dined alone together, they usually had one cocktail—his a scotch and water, hers a kir or Campari—and canapes before sitting down in the formal dining room. He wore a suit and tie, and she liked to dress in a filmy floor-length caftan. "She never let down on her appearance," said Michael Kuruc. "It was always to please him." When there was a political program on television, they might eat dinner on trays in the upstairs library. Afterward she would do paperwork for PamPAC, and when the Governor went to sleep she diverted herself by reading mail-order catalogues. "She loved those catalogues," recalled Kuruc.

Although they had separate bedrooms, they usually slept in Pamela's unless Harriman wasn't feeling well. Like the Duchess of Windsor, Pamela insisted that her Porthault sheets be perfectly pressed, with absolutely no wrinkles. Averell and Pamela rose early, and by 8:00 A.M. the maid brought them breakfast in bed on trays while they read the *New York Times* and the *Washington Post*. "Pam was very warm with him," said Harriman's longtime physician Edmund Goodman. "He loved this, and I don't think he had ever had it. As a result, he was warmer with her. He was affectionate. I had never seen him that way."

Both Marie and Pamela understood Harriman's unceasing need for company and both organized his life accordingly. But whereas Marie had been open and relaxed in social settings, Pamela was even more controlling than she had been with Leland Hayward. When visitors were expected for lunch, tea, or dinner, the social secretary posted a guest list in the morning. "That was the bible and you knew what to do," said Kuruc. With Pamela there always seemed to be a hidden agenda; few guests were invited to the Harriman house without a reason. "People loved Marie and feared Pam," said a woman who knew each well.

The fundamental problem was that Pamela and Harriman were too much alike: determined, literal-minded, earnest, and humorless. Marie's wit had tempered her husband's arrogance, but Pamela reinforced it by taking herself so seriously. Pamela's overarching ambition also matched her husband's, making them both more vulnerable to insinuating sycophants that Marie sent packing. "Marie was a much more settled woman than Pam," said Mary Warburg, who was friendly with both women.

Yet even Marie's partisans acknowledged that Pamela's ways worked to Harriman's advantage as he grew older. "Grandmère's style humanized Ave," said Marie's granddaughter, Alida Morgan. "Being able to schmooze with the gang worked well politically, and his access through Grandmère made things easier. They had a great mix, and she kept it exciting and irreverent. But Pamela's more formal way worked better at the end of his life. It suited the times, the politics, and keeping Ave accessible. At the PAC he could bask in the glow."

Harriman was extremely proud of Pamela's achievements, which reflected directly on him as his had once reflected on her. To Harriman, Pamela was his greatest acquisition. "He loved her with a burning passion concealed under that Victorian exterior," said one of Harriman's old friends. "He wanted her to succeed, and he gave her everything, not only money but training, access, and tutelage. He watched her pick it up slowly and carefully as he declined, and while he was alive she made few mistakes."

One clear measure of Harriman's confidence in Pamela could be seen in the spring of 1983 during their visit to the Soviet Union, where he was scheduled to meet the former chief of the KGB, Yuri Andropov, who succeeded Leonid Brezhnev as Secretary General of the Communist Party. This time Harriman brought her in as a full partner, along with his four aides who attended the meeting. According to his former State Department deputy, Peter Swiers, Harriman told Andropov, "I am grateful to my wife, Pam, for coming with me. I hope she will continue my work when I am no longer able to." As Richard Holbrooke later told *Vanity Fair,* "That was, I believe, the moment when Harriman passed the torch to Pam."

Back home, according to *Women's Wear Daily,* one of Pamela's favorite outlets for news of her comings and goings, she took to "lyrically and at length singing the praises of big bear Andropov. Doubtless, were it left in Pamela's capable hands, Soviet–U.S. entente would be reached immediately." The reality was less than inspiring. On their return, Pamela called Secretary of State George Schultz and asked if she and Harriman could brief him on the trip. "Pam handled the briefing," recalled a man who was present. "It was not impressive. It was all banalities, and there was no substance. She said things like, 'The Soviets really want to be our friends.' Schultz got irritated and shot back, 'Well, what proof do you have? Why do they keep building SS-18s?' She would turn to Averell and say, 'You explain, dear.' I could tell she was annoyed."

Later that year, during a Christmas vacation in Barbados, Harriman fell in the ocean and broke his leg. Until the bone healed, he couldn't risk returning to Washington, even on their private jet, so they settled in for an extended convalescence on the island. After a few weeks, Pamela persuaded Averell to buy Mango Bay, a four-bedroom house that was almost fully furnished, for $1.2 million. Pamela loved Barbados, a favorite retreat for the wealthy Europeans whose company she enjoyed. The principal inducement for Harriman was a pool where he could swim safely; to ensure his comfort, Pamela immediately had a heater installed.

A beachfront property set in a garden of orchids and fruit trees, Mango Bay was one of the island's showplaces. Its architect was Oliver Messel, the renowned London stage designer, whose theatrical touches included an inconvenient outdoor staircase that required guests to carry umbrellas in foul weather to reach their rooms. "Constructed of pale coral stone, the house could be a villa in the south of France or, with a little imagination, the setting for 'The Two Gentlemen of Verona,' played on the terraces and upper loggia," wrote

William Walton, whom Pamela enlisted to create rhapsodic articles in *Architectural Digest* about each of her homes. Pamela imported the top Manhattan designer Bunny Williams to redo the interior in tones of apricot and beige, paying special attention to her bedroom and study on the second floor overlooking the ocean. Harriman's quarters were located in a nearby cottage, with his nurse in an adjacent room.

It was evident to everyone that Harriman, now ninety-two, declined after the accident. Pamela took steps to move their principal residence to Middleburg, where inheritance taxes would be considerably less than in the District of Columbia. They needed no special dispensation from the District to do so, but they had to make some ownership changes on their properties, switch their voter registration, and begin paying Virginia income tax. On January 8, 1984, Harriman signed a deed, witnessed by the U.S. Consul General to Barbados, that transferred the ownership of his Georgetown property to a shell partnership called Highlands L.P. Shortly after their return to Washington, Pamela moved Harriman out to Middleburg. To help establish their legal residency, Harriman wrote to friends telling them that his address was now at Willow Oaks. Pamela, who had previously owned Willow Oaks entirely in her name, signed documents that June transferring half the ownership to Harriman as a gift. On Harriman's death, Willow Oaks would automatically be hers again.

To ensure that her husband was never alone, Pamela kept a roster of friends she would invite to Willow Oaks for lunch or dinner when she was in Georgetown or traveling on PamPAC business. She even furnished her car and driver to transport her guests out from Washington and back home. "I know why you came here," Harriman said after a luncheon with Clayton Fritchey. "She asked you to. It's like that every day. You know, I really love her."

Harriman's most frequent lunchtime companion was his former secretary, Pie Friendly, who had left the family office after a falling out with Janet Howard. Nevertheless, when Pamela called, Pie Friendly came, usually twice a week, serving almost as a nanny to the aging diplomat, reading to him and entertaining him with gossip about political Washington. Friendly was paid by the hour. Before her visits, she would go through the Harriman archives and pull out an old forgotten letter or a Groton report card that might amuse him.

Still, Harriman missed Pamela's daily presence. He would telephone the PamPAC office and thunder, "Where's Pam? When is she coming home?" and he would wait impatiently for her return to Willow Oaks. "When she arrived home he would be very happy, like a puppy dog," said Michael Kuruc. " 'Oh, hello, Averell,' she would say. 'How are you, dear?' And she would run into her bedroom and change." Many evenings she spent hours on the phone. "Damn telephones," he would bellow. But he couldn't really complain after she reassured him that she was doing her work for the Democrats.

Pamela was accustomed to difficult men, but Harriman posed the greatest challenge in her long experience. Conversations with him were arduous. "He was totally compos but his hearing was so bad, and he was so abrupt. He was either stopping you or keeping you going," said Charles Maechling, an old State Department crony who periodically came for visits. "After one and a half hours I would go home and head for the bar. I could barely talk. It was a terrible strain, shouting, then toning down." Pamela spoke slowly by nature, and she modulated her deep voice, raising it slightly and speaking loudly to register on Harriman's hearing aid. To the amazement of their friends, he was able to pick her voice out of a crowd, and his nearly sightless eyes would obsessively follow her around the room. "Where are you going?" he would demand if she stood to leave the room. "Why are you leaving?" Whenever he had to sit alone for any period, Harriman's voice boomed, "PAH-MAH-LAH," like a wounded animal.

For all his devotion to Pamela, he could be impossibly cranky. "You don't know what you're talking about," he might blurt out after Pamela ventured an opinion, or, "You don't have any feel for politics." "I would go down to Barbados to spell her," said Walton, "and he would slap her hands away at the table and accuse the guests of trying to steal his food. She was very stiff upper lip." Sometimes she lost her temper, but usually she retreated to an upstairs study where Harriman couldn't reach her. Throughout their marriage, she had been accustomed to sitting in on Harriman's interviews with journalists, helping remind him of names and dates and incidents, and protecting him from too-probing questions. Once in Harriman's last years, Rudy Abramson was questioning him about his childhood when Pamela tried to assist. "Please, I'm being interviewed," he snapped. "I will answer the questions as I wish." Abramson recalled, "She was totally meek. There was no arguing. Later she told me, 'You won't believe this, but he has never really talked to me about his family or his past.' "

From time to time she brought him to political events in town. She would settle him into a chair, zero in on a woman she knew Harriman liked, and say, "Oh, Ave adores you. Won't you sit with him for a while?" and then disappear into the crowd. She carefully selected his dinner partners, choosing women with clear voices. Carol Williams was a particular favorite. "She told me he could hear my voice better than others, and she asked me to tell him what the speaker was saying," recalled Williams. Some felt discomfited by the sight of Harriman sitting in a corner while Pamela fluttered about. But others maintained that Harriman was happy enough being part of the action. "She was good about protecting him," said a former PamPAC staff member. "She was selective about what he could do."

Pamela's management of Harriman was attentive and skillful, but she was no nursemaid. "She looked after him the way a rich lady would," observed Michael Kuruc. "She would see that all the comforts were there. She didn't have to do anything herself. There was always somebody to take care of him." Pamela let it be known to everyone how well she catered to her husband, all the while working indefatigably for the Democratic cause. "The many days on the road and tug of competing demands for her time, not to mention the daily commutes that she makes between Washington and the Harriman home in Middleburg have taken their toll," wrote the *National Journal* in April 1986. In order to pay income taxes in Virginia instead of D.C., Pamela had to spend 183 nights each year at Willow Oaks.

Despite Harriman's physical infirmities, he remained mentally alert until the last year of his life. One focus of his attention was managing his fortune and planning his last will and testament. Although he had left the business world at a young age, he had long been preoccupied by his personal finances in general and avoiding taxes in particular. The great New Deal Democrat simply hated giving money to the government. "Averell viewed taxes as a deterrent to hard work," explained Guy Waltman.

For decades the Harriman fortune had been supervised by professionals at Brown Brothers Harriman. Elbridge Gerry, Jr., the Brown Brothers senior partner in charge of investments and the son of Averell's sister Cornelia, served as trustee, along with his colleague John Madden, of the various family trusts set up by Averell for his daughters and grandchildren. The Harriman office was run by a series of managers who handled the accounts, paid the bills, and kept track of investment portfolios. Daniel Cook served Averell Harriman and his family for twenty years, followed by Guy Waltman, who replaced Cook in the mid-1970s.

Waltman had daily conversations with Gerry, who was known as a savvy yet conservative investor. If Waltman had an investment recommendation, he would present it, Gerry and Madden would offer their advice, and Waltman would proceed accordingly. "They were very involved and capable," said Waltman. Averell Harriman kept in regular touch with the family office, and he traveled to New York City once a month for a marathon two-day session with Waltman. They would begin each day at 8:30 A.M. and work straight through until 5:00 P.M., with a short break for lunch together. Harriman would sit across the desk, sometimes reading the charts upside down. As they went over reports line by line, Harriman asked a multitude of detailed questions. "I dreaded these meetings," recalled Waltman. "I would get my whole staff to think of every possible question Averell would ask. He always asked a question we were unprepared for."

In the late 1970s Harriman's estate had been worth about $150 million. As soon as he had figured out his annual income taxes, Harriman would call Nash Castro, his contact at the Palisades Interstate Park Commission, and tell him he needed to give away several million dollars' worth of real estate for tax purposes, leaving Castro the task of figuring out which acreage would work best. Once an expanse of 40,000 acres, Arden became less an estate than a tax dodge, eventually shrinking to 3,500 acres, which were divided between Averell and Roland Harriman and their families. Harriman also gave his 10,000-acre ranch in Sun Valley to the state of Idaho to take advantage of the tax laws. As a result, the value of Harriman's estate declined to around $100 million.

When Roland Harriman died in 1978, his similarly substantial estate was divided equally between his wife and his children, a move that meant paying a hefty estate tax. Averell Harriman would have none of that. Under the law at the time, only half of an estate could pass tax-free to a surviving spouse, so when Harriman drew up a new will in 1979, he left half to Pamela and the other half to charity, an arrangement that would prevent the government from collecting a penny. By setting up various trusts for his daughters and grandchil-

dren over the years, Harriman believed, said Waltman, that "they were adequately provided for. They were wealthy, not as wealthy as he was, but wealthy
enough." Still, Harriman declined to give his children and grandchildren the
bad news about the will himself. It fell to Waltman to do the job. "They
listened," recalled Waltman. "Most were not happy but said, 'If that's what Ave
wants to do about it, obviously he can do it.' "

When Waltman left in 1979 for another firm, Harriman hired William Rich
III, a thirty-four-year-old lawyer from the trust and estates department at Morgan Guaranty. Heavyset and unassuming, Rich had been educated at Hobart
College and Fordham University and lived in unfashionable Jackson Heights,
Queens. But he had made a name for himself at Morgan, which prided itself on
prudence and discretion. These were traits that suited Harriman, who wanted
someone to watch over his estate and to help structure his finances to minimize
taxes. Rich seemed the epitome of the cautious steward dedicated to preserving
the Harriman millions and avoiding risky and aggressive investments.

Not long after Rich's arrival, Harriman switched his legal representation
from his experts in trust and estate law at Manhattan's Davis Polk & Wardwell
to Clark Clifford and his law partner Paul Warnke, former Assistant Secretary
of Defense under President Lyndon Johnson and chief U.S. arms control negotiator under President Jimmy Carter. "Pam never really liked the fact that
Averell had a New York law firm," said Guy Waltman. "She wanted Clark
Clifford." For power and influence in the nation's capital, the Harrimans could
find no better representatives, but neither man had much experience in managing a complicated family fortune.

Changes in federal tax laws in 1982 resulted in a windfall for Pamela. Under
the new provisions, one spouse could make unlimited gifts to the other without
paying any gift tax. In addition, an entire estate—instead of just half—could
pass to a surviving spouse tax-free. Harriman acted fast, giving his art collection
to Pamela that year, a boon worth an estimated $45 million. In 1979, the van
Gogh *White Roses* alone had been appraised at $10 million, but it was thought
to be worth three times that amount.

Harriman's original plan had been to donate the paintings to the National
Gallery as he had done with the Marie Harriman Collection. When he gave
them to Pamela instead, it was with the understanding that she would have
them for her lifetime and then transfer them to the National Gallery according
to his wishes—at least in part so she would enjoy a handsome tax deduction.
"Averell trusted her implicitly, that if she made. a promise to him, she would
keep it," said Guy Waltman. Still, Harriman's family was taken aback that he
had parted with all of his art treasures. "Can't you leave me just one picture?"
Kathleen Mortimer asked her father. "I can't afford it!" he said, referring to the
taxes he would have to pay.

A year later, Pamela established a trust fund for herself at Harriman's
direction, with 120,000 shares of Union Pacific stock he had given her. Under
the terms of the trust, Pamela would receive $350,000 a year for twelve years;
at the end of that period, Harriman's grandchildren would divide whatever
principal might remain. In April 1984, after he returned from his Barbados

convalescence, Harriman told his family he wanted to reorganize eleven of the trusts that he had set up for them at intervals since 1935. His reason, he said, was that the investment portfolios were not growing enough under the direction of Gerry and Madden.

According to Harriman's plan, he would pool the assets of the trusts into two family partnerships, called "Oldfields" (after the Arden home of Mary Fisk) and "Southfields" (after a tiny town near the Arden estate). Three investment firms were appointed to manage the portfolios, and Brown Brothers Harriman was not one of them. Harriman named Clifford and Warnke trustees with ultimate responsibility for the Harriman funds, replacing Gerry and Madden. One of the conditions, Clifford recalled, was Harriman's helpful assurance that "you don't have to see the grandchildren." Not only had Harriman chosen two lawyers who hadn't specialized in trusts and estates, he now had them as his trustees as well. "The puzzling thing," said Waltman, "was that Clifford and Warnke couldn't lay claim to investment expertise."

Two of the Harriman grandchildren, Kitty Ames and Averell Fisk, balked at the proposed reorganization. Young Averell had been an irritant to his grandfather for years, bluntly questioning the way his money was being managed. He asked that his trust be removed from the plan so that he could invest in Palm Beach real estate. Kitty touched off a furor with Pamela by questioning the competence of Clifford and Warnke, as well as their level of interest in the grandchildren. She suggested that an independent trustee be named instead. Pamela found Kitty's inquiries "offensive," she said, and Harriman refused to answer them. Finally Kitty visited her grandfather and persuaded him to release her trust, along with her brother's, from the family partnerships.

The nine trusts put under the supervision of Clifford and Warnke were worth $13 million in 1984. The shares for Harriman's daughters Kathleen Mortimer and Mary Fisk were $2.6 million each, yielding some $130,000 in annual income. Each grandchild's trust was worth $1.6 million, throwing off about $75,000 apiece, which gave them a comfortable financial cushion. All the beneficiaries professed satisfaction with the new arrangement, and Harriman considered his duties to the family trusts discharged.

After further consultation with Clark Clifford, Averell Harriman signed a new forty-seven-page will on September 12, 1984, in a shaky but legible scrawl. (A ten-page codicil added a year later clarified several provisions but did not alter the main outlines of the will.) Harriman made Pamela his principal beneficiary, entitled to the bulk of his real estate, securities, and other investments. He left nothing to his daughters, "not from any lack of love and affection for them," he wrote, "but because I know them to be otherwise provided for." For his six grandchildren he earmarked $600,000, and through three new trusts he provided that his grandchildren and great-grandchildren could divide some of his millions down the line after Pamela's death. He named Pamela his sole executor as well as a trustee, along with Clifford and Warnke, of the new trusts created by the will. By consigning a portion of the estate to trusts, Harriman was theoretically putting some restrictions on what he knew were Pamela's lavish spending habits. Yet by giving her discretion as a trustee, he set up the potential for a conflict of interest and undercut his own good intentions.

He also gave her a major responsibility for which she had neither the inclination, the talent, nor the training—and Harriman's attitude was as patronizing as it was foolish. "She'll take care of herself," Harriman told the *Washington Post* in 1983. "Fortunately we can provide her something to eat and a place to lay her head." Harriman's one halfhearted effort to acquaint Pamela with the business world had been securing her a place on the Braniff board, where she had learned little. "Ave had a strong financial background and a keen interest," explained Guy Waltman. "But Pamela wasn't interested in financial affairs at all. She was not interested in the investments, and she didn't even ask questions. . . . We talked about her projects, her plans and the costs. But I never talked about investments. . . . She didn't seem to care."

Pamela had always relied on men for money, and as her spendthrift years with Hayward showed, she had no impulse for financial planning, much less living within her means. She had been angling for the security of a large fortune since her girlhood, when she lived in luxurious surroundings with little cash. Yet she spent money as if the supply of funds was bottomless, with the confidence that a man, and on occasion a sympathetic woman such as Kathleen Mortimer or Kick Kennedy, would pay the bills. If one source went dry, she knew she could secure another.

Pamela's attitude was grounded partly in her personality; whenever her cash ran low, she would worry briefly before slipping into denial and assuming that the money would mysteriously reappear. This impulse was reinforced by a sense of aristocratic entitlement. As the daughter of the eleventh Lord Digby, she simply believed that she would always have a safety net.

Harriman never explained to her the intricacies of his fortune, never taught her how to read financial reports, never included her in discussions of investment strategies. When Harriman brought in William Rich to manage the family office, he expressly told Pamela that he was the handpicked man, that she should trust him completely and abide by his decisions. To Pamela, this was welcome news. Now that she was married to a wealthy man who could afford the best advisers, she could concentrate on what interested her and let someone else keep her supplied with an endless flow of cash. The hired hands would worry about the tiresome financial details.

As Harriman put his estate in order in 1984, he gave little evidence of how ill he really was; the miracle was that he had lived so long. He had been diagnosed in the early 1970s with prostate cancer. At the time, various specialists had urged him to have radical surgery and radiation therapy, while his family physicians, Edmund Goodman and Alvan Barach, had strongly recommended that Harriman be treated instead with the female hormone estrogen. With Pamela's concurrence, Harriman chose the estrogen therapy, which worked very well. "He had no real side effects," said Goodman, "but at age ninety-three the cancer manifested itself again." This time it was debilitating bone cancer, and once again Harriman refused to be treated with radiation or chemotherapy. "If he was in pain," wrote Rudy Abramson, "he never admitted it."

Forced to use a walker, Harriman nevertheless continued to swim laps, riding in his golf cart to the pool where his nurse Bonnie helped him into the water. Pam threw a ninety-fourth birthday party for him in November 1985, a luncheon at the N Street house attended by fifty of his old friends, including Clark Clifford, Arthur Schlesinger, Jr., and an assortment of former colleagues from the State Department. "He talked of his impending death," said one man who was there. "He said two years from then he wouldn't be around."

Through the following winter and spring Harriman kept up with his correspondence and entertained his stream of visitors. When one old friend asked him if he had any regrets in life, Harriman growled, "Not marrying her the first time." Two unlikely guests invited by Pamela were Peter Duchin and Brooke Hayward, whose marriage took place on Christmas Eve 1985—and to whom the Harrimans gave $10,000 of Union Pacific stock as a wedding gift. "You'll never guess who is coming to lunch, Brooke and Peter," Pamela told a friend, who wondered aloud whether they would speak ill of her afterward and question her motives. Recalled the friend, "She knew if she didn't have them Peter would have a legitimate beef—that she had kept him away when Ave was dying."

Brooke and Peter met Pamela in Georgetown, where she proudly showed off the PamPAC offices and introduced her staff. She drove them out to Middleburg herself, and they all had lunch with Harriman. "She was extremely cordial," recalled Duchin. "Really impressive. She really put on a show. She lectured us about politics, she asked about the children. We knew we were driving with this woman who hated us, but she kept up the patter, showed us land she had bought, showed us her hunters and introduced us to her trainer." During lunch, said Duchin, "she was taking care of him as an English nurse would. 'Eat your cookie,' she would say in her deep voice. He would drift in and out. If he wanted to move two inches, she would move him two inches." Some sort of peace was struck that day. "They all made up," said Bill Hayward.

The truce fell apart less than two years later. During an interview Pamela gave to *Women's Wear Daily* in November 1987, she had this to say about her former stepdaughter: "One of Brooke's problems is that she and Jane Fonda were brought up together, and Jane became a very successful actress, and Brooke wanted desperately to be a good actress and it didn't work out for her. She also wanted to become a very good mother and I don't think that really worked out. So I think there were a lot of frustrations within her about her own life. I just hope now, with Peter, everything works out fine." Brooke, quite understandably, was apoplectic. "I have never heard Brooke so angry," recalled Bill Hayward. "Since then she has been collecting every awful thing about Pamela that she can find. After that piece, she would call me and say, 'Now listen, I gave your phone number to X. I want you to really nail her this time.'"

Even as Harriman was deteriorating, Pamela kept up a furious pace, beginning many days with political appearances and ending with fund-raising events in Washington and around the country. By 1986, Janet Howard had finally taken over as director of Democrats for the 80's, and she was working her staff of a half dozen around the clock. From April through July, she and Pamela organized a dozen receptions and dinners at N Street in an effort to raise $1 million to help recapture the Senate. PamPAC raised $245,958 for its own coffers during that time, and the events for individual Senate candidates such as Tim Wirth of Colorado and Brock Adams of Washington were well enough attended to reach Pamela's financial target.

In April, Pamela also decided that her husband would have, in effect, a state funeral in New York as well as a memorial service at the National Cathedral in Washington. Janet Howard already had in hand a file of information she had been collecting over the years on important funerals. She prepared three "funeral notebooks" filled with invitation lists, phone numbers (divided into A, B, C, and D lists), seating plans for the services, table-seating charts for the receptions, and the makeup of the military guard. Pamela closeted herself with Clark Clifford to go over the readings for the services. Some staff members found the exercise macabre. They became even more discomfited when they had to call the offices of senators, governors, and diplomats to find their whereabouts in case Harriman died. On Capitol Hill, these inquiries were known as the "get out the dead vote calls."

That year Pamela gave a Fourth of July party at Willow Oaks. Harriman was too ill to join the festivities. Within days, Averell and Pamela flew on her Westwind from Dulles to Westchester County Airport. From there they drove to Birchgrove and the prospect of cooler weather. Harriman rebounded briefly, even mustering the strength to swim in the pool again. He came down with pneumonia toward the end of July, and Pamela summoned Kathleen and Mary, who were vacationing in Alaska, as well as her son Winston, to join her at Harriman's bedside. "Kathleen sat by his bed reading to him from the chapters of a new biography of General Ira Eaker," wrote Rudy Abramson, "recounting the Fifteenth Air Force leader's arrival at Poltava after the first shuttle bombing of Hitler's eastern strongholds in June 1944." Shortly after midnight on July 26, Harriman succumbed to kidney failure in the same house where Leland Hayward had died fifteen years earlier. Averell Harriman, said Pamela, "just decided that enough was enough."

Three days later, nine hundred mourners filled St. Thomas's Episcopal Church on Fifth Avenue in Manhattan, where Harriman's mother had been a loyal parishioner. The crowd included ambassadors, business leaders, senators, four New York mayors, three New York governors, and other luminaries from five Democratic administrations. Episcopalian Bishop Paul Moore, Jr., whom Pamela had flown in from Martha's Vineyard on her plane, conducted the service, and Pamela, barely visible behind a heavy black veil and mantilla, led the recessional with an open hymnal, lustily singing "The Battle Hymn of the Republic."

"There was this proud English beauty holding her head high, her bosom fully inflated, and trailing behind her were all these power brokers and captains of industry," recalled one prominent New Yorker. Harriman's five grandsons—three Mortimers and two Fisks—as well as Peter Duchin and Winston Churchill, carried out the coffin. Led by New York State troopers, the funeral cortège transporting sixty friends and relatives drove for an hour to Arden, where everyone gathered at the Harriman family graveyard shaded by hemlock trees. There Harriman's coffin sat beside a freshly dug grave between the headstones for his mother and Marie. Bishop Moore gave a blessing and sprinkled the coffin with sand, and the mourners departed.

The memorial service in the main nave at the Washington National Cathedral was similarly majesterial and impeccably organized. The mourners were even seated in sections—former State Department officials in one place, media figures in another. With all her elaborate planning, Pamela had not stinted in honoring her late husband with dignity and sweeping ceremony. When the final bill for the funeral came in, she had spent $171,082.

Two months later the *Washington Post* got a fascinating tip: Averell Harriman had never been buried beside his second wife Marie in the family plot because Pamela had arranged to prepare a grave for him elsewhere at Arden. Executive editor Benjamin Bradlee immediately called Katharine Graham, who had attended the funeral and the burial. "Well, where *is* he?" Graham exclaimed. "Stashed at the Frank Campbell Funeral Home in White Plains!" said Bradlee. "Oh, for God's sake, Ben, how ghastly. You don't have to publish that!" Graham said. "Of course he couldn't wait," she added.

That evening, Graham was having a party in honor of Philippine President Cory Aquino which Pamela was planning to attend. As the newspaper was about to go to press, Pamela had Richard Holbrooke, who was staying for the night with CBS correspondent Diane Sawyer, call Bradlee, who lived a few doors away in Georgetown. "You can't publish that story, Ben," said Holbrooke. "Yes I can," replied Bradlee. Pamela then called Graham, who backed up her editor, prompting Pamela to announce that she wasn't coming to the Aquino dinner. "Pamela was so furious about the burial story," said one of her friends. "She kept calling the *Washington Post* 'that paper,' and she wouldn't talk to Kay Graham for the longest time."

The article provoked guffaws from New York to Washington—and certainly cast the Governor in an undignified light. The *Post* cited several family members who "appeared startled" that Harriman had not yet been interred. William Rich was quoted as saying that "Averell Harriman had decided several years ago to be buried at Forest Lake, a mile long lake about three miles from the cemetery," but that "Pamela Harriman and other family members" had only selected a site that summer after Harriman became seriously ill.

According to Rich, the paperwork for the necessary excavation was not complete when Harriman died, so the day before the funeral "the family" decided to store the body instead of burying Harriman and exhuming him later. Since so many funeral guests planned to attend a burial, Rich explained, "the family also decided at that time to go ahead and hold the service at Arden." "We were trying to keep the religious ceremony as normal as possible," he continued. "You had to go somewhere [after the funeral]. You couldn't just leave the body in the church. I know for a fact that Mrs. Harriman wasn't saying, 'Don't tell so and so.'" Rich did acknowledge that the hole in the ground "was the complicating thing." As for Bishop Moore, he said he had buried Harriman "liturgically" if not physically. Members of the Harriman family contradicted Rich's account, saying that Pamela alone had orchestrated the burial charade.

If Harriman had selected, as Rich claimed, a Forest Lake site "several years earlier," he never told his daughters or grandchildren. Nor did he and Pamela —both meticulous planners—take any steps to carry out such a wish. According to the family, it was Pamela who made the decision—and not until the last month of Harriman's life. After Kathleen Mortimer and Mary Fisk left for their Alaska vacation in early July, Pamela called David Mortimer, the grandchild who had the closest relationship with her, and told him that his grandfather wanted another grave site. She persuaded him to help her find one without telling either his mother or aunt, both of whom would have vehemently opposed such a move. "This was what Pam had decided and David went along with it. *She* did not want to be buried in the church graveyard," said a family member. After driving around Arden together, David and Pamela chose a plot within view of the boathouse where Harriman had learned to row as a young man.

When Kathleen and Mary came home from Alaska to attend their dying father, the arrangements were "a fait accompli," said one family member. Pamela told Kathleen that her father had said specifically he did not wish to be next to Marie. Kathleen didn't believe her; she knew Pamela was determined that Harriman not be buried near the woman she had so carefully excised from his life. Still, the family assumed that Harriman would be interred and moved later. At the last minute they learned of Pamela's plan to put Harriman on ice for two months. "She was in the wrong," William Walton said later. "She wasn't going to tell the family what she had decided to do or Averell had decided to do, and she did not come off well." In the fall of 1986, after the embarrassment of the *Post* story had subsided, Harriman was finally laid to rest, his solitary grave marked by a simple stone inscribed: "PATRIOT, PUBLIC SERVANT, STATESMAN."

At sixty-six, Pamela was once again on her own, but this time there seemed little likelihood that she would launch a search for a new man. Harriman had given her everything she needed, including his prestigious name. Yet constructing a life without a man posed a challenge for Pamela. Until then, she had followed a fairly predictable pattern: She would seek out men to support her, men of power and wealth who came across as strong and vibrant. Her secret was that she knew how to find their weaknesses, and before long, the roles were reversed. She became the psychologically dominant force and the men fell into dependence. Both Hayward and Harriman succumbed quite happily to such circumstances, and the relationships endured. (The wild and wayward Randolph Churchill was the exception who proved the rule.) When she failed, as with Murrow, Agnelli, and Rothschild, she bolted after the men refused to marry her —although her cultivation of friendships with former lovers showed her ability to keep them connected by making herself useful and making them feel guilty. Now the circumstances were very different. She had stature as well as financial security, which allowed her to break the pattern. Pamela Churchill Harriman no longer needed a man in her life.

CHAPTER

Twenty-nine

O~N~ HER HUSBAND'S DEATH, Pamela, for the first time in her life, became very wealthy in her own right. Harriman's estate was valued at $65 million, and Pamela received nearly $37 million of that directly. A total of $13.2 million came in direct bequests from Harriman, including the N Street homes valued at $1.5 million, the six-bedroom Sun Valley "cottage" worth $905,000, and more than $10 million in cash. In addition, she received Mango Bay, valued at $927,660 (for whatever reason, some $300,000 less than the Harrimans paid only two years earlier), oil and gas interests worth $5.8 million, and $1.9 million in venture capital investments.

The "residuary estate"—what remained after subtracting the direct bequests (besides Pamela's, there was $6 million for philanthropy and $600,000 for the grandchildren) and the $10 million in taxes, expenses, loan repayments, and other creditors' claims—was valued at about $24 million, and Pamela was entitled to half of that outright. One of the more mysterious disbursements to Pamela was a $3.8 million "loan" that was repaid to her before any other payments were made out of the estate. Just as Averell Harriman had planned, the estate tax bill on his $65 million was a mere $714,428, of which only $526,000 went to the federal government.

What Pamela received from Harriman's estate was only part of her fortune. She owned some $78 million in valuable property that was not provided for in Harriman's will; this consisted of gifts he had made to her before his death, or homes and land they had owned jointly. Among these holdings were the Westwind jet ($2.8 million); Willow Oaks ($1 million); 414 acres of Arden real estate, including horse stables and five homes ($762,000); Harriman's Sands Point acreage, subdivided for development ($23 million); and of course Harriman's art collection, which was worth approximately $50 million when he died. As for Birchgrove, the only property Pamela had from her Hayward years, she would sell that late in 1986 for $1,250,000 to Philip Friedman, a political consultant to PamPAC. From all these holdings as well as her portion of Harriman's estate, Pamela was worth about $115 million.

Harriman's family was not entirely forgotten in the will. Besides their $100,000 bequests, each of the six grandchildren could anticipate receiving larger amounts after Pamela died. The other half of the "residuary estate," placed in a "marital trust" worth $11.6 million, to pay Pamela income during her lifetime, was to be divided after her death among the Harriman children and grandchildren. In addition, Harriman had created $6 million worth of trusts to fund the W. Averell and Pamela C. Harriman Foundation (formerly the W. Averell Harriman Foundation) at $600,000 a year for twenty-five years. In the year 2011, his great-grandchildren could divvy up the remaining principal.

But Harriman's limited provisions for his family were clouded by two potent clauses in his will that gave Pamela considerable power. First, she had the right to name the beneficiaries of the marital trust after she died, which meant that she could exclude whichever Mortimers or Fisks she chose. Second, Harriman also stipulated that she could cut off without a cent anyone who tried to challenge the will.

When the family gathered for the reading of the will, no one was surprised by its contents. "We had a pretty good suspicion beforehand," said one family member. "She got everything she could get." But after they digested the magnitude of what Pamela received compared to the relatively small sums left to them, they were deeply disappointed. Kathleen, who had been closer to her father than her sister Mary, felt especially betrayed. She had been a devoted daughter. In Harriman's last years, Kathleen had called him two or three times a week, and she had come for weekends when Pamela went away. "Stan [Mortimer] said the only time he's seen Kathy cry was after she felt let down by her father," said a Mortimer relative. "My father was furious," recalled Amanda Mortimer Burden. "He said, 'How can you not get angry? How can you not say anything?' Kath said, 'It is my business and I am not going to say anything.' "

Nor did Pamela, who missed a great opportunity to create goodwill when she offered no mementos, much less valuable artwork, to any of Harriman's family. (Only when Kathleen Mortimer asked, did Pamela hand over a book of prints that Harriman had promised to his daughter.) "It's not that she's stingy," explained a woman who knew her for decades. "It just never crossed her mind. The trustees should have said, 'Make something over to them.' " As Kathleen Mortimer considered the situation, she recounted to her children the dark time after the war when she had given her weekly *Newsweek* paycheck to the struggling Pamela Churchill. Two of her sons, David and Averell Mortimer, talked about filing suit. But Bill Rich reminded them of Pamela's ability to disinherit them. "You will be committing slow financial suicide," he told them.

One of the biggest frustrations for Harriman's daughters and grandchildren was not inheriting the house in Sun Valley. The Idaho resort developed by Harriman during the 1930s had long been an anchor for their family life. Now the cottage belonged entirely to Pamela, who set the schedule for the family's annual winter skiing and summer hiking holidays and always had first call on the house.

She also controlled Arden, the other great Harriman redoubt, since she had taken over the costs Averell had shouldered—a substantial part of the maintenance and real estate taxes as well as salaries and pension payments for family retainers. Those expenses totaled nearly $1 million a year, of which Harriman had assumed 35 percent. The remaining 65 percent was divided among various Mortimers and Fisks, as well as Ned Northrup, a grandson of Roland Harriman.

Before he died, Averell Harriman assured his daughter Kathleen that Pamela had agreed to continue funding Arden for her lifetime. Pamela's annual share came to more than $300,000, compared to $75,000 apiece for Mary Fisk and Kathleen Mortimer. Both daughters owned their small cottages at Arden, along with more than three hundred acres apiece. But they were acutely aware of their dependence on Pamela's continuing subsidy of, among other things, the stables for their horses, which stood on her 414 acres.

Pamela likewise continued Harriman's practice of dispensing $10,000 worth of Union Pacific stock each year to his daughters, grandchildren, and great-grandchildren. By the late 1980s there were twenty-four of them in all, which meant an annual outlay of $240,000. "In accordance with Averell's wish," Pamela would write in her letter to the heirs each year, "use this as capital not income." Harriman had been free with his Union Pacific stock for one reason: He had bought it for such a low price that to liquidate his holdings would have triggered a large capital gains tax. He much preferred to give it away in tax-free increments. If the recipients wished to sell the stock, *they* would have to pay roughly a third of the proceeds in taxes.

One might reasonably conclude that Pamela's yearly payment of more than $500,000 to benefit Harriman's heirs was a sufficiently magnanimous gesture. Yet she got little credit for doing it, primarily because she was simply maintaining a family entitlement. "The family view, like all views of Pamela, varied from one individual to another," said one source close to the Mortimers and Fisks. "Some felt it was generous. Others felt that she was doing it because Ave insisted on it, that it was less an act of generosity than an act of obedience to his wishes."

Pamela didn't help matters by never quite letting the Harriman heirs forget her dominant position. "I get the feeling," Amanda Mortimer Burden said at one point, "that Pam somehow makes them aware that she is picking up the tab." Nevertheless, they buried their resentment, because it was the proper thing to do, because they were grateful that she had taken good care of Harriman in his final years, and because they had no other choice.

They had to be nice to her so they could benefit from the marital trust. They needed her help with Arden and her access to Sun Valley because both places allowed the Harriman clan to appear prosperous way beyond their bank accounts. As their share of the great fortune diminished, their idyllic retreats let them maintain their social position and cling to the notion of privilege and wealth, in short, to act as Harrimans.

Despite Kathleen's bitter feelings about her father's will, she and Pamela maintained an amicable relationship, finding common ground in their love of riding and their shared memories of Ave. They talked on the telephone every week or so, and Pamela invited Kathleen—and her sister Mary as well—to stay with her in Barbados. When Kathleen wanted an "eyelift," she chose a plastic surgeon, Sherrell Aston, recommended by Pamela.

Kathleen was a loyal donor to Pamela's Democrats for the 80's, giving

$22,500 over ten years. Despite their more distant relationship, Mary Fisk donated $12,000 during the same period. Pamela reciprocated as head of the Averell and Pamela Harriman Foundation, earmarking annual gifts to Harriman's daughters' special charities, including the New York City School Volunteer Program, which received $20,000 a year. Still, Kathleen could be sarcastic about Pamela, grumbling about the high opinion she had of herself and making remarks such as, "With Pam you never can tell if she is saying what she means." For her part, Pamela complained to friends that Kathleen's interests were "very limited."

Among the grandchildren, Pamela was never very involved with either Jay Mortimer or Robert Fisk, and she adopted her late husband's opinion of the sharp-tongued Averell Fisk as a spoiled spendthrift living the high life in Palm Beach. The only grandchild to openly disparage her, Averell Fisk kept a wary distance. Nor did Pamela have much to do with Kitty and Charles Ames, although they once came to stay in Barbados. It was a pleasant enough visit, but Pamela and her friends took a dim view of Charles Ames. Though he was bright and had the right pedigree, Ames came off as a politically conservative, dour, and somewhat old-fashioned character who was evidently immune to Pamela's allure. "He was not charming, and he was not fun to be in the room with," said one of her friends who met him in Barbados.

David and Averell Mortimer, the two heirs who thought most seriously of challenging the will, also made the biggest effort to get along with their powerful step-grandmother. Both had the same sort of chiseled good looks that could decorate any stylish dinner table. Averell Mortimer's wife Gigi was blond and very pretty—"too good-looking," concluded a friend who sensed that Pamela felt slightly threatened. Pamela had a natural affinity for David, partly because of his public affairs work at Columbia University, but also because of his social circle. His wife, a book editor named Shelley Wanger, was attractive and well connected, the daughter of the film producer Walter Wanger and the actress Joan Bennett.

David Mortimer was drawn to Pamela and her glittering world, although he had mixed feelings about her—especially after his unfortunate role in the Harriman burial fiasco. When Pamela traveled to China in 1987, she invited David to join her group, all expenses paid, including business-class airfare. David and Shelley regularly visited Mango Bay during the winter, but on their return they complained quietly that they found Pamela tedious. Nevertheless, they dutifully included her in family gatherings such as christenings and holiday parties.

While the Harriman family depended on Pamela's continued beneficence, the financial picture for young Winston and his children was brightening. "Clearly," noted Women's Wear Daily in November 1987, "Winston . . . seems to have come into some money." During the 1980s, he took the $1 million trust set up by Harriman—which was intended to provide a cushion of income—and used the proceeds to buy a ski lodge in Klosters, Switzerland, as well as an apartment in Portugal. Both purchases, he explained, were "so the whole family could enjoy it [the trust fund money]."

After Harriman's death, Winston sold the farmhouse he had owned since he married Minnie and bought a grand country house in Kent near the Churchill home at Chartwell. The financing, he said, came from the foreign rights to his grandfather's *History of the English Speaking Peoples*. Pamela, according to Winston, "generously gave us decoration of the three main rooms" in the new house. Asked how he felt about receiving so much Harriman largesse, Winston denied that he got "a lot of Harriman money," although he acknowledged, "I didn't ask her where the money came from."

Pamela also bought apartments in the Pimlico area of London for three of her four grandchildren—Randolph, Jennie, and Marina—and gave each of them a Volkswagen on their seventeenth birthday. She gave Winston, Minnie, and the four grandchildren $10,000 apiece each year tax-free, and she paid school and college tuition for all of them. When Randolph was engaged to be married, Pamela found a collection of silver Churchill plates that she bought at auction as a wedding gift. But when she called Winston to tell him, he confessed that it was he who had sold the plates to help pay for the wedding. Pamela was extremely annoyed, in the words of a friend, "that she got suckered into buying them." She ended up keeping half of the collection for herself and giving Randolph the other half. It was a petty episode, but it symbolized the frequent frustration Pamela experienced with her only son.

With his name and his connections, "young" Winston—as he was unfortunately known even in middle age—had seemed destined for great things. His goal, he once said, was nothing less than Prime Minister. "His single greatest asset," observed the *Guardian* three years after his election to Parliament in 1970, was "the natural confidence of his expectations." During his first few years in Parliament he kept a low profile, and in November 1976 Margaret Thatcher, then leader of the Conservative Party, tapped him as one of her deputies to speak on matters of national defense in the Commons.

"I was over the moon," Winston said. "Defense was breakfast, lunch, and dinner for me." Although he wasn't a member of Thatcher's shadow cabinet, his position on the "front bench" of the opposition party in Parliament gave him a chance to move up the ranks. He lashed out against Soviet communism and crusaded for an array of right-wing causes in foreign policy—positions that seemed to suit his party leader.

But in November 1978 he rebelled against Thatcher by opposing economic sanctions on Ian Smith's minority white government in the former British colony of Rhodesia. The southern African nation was embroiled in civil war, and sanctions had been enforced by both the Tory and Labour parties to pressure Smith into relinquishing power to an independent, democratically elected government. Young Winston's defiance allied him with the obstructionist Rhodesia Lobby, and he came across as a racist. Thatcher fired him from his position on the front bench—a move he referred to as being "cast into the outer darkness." He seemed to share his mother's fondness for publicity even when it was bad as he cheerfully posed for news photographs in front of his grandfather's statue.

When Thatcher was elected Prime Minister in May 1979, Winston still expected her to appoint him to Defense Secretary or some other top position in her government. Thatcher was a great admirer of his grandfather and might have welcomed the illustrious name to her cabinet despite his Rhodesia transgression. Her unwillingness to do so proved prescient less than a year later when Winston was forced to admit publicly that during his two years as Tory defense spokesman he had an extramarital affair with Soroya Khashoggi, the former wife of international arms dealer Adnan Khashoggi. In his position Winston had not been privy to state secrets, but the affair made embarrassing headlines and prompted his Labour opponents to demand inquiries into possible security breaches. In the end, wrote the *Daily Express,* "It was not, after all, anybody really powerful, only young Winston making himself look a bit of a chump."

The scandal closed the door on Winston's prospects for high office, and he settled into a middling career as a Tory "backbencher," a member of the Conservative Party rank and file in Parliament. He was always on the go, his schedule crammed with appointments—like his mother, he was blessed with a high level of energy—yet his activity seemed to lack purpose. The fault was not so much his intelligence, which was certainly adequate, as his temperament. He was afflicted by poor judgment; his political decisions, such as the maneuver on Rhodesia, were rash and insensitive. Not only was he unwilling to do sufficient background preparation, he was naturally impulsive. He lacked his mother's famous focus, as well as her careful attention to detail.

In Parliament, as at school, he remained a loner with few political allies, much less friends. He had no instinct for compromise, staking out rigid positions and refusing to back down even when he was wrong. In true Churchillian style, he loved to talk and argue with a certain degree of swagger, yet he lacked the flair of his father and grandfather; his pronouncements, delivered in a booming voice, could be comically grandiose. "He is a bit of a robot figure," said Peregrine Worsthorne, a columnist for the conservative *Sunday Telegraph.* Try as he might to exploit his famous name, Winston was destined to come up short compared to his heroic grandfather. It was, the *Sunday Telegraph* once noted, a "melancholy destiny."

Well into his fifth decade, Winston remained slender, and although balding he kept the blond good looks that resembled his mother more than his father, especially in the set of his mouth, the anticipatory smile, and the locking gaze of his deep blue eyes. His looks, Alastair Forbes once wrote, "have always struck me as curiously two dimensional, as if he were a comic strip hero." He took pride in his wardrobe, described in the British press as "swanky," and he was known for such flamboyant touches as wearing a gold bracelet on one wrist.

Like Pamela, Winston was preoccupied with money, and when it ran short he supplemented his parliamentary salary—less than $50,000 a year—by lecturing in the United States, where he readily found audiences willing to pay a hefty fee—usually $10,000 per lecture, plus expenses—to hear tales of the Churchills. "When the bank manager puts the squeeze on and funds look tight," he once boasted, "I go on a lecture tour and earn more in ten days than I do annually as an MP."

Pamela had shared her son's hopes that he might someday be Prime Minister. When he faltered, she publicly supported him. Recalling his ill-conceived stand on Rhodesia, she said, "I like that. He believes what he believes." Privately, however, she expressed disappointment that he had not made more of himself. Winston talked to his mother once a week on the telephone and saw her two to four times a year in the United States and England. He turned up in Washington during lecture tours and his annual visits with the Parliamentary Defense Committee, and she periodically invited him to bring Minnie and the children to one of her vacation homes. In Middleburg, Pamela and Winston would ride together, and he enticed her at age seventy-one to start skiing again in Sun Valley. They took his children pony-trekking in the Sawtooth range of the Rocky Mountains, and she often invited the family to Barbados during Christmas vacation.

Yet Pamela's relationship with Winston ran hot and cold, not only because of political differences but temperamental clashes. Despite expressions of mutual devotion, their dealings had an edge that originated in Winston's unorthodox childhood of material indulgence and emotional distance. In public comments, Winston frequently disparaged his mother's political instincts, calling her a "chameleon." "Had she married Ronald Reagan," he observed, "she would have been an arch-Republican."

Pamela's financial hold over Winston caused considerable unease. "Winston it seemed to me was always taking with one hand and complaining with the other," said Cheray Duchin Hodges (who had married banker Luther Hodges Jr. after her divorce from Peter Duchin). Whenever Pamela traveled abroad, Winston and his family had to hop to, helping her arrange her social calendar or flying to meet her for lunch in Paris. During vacations, she organized every activity down to the minute, but according to her interests and not theirs. As a consequence her grandchildren were often intimidated by her.

There was particular tension between Pamela and Minnie—in virtually every respect her mother-in-law's opposite. A handsome, large-boned woman, not the least bit glamorous, Minnie was a solid, almost maternal presence in Winston's life. After the Soroya Khashoggi incident, Minnie stood by Winston, never faulting him. Publicly at least, her heart never missed a beat. Yet for all her charm and sweetness, she seemed to displease Pamela. "Minnie had a difficult time because Pam was cool to her," said a woman who knew Pamela for many years.

The main issue between mother and son was the same one that marred Pamela's relations with the Harriman children and the Hayward children before them: Her need to be in charge. "Winston is resentful because she is so powerful and he is not," said New York socialite Jan Cushing Amory. Yet many of his actions seemed designed to get her attention, to show that he was stronger, more gutsy, than he appeared to be. His tone in discussing her was matter-of-fact, dutiful, yet not entirely careful. Asked once to characterize their relationship after his childhood, he said simply, "Since I have been an adult we have been divided by the Atlantic Ocean."

CHAPTER
Thirty

PAMELA WAS BLESSED with good health and took care of herself. Aside from occasional episodes of diverticulitis, her only physical complaint in late 1986 was the weight she had put on during Harriman's final illness. With typical determination, she embarked on a self-improvement program, following a strict diet consisting largely of fruits and vegetables. For snacks during her travels, her chef would prepare salads or tea sandwiches with the crusts removed. By early 1987 friends began to notice how much she had slimmed down.

Tended by Kenneth in New York, the ever faithful Alexandre in Paris, and Eivind, who brought his equipment in suitcases to her home, Pamela's hair had been transformed from auburn to a softly flattering champagne blond. Although personal trainers were not her style, for a short time she donned a sweatsuit to work out on a stationary bicycle on the third floor of her Georgetown home. For exercise she preferred swimming, taking long walks, and riding.

Most weekends in the fall and winter she rode with the Middleburg Hunt on Prospect, an English mare bred near Minterne. Beautifully turned out, she would step from her car while a groomsman readied her mount. She was usually accompanied by Jimmy Hatcher, an expert trainer who kept her horses in perfect shape. The terrain around Middleburg was tough, with hills, ravines, streams, and difficult fences, but Pamela was undaunted, even in her late sixties.

"I like to hunt up front," she once said, and those who rode with her attested to her boldness. One avid hunter named William Abel-Smith liked to recount the time that he was reluctantly approaching a large fence when suddenly from behind him a small horse with a small woman came roaring past him and over the jump. It was Pamela, and she shamed him into taking the jump as well.

Away from the hunting field, Pamela devoted time and considerable funds to raising top show jumpers, and she hired one of the best riders in the business, Katie Monahan Prudent, to compete on her behalf. Many mornings Pamela herself would be out in the ring by seven-thirty, taking the jumps with style and precision. "That's for me," recalled a man who watched her workout during one weekend visit. "That is why she looks good. She is physical, athletic, and she takes care of herself."

But by sixty-seven, Pamela was dissatisfied with the heavily lined and somewhat jowly face that she saw in the mirror. So early in 1988 she went to New

York City for a face-lift. Her doctor, Sherrell Aston, was one of the country's foremost plastic surgeons—"a miracle worker . . . who can erase years," in the words of *Town & Country* magazine. He taught at New York University School of Medicine and contributed to the principal "aesthetic plastic surgery" text-book.

Admired as much for his discretion as his surgical skill, Aston was a sooth-ing, sympathetic presence who tactfully referred to a patient's need to "freshen up." "Some consider it to be inconsistent to wear a designer dress, have the latest hairstyle and color, the latest makeup and, at the same time, walk around with droopy eyes and a sagging neck," he once said. Small, handsome, and dapper, with the courtly manner of a Virginia gentleman, Aston considered himself an artist and each face his canvas.

Pamela checked into Manhattan Eye, Ear and Throat Hospital for the procedure: major surgery of two to three hours. While Aston declined to discuss Pamela, other knowledgeable sources said that she had a face-lift as well as an eye-lift. First she was sedated with a combination of tranquilizers and analgesics, then her hair was tied in a topknot and cut away along the areas of planned incision, and her face and scalp marked with a purple "skin skribe" indicating where Aston would cut.

The classic Aston operation involved large incisions on each side of the face, beginning behind the hairline along the temple, down along the front of the tragus (the small knob of cartilage at the front of the ear), underneath the earlobe, and back into the scalp. There were incisions as well under the chin, and above and below the eyes. Using scalpels and scissors, he would lift up the skin down into the neck and across the cheekbone to the edges of the mouth and nose. Aston would then perform a "deep tissue dissection," cutting into and tightening the facial muscles in the cheeks and neck. In describing the procedure to patients, he would ask: "Would you put a clean fresh sheet over a lumpy and worn mattress and cover? Neither should you put your skin over muscles that are lumpy."

After reconstructing the musculature, Aston would remove the subcutane-ous fat around the eyes and below the jawline, cut off the excess skin, pull and "redrape" the facial skin back and upward, and stitch the incisions closed. The operation completed, Aston would place a surgical stockinette on his patient's head and wrap gauze bandages from her forehead to beneath her chin.

Pamela spent the night in the hospital, tended by a private nurse who applied constant ice compresses to reduce swelling, before moving to the apart-ment of her friend Kitty Carlisle Hart. Several days later, Pamela flew on her Westwind to Virginia for a recuperation of two weeks at Willow Oaks. Between the stitches and the inevitable swelling and bruising, her face looked monstrous at first. She stayed in bed, keeping her head elevated at all times, sleeping propped up by several pillows. Face-lifts are not usually characterized by postop-erative pain. Instead, there is often a disconcerting numbness, and a sensation, according to another Aston patient, of "having a rubber band around your face. Your scalp feels tight and your jaw feels tight." (Not long after Pamela's lift,

Kitty Hart had one; when she complained to her nurse that the bandage was too tight, the nurse said, "That's not the bandage, it's your skin.")

Pamela's new face was a masterpiece, the talk of society women in Manhattan and Washington. Gone were the crow's-feet, the puffiness under her eyes, and the drooping eyelids. Her jaw looked newly sculpted, her deep blue eyes wider and brighter, and her face seemed more angular, with greater contour around her cheekbones but without any telltale tightness. Although she still had fine wrinkles, evident mainly in the light, the effect, remarked Irene Selznick, was "as though time and magic and not the knife did it all."

The result was a tribute to Aston's surgical philosophy as well as his talent. He was, according to one of his patients, "a naturalist. He doesn't believe in doing too much. He doesn't make you look like your skin has been pulled back with a pigtail." Pamela's genetic contribution made a difference as well. She had good bone structure, and enough flesh in her round face to permit a softer look. In the end, as designer Karl Lagerfeld once said, "Looking great, at a certain moment, is also a question of budget." For Pamela's transformation, according to a woman familiar with the operation, the cost was more than $20,000.

Though Pamela declined publicly to acknowledge having had the face-lift, she proudly showed off her new look to certain friends and did not hesitate to solicit their approval. Such candor was unusual in her relationships with women, which were not known for either intimacy or intensity. She always had many woman acquaintances but few woman friendships. When she was a girl, schoolmates complained of her self-centered and manipulative ways. In her teens, fellow debutantes mocked her plumpness and her pushiness. Later on, her peers resented her brazen reinvention as a femme fatale. With the exception of her mentor Lady Baillie, Pamela only paid serious attention to men. When she began pursuing prominent husbands, women were her harshest critics. Pamela reacted to their hostility with a self-protective aloofness.

Women meeting her for the first time were amazed by her cool manner. When she entered a room, Pamela gravitated instinctively toward the men—to the point of rudeness. "She sails in, pushes between you and the man you are talking to, and suddenly you are looking at her back," protested one prominent Washington woman. The wives of Pamela's male friends such as Sandy Berger, media adviser Robert Squier, and former CIA director Richard Helms felt doubly rebuffed because Pamela tended to view them as appendages of great men, conveniently forgetting that she herself occupied that position for most of her life.

In Washington, Pamela would simply invite the powerful husbands alone to dinner on the assumption that their wives would have nothing to offer. When Richard and Cynthia Helms came to stay with her in Barbados, she planned a daily walk with him, leaving Cynthia behind. "It's not so much that she looks down on women," explained one wife who was ignored. "It is more that she sees women as an impediment to men." Even when Pamela entertained a couple, she tended to converse only with the husband, allowing the wife to listen politely, a virtually invisible presence. "Why should I go?" Prudence Squier complained to a friend about an invitation to Pamela's. "She doesn't have anything to do with me."(Prudence Squier eventually won Pamela's favor by writing a lengthy newspaper article praising the gardens at Willow Oaks.)

Lacking a natural rapport with other women, Pamela seemed to assign her friends specific roles, often based on their usefulness, as she had with Kathleen Harriman and Kick Kennedy in London, and with socially beneficial women in Paris and New York. "Pam has a way with her," said Lauren Bacall. "If she wants to be your friend, she is charming with you. It all has to do with whether it suits her." Moreover, added Bacall, "She doesn't want anyone hanging on. She cares about doers."

If a woman was powerful enough, or had something interesting to offer, she attracted Pamela's attention. When Diane Sawyer was dating Richard Holbrooke, she grew close to Pamela and later sealed the friendship with an admiring two-part interview on the CBS Morning News. Pamela befriended Democratic Party activist Madeleine Albright, later Ambassador to the United Nations, and Judith Kipper, a foreign policy specialist; both had expertise and connections that were helpful to her.

One of Pamela's oddest friendships was with Heather Foley, wife of the Speaker of the House. Heather was blunt-spoken and aggressively unstylish, wearing sandals on bare feet to social engagements and pulling her long, lank hair into a ponytail. But as the unpaid major domo of her husband's office, she wielded considerable power behind the scenes and granted favors to Pamela such as a choice seat at the State of the Union address. In return, Pamela invited the Foleys to stay in Barbados each year and enjoyed talking to Tom Foley, an unabashed Anglophile.

In Washington, Pamela's small circle included women of social as well as professional standing. Diana Walker was a *Time* magazine photographer who took flattering pictures of Pamela and whose well-heeled husband Mallory served as Pamela's occasional escort. The Walkers owned a home in Sun Valley, where Diana kept Pamela company on long mountain hikes. Diana was socially prominent and as non-judgmental as she was devoted. Pamela also was friendly with Wren Wirth, wife of former Colorado Senator Tim Wirth; Patsy Preston, the socialite wife of Lewis Preston, the former head of Morgan Guaranty who became chairman of the World Bank; and Teresa Heinz, the wife of Pennsylvania Senator John Heinz, another Sun Valley companion. These women resembled ladies in waiting, although Teresa Heinz assumed equal footing when she inherited $600 million from her husband after he died in a plane crash in 1991.

Pamela chose her friends with the same care as she had picked her lovers, and she dominated these relationships. She expected complete loyalty; there was little of the give and take that marks friendship among equals. At the same time, she was diligent about staying in touch, and fiercely protective of her circle. Once when Manhattan blueblood Minot Amory derided Diane Sawyer at Pamela's luncheon table, she snapped, "Young man, you are talking about one of my best friends. Keep silent or leave the table."

The most common observation among women who knew Pamela well was that she was not warm or confiding. Perhaps to reinforce her mystique—and to protect her secrets—she kept much of her life private. "When I see Pam, we never talk about personal things, only about politics," said a New York friend. "The interesting thing about Pam and women friends is that she reveals one side to one kind of woman and another to another kind of woman. Each person has a small scoop of her." The talk tended to be about her interests and experiences—and to a limited degree, her problems. Even though she kept the attention on herself, Pamela revealed little. She rarely discussed her past, except in an impersonal, anecdotal way, spinning out stories drawn from her mythology.

Pamela did not show much interest in the lives of her friends. If she asked personal questions, they were perfunctory. One longtime Washington friend said that Pamela didn't seem to know how many children she had. "It is not easy to sit down and chat with her," recalled another woman who had known her for years. "She asks a few questions—tell me this, tell me that—and that is it. She is always thinking of something else. She is caught up in her world. She is not cozy, but she looks after people well. It seems like a contradiction."

The reward for befriending Pamela was impressive generosity: flights on her private jet, thoughtful gifts and notes, and invitations to Barbados, Middleburg, and Sun Valley. "She has great follow-through," said Ann Jordan, a Washington friend. "She keeps you informed. If she knows you are interested, she sends you clippings. If you talk about something, she remembers." From her days in war-torn London and as the "universal aunt" who ferried English dowagers around Paris in her Bentley, Pamela relished doing favors for certain people, and letting them know that nothing was too much trouble.

Such gestures sometimes seemed less a matter of closeness than the brisk efficiency of a top concierge who took professional pride in a job well done. In this she resembled her early consigliare, Max Beaverbrook, who derived power and self-satisfaction by pulling strings for his friends or helping them out financially. "If you asked Pam to contribute to something or grease the way for you, almost by return mail you would get an affirmative answer, but you would know you would be asked to do something in return," said Barbara Howar. "She saved favors, so you thought twice about asking." Pamela's houseguests felt their obligation most keenly. "You do what she wants to do at her house," said one. "In Idaho, you have to go for long walks. You can't go fishing because she doesn't fish. She doesn't want you to go off on your own and see other friends if they are not hers. It is a great pity because she doesn't see this. It is very confining. She is very self-centered in that way."

Pamela's most enduring friendships—with Kitty Carlisle Hart and Leonora Hornblow—dated from her Hayward days. The two women were as friendly with each other as they were with Pamela. They both had a knack for accentuating the positive, and they were steadfast supporters of Pamela's through difficult times. "Leonora and Kitty are not looking for trouble," said novelist Nancy Holmes. "Leonora understands social clout and power. Neither makes waves. They are from a certain enclave, they don't break the rules and are very safe friends." As Kitty Hart herself once observed about her contemporaries, "We were all very disciplined. . . . We never said anything harsh that could be repeated. We were very careful."

Hornblow was born Leonora Schinasi—and nicknamed "Bubbles" almost immediately. She was the daughter of a Turkish tobacco mogul whose wife Ruby, a noted hostess in the thirties, threw parties at a large brick house on Riverside Drive in Manhattan. Leonora worked as a journalist and wrote two novels in the fifties, *Memory and Desire* and *The Love Seekers*. Sophisticated and witty, she was friendly with the great Hollywood and Broadway stars of her generation. Leonora's second husband, the film and Broadway producer Arthur Hornblow, Jr., was twenty-seven years her senior and previously married to the actress Myrna Loy. Every bit as smooth as his close friend Leland Hayward, Hornblow was a lawyer with an Ivy League degree who spoke fluent French and learned about Broadway from his father, a well-known theater critic.

Leonora and Arthur Hornblow were the first friends to whom Leland Hayward confided his infidelity with Pamela, and when the scandal broke, Leonora faced the "firing squad" of New York society to defend Hayward's new wife. Leonora and Pamela had good rapport from the start; as Harry Kurnitz once remarked, "The two man-pleasers got along." They remained close throughout Pamela's marriage to Hayward, even as Leonora stayed on good terms with his former wife Slim. Although Pamela's move to Washington and involvement in politics drew her out of Leonora's realm, they stayed in touch. Pamela would call when she came to New York and invite Leonora—a widow since Arthur died in 1976—for visits from time to time. On holidays and birthdays, Pamela would phone with a fond greeting. Whenever Pamela's behavior caused unfavorable comment, Leonora would quickly come to her defense.

By all accounts, Kitty Carlisle Hart was Pamela's "best" friend, and certainly her friend of longest standing. They had met in 1951 at the castle of Fulke Warwick, who had boasted about sharing Pamela's bed before she married Randolph Churchill. Pamela was thirty-one, and Kitty around ten years older, already a grande dame of Broadway. "She was fascinated by Moss and me and our lives and the theater," recalled Kitty. "She was so pretty, and I like pretty people."

The tone of their subsequent friendship sustained that simple note. "I have no idea if she is a complicated person," said Kitty. "No clue, never thought about it. I never analyzed her character. She has always charmed me. I love her, and I accept what meets the eye. That is the way I am. I tend to accept people as I find them." Moss Hart once called his wife "the most incurious woman I know."

Kitty Hart was herself an exquisite self-creation. She transformed herself from Catherine Conn by selecting the name "Carlisle" out of the Manhattan phone directory. She grew up in New Orleans under the strict tutelage of an overbearing and volatile mother, who gave her only child music lessons and drilled her in high society manners. When Kitty was ten her father died, and Hortense Conn whisked her daughter off to Europe, where they always stayed in "the worst room in the best hotel." Kitty went to finishing school in Switzerland and France, but Hortense was unsuccessful in her efforts to marry her daughter to a rich aristocrat. Instead, she launched Kitty on a stage career in London and New York that never took off. After a short and unproductive stint in Hollywood, Kitty returned to New York. In 1946 she met and married Moss Hart, the gifted playwright *(You Can't Take It With You, The Man Who Came to Dinner)* and director, known as "the prince of Broadway."

Kitty had found the role that suited her best: the fashionable wife of a theatrical legend. Hart, who used to rehearse lines in front of the bathroom mirror before dinner parties, orchestrated their life, which Kitty compared to a "continuous drawing room comedy. . . . Moss directed my clothes the way he directed a play." Although they had two children, Hart was homosexual, and he suffered from manic depression. But these aspects of her life she chose to put out of her mind.

"I believe in denial," said Kitty. "Denial is a marvelous thing"—a sentiment shared by her best friend. Both Kitty and Pamela were taught early to conceal emotion from the world, to be cheerful and charming whatever the circumstances. When Moss Hart died of a stroke in 1961, Kitty continued her career as a panelist on the popular television quiz show *To Tell the Truth,* where she essentially played herself, smiling like a minx and engaging in repartee with the show's mystery guests. In the following years she became chairman of the New York State Council of the Arts, until January 1996, when she was replaced by Republican Governor George Pataki.

Behind her feathery facade, Kitty Hart was every bit as sturdy as Pamela Harriman. Shaped by domineering mothers, Kitty and Pamela were both resilient and energetic, attentive to appearances, resolutely youthful, and wary of introspection. "We weren't encouraged to sit around and probe our soul," said Kitty. "We were encouraged to get on with it." Never did they discuss what they had in common—not even their strong mothers—and hardly ever what Kitty called Pamela's "fellas."

What Kitty cherished most about Pamela was that "she puts herself out for you if she loves you"—almost as if such effort was a rarity in a solid friendship. "Kitty is thrilled to have Pam for a friend," said Lauren Bacall. "Pam includes her in a lot of her life." Whenever Pamela came to New York, she would stay with Kitty, who always had a bedroom ready. Pamela in turn "really admires Kitty for her inner serenity, her grace and beauty," observed another friend of Pamela's. And as women in the limelight, each friend also derived considerable satisfaction from the prestige of the other.

If Pamela missed having a man in her life, she didn't let on to her women friends. "She is not really secure enough to confess that she is lonely," said one. "She may hint at it, but she doesn't really allow that because she doesn't want to admit vulnerability. She considers it a failing to be alone." For the first year or so after Harriman's death, she contented herself with various escorts that she might "borrow" from their wives—Mallory Walker, Tom Foley, and Clark Clifford, among others. She was also seen with single men-about-town like Thomas Quinn, a wealthy contributor to the Democratic Party with social connections in Newport. When asked in June 1988 by a magazine reporter if she would marry again, Pamela said, "No, absolutely not. I've had a wonderful life and I've been married to wonderful people, and I couldn't top it. Also I realize how tremendously lucky I am. I can afford to do what I want."

Her answer came at a time when everyone was buzzing about her involvement with John Carter Brown, director of the National Gallery of Art. Their relationship had begun shortly after he and his second wife, Pamela, had separated in August 1987. At fifty-four, Carter Brown was fourteen years younger than Pamela Harriman. He was a tall man, with an austere, almost gaunt face, straight nose and thin, prominent cheekbones, pale blue eyes shaded by sparse sandy lashes, and wiry brown hair carefully brushed back off his forehead.

Unlike Agnelli, Rothschild, Hayward, and Harriman, Brown seemed to operate at the margins of Pamela's life, and the extent of their physical involvement caused considerable speculation. In any event, Brown was a suitable companion, as close to Pamela's aristocratic background as any American—even more so than Averell Harriman, whose family were parvenus by comparison. The Browns arrived in New England in 1638 and built a substantial fortune in a variety of businesses: shipping, manufacturing, land development, banking, and railroads. When Carter Brown's father, John Nicholas Brown, graduated from Harvard in the early 1920s, he was worth $30 million. Carter Brown, along with his older brother Nicholas and younger sister Angela, grew up in an "extraordinary household," Carter recalled, "where we had chamber music and books and old master paintings."

With a master's degree in art history and an impressive fluency in Greek and Latin, John Nicholas Brown was the consummate aesthete. His wife Anne, the daughter of an Episcopalian priest, was intimidating and opinionated, though no less committed to culture. The Browns dined in formal dress each evening and lived in three luxurious homes—an eighteenth-century Georgian mansion in Providence, where the family had founded Brown University; a sleek modern summer home on Fisher's Island; and a "cottage" in Newport that resembled a French château. There were servants and governesses who taught the children French, and numerous trips abroad to explore Greek ruins and make the rounds of museums.

As the middle child, Carter Brown felt he was "slightly ignored." According to longtime family friends, he had a difficult relationship with his strong mother, who sharply criticized him. Carter "always wanted to demonstrate to her he was very capable," according to one friend. Carter was intellectually precocious, by far the brightest of the three children, and he was fascinated by visual style. When Carter Brown was nine, his parents packed him off to boarding school in Arizona. Several years later he moved on to the great WASP training ground Groton, where he graduated first in his class at age sixteen. Before entering Harvard, he spent a year at Stowe School in England, the beginning of a lifelong Anglophilia.

Carter graduated summa cum laude and phi beta kappa from Harvard, majoring in history and literature. He had already started, he said, on his "life plan" to be director of the National Gallery. He earned an MBA from Harvard Business School—to get "a sense of the practicalities of the world" and "an ability to speak the language of business"—skills that could benefit his goal as an arts administrator. During a trip to Europe, he spent several weeks in Italy with the famous connoisseur Bernard Berenson, studying the collections of the great museums, and he audited museum training courses in Germany, Holland, and France. Back home he received a master's degree in fine arts from New York University and was hired in 1961 to be the assistant to the director of the National Gallery, John Walker, an old family friend from Fisher's Island.

"Ever since he was a young genius," noted *The New Yorker's* Brendan Gill, Carter Brown "flawlessly proceeded upward." As Walker's handpicked successor, Brown took over as director of the gallery in 1969 at age thirty-four. His background and intelligence were ideally suited to the role of a museum administrator. He successfully competed against other museums with what *New Yorker* writer Calvin Tomkins called "aggressive aplomb," cultivating wealthy donors as well as high-ranking diplomats. "Carter has snowed everybody," said S. Dillon Ripley, the former secretary of the Smithsonian Institution. Brown transformed the National Gallery from a provincial collection dependent largely on its wealthy benefactors, Paul Mellon and his sister Ailsa Mellon Bruce, to an internationally recognized museum with a $50 million budget subsidized by the federal government. With its stylish exhibitions and its black-tie opening night parties, the gallery became synonymous with the elegant persona of its chief impresario.

In fact, Carter Brown had virtually no identity outside the National Gallery. When he was thirty-six he married Constance Mellon Byers, the adopted daughter of Richard King Mellon, a cousin of Paul Mellon. Connie "was quite mad but rather splendid," said Alan Pryce-Jones, the brother-in-law of Elie de Rothschild, who got to know the Browns when he moved to Newport. Connie had evident misgivings about Carter from the outset when she canceled their original wedding date and then hastily—and under some pressure from Carter's mother—married him with only immediate family present. Connie had grown up in a world of luxury, and she brought a fortune to her marriage. Although Carter Brown's family had been very wealthy, his father, according to Nicholas Brown, "was embezzled twice and died a relatively poor man." ("Relatively" is the operative word; the inheritance each of his children received could be measured in seven figures.) Still, Connie was worth substantially more than Carter, which was but one damaging factor in a marriage that quickly went bad.

Connie was deeply insecure and had serious physical problems, including premature osteoporosis. "She kept breaking bones. She was in a lot of pain," explained Nicholas Brown. "You start to do things to dull the pain. She started with drink, and drugs eventually got her." Connie Brown complained to her friends that her husband was remote and manipulative. "He would take yachts in Greece and invite everyone and have it all his way while she paid the bills," said a friend of the couple. "She said he spent her money and didn't care about her. She was very bitter. She felt taken advantage of. She told me this. She felt he married her because of the Mellon connection." Once, when Brown gave the captain a meager tip after a cruise, Connie announced, "I really don't mind Carter being cheap, but I can't stand his being cheap with my money."

Bound up in his work, Brown had neither time nor patience for Connie's alcoholism and drug dependency, and he resented her high-handed ways. According to his brother, "Carter felt ill-used by Connie and her family. She was very very headstrong. She was a Mellon, and her whole attitude was, 'Aren't you lucky to be married to me?' " With that much mutual resentment, Carter and Connie divorced in 1973 after only two years of marriage. Connie was so furious when they separated that she had all his belongings dumped in front of the employee's entrance at the National Gallery. "It was her way of helping with the move," Carter Brown recalled. "It was quite amusing to walk past and see all my clothes there." Several years later Connie was diagnosed with cancer, and she died in 1983, embittered about her former husband to the end.

In 1976 when Carter Brown was forty-one, he married another product of his monied world: Pamela Braga Drexel, a pretty twenty-eight-year-old brunette whose first husband, Nicholas Drexel, was a socially prominent investment banker. Carter's parents had been friends with the Bragas, and he and Pam had been acquainted for years. After their wedding at the Henry VII Chapel in Westminster Abbey, they settled into a comfortable life in a Georgetown home and a Middleburg farm where Pam Brown pursued her interest in show jumping. Carter Brown was forty-three when Pam had their first child, a boy named John Carter Brown IV, in 1978. Their daughter, Elissa Lucinda Rionda Brown, was born in 1984. When their son Jay was two he was diagnosed with a cancer known as neuroblastoma, which doctors treated successfully. But the boy developed a severe curvature of the spine, leading to two major operations to fuse his backbone and straighten it with steel rods. It was, Brown said with typical understatement, a "rough patch."

The ordeal strained a marriage that had begun to fray after only a few years as Carter and Pam Brown discovered how different they were. Pam loved the country life, her dogs and her horses, and Carter did not. He found it difficult to relax, much less to spend an evening at home with his family. She resented the demands of his social and professional life. Brown was accustomed to going out every night of the week, sometimes to several events an evening, and he thrived on his heavy travel schedule for the gallery. His wife found the socializing "burdensome," said Brown. "My poor brother," observed Nicholas Brown. "He can't seem to hang on to anyone. He is very single-minded in his business. . . . He is bloody brilliant but with interpersonal family relationships he has had bad luck. He married two women who didn't measure up to the standards of our world."

Beyond his preoccupation with the gallery, Brown did not seem to have the temperament to make a happy marriage. "I don't think he understands women well," said one woman who knew him for a number of years. "Women are considered emotional and in Carter's eyes, that is disruptive." He was conspicuously guarded. In conversation he often spoke in a near whisper, and his eyes tended to flutter shut for uncomfortably long intervals. Friends and family attested to his reluctance to speak about intimate matters to anyone. He said, for example, that his brother Nicholas was his best friend. Yet according to Nicholas, Carter rarely confided in him. "It is one thing to be a good friend," said Nicholas, "and another to be communicative about personal matters."

For reasons known only to himself, Carter Brown "put on his suit of armor a long time ago," in the words of someone close to the family. "That way he could be protected. You don't spill the beans, no one can get to you." Although they worked together for eight years, John Walker once recalled, "I didn't know him any better at the end than I did at the beginning."

As his relationship with Pam Brown grew more difficult, she turned to an older man from Middleburg, George Ohrstrom, a breeder of racehorses with whom she had more in common. In the summer of 1987 she told Carter Brown she wanted a divorce.

Brown refused to move out of their Georgetown house. In part to make it easier for their young children, Carter and Pam contrived to live separately under the same roof for more than three years until Pam bought her own home down the block. After his wife discouraged him from coming to their farm in Middleburg, Brown was understandably receptive when Pamela Harriman offered to lend him her guest cottage at Willow Oaks and invited him to bring his children and their nanny for weekends.

Brown had come to know Pamela through her husband's connection to the National Gallery. "Averell and Marie were great friends," said Brown. "I had been a familiar spirit in the house on N Street. I had a key to go and use the pool." Within days of Pamela's marriage to Harriman in September 1971, Brown laid the groundwork for a relationship with a note of congratulations, remarking on Pamela's beauty and graciousness, mentioning that he too had just married, and hoping that the newlyweds would see each other frequently. He was delighted, he said, "to see such corroboration of the whole matrimonial idea." Brown also reiterated the gallery's interest in Averell Harriman's "fabulous collection." Only months later Brown helped clinch Harriman's gift of Marie's twenty-two artworks.

Pamela Harriman and Carter Brown traveled in the same social set, although he had little contact with her political life. In 1982 he named her to his exclusive Trustees Council. "The thing was to involve her as much as possible in the museum," said a source familiar with Carter's decision. "Most people knew she liked money, so there was a certain worry the Harriman paintings might not get to the gallery eventually." Four years later Pamela donated $20,000 to the National Gallery through the Averell and Pamela Harriman Foundation, followed by an equal amount the following year. After Brown and his wife officially announced their separation early in 1988, Pamela began appearing on his arm at public events.

With her newly svelte figure and "freshened" face, Pamela at sixty-eight seemed younger when she was with Brown. Though she said little publicly about her involvement with him, she encouraged the impression that it was a full-blown romantic affair. When they took a cruise along the Turkish coast with friends, they shared a stateroom, and during visits to Middleburg, Sun Valley, and Barbados, he stayed in her bedroom. "She certainly made one think she was hopping into bed with him," said a woman who accompanied them on a National Gallery tour of European art collections. "I don't know where she gets the energy and drive."

Yet those who knew the couple detected no sparks of passion or evidence of genuine devotion. At parties Pamela sometimes made proprietary gestures—holding Brown's hand or linking her arm through his—but that was her way with all men who caught her interest. "She was a very good friend," explained Brown, adding that "it was not a romance," and it was "not the case" that they were physically intimate. Because they were both single, and because of her past, "people assumed so much drama," said Brown. "If you are grown-up, you don't have to be that way, you can be just friends."

Some observers tried to explain the relationship by suggesting Brown was homosexual or bisexual. "I have never understood where that idea could have come from," said Brown. "It is absolutely without foundation. These days it is chic to admit being homosexual, but I can't claim it." The stories, which circulated through the arts community, were a result, according to Brown's brother Nicholas, of "jealousy, and the stereotype of the single person in the art world, someone who is fastidious as to dress and aesthetics."

More than anything, Pamela Harriman and Carter Brown had the sort of mutually advantageous arrangement that marked so many of Pamela's partnerships. "Being in a common world was a big factor, and in all honesty there was a consanguinity," said Nicholas Brown. "He was pursuing his goals and she was pursuing hers. They were not the same goals, but they could be pursued in tandem. Both of them tend to do useful things. . . . It was not an exclusive relationship for my brother. He was seeing other people, I know for a fact. It was what the French call a marriage of convenience. She needed a squire who was not threatening, and he liked having someone with an airplane and a house in Barbados."

For Pamela, Brown was an ideal escort. Brimming with erudition, he was a natural performer who delivered well-turned phrases with obvious relish. Although not a scholar, Carter Brown was comfortable around intellectuals and could readily synthesize their ideas. His brother called him the "black box who has the ability to convert the visual to the verbal." Carter Brown undertook to broaden Pamela's artistic horizons, and she was mildly diverted, although not completely engaged. She was thrilled, however, to accompany Brown to the opening of I. M. Pei's addition to the Louvre, where she could make an entrance as a wealthy woman with a distinguished companion.

Brown also assisted Pamela in a more personal way. When Pamela sold Marie Harriman's Degas bronze for $7 million in the late 1980s to fulfill her late husband's pledge to Columbia University, she had money left over that she wished to use to buy some more art. Following a consultation with Brown, she bought a John Singer Sargent painting, *Stairway in Capri*, at a gallery in New York. But for the first time, Pamela did not assume the interests of the principal man in her life. With her own money, power, and identity she didn't have to, so she remained committed to her political activities and treated the art world as an avocation.

The relationship was rewarding for Carter Brown as well. Besides sharing the trappings of her luxurious life, she opened doors for him, not only through her political connections but by way of introductions to prospective donors in Europe. Pamela and Brown understood each other and shared some character traits. "Carter is a tough guy, very categorical," said a man who knew him for decades. "He wants, he gets, and when he is finished, he kicks out. He doesn't have time to waste. He is very efficient." Much the same could be said of Pamela. Doubtless her sang-froid allowed her to cope with Carter Brown as she had with Averell Harriman and other emotionally distant and challenging men. By background, values, and personality, Pamela Harriman and Carter Brown seemed well matched.

The ultimate prize in Carter Brown's relationship with Pamela was the famous van Gogh *White Roses* that Averell Harriman had given his wife in 1982. At that time, Pamela had promised to fulfill her husband's wish that she donate the painting at some point to the National Gallery. In June 1989, Brown persuaded Pamela to officially pledge the van Gogh, kicking off a campaign to mark the National Gallery's fiftieth anniversary in 1991.

Pamela promised to give 20 percent of the painting's value for the anniversary and to donate the remaining 80 percent on or before her death. Until she completed the gift, she could keep the painting for 292 days each year, and the National Gallery could have it for 20 percent of the year, or 73 days. Brown arranged for a beautifully executed copy to hang in her living room when the real thing was at the gallery. Using the *White Roses* example, Brown was able to entice many other wealthy collectors to donate works of art.

The van Gogh was a major coup. By 1989, at the peak of the booming 1980s art market, its value was estimated at $60 million. Pamela didn't actually give the painting at that moment, largely for financial reasons. Tax reforms instituted in 1986 had forced donors to value their gifts at the original purchase price instead of the appraised value at the time of the donation. So if Pamela bought a painting for $100 that had appreciated to $1,000, she could only take a $100 income tax deduction when the gift was made. What's more, she would be obliged to pay capital gains tax on the increase in value of $900.

Pamela made her pledge at a time when the arts community was lobbying Congress to change the law and restore deductions based on current market value. In the following months she worked her political connections behind the scenes to help arts administrators make their case—bringing to bear her fund-raising clout on an issue of clear self-interest. "She was wired in. She said she would like to be helpful," said one arts administrator familiar with her maneuvers. After being briefed on the argument, "she spoke to two or three different senators on the Finance Committee," said the arts administrator. "She knew this would help her make the gift to the National Gallery possible." In October 1990 the Senate Finance Committee reached agreement, and later that year Congress passed a bill allowing a one-year "window" in 1991 during which donors could not only deduct the market value of their gifts but spread the deduction over five years to significantly reduce their taxes.

In January 1991 Pamela signed a contract with the National Gallery and gave 20 percent of the van Gogh, which by then had dropped in value from $60 million to $50 million, according to David Rust, former curator of French paintings at the gallery. The new law allowed her to deduct approximately $10 million, or about $2 million a year, from her income in 1991 through 1995. (In 1993, Congress passed legislation to restore the market value deduction permanently, which gave Pamela the option of donating additional increments and taking further tax deductions if she chose; three years later, she still had not increased her gift.)

The van Gogh not only yielded Pamela tax breaks but a flood of warm publicity for what Carter Brown publicly described as a "magnificent act of generosity." "I've been so very upset to see so many private collectors whose pictures we thought were going to museums and were instead put into foundations or sold," said Pamela. "I think it's very important a work of art of this quality is kept within the United States." Missing from the announcement was the fact that Marie Harriman had originally selected *White Roses* on her honeymoon with Harriman in 1930, that Averell Harriman and his mother had split the $72,000 purchase price, and that Mary Harriman had then given the painting to Averell and Marie as her wedding gift.

If Pamela had misgivings about relinquishing her biggest single asset, she gave no hint. But if Carter Brown had not been her companion, it's doubtful she would have donated the painting when she did. "Carter influenced her," said a longtime friend. "Averell did ask her to donate it, but she would have done it later, probably on her death."

The divorce of Carter and Pam Brown became final in December 1991, ending a long and acrimonious negotiation over his two conditions: joint custody of the children and a financial settlement with his ex-wife, who had come into a substantial inheritance. Brown pressed for an advantageous division of their assets because he said he needed the money. "The irony is, she was better off than I was," said Brown. Sources close to the family estimated his net worth between $5 and $10 million, although he was always tight with his own money. During his marriage, Pam Brown paid for her own clothing, most household expenses, and half the school tuitions for their children. The National Gallery covered nearly all his travel and entertainment. In the end, Pam Brown settled because friends told her he would not be satisfied unless he got something. He kept their Georgetown house, and she gave him a seven-figure sum for his share of the Middleburg farm.

Pam Brown went on to marry George Ohrstrom, but there was never any suggestion that Carter would marry Pamela Harriman once he was free. In fact, their relationship was already winding down. They finally parted company late in 1992 after he resigned as director of the National Gallery. The previous January he had stunned the art world when he said he would step down at age fifty-seven after twenty-three years in the job. He said he wanted to devote "more time and energy to responsible parenting," and give greater attention to his membership on numerous boards.

The night he had announced his intended departure to the trustees, he had asked them all for dinner at his Georgetown home. As he disclosed his plans, Jay and Elissa were with him to underscore the sincerity of his words. "Upstairs you go," said Brown afterward. "Time to do your homework." The children bounded up the stairs, then climbed down the back steps and returned to their mother's house—a scene from the pages of a Henry James novel. Pam Brown later told friends that she was "amused" by the charade.

In a city as status-obsessed as Washington, it seemed inconceivable that someone would willingly give up a position as prestigious as director of the National Gallery. Carter Brown in fact felt strongly about leaving on a high note. He had just completed his most elaborate exhibition, "Circa 1492," and he faced an era of possible budget constraints and more modest shows. He also seemed to want a less public if not less busy life; he signed on as chairman of a new fine arts cable channel, and he organized an ambitious exhibition to celebrate the 1996 Olympic Games in Atlanta. "He hasn't retired," said Nicholas Brown several years after his brother's resignation. "If anything, he is working harder than ever. Leaving the gallery was about being there thirty-one years and needing something else."

To Pamela Harriman, the loss of the National Gallery affiliation made their partnership less interesting. For five years Carter Brown had enjoyed her hospitality and her fortune. In addition to the van Gogh, the Averell and Pamela Harriman Foundation had donated $12,000 to the John Carter Brown Library in Providence from 1989 through 1992. She had flown Brown around in her jet, treated him to countless weekends and vacations, and given many gifts to his children. But the generosity was not mutual.

Winston Churchill complained to his mother that Brown was using her. "It was pretty one-sided from the financial point of view," he said. After a while, she appeared to agree. "I don't know what one would expect by way of reciprocation," countered Brown. "I don't have too many planes or homes myself. I tried to hold my end up, paying for meals and Christmas presents. There was a basic disparity between what she was able to do and what I could do." For his part, Brown also showed signs of ennui with the relationship. According to one friend, Brown "got bored when he saw Pam go through the same routine about Russia over and over again with new groups of people."

In predictable fashion, Pamela broke free and moved on, as unscathed as he was. Though there was no obvious ill-will, the two former partners didn't show signs of a lingering friendship either, a departure from Pamela's usual pattern. They had benefited about as much from each other as they could, and both of them had plans that they could no longer pursue as a team.

CHAPTER

Thirty-one

B Y THE EARLY 1990s, Pamela Harriman had accumulated more titles than any of her illustrious aristocratic ancestors. In newspaper and magazine accounts, her status had risen with each passing year: from "mother superior" and "godmother" of the Democrats to their "duchess," "queen," and finally "empress." Democratic politicians routinely lauded her as their "saviour" and their "heart and soul." She was said to have ascended to the "upper reaches" of the party, where powerful politicians would "seek her political advice regularly." When she joined the prestigious Century Association in 1990, she listed herself as a "politician." Theodore Sorenson, John F. Kennedy's speechwriter, who for a time served as Pamela's lawyer, proclaimed that "among people who matter, people who think, . . . she is considered a great woman who has made a distinguished life and is all the more interesting and respected for all she has done." But it took a sophisticated European woman to understand the magnitude of Pamela's transformation. "She has made herself virginal again," said Cynthia Sainsbury, a socialite who had met her in Paris when Pamela was the mistress of Elie de Rothschild.

In large measure, Pamela owed her new respectability to diligent self-promotion. When Joan Kroc, widow of the founder of McDonald's, gave $1 million to the Democratic National Committee in 1987, no one called her "empress" of the Democrats, nor did the party name a communications center after her. The difference lay in Pamela's uncanny knack for publicity, and the way she exploited her mystique to become a glamorous symbol of the Democratic Party. Pamela was perfectly suited for Washington, a city where perception *is* reality.

Pamela's campaign to be taken seriously gained momentum after Averell Harriman's death. As the newly appointed president of the W. Averell and Pamela C. Harriman Foundation, she controlled some $400,000 a year in grants, and as a director since 1984 of the Mary W. Harriman Foundation she had a say in the dispersal of another $700,000 annually. She used these two resources to donate large sums of money to public policy organizations that rewarded her by admitting her to membership and placing her on their boards.

In 1987, for example, the two Harriman funds donated $20,000 to the Brookings Institution, a liberal think tank, and in 1988 she was named a trustee. From 1989 through 1993, the Harriman foundations gave Brookings an additional $1,100,000 and pledged $600,000 more. In 1985 Pamela signed on with the Atlantic Council, a bipartisan organization dedicated to promoting the alliance between the United States and Western Europe. The following year the Mary Harriman Foundation pledged a $125,000 gift to the council, and the Averell and Pamela Harriman Foundation gave $6,500. Pamela was elected vice chairman of the Atlantic Council in 1989 after she donated $25,000 more. She gave an additional $104,000 in subsequent years.

Proof that Pamela had been embraced by the establishment came in 1987, when she was invited to join the Council on Foreign Relations. The membership included diplomats, former government officials, prominent lawyers, journalists, and business leaders, but the council was short on women. Averell Harriman had joined in 1922 and was a director from that year until 1953. Pamela and Averell had given the council $3,800 in 1983, and the Mary Harriman Foundation had donated at least $20,000 each year. After Pamela became a member, the Council on Foreign Relations received $255,000 from the Harriman funds in six years.

Following her late husband's example, Pamela set herself up as an informal ambassador at large, bankrolling trips with groups of experts to foreign capitals to meet with political and business leaders. The first trip was to China in the summer of 1987. The "delegation" included her step-grandson David Mortimer, Arthur Schlesinger, Jr., her political confidante Sandy Berger, and China expert Harry Harding from the Brookings Institution. Richard Holbrooke, then an investment banker with Lehman Brothers, scheduled a business trip so he could join Pamela's group in Beijing. Before they left for China, Pamela studied written material prepared by Harding, who also gave her a thorough oral briefing. She acquitted herself well during the visit, presenting prepared opening remarks, initiating discussions, and making toasts.

Pamela undertook the same sort of intensive preparation before subsequent trips: to Japan with a group from Virginia headed by Governor Gerald Baliles; to Turkey with the Atlantic Council; and to the Soviet Union before and after its breakup. On each visit to Moscow, she represented the Harriman Institute at Columbia University, which had been established with Averell Harriman's $11.5 million gift. Strobe Talbott, then the diplomatic correspondent for *Time* magazine, who would later be named Deputy Secretary of State, was a member of the traveling party on the first trip. Robert Legvold of the Harriman Institute, and Ed Hewett and Judith Kipper of Brookings, came both times. Holbrooke joined Pamela for the second trip.

Pamela left nothing to chance. If she wanted to ask questions in a meeting with Soviet officials, she would run them by Legvold first. "I think there is a certain insecurity in her about these issues," said Legvold. "She didn't want to risk vulnerability on things she didn't know about." Pamela often fell silent in meetings, contenting herself with listening to the professionals. Afterward, she quizzed her colleagues on their views and digested the notes they prepared as a record of the trip.

In 1990 she met one-on-one with Raisa Gorbachev, wife of the Soviet president. Pamela asked Raisa simple and straightforward questions such as,

"What do you want from us? How can we help you to accomplish what you're trying to accomplish?" Afterward, she reported her impressions back to her colleagues: Raisa was charming and confident, as well as tough-minded about resisting American attempts to interfere in Soviet affairs.

The two women had met previously in late 1987 when Pamela upstaged First Lady Nancy Reagan during a summit meeting by inviting Raisa to tea with a high-powered group of women, including Katharine Graham and Supreme Court Justice Sandra Day O'Connor. "She had cultivated Dobrynin [the long-time Soviet Ambassador to the United States] for years at little lunches on N Street and dinners alone where Pam could show off her knowledge of Soviet affairs," recalled William Walton. When the time came, said Walton, "she was the woman who the Russians chose."

During Pamela's gathering, Raisa had been "belligerent and condescending," according to a participant, but "Pam was very friendly toward her. They met the press hand-in-hand, and Pam was understandably pleased." Afterward, Pamela's "coup" with Raisa was hailed as evidence, according to one news account, of "how seriously the Kremlin took her."

Several weeks after each of her missions abroad, an opinion piece would appear under Pamela Harriman's byline on the op-ed page of the *Washington Post* or the *New York Times:* on the Chinese view of the Soviet Union, for example, or the strategic importance of Turkey for the Western Alliance. Other columns on domestic issues, such as her opposition to Republican proposals for reducing the capital gains tax—written as she was maneuvering for her multi-million-dollar tax deduction for *White Roses*—also carried her byline in the nation's leading newspapers.

These essays, along with speeches and policy statements, were ghost-written by a wide array of advisers. "Pam wouldn't sign her name without conferring with her consultants," said one of her former employees. "Nothing was written without five rewritings. If it had to do with the Soviet Union, it was done by Marshall Shulman. If it had to do with domestic politics it was Arthur Schlesinger."

Alfred Friendly, Jr., husband of Averell Harriman's onetime secretary Pie Friendly and formerly a foreign correspondent for *Newsweek,* worked as a ghost-writer for Pamela off and on for nearly five years—although for small jobs, "I didn't send her a bill," he said. For a period in 1986 Pamela had the political consulting firm Squier Eskew on a $5,000-a-month retainer for help on position papers and speeches. "She wanted to pay me $1,000 for an op-ed piece on the New Right after I left the PAC," said Peter Fenn, who lent a hand for no charge. Like Fenn, many who had worked on PamPAC's *Fact Books* donated their expertise out of a sense of gratitude because she had included them in PamPAC activities. Pamela rewarded some advisers with free trips to foreign countries, while others accumulated credits in Pamela's elaborate favor bank. In Arthur Schlesinger's case, the reward came in the form of frequent invitations to Barbados and Sun Valley.

Political consultant Robert Shrum—"Shrummie" to his friends—was one of Pamela's favorite writers. "She didn't pay me for my work," said Shrum. "I did it as a favor. I helped her with political strategy, press relations, messages and speeches. During the eighties we talked all the time, and I saw her all the time. We became very good friends. I went to Barbados several times. I like her, and I am on the same wavelength with her." Shrum wrote everything from thirty-second introductions to full-scale speeches, some of them scrawled on cocktail napkins to be transcribed by Pamela's secretaries. His most noted effort was an address Pamela gave to the 1984 Democratic Convention that included a line she used over and over in the following years: "I am an American by choice—and a Democrat by conviction."

In her effort to get top-quality work, it was not unusual for Pamela to hire three speechwriters for the same assignment. After catching on to this practice, one of them would sometimes call Janet Howard and say, "Should I take this assignment seriously or is Shrummie doing it too?" Howard would either reply, "Shrummie is doing it, so don't bother." Or she would say, "You're the only one, so you better get to work."

Public speaking did not come naturally to Pamela. When she was behind a lectern, she would plant her legs far apart, as one friend observed, "like two stalks of asparagus," making her seem almost mannish. Even for the briefest remarks, every word had to be typed out on an index card. Her manner was wooden, and she spoke with a portentous Churchillian cadence.

Both Robert Shrum and Robert Squier coached Pamela on her delivery; she even had a lectern moved into her office. Before the 1984 convention speech, Shrum worked with her intensively. She went over the text many times and practiced on the TelePrompTer in the hall. "It was a high-detail project," recalled one of her aides. She spoke in the late afternoon before a mostly indifferent audience of milling and chatting delegates. Her speech was unmemorable, but she did well enough to feel confident that she had been a success.

Sandy Berger, Pamela's principal adviser on PamPAC, had a hand in nearly everything produced on paper for Pamela. He was the lead writer of the speech that the *Washington Post* billed as her "diplomatic coming out." She had been invited to give the Samuel D. Berger Memorial Lecture (no relation) at Georgetown University on April 27, 1988. It was her most conspicuous effort, said Stuart Eizenstat, "to be seen as something other than a major fundraiser, something other than a social figure." Previous lecturers included the British politician Roy Jenkins, a brilliant speaker, and the Middle East envoy Philip Habib, who had been instrumental in bringing together Israel's Menachem Begin and Egypt's Anwar Sadat.

The topic Pamela chose was bipartisanship in foreign policy, a noncontroversial idea that she had embraced since her World War II days and that her late husband and other postwar "wise men" had worked to achieve. For several weeks, Pamela had Sandy Berger and Alfred Friendly working nonstop on the speech, passing drafts back and forth. Shrum and Eizenstat both chipped in with advice as well. Pamela changed a few things, and threw in several of her favorite stories about Churchill and Harry Hopkins.

Some three hundred guests—diplomats, socialites, and political figures— filled the auditorium, some of them summoned by Pamela's staff to ensure a capacity crowd. She lectured earnestly and deliberately, in a deep monotone. For all the writing and rewriting, the speech was dull and didactic, complete with a list of diplomatic do's and don'ts and banal exhortations: "We can, and I believe we must, forge a new sense of mutual trust and comity." Stephanie Mansfield of the *Washington Post* reported "scores of stifled yawns."

Pamela's courtiers were nevertheless full of praise at a wine and hors d'oeuvres reception she organized afterward. "Let me be the first to congratulate you," said Eizenstat, his "eyes shining," according to Mansfield. Pamela's old friend, Rhode Island Senator Claiborne Pell, had the speech read into the *Congressional Record*. At a dinner party afterward, hostess Evangeline Bruce "regaled the table with details not of what Harriman had said, but of what she had worn and how seriously she seemed to take herself," according to *Vogue* writer Julia Reed, a guest at the dinner.

Mansfield's account in the *Washington Post* the next day dismissed Pamela Harriman as "the only Washington hostess with her own foreign policy," and noted that she wore a "short, tight-fitting black silk cocktail dress, a gold necklace and sheer black stockings," with her hair "coiffed into a Washington power helmet." Pamela complained to Katharine Graham, who, according to a mutual friend, "could only say she had no control." Indignant letters to the editor followed. Of the three that were published, one noting Pamela's commitment to "high standards of statesmanship" was from Carl Anderson, a consultant who had received $10,226 in fees from PamPAC. Another protester, Iowa Senator Tom Harkin, had benefited from a $10,000 PamPAC contribution as well as fund-raising help from Pamela in 1984 when he challenged an incumbent Republican.

The toughest judgment of Pamela's performance was rendered by a British writer, Henry Fairlie, in *The New Republic*, who described the speech as a "memorial to Pamela Harriman's apotheosis," in which "sentence by sentence the bromides issue with lapidary unction. . . . One is left wondering why she was invited to speak and why she was willing to perform the charade." The answer to the second why was her eagerness to strengthen the impression that she was a woman of substance. As for the first, Pamela's money surely played a role. In 1988, she made a donation of $5,000 to Georgetown University through the Averell and Pamela Harriman Foundation, and Averell had previously contributed financially to the Berger lecture series, named after a longtime diplomat who had been his colleague since Lend-Lease days.

Pamela continued to speak at fundraisers and at less visible gatherings. In February 1989, she addressed students at Groton, the alma mater of her late husband, where she was misleadingly introduced as having "graduated from Downham College" and done "postgraduate work at the Sorbonne in Paris." "How wonderful it is to see so many women. I can't help but observe that if I had been born later, I might have gotten here on my own," said Pamela, borrowing from Winston Churchill's famous quip to the U.S. Congress in 1941: "I cannot help reflecting that if my father had been American and my mother British, instead of the other way round, I might have got here on my own." Pamela's speech, which was written by Robert Shrum, recycled several of her anecdotes about Churchill, along with the line about being "American by choice—and a Democrat by conviction." Pamela urged her listeners to embrace "true public service—the belief that there are things more important than the amount of money one makes, or keeps."

Pamela's public image was sharpening as an independent, highly respectable woman of the world. At the same time, she was growing more dependent on her cadre of male advisers. Pamela always enjoyed the act of consultation, not only for the information it could yield but because it stroked her ego. She gloried in having Washington's "big men," as one friend called them, sharing their wisdom with her.

Among the men surrounding her, Clark Clifford assumed her husband's role as "wise man" in her life. He was fifteen years younger than Averell Harriman, and they had been friends since they first served together during the Truman administration. A fixture in Washington for a half century, Clifford had a reputation as the "ultimate insider." Not only did he play a prominent role in Pamela's political action committee, he counseled her on nearly every day-to-day decision she made. "Her umbilical cord was to Clifford," said a former PamPAC employee. "He got involved in lots of little things. She would ask, 'Should I do this event in Cleveland? Should I deliver this speech?' " Clifford edited all of her speeches, concerning himself even with grammatical matters such as split infinitives. "Clifford made it a point to know everything," said the former employee.

One of Clifford's favorite gestures was forming a steeple with his fingertips as he pondered a problem, and he spoke in a velvety, resonant voice, with a deliberate, slightly sanctimonious air. His attentiveness was seductive to Pamela, just as hers was to so many men. As a consequence, he rose even further in her estimation. She told Washington journalist Marjorie Williams that she was "in awe" of Clifford's "high principles," that she had "total confidence" in his advice, that she was impressed by his "style" and his "presence," which she called "rather theatrical." Pamela seemed to know little about him as a person, but she fully understood his value to her. "I bore him a great deal with unimportant things I need advice on," said Pamela. "I've never known someone who always has time, even for the most trivial things. . . . It doesn't matter how trivial your problem is, he seems to embrace it with total concentration."

Pamela might as easily have been talking about Max Beaverbrook. Yet she had changed significantly since her days at the feet of the manipulative press lord. As one of her close friends noted, "She has a great capacity for growth that is continuous and remarkable. She is a hard worker, and she has seriousness about understanding subjects." That was certainly true—but only up to a point. Her intelligence had never evolved from the reactive to the creative. She was practical by nature, and her growth was guided by ambition, not intellectual curiosity. "Pamela would line up the judgments of others and make choices from what was laid out," said the Harriman Institute's Robert Legvold. Those choices drew more on instinct than deliberation in the face of conflicting advice.

With her advisers, her think tanks, her speeches, her articles, and her elaborately planned trips, Pamela was furnishing her mind as if it were a room in one of her homes, selecting ideas as she would Louis XVI chairs, arranging them quite formally, so that they would not be disturbed. Unlike genuine autodidacts, she did not read much. Pamela could frankly admit, "I don't like things that I don't know. I like to know how things work that I'm interested in." She was most comfortable digesting information that had been packaged for her by experts she trusted—and the views she espoused consequently followed their liberal Democratic beliefs. When Sandy Berger or Robert Shrum or Richard Holbrooke called on the telephone, she sometimes had their conversations taped so they could be transcribed for her to study. Recalled one friend, "She will listen to people like Tom Foley, and then in the next conversation you will hear her spouting things that Tom Foley said," just as she had picked the brains of American generals and diplomats at 49 Grosvenor Square and passed along unfiltered recapitulations of their observations.

With those whose opinions she regarded as inferior, Pamela could be quite imperious. "She expects people to do as she says or think as she thinks," said one woman who knew Pamela for many years. "You could say she is carried away with power." But she also seemed to be genuinely wary of anything contradictory that might jostle her carefully ordered universe. "You can't have a discussion with her on the pros and cons of the budget," said a Washington friend, "because she doesn't read or analyze opposing viewpoints. It is another form of her denial. If it doesn't fit in, she won't consider it. She has a closed mind, which limits her, and limits your discussions." Though Pamela may have believed her store-bought opinions mattered, few others could imagine that her campaign would one day lead to an appointment as the American envoy to France.

Thirty-two

Now SHE HAS the image of power," said Pamela's old friend William Walton. "She loves the meetings, the constant detail work, the tight focus of the minutiae and the power plays of government life." Perhaps inevitably, she also developed an imperial style. At public events, she was flanked by aides. One of them usually stood behind a pillar or a potted plant, holding Pamela's powder and lipstick in case she needed to freshen her makeup. Her Georgetown home had a telephone system with nearly a dozen lines, and her office and domestic staff were instructed to answer after only one ring. She kept five separate calendars that her staff coordinated daily, along with computer printouts of each day's schedule that included names as well as suggested attire. She was so heavily booked that when a friend asked her in October 1987 to a "quiet dinner," Pamela's first available date was July the following year, nine months away.

For her regular trips from Georgetown to Middleburg on weekends, to Sun Valley for her August vacation, and to Barbados for winter and Easter holidays, she kept each house fully staffed and in readiness for her arrival. Women servants wore white for daytime and black for serving in the evening; the butler dressed in black tie. The upstairs maid pressed all her clothes and laid them out. The ladies' maid drew Pamela's bath and packed her suitcases for trips. The chef was required to write out the day's menus each morning in French. Pamela's son Winston joked to a friend that he had counted up all the people who worked for Pamela and found that they numbered more than a hundred. Watching her leave Georgetown, a *Washington Post* reporter described her coddled existence: "Her maid scurries upstairs with a last minute glass of orange juice. An assistant carries her papers as the butler opens the front door. 'Goodbye!' she calls gaily. Her chauffeur drives to the airport, the jet pilot shakes her hand, a young staffer holds her umbrella."

She treated her employees with the aristocratic paternalism that she learned in her youth. The help never had to make do with sandwiches from the corner deli. Pamela's chefs—at one point she employed two simultaneously in Georgetown—prepared delicious meals for all staff members. Each Christmas, PamPAC employees received identical expensive items such as Gucci pocketbooks or plush terrycloth robes that Janet Howard would order in bulk. While crediting Pamela for good intentions, one former PamPAC employee couldn't help observing, "I think the staff would rather have been paid for their overtime."

Pamela rewarded her domestic staff more modestly, with gifts of gloves or heavy woolen socks purchased from a military surplus store, along with small cash bonuses.

When it came to larger obligations, Pamela could be cold-hearted with her help. For all his tightfistedness, Averell Harriman had taken care to establish pension plans for his longtime employees at Arden, and on his instructions, Pamela had continued the payments. Following Harriman's death in July 1986, Clark Clifford wrote a letter to Michael Kuruc, the Harriman butler, with several hundred shares of Union Pacific stock, worth around $13,000 before taxes, a gift that the governor had asked Clifford to make on his behalf.

Shortly afterward, Kuruc decided to ask Pamela what benefits he might expect down the line. He had been employed by the Harrimans for more than twelve years, and he was in his sixties when Harriman died. Averell Harriman had been especially fond of Kuruc, who had waited on him impeccably and had taken care of his household very much in Old World style. Kuruc had traveled with the Harrimans to Barbados and Sun Valley, and he had spent hours keeping the Governor company in Middleburg when Pamela was away, frequently working overtime for no extra pay. But Kuruc had never minded, because Harriman had assured him on several occasions that he would be provided for—although he never put anything in writing.

Perhaps in deference to her husband, Pamela had been unfailingly considerate to Kuruc. "I modeled myself after the guy in *A Star Is Born*," Kuruc recalled. "I wanted to do everything to please Madam. That was my role and she appreciated it. She was very nice to me." Kuruc fondly remembered the time Pamela rented a home for him one summer near Birchgrove so he could see his family in the evenings. "There was even a fruit basket when we got there," he said. But when Kuruc questioned his newly widowed employer about his long-term security, he encountered a different boss.

"I didn't use the word 'pension,' " recalled Kuruc, "but I decided I had a right to find out, to make sure. She did a 180-degree turn. It wasn't that suddenly I was out. It was, 'You can stay but you are not going to get anything.' I replied, 'I guess I am getting older so maybe I'd better look around.' She said, 'When are you leaving?' I can still remember her say, 'When are you leaving?' To me it was not ladylike. I found it very rough. Since there were no benefits, I left."

Pamela's most privileged and well-paid employee was Janet Howard, whose power had grown dramatically when she became director of PamPAC in 1985. Their relationship was close, but complicated and troubling at times. "Janet and Pam have a chemistry that is very very strong and has built up over time," said John Bowles. Their bond deepened in the immediate aftermath of Averell Harriman's death, when Howard had worked night and day to put together the funeral, mock-burial, and memorial service. Not long afterward, Howard collapsed at Arden and was rushed to a Manhattan hospital. Pamela stayed by her side in the emergency room, and after Howard's subsequent hysterectomy. Howard fully recovered and resumed control of PamPAC in the early autumn of 1986.

Four years after she was hired in 1980, according to a former PamPAC staffer, Howard's salary had risen from $40,000 to around $100,000 a year. Only a portion came from PamPAC, which reported an amount that fluctuated from around $4,000 to more than $9,000 annually. Most of her salary was paid through Brown Brothers Harriman—"As if I'm a bank manager!" she once exclaimed—and some came from other PamPAC accounts that the Federal Election Commission was not permitted to monitor. Pamela paid Howard bonuses in Union Pacific stock, including $50,000 worth after Harriman's death. Without any financial responsibility for room, board, or transportation, Howard's expenses were minimal.

Janet Howard became omnipresent in Pamela's life, the first person she spoke to in the morning and the last at night. Howard routinely worked fifteen-to eighteen-hour days. A former Harriman employee remembered the time that Pamela "called Janet at 1:00 A.M. to give her some instructions. She had caught her asleep with a magazine dropped on her lap. The next day I saw Janet's scribble all over the magazine pages." Pamela counted on Howard to carry out her detailed instructions to the letter. What distinguished Howard was her eagerness to meet Pamela's mountain of demands.

To the Washington political world, Howard was "almost an extension of Pam," recalled Stuart Eizenstat. "Janet is a human Rolodex," said political consultant Bill Carrick. "She knows everyone and keeps track of people in a way Pamela doesn't." To Robert Shrum, she was "a great chief of staff, very good at organizing." Howard curried favor with powerful contributors and elected officials to whom she distributed expensive Christmas gifts, usually cases of wine purchased with what was known as her "Christmas patronage fund." "Janet was a good representative for Pamela Harriman," said a former PamPAC employee. "To the donors and the senators, Janet busted ass."

But she alienated many others with her officious and sometimes belligerent manner. For all her quickness and native intelligence, Howard did not wear well. Her principal flaw, said a former colleague, was that "She doesn't think anyone is as smart as she is." Those she crossed called her Pamela's "hatchet woman," "dragon lady," "guard dog," and "ax lady." After her surgery she gained weight, which made her seem that much more formidable when she went on the warpath. "She comes at you like a tidal wave," said a former PamPAC consultant. " 'How dare you do this?' is a typical phrase for her. One guy once said she could start a fight two minutes inside heaven's gate."

At political fundraisers, Howard would keep a wary, somewhat anxious eye on Pamela while bustling around to ensure the perfection of the arrangements. From the outset, she clearly idolized and sometimes tried to emulate the woman she called "PCH." When Pamela wasn't around, Howard "would try to assume the sophistication and air of supremacy that Mrs. Harriman had by nature," recalled one top Democratic operative who worked with PamPAC. In Pamela's presence Howard often adopted the guise of adoring daughter, fussing about her comfort and her health. Yet on matters of policy or political strategy, Howard was capable of challenging her boss. A former PamPAC consultant recalled watching Janet "jabbing the air and leaning in toward Mrs. Harriman, and Mrs.

Harriman was doing it back. But Mrs. Harriman knows Janet would fall on her sword for her."

Some former employees, friends, and members of Pamela's family worried about the relationship. "Their lives are quite intertwined. It is a case of too much overreliance on both of their parts, they are too dependent on each other," said a former PamPAC employee. The predominant concern was that Pamela gave Howard too much power, and that Howard's abrasive style caused problems for her employer. Several people came forward, including one high-ranking Democratic Party official, to tell Pamela that the negatives were not worth it.

But Pamela's needs overrode any concerns she might have felt. Janet Howard knew virtually everything about Pamela, and she was completely loyal and protective. "She knows the institutional history, and she delivers for Pamela's daily life," said one of her former subordinates. She would willingly do Pamela's dirty work and engage in confrontations that her boss wanted to avoid, allowing Pamela to profess innocence.

As director of Pamela's political action committee, Howard enforced a meticulous code of do's and don'ts that Pamela had established. But with her boss branching out into foreign policy activities, Howard was increasingly left on her own. "Pamela did float above it all," recalled a former PamPAC employee. "She gave the directions, she worked hard and was always busy. But she had other things going on. If a major thing went wrong, she would be briefed in cursory fashion."

For a PamPAC dinner in California in the mid-1980s, Howard had couriers and secretaries flying back and forth with drafts of Pamela's speech, while in Washington Clark Clifford was correcting typos, and more than a dozen PamPAC staffers worked from 7:00 A.M. to 3:00 A.M. the following morning on seating charts. But Pamela, like the donors and politicians, saw only the product of Janet Howard's efforts: fundraisers that came off without a hitch. "Pam could see an enormous amount of work being done by very few people with helluva good results on the surface," said a former PamPAC consultant. Yet the public record indicated that from 1986 onward, PamPAC became less efficient and less focused on its mission of getting Democrats elected.

Political action committees were not known as cost-effective organizations. The bulk of their money went to administrative expenses rather than political candidates. In its early years, Democrats for the 80's kept its operating costs under some control. In the 1983–84 election cycle, for example, 44 percent of the money PamPAC raised went to candidates, but by 1989–90 that amount had dropped to 25 percent—a mere $129,000 of the $511,222 that was raised.

One reason for the rise in operating costs was the decision by Pamela and Janet Howard to spend more on consultants and political polling. In 1983–84 those expenses came to around $33,000, according to Federal Election Commission (FEC) records. By 1989–90 they had risen to nearly $255,000. In 1989, Pamela touted her new "national polling operation" to "take the public pulse on a regular basis." Although the impact of the polling could not be measured, the purpose was to provide data to Democratic members of Congress to guide their votes. The operation was also designed to impress Democratic leaders with Pamela's knowledge. "The polling was to keep Pamela informed, to provide information," recalled one PamPAC consultant. "She could hand it out like patronage to House and Senate members. The idea was information equals power."

The figures reported to the FEC told only part of the tale of PamPAC's spending. Beginning in the mid-1980s, PamPAC had moved increasingly into raising non-federal or "soft money" that supposedly went to state and local Democratic Party activities but actually ended up helping candidates for national office. As these activities expanded, in order to keep track of the money PamPAC kept six sets of books—three for federal contributions from individuals, labor unions, and corporate political action committees, and three for soft money from individuals, corporations, and labor unions—all with different-colored checks.

None of the soft-money accounts was subject to government scrutiny, so it was impossible to tell how much in non-federal funds flowed through Pam-PAC in the late 1980s. Regular federal fund-raising peaked in 1981, when Pam-PAC pulled in $600,108. By 1989, only $268,381 in federal money was raised, but former PamPAC staff members said at least an equal amount came in soft money. In addition, many of the committee's burgeoning expenses—including the cost of couriers crisscrossing the country with Pamela's speeches—were recorded in the soft-money books where they couldn't be tracked. "The expenses were always a big secret," said a PamPAC staff member who worked for Janet Howard. "No one knew how much was spent, but there were enormous billable hours as invitations were done over and over, and seating charts were done over and over."

In February 1989, PamPAC renamed itself Democrats for the 90's. Pamela had been thinking of closing the operation but had decided to continue, according to Stuart Eizenstat, because "it was felt that it was important for her to have something to do. . . . It was important to have her engaged." Pamela announced the transformation at a $1,500-a-plate dinner in her honor during the National Governors' Conference, and the crowd saluted her with a song called "Just Wild About Harriman." But with the exception of the polling project, Pamela seemed to be losing her enthusiasm. "Like many prominent local Democrats who have grown increasingly disgruntled after almost nine years of Republicans in the White House, Harriman plans to flee to her country house whenever possible," *W* magazine noted toward the end of the summer.

Pamela had also reached a point of diminishing returns with her fund-raising. "The game had caught up to her," said a prominent Washington lobbyist. "She wasn't bringing in enough money, and people who were willing to play her game in the beginning were no longer willing to do so." The issues evenings had lost their cachet, and Pamela's staff often had to invite people to fill out the room. "Typically we'd only raise fifteen thousand even with forty people," said a former PamPAC staff member. Pamela tried to revive interest by taking to the road and organizing evenings in Chicago and Los Angeles. *W* called it her "floating salon with the help of her private jet and a lot of desperate

Democrats." But when the idea failed to take off, PamPAC seemed on the verge of sputtering into irrelevance.

As the pressure intensified to revitalize the operation, tensions erupted between Pamela and Janet Howard. "Pamela would disappear for days on end to Middleburg," said a former staff member. "Janet would call her once a day, and Pamela wouldn't even want to talk." In June 1989, PamPAC sponsored a dinner at Washington's Madison Hotel. "We expect the dinner to raise over $300,000 to help win the 1990 Senate races," Pamela announced in a press release. There would be twenty-five tables, each hosted by a Democratic senator, and the cost was $1,000 per person, payable either to "Democrats for the 90's" or "Democrats for the 90's/Non-Federal Account."

Federal records indicate that from January through June 1989, PamPAC attracted $206,670 in contributions, most of them for the June dinner. The costs shown for the evening included strikingly small amounts: some $7,000 in catering costs at the Madison Hotel for a dinner attended by more than 250 people. With most of the expenses evidently buried in PamPAC's soft-money accounts, it was difficult to gauge the success of the event. The public record did show, however, that by year's end only $38,500 went from PamPAC to Senate candidates—far short of the $300,000 Pamela had promised.

Pamela participated in other big dinners for the Democratic Party that year, but the pace of her committee's activities had slackened considerably. In early 1990, Pamela and Janet Howard hatched a new idea to attract attention. PamPAC would organize a concert at the Kennedy Center, a gala event to be co-sponsored with the Democratic Senatorial and Congressional Campaign committees as well as the Democratic National Committee. Pamela asked Time-Warner chairman Steve Ross to line up some of his company's top entertainers; her first choices were either Linda Ronstadt or Paul Simon. Neither was available, nor were many other popular singers. Simon did phone his friend, *Saturday Night Live* producer Lorne Michaels, to say he should help Pamela. Michaels recruited the comedian Dana Carvey, as well as Roberta Flack and the rock group Crosby, Stills, and Nash. "I have a background in the theater and lots of friends," Pamela proudly explained when the lineup was announced. The aim, she said, was to raise $1.5 million to benefit Democrats running for the House and Senate.

The anticipated "party of the decade," as Pamela called it, generated effusive publicity. The *Boston Globe*'s John Robinson was Pamela's biggest cheerleader, praising her for being "defiant in defeat, insisting that the whipped and troubled Democrats have a glorious future," and quoting DNC treasurer Robert Farmer's claim that "she has a big success on her hands."

Behind the scenes, however, PamPAC was in a frenzy as costs spiraled out of control and fund-raising lagged. The Democratic Senatorial Campaign Committee (DSCC), facing a tough election campaign with limited resources, became concerned that its funds would be imperiled by the event. Committee officials suggested that costs for the concert be held to $100,000 and pressed Janet Howard for a budget. When she refused, the committee scaled back its involvement to limit its financial liability—a bold act of defiance that prompted

Howard to spread the word that the committee had "mistreated" Pamela and was "disloyal" to PamPAC. Pamela remained silent as her underlings dealt with the conflict.

The night of the concert on June 20, 1990, Pamela "was still going strong" at midnight, according to *W* magazine, "wearing a black Givenchy cocktail dress, a silver choker made from hundreds of tiny silver Turkish coins she picked up in a bazaar in Istanbul, and a huge emerald ring she twirled nervously on the finger of her left hand. . . . She spent the night chatting with everyone, it seemed, except her pal Carter Brown." Afterward, PamPAC said that the "Democratic Decade" event raised more than $1 million; but the cost overruns left a bad aftertaste. "Party regulars fretted," according to *Newsweek,* that the "lavish bash struck the wrong note after a decade of Republican excess." *Newsweek* also noted the DSCC's complaint that "the gala's $400,000 cost was too steep."

Records filed with the FEC showed that the event did indeed take in over $1 million: $704,498 in non-federal funds and $393,509 in federal contributions. But after expenses that actually came close to $500,000, little remained for the candidates. PamPAC received a measly $75,000 in federal funds, the Senate Committee $51,235, the Congressional Committee $75,000, and the Democratic National Committee a minuscule $10,000. (Soft-money dispersals to the various participants were not recorded, although it appeared that the DNC received the lion's share.) As usual, most of the expenses seem to have disappeared into non-federal accounts; FEC reports showed only $169,044 of the costs. In the period between the concert and the end of the year, PamPAC had distributed just $55,500 to Senate candidates. "The Democratic Decade event was when PamPAC cratered," said a former PamPAC consultant. "It was a disastrous event financially and a big unhappy experience."

Six months later, Pamela announced that PamPAC would disband. "I think I've paid my dues," she told the *Washington Post. Newsweek* reported that party activists were "distraught" and quoted courtier Robert Squier: "It's as if someone announced we were going to dissolve the DNC." But the magazine also alluded to Pamela's pique, noting that she "told friends she felt unappreciated. 'Pam has been treated very badly by the men in this party,' said one. 'They felt it was fine for her to have dinners and raise money, but when it came to controlling budgets, they didn't want her around.' "

Once again, Pamela took solace in denial, ignoring PamPAC's problems and blaming others by saying, "They don't appreciate me." Before shuttering the committee, she had naturally consulted with her advisers. Stuart Eizenstat urged her to keep going, but Sandy Berger advised her to close down. Political action committees had fallen into disfavor generally, and the FEC was about to impose new reporting requirements on soft money beginning in 1991 that would have complicated PamPAC's operation.

By the time of PamPAC's demise, Pamela's fund-raising ability had achieved mythic status. She repeatedly claimed that her committee had raised and distributed $12 million to the Democratic Party over ten years, a figure that many press accounts accepted uncritically. *Newsweek* went even further, reporting that she had spent the decade "doling out some $14 million to Democratic congressional and gubernatorial candidates through her PAC and raising more than $10 million more for the party with her galas and soirees."

Pamela actually raised nowhere near $24 million, or even $12 million, and she parceled out far less. Of the $3.9 million in federal funds collected by PamPAC from 1980 to 1990, $1.3 million went directly to candidates, according to the Federal Election Commission. From 1986 onward, the committee gathered an estimated $1.5 million in additional soft money, and Pamela's fundraisers for individual senators accounted for some $2 million more.

At best, Pamela's personal fund-raising—excluding the lavish Democratic galas to which she lent her prestigious name—totaled some $7.5 million, and she probably gave candidates around $3 million of that amount. Broken down over the decade, that would be $300,000 a year of other people's money, considerably shy of the million-dollar annual figure often cited.

Pamela also took credit for having "masterminded" important campaigns. She claimed, for example, that her fund-raising "saved the seat of Paul Sarbanes" of Maryland during his 1982 Senate race. Sarbanes in 1982 raised a total of $1.6 million for his campaign, and neither PamPAC nor Pamela individually made a contribution. PamPAC did pay $20,104 in April 1981—nineteen months before election day—to make the radio ad attacking the National Conservative Political Action Committee's $500,000 assault on Sarbanes as a free-spending liberal. The resulting publicity put Pamela and her fledgling committee on the map and emboldened Sarbanes, but it didn't exactly "save" him.

The turning point for the Democrats during the Reagan-Bush years was recapturing the Senate in 1986, and Pamela assigned herself a key role in that victory. On a purely financial basis, with large contributions flowing to Democratic candidates from so many other sources, Pamela's image as a financial linchpin didn't hold up. In the 1985–86 election cycle, PamPAC contributed $304,250 to 83 House and Senate candidates—a trifling total compared to the more than $100 million the candidates received from other sources. Pamela personally gave $19,000 in Harriman money to 25 candidates. Even when she raised a six-figure sum for a senator at one of her special fundraisers, her net contribution was only a small piece of a multi-million-dollar budget, and her dollars certainly didn't swing any elections.

But Pamela had found a new way to shake the political money tree. When she was throwing weekly fundraisers for individual senators in 1986, no one else was operating at that level of intensity, and her commitment helped make recapturing the Senate a cause célèbre. "She was right in the middle of things," said Bill Carrick. "She provided an easy way, especially for non-incumbents, to get plugged into Washington fund-raising, to have an event and not worry about logistics. It was very much her cachet that made a difference. It became social as well as political, and people came in from all over the country."

More than anything, though, Pamela's political action committee was a triumph of hype. "It gave more visibility to the Democrats," said labor leader Jesse Calhoon. "In the media, the party had moved to the fringes. Her organization brought the Democratic Party, at least public relations wise, to a more centrist position." Pamela liked to perpetuate the notion that PamPAC had an impact on the Democratic Party's ideological agenda. One magazine account called her home a "clubhouse cum think tank." But out of some one hundred issues evenings over the years, no new ideas emerged for the party, even in the PamPAC *Fact Books* that served as "Cliff Notes" for candidates. The crucible for the new Democratic centrist platform was across town, at the Democratic Leadership Council's Progressive Policy Institute on Capitol Hill.

The unstated mission of PamPAC all along had been Pamela's advancement. Her committee, said John Bowles, one of her original supporters, "did become a very unique activity, a stepping stone to Pamela's significant involvement in party activities." Her N Street home served as the headquarters for the Democrats' government-in-exile. "People liked going to her house," said Bill Carrick. "There was usually a stellar cast of characters. The truth was, it was useful. A lot of people who normally didn't talk to each other got together."

This was Pamela Harriman at her best, broker to the powerful, encouraging them to talk. "She ran the inn," said Gordon Stewart, a former Carter White House official. "She was warm and welcoming." Her willingness to "keep the lights on," as Stewart described it, for so many years automatically gave her a prominent position that she used to the utmost. She gave the party pizzazz as she helped boost its self-esteem, never for a minute letting anyone forget the importance of her role and the depth of her commitment.

To that end, Pamela knew how to spin the press. The "practical dreamer" who had spent a lifetime reinventing herself was never more effective than in creating her political image. She had come to understand the power of the "big lie": that if something—the dollars she purportedly raised, the politicians she supposedly elected—was repeated enough it would become conventional wisdom.

Pamela had been in the headlines for some fifty years, nearly always in extreme terms: the dazzling saloniste, the "international siren," the home-wrecker, the gold digger, the power broker. "If I had ever gotten bothered about what people thought, I would never have gone anywhere," she told a reporter for the *Washington Post* in 1983. "But if I say, 'I don't care,' and then suddenly in the papers it says, 'Oh, I don't give a damn about what people say about me,' they'll all say, 'Aahh! That's another reason why we think she's a bitch!' But I don't really care, no!" Yet while Pamela refused to surrender her freedom and her ambition to secure public approval, she also wanted—and eventually expected—to be noticed. Good publicity or bad, it was all the same to Pamela, because she couldn't bear to be ignored.

As she became a political figure, however, she grew more sensitive to negative publicity. She was determined to protect her new respectability. Pamela and Janet Howard worked unceasingly to burnish Pamela's image. Pamela didn't hesitate to whisper "enormous success" in a reporter's ear after one of her fundraisers for George Mitchell or to brag to *Vogue* writer Julia Reed, "I lunch only at Brookings." Once when Artemis Cooper, the granddaughter of Duff and Diana, was having lunch at N Street, Janet Howard summoned Pamela to the phone. Cooper could hear Pamela accepting congratulations on her work for the Democrats. After she hung up, Pamela said, "Janet, I hope you got every word of that."

Whenever Pamela was hosting an event, receiving an award, or traveling with one of her delegations, Janet Howard would call members of the press she considered friendly, most frequently Chuck Conconi, then a reporter at the *Washington Post.* Pamela was especially fond of *Women's Wear Daily* and its monthly magazine *W,* even though their articles often had an edge, because, explained a *Women's Wear* writer, "We don't forget her."

If an unfamiliar reporter called, Janet Howard would make detailed inquiries about bona fides and intended lines of questioning. "I had to do a dog and pony show," said one veteran writer for a leading national magazine. "She was vetting me." Reporters sometimes bristled at the treatment. When the *New York Times* assigned Felicity Barringer to write a 1,000-word profile of Pamela, Howard was "unnecessarily antagonistic and acting socially superior," recalled Barringer, who declined to pursue the story. But those who withstood Howard's hazing often seemed grateful when Pamela finally granted an audience, her own tape recorder cued up to provide her with a transcript. Articles often noted that she "rarely gives interviews," despite abundant evidence to the contrary.

Pamela managed her coverage by speaking in generalities and frustratingly thin anecdotes, deflecting questions about her earlier life with laughter and coy evasions. She was most effective on television. "Whenever we want Pamela for an interview," said a top network news executive, "Janet sets rules for what is off-limits and tries to control the shape of the interview, and she succeeds. She insists that Pamela Harriman be portrayed as a woman of history and that she never talk about her personal life."

With magazines and newspapers, Pamela applied different but no less controlling rules. She agreed to talk to *New York* magazine's Michael Gross, for example, on condition that *her* quotes be attributed to an "intimate." Here's what the "intimate" had to say about Pamela's relationship with Agnelli: "Their five years simply ran its course. She knew it would have never worked." Of course Agnelli had broken off the relationship when he decided to marry Princess Marella Caracciolo.

For years, Janet Howard collected Pamela's press clippings and faxed them to her when she was traveling. If Pamela was appearing on television, Howard would phone a list of people to alert them. Afterward, Howard would get a videotape for the collection kept in the basement at PamPAC, and Pamela would periodically show the tapes to visitors. Pamela often sent clippings to her friends, and she sometimes took copies with her to social events. When she attended the fiftieth anniversary of the Casablanca Conference in Morocco, she carried around a fax of Michael Gross's *New York* magazine cover story. "It was odd to see her holding it and showing it to people," recalled a conference participant.

The most unusual aspect of Pamela's self-promotion was her habit of reading letters aloud at dinner parties. She would begin with period pieces: her correspondence with Harriman, her father-in-law Winston Churchill, Harry

Hopkins, and assorted generals. "She kept them in her room, and she would go and get them," said the Harrimans' former butler Michael Kuruc. "She would read to people at the table like a performer. She did it if the conversation lagged. She was prepared." "I'd like to share this with you," she would usually begin. If it was a Churchill letter, she would summon forth her best imitation of the British statesman.

The wartime letters cast her in an exciting light simply by her association with great men. But her readings moved to a new level of vanity when she started sharing letters from important people congratulating her for reinvigorating the Democratic Party. These were particular favorites during her Barbados holidays, when she often entertained English visitors. "They were impressed," said one of her guests. "I found it sort of un-English and a little embarrassing."

"At this point in her life Pamela has evolved into a serious person," said William Walton in the late 1980s. "She doesn't make comments or jokes about her past." Yet she was selectively sensitive. If an account glamorized her parade of lovers and reinforced her legend, she seemed unconcerned. But if she was mocked or belittled, she was infuriated. When Rudy Abramson's comprehensive biography of Averell Harriman was published in 1991, she complained to friends about his statement that she had been rejected by Gianni Agnelli. She was equally vexed by a glancing reference, in a biography of the designer Christian Dior, to a period in the 1950s when Pamela was "between lovers."

Nothing upset her more than "Shamela," Henry Fairlie's article in *The New Republic* in which he skewered her Georgetown lecture in 1988. In addition to picking apart her speech, Fairlie had sarcastically portrayed her efforts to buy respectability. His tone reflected an ingrained British skepticism that had dogged Pamela since her disappointing debutante days. Discussing the piece with one friend, Pamela burst into tears. "She thought it was mean and unfair and that everyone would see it," said the friend. Pamela was most upset because it had appeared not in the society pages, but in a prestigious political journal that she hoped would take her seriously. "She generated letters of support," said one of her friends. "She got on the phone, got people to write and defend her." Among her champions were Congressman Tony Coelho and the journalist Leslie Gelb, who described her as a "loyal friend" and identified himself as a correspondent for the *New York Times*.

Ultimately, Pamela concluded that the best way to define her image was to tell the tale herself. Several writers had set out to write her biography but each time she managed to thwart them. She dispatched the powerful Washington lawyer Edward Bennett Williams to Lynn Nesbit, the agent for Brooke Hayward, who was considering a biography of Pamela as a follow-up to her best-selling *Haywire*. Williams told Nesbit that Pamela would sue if Brooke "wrote a single word about her." When award-winning biographer Doris Kearns Goodwin began gathering material in the mid-1980s, Pamela sent her a letter expressing thanks for her interest while declining to cooperate. Although Pamela was eager to discourage others, she never seriously contemplated taking on the task herself. "Arthur Schlesinger was always trying to get me to go up to the library in New York where you can dictate into something there, the archives," Pamela told one interviewer from the *Washington Star*. "But I never have. Life is so busy. I've always been moving."

After shutting down her political action committee, however, Pamela had a change of heart. In the spring of 1991 she signed on with New York agent Morton Janklow and began searching for a collaborator. Pamela asked Richard Holbrooke, who had worked with Clark Clifford on his well-received 1991 memoir, *Counsel to the President,* but Holbrooke declined. Arthur Schlesinger, Jr., was also unavailable, as was biographer Robert Lacey. Finally Pamela settled on Christopher Ogden, a forty-seven-year-old diplomatic correspondent for *Time* magazine who had previously covered the White House, served as the magazine's bureau chief in London, and had written a biography of Margaret Thatcher.

Tall, balding, and bespectacled, Ogden was the sort of man with whom Pamela felt comfortable. A woman who worked with him at *Time* said he reminded her of a "tightly rolled English umbrella," and he once described himself to an English friend as an "à la carte Catholic." He was the son of a newspaper editor in Providence, Rhode Island, and his Yale education and overseas posting gave him the patina of a "gentleman journalist."

In embarking on the project, Pamela had consulted with several of her advisers, including Richard Holbrooke, who introduced her to Ogden. For the first time, however, she did not have the full attention of Clark Clifford, who was mired in a banking scandal resulting from his tenure as chairman of the Washington-based First American Bankshares. Investigators had discovered that First American was secretly controlled by the Bank of Credit and Commerce International (BCCI), a $20 billion international operation involved in money laundering and other crimes. Clifford maintained he knew nothing of the link, "a strange defense," noted *Wall Street Journal* columnist Paul Gigot, "for a man whose life has been devoted to shrewd maneuvering in Washington." By the spring of 1991, Clifford had been badly tarnished by a government investigation.

Having chosen her collaborator, Pamela was eager to get out her book fast, so she plunged into interviews with Ogden before publishing arrangements had been made. "They did it against everyone's advice," said Morton Janklow. "She trusted and liked him and thought she could rely on their understanding." That understanding was based on the Clifford-Holbrooke model: She would speak freely and decide later what to print. "It was in the context of, we would discuss it, get it out on the table, go through and sort it out," acknowledged Ogden. "It was going to be her book, with her name six times bigger than mine."

Pamela wrote to friends and relatives that summer asking them to assist her with reminiscences. Mostly she talked into Ogden's tape recorder for what he described variously as forty or fifty hours. They had long walks in the woods at Willow Oaks and on the mountain trails of Sun Valley. She took him around socially and proudly introduced him to her friends. "She was like a girl, like a coquette, not a grown-up woman with her biographer," recalled Barbara Howar after encountering them at a party given by George and Liz Stevens in Washington.

Janklow, who represented both Pamela and Ogden, approached Random House president and publisher Harold Evans in June 1991 and asked for a $2 million advance. Evans countered with $800,000 and Janklow went elsewhere. In July, Janklow told Evans he was about to sign with Putnam but wanted to give Random House a second chance. After what a Random House executive characterized as a "long negotiation," Evans offered $1,625,000, and Janklow struck a deal for the 125,000-word autobiography to be completed by June 1993. Random House based its advance on the expectation that Pamela would provide intimate details about her lovers, her friends, and her marriages. As a result, Evans drafted a publishing contract containing tougher than usual language about the publisher's right to reject a manuscript that was not "a full and frank memoir."

Connected to the Random House document was a sixteen-page collaboration contract that Janklow, a lawyer, drew up for Pamela and Ogden. Based on the contract he wrote for Clifford and Holbrooke, the agreement generously split the advance 50–50 between Pamela and Ogden, and stipulated that all the interviews would be confidential, limited exclusively to her memoir, and would remain Pamela's property indefinitely. Pamela signed the collaboration contract in August 1991 and sent it along to Ogden, who had volunteered to take a lucrative buyout offer from *Time* magazine.

Ogden gave the collaboration agreement to attorney Alan Gelfuso, a high school friend from Providence. The lawyer asked for various changes to ensure that his client would be protected if the project was canceled through no fault of his own. By autumn Ogden still had not signed the document, and none of the parties had signed the publishing agreement.

On October 3, Pamela hosted a dinner at the fashionable Knickerbocker Club in New York. Among those invited were Harold Evans, as well as Ogden and Theodore Sorenson, whom Pamela had hired to help navigate her publishing project. Toward the end of the evening, Pamela asked Evans about a standard clause in the publishing contract stipulating that if Random House rejected the manuscript, she had to pay back the advance either out of her pocket or from the "first proceeds" of a subsequent sale to another publisher. "I don't see why I have to repay any money," she said to Evans. "I think that is very very unfair." Evans said there was nothing he could do about changing the clause.

Underlying Pamela's concern was her growing realization that Random House wanted her to divulge far more than she was prepared to tell. As a result of the big advance, Pamela "panicked," according to Ogden. Her anxiety was heightened by entreaties from her son Winston and other family members, as well as Kitty Hart, not to "lay herself open" by writing a tell-all book. Pamela told friends she really wanted to write a book about politics and public policy that would include her views on Churchill and other leading figures she had known.

She was actually quite determined to demonstrate her importance, especially in Anglo-American relations during World War II. Back in the early 1970s, former NBC correspondent Elie Abel had collaborated with Averell Harriman on a book about the diplomat's war years. At one point, Pamela surprised Abel by asking what he was going to do about her role. He explained that the book was intended to cover Harriman's career as a businessman and diplomat. Since she made no contribution to either undertaking, Abel told her she would be mentioned only in passing. Pamela was obviously displeased that Abel didn't judge her as significant as she felt she had been. Wisely, she declined to press her point with Harriman, but when it came time for her own memoir, she suffered no restraints.

"She wanted to write about what she wanted to write about rather than the things the publishers thought they wanted," said a woman who knew her for decades. In mid-October, Morton Janklow called Evans to explain the pressure Pamela was feeling and to convince Random House to accept a more narrowly focused book. Not surprisingly, Evans said no, and Pamela returned the Random House contract unsigned. Her explanation to friends came out of left field: While watching the televised confirmation hearings on Clarence Thomas's nomination to the Supreme Court, she had been so appalled by the furor over sexual harassment charges against him by Anita Hill that she felt "America is not ready for a serious book by a woman."

She informed Ogden of her decision, telling him she wasn't prepared to write a full biography. Sharing the news with a group of friends at dinner in New York, Janklow's partner Lynn Nesbit speculated that Ogden "will be handsomely paid off by Pamela." Ogden spent some time in early November trying to persuade Pamela to change her mind. According to Ogden, they even discussed "making it an unauthorized book. She said, 'That is an interesting idea,' but she was noncommittal." With the situation unresolved, she left for a two-week holiday in Barbados.

On December 6, Ogden visited her at N Street in an effort to settle their aborted collaboration. He found Pamela "peculiarly tense," he later said. He asked for a payment of $305,000 for his five months of work, including insurance and health benefits—the sum she had originally pledged to give him by that date. Ogden later said that Pamela lost her cool and exclaimed, "We had no contract. Give me back my tapes."

Ogden had no such intention because, as he explained to a friend, "I have no choice. They are the only leverage I have." He based his legal claim on the collaboration contract. "She had signed the agreement," he said, "so I operated on the basis of having an agreement." Sorenson advised Pamela that she had no legal obligation to pay Ogden because he had not signed the document. By holding the tapes hostage, Ogden hoped she would change her mind.

According to her friends, Pamela considered paying Ogden $150,000, which he would probably have accepted. "All I was looking for," he said at the time, "was a clean break. I was not out to break her bank." Although she made no official counteroffer, Pamela asked Holbrooke to request that Ogden return the tapes. Holbrooke urged him not to use them as bargaining chips, but to continue negotiating. By that time, however, Ogden had written Sorenson several times and had received no reply. "I felt I was being totally brushed aside," Ogden recalled.

"The tragedy for her is that Clark Clifford couldn't be on the case," said one of her friends. "This is the kind of case he was ideal for." In fact, Clifford later said he would have been able to persuade her to accommodate Ogden and retrieve the tapes. Several advisers did urge Pamela to settle, but she chose instead to follow Sorenson's hard line: "Winston Churchill's daughter-in-law should never submit to blackmail!" One of her friends recalled, "That got her, invoking the old man." Pamela concluded that Ogden was trying to hold her up, and decided not to pay him a penny.

When Sorenson finally contacted Ogden in mid-January 1992, he handed over the tapes with another plea to resolve their differences. But he kept his own copies, claiming "those interviews are my work." By then Ogden planned to use the tapes to write his own biography of Pamela Harriman. In early January, Richard Stolley, a top *Time* editor, had contacted Little, Brown publishers, also a subsidiary of Time-Warner, on Ogden's behalf. As he continued negotiations with Sorenson, Ogden worked out the terms of his new book deal. "At first Sorenson was very aggressive; there would be no book whatever," said Ogden. "Eventually they did not try to obstruct me from doing a book." In May, Ogden had a contract and what the *Washington Post* called a "hefty six figure advance." (He also reconnected with *Time* as a part-time writer contributing primarily to the overseas edition.) Under the terms of his Little, Brown deal, Ogden would not quote directly from his interviews, but he could use the material in his own words.

Pamela had spoken to Ogden on a privileged basis, with the understanding that their conversations could only be used for her book subject to her approval. "I find it extraordinarily troubling," Janklow later said, "that Mr. Ogden would intend to use information given, in confidence, to him by Mrs. Harriman for use in his own book with Little, Brown." At the same time, many of Pamela's friends agreed that from an ethical as well as a practical standpoint she should have paid Ogden for his trouble instead of slipping out on the technicality of his unsigned collaboration agreement. "It was just stupid and cruel," said one of her bewildered friends. "Everyone has a blind spot."

Like her fights with Leland Hayward's children and her absence of benevolence toward Averell Harriman's heirs, the blind spot again appeared to be financial. "It has so much to do with her not being able to give money away," said Brooke Hayward after the memoir collapsed. Still, Pamela ended up spending more on legal fees to Sorenson than she would have paid to meet Ogden's request for $305,000.

The real problem was her poor judgment at almost every step of the way. "Whatever caused her to decide to do the book, then to jump into a relationship with Ogden prematurely, and then to jump out, she did on her own," said a friend of Pamela's. "She talked to people about what to do and each time she decided on her own and decided badly." Her legal strategy, on the other hand, depended entirely on Sorenson, who told her to be tough when they should have been negotiating and to cave when they should have been tough. Heeding Sorenson's advice was a characteristic mistake. As usual, she hired him based on her instincts, relying on his reputation as an important political figure and friend of the Kennedys.

Once Ogden decided to go forward with his own book, the price of paying him off or fighting him in court rose beyond what Pamela was willing to spend. She was fed up, according to friends, and she wanted to turn her full attention toward the 1992 presidential campaign. Pamela had lost control of her image at the very moment it mattered the most to her. Yet she clung to the idea that the resulting book might ultimately work to her advantage. Despite falling out with her collaborator, her ego would not admit that he might betray her. After all, she had chosen him, and he was a Yale man, like Averell Harriman, with the right credentials. In the summer of 1992 Brooke Hayward observed, "The information she gave him has to be self-serving. He is doing the work and she is letting him because she will be the ultimate beneficiary." Though it was surely self-serving, her account also contained more than she would have disclosed publicly once she had a chance to think it over. Whether through denial or self-delusion, Pamela's mistake, according to a woman who knew her for many years, was that "she didn't realize that he would put in what she didn't want."

Thirty-three

WHEN PAMELA SHUT DOWN her political action committee in December 1990, she told her board that she wanted to be involved in electing a Democratic President in 1992. Yet at the same time she seemed "terribly discouraged" about her role in politics, said a longtime friend. Her subsequent activities seemed to bear out that impression. Early in 1991 she spent most of her time in Barbados, traveling abroad and working with the various foreign policy organizations she supported. She was still involved with Carter Brown, and *White Roses* made her the center of attention at the National Gallery's fiftieth birthday party in February 1991. Beginning that spring, when Pamela turned her attention to her ill-fated memoir, friends began to murmur about a new, "non-political Pam." But as was often the case during difficult periods, Pamela was merely in hibernation, readying herself for the challenge of a presidential campaign.

Traditionally, her preferences for candidates had no ideological basis. She gravitated to personalities who seemed successful. She and Harriman had been on the periphery during the Carter years, and they had stayed aloof from the campaign of Walter Mondale in 1984 on the assumption that he couldn't win. Instead, Pamela focused PamPAC's efforts that year on electing Democrats to the House and Senate. During the primaries, Pamela contributed $1,000 apiece to Ernest F. Hollings and George McGovern even as Mondale, the early front-runner, courted her favor. Once when he was scheduled to meet her for lunch at the Four Seasons Hotel in Washington, she kept him waiting for ten minutes by the concierge desk—a sight that was duly noted in the *Washington Post.*

Pamela's only visible role in the 1984 presidential campaign was her speech at the Democratic Convention in San Francisco—a political payoff for her PamPAC work from Democratic chairman Charles Manatt—along with the brunch she hosted with Walter Shorenstein at his home overlooking the Pacific. Although the Harrimans ultimately backed Mondale as the party's nominee, they neither helped him with fund-raising nor contributed anything to his campaign.

Their single gesture was asking him to be the featured speaker at one of PamPAC's issues evenings in the early summer before the convention. Pamela invited the party's political pros, who expected Mondale to roll up his sleeves and speak candidly about the campaign. Instead, he gave a stock stump speech that deadened the room. "Everyone was dumbfounded," said one participant.

To enliven the follow-up session after dinner, Janet Howard suggested a fifteen-minute talk by one of the guests, Arkansas Governor Bill Clinton, who had served on the PamPAC board in 1981. Clinton spoke passionately about educational reform, thoroughly upstaging the presidential nominee. "Mondale responded by becoming much better," recalled one participant. "But it was Clinton's evening." Afterward, Robert Strauss was heard to say to Harry McPherson: "When I run you for President, I'm not going to let that boy speak the same night you do!" The following November, Mondale lost in a landslide to Ronald Reagan.

After Harriman died in 1986, Pamela could of course decide for herself whom to support for the 1988 presidential nomination to run against Vice President George Bush. Seven Democrats were in the race: Senators Gary Hart of Colorado, Albert Gore, Jr., of Tennessee, Joseph Biden of Delaware, and Paul Simon of Illinois; Massachusetts Governor Michael Dukakis; Missouri Congressman Richard Gephardt; and the Reverend Jesse Jackson. For many months, none of the candidates caught her interest. "Her circle of advisers was all over the map," said Bill Carrick, who ran Gephardt's campaign with Robert Shrum as media adviser. "She had different voices telling her different things."

The field was narrowed before the first primary. Barely a month after he announced his candidacy in April, Gary Hart withdrew when reports of his marital infidelities appeared in the press. Joseph Biden also dropped out after he was accused of plagiarizing a speech by British Labour Party leader Neil Kinnock.

Throughout 1987, Pamela placed bets on all the remaining leading candidates except Dukakis. She made personal contributions of $1,000 apiece to Gore (in July), Simon (in October), and Gephardt (in December). Democrats for the 80's also contributed $5,000 each to Gore, Gephardt, Simon, and Jackson. It was Gore, however, who held her attention.

Handsome, energetic, and focused, Al Gore, then thirty-nine, seemed like the son she had always wanted. His father, Albert Gore, had served three terms as a liberal senator from Tennessee, and young Al had graduated from Washington's prestigious boys school, St. Albans, and Harvard before serving a six-month stint as a journalist for Army publications in Vietnam. He was married to Mary Elizabeth "Tipper" Aitcheson, a vivacious and strong-minded woman he had met as a teenager. Gore won a seat in the House in 1976 and in the Senate in 1984. He compiled a liberal voting record and built a reputation as an expert on defense and environmental issues. Pamela contributed $1,000 to his Senate campaign, and PamPAC donated $10,000.

Gore had been "around quite a bit" at PamPAC's issues evenings, recalled Peter Fenn. He was always respectful of Pamela, although he and his wife were not close to her. Pamela was impressed by Gore's interest in foreign policy. "She likes comers," recalled a Gore consultant. "People she respected said he was really smart, and he staked out issues like arms control. For Al she has a genuine fondness."

Richard Holbrooke and Sandy Berger both got behind Gore's candidacy, and they urged Pamela to do the same as he headed into the New York primary in late April. Michael Dukakis and Jesse Jackson were the front-runners, although Gore had concentrated his efforts on the southern primaries and had done reasonably well there. After his endorsement by New York Mayor Ed Koch, Gore was swept up in Koch's bitter attacks on Jackson, who had alienated many New Yorkers four years earlier by calling the city "Hymietown" and Jews "hymies." Koch said that Jews would have to be "crazy" to vote for Jackson, while Gore accused Jackson of equating the Palestine Liberation Organization with Israel and of naively allying himself with Yassir Arafat and Fidel Castro.

At that moment, Pamela decided to join with Gore on what one of his advisers called "the single worst day of his political life to that point." With the primary less than three weeks away, Gore said in a speech: "We're not choosing a preacher, we're choosing a president." The remark drew an indignant reaction from Jackson, who said, "The Senator should not discriminate against someone because they are a preacher, a priest or a rabbi," and caused New York Governor Mario Cuomo to rebuke Gore for negative campaigning. After the speech, Pamela took her place at Gore's side to announce her endorsement. Her last-ditch gesture went appropriately unnoticed in the New York press; in any case, Gore finished a poor third to Dukakis and Jackson.

When Gore withdrew two days later, Pamela moved to Dukakis. "She's a pragmatist," noted Democratic donor John Hechinger. "She's not lamenting Gore anymore." She did help Gore retire his $2.5 million campaign debt with a fundraiser that reportedly produced $250,000. Still, party professionals remembered Pamela mostly for what seemed a miscalculated and belated endorsement.

Pamela tried to ingratiate herself with the Dukakis camp by giving the winning candidate a dinner at N Street before the July convention. She invited what *Boston Globe* reporter John Robinson termed the "former power crowd, those who have tasted being in but who have been out now these long anguishing years of the Reagan ascendancy." Among the guests were former Secretaries of State Edmund Muskie and Cyrus Vance, former Secretaries of Defense Robert McNamara, Harold Brown, and Clark Clifford, as well as assorted power brokers including Vernon Jordan, Robert Strauss, and Harry McPherson. "There's a lot of advice in this room, and everyone is dying to give it," Strauss told Dukakis during dinner.

But Dukakis chose to ignore Strauss's nudge, staying with his own cadre of advisers. "He never called those people," Janet Howard later complained. More to the point, Dukakis never contacted Pamela, except for money. According to Democratic fundraiser James C. Calaway, Pamela donated $100,000 in soft money that year to the "Democratic Victory Fund," which raised a record $53 million for the campaign. Gifts of that magnitude had become essential to keep her place as a big-time party activist. Her $150,000 for the communications center two years earlier was ancient history. In the world of political fund-raising, well-heeled donors were expected to continue paying their six-figure dues. Pamela's donation made her one of 197 "trustees" who gave $100,000, a group that included Smith Bagley, Blanchette Rockefeller, Thomas Watson, Jr., Walter Shorenstein, and the newspaper heiress Anne Cox Chambers. During the 1988 convention in Atlanta, they were entertained at a series of dinners, took private tours of the Carter Presidential Library, and saw the sights on special trains.

In the autumn Pamela convened a group of party stalwarts for lunch. When she inquired what Dukakis had asked them to do, they each replied, "Nothing." "What did they ask you to do?" one guest asked the hostess. "Nothing," Pamela said. "Mrs. Harriman, in fact, is so offended by the way Dukakis has treated her that she has deliberately gone off to Italy for the duration of the campaign," the *Washington Post* reported.

Pamela had actually harbored some hopes for a reward from Dukakis for her service to the party. When asked back in 1983 what she wanted, Pamela had declared, "Why should there be anything in it for me? To me, if we can get a Democratic Senate and a Democratic President I'm going to retire for the rest of my life." A year later, she switched signals when she responded to speculation that she might become U.S. ambassador in London. "That would be a fun idea, wouldn't it?" she told London's *Daily Mail*. "I doubt if it would happen, but it would be rather amusing to return to one's country of origin." By 1988, however, Pamela had set her sights even higher: a cabinet post, perhaps, or Ambassador to the United Nations. "Now she tells people that she doesn't just want an embassy because the social job has no charm for her," William Walton told *Vanity Fair*'s Marie Brenner that spring.

With George Bush's election, Pamela put her expectations on hold. She continued her PamPAC work through the mid-term elections before shutting the committee down at the end of 1990. For much of 1991 the Republican President seemed invincible following the Persian Gulf War. Only one Democrat, former Massachusetts Senator Paul Tsongas, had announced his candidacy on May 1 as others nervously weighed their options: Gore, Gephardt, and Jackson, along with current and former governors Mario Cuomo of New York, Bill Clinton of Arkansas, Jerry Brown of California, and Douglas Wilder of Virginia, and Senators Tom Harkin of Iowa, Bob Kerrey of Nebraska, and John D. "Jay" Rockefeller IV of West Virginia.

In June, Pamela was telling friends that her candidate was Jay Rockefeller, who had just begun exploring a presidential bid. Al Gore was dealing with the recovery of his eight-year-old son, who had nearly died after being hit by a car two years earlier.

Rockefeller was the nephew of Averell Harriman's old Republican nemesis, Nelson Rockefeller, but the fifty-four-year-old West Virginia senator was a Democrat to the core. As the scion of a great family, Jay Rockefeller embodied the same sort of dogged patrician commitment to public service as Pamela's husband. (Part of that public service included Rockefeller's $34,000 in donations to PamPAC over a decade; PamPAC played the shell game by giving him $10,000, which he hardly needed.) Rockefeller, who stood six feet six, was a graduate of Harvard and played classical piano for relaxation. He showed none of the arrogance that often seems to go with great wealth, but he didn't hesitate to use his fortune to advance his political ambitions. After serving from 1976 to 1980 as governor in West Virginia, he spent a staggering $12 million of his own money on his reelection for another four-year term and an equal amount to capture a Senate seat in 1984. Senator Rockefeller studied diligently and established himself as a leader in health care and family issues. After his reelection in 1990 he emerged as a presidential prospect. To Pamela, he had "leadership quality."

In mid-June 1991, Pamela hosted a conference at Willow Oaks bringing together party strategists, twenty-five major Democratic fundraisers and donors, and a dozen potential presidential candidates. The conference was the inspiration of Democratic National Committee chairman Ronald H. Brown, who organized two days of briefings outlining a strategy for winning the White House. Political strategist Paul Tully used charts, slides, and poll results to show that "George Bush's support is an inch deep," recalled one participant. The party leaders also assured the donors that Democrats would no longer be identified mostly with labor but would represent business as well.

The candidates did not speak formally, although they participated in the general discussions. The donors, who included Shorenstein, Hollywood producer Ted Field, health care executive Hugh Westbrook, Massachusetts manufacturer Steve Grossman, Jay Rockefeller's sister Alida Messinger, Goldman Sachs chairman Robert Rubin, and heiress Penny Pritzger from Chicago, were asked to give or raise $200,000 apiece in soft money.

All twenty-five made the financial commitment and earned the designation of "managing trustee." "Almost everyone gave a minimum of $100,000," said a conference organizer. "A handful wrote out checks for $200,000." Pamela was among those who pledged only to raise the $200,000. She wrote no checks of that magnitude in 1991—the first year in which soft-money contributions had to be disclosed to the Federal Election Commission—or in subsequent years. Her largest single donation was $30,000 in soft money to the DNC in October 1991, and her aggregate contributions to individual federal candidates and party committees amounted to $40,250, bringing her total of hard and soft donations to some $70,000 during 1991 and 1992.

At the meeting's conclusion, Ronald Brown held a press conference outside her house to announce that a "preliminary strategy" for the 1992 campaign had been developed. During a Republican fund-raising dinner that night, President Bush immediately took a shot at "frantic Democrats" who "all go down to Pamela Harriman's farm down there—the bastion of democracy—and come back and tell me that we don't have a domestic program." Pamela seemed to relish her return to the spotlight, even when liberal commentator Michael Kinsley observed that there was something "comical" about the "daughter of a British lord, ex-wife of a Tory prime minister's son," and "widow of a robber baron's son" as "mother superior of the Democratic party."

Jay Rockefeller, meanwhile, seemed to be gaining momentum. He had been received well on a tour of twenty-two states, and polls showed him in second place behind Mario Cuomo, another undeclared candidate. (At the time, Tsongas was still the only official candidate.) But in early August Rockefeller suddenly withdrew from the race, saying that he needed more time to prepare for the presidency. Pamela was in Sun Valley then, and Janet Howard reported to one Democratic donor that she was "very depressed." Soon afterward, however, Pamela's view had shifted to the steely judgment that Rockefeller's rationale showed his weakness.

"I'm helping all of them," Pamela said, when asked by a reporter that September about a possible endorsement. "I push and shove from behind." Although she shied away from a public position, she was focusing on Mario Cuomo, who had coyly declined to attend her Middleburg meeting. (Two weeks after Rockefeller had pulled out, Al Gore quelled speculation about his possible candidacy by declaring he would not run, citing concern for his family.) Governor of New York since 1983, Cuomo was one of the party's most outspoken liberals, highly regarded for his intelligence as well as his eloquence. Pamela had been a fan since Cuomo had given the moving keynote address to the Democratic Convention in 1984 that made him an instant political star—and possible national candidate.

Shortly after the speech, Pamela had called on Phyllis Cerf Wagner, the widow of Leland Hayward's friend Bennett Cerf. Phyllis had gone on to marry former New York City Mayor Robert Wagner and had become active in state Democratic politics. Pamela sought her help in arranging meetings with Cuomo to cement her friendship with the governor. Pamela also gave $25,000 to restore the New York governor's mansion, according to Louis Auchincloss, who chaired the restoration drive. "It was the minimum you might give to the renovation," recalled Auchincloss. "She flew to Albany for a dinner, obviously to give the once-over to the great Cuomo. This was when he was first in the news as a contender. She didn't give $25,000 for nothing. She came to the table to talk."

Pamela began boosting Cuomo as a candidate after he suggested in early October 1991 that he might indeed run. She made only one public utterance on his behalf, however, when Texas Senator Phil Gramm wondered how well the New York governor's ethnicity would play in the South, where "we don't have many Marios." In a remark that showed she didn't understand Gramm's subtext, Pamela lamely retorted that the popularity of the "Super Mario Brothers" video games made voters familiar with the name. On December 20, after more than two months of the public wavering he is famous for, Cuomo announced he would not seek the nomination: New York State's budget problems required his total attention.

The new front-runner was William Jefferson Clinton, who had formally entered the race in October, along with Harkin, Wilder, and Kerrey, once Rockefeller and Gore had bowed out. Pamela had known Clinton for a decade, and she had fond memories of his bravura performance during her Mondale issues evening in 1984. Even more important, Sandy Berger was one of his longtime advisers. After Clinton had been nearly booed off the podium during an interminable speech at the 1988 Atlanta convention, it was Pamela and Berger who took Clinton and his wife Hillary to dinner and offered them words of encouragement.

In the meantime, Clinton had shown himself an accomplished politician with an agile intelligence, a gregarious manner, and a moderate stance on social and economic issues. Like Pamela, he had the ability to create instant intimacy and make someone feel like the most important person in the room. He was also a master of reinvention, a man whose views, according to political columnist Joe Klein, were "always subject to further revision." Pamela compared Clinton's "resilience and inner strength" to the determination of Churchill.

Even as Pamela had quietly advocated Cuomo, she had hedged her bet by donating $1,000 to Clinton on October 18, 1991—her only contribution to a declared candidate that year. Nevertheless, as did many, she had serious doubts about Clinton's electability because of the stories of his extramarital affairs that had followed him publicly since he first considered running for President in 1987. "She was skeptical about Clinton because he had not abided by the Sixth Commandment," said one of his old friends. "There is a certain ironic piquancy to that." But Pamela's concern was more pragmatic than moral. In a conversation with a fellow fundraiser that October, Pamela brought up what she called "the silver zipper question." The fundraiser recalled, "She was not judgmental but sympathetic, and concerned that it would be a problem and that it should go away."

When Cuomo withdrew, Pamela committed to Clinton and began offering him advice about personnel and fund-raising strategies. He seemed headed for a big win in the New Hampshire primary in February 1992 when Gennifer Flowers, a former cabaret singer, announced that she and Clinton had had an affair for twelve years. She made public tape recordings of their telephone conversations. Fearful of another Gary Hart debacle, some leading Democrats discussed bringing in a new candidate like Gephardt, a veteran of the 1988 race, or Texas Senator Lloyd Bentsen, who had been Dukakis's running mate in 1988.

As Clinton aides struggled to contain the damage, Pamela distanced herself from his campaign. When a Clinton worker called to ask for lists she had promised for a Clinton fundraiser, Pamela said, "Let me think it over for forty-eight hours and I'll get back to you." By then Bill and Hillary had gone on *60 Minutes* and he had denied the affair with Flowers. As he admitted that he had caused "pain" in his marriage in the past, Hillary sat stoically at his side. Clinton's apparent candor, and his wife's support, kept his political hopes alive, and he posted a respectable second place in New Hampshire to favorite son Tsongas, with Kerrey, Harkin, and Brown trailing far behind.

Pamela climbed back onto the bandwagon and became one of Clinton's most ardent supporters. In April, she invited him to dinner at N Street, and two months later she hosted a brunch in his honor for major donors and members of his finance committee. "She is pretty starry-eyed about Clinton," said a longtime friend that June. "She says she has always backed him, she has always been a great supporter." "She was not present at the creation, and she had deep misgivings about Clinton all along," said another. "But she can suppress memories of early doubts. She simply will not remember them. Is this self-deception, or is it iron will and the knowledge that she must move on?"

ASIDE FROM THE DISTRACTION of her collaboration and subsequent dispute with Christopher Ogden from May until December 1991, Pamela had been preoccupied throughout the months of the primary campaign with family matters. The high point was a one hundredth birthday celebration she gave in Averell Harriman's memory in mid-November 1991, a round of lunches, dinners, and panel discussions to celebrate the noted diplomat. She commissioned a hagiographical film narrated by Walter Cronkite that excluded any reference to Marie's role in Harriman's life for forty years but included footage of Averell and Pamela looking like lovestruck teenagers. She had financed the film by setting up a "Centennial Film Foundation" with contributions of $46,100 and $25,000 from the Averell and Pamela Harriman Foundation and the Mary Harriman Foundation. For the celebratory dinner, Pamela invited ABC anchorman Peter Jennings to be her master of ceremonies.

An uncomfortable moment came during an afternoon symposium at the Library of Congress when Senator Daniel Patrick Moynihan cut through the encomiums to say that Harriman, his former boss, had been a lousy politician who had badly divided the New York Democratic Party. Some observers recalled Pamela's affront to Moynihan when he had run against Bella Abzug for the Senate and wondered if this was his revenge. Behind the scenes, Pamela fumed that Moynihan had insulted Harriman's memory, and Janet Howard muttered that she would try to erase the Moynihan section from the videotape that she was preparing. That night at dinner, "people were certainly talking sotto voce about what Moynihan had said," recalled a prominent Washingtonian. "Pamela was trying to keep up appearances but you could see the anger still there." To Pamela's relief, the incident never surfaced in any of the glowing newspaper accounts about the celebration.

In March 1992, Pamela traveled to England for the marriage of her twenty-six-year-old grandson Randolph Churchill, an accountant known for his unassuming manner. The service was held at Westerham Church near the home of Winston and Minnie, with a seated wedding luncheon for 250 at Chartwell. The event brought together an assortment of Digbys and Churchills: Pamela's former sister-in-law Mary Soames and her children; Winston's half sister Arabella and her husband, a professional juggler; Pamela's brother Eddie and her younger sister Jaquetta, whom Pamela had not seen in so many years that she failed to recognize her when they met. With her "slightly overemphatic makeup, immaculate clothes and extremely good jewels," as one newspaper described her, Pamela was the inevitable center of attention. Jaquetta Digby James, eight years Pamela's junior, was plump and white-haired, wearing tweeds and sensible shoes. "They were like chalk and cheese," recalled a wedding guest. Jaquetta, a widow with six children, had traveled to England from her home at Torosay Castle on the Isle of Mull in Scotland where she had built a successful tourism business (40,000 visitors a year) presiding over a tea room, gift shop, and miniature railroad.

The wedding was a model of family harmony, but there was an undercurrent of trouble that blew up less than a month later with a headline in Nigel Dempster's *Daily Mail* gossip column: TONGUES WAG OVER CHURCHILL'S BLONDE. Winston Churchill had strayed from his wife again, this time with a forty-four-year-old Manhattanite named Jan Cushing Amory, who was separated from her fourth husband, the socially prominent Minot Amory. They had met the previous August at the Volpi Ball in Venice, where they danced— ironically enough—to the music of Peter Duchin. "We had automatic physical attraction," Jan Amory recalled. "Winston was kissing me on the cheek. Peter Duchin was looking, and Winston was rubbing it in. They were all staring."

The romance played out in the following months with trips to Germany, Belgium, Florida, and Texas, as well as assignations in London and a country hotel at Cliveden, formerly the home of William Astor where John Profumo, British Minister for War, was caught with party girl Christine Keeler in 1963, creating a long-running scandal for the government of Harold Macmillan. "Winston would go on these trips when he was supposed to be in Parliament," said Amory. "He would call his aides and ask what the vote was that day. Then he would call Minnie and she would say, 'What did you vote on?' and he would read it to her."

Pamela had learned of the affair in October 1991 when Winston and Minnie visited her in Washington. Amory had given Winston a pair of David Webb cufflinks—frogs with ruby eyes—that he couldn't wear because they were so distinctive. When he arrived at N Street, he took his mother aside and said, "Hand me these in two days." Pamela replied, "On one condition. You tell me who gave you these." Winston told her, and two days later when he turned fifty-one, she complied, saying, "Happy birthday, Winston darling." Minnie, according to Amory, "kept saying they were the best gift his mother ever gave him." Pamela didn't know Amory, although they had met once at a luncheon in Barbados several years earlier, and Amory had been an early backer of Pam-PAC with a $1,000 donation to the committee's ninetieth birthday party for Averell Harriman.

Pamela maintained her aplomb for a while as Winston brazenly called her from his travels with his lover. "I don't know whether it was to get her approval or what," said Amory. Their phone calls would begin almost flirtatiously; after he inquired how she was, Pamela would reply: "Winston, darling, all the better for hearing your wonderful voice." But the tone would quickly shift when he made his whereabouts known. "He would say, 'Mother, I am here with Jan in Dallas,' " recalled Amory. "Her only comment was, 'Enjoy it while you can.' "

Three weeks before Randolph's wedding, Winston pushed his mother too far when he met her at Claridges in London to announce his intention to divorce Minnie and marry Amory. "When he told his mother, she turned dead white and started to shake," said Amory. " 'You will no longer be welcome in my house,' she said." When she regained her composure, Pamela tried a differ-ent approach, reminding him of Minnie's skills as a mother and parliamentary wife popular with his constituents. "Winston told me it was the first time Pam raved about Minnie," said Amory. Pamela told Winston he needed Minnie for the upcoming parliamentary election, and she urged him to concentrate on his son's marriage.

Back in Washington Pamela called Arthur Schlesinger, who was also an old friend of Jan Amory's. "She told Arthur she didn't approve of me," said Amory. "Even Arthur doesn't say anything nice about Jan," Pamela later told Winston. "Pamela was very nervous about the affair," said one of Pamela's Washington friends. "She was upset, and she was concerned about Winston's career." Pamela asked Schlesinger to convey her disapproval to Amory, which he did over lunch in Manhattan. Amory chastised Schlesinger for failing to defend her to Pamela. Instead of backing down, Amory renewed her determination.

Nigel Dempster had raised the stakes by making the affair public. At that point, according to her friends, Pamela played the financial card, telling Winston that if he proceeded she would disinherit him and leave everything to his children. Although ready to break up his family and sacrifice his political future, the thought of being cut out of Pamela's will gave Winston pause. He was feeling particularly vulnerable financially at the time. As an investor in the Lloyds of London insurance company, he had lost $300,000 that he was only partly able to offset, he said, by "hitting the American lecture circuit and writing articles."

For the next several weeks, Winston equivocated with Amory while Minnie offered her forgiveness. Amory took the Concorde to London in late May for dinner with Winston at Mosseman's, a luxurious dining club. When they met at the entrance, a *Daily Mail* photographer caught them kissing, a scene Dempster described in his column as "a pleasing sight of passion." A furious Winston called Amory to accuse her of setting him up. With that, the relationship ended, much to Pamela's relief. "Like mother, like son, he comes by it honestly," she remarked to one Washington friend, who said it was the only time she had heard Pamela say anything witty, much less self-deprecating. What Pamela would not —or could not—admit was the extent to which Winston's dalliance with Amory brought out the differences between mother and son: his need for approval and her emotional aloofness, his callow impulsiveness and her keen calculation, his weakness and her strength.

BY THE TIME of the Democratic Convention in July 1992, Pamela was fully focused on the Clinton campaign. She was thrilled that Clinton had chosen Al Gore as his running mate. When asked some months later if she had suggested Gore to Clinton, the *Washington Post* noted, "She's almost too quick in saying 'no.' 'I mean,' she teases, laughing, 'You mustn't ask that question.' " Her coyness aside, there is no evidence that she played a decisive role in Gore's selection. He was one of five finalists chosen by Clinton from a list of forty names assembled by a search team. Clinton sought the opinions of his advisers and party leaders before a consensus crystallized for Gore. Pamela was among many who were asked.

Pamela arrived at convention headquarters in New York City as a member of the Virginia delegation, but her role was Democratic Party big shot. As a managing trustee of the party, she had access to Room 200, a private lounge off the convention floor where she could mingle with other wealthy contributors. "At first it was very limited," said a fellow trustee, "but by Thursday everyone had heard of it and somehow everyone was there. Pam dropped by and found out it wasn't exclusive enough."

But she turned up at one party after another. She started the social whirl with a Sunday morning brunch she gave in honor of Robert Strauss, whose Democratic credentials were undiminished by his status as George Bush's Ambassador to Russia. She sat with her delegation on the convention floor, she and Al Gore gave talks to the Democratic governors, and she appeared on television, seated with the Clintons, flashing her 150-watt smile. "I haven't felt this good in a long long time," Pamela told a *Washington Post* reporter.

Though she was certainly not a part of their inner circle, Pamela had developed an easy relationship with the presidential nominee and his wife. During the campaign, they "sought her views on people or jobs or positions where they had reason to think she was knowledgeable," said one high-ranking Clinton campaign aide. "They did this with a wide range of people. It would have been dumb not to ask Pamela. They cut a broad swath, and Pamela was part of that." Both Clintons, said the aide, "treat Pamela with respect and appreciation and affection, even though she is not their oldest and best friend. Bill and Hillary didn't sit down and track when her involvement began. They don't keep score in even a larger sense. They understand that even if you take a different viewpoint, there is always a tomorrow." The essential link between Pamela and the Clintons was Sandy Berger. "At every point in 1992, Sandy was key," said a friend of Berger's, "preventing her from making mistakes, representing her in the best light to the Clintons, creating possibilities, protecting her."

Typically, Pamela had not focused on Hillary in the beginning, but during the presidential campaign Pamela would acknowledge her powerful position. With an age difference of twenty-seven years, the two women seemed to have little in common besides a fierce allegiance to the Democratic Party. Educated at Wellesley and Yale Law School, Hillary was a committed professional and longtime feminist. She had grown up in a closely knit midwestern family rooted in traditional values that were far removed from Pamela's aristocratic origins and the fast life in London and Paris. Hillary also possessed the analytical capability and intellectual self-confidence that Pamela lacked; her sureness contrasted with Pamela's reliance on the views of others.

Yet they shared certain important traits that created mutual respect: discipline, focus, industriousness, pragmatism, and an appetite for power. Consequently, Pamela came to regard Hillary "more as she would a man," according to a campaign aide who observed them together. Hillary was accustomed to equal status with important men; in that way she was unlike the wives of other prominent politicians Pamela had cultivated. The two women "have good rapport," said the campaign aide. "Rather than getting distracted that someone's manner might not be hers, Hillary is not irritated or put off by stylistic differences." Another aide who spent time with them noted, "Hillary was not sucking up to or intimidated by Mrs. Harriman."

That summer Pamela made her N Street home available to the Clintons several times for meetings. During one August afternoon, Clinton met with the Senate and House leadership in a downstairs parlor while Pamela sat with Hillary and her principal aide Brooke Shearer in the upstairs sitting room as they discussed press coverage of the campaign. (Shearer and her husband Strobe Talbott, then Washington bureau chief for *Time,* were longtime friends of the Clintons.) "Mrs. Harriman was just listening," said another visitor. "She was sympathetic." Noted a Clinton campaign official, "Pamela calls the Clintons by their first names, makes them feel welcome in her home, and feels comfortable enough to come in and out of rooms where they are, to sit and talk, but also to allow privacy when she feels they want it, to make phone calls, to rest, take a shower, have private meetings."

Pamela was working hard on her biggest and most elaborate fundraiser ever—a two-tier event in Middleburg on Saturday, September 12, that was intended to raise more than $1 million in hard and soft funds for the Clinton-Gore campaign. The biggest donors—those who gave $10,000 and above to the "Democratic Victory Fund"—would attend a luncheon and afternoon briefing with senior campaign advisers at Middleburg's Red Fox Inn. That evening they would gather at a cocktail reception and dinner on the lawn at Willow Oaks along with a substantially larger group of donors at $1,000 a ticket.

The event was to be the capstone of a highly successful Democratic financial drive. By September, the Democrats had taken in more than $43 million, largely in soft money, $18 million of that in August alone. Robert Farmer, treasurer of the Clinton-Gore campaign, was predicting they might exceed the $53 million in soft money collected in 1988. The campaign was so "flush with cash," Democrats told the *New York Times* in early September, that "Clinton would not have to appear at any fund raising events after this month." Four days following Pamela's event, Ted Field—one of the party's top five individual contributors—was planning to raise another $1.1 million at a Clinton-Gore dinner featuring a performance by Barbra Streisand at Greenacres, his $39 million Hollywood estate.

The Middleburg event was underwritten by the Democratic National Committee, but Janet Howard handled the planning. Some seven hundred guests were expected, and Howard threw herself into the maze of "interior seating" for each table at the dinner. Overseeing a staff of fifteen at N Street, she spent the three weeks before the event "working more intensely than any human could," recalled a volunteer. With a week to go, more checks were coming in than had been anticipated, and Howard collapsed from the strain, suffering from tremors and paralysis in her right arm. When the ambulance arrived and Howard was strapped into a stretcher, "they took her down the steps," recalled a staff member, "and she was grasping the rails and shouting, 'This is my event and I am in control.' " At that point, Melissa Moss, finance director of the Democratic National Committee, stepped in with her own people. Howard returned to work with her arm in a sling, determined to assign everyone seats at the dinner even as the guest list ballooned to twelve hundred.

At noon on the 12th, a cool and bright late summer day, more than 150 elite donors sat down for lunch at the Red Fox Inn. Between them they had contributed or pledged $1.7 million. Among the most generous were IBM's Thomas Watson ($50,000); Joan Challinor, an heir to the Knight-Ridder newspaper fortune ($40,000); cellular phone mogul Mark Warner ($20,000); auto manufacturer J. J. Cafaro ($20,000); and George Krupp, a defector from George Bush's team of big donors, who gave $50,000 at Janet Howard's urging. New York financier Felix Rohatyn gave $10,000 on top of the $100,000 in soft money he had hurriedly donated in August when his candidate, Ross Perot, quit the race. After briefings by Bob Squier, Robert Reich, Sandy Berger, Ira Magaziner, and more, the elite group repaired to Willow Oaks for a private reception in Pamela's house with the Clinton-Gore staff. Dressed in a black and white silk dress, her ears glittering with large diamonds, Pamela was gracious and welcoming, seemingly unruffled by the logistical problems unfolding nearby.

At that moment, more than a thousand guests were standing in lines for as long as an hour in the dusty fields at the Glenwood Racing Course several miles away, waiting for shuttle buses to take them to Willow Oaks. There they trooped around Pamela's swimming pool and gardens and milled under a large white tent for drinks and skimpy hors d'oeuvres. Despite all of Janet Howard's efforts, the seating plan collapsed, and guests thronged to an adjacent tent to find places for dinner. Many guests were stranded outside the tent with no seats until extra tables and chairs were brought in, and the caterer came up with several hundred more dinners.

Pamela avoided the cocktail tent. As she stood in her living room watching one bus after another disgorge the crowds, she said, "What is going on with all these people? Why is there such a backlog?" She seemed unaware until that moment that the dinner was oversubscribed. She paced the floor, studying her remarks, and brightened only with the arrival of Al Gore. But when he left to greet the crowd in the tent, she remained. "She didn't work the crowd at all," said one organizer of the event. "She was in a bad mood all night."

Out in the dinner tent, Washington lawyer Vernon Jordan, Clinton's closest African-American adviser, stood before the boisterous crowd and urged everyone to sit down. "Now this is one plantation I'd like to buy," he said. "Maybe if Clinton wins, I can do it." Pamela finally made her way to the microphone for introductory remarks. Her hands pressed against the Plexiglas podium, she read slowly from a prepared text, observing that the Democrats had been "through the fire" as she affected a Churchillian curl of her lip for emphasis. During dinner she sat between composer Marvin Hamlisch, who later sang several of his own songs, and Congressman John Dingall, while Clinton—minus Hillary, who was campaigning elsewhere—was seated with Felix Rohatyn, Joan Challinor, and retired Arkansas Senator J. William Fulbright. Even after the main course was served, the guests wandered, and Pamela tried to quiet them. "Bill, you can sit down too," she said, smiling through her stern nanny voice as Clinton chatted with a group of well-wishers near his table. Her familiarity seemed a mark of triumph: Who could speak to the Democratic nominee that way before a crowd of one thousand?

Clinton and Gore praised Pamela effusively. Gore called her "the first lady of the Democratic Party of America." Perhaps mindful of the week's calamities, both men also singled out Janet Howard, "someone whose name is rarely mentioned," for commendation. Gore spoke smoothly without notes, rolling out a quote from Gandhi and recounting anecdotes from the campaign trail. Confident and relaxed, Clinton invoked the difficulties that faced Abraham Lincoln and Franklin Roosevelt and pointed toward the opportunities of the post–Cold War era. The Bush people were the "things could be worse" crowd, he observed, while the Clinton-Gore people were the "things could be better" crowd. "It's time for America to reward those who work hard and play by the rules," he said. Yet just a few feet away was Clinton's hostess, who had told an interviewer only the month before, "It's a great thing in life if you make your own rules. People respect you for it and abide by it."

Throughout the evening, Pamela seemed curiously anxious and disengaged. At the conclusion of the speeches, Ron Brown, Al and Tipper Gore, and Bill Clinton wrapped their arms around each other's waists and swayed to Ray Charles's "America the Beautiful" while Pamela stood slightly apart, grinning and clapping mechanically. Finally, when Brown pulled her into their foursome, she threw back her head and let loose her famous wide-open-mouth laugh. The tension had broken, and she knew she had a significant financial success that sealed her prospects. She had fulfilled her compact as a "managing trustee" and then some.

"We raised $3.2 million in one night!" Pamela later proclaimed. She was off by more than a million. By the evening of the 12th, the Democratic National Committee had received $1,386,266 and had pledges for an additional $1,170,500, for a total of nearly $2.6 million. But $400,000 of that came from a group of Floridians whose own fundraiser had been canceled because of Hurricane Andrew, so the actual amount raised by the Middleburg evening was $2.2 million. The DNC controlled the budget and kept expenses low by using numerous volunteers and offering few frills; local vineyards donated the wines, and the flowers for the centerpieces came from Pamela's gardens. Even at $2.2 million, however, Pamela's haul for the Democrats was one of the biggest ever, and her achievement pointed once again to the power of her mystique.

Pamela remained in the campaign limelight largely through her position as a director on the Presidential Debate Commission. She traveled to Kansas City, Richmond, Virginia, and East Lansing, Michigan, for the three televised match ups between Clinton and Bush—the only director to do so besides the two commission chairmen. She would arrive early in the afternoon to inspect the set, introduce herself to technicians, and make herself available for press interviews. Before the debates began she would be seated front and center, ready for her introduction as a commission member to the audience. She took her role very seriously and spoke of it often to Washington friends.

After voting in Middleburg on November 3, Pamela and Janet Howard flew to Little Rock, where Pamela watched the election returns with the Gores and a group of major Democratic contributors. Because of the presence of independent candidate Ross Perot, Clinton's victory in the popular vote was narrow, with 43 percent compared to 38 percent for Bush and 19 percent for Perot. But Clinton got 357 electoral votes to Bush's 168, and for the first time in a dozen years, a Democrat had captured the White House. The next morning Pamela went to breakfast with Clinton's finance council, a gathering that one participant described as a "love-in." But Pamela didn't tarry. She had important business to attend to in Washington: an interview with the *Washington Post*.

The resulting article two days later had a banner headline in the newspaper's Style section: PAMELA HARRIMAN, LIFE OF THE PARTY, a punning description that later turned up as the title of Christopher Ogden's book. Illustrated with a large photograph of Pamela and the President-elect, the article celebrated her work for the Democrats when they were out of power and her role in their resurgence. "The phones haven't stopped ringing at her Georgetown offices, people calling to congratulate her for having the passion, the commitment, the instincts that brought the Democrats back from the dead," reported the *Post*. "She was the one, they keep telling her with unqualified praise, who had hung in there so long." More than just a fundraiser, she was portrayed as a major player who was being taken very seriously by no less than the President-elect. It was the story line that Pamela had been honing for years. "The *Post* story helped her recreate herself," remarked one of her old friends. "Everything about her was told in a more respectful manner. It was as if she had stepped through a door."

CHAPTER
Thirty-four

WHILE TAKING HER BOWS in the *Washington Post*, Pamela disavowed any desire for a position in the Clinton administration. Asked about the oft-repeated question, "What's in it for her?" she retorted, that was "the sort of thing I'm up against. I really hate that." As for her statement a decade earlier that if the Democrats recaptured the White House, she would retire, she replied, "I think that's probably about right. I certainly don't want to leave Washington. I mean, I haven't waited to get a President for 12 years and then leave Washington."

Pamela had already let top Clinton advisers know that she wanted to be named Ambassador to France. Although there was speculation in the newspapers that she would be tapped for Ambassador to Britain, Pamela told friends privately that London was out of the question. She didn't feel she would be taken seriously there, and her unpredictable son Winston could have caused her problems.

Pamela spent Thanksgiving with her stepdaughter Kathleen and family at the Harriman estate at Arden. When asked if she were interested in Paris, she said, "Good God, no, it would be difficult to go to Paris as a single woman. The action will be in Washington." Yet the same weekend Pamela had a long conversation with Robert Shrum. "I told her I thought she would be offered France, and she didn't quarrel with me," recalled Shrum. "She seemed interested in taking it. She knew that it seemed inevitable."

Since no one had paid any attention four years earlier when she floated the idea of a cabinet post, Pamela had decided that what she once called a "social job" in France would suit her very well. The decade she had spent in Paris during the 1950s had not been entirely happy or successful. To return as ambassador would be sweet vindication. "It would be such a revenge over the very people who didn't think she was fit to be seen," said Sandy Bertrand, her Parisian friend from those days. By the time Clinton was elected, many French socialites and politicians had adopted a tolerant and even admiring view of her earlier days in Paris. Now they were fascinated by her wealth and her glamour.

In the years after Harriman's death, Pamela had visited Paris frequently, keeping old friendships in good repair and making new contacts. The night of her Middleburg fundraiser, one top contributor was struck by how intensely she was following the upcoming referendum in France on the Maastricht Treaty to unify European economic, political, and defense policies. "She felt the French would squeak by with a yes vote," said the contributor—a prediction that turned out to be correct. "It is signed and sealed for her to go to Paris," said a longtime friend several days later.

That may have been an overly optimistic assessment, but Pamela's campaign for the job was certainly steaming along. Once Sandy Berger knew Pamela wanted the job and was willing to undergo the confirmation process, he began lobbying Clinton on her behalf. Pamela made her wishes known to her close allies on Capitol Hill, who in turn would call key Clinton aides to say that she had to be taken care of. "It was nothing as overt as her calling up and asking them to make the call," said a source close to the Clinton-Gore transition team. "It was done lightly. She didn't need to do much. The key was Sandy, and that she had so many friends." Berger, continued the same source, "got the job for her. He bypassed the system, as an assistant to Clinton with a personal relationship stretching back twenty years. He put it on the line and it moved very fast." For Berger, securing the job of Pamela's dreams was the least he could do for the benefits he had derived from associating with her; he would get his reward too, an appointment as Clinton's deputy national security adviser.

It was essential that Pamela not go public. Other Democratic benefactors such as billionaire Anne Cox Chambers, who had previously served as Ambassador to Belgium, were on the short list for Paris as well. Pamela "had to never appear to be seeking it because if she was turned down, she had to reserve her position at the best table in town," said one of her friends. So she used the Court of St. James's job as a straw man, knocking it down by pretending that she wanted to stay put. "She will have impact and influence without a job," Robert Shrum told *New York* magazine in January. "There's no reason to think she'll do anything besides talk to the President—which is pretty important." Nevertheless, Washington continued to buzz with possible positions she might take—from chief of protocol to membership on the foreign intelligence advisory board. The conventional wisdom in press accounts was the certainty that she would continue to be a "leading host" in the Clinton administration.

As if to underscore that role—one that she had ironically been seeking to escape for many years—Pamela threw a highly publicized buffet dinner on Thursday, November 19, in honor of the Clintons. It was the second in a pair of parties for the President-elect on his maiden trip to Washington following his election. The first, the night before hers, was at the home of Vernon Jordan, now the chairman of the administration's transition team. That gathering, for forty friends and political allies, was described as "warm and private," and featured heartfelt toasts by Clinton and Jordan.

Pamela's party had started out small but quickly ballooned to nearly one hundred guests as "scores of VIPs clawed and scratched . . . to get themselves on the invitation list," according to the *Washington Post*. To accommodate the overflow, Pamela had a heated tent installed on her terrace. In contrast to the Jordan evening, which she had not attended, Pamela's party had an "official" feel, with two-thirds of the guests from the Democratic ranks in the House and Senate, along with such old-line Georgetown stalwarts as Evangeline Bruce, who Pamela could count on to provide a detailed account to her British upper-class friends. Wearing a form-fitting black dress spangled with amber sequins, Pamela greeted Bill and Hillary Clinton at her door in a blaze of television lights. Hillary spun off to work the crowd on her own as Pamela stuck with Clinton for the entire night, "clasping his hand firmly in hers," according to the *New York Times,* steering him from room to room, her "pink-faced and smiling" trophy.

It was Pamela, not the President-elect, who occupied center stage, simply for having him in her home. "In many ways the two parties were celebratory for Pam and Vernon," said a top Clinton campaign official. "Really it was a coming-out party for the two of them, an expression of their delight and enthusiasm at the outcome." The next morning's *Washington Post* quoted one "non-invitee" who called Pamela's dinner "the night of the living dead. It is the old line Washington establishment, that's all it is. It's a visit to Madame Tussaud's." The *Post*'s coverage threw Pamela into a swivet. "She was unhappy because they did such a nice thing about the Jordan party," said a friend who spoke to her that day. "She had opened up her house to more people and had been criticized. She didn't think the party went that well because it reinforced the stereotypes. The import was that she wasn't part of the new social scene, the Clinton social group, but was one of the has-beens, and not at the center. The Jordan party was the happening crowd, and hers was yesterday's people."

Pamela's disappointment only reaffirmed her desire to head for France as soon as possible. By the time of the inauguration, she was winking and nodding to friends that Paris was imminent. "I knew there was a suggestion of it, I guess, in January, and I was surprised," she later fibbed to the *International Herald Tribune*'s Joseph Fitchett. Publicly she continued to insist that she had no special ambition.

On March 23, 1993, Clinton announced Pamela Harriman's nomination as U.S. envoy to France: the first woman named to that post. The *New York Times* described her as "an accomplished political operator with long established networks of rich and powerful friends on both sides of the Atlantic." The *Washington Post* reported that she was already "winning hearts" in Paris, where she was regarded as "the most important grande dame in Washington after the *Post*'s Katharine Graham." Tom Foley exulted to *People* magazine that "no one in this country can take greater credit for winning the White House than Pamela," a burst of hyperbole that seemed to ignore the role of such strategists as James Carville, not to mention the political skills of Bill and Hillary Clinton.

Other early press reports dismissed Pamela as a socialite with few credentials other than service to the Democratic Party. "She has no diplomatic experience of her own and will be going to Paris at a time of rising trade tensions between the U.S. and France," noted the *Wall Street Journal*. Ross Perot denounced the appointment as an example of "what's wrong with the system." After castigating his Republican predecessors for rewarding political fundraisers with ambassadorial positions, Clinton appeared to be doing the same thing. "Mrs. Harriman's most obvious asset," wrote Deborah Orin in the *New York Post,* was "her skill at raising political megabucks . . . a skill that you'd think would be devalued in the Ross Perot era of outrage over the corrupting influence of money in politics."

In a front-page story, France's *Le Figaro* hailed her as a "powerful king maker," while much of the French press couldn't resist zeroing in on her titillating past, with *L'Express* describing her as "a cross between Lady Hamilton and Moll Flanders" and *Paris Match* calling her "one of the most subtle seductresses of the century." Given the inbred French antipathy for the English, there was surprisingly little grousing about Pamela's country of origin—perhaps because she had become so thoroughly American.

Pamela adored the publicity. When a Parisian friend wrote to congratulate her, she responded by sending the November 1992 profile from the *Washington Post*. "After the nomination she spent a lot of time collecting press clippings and reading them to people," said one of her friends.

Reaction among the Parisian upper crust ranged from amusement to dismay to giddy expectation. One joke had Pamela "sleeping in a Rothschild bed legally for the first time," a reference to the U.S. Embassy Residence at 41 rue du Faubourg St. Honoré, which had been built by Elie's great-uncle, Baron Edmond de Rothschild, and which still displays the Rothschild monogram on its doors. A favorite Pamela joke at the exclusive Traveller's Club was off-color: "A Greek tycoon told Pamela Churchill, 'If I had everything I spent on you I could buy a tanker,' to which she replied, 'If I had all that you spent *in* me I could float it.' "

"A lot of French were puzzled," said an American with numerous friends in Parisian society. "Old French conservative families thought it was insulting not to find a decent American. Why send an English woman of notorious background?" Prominent among those offended were friends of Liliane de Rothschild, who announced with a laugh, "That makes one embassy where I don't have to go!" Others who knew Pamela in the old days welcomed her arrival. "Pam had many romances, but French people are very permissive," said a well-born Parisian acquaintance. "As long as you are elegant, Paris is not a city that will judge."

Shortly after the announcement, Pamela began cramming for the job like a studious schoolgirl. Each day, often accompanied by Jean Kennedy Smith, the ambassador-designate for Ireland, she went off to Foggy Bottom for the standard course of studies for new envoys. She buried herself in her briefing books, toting them out to Middleburg when she had company for the weekend. "She stunned all the pros with her seriousness and commitment," said a veteran diplomat who met with her. "She was deeply into doing her homework, and she was not only interested in the glamorous things but in corn glutens and civil aviation." She met with former ambassadors Arthur Hartman, who had served under Jimmy Carter, and Walter Curley, George Bush's appointee. Her first priority in debriefing Curley was finding out the cost of running the embassy, particularly how much she would be required to spend personally.

To supplement her schoolwork, Pamela set up day-long seminars with French experts Stanley Hoffman of Harvard and Nicholas Wahl of New York University. Wahl, whose duties included familiarizing her with trade and economic issues, shrewdly observed, "She has this inborn intuition about power and what's on people's agenda." At the suggestion of Hoffman and Arthur Schlesinger, Jr., Pamela took the unusual step of hiring a private bilingual speechwriter to work for her at the embassy. She arranged to bring Janet Howard as her executive assistant. At first, Pamela balked at keeping the highly respected deputy chief of mission, Avis Bohlen, whose father, Charles "Chip" Bohlen, had worked for Averell Harriman in Moscow and later served as Ambassador to the Soviet Union and France. Pamela told her various advisers that she preferred a man in that position, but they persuaded her to hang on to Bohlen.

On May 4 at 2:15 P.M. Pamela entered Room 419 at the Dirksen Senate Office Building, a large, sterile chamber with an arched ceiling and walls paneled in blond wood. Immaculately groomed, she wore a kelly green linen suit, a long paisley silk scarf in shades of muted green and brown, a choker of gray pearls and matching gray pearl and diamond earrings. On her right shoulder she had fastened a gold brooch in the shape of an eagle. Janet Howard followed, holding her boss's briefcase, along with two aides, Peter Swiers of the Atlantic Council and Wendy Sherman of the State Department.

As she settled into her chair, the television lights snapped on, and two TV cameras aimed toward her as seven photographers clustered around with strobes flashing. Pamela seemed unperturbed, twinkling and chatting with well-wishers, holding her smile in a state of suspended animation, rotating her head slightly to offer various camera angles. Observing her closely from the audience was a lineup of Washington socialites that included Oatsie Charles and Nuala Pell, wife of committee chairman Claiborne Pell. With two of the women in sunglasses, they looked like the front row at a Bill Blass fashion show. None was a close friend of Pamela's; they had come to watch her perform. At a nearby table Lady Renwick, the French wife of the British ambassador, scribbled notes and whispered to Pamela's friend Patsy Preston.

As the Democratic senators filed in, Pamela rose to greet them at their horseshoe-shaped table in the front of the room. Virginia's Charles Robb planted a kiss on her right cheek. Joseph Biden said loudly, "Madame Ambassador, how are ya? It'll be a piece of cake." Paul Simon patted her on the shoulder. Claiborne Pell was in Moscow, so Biden would chair the proceedings. The only other significant absentee was Daniel Patrick Moynihan, estranged from the widow of his onetime mentor.

Pamela had greased the way with her campaign contributions to the committee's Democrats—an aggregate of $112,704 from 1980 through 1992. PamPAC had given Pell $10,000, Biden $15,000, Moynihan $5,100, Robb $6,000, Christopher Dodd $11,000, John Kerry $4,000, Harris Wofford $1,000, Paul Simon $27,000, and Paul Sarbanes $25,104. From her own pocket Pamela had given $3,000 to Kerry, $2,000 to Wofford, $1,000 to Pell, $2,000 to Simon, and $500 to Dodd. She also claimed to have raised $100,000 at a fund-raising reception for Kerry at her Georgetown home in 1989. Only two senators missed out on Pamela's charity: Harlan Mathews, appointed the previous year to fill Al Gore's seat in Tennessee; and Wisconsin's Russell Feingold, an unconventional long shot elected in 1992 after PamPAC closed. At one point during the hearings, Republican Jesse Helms read out a list of Democratic senators supported by PamPAC that failed to include Biden's name. "Where's Biden?" asked Biden. "I'll have to reconsider my position!" "You didn't ask!" Pamela retorted playfully as laughter rippled through the hearing room.

Pamela knew she would sail through the proceedings easily, that her Senate friends would band together and protect her from even the hint of a tough question. In her opening statement, she emphasized the foreign policy credentials she had accumulated: her membership in the Council on Foreign Relations and other policy organizations, her speeches and writings on international issues, and her "many meetings" with foreign leaders.

"My own firsthand knowledge of France goes back to 1936–1938 when I studied at the Sorbonne in Paris," she said of the period that actually lasted about six months. She spoke with comparable drama about World War II, when she "watched . . . Charles de Gaulle fight for the fate of France," and about her postwar decade in Paris "when NATO and the Marshall Plan were born." No matter that the closest she got to these momentous events was the odd dinner-party conversation in Paris and London.

The senators were fawning, but she was still visibly nervous; she told a friend that she had hardly slept the night before. Addressing the committee, she spoke with minimal expression. Her basso Churchill voice seemed stilted and at times halting, her manner somehow vulnerable. The Democratic senators responded with fulsome praise.

Charles Robb, son-in-law of Lyndon Johnson and no stranger to bombast, gave her an effusive introduction that knowing observers interpreted as a kind of penance. Following the acrimonious Clarence Thomas–Anita Hill battle in 1991, Robb had voted to confirm Thomas as a Supreme Court Justice, a Democratic apostasy that prompted Pamela to condemn him publicly. "I think he's dug his own grave," she growled to a *Washington Post* reporter at the time. Climbing out as fast as he could, Robb told the Senate Foreign Relations Committee that Pamela was "extraordinary," "distinguished," and possessed "charm, intellect and grace." He concluded by observing, without a hint of levity, "I suspect there are many world leaders that would envy the career that Pamela Harriman has had in terms of the contact with the people who shape and mold history over the course of most certainly the last half of the 20th century and even beyond that."

Biden, lacking any evident irony, struck an accidentally suggestive note with his first question: What was Pamela's opinion of what "only the French could call . . . cohabitation?" He was referring to the divided government that followed French elections the previous month, resulting in a Socialist President, François Mitterrand, and a conservative Prime Minister, Edouard Balladur. Fixing her intense gaze on Biden, Pamela replied, "I think the . . . uh . . . Balladur government . . . has expressed its opinion that it will continue the foreign policy . . . uh . . . principles of the last government, and there is no reason to think that there will not be perhaps even be a betterment of our relations." She was measuring her words by the teaspoon, taking care to avoid any gaffes that would produce headlines. Biden obligingly led her through a series of safe questions that allowed her to show some knowledge of trade and economics. "I believe in this world of instant communications, sometimes voice to voice is better than fax to fax," said Pamela.

Even Jesse Helms, the fierce conservative Republican from North Carolina, turned to Jell-O in Pamela's presence. One of his favorite ploys was needling and obstructing ambassadorial appointees who seemed too liberal, but on this day he rambled on about his trip to the grave site of Winston Churchill and complimented Pamela on her son, "a very handsome and dashing young member of Commons." Not once but twice he told her he thought she would do a "good job." He confused her membership in the Monet Society with support for Jean Monnet, the French diplomat who helped organize the European Economic Community. Pamela looked bewildered until Janet Howard tore over and whispered in her ear. *"Ohhhwwww, it's Claude* MOH-nay," Pamela said, her voice suddenly booming with gleeful condescension. "Senator, it's the *painter,* the *artist.* His home is in France. It's called Giverny, where Claude Monet lived and painted, and I have given a contribution to Giverny to help restore his home." When the laughter subsided, Helms offered several perfunctory queries. The last of these seemed innocuous enough, but it spoke to a matter that Pamela would never admit was already nagging her. Calling her a "delightful and generous hostess," Helms asked, "Are you prepared to supplement with personal funds?" "Yes, Senator," she replied, "whatever is necessary." "It will be necessary," said Helms.

Less than an hour after she sat down, Pamela's hearing ended with a salute from Biden, who predicted she would do a "phenomenal job." "Thank you, Senator," Pamela replied. "I'll do my best." Pamela hosted a small reception in an adjacent room, where a line of people waited patiently to shake her hand. "Pam seemed rather emotional," said Ina Ginsburg, a Washington writer and socialite. "I could see it in her face. It was unusual, almost tearful. She seemed genuinely moved." Later that day the committee unanimously recommended her appointment, and the Senate approved it three days later.

The long goodbye began with a string of celebrations in Pamela's honor. She had her hairdresser Eivind at the house every day, and even her dermatologist Thomas Nigra, a specialist in treating wrinkles, made some house calls. Investment banker John Whitehead and his wife Nancy Dickerson led off the festivities with a dinner at the Hay-Adams Hotel. Katharine Graham, Vernon and Ann Jordan, French Ambassador Jacques Andreani, and Washington lawyer Lloyd Cutler and his wife Polly also hosted parties; but the biggest event was a dinner dance given by Sir Robin Renwick at the British Embassy.

Renwick toasted his former countrywoman as a "great lady," and Pamela made a disjointed speech about going to Paris "for the third time." She began with her familiar touchstones, her two previous sojourns in Paris, along with the "woah" against the "Nahzis" with Churchill, and ended by reading, in surprisingly rusty French, a 1941 letter from "my great friend" Charles de Gaulle that had accompanied a biography of the Duke of Marlborough for her infant son, a descendant of the duke. The book, de Gaulle had explained, was "one of the few possessions that a general brought with him when he left France in this dark hour." Veteran Pamela-watchers were tickled to recognize the letter from her dinner-party readings. Still, Pamela's overall message came through: She was perfect for this job because she had historical perspective, even if from an unusual vantage point, and she knew most of the important figures in France. "The French are difficult to understand—the culture and customs and habits and inner instincts," said Jack Valenti afterward. "Pam knows what is in the bones of Frenchmen."

To herald her May 17 swearing in as the nation's sixty-fourth Ambassador to France, Pamela sent engraved invitations—stiff écru cards edged in dark green—to virtually everyone who had played a role in her life. "Oh Mummy, do I have to come over?" exclaimed Winston when his mother called with the date. "It's the most important day of my life!" said Pamela. And so it was, her crowning achievement—the ceremonial symbol of the wealth, power, and respectability that she had finally acquired. And unlike her previous successes, she had secured this one at least partly in her own right. The Harriman wealth and position were essential, of course, but she had pursued her goal shrewdly through hard work and concentration.

The morning of the ceremony, Pamela awakened early, Eivind came at eight to comb out her blond bouffant, and she arrived at the State Department three hours later. The setting was the ornate Benjamin Franklin Room, with its gilded plaster, eight crystal chandeliers, and deep red scagliola Corinthian columns. Randy old Ben, America's first ambassador to France, might well have smiled at the notion of a former courtesan assuming his role. More than three hundred guests showed up for an occasion that normally would attract a crowd of fifty at best. The room overflowed with Washington luminaries, including Katharine Graham, Carter Brown, Lewis and Patsy Preston, Richard and Cynthia Helms, Sandy Berger, Tom Foley, Bob Strauss, and George and Liz Stevens. Winston and Minnie Churchill came in from London, and Kitty Hart flew in from New York, as did Helen Worth, who had taught Pamela cooking back in 1962.

Prominent among those who crowded the room were Averell Harriman's two daughters, Kathleen Mortimer and Mary Fisk, both conservatively dressed, their hair tidily but simply styled, their handsome patrician faces lined with age. Surrounding them were the six Harriman grandchildren. The Harriman progeny offered a portrait of familial solidarity; all of them seemed pleased by Pamela's honor. Pamela had flown the Bostonians and New Yorkers to Washington on her Westwind.

She appeared confident as she stood on the dais, a trim, delicate figure in a peach suit. She looked radiant, her face suffused with pleasure as her blue eyes raked the crowd. Each time she made contact with a friendly face, she tilted her head or dipped from her waist, smiled or laughed. She stepped to the podium to face Vice President Al Gore, with Winston standing between them, holding the Bible that had belonged to his American great-grandmother Jennie Jerome, inscribed to her son Winston Churchill on his marriage to Clementine Hozier in 1908.

After Gore administered the oath, he and Secretary of State Warren Christopher gave short speeches. Christopher called her appointment a "perfect fit," and noted that "anyone who has proven capable of unifying the Democratic party . . . would find the problems of the United States and France to be well, just a piece of cake." Gore remarked that he and Tipper would miss the friend they had come to "admire and love." "To paraphrase Voltaire," he said, "If Pamela Harriman did not exist, we would have had to invent her."

Pamela spoke briefly and with evident feeling, addressing "all my friends in the world now gathered in this room. . . . Now my home in Paris will be your home too. Please come . . . [as the laughter rose] but *not all at once!*" Applause filled the room, Winston guffawed and clapped, and Warren Christopher gave her a kiss. Afterward Pamela presided over a champagne reception, standing in the receiving line almost the entire time. That night, Bill and Hillary Clinton gave a small dinner in the family quarters for Pamela and some of her friends, including the Schlesingers, the Foleys, and the Bergers. For those who missed the swearing in, Pamela sent videotapes produced by the Harriman Communications Center at the Democratic National Committee. As usual, she had thought of everything.

CHAPTER

Thirty-five

On May 27, 1993, Pamela touched down in Paris with her publicity machine already in overdrive. In the American and French press she appeared as a bundle of energy who plunged into her job within minutes of her arrival on an overnight flight. In one interview after another, she described in detail her punishing schedule: up at six-thirty to watch the previous night's CBS Evening News and read four newspapers, in the office by eight-thirty, rounds of meetings, events, and speeches followed by phone calls after midnight to her key contacts in Washington, and then to bed as late as one-thirty. "When the adrenaline is running you don't need so much sleep," she explained to *Vogue*. Each morning, she added, "I have press briefings from my staff in both French and English, and then I start on the cables that have come in from all over the world. There are stacks of them, and you're expected to master every word—classified, confidential, or secret—and the print is very very small."

She had also introduced what she called "working" breakfasts, lunches, dinners, and receptions, where she discussed substantive issues with diplomats, businessmen, and other officials. "One of the things I've been trying to do is to explain to the French the power of Congress," she told the *New York Times*. Following a quick trip to Washington, she bragged about a luncheon she arranged for Balladur with Tom Foley and other congressional leaders. "I'm happy to say they've seen more Frenchmen in Washington in the last three months than they've seen in a long long time," she told *Vogue*. At every opportunity she mentioned her closeness to Bill Clinton. In an interview with Joseph Fitchett for *Town & Country*, she said, "The one thing the President said to me: 'Call me anytime, whenever you feel like it,' " as she turned to her aides and added, "and we've been able to do that, haven't we?"

Professional diplomats were unimpressed. Pamela's dawn-to-midnight routine mirrored that of her predecessor, Walter Curley, who managed Franco-American relations during the Persian Gulf War, the collapse of the Soviet Union, and the transformation of Eastern Europe. Many other ambassadors conducted business during meals; they simply didn't give the practice a name. Duties such as arranging meetings for French leaders with American senators and representatives were also commonplace for an American ambassador. "It was all standard procedure," said one experienced diplomat. "The problem is that all this was new to her. If you've never worked or been in charge of a big organization before, it is brand new. This is what is so irritating."

Nor, for that matter, was Pamela's relationship with Clinton unusually close or her access remarkable. Many political appointees have had good relations with the President who had chosen them, especially in important capitals like Bonn, London, and Paris. Walter Curley had been close to George Bush for many years, and French leaders were well aware that Curley could reach the Oval Office whenever he wished. A longtime investment banking partner of Pamela's former lover Jock Whitney, an ex-Marine and former Ambassador to Ireland, Curley also had ties to American business as well as the State and Defense departments. Curley, however, was an old school sort who didn't flaunt his access as Pamela did.

Pamela's knowledge of the language gave her an undeniable advantage; from the beginning, she was delivering speeches in French, which flattered her listeners. American press reports frequently referred to her French as "fluent" and "elegant," neither of which was quite accurate. Although she spoke with great confidence, her accent was that of a typical British aristocrat who wouldn't deign to accommodate French pronunciation or conform to the dynamics of the language. "Contrary to much press," said an American Embassy official in Paris, "her French is not at all strong and nimble."

Nearly every newspaper and magazine account made much of the "major collection" of Impressionist and Post-Impressionist paintings that Pamela brought to the embassy residence, an assemblage worth "something like a hundred million dollars," according to one London newspaper. Most other ambassadors, by contrast, borrowed art from museums through a special State Department program. She even went to the trouble and expense of enlisting Phillips Collection director Charles Moffett to hang her paintings in return for a plane ticket and a free room while he did his work.

As in Washington, Pamela's "fabulous paintings" contributed to her aura of great wealth and aristocratic style. In fact, only a handful of significant paintings belonged to her by way of Averell and Marie Harriman: the famous van Gogh *White Roses* (of which 20 percent was already owned by the National Gallery); *Mother and Child,* by Picasso; *Woman in a Blue Hat,* by Matisse; and *Portrait of Mademoiselle Demarsy,* by Renoir, along with three lesser works by Renoir, Seurat, and Daumier, the pretty Sargent that Carter Brown had helped Pamela select, and more than two dozen minor drawings and paintings by Paul Helleu that she had acquired when she was Elie de Rothschild's mistress. (Pamela left the 1975 oil portrait of Averell Harriman by Gardner Cox in the N Street Library, which surprised Harriman's daughters and grandchildren.) The rest of the important paintings hanging in the residence, including several beautiful Cézannes, a Henri Rousseau landscape, a Derain, and four Walt Kuhns, were all lent by the National Gallery—from the Marie Harriman Collection.

Pamela and Janet Howard had begun mapping out their public relations strategy well before arriving in Paris. Immediately after her nomination, Pamela made inquiries about the press officer at the embassy. "Is he really good?" she asked. "I need somebody good." Under ordinary circumstances, ambassadors are given explicit instructions to avoid the front pages, not to mention gossip columns and celebrity magazines. But she had a different agenda. "She made a conscious effort," explained a former Paris Embassy official. "It was a political thing, to make her appointment as ambassador inarguable. Somebody could say she was just a big money raiser, a courtesan, a charmer, and a rich woman. But she and her people wanted her to look like a statesman born."

In Paris, she confined herself to tightly controlled briefings for the press where she could address friendly queries on specific topics. She shunned free-wheeling French radio and television shows, which were known for hard questions. Instead, she agreed to a cozy chat with Barbara Walters, and reminisced about World War II on *Face the Nation* and *This Week with David Brinkley*. Once during an off-the-record luncheon at the Anglo-American Press Club she lost her cool when a female journalist asked her about the increasing tendency of the United States to inject moral issues into foreign policy. "I don't know what you are talking about," she snapped.

Pamela sought to cultivate selected influential journalists. She worked closely with Benno Graziani, a sometime escort whom she knew from her Agnelli days, on an eight-page spread in *Paris Match* that included four full-page color photographs by fashion designer Karl Lagerfeld. Graziani, said a longtime embassy employee, "has been a very good adviser who can pull strings. When she wants to counteract bad publicity he knows whom to contact and can pull someone out to praise her." She entertained these journalists at lunches, dinners, and movie screenings, rarely missing a chance to disclose some self-serving information. She told *Washington Post* correspondent William Drozdiak that Mitterrand had gone out of his way to meet with her for a half hour after receiving her credentials, and that Balladur "was grateful to me" for setting up his Capitol Hill meeting.

Almost lost amid all the superficial publicity were her genuine achievements and her operating style. Contrary to her persona as a player in the policy world, Pamela understood from the beginning that if she were to try developing strategies on crucial issues, she would fail in the job that meant everything to her. "She will send cables drafted by her political counselor," said a veteran diplomat as she started her term. "They will be read, and she may even be in the room where issues are discussed, but her views won't count because there is no merit in what she says. Her weakness is substantive. She cannot go through the complicated pros and cons of an issue memorandum that says if we do A, the outcome will be B or C, or if we do B, the outcome will be something else."

Nevertheless, her State Department bosses gave her high marks. "She knows her limitations, which is one reason she is effective," said a senior administration official after Pamela had been on the job for about a year. As ambassador, she was savvy enough to take her skills—gathering and trading information, creating an atmosphere for discussion, sizing up the strengths and weaknesses of men in power—and apply them well. By tailoring her job to match her talents, Pamela helped improve Franco-American relations.

There was a time when the American envoy in Paris could—and did—shape policy. Career diplomat David Bruce, who served during the 1950s, would "fly straight to Washington, get the government together, and get from them the decision he wanted," according to former Ambassador to France Arthur Hartman. With the centralization of power in Washington, along with the ease of modern communications, the role of the ambassador was greatly circumscribed. Much of the job—perhaps three-quarters—was devoted to obligatory ceremonies and official meetings. While most top-level dealings occurred directly between Washington and the French government, the American envoy was still expected to deliver and receive messages, to read the mood of the French leadership and transmit those impressions back to the U.S. government, as well as to advocate American interests in France. "The ambassador's job is weird," said a top State Department official. "It has enormous prestige but little policy impact. It is just right for Pam."

Pamela was well suited to the ceremonial role. She had automatic standing because she had lived in Europe during and after the war, and because she knew many leading figures in politics and society. Instinctively guarded, she spoke slowly and carefully, and she stuck to generalities, a practice that played well in diplomatic circles. She also thrived on her busy schedule, filled with meetings and briefings. Each day she tucked into her Chanel shoulder bag small cards outlining her schedule, as well as brief profiles of the people she would meet. One friend recalled the time in December 1993 when Pamela was the guest of honor at a Sunday lunch outside Paris. "Halfway through the lunch she got a phone call saying she had to go to the embassy to take a call," said the friend. "She rushed back to get the call. She loves all that."

At first her judgments on the French political scene were only moderately helpful. She "regularly appears a little overwhelmed," reported a Paris embassy official in January 1994 after she had been on the job about six months. "Mrs. Harriman doesn't have—despite earlier years in France—a helpful sensitivity for the Gauls. Her insights, when they are offered, do not illuminate beyond what is offered in the French press." But the State Department recognized that her star quality could be exploited. "She was able to use her convening power well," said a former State Department official. "She could have dinner at the embassy, and they would come at the highest level because she is Pam."

Pamela employed this "convening power" wisely by avoiding the ostentatious entertaining that everyone expected of her and concentrating on small gatherings. Such social contacts with the President, Prime Minister, and Foreign Minister could yield useful nuances about their views on important policy questions. "The French cannot always be talked to directly," she once said. "They like a little buildup before the point emerges. They can react badly when visitors from across the water simply plop down and say, 'Okay, here's the problem and here's how we're going to fix it.' One needs a different approach to get people here to show what they have on their minds."

Pamela identified the comers in the French diplomatic bureaucracy and developed relationships with several, including the Secretary General of the Quai d'Orsay, who was the leading professional diplomat under the Foreign Minister. As a result, she learned where to go to get information quickly. She carefully charted the realignments among top French leaders, telling Washington who was up, who was down, and how various personalities fit in the Parisian political scene. All the while, she made certain to protect her flanks. When Balladur was Prime Minister, she saw him regularly, while at the same time she was entertaining Jacques Chirac, Balladur's political rival. "She knew it was a very subtle game," said one American journalist. "Would Balladur run for President and challenge Chirac, his best friend? She followed the game closely."

In her dealings with the French, Pamela was sometimes transparently manipulative, as several American friends witnessed while visiting her at the embassy. "She was on the telephone with [U.S. Trade Representative] Mickey Kantor, thanking him for sending a letter because it would give her a chance to see Mitterrand," recalled one of the visitors. "She called Mitterrand to say she was coming to deliver a letter from President Clinton. She went over and did it. Later a Frenchman came for a drink, and she was saying that she had a one-on-one meeting with Mitterrand for fifteen minutes. The Frenchman was so impressed. He said Mitterrand must have really wanted to see her, because no one sees Mitterrand for a fifteen-minute one-on-one. Anyone else would have admitted she had only seen him for a couple of seconds to deliver a letter, but she totally exaggerates, and creates a perception of her importance. She is an absolute master."

Pamela quickly grasped that to be taken seriously in Washington, she had to work the phones constantly. "To be a player, you have to be on the phone every day well into the evening, with State, with the White House, with Defense," said one former State Department official. "She knew that if she didn't, she would be forgotten." In addition to reporting on events in France, she kept up with events in Washington. "She knows more than almost anyone what's going on in the State Department," said another official there. She stayed in closest touch with two of her key advisers from Washington days, Sandy Berger at the White House, and Peter Tarnoff, Under Secretary of State for Political Affairs, who had previously headed the Council on Foreign Relations, a major beneficiary of Harriman Foundation funds. She also consulted frequently with Richard Holbrooke, first when he was Ambassador to Germany, and then after he returned to Washington in mid-1994 as the Assistant Secretary of State in charge of Europe and became her boss. She continued to ask her longtime advisers for guidance, but she became a source of information too.

During Pamela's first six months in Paris, Franco-American relations were dominated by the GATT, the comprehensive world trade agreement completed in December 1993 after seven years of negotiations. She had been studying trade issues since her nomination was announced, and though she took pride in the number of speeches she made promoting free trade to French businessmen, it was her moves behind the scenes that had an impact.

The most important hurdle in the negotiations was French resistance to U.S. efforts to open Europe to American farm exports. An agriculture deal had been negotiated by the Bush administration, but the Clinton administration modified that agreement, yielding on several provisions to placate belligerent French farmers. Then, during the final weeks of negotiations, the United States tried to abolish a French tax on Hollywood movies that subsidized French filmmaking, and to loosen quotas on the number of American programs that could be shown on French television. Although Bill Clinton vowed to stand firm on these "audiovisual" issues, at the last minute he agreed to exclude them from the overall GATT agreement to ensure that the treaty would go forward.

U.S. Trade Representative Mickey Kantor and the European Community's chief trade negotiator, Sir Leon Brittan, worked out the final framework of the World Trade Accord during marathon negotiations in Brussels and Geneva. Neither Pamela nor any other ambassador played a role in those meetings. But she did give Kantor some useful guidance, especially on the need to work directly—and privately—with French leaders on the agriculture provisions instead of through the German government as the Bush administration had done. When the French farmers were protesting in the summer of 1993, Pamela arranged a dinner at the residence of the French Ambassador in Brussels for Kantor and Yves Galland, the French Minister-Delegate for Finance and Foreign Trade. "After that," recalled Kantor, "Galland came to Washington and met with me privately, and we were able to work it out."

Throughout the GATT negotiations, "Pamela and I were talking two or three times a week," said Kantor. "She was trying to keep me informed on what the French were saying to the European Union, and I was giving her a running account of what Leon Brittan was saying." Because they had worked together for the Democratic Party, Pamela was a known quantity to Kantor: "I knew that what I was getting was careful and considered advice, and that the information was relevant. If someone else had been there, I might have worried about the quality of the information, about the access or what filter the information was coming through."

Publicly, French officials were implacable on the "audiovisual" question, accusing the United States of cultural imperialism. Culture Minister Jacques Toubon called the film *Jurassic Park* a "threat to French identity." As Franco-American relations frayed, Pamela declined to address the issue in her speeches —missing an opportunity, in the view of some observers, to have an impact on the debate. "I wish she would have done something to promote American culture," said Jack Valenti, the chief lobbyist for Hollywood interests during the GATT talks. At the very least, said one American correspondent, "she could have had popular entertainment figures come over to make the case that this was nothing threatening and to emphasize cultural universality."

That sort of open advocacy would have violated Pamela's habitual caution; if she stumbled, she could have subjected herself to ridicule. What's more, noted Kantor, "You can shove only so much down anyone's gullet. We made enormous strides in agriculture, which is our largest export product." Kantor said it would have been "an act of irresponsibility" to scuttle a worldwide trade agreement because of differences over movies and television programs. Pamela, he said, "knew if we couldn't move the French in the appropriate way, we were not going to conclude the treaty. She knows when to hold 'em and when to fold 'em."

To a lesser degree, Pamela involved herself in the debate over the war in Bosnia. After Jacques Chirac was elected President in May 1995, he broke the impasse in the war by calling on the United States and Britain to help France with a "rapid reaction force" to back up the UN peacekeeping troops in Bosnia. With U.S. policy makers caught off guard, Pamela saw an opening. In a meeting with State Department officials she said nothing until she was asked whether the French were trying to withdraw or to get further involved. "She said they were looking for a way out," recalled a participant at the meeting. "It was her intuition, well informed."

Pamela followed the twists and turns in the Bosnia crisis. When Holbrooke came to Paris as the U.S. negotiator in July 1995 with a message from Clinton, Pamela had him over for lunch, where she ticked off questions from a leatherbound portfolio and wrote down all his answers. Before they went off to meet with Chirac, Holbrooke drilled her in the few things she was supposed to say. Pamela stayed with the script.

She proved adept at carrying straightforward messages back and forth between French and American leaders. Pamela "has learned enough about the core issues that she can keep up with the jargon on Bosnia, NATO, and Algeria," explained a State Department official. "But if there is an extra complicated message to Juppé or someone like that, she brings Avis Bohlen on the phone to assist her. The policy and technical decisions are done by Avis and her political counselor." Bohlen, noted an American correspondent in Paris, "has had a lot to do with keeping Pamela well oriented. Having Avis alongside has given Pamela an image of professionalism." When Bohlen's term came to an end late in 1995, Pamela replaced her with Don Bandler, a highly regarded career professional who had worked under Holbrooke in Germany.

As the overseer of 1,100 employees at the embassy, Pamela respected the chain of command and used her time efficiently, leaving the detail work to others. She and her staff spent six months preparing for Bill and Hillary Clinton's first visit to France in June 1994 for the fiftieth anniversary of D-Day. She selected a group of thirty French and American businessmen to have breakfast with Clinton at the embassy, and she gathered twenty-eight prominent French women to meet with Hillary at the Ledoyen restaurant. During the visit, Pamela sensibly stayed in the background. "She knew it was the visitors' show," said a White House official. "She was in all the meetings, but the only people who were talking were the President and his opposite number."

Pamela had not lost her knack for responding instinctively to the needs of powerful men. When Bill Clinton wanted to wander the streets of Paris after a state dinner at the Elysée Palace, Pamela swung into action, calling on Culture Minister Toubon to help her open the Louvre for a midnight tour. A year later, during Chirac's first Washington visit as President, Pamela was dismayed to see that his schedule contained no social gathering with the Clintons. She jumped official channels, called Hillary, and helped organize an informal White House dinner for twenty, including the Vice President, the Secretary of State, and several key French officials. "She saw that the schedule was outrageously rude," said a State Department official. "Chirac was beginning a seven-year presidency, and he is crucial to our future in Europe. Any ambassador would have known it was a disaster, but dealing with it was not axiomatic. Pamela created an opportunity. The President knew what she had done, and she did it beautifully."

Such attention to detail enhanced Pamela's rapport with Clinton, who viewed her as one of his successful appointments. During her visits to Washington, he made time to meet with her in the Oval Office. Once she conferred with both Bill and Hillary Clinton, without the participation of any aides. "It was unusual for Mrs. Clinton to be there," said a White House official. "There were big smiles." Another time, according to a State Department official, "Clinton cleared out his office and spent a long time with Pam getting some rumint," an intelligence community term for gossip.

Nearly two years into the job, Pamela was caught in a messy controversy but managed a fast recovery. On January 26, 1995, French Interior Minister Charles Pasqua summoned her to his office—an unusual request, since the ambassador usually dealt with the Foreign Minister. Pamela walked into a trap by agreeing to see Pasqua, which was the equivalent of the French ambassador in Washington meeting with the head of the FBI. Some of her staff cautioned her not to do it, but she went ahead, prompting them to speculate that she believed she could handle the wily bureaucrat with her famous persuasive powers.

Pasqua presented Pamela with evidence from a two-year-long sting conducted by French counterintelligence agents: five CIA operatives, four of them working inside the American Embassy in Paris, had been bribing French officials to obtain information about their government's position on the GATT negotiations and on the telecommunications business in France. Pasqua demanded that the spying be stopped.

Taken aback by the details of the operation, Pamela assured Pasqua that she would investigate the matter. On her return to the embassy, she told the CIA agents, including Richard Holm, the Paris station chief, that they had a serious problem, and she needed a full report. Pamela asked Washington for direction as CIA operatives in Paris tried to sort out how the spying scheme had been compromised. She answered another summons from Pasqua on February 10, when he gave her two more names of American agents and showed her some photographic evidence.

As the CIA and French intelligence service worked in their customary fashion to handle the matter behind closed doors, Pasqua leaked a detailed account of the sting to the French press on February 22. French newspapers played up the story, characterizing the dispute as "the most serious trans-Atlantic rift in several years," according to the *Wall Street Journal*. The *New York Times* and *Washington Post* ran front-page stories—with photographs of Pamela looking stoical—and called the incident a "rare public humiliation" that caused "spectacular public sparks."

Nobody was denying Pasqua's allegations. The State Department would only say they were "unwarranted," "unnecessary," "unprecedented," and "overblown." Pamela tried to recover with an embassy statement that Pasqua's account of his conversation with her was "inaccurate and incomplete." For her, the disclosure was what one experienced diplomat called a "lose-lose" situation. "In that position you can't win. If you say you were innocent, and didn't know, that is the worst because an ambassador is supposed to know. If you say, 'I knew,' then you are to blame." Pamela actually knew more than the press accounts indicated. Since her arrival in 1993 she had been briefed twice a week by Holm, who was precluded by law from giving her specifics on what the CIA calls "sources and methods." But she was generally aware that agents in the Paris embassy had been gathering economic intelligence, that the operation had been authorized in Washington, and that the "customers" for the information included the Commerce and Treasury departments.

Economic espionage between allies had been commonplace for a number of years, and heads of American companies had been complaining since the 1980s about French attempts to infiltrate their operations and steal industrial secrets. During the Bush administration the CIA began trolling for information on French strategies in the world trade talks. But starting in 1993, the agency's efforts intensified as the GATT negotiations moved down to the wire. "President Clinton made gathering economic intelligence a high priority" as American foreign policy increased its emphasis on commerce and trade issues, according to the *New York Times*. "In 1993 the Clinton administration asked the CIA for dramatic improvement . . . in supporting trade negotiations . . . where it had previously played only a bit role." Nevertheless, Pamela had been so concerned about the potential diplomatic damage from being caught spying on an ally that she had voiced her disapproval to Anthony Lake, the President's National Security Adviser. Even as the operation continued, she periodically expressed her worries to Holm during his briefings. When the scandal broke, said an embassy official, "it was embarrassing because it rained on her parade, but she was a professional. She tried to understand what had happened."

In the aftermath, Washington issued its public statements, the agents were quietly sent home, and Pamela did what she does best. She quietly raised questions with the French press about Pasqua's motivation for leaking the story. It turned out that the Interior Minister had been involved in a wiretapping scandal that had tarnished Balladur's campaign to become President of France, and Pasqua was using the sting to divert attention from Balladur's troubles. "Pam understood early what needed to be done," said Robert Shrum, who was visiting her at the time. "Without directly saying so, she gave French readers and voters room to interpret that this was done for French political purpose." Within a week the squabble subsided, and in March, Balladur lost the election to Chirac, at least in part because Pasqua's leak backfired.

By that time Pamela Harriman had established herself as a popular presence in French politics and society. To a greater degree than her predecessors she permitted her official duties to dictate her social life. She had no obligations to a husband or children. "I'm available the whole time," she told one interviewer. "It makes things much simpler. You can concentrate absolutely, totally on what you're doing. When I'm working, which is just about all the time, I have blinkers on." During a visit to Paris, Kitty Hart asked her why she worked so compulsively. "I don't want them to think I'm not serious," she replied.

Yet Pamela managed to find time to see old friends from her café society days, including the playwright Jean-Pierre Grédy, the writer François Valéry, the decorator Henri Samuel, the perfume magnate Hélène Rochas (who, like Pamela, had had an affair with Stavros Niarchos), Gerald and Florence Van der Kemp, and Pierre Bergé, the flamboyant business partner of Yves Saint Laurent. "She has the same French friends she knew here thirty years ago," said Bergé. French socialites competed for Pamela's attention by fêting her with a series of lavish dinners; W described her residence as "looking like the world's best flower shop. It's all those bouquets the beau monde insist on sending her." When Jean-Charles de Ravenel and his wife Jackie decided to "christen" their "fabulous new flat," W reported, they gave a buffet dinner for thirty in Pamela's honor. Those who knew her in her previous incarnation took a proprietary pride in her success. "Her past?" said François Valéry. "Everyone has a past. It is who she is today that counts."

Her friends also said she was too preoccupied with her duties to have a romance. She often went out alone, or she was accompanied by a familiar figure such as Benno Graziani. "She changes escorts all the time," said a man who knew her for many years. For a while she was accompanied by Claude Roland, a well-connected public relations man. "Claude Roland knows the little intrigues of the Quai d'Orsay," said a knowledgeable Parisian. "He is not good-looking; he resembles a parrot. But he is someone ready to go, always free, a shameless social climber." Pamela periodically imported escorts from America; during the D-Day fiftieth anniversary celebrations, she had Washington man-about-town Thomas Quinn on her arm.

Now that she was living barely a mile down the Seine from her old Avenue de New York apartment, Pamela's relations with the two men who once supported her there made a fascinating contrast. Elie and Liliane de Rothschild gave Pamela wide berth. They had been frequent guests of Walter Curley and his wife, but they strictly adhered to Liliane's vow to avoid the embassy during Pamela's term there. For Elie, this proved no hardship. Mostly because of Liliane's animus, Pamela and Elie had not remained friends.

Gianni Agnelli, on the other hand, had kept up a companionable relationship with Pamela over the years, as Marella Agnelli maintained a discreet distance. "Gianni remains very loyal with all his ex-mistresses," Marella once explained. "They are friends." "Gianni would still come and see Pamela, not for sex but because he liked her," said one of his longtime cronies. "Pamela is very much a good souvenir"—meaning a good memory, in the French sense of the word. During her marriage to Leland Hayward, Pamela had entertained Agnelli over lunch at her Fifth Avenue apartment, and she continued to make herself useful to him. "When Gianni was having a new yacht built," said interior designer Paul Manno, "Pam asked me to meet with him and discuss how to decorate it." Agnelli reciprocated with favors. Jeanne Thayer recalled the time in 1962 when she was planning a trip to Italy: "Pamela said, 'If you are going to be in Forte dei Marmi, give me your address there and I will get you a car from Fiat. I will cable Gianni and he will see that you get a car.' She was very matter-of-fact. Gianni answered right back by a hand-delivered note, and we got a top-of-the-line Fiat."

Pamela had been in Paris only a few months when the Agnellis invited her for a brief vacation at their chalet in St. Moritz. Agnelli, who had an apartment in Paris near the American Embassy, was spotted from time to time dining with Pamela at Brasserie Lipp, and he made quiet visits to the embassy residence. One weeknight when he arrived, the guard didn't know who he was because Pamela had kept her plans for the evening secret. Another embassy employee recognized Agnelli and ushered him in.

Although Marella Agnelli had little fondness for Pamela, she not only entertained her with Gianni but on her own. They had one awkward encounter. Marella had invited Liliane de Rothschild to see the artwork in the Agnellis' New York apartment in 1990. According to a much-repeated account, Liliane arrived as Pamela was having a drink with Gianni; upon seeing Pamela, Liliane supposedly fled into Marella's bedroom, where she stayed until Pamela left. In fact, Marella was conducting Liliane around the living room when Pamela appeared unexpectedly for her appointment with Gianni. Liliane and Pamela exchanged a brief but courteous greeting before Liliane continued her tour with Marella in another room, leaving Pamela with Gianni and Oscar de la Renta. Liliane asked many detailed questions about the paintings, so it was a half hour before the two women returned to the living room. By then Pamela had left.

Pamela entertained Agnelli and other friends from her former life in elegant style at the twenty-room embassy residence. In addition to official functions and two or three small dinner parties each week, she gave Sunday brunches that were followed by first-run movie screenings. After two weeks of sampling meals at the residence, Pamela decided to fire the chef; not only did she dislike his cooking, she resented his complaints about dealing with Janet Howard instead of Pamela herself. By the fall, Pamela had a new chef.

The residence had been expertly run for twenty-five years by a French-woman named Denise Cardinet, who had studied at the Sorbonne, Cambridge, and Brown University, and had worked for eight American ambassadors in Paris. Although Pamela publicly described Cardinet as an "indispensable ally," she began undercutting the longtime employee shortly after moving into 41 rue du Faubourg St. Honoré.

The impetus for Pamela's campaign came from Giuseppe Santos, the butler who had served her at Avenue de New York for three years when she was Gianni Agnelli's mistress. On hearing of her appointment, Santos wrote Pamela a letter offering his services again; he was still vigorous at age sixty-five, and his most recent employer had been the Aga Khan, the elder son of another of Pamela's lovers, Aly Khan. Pamela immediately hired Santos on her personal staff.

He formed an alliance with Janet Howard, who was staying in a room in Pamela's private quarters and had assumed the spousal role of communicating with the residence staff. At Pamela's direction, Santos and Howard closely monitored the household staff of sixteen and added to their duties. Pamela also asked all the employees to sign contracts pledging that they would not disclose anything about working conditions at the residence.

Eventually Pamela replaced half of the workers with her own handpicked employees, and Cardinet left as well, nearly a year before her official retirement date. "Denise Cardinet was an attractive, nice, loyal woman who ran the embassy very well, but she was run out by Pam," said a former embassy employee. Following Cardinet's departure, Giuseppe Santos became major domo for the residence. Balding and good-looking, Santos was beautifully trained and full of self-assurance. Visitors often compared him to the butler played by Anthony Hopkins in the film *The Remains of the Day*. "He is a marvel," said one of Pamela's friends, "sweet but not fawning. He reads her very well."

With Janet Howard and Giuseppe Santos making a multitude of decisions on her behalf, Pamela had every detail of her daily life covered. Working out of Pamela's embassy office, Howard was now served by secretaries and assistants, although she continued, as one embassy official delicately observed, "to express the ambassador's displeasure or anxiety."

Beyond the customary $65,000 annual stipend from the State Department earmarked for entertaining, Pamela spent $10,000 to $15,000 a month of her own money—an additional $120,000 to $180,000 a year. "You would have to be doing a lot above and beyond to spend that much," said a veteran diplomat familiar with the Paris embassy. Pamela had other substantial out-of-pocket expenses as well. Janet Howard was paid as a political appointee by the U.S. government, but Pamela drew from her own funds to pay Santos, as well as her personal speechwriter, and her maid Iris, who earned $40,000 a year. Pamela spent $500,000 of her own money to have Mark Hampton, the Manhattan interior designer, redecorate six rooms in the twelve-room ambassador's private apartment. The work, which took five months, included silk curtains on all the windows, new carpets, new upholstery, and what Hampton described as "a lovely paint job with many coats to build up a nice patina."

Such improvements were routine for well-heeled ambassadors. Reagan appointee Joseph Rodgers replaced the plumbing and bathrooms and built a kitchen and dining room in the private quarters, and Walter Curley renovated both the screening room and library in the public part of the residence—using his own funds as well as contributions from other wealthy individuals. Pamela's ability to finance her Paris embassy expenses seemed beyond question.

But when Pamela unexpectedly put her two Georgetown houses on the market in May 1994, her friends began to wonder if she was as rich as she seemed. These were the famous Harriman properties, the symbol of Pamela's ascent in Washington society, the site of her political salon and presumably her permanent base of operations once she returned from Paris. The asking prices were $3,695,000 for "The Harriman House" and $1,495,000 for "The Statehouse," which had served as PamPAC's offices. When asked about the planned sale, Pamela offered vague replies about no longer needing the houses. "That house on N Street was never her house," one of her friends explained. "There is something dreary about living in it now." But Pamela had never operated on the basis of needing; with her, it was always a question of wanting.

The notion that she planned a more modest style of living didn't ring true. "She is desperate to sell those houses," reported a friend after talking to Pamela in July. "She didn't say why she is desperate. It's funny. She says one thing to one person, and something different to someone else." But a woman who had known her for a number of years offered an explanation: "Don't say I told you so, but she is short of money. She has spent an awful lot."

Thirty-six

BY MID-1994, Pamela Harriman had been under growing financial pressure for more than a year and a half. The first indication of her difficulties came in early 1993, even before she was nominated as ambassador, when she sold Mango Bay so hastily that, as one friend put it, "she walked out with her photographs at 9:00 A.M. and the new owners walked in at eleven." The sale price was $3.3 million, and Pamela netted $2.8 million before taxes. On March 5, she took out $1 million in mortgages on Willow Oaks and her two Georgetown homes—transactions that were recorded in her financial disclosure forms submitted before her confirmation hearings. The conflict between maintaining appearances and raising cash was aptly symbolized by her invitation to the Fisks and Mortimers to fly down on the Westwind for her swearing-in. It was the last time she used the plane. Three days before, she had committed to sell it for $1.6 million.

Pamela explained away the Barbados and the airplane sales as necessary steps toward putting her financial affairs in order before her stint abroad. She loved Mango Bay and had relied on it as a place to impress her wealthy friends and to unwind each winter from mid-December to early January and again at Easter. Yet when she unloaded the house, she said with typical unsentimentality that it had really been "for Averell" and had become a "chore." It was, she told one friend, "a phase of my life that's now over." The airplane was her favorite perk, but she logically argued that she could far more readily use the Concorde for transatlantic travel.

The fact was, the Barbados house and the Westwind were the easiest assets to liquidate without drawing attention to her financial difficulties. After all, why would a woman worth $115 million on her husband's death only seven years before sell a vacation house and a plane except for the sake of convenience? The real reason was quite simple: Pamela had always been a free spender, and now that she had a lot of money she was spending even more.

Pamela's problems stemmed from the fact that she always wanted to keep up with the Joneses—only the Joneses were named Agnelli and Niarchos, and had hundreds of millions to burn. Of the $115 million Harriman fortune, about $27 million was liquid—a staggering amount to ordinary people—and the rest tied up in real estate and other investments.

Assuming this money generated a 5 percent return—the conservative number customarily used to project an assured income—Pamela could count on after-tax annual earnings of about $1 million. The trouble was, she was spending well over $2 million a year. Only she knew how she spent all that money, but a partial accounting is possible. Her most important fixed cost was the price of fulfilling the bargain she had made with her late husband: the $240,000 in Union Pacific stock she gave the Harriman heirs each year, along with her annual $300,000 contribution to maintain Arden. Winston Churchill and his family received their maximum of $60,000 in annual tax-free gifts as well. That meant she was down $600,000 before she spent a dime on herself.

In the year before she sold Mango Bay and the Westwind, Pamela was spending about $70,000 annually on the Barbados property, which she visited barely two months a year, including roughly $48,000 to keep a half-dozen servants (butler, maid, cook, laundress, and two gardeners) employed year-round. Her private jet cost more than $1 million annually in upkeep, which she was able to cut somewhat by periodically leasing the plane to companies and wealthy individuals. Willow Oaks, according to one of her advisers, cost her $300,000 a year (excluding her outlay to maintain four horses for hunting and show jumping); the two Georgetown homes and her domestic and office staff another $300,000; Sun Valley around $10,000; and the Sands Point development about $25,000 in taxes. These expenses added up to around $1.7 million, in addition to her $600,000 in family commitments. In 1992, Pamela also made $11,900 in political contributions and paid more than $300,000 in fees to Theodore Sorenson, her attorney in her dispute with Christopher Ogden.

Bill Rich, the financial manager hired by Averell Harriman, had the unenviable task of keeping Pamela supplied with cash. He earned $250,000 a year as head of the fifteen-person Harriman office at a time when hot-shot lawyers in corporate finance pulled in millions. In somewhat Dickensian fashion, he arrived at his office on the twenty-third floor of 63 Wall Street before dawn and wore a telephone headset while fielding calls at his desk. Though Harriman's former lawyer James Dolan of Davis Polk had closely supervised the family office, Clifford and Warnke gave Rich considerable latitude after Harriman's death. Fellow Harriman employee Thomas Richardson recalled that he noticed in Rich a "lack of judgment and an unwillingness to listen to other opinions," along with a susceptibility to flattery and "ego massage."

Although Rich was charged with estate planning and financial services for the heirs of Averell and Roland Harriman, his main job was as "Pamela's personal service provider," according to a source close to the Harriman family. "He spent most of the time worrying about how many bulbs were planted in which garden, and how much fuel was available for the plane. That was his preoccupation." In Pamela's presence, he was self-effacing and loyal. "He was civil to Pamela," recalled one of her friends, "always respectful and professional."

But behind her back, he would roll his eyes and complain about her spending to Harriman's daughters and grandchildren. "Pamela has had cash flow problems forever," said a friend of William Rich. "Bill said she is a spendthrift. He would have long discussions with her, and she would do relatively minor things like switch the fountain pens for her secretaries at N Street. Then she would take a trip to Europe and spend $75,000 for clothing, and she could not understand why there was not enough to pay the bills. She thought Bill should be able to figure out how to afford everything."

Others insisted that whether out of weakness or poor judgment, Rich encouraged Pamela's irresponsible attitude toward money. "Rich gave her optimistic forecasts," said one of Pamela's advisers. "She was running a deficit every year and he was reassuring her, telling her, 'You can do this. You can do that.' He was not rigorous."

An example of how Rich encouraged Pamela's extravagance was in the way she used her Westwind. "She would commute to New York on her jet, which was insane," said one of her friends. "She spent a few thousand just because it felt good. Even Warren Buffett takes the shuttle. Rich fed that part of her that wanted to live this way, the overreaching part that wanted this unnecessary luxury."

Not long after Harriman's death, Pamela had begun invading capital to cover her structural deficit. Beginning in 1992, she started to borrow substantial sums. That year she took out an $8 million line of credit from Morgan Guaranty for "living expenses," as well as a $3 million loan from a trust Harriman had set up for his great-great-grandchildren and $2 million pledged against her property at Sands Point, followed in 1993 by her $1 million in mortgages on the N Street and Willow Oaks properties. The interest on these debts ran well over $500,000 annually.

By the time Pamela sold Mango Bay and the Westwind in 1993, one of her advisers said, she knew that "she had to make adjustments." Yet even then she had grand plans, asking Rich to set aside the money so she might use it to buy an apartment in Paris. When she had quizzed Walter Curley about the expenses of the embassy, thoughts of retrenchment were on her mind, but by the time she got to Paris, she was arranging for the expensive renovation of her private quarters. "She put aside everything and went on living her *foie gras* life when she should have been going down scale," said an old friend. In effect, she was doing the same thing she and Leland Hayward had done after they sold their Fifth Avenue apartment: using the proceeds to continue living at the same high level.

Aside from Pamela's personal expenditures, there was another major drain on her funds, as well as those of the Mortimers and Fisks. Averell Harriman had hired Bill Rich because he seemed the kind of man who would manage trusts and estates in a prudent way. But over the years Rich had become a speculator in real estate and other high-risk ventures. The investments came to light almost by accident in late 1992, when an accountant working for David and Averell Mortimer discovered a discrepancy in their tax returns for the previous year. While they had been paid the customary distributions from their Harriman trust funds, the amount of income reported to the Internal Revenue Service was considerably lower—reduced, it turned out, by interest on a mysterious multi-million-dollar loan. The family hired Henry S. Ziegler, the Mortimer family's attorney at the New York law firm of Shearman & Sterling, to investigate.

While Ziegler and his associates conducted their probe, Clifford and

Warnke became embroiled in the BCCI scandal, which forced them to resign as trustees for all the Harriman trust funds and disband their law practice. Clifford and his partner Robert Altman had been indicted in July 1992 and were ordered to stand trial early in 1993. Due to his poor health, prosecutors declined to try the eighty-seven-year-old Clifford, and Altman was acquitted the following August. But both men, as well as Warnke, had plenty to worry about as defendants in civil suits that were seeking more than $100 million in damages for negligence and breach of fiduciary duty in the BCCI matter.

Throughout Clifford's ordeal, Pamela remained loyal. At one point she even threw a party for several hundred guests at N Street to celebrate the memoir he wrote with Richard Holbrooke. After Clifford's indictment, Pamela tried to cheer him up by hiring a Chinese chef to prepare a special eight-course dinner at his home. But his legal troubles spelled the end of their professional relationship. He withdrew as her personal lawyer early in 1993, and she switched to seventy-five-year-old Lloyd Cutler, a Yale man who had been White House counsel in the Carter presidency and was a stalwart of the Washington legal establishment.

In September 1993, Henry Ziegler presented his report to the Mortimers, and it was extremely bad news. He told them that $21 million from the family trusts had been invested in the failing Seasons Resort and Conference Center at Great Gorge, a hotel and condominium complex on 293 acres in northern New Jersey that had been built by Hugh Hefner as a Playboy Club in 1971—and was widely regarded by real estate professionals as a lemon. The family trusts still had their portfolio of stocks and bonds, but all those securities were locked up as collateral on an $18 million loan that had been used to buy the property. To their horror, the Mortimers learned that the interest payments on the loan ($4.2 million from 1990 through 1993) had canceled out the income from the portfolio. Pamela, it turned out, had personally guaranteed the loan.

Averell Mortimer called in Kitty Ames's husband Charles for assistance. An expert in real estate law, he had some distance from the situation since Kitty and her brother Averell Fisk had kept their individual trusts under separate supervision after Harriman reorganized the family holdings in 1984. Ames and Mortimer met with Bill Rich in October 1993 and learned that at least $8 million more from various family trusts had disappeared into yet another floundering business, a plastics company based in Allentown, Pennsylvania, called Polymer Dynamics (PDI). All told, the family was out some $30 million.

THE GRIM SEQUENCE of calamitous investments had begun five years after the trusts had been restructured in 1984. During that initial period, the trusts had prospered, surviving even the stock market crash of 1987 to grow from $13 million to $25 million in 1989. The stock and bond portfolios were capably managed by two investment advisory firms that were overseen by a third investment consultant. Yet the grandchildren, according to Clark Clifford, "were pressing Bill Rich to have the assets throw off more income" as their financial needs grew. With the arrival of their own children came tuitions for private schools and camps, ambitious vacation plans, and a yearning for larger homes.

Like Pamela, Averell Harriman's heirs were accustomed to living rich and maintaining appearances, although at a less extravagant level.

The heirs' attitude toward Bill Rich and his staff also mirrored Pamela's view: Let others attend to the boring details and keep the supply of funds coming. In the Harriman world, a financial administrator was not much different from the man who mucked out the stables. If one of the grandchildren ran short of cash, Rich could advance it. The family office staff knew they were being patronized, and they resented the attitude of the heirs, especially David and Averell Mortimer, whose demands were the most insistent. "They had no patience," said Tom Richardson. "It was never, 'What did you do for me yesterday?' but, 'What're you going to do for me tomorrow?' "

Aware of the heirs' pressure, Clifford urged Rich in 1989 to diversify beyond the stock market into real estate—a seemingly odd choice when the goal was a reliable source of income. Whether Clifford knew it or not, he was encouraging Rich to dabble in an area where he had little proven expertise. Harriman had hired him for personal financial planning and general administration, not as an investment adviser, although he had given Rich some limited authority over "private investments" in oil, gas, precious metals, and minerals that were not traded on the open market. With the apparent acquiescence of Clifford, Warnke, and Pamela, Rich greatly expanded this "private investment" responsibility. "I am astounded that he even got involved and made decisions on investment on his own," said a friend of Bill Rich. "If you don't have expertise, you go with someone who does."

Rich, however, decided to go it alone, emboldened by a successful real estate investment he had already made for the grandchildren's venture capital partnership. In 1987, he had spent $1.4 million on ten acres in Hunters Point on the East River in Queens, New York, and sold the property two years later for $4.5 million. Out of the $3.1 million profit, he distributed $230,000 to the six grandchildren and set the rest aside for reinvestment. One of the dealmakers who brought the property to Rich was a glib real estate entrepreneur from New Jersey named Eugene Mulvihill. Mulvihill's financial exploits were well known in his home state; five years earlier, he had pleaded guilty to six felony charges of fraud.

In 1989, Mulvihill alerted Rich to an investment opportunity in the Seasons Resort, which Mulvihill had bought the previous year for $11 million. Mulvihill took him to visit the resort on a fine autumn day and sold him on its possibilities. The hillside setting had a certain appeal, but the hotel itself was a gloomy structure of wood and stone, poorly designed and rundown. Although the hotel had twice failed in the go-go eighties, Rich, according to Clark Clifford, saw "great potential" in an apparently undervalued property. Rich's plan was to turn it into a first-class conference center for corporations. Unlike many in the financial community, he was evidently unaware that by 1989 the hotel industry was overbuilt, suffering from $2 billion in annual losses, and headed for a collapse.

Clifford shared Rich's enthusiasm for Seasons and so evidently did Pamela, who according to Clifford was "greatly taken" with the investment and "put some of her own money in it." But Clifford, Warnke, and Rich neglected to do the homework that would have raised numerous red flags about the hotel's indebtedness and a host of environmental and tax problems. Nor did they bother to check the background of Mulvihill or his partner Robert Brennan, a flashy New Jersey financier who had been under investigation by the Securities and Exchange Commission for stock manipulation since 1974. Brennan's face had appeared in commercials for his New Jersey bank on the Super Bowl and *60 Minutes,* and his battles with regulators had been hashed out in magazine cover stories and newspaper front pages for years. Nevertheless, when Rich first presented the investment to Clifford, Warnke, and Pamela in 1989, according to Clifford, "I had never crossed paths with Brennan and Mulvihill, nor did their names mean anything to me."

Rich invested a quick $5 million, and this time instead of using the family's venture capital funds, he took $4.4 million directly from the Harriman trusts, as well as $600,000 from Pamela and the grandchildren of Roland Harriman, whose assets he oversaw as manager of the family office. When his initial investment failed to turn the expected profit, Rich borrowed increasing amounts, throwing good money after bad, as he tried to turn the investment around. In an effort to recoup some funds in 1990, Seasons sold its golf course for $20 million to Japanese investors, but all the proceeds went to Mulvihill and various creditors, and nothing to the Harriman interests. Among the debts Seasons repaid was a $5.5 million loan from First American Bank of New York—one of the Clifford-Altman banks in the BCCI case. Clifford was chairman of the New York bank's parent company, although he said later that he "never knew about the loan." Rich, however, sat on the First American board that authorized it.

By the spring of 1991, the Harriman family owned all the stock in Seasons, and the losses were running several million dollars a year. Rich needed more cash to keep the operation going, so in March he secured an $18 million line of credit from Morgan Guaranty. For that amount, the pledge of the trust assets as collateral was insufficient, so Pamela agreed to sign the personal guarantee for the loan. Clifford, Warnke, and Pamela put their names to all the remaining loan documents.

"Why did Bill Rich arrange the eighteen million dollar loan?" mused a lawyer familiar with the situation. "Because he had gotten in way over his head and wanted to make sure enough money was available to power through the problem. Why did Pamela, Clifford, and Warnke sign? They must have bought Bill Rich's explanation that it was a good sound investment, and the recovery was around the corner." No one thought to inform the Mortimer and Fisk families as Rich imperiled their trusts by running the credit line to the limit while paying off loans and other liabilities.

An investment in Polymer Dynamics was equally troubling. Ironically, it was Averell Mortimer who had first identified Polymer as a hot startup company back in 1984 when he borrowed $150,000 from his grandfather to buy some stock. PDI made soles for athletic shoes, and both Mortimer and Rich were such true believers in its potential that they sat on the company's board. "They thought it was going to be the next Xerox," said one family member.

During the eighties and early nineties, Rich sank some $15 million into PDI, pulling money from a variety of sources: Pamela's accounts, family venture capital funds, and family trusts. Even Clark Clifford invested $1 million in the company. By 1993, PDI was struggling to stay afloat and the Harriman investment had vanished.

As CHARLES AMES and the two Mortimer brothers digested the magnitude of the losses in the fall of 1993, they asked Henry Ziegler to take over from Bill Rich as their trustee, but he declined. Any new trustee, Ziegler told them, would have to sue the investment partners for their poor handling of the estate. That would mean taking on Pamela, Clifford, and Warnke, who had presumably approved the outlays since they were partners in the Oldfields and Southfields investment companies that controlled the family trusts.

During their meeting in Rich's office in October 1993, Charles Ames and Averell Mortimer proposed that Pamela take on the $18 million loan as her liability. They assumed, of course, that she had the financial resources to do so, and it seemed a reasonable solution since she had guaranteed the loan. At the same time, she would become owner of the hotel. According to a family member, Rich reported back that when he recommended that course of action, she replied, "Why should I do that?" "She is so concerned about raising money for an apartment in Paris that I am having trouble getting her to focus," Rich explained.

In a gathering at Arden early in December, Charles Ames and Averell Mortimer briefed the rest of the family. The newly discovered investments had dealt the Harriman heirs a severe blow. Kathleen Mortimer and Mary Fisk had each lost $200,000 in annual income. Although Mary Fisk still had more than $1 million in other income-producing assets, she spent around $250,000 a year, which had already forced her to invade capital. Kathleen Mortimer's husband Stanley had his family inheritance that generated several hundred thousand dollars a year, prompting one of his relatives to remark, "Imagine, to be one of Averell Harriman's only two children and to have to live off your husband!" Four of the six grandchildren had lost more than $100,000 each in annual income; for Kitty Ames and Averell Fisk, who still participated in several all-family trusts managed by Oldfields and Southfields, the amount was around $50,000 apiece. None of them was in danger of going hungry, however. All the grandchildren earned a living except Kitty Ames, whose husband had an ample salary, and all could draw from several more modest trusts.

The family decided to make a direct plea to Pamela. Charles Ames sent a fax to her in Paris describing his meeting with Rich and asking for her assistance. Pamela invited him and Kathleen Mortimer to stay with her in Paris and discuss the matter. They met in her large, elegant office overlooking the Place de la Concorde. Settling in behind her enormous mahogany desk, she gestured toward Ames's fax and said coldly, "These are quite some accusations." It was a disquieting beginning, as there had been nothing accusatory in the Ames memo, merely a summary of the meeting.

Ames presented a slide show outlining the investments and the losses sustained by the heirs. According to sources close to the family, Pamela expressed shock but seemed oddly detached, almost as if she didn't quite comprehend what she was being told. At no time did Ames specifically mention the $18 million loan, and when he asked for her help in replacing Rich as trustee and avoiding further financial losses, she was characteristically guarded. She said that she had retained Lloyd Cutler, who had read Ames's memo. Cutler needed to do further analysis, but Pamela told them he would be in touch.

Despite Ziegler's advice about legal action, the family had no desire to move against Pamela. The fact remained that they were heavily dependent on her, and a hostile lawsuit could backfire. She not so subtly reminded them of her superior position when, at the end of the Paris meeting, she handed over a stack of envelopes, each containing $10,000 worth of Union Pacific stock for each of the twenty-four Harriman heirs—two daughters, six grandchildren, and sixteen great-grandchildren. That evening the trio dined in the residence. The conversation was polite but awkward, and during the night Kathleen Mortimer succumbed to the strain and became sick to her stomach.

The family was unnerved that Pamela had brought in her own lawyer, but Ames began working with Cutler. In late December, Kathleen Mortimer, Mary Fisk, and the six grandchildren asked Bill Rich to resign from the investment partnerships and step down as trustee. "You have acted in disregard of the investment policies and safeguards," they wrote, "and in violation of the trust and confidence that we placed in you." Cutler meanwhile interviewed Rich, Clifford, Warnke, and others who had assisted them to elaborate on the information Ziegler had gleaned.

With Cutler's assistance, the family finally pushed Bill Rich to resign as trustee in February 1994, when he was replaced by Ames and fellow Bostonian Nicholas Thorndike, a professional corporate director and trustee. At that point Ames revived the proposal that Pamela take over the $18 million loan. First he argued on moral grounds that if Averell Harriman were alive he would have made it up to his family, and she should do the same. When Pamela was unmoved, Ames shifted to a legal line, insisting that her personal guarantee meant she was responsible for repaying the loan—a notion Pamela found equally unacceptable.

With the lines drawn, Ames and Cutler began discussions about a possible settlement. In April 1994, the heirs were forced to liquidate their securities portfolio to pay off the $18 million Morgan loan, leaving them just $3 million in their trusts. The heirs were furious that Pamela stood by as their fortune was ravaged. In their view, she could well afford to bail them out, and they had difficulty muzzling their criticism of her.

Even Kathleen Mortimer, Pamela's friend since 1941 with whom she shared many fond memories, turned against her. Kathleen began complaining to friends about the cars and London apartments Pamela had given Winston's children when she should have been helping David Mortimer buy a bigger place in Manhattan. (He bought a $1 million Park Avenue apartment anyway, assuming a large mortgage in the process.) Her worry, she said, was that Winston and his family would get the remainder of the Harriman fortune. The

Mortimers and Fisks were also disquieted to hear that Pamela had expressed an interest in buying a Paris apartment. Nevertheless, Kathleen kept the lines of communication open and continued to talk to Pamela weekly on the telephone.

The family had no idea how badly Pamela's own finances had deteriorated. Her spending aside, she had lost significant amounts in the two investments as well. Although some estimates pegged her losses as high as $25 million, her own advisers said the actual amount was around $4 million in Seasons and about $5 million in PDI. When Lloyd Cutler grasped the dimensions of Pamela's financial predicament, he moved to reduce her overhead sharply.

On Cutler's advice, Pamela signed up fellow Democratic Party patron Felix Rohatyn of Lazard Frères as her financial adviser. She sold tens of thousands of shares of Union Pacific stock in the spring of 1994 to pay off her $8 million line of credit, as well as another $1.3 million loan secured by the property at Sands Point. That left her with only $3.3 million in cash and marketable securities— half of which were pledged against a loan to PDI. Her unencumbered liquid assets had dropped from $27 million to $1.65 million in less than ten years.

When Pamela put the Georgetown houses on the market in early May, she was not only trying to raise money; according to a friend, "she wanted the Harriman family to know that she was cutting back. They felt she was living in a big way, which she was, and they weren't." Pamela still had significant assets in her art and real estate in Middleburg, Sun Valley, Arden, and Sands Point, as well as some investment properties in Riverhead, New York, and the Caribbean. Nevertheless, by her standards, she was all but impoverished.

Pamela recounted her travails to Kathleen Mortimer in a series of tearful telephone calls in May and June of 1994, explaining, according to a sworn statement from Charles Ames, that she was in a "precarious financial state, was insolvent, and might have to declare personal bankruptcy." During a home leave visit that July, Pamela went to New York to see Kathleen Mortimer. With her current financial statements in hand, she told Kathleen over lunch in a Manhattan restaurant that she could not afford to help the family. Visibly distraught, Pamela said she had no money and that everything was mortgaged.

After she had removed her horses from the stables at Arden (where she had put them when she went to Paris) and shipped them back to Middleburg, Pamela's lawyers told the family that she could no longer afford to help with the upkeep of Arden, despite the promise she had made to her late husband. She was already in arrears for $165,000, about half of her annual subsidy. Her representatives said she planned to shut down the Arden stables and to sell her 414 acres. She also announced her intention to put the Sun Valley cottage on the market—contrary to the heirs' understanding that Harriman wanted it to go to his grandchildren. Pamela had even begun to pass ownership to them by giving them five percent of the stock in Suvalo Corporation, which held title to the house. Unfortunately for them, she controlled the other 95 percent. When the family vigorously objected, she replied that it was her property and she could dispose of it however she liked.

To Pamela, these moves were purely pragmatic. "She came to the realization that she was spending large amounts on things she was making almost no use of," explained one of her advisers. "It is fair to say she focused more on what she wanted to spend her money on." By hitting the Mortimers and Fisks where it hurt the most—the country homes that symbolized what it was to be a Harriman—she tipped the family over the edge.

In May 1994, the Harriman heirs had hired a tough-minded Manhattan litigator, Paul Curran, to investigate how they might sue Pamela, Clifford, Warnke, and Rich. Curran took over from Ames and continued settlement discussions throughout the summer. Cutler was also serving a six-month stint as Clinton's White House counsel, helping the administration deal with accusations of financial improprieties by Bill and Hillary Clinton when he was Arkansas governor. A waiver from the government ethics office permitted Cutler to continue working with several then unnamed private clients, including Pamela, on what he described as "family property matters."

The heirs argued that Pamela should sell other assets that didn't mean anything to them—specifically, the art Harriman had given her and especially the *White Roses* that adorned the Louis XVI sitting room at the embassy residence. No comparable van Gogh had gone on the market since 1987, when *Irises* had sold for $53.9 million and *Sunflowers* for $39 million, and art experts agreed that the worth of *White Roses* seemed reasonably within that range. If so, the sale could have greatly eased the financial difficulties of Pamela and the family. As for the promised gift to the National Gallery, the heirs contended that the pledge was not enforceable, although reneging on such a highly publicized promise would probably generate an enormous amount of negative publicity for Pamela. The family also had its eye on the balance of the art collection, worth between $10 million and $20 million.

Pamela retorted that any art sale would be an "inappropriate" way to compensate for what had happened to the trusts. But while she considered the van Gogh out of the question, she seemed to come around to the idea of selling some art, without specifying which paintings, along with the Georgetown properties. In an effort to accommodate Pamela's lack of cash, the family proposed that she pay their trusts $9 million up front—about half what they felt she owed them—and she would become a half-owner in the Seasons Resort, with the family retaining the other half. She would place the remaining proceeds of her art and real estate sales into new trusts that would give her income until her death, when an additional $9 million would go to the heirs. Ames also asked her to devise a plan to pass the Sun Valley cottage to the family and deal with her share of Arden, and to release the heirs from various debts they owed to the Harriman estate—some $2 million in loans that Harriman had made to them before his death for various venture capital investments.

Cutler countered by offering a cash settlement of under $10 million along with the possibility of forgiving the heirs' debts. The heirs continued to maintain that even if her ultimate objective was to pass her money to Winston Churchill or to charity, her first priority should be covering the Harriman family losses. But Pamela dug in, maintaining that she was not responsible for the heirs' financial problems and insisting that she individually had lost more than anyone. What's more, she said, she had been exceedingly generous in her support of

Arden, in her annual gifts to the heirs, and in letting them use Sun Valley. The heirs interpreted her attitude as "very hardball," according to one family member. The family never explicitly mentioned the bad publicity that a lawsuit could produce, although Cutler went out of his way to say Pamela wasn't concerned about possible public reaction, which led the heirs to believe she was.

In August, all telephone contact between Pamela and Kathleen Mortimer ceased. The heirs put the Seasons Resort into bankruptcy, paving the way for the lawsuit that Curran began to assemble after reviewing thousands of pages of documents. Although Pamela was worried about her dwindling resources, her mood was defiant. As she had been parrying with the Harriman heirs, she had also been dealing since early spring with the upcoming publication of Christopher Ogden's book.

Titled *Life of the Party,* the biography had chapters named after men who had been her lovers ("Ed," "Gianni," "Elie")—as well as some (John F. Kennedy and Clark Clifford) who had not. The jacket photograph showed her leaning against a chair with one hand rakishly on her hip and her mouth open wide in an omnivorous laugh. She loved the photograph, which had appeared in *Vogue.* As Ogden was completing his manuscript at the end of 1993, she had called him out of the blue to ask how the book was going. When he told her he wanted to use the photo on the cover, she readily agreed to sign a release—and even called back several weeks later to make sure he had obtained the picture. But the jacket was about all she admitted to liking in the book, which became a national best-seller.

When the Mortimer family was still on speaking terms with Pamela, David's wife Shelley Wanger had tapped her publishing industry sources and helpfully sent her a set of galleys in March. During the weeks before the May publication, Pamela talked to friends about her distress; in at least one conversation, she dissolved in tears. Pamela said she was extremely upset by the emphasis on her love affairs. Theodore Sorenson's firm issued a statement that the book contained "an extraordinary number of inaccuracies and falsehoods, many of which are defamatory." Still, Pamela couldn't entirely get around the fact that she had been an initial key source for the author—which served to undercut her objections. The portrait created by the book ran directly counter to Pamela's carefully constructed new image as a diplomat, which bothered her more than anything.

By summer's end, it was clear to friends that Pamela had survived the book. At the peak of its publisher's promotional campaign in May, she had even traveled to Washington to receive an award. She had kept up the pace in Paris, holding her head high throughout the D-Day celebrations, making appearances on American television, and organizing dinners for visiting dignitaries. "For the first time, she looked her age," reported one visitor to Paris that summer, "but she was poised and contained." She was hunkered down to fight the family in a lawsuit that she told friends was inevitable.

On September 15, the trustees for the Harriman daughters and grandchildren filed a 118-page complaint in Manhattan Federal Court. Seeking a minimum of $30 million in damages and a maximum of three times that amount, they charged Pamela with being a "faithless fiduciary" who had squandered the family's inheritance. At the same time, they accused William Rich, Clark Clifford, and Paul Warnke of mismanagement, fraud, conspiracy, and racketeering. All four defendants vigorously denied the allegations.

It was an extraordinary moment for an old-line WASP family that had always kept its disagreements out of the public eye. To go to the mattresses with an embarrassing and messy lawsuit indicated a grievance that reached deeper than any legal document could possibly show. The money was important, of course, but what was really at stake was the family's image and the family's pride. Harriman had given Pamela his name, and he had given her his patrimony. He had also given her responsibility for his heirs. In her self-absorption, she had failed them. When the settlement talks finally broke off the day before the family filed the lawsuit, the sticking point was her flat refusal to accept responsibility. Once again she had overreached, and once again she stumbled.

CHAPTER

Thirty-seven

THE LAWSUIT NATURALLY was front-page news. It was filled with the most private details about family finances and acrimonious allegations of greed and a "conspiracy to breach fiduciary duties" that was undertaken "maliciously, willfully, and wantonly." The overall effect, said a woman close to the family, was "like waving their underwear." Friends and relatives of the defendants groped for explanations, while enemies gleefully faxed clippings back and forth. "It was with real pleasure that I tell you my worst fears were realized," said Pamela's longtime antagonist Brooke Hayward. "I want her flogged alive."

Pamela was "outraged" by the lawsuit, said her New York attorney Roy Reardon of Simpson, Thacher & Bartlett. She bitterly complained to one friend that "Kathy Mortimer turned on me," and lamented, according to another ally, that "she had thought David and Shelley [Mortimer] really loved her." Lloyd Cutler let it be known that Pamela had actually planned in her own will to leave most of her estate to the Mortimers and Fisks and something less to Winston, but all that would now change. Pamela blamed Charles Ames for "stirring up" the family and instigating the legal action. "I think Charlie Ames wants to see her in a bed-sitter in Kensington," said one of her friends.

Partisans of the Mortimers and Fisks maintained that only extreme provocation could have pushed them to such action. "I cannot be more strong that this goes so much against their grain," said Brooke's husband Peter Duchin. "I know they feel terrible about having to do this." Despite David Mortimer's Park Avenue co-op and Averell Fisk's $2 million Palm Beach home, Duchin and others insisted that the family lived modestly, traveling tourist and riding city buses. Their cottages at Arden, friends said, were really quite small.

The family had always projected an image of easy grace and civility, but now allies of Pamela accused them of avarice and indolence—the very opposite of the values Averell Harriman had impressed on his progeny. "The grandchildren naturally looked forward to coming into an inheritance," said Clark Clifford. "All seemed clear, the sky was fair, hardly a cloud. It never occurred to them that their grandfather would marry again when he was age eighty. Governor Harriman in his lifetime and in his will was quite generous to Mrs. Harriman, which was a source of great concern. They felt it was theirs." Noted Kitty Carlisle Hart, "They didn't get what they expected. They expected vast sums." Tom Richardson of the Harriman office sneered that David and Averell Mortimer were mere "remittance children." Lloyd Cutler articulated Pamela's main line of attack: "There are very few people in that family who earn their own living."

It didn't matter that these characterizations were only half true; most of the grandchildren had salaries, but they needed their unearned income as well. The tawdriness of the litigation tarnished the family's reputation along with Pamela's, although she had a higher and more visible perch from which to fall. After two years of glowing coverage in the press, one article after another now depicted Pamela as the evil stepmother, chipping away at her new identity as a respectable woman of limitless wealth, generously devoting herself to public service. The heirs were as intent on depicting her as a spendthrift as she was to paint them as high society layabouts.

What the family misjudged was Pamela's apparent obliviousness to shame. If the cycle of triumphs and setbacks in her life had taught her anything, it was that she could endure bad publicity. She might shudder privately when she took the first hits, but after that she seemed immunized to attacks that anyone else would find mortifying. "Our woman in France," wrote *W*, "is playing it cool as a cuke. . . . Those who have seen Pamela lately say she never refers to the legal imbroglio, that the Harrimans might as well not be suing for squandering their trust fund." Pamela went on the offensive, almost as if adversity fueled her in some strange way. "The family very seriously miscalculated how she would react under pressure," said her son Winston. "There is quite a lot of steel in that velvet glove."

Her nonchalance played well in France, which was well known for tolerating and often simply ignoring personal scandals. A few brief stories about her legal troubles surfaced deep inside French newspapers, but her Parisian friends considered it in poor taste to ask her any questions. "She is a great lady because she doesn't show any strain," said one admiring member of her circle.

Privately, however, she was in considerable turmoil over her own financial losses, if not those of the heirs. For counsel and support, she continued to lean on advisers in New York and Washington. Said one, "She has this capacity to win your sympathy and make you think you are her only friend. Each person thinks she is relying on him or her alone." She also called on Gianni Agnelli for advice. "She was in very deep trouble when she talked to him," said an Agnelli confidante.

Her lawyers dismissed "accusations of insolvency" as "unattributed hearsay." It was not Pamela's "recollection," they said, that she had told Kathleen Mortimer she was on the edge of bankruptcy. Acknowledging her low cash reserves, they emphasized that most of her assets were tied up in art and real estate: paintings valued between $10 million and $20 million, other fine art and furnishings valued at $3.9 million, sixteen Sands Point lots at $5 million, the N Street homes on the market for $5 million, Willow Oaks worth $1.4 million, $500,000 for her share of the Arden acreage, Sun Valley $1 million, the property in Riverhead, New York, $400,000, and oil and gas interests of $3.5 million.

When the heirs tried to freeze Pamela's assets, her lawyers argued vigorously that she needed the cash in her various New York accounts "to meet her living expenses." In other words, she was dipping into her already diminished capital to support a style of life that even well-to-do people would consider extravagant.

Shortly after filing their lawsuit, the heirs launched a second offensive in Virginia, this time asking the commissioner of accounts in the Loudon County Court to remove Pamela as executor of her late husband's estate and trustee of the three trusts established under his will. They charged that Pamela had borrowed extensively from the estate, engaging in "wrongful self-dealing" that violated her role as trustee, and that she had condoned investments in "speculative illiquid assets." All told, the heirs claimed, they were out more than $10 million from the Virginia estate in addition to the $30 million from the nine New York trusts. The heirs further asked the court to make her repay the loans and restore the losses resulting from "negligence, lack of prudence and dereliction" of her duties. Pamela, the heirs contended, was "the individual most responsible for this reprehensible state of affairs."

The $12 million marital trust that Harriman had set up in his will to give Pamela income and be divided among the heirs at her death had dwindled to $500,000 in liquid assets. Instead of blue-chip securities that could grow in value as well as produce interest and dividends, the marital trust was filled with "imprudent investments," overvalued properties, and a variety of loans to Seasons Resort and Polymer Dynamics as well as to Pamela herself, who had taken $1.8 million "for her personal use and enjoyment." While allocating cash to herself, Pamela had put the rest of the marital trust into investments of dubious worth.

The marital trust's portfolio included 349 undeveloped acres in Middleburg that had been bought only months before Averell Harriman's death. The property had been carried on the books with a value of $1.5 million until the amount was suddenly raised in 1991 to $3.7 million. Any evaluation of the acreage, however, was difficult because its worth depended on the outcome of a long-running controversy over a proposed highway around the town. Even more disturbing was the disclosure that the trust owned the building occupied by PDI rent-free. The building, worth roughly $3 million, had been purchased with $1.2 million from a $2.5 million Brown Brothers Harriman loan taken out by the trust, with $1.1 million from Pamela's sale of Mango Bay and $486,000 from her mortgage on the N Street properties.

The two "charitable lead trusts" were also a mess. Established by Harriman's will with $6 million to underwrite the Averell and Pamela Harriman Foundation for twenty-five years, by 1994 they had only $206,000 in cash and marketable securities, along with $4.5 million in an array of speculative investments in Seasons, PDI, and other money-losing operations. Though the trusts were actually receiving interest from one $2.5 million mortgage on Seasons, only part of the trusts' 1994 payment could be made to the foundation. As a result, the foundation had to tell the Brookings Institution it could not honor that year's installment of the $1.5 million pledge Pamela had made in 1991.

Pamela claimed not to have known that any of the Virginia trusts were used for risky investments, and her lawyers contended that what the heirs called "loans" from the estate were in fact "advances," to which Pamela was entitled. They could not adequately explain, however, either her personal loan from the marital trust or her role in buying the PDI building. In the New York lawsuit Pamela's attorneys argued that, as just one of three partners in the investment companies controlling the nine trusts, she could not be held solely responsible for their financial oversight. As a trustee and executor in the Virginia trusts, however, she had an undeniably central position in administering her late husband's estate.

The Virginia action kicked off another wave of unflattering publicity for Pamela. In an effort to generate better press coverage, she hired the Manhattan public relations firm of Howard Rubenstein Associates for three months beginning in November. "We acted like middlemen," explained James Grossman, the Rubenstein executive who worked on the account, "putting together journalists with people who said nice things about Ambassador Harriman, friends like Arthur Schlesinger who did speak to the press a lot." The firm also advised Pamela's attorneys on how to deal with journalists, and by the end of the year news accounts were downplaying Pamela's spending habits and emphasizing the size of her investment losses as the chief cause of her troubles.

The heart of her defense was that she was a victim and therefore absolved of responsibility. "The Governor always said, 'Rely on Bill Rich,' " she kept telling people as she now rued having trusted her husband's handpicked adviser. Absorbed by her own difficulties, she showed no sympathy for the Harriman heirs. "I don't really think I deserve this," she fretted to Dr. Isadore Rosenfeld, her personal physician.

Pamela's claim that she was an innocent bystander seemed plausible—up to a point. Averell Harriman had often told friends that Pamela had "no head for business." He "didn't really think women were capable of financial responsibility," said a woman who had known him since the war years. Rather than feeling slighted, Pamela had been relieved when Averell Harriman told her to leave her financial affairs to others so she could tend to her own interests; in the same spirit, she had ceded details of her political action committee to Janet Howard. Perhaps it was true that Harriman instructed Clark Clifford, the man who had been consumed with Pamela's most trivial problems, not to bother her pretty head with details of multi-million-dollar investments.

Yet no amount of naiveté or indifference could convincingly explain why her signature was on so many important documents, including the $18 million loan guarantee. "She was signing things she should have never done with the children's trusts," rationalized her son Winston, "but she was mortgaging her own property too." Offering an insight into his own financial ups and downs, Winston continued: "I hate to think the number of times I have taken things on trust. You have no reason to suspect the integrity and motives of your advisers, so you are liable to sign a stack of twenty or thirty complicated documents without reading them in detail." That is precisely what Pamela admitted doing, along with giving Bill Rich power of attorney to sign on her behalf. A man who had known her for decades explained, "You don't know how to make candy, but you know a lot about eating candy and you like candy. She likes money, which is candy to her. She didn't have to know how it worked."

By apparently signing without reading—and by supposedly failing to monitor what Rich was doing in her name—Pamela had put her imprimatur on crucial papers that contained inaccuracies and from which important information was omitted. Among these documents were eight years' worth of incomplete accountings for her husband's estate in Virginia, as well as her 1993 Federal Disclosure Form required by the Ethics in Government Act to qualify for the job as ambassador. It appeared that some of her obligations to the estate and marital trust were not fully disclosed on the 1993 form, which could have presented political if not further legal problems for Pamela if someone had chosen to press the matter in Congress.

Moreover, what one attorney for the heirs called Pamela's "sleeping beauty defense"—her insistence that she was unaware of any problems with the trusts and the Harriman estate until she awoke in late 1993—didn't completely hold up. Bill Rich told family members, for example, that after Averell Harriman's death he regularly reviewed investments with Pamela, presented her with thick briefing books and believed she was "tuned in" to her financial affairs. "I was told that Pam put some pressure on Rich to do more sexy kinds of investing," said a friend of Bill Rich.

There was also some clear evidence that Pamela was more alert about the Seasons Resort and PDI investments than other aspects of her finances. According to court papers, she knew about the initial $5 million investment in Seasons—the heirs' attorneys called it a "personal commitment"—and that she had only contributed $50,000 of her own money at that stage. As the investments in both Seasons and PDI grew, Pamela was well aware that she had several million dollars of her own committed to each venture, which made her pleading ignorance about the involvement of the family trusts less believable.

The pivotal point in evaluating Pamela's defense had to be what she knew and when she knew it. If the briefings she received from Rich were meaningful —if she actually followed her late husband's example of questioning the assumptions and performance of his advisers—and she still approved the investments, she could be blamed for financial mismanagement. If she had let Rich's words wash over her and put her rubber stamp on everything he proposed, then she was simply negligent.

The inescapable fact was that Pamela had taken on the important roles of executor, trustee, and investment partner that carried legally enforceable requirements for behavior. Given the size and complexity of Harriman's estate, Pamela should have granted those responsibilities her full attention. "It is her fault," said one of her longtime friends. "She said she gave proxy and never checked, but she doesn't see why that makes her culpable." According to this friend, some of Pamela's advisers "tried to tell her that she bears responsibility. But she feels she is a victim, she only sees half. She is not into self-analysis in general, least of all on this issue."

As one of America's most visible diplomats, Pamela's explanations put her in an especially awkward spot. She was responsible for promoting her country's business interests abroad and for understanding and conveying messages about world trade—a role that seemed ironic for someone who claimed not to have a clue about her own financial affairs. "The question I have," said one attorney representing the family in the Virginia lawsuit, "is how can she be a public servant and sign things she certified as true but never read?" As usual, Pamela was trying to have it both ways, claiming ignorance in one area of her life, and extraordinary competence in the other.

Toward the end of 1994, Pamela got an infusion of money: $1 million from the sale of an oil field that Harriman had bought years earlier, $800,000 from lot sales at Sands Point, and $350,000 from her 1983 trust. But with legal bills already pushing $2 million, her available cash still stood at around $1.5 million, which was less than she had been spending each year since the late 1980s. "She is a bit strapped," said a woman who had known her for many years. "She may have to sell a painting."

Her advisers had already told her that whatever happened in the lawsuit, she had to liquidate some of her property, as Lloyd Cutler put it, "to build up some income-producing assets." In November she had quietly removed the *Mother and Child* by Picasso from the walls of the embassy residence and shipped it to the Pace Wildenstein Gallery in Manhattan. Starting with a lofty asking price of $25 million, the gallery privately shopped the painting to wealthy collectors, but there were no takers even when the price dropped to $16 million. Concerned that the work would lose its desirability and be "burned" if the gallery continued to push it, Cutler recommended that the Picasso be offered to either Christie's or Sotheby's for auction.

Representatives from the auction houses inspected the Picasso and visited Paris to see the other two valuable paintings Pamela had decided to sell: Renoir's *Portrait of Mademoiselle Demarsy,* a radiant rendering of an auburn-haired young girl, and Matisse's *Woman in a Blue Hat,* a scowling matron painted against brown patterned wallpaper. The Picasso and the Renoir had been picked out by Marie Harriman, and Averell had bought the Matisse at a Paris auction in 1948 for $20,000. Pamela had promised Averell Harriman that she would give all three to the National Gallery on her death; only five years earlier she had publicly scolded "private collectors whose pictures we thought were going to museums and were instead . . . sold."

Sotheby's and Christie's each sent top-level delegations in early January to court Pamela's business. She chose Christie's because Christopher Burge, the smooth-talking British-born chairman of American operations, valued the Picasso between $7 million and $10 million compared to Sotheby's estimate of $4 million to $5 million. Although an undeniably pretty painting, the Picasso was limited by its scant coloring and unfinished feel—sepia outlines with only a patch of pale blue on the child's sweater. Both houses placed the same value on the Renoir ($5 million to $7 million) and the Matisse ($2.5 million to $3.5 million).

The Christie's pitch also included a six-figure promotion campaign before the sale on May 11: *Mother and Child* would be on the auction catalogue cover, the paintings would travel to Los Angeles, Frankfurt, Paris, Seoul, and Tokyo for public and private exhibitions for prospective buyers, and they would be featured in a two-page ad in *Town & Country* magazine. Even more important than estimates and marketing, Christie's offered Pamela an unusually generous guarantee: $14.5 million for the three paintings, instead of the $11.5 million that might have been expected. The guarantee meant that if the price fell below $14.5 million, Christie's would make up the balance and take a loss. In return for assuming that risk, the auction house would take a portion of any proceeds above the guarantee.

Once Pamela signed the consignment agreement in mid-January 1995, Christie's transferred the three paintings to a vault in its Park Avenue headquarters. "She is not sad, not really," said one of Pamela's friends after discussing the planned sale with her. "They were lovely paintings but they weren't her special favorites." Her son believed otherwise: "It was a hard decision," Winston said. "She was very fond of those paintings. It is a blow to her." Pamela's artwork had in fact become an important part of her identity. As evidence of her strong attachment, one of her favorite routines for visitors viewing the art collection at the residence had been to declare that the Renoir was her "laughing picture" and the Matisse her "frowning picture." "When I get in one of those moods," she would say, "I come and sit in front of the right picture."

With the prospect of at least $14.5 million from the art sale, Pamela was now in a position to reach a settlement with the Harriman family. During a conference on January 24, 1995, in Manhattan Federal Court, Cutler offered the heirs $15 million, most of which would come from Pamela. Nevertheless, the following day the family intensified its attack in Virginia by filing a full-scale lawsuit insisting that she repay $11 million in trust losses as well as millions more in loans—in addition to the $30 million they were already seeking in New York. A week later, Pamela fired back with stern letters from her attorneys to Averell and David Mortimer demanding immediate repayment of $430,000 and $230,000 in loans that their grandfather had made to them in the early 1980s.

Among Pamela's council of advisers, Lloyd Cutler had been the strongest advocate of a settlement, and as the pressure on both sides grew, he got the upper hand and began serious talks with the family in early February. Using Cutler's $15 million proposal as a starting point, the two sides traded offers and counteroffers for the next several weeks. The "central issue" on Pamela's side, said Charles Ames, was her "financial capacity" to meet her obligations to the heirs and still retain "sufficient assets to continue to live in the style to which she had become accustomed." According to Ames, Cutler's associate William Perlstein said her "objective" was to "maintain a net worth of at least $10 million and an annual income of at least $700,000 to $800,000." In the view of Pamela's lawyers, the "most contentious issues" were resolving the repayment of Averell and David Mortimer's loans, as well as dealing with the heirs' "insistence that they have guaranteed access to the cottage at Sun Valley."

By March 6, 1995, the two sides had settled on the framework of an agreement. The seven-page, single-spaced letter was signed by Ames and Cutler, who had received Pamela's approval of the terms. To finance a settlement, she agreed to use the proceeds from selling "all her readily marketable assets"—the three paintings, the two N Street properties, and her oil and gas interests. Eighty percent of what she received would go to the heirs outright—a sum anywhere between $13 million and $16 million. On Pamela's death, her estate would pay $6 million to restore the losses in the marital trust, an obligation that she would secure with a mortgage on the Sun Valley property as well as a second mortgage on Willow Oaks. In return, Pamela would assume sole ownership of the Seasons Resort and take over the family's interest in PDI and other venture capital investments.

Pamela also agreed to sell her Arden property to the heirs for 35 percent of the fair market value, which came to around $200,000. They would be able to use the Sun Valley cottage during Pamela's lifetime "on terms no less favorable than those offered to others," and on her death they could buy it for $950,000. One intriguing feature of the agreement stipulated that if Pamela failed to "honor her pledge of van Gogh's 'White Roses' to the National Gallery," and sold her interest in the painting instead, the heirs would be entitled to 25 percent (later negotiated down to 15 percent) of the proceeds.

The settlement was structured according to a range of possible results from the art and real estate sales, based on financial statements her accountant had given the heirs at the end of January. Set out as "worst," "low," "base," and "high" cases, the calculations listed Pamela's assets, liabilities, and potential income after settling with the heirs. At worst, Pamela would be left with a $12.5 million net worth, half of which would be "income producing assets" that would give her $619,000 a year. At best, she would have a $37 million net worth that would yield $1.5 million in annual income. Under all these scenarios, Pamela would presumably be able to continue living in her homes at Willow Oaks and Sun Valley.

Once the settlement commitment was signed, lawyers for both sides negotiated intensely during the following two months over details and supporting documents. Throughout this period, according to Ames, Cutler said "he was in regular contact with Pamela Harriman by telephone" and that "she had been sent copies of the drafts." Ames recalled that "Pamela Harriman had previously told me, in person and on the telephone, that she had turned over to Cutler the whole matter."

The lawsuit, the pending settlement, and especially her financial problems were very much on Pamela's mind. "She talked about the lawsuit endlessly," said one friend after a Paris visit. "This is a fine thing to happen to me at my age," Pamela remarked at one point. On the telephone to allies in New York and Washington, she vented her anger not only at the Harriman family but at Clark Clifford. For the first time, she openly criticized her late husband, complaining somewhat disingenuously about the choice of Clifford as her attorney, "Averell never asked *me* who I wanted," she fumed.

Around the embassy she dealt with her travails in her usual fashion, compartmentalizing them so she could get on with her life. "All day long she works her ass off and deals with the lawsuit at night," said one diplomat. "When I go to bed and turn out the lights," she confessed to a visitor over lunch, "it rips up my mind." In late February, when negotiations on the settlement snagged and she was talking to Lloyd Cutler frequently after midnight, she was dealing with the humiliating accusations that five CIA agents under her authority had been bribing French officials.

As if Pamela didn't have enough to worry about, her troublesome son was creating even more problems. During Pamela's Christmas visit with the young Churchills in 1994, Winston had told her that he was having an affair with a Belgian divorcée named Luce Danielson. The romance had been going on for more than a year, having begun not long after Winston dropped Jan Amory in May 1992. Unlike his flamboyant romance with Amory, Winston and Danielson had gone out of their way to be discreet. A jewelry designer in her mid-forties, Danielson was frequently on the road and kept offices in Belgium and London. Always mindful of the next potential customer, she "wore her own jewelry everywhere," reported an American woman after dining with the couple. "She did it in a major way, with bracelets of twisted gold and diamonds."

This time, Winston told his mother, he was really going to leave Minnie, and Pamela was again furious. "She did everything except physically sit on him to keep him quiet," said one of her friends. Although she was angry and wounded, Minnie tried once more to dissuade Winston from leaving her. Pamela flew over to England on the eve of her seventy-fifth birthday in March 1995 in a final effort to talk Winston out of it. She extolled Minnie's virtues as wife and mother and spoke of the need to keep the family together, but given her history she was in a weak position to criticize her wayward son. In the end, Pamela failed to dent Winston's determination, largely because her reduced circumstances removed her financial leverage. "Winston knew before that the money would stop if he didn't listen," said one of her friends. "Now he knows he won't get the money because she doesn't have it."

And Winston knew something else: At the moment his mother was losing her fortune, he was on the brink of inheriting his own. Four days after Pamela's birthday, lawyers for Winston and Minnie announced that the couple was separating after thirty years of marriage. Barely a month later, headlines across the front pages of London newspapers revealed that Sir Winston Churchill's personal papers—1.5 million documents from his childhood through the end of World War II—had been sold by the Churchill family for $20 million. Funds for the purchase came from an $18.4 million grant from a new national lottery, along with a $1.5 million contribution from John Paul Getty, the oil heir, that allowed the archive to remain at Churchill College in England instead of being sold abroad to the highest bidder—a possibility that had been floated for several years.

The proceeds went to a family trust old Winston had created back in 1946 for the exclusive benefit of his son Randolph's male heirs, who numbered four some fifty years later: Winston; his sons Randolph and Jack; and their sister Jennie's son, George. The announcement set off fierce condemnation in Parliament and the press over the size of the purchase price. Many critics insisted that the papers were the property of the state already. "While Sir Winston won the war, his heirs have won the lottery," declared the *Daily Mail*.

Everyone seemed to point a finger at Winston for "cashing in" at the nation's expense. Editorials bemoaned the prospect of his becoming a multimillionaire and derided him as a "socialite" with an "expensive and complex personal life," suggesting that he might use the funds to finance his divorce. But other commentators noted that Churchills had always made their own rules, and that Sir Winston had explained his own rich lifestyle by saying, "I like to be well mounted." As the furor subsided, eighty-two-year-old Peregrine Churchill, Sir Winston's nephew and one of the two trustees overseeing the money, snapped that they had "100 per cent discretion as to what to do with this money. . . . We may cut [Winston] off without a penny." That outcome was highly unlikely, but the trustees chose, at least initially, to invest the money and disperse the interest to the heirs. Even with that result, young Winston could look forward to his own unearned income of more than $200,000 a year—a prospect that inspired him to move to a large apartment near fashionable Belgrave Square.

Winston blithely ignored the criticism. A far more pressing concern was the certain loss of his seat in Parliament. The district he represented for twenty-five years was scheduled to be eliminated in the next election. He had been searching for a safe Conservative seat, but between the controversy over the Churchill Papers and the notoriety of his love life, he could not find a constituency that would take him. "He knows it could be the end of his political career, which is sad," said one of his relatives. "At fifty-four that can't be easy. It is also sad when your mother has been successful. That has been very hard on him."

Winston got no sympathy from Pamela, who could barely speak to him following their March showdown. After so many uneasy years, their relationship had finally ruptured. Pamela declined to meet Danielson, and in a curious reversal, made common cause with Minnie, to whom she was sweet and supportive. Her grandchildren found Pamela much changed as well. She gave young Randolph a festive thirtieth birthday party in Paris, and she frequently had the grandchildren to visit. During the time she spent with them, one source close to the family observed, "she was a different person, terribly nice to them all. She became much more human. She was being very cozy, which she has never been. She will never be maternal to anyone, but at least she is getting on with them."

Pamela also drew closer to her brother Eddie, the twelfth Baron Digby, calling on him frequently for advice on her legal problems and inviting his children to visit her in Paris. "When she is in adversity, she's at her nicest," he explained to a friend. Pamela's gestures were thoroughly understandable. For all her glamour and her energy, she was an elderly woman entering a period of physical and emotional vulnerability. After she had been let down by advisers and friends and in-laws, her British family remained the place she could go and be cared for without having to give much in return.

In mid-April, an unexpected development created a new obstacle for the lawyers refining the settlement agreement in Washington. The Averell and Pamela Harriman Foundation, which had been run by Kathleen Mortimer and Mary Fisk since Pamela resigned before moving to France, hired its own attorneys. Those representatives said that unless Pamela restored money to the charitable trusts that supplied the foundation's funding, they would file a lawsuit against her. In the settlement agreement the heirs had promised to kick in 30 percent of any funds needed to make the charitable trusts whole. But Pamela's lawyers were worried that after settling with the family, she might not have enough money to repay her 70 percent share plus possible taxes and penalties to the Internal Revenue Service growing out of the improper investments of the trusts—an amount that could have totaled an additional $3 million. Nevertheless, Cutler said there was "too little time" to resolve the issue until after the settlement had been signed.

Following a four-day marathon in Cutler's office during the first week of May, the lawyers for both sides completed the twenty-four-page settlement agreement. With its forty attachments, the document was more than an inch thick. According to Ames, everyone agreed that Pamela and the family should sign the papers before the auction on May 11. "Lawyers on both sides felt they had among their client group people who were a little squirrelly," said one man familiar with the settlement. "It was best to pin everyone down."

On Sunday night, May 7, Lloyd Cutler mingled with hundreds of other guests at Christie's auction preview party on Park Avenue. Pamela's pictures were only three among scores of top artworks on view. But the biggest crowd gravitated to the Picasso, Matisse, and Renoir at the end of a long exhibition room, set off by a sign saying, "From the Collection of the Honorable Pamela Harriman." No matter that without those three paintings Pamela's "collection" amounted to very little, or that the Christie's hype was a bitter irony to family members who knew that the paintings were really from the collection of Marie and Averell. All evening Manhattan socialites scrutinized and gossiped over the pictures, making wagers, and clucking over Pamela's fate. The crabby Matisse image drew the strongest reaction. "Mrs. Harriman meeting the family," quipped one browser.

As far as the Harriman clan was concerned, the settlement was a done deal, and over the next three days they all signed it with a sense of relief. As for Pamela, the original plan called for Cutler's associate William Perlstein to fly to Paris, as Ames later recalled, "to present the settlement documents to [her] for her signature." Instead, Pamela came to New York on Monday to attend a memorial service for World Bank president Lewis Preston, who had been one of her financial advisers. She settled in at the apartment of Kitty Hart, who as usual could divine nothing about the lawsuit from her old friend. "She probably knows I don't know a damn thing about legal matters," Hart later said.

The auguries were good for Pamela on Tuesday, May 9. An auction at Sotheby's the night before had been a "replay of boom times" that included $29.1 million paid for a Blue Period Picasso and a record $14.8 million for a Matisse. Pamela was hoping that her three would fetch from $20 to $25 million, well above the Christie's estimate. Perlstein spent that afternoon reviewing the settlement documents with Pamela, and as far as the heirs were concerned, everything was on track.

Wednesday morning brought a dark headline in the *New York Times:* THE

BIDDING FLATTENS OUT AT SOTHEBY'S. During the previous evening's auction, a "somber affair of bottom fishing and restraint," one Picasso was sold for well under its low estimate, and another Picasso went unsold. That morning Pamela showed up at New York Hospital to visit Gianni Agnelli, who had just undergone surgery. Her mood, according to another visitor who encountered her there, "seemed rather preoccupied."

She returned to the offices of her New York attorney Roy Reardon for the final briefing by Perlstein, and at that point, Pamela balked. After spending millions on a legal team that had worked incessantly for three months on the settlement, she refused to sign.

Pamela's escape hatch was the "contribution clause," a provision in the settlement that $3 million of the amount paid to the heirs would come from other defendants, principally Clark Clifford, whose estimated assets were more than $10 million. By the spring of 1995, Clifford was ready to pay $1 million to the settlement, and another lawyer involved in the Seasons purchase, Edmund Burns, had offered $500,000. In the weeks before the settlement deadline, Pamela had dispatched Janet Howard to Washington to persuade Clifford to raise his portion to $2.5 million. When Howard failed to extract anything, Cutler undertook to negotiate further with Clifford's representatives, but nothing came of his efforts either. With half of the contribution unfulfilled, Pamela took advantage of the loophole and announced she had a right to walk. In the process, Pamela roundly blamed Clifford, her longtime confidante and adviser, for failing to come up with the additional $1.5 million that would have closed the deal.

In fact, the "contribution clause" was merely a pretext. Faced with Pamela's reluctance, Ames had immediately offered to reduce the amount she owed the heirs by $1.5 million—the exact amount Clifford had failed to provide—if she would sign as agreed before the auction took place. Pamela declined that offer too, and shortly before midnight on Wednesday, the 10th, the settlement collapsed.

When Cutler had first called Ames at noon that day, he said Pamela believed the settlement could leave her "penniless" if the paintings sold near the $14.5 million minimum. She hated the idea of mortgaging Willow Oaks to the hilt and encumbering Sun Valley as well, and she was apprehensive about her financial obligation to the charitable trusts. She thought it was possible, according to Cutler, that she could "give up the bulk of her liquid assets and then the very next day face a possible lawsuit from the Harriman Foundation."

"The true reason for Pamela's refusal to sign," Ames later charged, was "she feared that if the Christie's auction results were disappointing, her obligation to the plaintiffs . . . and others . . . would impinge on her lavish lifestyle." "They wanted Middleburg!" she told one Washington friend. To others, she said she didn't sign because "it would have wiped me out." An auction result at the low end of the financial projections would have left her an annual income ranging from $600,000 to $800,000. If she factored in a payment to the charitable trusts, her available funds shrank further. When she confronted the prospect that her income might dip below $500,000 annually, she couldn't face it; her maintenance costs for Willow Oaks alone would have devoured half of her income. "To her, $800,000 is a shoestring," said one of Pamela's friends.

Pamela's lawyers later tried to rationalize her abrupt decision by saying that they had warned Ames and his associates that she would be a "hard sell" and that she "might have some objections." According to Perlstein, Ames had replied that he was confident in the Cutler firm's "persuasive powers." Yet all the information they discussed with Pamela on May 9 and 10 had been given to her in telephone briefings and by fax in the weeks before the closing deadline. Lloyd Cutler argued that "while we were in 'regular contact' with Ambassador Harriman, she has extremely time consuming official duties and is not well versed in the details of litigation settlement agreements drafted by lawyers."

In other words, Cutler was claiming that Pamela had never really listened at all to her high-priced legal talent. Given the number of late-night phone calls between Paris and the law offices in Washington and New York, that seemed implausible. But even if she had been tuning out, Cutler was excusing the very behavior that he claimed had led to her problems in the first place. Once again she was shifting the blame to the men she hired to represent her while she busied herself with other matters. Pamela Harriman was still a sleeping beauty.

Thirty-eight

THE FISKS AND MORTIMERS were shocked and incensed by Pamela's actions. "We got ambushed," fumed one of their representatives. Sources close to Cutler said that he had "tried every which way" to convince Pamela to sign. "You wouldn't want a client not to go through with something that went that far," said Fred Davis, an attorney for the heirs. "It was not a back of the envelope agreement."

The family had invested great hopes, not to mention time and money, in the settlement. "It is hard to tell who has the queen's ear," said one of the family's attorneys as he sought an explanation for Pamela's surprising turnabout. "Pamela falls under spheres of influence," Bill Rich once explained to a friend. "She gets infatuated with people she views as powerful and influential. To find out where she stands you have to talk to the last person, figure out his view, and then you will know her views." In this case, however, it wasn't a "he" advising Pamela but rather a "she" by the name of Linda Joy Wachner, the forty-nine-year-old chairman of two clothing companies, Warnaco and Authentic Fitness Corporation.

The two women had struck up a friendship when Pamela was staying at Felix and Liz Rohatyn's home in Southampton, Long Island, during July 1994. Restless and hard-driving, Wachner was quite plain but always impeccably groomed. She coincidentally was born with the same curvature of the spine as Janet Howard—and also spent more than a year in a body cast as a child. "It's very wearing to have a spinal disorder," Wachner once said. "Lots of people think I'm short, but it's just that I sit a lot. I can't stand for long periods of time."

Wachner came to prominence in 1986 as the first woman to buy a Fortune 500 company. She had studied economics and business at the University of Buffalo and kept her name when she married in 1973. Starting out as a ninety-dollar-a-week merchandising assistant in New York City, she jumped from one marketing job to another in the apparel business as she moved from New York to Houston to Connecticut to Hollywood and back to New York in fifteen years. As a protégée of Norton Simon chief David Mahoney in the 1980s she became chairman of Max Factor worldwide, which she tried to buy in 1984. Two years later she acquired Warnaco—a manufacturer of clothing lines by Warner, Ralph Lauren, Calvin Klein, Oscar de La Renta, and Valentino among others—in a leveraged buyout and took the company public in 1991. By 1994 her annual salary had climbed to $9.5 million.

Widowed in 1983, Wachner devoted herself to her work, traveling the world in her leased Gulfstream III to inspect Warnaco operations in twenty countries. "I have no family and I've worked like a dog all my life," Wachner would often tell new friends. "She's tough as monkey meat, but she doesn't put on airs or pretend she came from something she didn't," said a Manhattan friend. She was known as a demanding boss with a controlling personality, but her high intelligence and business skills were undeniable.

Socially, she was profoundly ambitious, and TV interviewer Barbara Walters gave her entree into the monied crowd that dominated the social worlds of Manhattan and Southampton. Wachner started collecting celebrities by flying them around on her jet, throwing lavish parties in their honor, and buying them imaginative gifts. When Sir Robin Renwick left as Britain's Ambassador in Washington in the summer of 1995, Wachner whisked him and his wife to Long Island for a dinner party for fifty with cabaret singer Bobby Short as the entertainment. The next month, she chartered a yacht for a Mediterranean cruise with a group including the Renwicks, Barbara Walters, and Senator John Warner. When Wachner showed up for a party at the Corsican home of Gianni and Marella Agnelli, Valentino's partner Giancarlo Giammetti announced mischievously, "Linda, you've finally arrived." "They use her and she uses them, and in that world nobody minds," said one observer of the social scene.

When Wachner attached herself to Pamela, no one was really surprised. "Between Linda and Pam there is a joining of interests," explained a woman who knew them both. "Pam can offer her social legitimacy. Linda has the resources. It is really a fine merger." Wachner put her jet at Pamela's disposal, and in the spring of 1995 they went together to one of Europe's most chic spas, the Institut de Thalassothérapie at Quiberon on the south coast of Brittany. As Pamela fretted about her financial and legal woes, Wachner came to the rescue, reading documents and giving her advice. On one occasion they spent an entire afternoon at the embassy residence, poring over papers together. "I helped her focus on the economics of the deal," explained Wachner.

Pamela had always entrusted her fate to men, but she now put herself in the hands of a high-powered woman who had become, in effect, her man of the moment. "Linda Wachner is the first women of any consequence to Pam," said one of Pamela's New York friends. Wachner stood firm for Pamela when Pamela was feeling abandoned by the men she had trusted. "There are no men to do this for her," said a friend of Pamela's. "She needs someone to listen to her, to say, 'Yes, you should do this,' or, 'No, you should not.' Linda is like a husband, but obviously there is nothing physical."

In a sense, Wachner was an unpolished version of Pamela's strong and pragmatic personality. Both were masters of the quid pro quo. Each appeared intensely self-involved, with an inflated self-image that masked a measure of insecurity. They shared one important friend, Pamela's political confidante Robert Shrum, who had known Wachner for a number of years and in 1995 formed a business partnership with her. "We are both women who set out to do what we wanted to do," said Wachner. "She has an enormous accomplishment as Ambassador to France. I have a pretty good accomplishment as the only woman CEO of a Fortune 500 company."

Politically, however, Pamela and her new adviser were at opposite ends of the spectrum—further proof of Pamela's adaptable nature. A registered Republican, Wachner gave $146,000 to GOP candidates from 1984 through 1995, including Michael Huffington for Congress in California, Senator Robert Packwood for his reelection in 1992, and New York Senator Alfonse D'Amato, scourge of the Democratic Party. Wachner supported George Bush in his race against Michael Dukakis, and in 1992 she gave $101,200 to the Republican National Committee while Pamela was giving a mere $11,900 to the Democrats. Starting in 1994, Wachner put herself behind Bob Dole for the 1996 Republican presidential nomination with $6,000 in donations. Hedging her bets from 1989 through 1995, she also gave $24,400 to a scattering of Democrats such as Bill Bradley and New York Congressman Charles Schumer.

When Pamela began expressing doubts about the settlement agreement on May 9, Linda Wachner reinforced her misgivings. Early that morning and the next as well, Wachner was on the phone to Pamela at Kitty Hart's apartment, first from her plane en route to Asia, and then from Hong Kong. Her advice was simple: Fight.

She convinced Pamela that her lawyers had sold her short and that she could do better. With the proceeds from the art, Pamela would have a war chest for a legal battle that far exceeded the reserves of the Mortimers and Fisks. They were using the remaining $3 million in their trust funds to pay their legal bills, and Pamela could easily spend them into submitting to a deal more to her advantage. "It was not an irrational decision on her part," said a lawyer for the heirs.

Pamela resolved to stay in New York until after the sale of her paintings, although she didn't make an appearance in the jammed Christie's auction room at seven-thirty that Thursday night. Lloyd Cutler was there, and so was Averell Fisk. Christopher Burge, elegant in black tie, stood at the podium flanked by several rows of Christie's employees on the phone with bidders as well as sellers, one of whom was Pamela, listening intently for the results. The Renoir went first, for $5.1 million, just above Christie's low estimate. "Tell Pamela Harriman to give me one of her famous lunches," cracked hard-charging corporate dealmaker Carl Icahn, the losing bidder. The Picasso was next, fetching a very respectable $10.9 million that exceeded the high estimate. The Matisse, however, posed real problems, inching up to a mere $1,020,000, less than half of the low estimate.

The total price, including $1.7 million in commissions paid by the buyers to Christie's, was $18.7 million. Ordinarily Pamela would have been entitled to the remaining $17 million. But according to her advisers, the $14.5 million guarantee enabled Christie's to take a cut of around $1 million, leaving her with $16 million. Pamela told Burge she was happy with the result of the sale, but her lawyers later said she was disappointed, or as Lloyd Cutler described the outcome to friends, "It was a two-base hit, not a home run."

If Pamela had settled that day, she would have been required to pay the heirs 80 percent of her net proceeds, some $13 million, along with contributions from her other asset sales, for a total to the Harriman family of around $15 million—although Ames had been willing to reduce that to $13.5 million. Still, according to court papers, Pamela's aggregate financial obligations under the terms of the settlement would have been more than $30 million, including the $6 million at her death, $3 million from the Sands Point lots to repay one of her loans, $4.6 million to the charitable trusts, and $3 million in taxes. She had an estimated $40 million to meet those payments, which during her lifetime would have left her with around $14 million in assets, many of which were "illiquid and speculative." Her fear of living on around $500,000 a year would have come true, a prospect that clinched her decision to keep what she had.

The morning after the auction, Pamela hopped on the Concorde and fled to Paris. The same day Lloyd Cutler entered the hospital for surgery that would require a recuperation of several months, and Roy Reardon, a dogged litigator, took charge. After a period of silence, there was a last spasm of negotiations in the weeks after the auction. Ames yielded more ground, agreeing to Pamela's new demand that the family pay half the amount—instead of 30 percent—to reimburse the charitable trusts for their losses, and that Pamela take out a life insurance policy instead of mortgaging her two properties to guarantee her estate's eventual payment to the marital trust. Pamela's lawyers then made a "final offer" several million below the $13.5 million Ames had suggested. At that point Ames said no. Perhaps he got too stiff-necked under the circumstances, but he reasonably believed that if he kept giving in, Pamela's side could nibble the heirs to death in a renegotiation.

"We returned to war," said one of Pamela's lawyers. "Someday we will return to settlement." In the meantime, though, legal skirmishes continued in New York and Virginia. The heirs filed yet another lawsuit in June, charging Pamela with breach of contract for rejecting the settlement. The new action brought out even more embarrassing details of Pamela's tattered finances, including the four sets of "worst" to "high" projections for Pamela's balance sheet that formed the basis of the aborted settlement—documents her lawyers sought unsuccessfully to keep under court seal. A New York judge dismissed the new lawsuit, but the heirs immediately filed an appeal.

Amid the turmoil of the legal battles the old Pamela, the femme fatale, incongruously reappeared in the headlines. As ambassador, it had been widely assumed that, as one of her French friends put it, "Her man is politics, Mr. Politics." Yet during much of June and July, gossip columnists amused themselves by linking Pamela romantically to Prince Rainier of Monaco, the widower of Grace Kelly, whose tiny principality fell under the United States ambassador's portfolio. Pamela had turned up in May at the Bal des Roses gala in Monte Carlo. When photographs of her with Rainier appeared in an English magazine, speculation swept through European capitals that she might marry the seventy-two-year-old prince and restore her fortune in the old-fashioned way. The *New York Post* called Pamela and Rainier "mutual objects of desire," even after an embassy spokeswoman dismissed the story as "absolutely false." Lloyd Cutler griped to the *Washington Post,* "For heaven's sake . . . that rumor ought to be sat on."

Pamela had known Rainier since her days on the Riviera after the war. When asked about the romance chatter, she said it was "nutty," and explained that his daughter Princess Caroline had actually asked her to the ball. Rainier, she noted to one friend, was "a very dull man." Nevertheless, those who had known her for many years couldn't help being titillated by the idea of a dramatic rescue, even if the prince was something less than charming. "I laughed like hell when I heard it," said Kitty Hart. "It seems ludicrous, but you can't rule anything out. Who knows, it might be fun for her." Even as the rumor fizzled, it seemed quite remarkable that a seventy-five-year-old woman could generate that kind of excitement.

Through the summer months Cutler's staff worked on settling matters with the Harriman Foundation. Pamela's impulse was neither a philanthropic act nor a way to reach out to the family, but a recognition that the charitable trusts were her point of greatest legal and personal liability. From an image standpoint, any default on her pledge to Brookings would hurt her position in the foreign policy establishment. If she restored money to the trusts she would face only nominal fines from the Internal Revenue Service, but if she did not, her penalties could run to 200 percent of the amount lost by the trusts. "It is a serious problem," said a lawyer for the heirs. "She is the sole trustee of two trusts with virtually no assets. If they made her pay interest and penalties it could run over ten million."

A financial consulting firm hired by the foundation estimated that if the assets of the charitable trusts had been managed prudently, there would have been $4.7 million available in 1995. Pamela offered to restore between $2 million and $3 million to the trusts, which would be added to the $2.2 million net proceeds anticipated from selling one of the mortgages the two trusts controlled at the Seasons Resort. With that amount of endowment, however, the trusts would be exhausted in 2002 instead of 2011 as envisioned in Harriman's will, and there would be nothing left for his great-grandchildren to share.

The foundation then raised Pamela's required ante by several million more to ensure that the annuities would stretch to the full twenty-five years and some principal would remain. When Pamela said she couldn't afford that, negotiations broke down in late July. She charged the heirs with "intentionally derailing the agreement . . . that would have made the foundation whole" because they believed that funds she paid to the charitable trusts "would no longer be available to settle the New York action." A month later the foundation entered the legal fray in Virginia by joining the heirs against Pamela, repeating their charges of mismanagement. As of August 1995, according to the foundation's legal documents, the charitable trusts had "less than $600 in cash" and the pledge to Brookings was imperiled.

Whatever chance Pamela had to make a graceful settlement and repair relations seemed hopelessly out of reach as positions hardened by the day. The stigma of embarrassing publicity had disappeared for both sides; they had already shed their privacy and appearance of amity. Lawyers used terms like "trench warfare" to describe the intrafamily conflict.

With the legal battle entering its second year, the Harriman heirs tightened their belts—in their own fashion. Early in 1995, Averell Fisk had put his four-bedroom lakefront Palm Beach home on the market for $2.8 million, but by year's end he still had no takers. Arden had to shut down some of the stables and dismiss several workers, including Kathleen Mortimer's gardener. On weekends, the thin, refined figure of David Mortimer could be seen riding about on a tractor to help keep the estate going. "He does an enormous amount of work every weekend," said one of his sympathetic friends, "cleaning out the stables, doing all the work Pamela had promised to have done." The Arden overhead had been reduced by about a third, which enabled the family to lessen its contributions, although Mary Fisk and Kathleen Mortimer were still obliged to pay about $50,000 apiece for upkeep and taxes. Mary Fisk continued to drain her reserves of capital as she let her cook go and started preparing meals for herself. When a friend saw Stanley Mortimer at the races in Saratoga in August, she asked, "How are your horses doing?" "I don't have any now," he groused. "I can't afford it until this thing is settled."

By 1995 Pamela had cut her overhead as well—by 35 percent, according to one of her advisers. She no longer employed a private speechwriter at the embassy, using State Department aides instead, and she dismissed her personal maid Iris. Even so, her expenses in Paris were running several hundred thousand dollars a year. She continued to honor one commitment she made to her late husband by allocating some $100,000 annually to fund the pensions of retired Arden retainers "to preserve the family's tradition of caring for its staff," according to Lloyd Cutler. All told, she was still spending nearly $1 million a year.

Always resourceful, Pamela figured out new ways to pay some of her embassy expenses. Before her annual Fourth of July reception she sent letters to prominent Democratic Party contributors back in the United States soliciting donations. Janet Howard worked the phones with her old contacts, asking for help in return for an acknowledgment in the program. Friends and guests on private business who stayed in the official suites at the residence were presented on the morning of their departure with cards in elegantly written calligraphy stating the charges for their accommodations. Such costs, according to a veteran diplomat, were traditionally at the discretion of the ambassador, who otherwise had to pay out of pocket. Pamela also became adept at having corporations foot the bill for events at the residence, as Gulfstream Corporation chairman Theodore J. Forstmann did in the fall of 1995. "It is not out of the ordinary to have a reception at the residence for your directors and invite French business people," explained one diplomat. "It is only prohibited if one corporation is favored over another. Pam has done it a lot, making the residence available to everyone."

She had sold the smaller house on N Street for $990,000, one-third below the asking price, netting her $330,000 after paying off the $500,000 mortgage, taxes, and expenses. She had reduced the cost of keeping up the main house by dismissing her staff. She kept a live-in caretaker there, and her gardener looked after Willow Oaks, where Patsy Preston rented the guest cottage—although maintenance still ran several hundred thousand a year. She also had a new source of income—easily more than $100,000 a year—from letting out her cottage in Sun Valley to anyone who could afford the $850 nightly tab. She sold several more lots at Sands Point, bringing in nearly $1 million by the end of the year.

In September 1995, Pamela took the main N Street home off the market. From the start, the asking price seemed based more on the Harriman name than on the house's true worth. With an assessed value of $1.9 million, most realtors considered the price tag of $3.7 million to be inflated. Prospective buyers had to be financially vetted by Lloyd Cutler's law firm before they could even see the property. Despite its swimming pool and beautiful garden, the house needed considerable renovation, especially the bathrooms and the anti-quated kitchen. "Without her glamour, it is an ordinary old house," said realtor Ann Brower. Pamela had briefly dropped the asking price to $2.9 million in the spring of 1995, but then raised it to $3.3 million when friends told her to hold firm. But in sixteen months, there had been no serious offers. By taking the house off the market altogether, Pamela figured that if she had some work done on the kitchen and waited a while, she could do better.

Thanks to the kindness of friends—and Pamela's irresistible ability to wine and dine them in the Paris embassy—she still managed to live the high life. Anne Cox Chambers invited her to stay at her home in the South of France, and Linda Wachner ferried her from country to country. Pamela tried to stay fit by swimming on Sundays in the pool at the Ritz Hotel, where prominent socialites liked to congregate. She continued to use the Sun Valley house for her own pleasure but banned the Mortimers and Fisks from the premises. She took a three-week vacation there in August 1995, finding solace in long walks and slipping away just once to Southampton for a weekend with Wachner, who flew out for several days in Idaho as well. Patsy Preston, still mourning her husband's death, also came for a visit. To her friends and guests, Pamela raged about the Harriman relatives. Pamela had persuaded herself, as one friend de- scribed it, that they were bent on revenge and wanted to "destroy her." "I won't even be able to afford to buy one dress," she complained as she vowed to "fight them till I die." Perhaps for inspiration, Pamela had as her bedside reading a new biography of the intrepid Jane Digby.

Back on the job in September, Pamela showed no sign of slowing her pace or reducing the scale of her entertaining. When Microsoft billionaire Bill Gates came to town, she threw a dinner for sixty that included French computer and economic experts as well as American journalists. In October, she hosted a gala at Versailles to raise funds for the American Library in Paris. Pamela's invitation asked prospective donors to remember their childhood in an enchanted castle and then come and relive it at Versailles at a cost of $600 a head. The message seemed unfortunate, given Pamela's circumstances. "Nobody I know spent their childhood in a castle—except maybe Pamela Harriman," said one Paris-based journalist.

When Pamela had been especially weighed down by the legal imbroglio back in the spring, her staff had begun saying that the strain was so intense that she might bow out of her job early. But by late 1995 Pamela had bounced back and served notice that she intended to stay through the end of Clinton's first term—which had been her plan all along. "She feels she has to stay so she can hold her head high," said a Washington friend.

Not long after her arrival in Paris she had told *Vogue* magazine, "It's not the accolades when you arrive, it's the judgments when you leave." Mindful of those judgments, Pamela focused on doing everything possible to ensure she would be remembered as one of America's best envoys. "She's not thinking beyond that," said Robert Shrum. "She has a certain fatalism. She wants to pay attention to what she is doing now and when she gets to tomorrow she'll deal with it."

She had fulfilled her professional ambitions, yet Pamela seemed vaguely unsatisfied. It had been a decade since Averell Harriman's death had embold-ened her to go it alone. "I don't think she's ever truly happy without a man in her life," said her son Winston. "Since Averell there has been nobody to fill that particular vacuum. There's not too much time for it now, with her sixteen-hour-a-day job, so it is not front burner at the moment." But after stepping down from her post, according to Winston, "I would think there would be another man."

Where she might end up living afterward became an intermittent guessing game among longtime Pamela-watchers, although nobody seemed inclined to hold her to anything she said. "She is trying to figure out where her roots are," one of her friends said late in 1995. Before the money troubles she had planned to shuttle between her estate in Virginia and an apartment in Paris, and even after a year's worth of legal battles she hadn't entirely abandoned that prospect. "She wants to live in as many places as she can afford," said one of her advisers.

She had grown closer to Minnie and the Churchill grandchildren, but there seemed little likelihood she would settle in England. "I don't feel at home in England," she told a Washington friend. Paris would surely be the most hospita-ble place. Even after she lost the power of the ambassadorship, she would be noticed and admired as only the French can appreciate a woman of a certain age. "She very much loves her Parisian existence," said Winston. "She feels very comfortable there."

Yet while her standing in Paris remained high, her reputation back home had taken a beating because of the publicity over the lawsuit. Pamela had no desire, said one of her friends, to return to Washington for an encore as "den mother of the Democrats," nor did she have the financial resources to be a big-league donor. But she did seem intent on proving she had not been defeated by the Harriman family and on regaining the respectability she had battled so hard to acquire. Some Washingtonians who knew her well speculated that she would be appointed to a prominent government commission. Others predicted she would serve as a corporate director, a position that could offer her substan-tial fees and benefits as well as prestige. "She would be a great addition to Warnaco or any board of any company," said Linda Wachner.

In October 1995, Pamela launched a breathtaking legal counterattack, not only against the heirs, but also against her former advisers: Rich, Warnke, and

Clifford, the man whose "high principles" once held her "in awe." She even sued Brown Brothers Harriman, the Wall Street firm that had symbolized the family fortune for decades. Pamela said that Rich had made numerous investments without her knowledge; she accused Clifford and Warnke of "legal malpractice"; she condemned Brown Brothers Harriman for "negligence" and "breach of fiduciary duty" by permitting unauthorized withdrawals from her accounts. She further charged that her stepdaughters Kathleen Mortimer and Mary Fisk had "unclean hands" for thwarting her efforts to settle with the foundation. And she went after all six grandchildren, demanding repayments of the $2 million in principal and interest on the loans they had received from Averell Harriman. She somewhat justifiably singled out Averell Mortimer for getting the Harriman family involved in the ruinous PDI investment.

In a front-page story, the *Washington Post* called the legal actions a "nasty new phase" of the feud. But there was method to Pamela's anger: By bringing in such affluent defendants as Brown Brothers Harriman and several law firms that had worked on the trusts, she was enlarging the number of potential contributors to a settlement and possibly reducing some of her own financial liability.

The best hope for restraint on both sides was the vast amount the lawyers were draining from what remained of the Harriman fortune. While Pamela had more money, she also employed the highest priced talent. By the end of 1995 Pamela's legal tab from Cutler, Reardon, and her Virginia law firm of Hunton & Williams had climbed to $4 million. The family also had legal bills of more than $1 million that further depleted the family trusts. The heirs relied heavily on the services of family member Charles Ames, who charged them a cut rate, they employed fewer attorneys, and as plaintiffs they could more easily control costs, offering bonuses, for example, from a settlement or court judgment. The family war chest grew by $2.2 million in October 1995 when one of the Seasons Resort mortgages was paid off, entitling the family trusts to half the proceeds. (The other $2.2 million went as expected to the two charitable trusts, which were able to resume their annual payment to the Harriman Foundation as a result.)

The fees for full-scale trials in New York and Virginia could only multiply. Depositions for Clifford and Warnke were scheduled for January 1996, and for Pamela in February. The case was assuming "Bleak House" proportions, a spectacle of waste, delays, and legal maneuvering. One courtroom appearance in September 1995 might have been mistaken for a trial lawyers' convention, with numerous representatives from nine law firms on hand. "Never in my career have I seen so many lawyers involved in a lawsuit," said an experienced litigator familiar with the case.

In early December, Brendan Sullivan, the prominent trial lawyer representing Clark Clifford, had two hourglasses made. On the top of each was printed: "$ OF PAMELA & HEIRS," and on the bottom it said simply: "LAWYERS." He sent one to Lloyd Cutler and one to the family's Washington lawyer, David Boyd. At the same time, the heirs suffered several legal setbacks, including a ruling by the judge in the Virginia case to disqualify the family's lawyers at Shearman & Sterling in New York, since the firm had once advised Averell

Harriman on estate planning matters. The decision guaranteed further delays and additional costs as the family scrambled to find new representatives.

Behind the scenes, settlement talks between Ames and Pamela's lawyers had resumed after Pamela's legal offensive. This time Lloyd Cutler was working in close consultation with Linda Wachner, who now recognized that Pamela had to settle. Wachner was on the phone daily with Pamela's attorneys—and sometimes several times a day. Although she was operating "as a friend," Wachner was retained by Simpson Thacher & Bartlett "as a professional," she said, adding, "I was not paid." For weeks the two sides remained far apart; around Thanksgiving, Pamela complained to a friend that every time an agreement seemed within view, *"they* would want more the next day."

Maybe it was the image of sand slipping through the hourglass, or the multimillion-dollar payment Pamela made to her attorneys in November, or sheer battle fatigue on both sides, but on December 13 Charles Ames was once again shuttling between Boston, Washington, and New York. The reason for the urgency, it turned out, was the opportunity for both sides to reduce their taxes if they settled by the end of the year—which would surely have made old Averell proud. With the structure of the settlement already in place, one lawyer for the family predicted that given good faith on both sides, an agreement could be reached in a matter of days.

Ambassador Pamela Harriman was very much in evidence during the signing of the Bosnia Peace Accord on December 14 in Paris. The accord had actually been hashed out in Dayton, Ohio, with her friend Richard Holbrooke as stern mediator. The Clinton administration had reluctantly chosen Paris for the signing to soothe the feelings of the French, who had taken the lead the previous spring in trying to end nearly four years of war. At first, the petulant French weren't going to allow Pamela to attend the signing in the Elysée Palace overseen by Bill Clinton, France's Jacques Chirac, Britain's John Major, Germany's Helmut Kohl, and Russia's Viktor Chernomyrdin. But Holbrooke raised a fuss and secured a place for her in the audience, where they sat together in the fourth row. Pamela was once again on the evening newscasts, smiling her big smile, shining in the reflected glory of world leaders.

In the week before Christmas, both sides in the Harriman legal wrangle began expressing guarded optimism about the prospects for a settlement. After spending the holidays with Minnie and the grandchildren, Pamela flew to New York, and on Friday, December 29, she arrived at the thirtieth-floor office of Roy Reardon to sign the new settlement agreement. At 2:30 P.M. Ames appeared with Kathleen and David Mortimer, the two family members who had been closest to Pamela. (The other Mortimers and Fisks were out of town, including Averell Mortimer, who was vacationing in Mustique.) It was only when they stepped off the elevator that "they knew it was on," said a source close to the family.

Confronting one another for the first time in a year and a half, the Harriman heirs and Pamela coolly shook hands, presumably no longer "unclean." They exchanged small talk about the effects on the Paris embassy of the federal goverment shutdown created by the budget impasse between President Clinton and the Republican Congress. But the atmosphere was businesslike as the group sat down to sign stacks of documents. "We weren't there for a cup of tea," one family member later reported to a friend. Out in the hallway stood Linda Wachner, waiting to fly Pamela back to Paris on her Gulfstream.

The settlement was similar to the earlier agreement, but with lower dollar amounts for both sides from a money pot diminished by legal fees and other expenses. Instead of $15 million, Pamela had to pay $9 million to the heirs outright and $2 million to replenish the charitable trusts and assure funding for the foundation. On her death she would pay several million more—the exact amount would depend on the value of various assets—to the marital trust from her estate. She guaranteed the estate payment by taking out a $1.5 million term life insurance policy and signing a security agreement giving the heirs up to $2.14 million from any sale of Willow Oaks if her estate could not satisfy her obligation to the marital trust. Between the $500,000 mortgage already in place and the new security pledge, Pamela's banker (J. P. Morgan, Delaware) and Harriman's heirs essentially controlled Pamela's beloved Virginia property— and precluded her from selling it in her lifetime unless she gave an alternate guarantee for her estate's payment. At the same time, Pamela renounced the power Harriman had given her in his will to choose which of his heirs would receive the marital trust proceeds.

Pamela also forgave the more than $2 million in loans she had been seeking to collect from the Mortimers and Fisks. The family retained their options to buy Pamela's Arden stake as well as Sun Valley, which they could once again use for vacations. And they still stood to receive 15 percent of any proceeds from *White Roses;* even if she didn't dare to sell it, the possibility remained that she could lease it for periods of time to museums or galleries.

"It was a tough compromise," said a source close to the family. "Everyone had to take less." Pamela was left with an estimated $9 million in cash, which could yield around $700,000 with an investment return of 8 percent—a reasonable annual income under the guidelines developed by her advisers. Nevertheless, it was hard to imagine the Pamela Harriman of legend confined to a two-bedroom apartment. She seemed destined to continue living beyond her means. Pamela still had some $12 million tied up in real estate and oil and gas interests. She also had the slender prospect of recovering some money from Seasons as the value of resort properties in general moved upward. And she retained her majority interest in *White Roses,* her ace in the hole.

By forcing the family to settle for less, Pamela had won a Pyrrhic victory. She had to relinquish millions of dollars to end what was becoming an enormously costly war of attrition. "It was never serious litigation," said one courtroom veteran. "There was no real discovery, just filing one lawsuit after another like dogs in a park marking out their spaces. The settlement was just a matter of dollars. It was based on fear that all the dollars would be sucked up and neither side would have anything."

In their public statements, Pamela and the family emphasized that together they would pursue lawsuits against Clifford, Warnke, Rich, and other defendants to recover more money. Privately each side pledged $500,000 to go after these "third parties," and at Linda Wachner's urging they hired New York litigator Stanley Arkin. But their saber rattling seemed primarily a face-saving device that enabled both sides to point the finger of blame at someone else. The settlement only made sense if Pamela and the heirs could end all the litigation. Otherwise they would face spiraling legal fees and the time and agony of depositions and trials. The real aim was to maneuver toward a settlement with Clifford—the only individual with financial resources in the millions—and perhaps Brown Brothers Harriman and two Manhattan law firms involved with the trusts.

The settlement with Clifford, ailing and bedridden, finally was worked out in the summer of 1996. After Clifford's offer of $750,000 sat on the table for months, Arkin concluded that pursuing him in court would be costly and counterproductive, so he asked Federal Judge John Martin to act as a mediator. Martin summoned all parties to his courtroom on June 3. Several days before the court date, Pamela called Clifford to plea for $2.75 million, invoking their friendship of many years. He listened and responded politely, but he was un-moved by her persuasive powers. During the court conference, Martin an-nounced that Pamela and the heirs, represented by Arkin, Ames, and Linda Wachner, would accept $1.5 million from Clifford. Brendan Sullivan replied that his client would pay nothing more than $1 million—the precise amount Clifford had offered a year earlier. After further discussions, Pamela and the heirs agreed to $1 million along with $100,000 from Clifford's former partners, including Warnke, who could contribute less than $50,000. Attorney Edmund Burns stood by his earlier offer of $500,000, and the second Manhattan firm, Brown and Wood, offered $100,000. Bill Rich ultimately agreed to pay a token amount to put his legal problems behind him.

The notion of Pamela and the heirs as legal colleagues did not mean that they had become one big happy family. "Thank God it's over, and I don't have to see any of them again," she had remarked after the December settlement. The terms included a strict confidentiality agreement that reimposed Pamela's control over the Harriman heirs. If any of them talked to an outsider not only about the terms of the settlement but the steps leading up to it, future payments from Pamela could be jeopardized. "It won't be a case of pretending this has never been," said Winston. "It was a quite unpleasant case all around." On January 6, 1996, eight days after the settlement between Pamela and the heirs was signed, Mary Fisk dropped dead of a heart attack at seventy-eight. Pamela sent a gracious note of condolence to Kathleen Mortimer, but otherwise did not resume communicating with the family.

Pamela had survived another of the Perils-of-Pauline episodes that had punctuated her life. "It is a sinister pattern," said a wealthy European woman who knew Pamela for more than three decades. "She is always after financial security, and it seems the moment she has it, it disappears. The fact that she has looked for that sort of security her whole life shows how insecure she is."

Pamela had used everything she had—her wiles, her body, her brazen ambition, her association with the Churchill family—to achieve a place in the world of wealth and power that she had coveted since childhood. She had weathered fifty years of tumult and striving, of being rejected by the likes of

Murrow, Agnelli, and Rothschild, of enduring three difficult husbands, two of whom left her financially threadbare, of fighting with stepchildren, of being written off time after time only to scrape her way back into prominence. But Pamela Churchill Harriman had never been satisfied by her triumphs or defeated by her setbacks. She always wanted something more.

When Averell Harriman died in 1986, Pamela was free to pursue her own ambitions without checking with the man of the house. She had inherited a fortune, she had social position, she had political respectability. She used all three to secure a highly prestigious diplomatic post in an elegant European capital where, because she knew the language and culture, she stood the best chance of making a great success. All she had to do was proceed with a measure of prudence. But she always had a streak of grandiosity, which was now magnified by the Harriman fortune. True to form, she overreached. She spent extravagantly, and acted cavalierly toward her Harriman relations.

"She probably didn't think about it or realize the Fisks and Mortimers weren't as well off as she," said a woman who knew her for many years. "She has always wanted money and she has lived very high. She didn't realize she was living much better than the others. I don't know if she really realized how others live. She has never really come down to earth."

In what should have been her moment of public triumph and personal vindication, she found herself struggling with the same sort of conflict and uncertainty that had always played beneath her dazzling surface. She had a big house and considerable status, but still lacked the financial security of the truly rich. The long journey from London to Paris to New York to Washington to Paris seemed destined to end as a zero-sum game. In her eighth decade, Pamela Digby Churchill Hayward Harriman was still the young girl from Dorset: secure in her bloodlines, toughened by the hunting fields, entranced by glamour and wealth, and always ready to fight—again, again, and again.

A Note on Sources

This book was researched and written without the cooperation of Pamela Harriman. The principal advantage in writing about a living subject was the opportunity to interview friends, relatives, and others who have known her throughout her life. On the other hand, for a variety of reasons—mainly a reluctance to offend someone perceived to be powerful and influential—not everyone was willing to be quoted by name. Of the more than four hundred people I interviewed over a five-year period, roughly one-quarter preferred anonymity. I relied on such sources only when they had direct knowledge of people and events. Since I could not name these sources, their quotations appear without footnotes. All unattributed quotes came from my interviews, with one exception, which is noted below. Otherwise I did not use anonymous quotes that have appeared in newspapers, magazines, or books.

Life of the Party, by Christopher Ogden, published in 1994, was based largely on about forty hours of interviews the author conducted with Pamela Harriman. The book was originally intended as an autobiographical collaboration, but the author proceeded on his own after Pamela Harriman balked at including certain information about her private life. For legal reasons, Ogden was prevented from using direct quotations from their interviews. While unable to confirm the source of specific information, Ogden told me, "If you look up something and see no footnote, and you draw the conclusion that this must be from her, it wouldn't be far wrong." Based on this guidance, as well as my own knowledge, I have used his book as a reference for Pamela Harriman's version of some events in her life. I have only quoted directly from the Ogden book when he expressed her feelings or views because, he said, "Whenever I attribute belief I had a pretty strong reason to say that."

I also consulted various archives for letters, memos, diaries, and financial records. The most important of these are listed below with the abbreviations I have used in the notes. Also listed are abbreviations for legal documents and periodicals frequently mentioned. In citing periodicals, I have listed only publication names and dates unless the article is a long feature in a magazine or newspaper, in which case I have included the title and author as well. Conversions from British sterling to American dollars were based on International Financial Statistics (tables of foreign exchange rates) from the Board of Governors of the Federal Reserve System. Computations of current dollars were based on the U.S. Department of Labor's Bureau of Labor Statistics Consumer Price Index from 1913 through 1995.

ABBREVIATIONS

AD	*Architectural Digest*
BG	*Boston Globe*
CRP	Center for Responsive Politics, National Library on Money and Politics (Washington, DC)
DM	*Daily Mail*
ES	*Evening Standard*
FEC	Federal Election Commission (Washington, DC)
	RRD Report of Receipts and Disbursements
FCL	Foundation Center Library (Washington, DC)
	APHF: W. Averell and Pamela C. Harriman Foundation
	MWHF: Mary W. Harriman Foundation
HH-GU	Harry Hopkins Papers at Georgetown University (Washington, DC)
HH-FDR	Harry Hopkins Papers at Franklin D. Roosevelt Library (Hyde Park, NY)
LH-NYPL	Leland Hayward Collection at the Library and Museum of the Performing Arts, the New York Public Library at Lincoln Center (New York, NY)
MB-HLRO	Papers of Max Beaverbrook, the first Baron Beaverbrook, at the House of Lords Record Office (London, UK)
	MB-DD: daily engagement diaries
	CVB: Cherkley Court visitor's book
NY	*New York* magazine
NYHT	*New York Herald Tribune*
NYJA	*New York Journal-American*
NYT	*New York Times*
TAT	*The Tatler*
T&C	*Town & Country*
TNR	*The New Republic*
TNY	*The New Yorker*
TT-L	*The Times* (London)
USNY	United States District Court, Southern District of New York
VCLC	Virginia, Circuit Court of Loudoun County
	RE: Residuary Estate
	MT: Marital Trust
	CLT: Charitable Lead Trusts
VF	*Vanity Fair*
W	*W* magazine
WAH-LC	W. Averell Harriman Papers in the Library of Congress (Washington, DC)
	WAH-DD: daily appointment diaries
WP	*Washington Post*
WSJ	*Wall Street Journal*
WWD	*Women's Wear Daily*

Notes

Introduction

13 On the stage: Author's observations.
13 "one of the great women": Charter Day speech by Pamela Harriman, 2/3/96.
14 "powerful and penetrating": Remarks by Timothy J. Sullivan.
14 Since then she had donated: APHF annual reports, 1988–93 (FCL).
14 "great influence on both": Introduction by Margaret, The Lady Thatcher.
15 "faithless fiduciary": USNY, *Charles C. Ames, et al.* v. *Clark M. Clifford, et al.*, complaint, 9/13/94, p. 2 (cited hereafter as USNY complaint 9/13/94).
15 "golden chain of lovers": Joanna Richardson, *The Courtesans* (1967), p. 52.
16 "There are certain women": Gerald Clarke, *Capote* (1988), p. 486.
17 Both Jacqueline Kennedy Onassis: *Washington Times*, 10/12/95; interview with Evangeline Bruce.
17 "[Women] arc rooting": William Drozdiak, "From Power Hostess to Effective Envoy," *WP*, 4/25/96.
17 "We had to be fairly creative": Interview with Rear Admiral Daniel J. Murphy.
17 "The scandal of her life": Maurice Druon, *The Film of Memory* (1955), p. 134.
18 "50 Most Beautiful People": *People*, 5/3/93.
18 a "marvelous primitive": Clarke, p. 486.
18 "What is your secret?": Interview with Mandy Grunwald.
18 "Don't underestimate her confidence": Interview with Peter Glenville.

Chapter One

19 Edward Kenelm Digby was: Among the sources for the descriptions of Lord and Lady Digby were *The Complete Peerage*, Vol. 4 (1916), pp. 353–357; interviews with Edith Foxwell, Esme Cromer; Rudy Abramson, *Spanning the Century* (1992), p. 307.
19 She was not beautiful: Interviews with Edith Foxwell and Esme Cromer.
19 A patch of white streaked: *W*, 3/14–20/80.
20 In the hierarchy of English nobility: The description of Digby family history and its place in the aristocracy draws from *The Complete Peerage*, Vol. 4, pp. 353–357; Sir Egerton Brydges, *Collins's Peerage of England; Genealogical, Biographical, and Historical*, Vol. V (1812), pp. 348–385; David Cannadine,

The Decline and Fall of the British Aristocracy (1992), pp. 10, 22, 570; Winston S. Churchill, *Memories and Adventures* (1990), p. 67.

20 while Pamela would boast: NYT, 3/2/77.

20 As was customary for peers: Cannadine, pp. 10, 55, 547.

20 In the late nineteenth century their land: *The Complete Peerage,* Vol. 4, pp. 353–357.

20 Given Pamela Digby's lifelong: Brydges, p. 385.

20 The most heroic Digby ancestor: Churchill, pp. 68–69; *The Complete Peerage,* Vol. 4, p. 356; Clive Aslet, "Minterne Magna, Dorset: The Seat of Lord Digby," *Country Life,* 2/21/80 and 2/28/80.

21 The most infamous Digby was: The account of Jane Digby's life relied on two sources: E. M. Oddie, *The Odyssey of a Loving Woman* (1936), and Margaret Fox Schmidt, *Passion's Child* (1977).

21 "perfect oval": Schmidt, p. 25.

21 "wild rose": Oddie, p. 33.

21 "wild, impetuous": Ibid., p. 28.

21 "the Byronesque lover": Ibid., p. 60.

22 "My heart warms towards": Ibid., p. 177.

22 "the magnificent, large-hearted": Ibid., p. 187.

22 "It is now a month and twenty": Ibid., p. 318.

22 "Judge not, that ye": Ibid., p. 324.

22 When Jane's brother: *The Complete Peerage,* Vol. 4, p. 356.

22 Four years later: *Country Life,* 2/21/80 and 2/28/80.

23 Kenny Digby—the name: TT-L, 1/30/64; Churchill, p. 64; *The Sketch,* 6/26/34; interviews with Sarah Norton Baring, Winston Churchill.

23 Pamela Bruce was of Welsh: *The Complete Peerage,* Vol. I (1910), pp. 13–14; *Dictionary of National Biography,* Vol. IV (1973), pp. 1102–1113; *Who Was Who, 1929–1940,* p. 2.

23 Her oldest sister Margaret: TAT, 10/11/18, 3/26/19; *Debrett's Illustrated Peerage* (1960), pp. 114–115; *The Complete Peerage,* Vol. 2 (1916), pp. 112–113; *Debrett's Illustrated Peerage,* pp. 1050–1051; *The Complete Peerage or a History of the House of Lords,* Vol. 11 (1949), pp. 133–139; *Who Was Who, 1971–1980,* p. 685; Cannadine, p. 225.

23 On March 20, 1920: Pamela Beryl Digby, Birth Certificate #278; TAT, 4/7/20.

23 Several months later, old Lord Digby: TT-L, 5/12/20; "The Late Lord Digby's Fortune," TT-L, 12/20/20; last will and testament of Edward Henry Trafalgar Lord Digby, 12/2/19.

23 Instead of moving into Minterne: The description of the Digby family's fortunes in 1920 and the changes in the British aristocracy drew on Cannadine, pp. 11, 48, 65, 70, 89, 97, 265, 486, 595, and 598; interviews with Julian Pitt-Rivers, a Dorset neighbor, and with Mary Dunn.

24 Lord and Lady Digby set sail: *The Illustrated London News,* 8/28/20; TAT, 9/1/20; Serge Obolensky, *One Man in His Time* (1958), p. 249.

24 Pamela's memories from that period: Interview with Nicholas Haslam.

25 When Lord Digby's term ended: TAT, 6/27/23.

25 Sheila was impossible: Marie Brenner, "The Prime of Pamela Harriman," *Vanity Fair,* 7/88.

CHAPTER TWO

26   The estate at Minterne Magna unfolded: Author's observations.
26   The main hall rose: "Current Architecture: Minterne House, Cerne Abbas," *Architectural Review,* 25 (1909)(1), pp. 143–150; *Country Life,* 2/21/80 and 2/28/80; Clive Aslet, *The Last Country Houses* (1982), pp. 54–55, 107, 111, 146–153.
26   "always impressed": C. L. Sulzberger, *The Last of the Giants* (1970), p. 455.
27   Like most aristocratic households: Angela Lambert, *1939: The Last Season of Peace* (1989), pp. 40–41.
27   Several miles away from Minterne: Rodney Legg, *Cerne's Giant and Village Guide* (1990), pp. 7–9.
27   The girls loved to tear: Interview with Edith Foxwell; Pamela Churchill, "The Giant of Cerne Abbas: Aperitif for a Country Weekend," ES, 6/15/46.
27   In recalling her childhood: Christopher Ogden, *Life of the Party* (1995 ed.), p. 41.
27   the only hunt ball held: TAT, 1/25/39.
28   Wages were low: Lambert, p. 127.
28   "always reflected what had been": Pamela C. Harriman, "How can I start with a clock? I can't sit on it, I can't eat off it," AD, 6/84.
28   They also served as: Interview with Esme Cromer.
29   From spring to late summer: TAT, 6/27/23, 5/8/29, 4/2/30, 5/14/30, 7/2/30, 7/12/33, 8/23/33, 10/4/33.
29   The Digbys were blissfully: Interview with Sarah Norton Baring.
29   Women invariably called Kenny: Interviews with Katharine MacMillan, Edith Foxwell, Sarah Norton Baring.
29   "hedging and ditching peer": Interview with Alan Pryce-Jones.
29   "Pansy Digby was the most": Interview with Louise de Waldner.
30   Pansy Digby sensed: Interview with Esme Cromer.
30   Although she was eighteen months younger: Interviews with Katharine Mac-Millan, Sarah Norton Baring, Linda Mortimer.
30   Later in life, Pamela: Ogden, p. 38.
30   a daughter named Jaquetta: *Debrett's Illustrated Peerage* (1960), p. 380.
31   On late summer mornings: Churchill, pp. 74–75.
31   "Your nose was your best": W, 4/29–5/6/91.
31   That evening, she stood: Interviews with Stuart Scheftel, Edmund Goodman.

CHAPTER THREE

32   The Digby fortune was very much: Interview with Mary Dunn; Cannadine, pp. 91–92, 650.
32   During the Depression: Cannadine, pp. 126–131, 723–725.
32   After World War II: Churchill, pp. 63–64.
32   Far from London: Interviews with Mary Dunn, Zara Cazalet, Lydia Redmond; Cannadine, pp. 404–406.
33   the Digby girls saw little cash: Interviews with Clay Felker, Stuart Scheftel.
33   "The Digbys didn't have": Interview with Mary Dunn.
33   The Digbys and other provincial: Cannadine, 345, 347, 352.

33 The Countess of Bradford presided: James Lees-Milne, *Prophesying Peace* (1977), pp. 61, 237 (cited hereafter as Lees-Milne 2).

33 "great mock English Renaissance": TT-L, 1/28/77; *Chips,* ed. Robert Rhodes James (1967), p. 453.

33 Auntie Eva's second husband: TT-L, 6/1/74; Andrew Barrow, *Gossip* (1979), p. 109.

33 "under her capable thumb": Venetia Montagu letter to Lord Beaverbrook, 6/1/48 (MB-HLRO).

33 "had very much the same sort": Interview with Esme Cromer.

33 "Eva was ruthless": Interview with Alan Pryce-Jones.

33 "Even as a girl she wanted": Interview with Edith Foxwell.

34 Over the years, Pamela constructed: Abramson, p. 307; Ogden, pp. 30–52.

34 She was an obedient daughter: Interview with Esme Cromer.

34 "Pam liked to be the center": Interview with Edith Foxwell.

34 "very determined, quite calculating": Ibid.

34 called her "carrots": *W,* 3/14–21/80.

34 "I would have loved to have": Alice Steinbach, "Pamela Harriman: History to Hardball," *The Sun,* 7/4/82.

34 A one- or two-year stint: Lambert, p. 42.

35 Downham in Hertfordshire: *Schools Directory—England, 1937,* p. 77; *Schools Directory—England, 1966,* p. 485.

35 "I was always the one": Joy Billington, "The Aristocrat with the Democrat Touch," TT-L *(Sunday Magazine),* 10/31/82.

35 Pamela received her certificate: *The Bystander,* 10/4/39.

35 That fall, at age sixteen: TAT, 9/16/36, 10/7/36.

35 In the year after Downham: Ogden, pp. 49–52, places Pamela in Paris for a year, from the autumn of 1936 to October 1937. Those who knew her then said she was only in Paris in the fall of 1936, and that after a break in London, she returned to the Continent for several more months in Germany.

35 "a light dusting of culture": Lambert, p. 43.

35 Instead of a finishing school: Ibid., p. 43; interviews with Katharine Mac-Millan, Stuart Preston.

35 "On weekends my friends": Martha Duffy, "And Now, An Embassy of Her Own," *Time,* 7/5/93.

36 In later years Pamela recalled: Anne Trebbe, "It's Her Party: British-Born Pamela Harriman Is the Democrats' Unofficial First Lady," *Savvy,* 6/88.

36 After returning to England in February: *The Sketch,* 2/3/37.

36 In the years before the war: Interviews with Mary Dunn, Zara Cazalet; David Pryce-Jones, *Unity Mitford: A Quest* (1976), p. 85; Schmidt, p. 92.

36 Like their French counterparts: Interviews with Sarah Norton Baring, Mary Dunn.

36 They were also escorted: Pryce-Jones, p. 93.

36 Pamela stayed with Countess Harrach: Ogden, pp. 56–59. According to Ogden, Pamela "fixes" her time in Munich following her trip to the U.S. and Canada in 11/37 and ending in 3/38. This was impossible for a variety of reasons, including the debutante season that began in late 1937, as well as contemporary periodical accounts that placed her in England during those months. Sources who knew her at the time said she was only in Germany for the spring of 1937.

36 "the most wicked Englishwoman": Sulzberger, p. 455.

36 Countess Harrach, known for: Interview with Mary Dunn; Pryce-Jones, pp. 93–94.

36 Pamela was alarmed by the goose-stepping: Abramson, p. 308; *Vanity Fair*, 7/88.

36 "It was a frightening": Diane Sawyer interview with Pamela Harriman, CBS Morning News, 3/1/83; Joy Billington, "The Americanization of Pamela Harriman," *Washington Star*, 10/21/76; Abramson, p. 308.

37 "an urge to get out the word": Laura Foreman, "Pamela Harriman's Role: Hostess to the Powerful," NYT, 3/2/77; interview with Sarah Norton Baring.

37 "Downham College": Official biography of Pamela Harriman distributed with Democrats for the 90's press release, 6/30/90.

37 "My own firsthand knowledge": Pamela Harriman statement to Senate Foreign Relations Committee, 5/4/93.

37 "still a student at the Sorbonne": Abramson, p. 308.

37 on another occasion saying: Ogden, p. 59.

37 during February and March she was safely: *The Bystander*, 2/23/38.

37 "becoming bright blue tweed": TAT, 3/30/38.

37 The coronation ceremony was a medieval: Channon, pp. 124–125.

37 After the usual round: TAT, 11/24/37.

38 With its capacious reception area: Susan Braudy, *This Crazy Thing Called Love* (1992), pp. 57–58, 68.

38 But what raised the Woodwards: Interview with Florence Van der Kemp.

38 dined at the '21' Club: *Spy*, 2/93.

38 "I was allowed to bring two evening": Elisabeth Bumiller, "Pamela Harriman: The Remarkable Life of the Democrats' Improbable Political Whirlwind," WP, 6/12/83.

CHAPTER FOUR

39 Back home in December 1937: *The Sketch*, 12/29/37.

39 Through a marathon of parties: Lambert, pp. 8–9.

39 "Never marry for money": Lambert, p. 17.

39 The debutante Season began: Ibid., p. 18; Doris Kearns Goodwin, *The Fitzgeralds and the Kennedys* (1987), p. 609; Lynne McTaggart, *Kathleen Kennedy: Her Life and Times* (1983), p. 29.

39 In 1938, more than: Lambert, p. 8.

39 Those called Lady Mary: Ibid., p. 50.

39 "hons," in the flippant vernacular: Nancy Mitford, *The Pursuit of Love* (1988 ed.), p. 14.

39 The wealthiest families gave: Lambert, pp. 10, 60, 91.

40 The subsequent sons were known: Cannadine, pp. 236, 238.

40 Yet by 1938: Lambert, p. 92; Cannadine, pp. 392, 397.

40 As a consequence: Lambert, pp. 9, 12.

40 Even before she had gone: TAT, 11/24/37.

40 "Little Season": Lambert, p. 54.

40 Preparing for the Season: Ibid., pp. 51–52; *The Bystander*, 4/6/38.

41 "I remember Pam came": Interview with Susan Remington-Hobbs.

41 before long they were seen: *The Bystander*, 2/23/38.

41 On a bet of ten shillings: Churchill, p. 71.

41 Home to the upper class: Michael Leapman, *The Book of London* (1989), p. 84; Reginald Colby, *Mayfair* (1966), p. 166; *London: Louise Nicholson's Definitive Guide* (1988), p. 144.

41 "Mayfair was not Dickens' ": Colby, p. 126.

41 Across the street was: Ibid., p. 163; Leapman, p. 82.

41 The mood in England: Martin Gilbert, *Churchill: A Life* (1991), pp. 588–592 (cited hereafter as Gilbert One Volume).

41 As if to defy: Aiden Crawley, *Leap Before You Look* (1988), p. 84; Lambert, pp. 70, 83, 86, 90; interview with Sarah Norton Baring.

42 The balls began at: Crawley, p. 84; Lambert, pp. 12, 45, 71, 96–97.

42 Many girls slipped out: Lambert, pp. 72, 151, 154.

42 The high point: Ibid., p. 57.

42 Pamela was part of: TT-L, 5/14/38, listing of debutantes presented at Second Court on 5/12/38; Lambert, p. 58; McTaggart, pp. 38, 58; interviews with Alan Hare, Katharine MacMillan.

42 Inside the courtyard: Lambert, pp. 58–59; *The Bystander*, 5/18/38.

43 "would speak to you as they would": Diana Cooper, *Autobiography* (1988 ed.), p. 86.

43 full-court curtsy: Lambert, pp. 8, 58, 174.

43 Some four hundred guests attended: Janet Morgan, *Edwina Mountbatten* (1991), pp. 223, 250–251; interviews with Susan Remington-Hobbs, Sarah Norton Baring.

43 The last of that Season's: Lambert, p. 133; Goodwin, p. 607; McTaggart, p. 39.

44 Lord and Lady Digby hosted: Lambert, pp. 56, 58, 69, 71, 83, 85, 175; McTaggart, p. 32.

44 "My clothes were not": Diane Sawyer interview with Pamela Harriman, CBS Morning News, 3/1/83.

44 "I yearned for the things": TT-L *(Sunday Magazine)*, 10/31/82.

44 she served on the prestigious: *The Sketch*, 5/25/38.

44 Her photograph, taken from an angle: TAT, 6/22/38.

44 But she always kept: Interview with Katharine MacMillan.

44 Nobody stayed in the city: McTaggart, p. 41; *The Bystander*, 6/10/38; Lambert, pp. 122, 138.

44 House parties helped organize: Lambert, pp. 122–123.

45 "It was terribly flirtatious": Interview with Sarah Norton Baring.

45 "rather touchingly tubby": Interview with Mary Dunn.

45 "Pamela Digby smiling": *The Sketch*, 1/26/38.

45 Certainly Pamela's two friends: Interview with Sarah Norton Baring.

45 "Popsie and Pam would talk": Interview with Susan Remington-Hobbs.

46 "I found it very frustrating": WP, 6/12/83.

46 "She was a red headed bouncing": *The Letters of Nancy Mitford*, ed. Charlotte Mosley (1993), p. 431.

46 "I can't remember what position": Interview with Sarah Norton Baring.

CHAPTER FIVE

47 Once Pamela was officially: Lambert, p. 142; David Pryce-Jones, p. 62.

47 In her embroidered recollection: Ogden, p. 63.

47 The more mundane truth: TAT, 8/10/38.

47 She zipped around: *The Sketch*, 10/26/38, 11/2/38.

47 Later in the year she caught: TAT, 1/11/39.

47 The frivolous young aristocrats: Cannadine, p. 353; Lambert, p. 36; Gilbert One Volume, pp. 594–595.

47 Upper-class dowagers: Channon, p. 168; Cooper, pp. 477, 479; Goodwin, p. 648; Gilbert One Volume, p. 597.

47 Duff Cooper protested: Channon, p. 172; Gilbert One Volume, p. 598.

47 "a disaster of the first": Gilbert One Volume, pp. 599–600.

47 "the deep repeated": Ibid., p. 604.

48 "Second Season": Pryce-Jones, p. 62; McTaggart, p. 76.

48 Not that men were: Lambert, pp. 154, 495.

48 While discretion was essential: William Manchester, *The Last Lion, 1874–1932* (Vol. I) (1983), p. 88.

48 "They went to bed a lot": Ibid., p. 89.

48 "After Pam came out": Interviews with Susan Remington-Hobbs, Ivan Moffatt.

48 In those early days: Interview with Esme Cromer.

49 "Pam's protector": Transcript of Marie Brenner interview with William Walton.

49 Olive Baillie issued: Interviews with Alan Pryce-Jones, Sarah Norton Baring.

49 "She really only liked": Interview with Ho Kelland.

49 Having spent much of her early: Interview with Susan Remington-Hobbs; Tim Forrest, "Lady Baillie: A Very Private Collector," *The Antique Collector*, 6/89 and 2/90.

49 "The big table in Monte Carlo": Interview with Aimee de Heeren.

49 Olive Baillie's husband: Interviews with Aimee de Heeren, Sarah Norton Baring, Susan Remington-Hobbs; Channon, pp. 20, 98, 137, 329.

49 "She thought Pamela was exceptional": Interview with Esme Cromer.

49 The turreted gray castle: *Leeds Castle Guidebook* (1989), pp. 4–74; Channon, pp. 335, 354.

50 "there was lots of corridor-creeping": Interview with Susan Remington-Hobbs.

50 David Margesson, handsome and impeccably: Ogden, p. 70.

50 Lady Baillie was a powerful: Interviews with Sarah Norton Baring, Alexis Gregory.

50 Chief among them was: Mark Hampton, *Legendary Decorators of the Twentieth Century* (1992), pp. 168–172.

50 "I never had a beau": TT-L *(Sunday Magazine)*, 10/31/82.

50 "I had the feeling that among": Interview with Sarah Norton Baring.

50 "I used to see her at the 400": Interview with Mary Dunn.

50 "Pam used to disappear": Interview with Sarah Norton Baring.

50 "If you were having an affair": Interview with Edward Morgan.

51 "Debutante of the Year": Barrow, introduction, p. 59; *The Letters of Ann Fleming*, ed. Mark Amory (1985), p. 131.

51 The twenty-eight-year-old earl: Gail MacColl and Carol McD. Wallace, *To Marry an English Lord* (1989), pp. 96, 116.

51 Naturally, he was a great friend: Interview with Susan Remington-Hobbs.

51 To maintain a semblance of propriety: Interview with Aimee de Heeren. After

meeting at Leeds, de Heeren recalled, "Pamela said she was going to Paris, and she asked me to chaperone her. I only was a little older, so I thought it was a joke. It was a little unusual for a girl her age to be going to Paris alone." When de Heeren arrived at her Paris hotel, she found a message that Pamela had called and left her number at the Plaza Athénée. But when de Heeren tried to reach her that night, there was no answer in Pamela's room. De Heeren asked the next day where she had been. Pamela replied, "I am not accustomed to answering questions." That afternoon, Pamela came to de Heeren's hotel with Warwick to have tea. "He didn't pay much attention to her," recalled de Heeren. "He was distracted by many sights. There were a hundred women after him."

51 a favorite of the Hollywood: Peter Viertel, *Dangerous Friends* (1992), p. 295.
51 Pamela recalled that her weekend: Ogden, p. 74.
51 Pamela also had a fling: Interview with Mary Dunn; *The Diaries of Sir Robert Bruce Lockhart,* ed. Kenneth Young (1973), Vol. I, pp. 17, 257, Vol. II, p. 449; Sally Bedell Smith, *In All His Glory* (1991), pp. 178–179; Cannadine, p. 401.
51 Eight years older: Interview with Mary Dunn.
52 "I was a very jealous": Ibid.
52 "I thought she was so grown up": Interview with Sarah Norton Baring.
52 In Sheila's honor: TAT, 1/25/39.
52 But by early April: Ibid., 4/12/39.
52 There had been hardly a ripple: Lambert, p. 65; Goodwin, pp. 663–664; Abramson, p. 308.
52 The Kennedys had a dance: Lambert, p. 133; McTaggart, p. 59.
52 Jean Norton threw a ball: Interview with Sarah Norton Baring.
52 The most memorable: Lambert, p. 171; Channon, p. 205; John Pearson, *The Private Lives of Winston Churchill* (1991), p. 276.
52 "I was loath to leave": Channon, p. 224.
53 Everyone left London as usual: *The Sketch,* 5/31/39; Lambert, pp. 185–186; Cooper, p. 488; McTaggart, pp. 61–62; Channon, p. 108.
53 "This country is at war": Goodwin, p. 681.
53 "London was generally deserted": Interview with Ivan Moffatt; Lambert, p. 206.
53 With the help of David Margesson: Ogden, p. 77; Churchill, p. 6.
53 The notion of being employed: Lambert, p. 211.
53 "There was a curious pall": Interview with Ivan Moffatt.
53 she could be seen in: TAT, 9/27/39.
53 "She had an atypical": Interview with Sarah Norton Baring.

CHAPTER SIX

54 Air-raid sirens wailed: Gilbert One Volume, p. 623; Channon, pp. 211, 214, 218, 221, 224; Goodwin, pp. 681, 686; Cooper, pp. 520, 530; Lambert, p. 208; Churchill, p. 7; Barrow, p. 100.
54 "He made the swinging": Interview with Mary Dunn.
54 "I said, 'If you'd like' ": Ibid.
54 "She was the first person": Ibid.
54 Lady Mary was scheduled: Churchill, p. 6; Abramson, p. 308.

55 "This is Randolph": Churchill, p. 6.
55 "What do you look like?": Brian Roberts, *Randolph* (1984), p. 189; Anita Leslie, *Cousin Randolph* (1985), p. 47.
55 "He's great fun": Interview with Mary Dunn; Abramson, p. 308.
55 With flaxen hair: Roberts, p. 2; Pearson, p. 133; John Colville, *The Fringes of Power* (1986), pp. 34–35.
55 a grand English family: Pearson, pp. 20, 48–49, 55, 120, 133, 244; Randolph S. Churchill, *Twenty-One Years* (1964), p. 12.
55 Winston Churchill had showered: Roberts, pp. 10, 78–79; Pearson, pp. 121, 126, 136, 184; Mary Soames, *Clementine Churchill* (1979), p. 315.
55 "I could never brook": Randolph Churchill, p. 12.
55 When Clementine tried: Roberts, p. 13.
55 "Winston never backed": Interview with Diana Mitford Mosley.
55 "No one seemed to notice": Pearson, p. 169.
55 On the plus side: Roberts, pp. 27, 33; Randolph Churchill, p. 17; Pearson, pp. 165, 231.
56 When Randolph was barely: Roberts, p. 32; Pearson, p. 108.
56 "It was not training for": Interview with Michael Foot.
56 "Winston drank": Interview with Diana Mitford Mosley.
56 By the age of twenty-two: Lockhart, Vol. I, p. 281.
56 Randolph was educated: Pearson, pp. 220, 225.
56 strolling across the quadrangle: Interview with Stuart Scheftel.
56 When Randolph was only: Roberts, pp. 43, 60.
56 Through his lively: Ibid., pp. 31, 37, 66, 88, 101, 137–154, 227; interview with Diana Mitford Mosley.
56 Winston Churchill had astonishing: Roberts, p. 88; Pearson, p. 231.
56 Everything came too easily: Interviews with Alan Pryce-Jones, Michael Foot; Pearson, pp. 231–232, 386.
56 "I wanted to have a show": Randolph Churchill, p. 123.
56 "As a writer, he was": Interview with Stuart Scheftel.
56 Randolph's earnings were: Roberts, pp. 114, 188; Pearson, pp. 37, 208, 231, 247.
57 "He was very vulgar": Transcript of Marie Brenner interview with William Walton.
57 He thought nothing of urinating: *The Diaries of Evelyn Waugh*, ed. Michael Davie (1976), p. 577 (9/1/44).
57 "He staggers into my room": Philip Ziegler, *Diana Cooper* (1981), pp. 221–222.
57 "Going out with Randolph": Virginia Cowles, *Looking for Trouble* (1941), p. 113.
57 He would lash out: Churchill, p. 346; Lockhart, Vol. II, p. 333.
57 "His tendency to monopolize": Roberts, p. 63.
57 Because he was a Churchill: Ibid., pp. 29, 44, 88, 169–170, 177; Pearson, p. 115.
57 While visiting newspaper: Roberts, p. 56; Pearson, p. 225; interview with Dorothy Paley Hirshon (formerly Dorothy Hart Hearst).
57 Whom Randolph considered "exquisite": Randolph Churchill, p. 80.
57 In the early 1930s: Ralph G. Martin, *Henry & Clare* (1991), p. 70.
57 "To the boy wonder": Ibid., p. 131.

57 While lecturing in: Roberts, pp. 75, 97, 124; Pearson, p. 230.

57 "the voice of Mr. Randolph": Roberts, p. 106.

57 Randolph's only lifelong: Ibid., pp. 175, 177; Pearson, p. 275.

58 "Randolph was a raging": Interview with Michael Foot.

58 Randolph disapproved of: Roberts, pp. 51–52, 174; Randolph Churchill, p. 120.

58 "The influence of women": Randolph Churchill, p. 119.

58 He was called "Randy": Roberts, pp. 72, 173; Pearson, p. 278.

58 At the time he encountered: *Daily Mirror*, 1/5/39; Roberts, p. 173; Pearson, pp. 275, 277–278; interview with Sarah Norton Baring.

58 "a pretty luscious little piece": Nancy Mitford Letters, p. 85.

58 "Edward then spent two hours": Ibid., p. 85.

58 "Ed Stanley called me": Churchill, p. 7.

59 "I had had no experience": Transcript of John Pearson interview with Pamela Harriman.

59 "You were treated as a child": Abramson, p. 310.

59 But mostly she cited her: WP, 6/12/83.

59 he impressed her by: Ogden, p. 86.

59 "At the time, he absolutely": WP, 6/12/83.

59 "I was getting so terribly": Churchill, p. 7.

59 "Winston's importance is": Transcript of John Pearson interview with Pamela Harriman.

59 "From April onwards": Mary Soames, *Winston Churchill* (1990), p. 124.

59 By July 1939: Pearson, p. 276; Roberts, p. 186.

59 "Winston was back in the news": Interview with Alastair Forbes.

59 She certainly wasn't alone: Lambert, pp. 202–204.

60 "She was not educated": Interview with Mary Dunn.

60 "He must have a son": Roberts, p. 189.

60 "he thought Pamela was": Interview with Mary Dunn.

60 he also asked Laura Long: Roberts, p. 190.

60 "She's too young": Churchill, p. 8.

60 But faced with Pamela's: Abramson, p. 308.

60 Randolph took Pamela: Pearson, pp. 192, 208, 279; Churchill, p. 77.

60 "He was a very large": TT-L (Sunday magazine), 10/31/82.

60 "a little overpowering": Transcript of British Broadcasting Corporation (BBC) interview with Pamela Harriman, 8/1, p. 2.

60 Perhaps it was his weakness: Churchill, p. 8.

60 "charming girl": Martin Gilbert, *The Churchill War Papers*. Vol. 1, *September 1939-May 1940* (1993), p. 174 (cited hereafter as *The Churchill War Papers*).

60 Not only did Churchill: Pearson, p. 279; Churchill, p. 8.

60 Both Winston and Clementine: Pearson, pp. 189, 261, 279.

61 "Every time Randolph disappeared": Churchill, pp. 7–8.

61 Using Churchill pull: Abramson, p. 309.

61 Most of their friends: Interview with Loelia Westminster.

61 The setting was several: David Gentleman, *David Gentleman's London* (1985), pp. 72–73.

61 "Wait a minute": Cecil Beaton Diary for November 1940, from The Library, St. John's College, Cambridge, copyright © the literary executors of the late Cecil Beaton.

61 "Good luck sir!": ES, 10/5/39.

61 Pamela wore a coat: TT-L, 10/5/39; *Daily Mirror,* 10/5/39; interview with Loelia Westminster.

61 "to assert my independence": Transcript of John Pearson interview with Pamela Harriman.

61 As Randolph and Pamela left: *Daily Mirror,* 10/5/39.

61 More than a hundred guests: TT-L, 10/5/39.

61 "Every smart person": Interview with Mary Dunn.

61 Each guest carried: *Daily mirror,* 10/5/39.

62 "the most romantic house": Cooper, p. 430.

62 The atmosphere was festive: ES, 10/5/39.

62 "at the end Randolph expressed": Ibid.

62 "It was a marriage done": Interview with Alastair Forbes.

CHAPTER SEVEN

63 The setting couldn't have been: Churchill, p. 9; Lockhart, Vol. II, p. 56; Channon, p. 21; Ann Fleming Letters, p. 68; Colville, p. 665; Diana Vreeland, *D.V.* (1985), p. 97.

63 He thought he could instruct: Churchill, p. 9.

63 the book that his own father: Manchester, Vol. I, p. 243.

63 "Are you listening?": Churchill, p. 9.

63 "Can you imagine!": Ibid.

63 For the first year: Abramson, p. 310; transcript of John Pearson interview with Pamela Harriman; Churchill, p. 9; Goodwin, p. 685; Gilbert One Volume, p. 630; *Harold Nicolson: Diaries and Letters 1939–1945,* ed. Nigel Nicolson (1967), p. 45.

64 Randolph and Pamela were unhappy: Churchill, p. 9; Roberts, p. 190.

64 "Randolph did everything": Roberts, p. 191.

64 "Randolph would promise": Transcript of John Pearson interview with Pamela Harriman.

64 "There was snow and more snow": Churchill, p. 9.

64 "He found little satisfaction": Transcript of John Pearson interview with Pamela Harriman.

64 "a certain musical comedy actress": Leslie, p. 48.

64 "Rubbish—I am tougher": Churchill, p. 11.

64 "In fact, it wouldn't": Ibid.

64 "I'm sure you will approve": *The Churchill War Papers,* p. 778.

64 Every day he took: Churchill, p. 11.

65 "the young officers greeted": Ibid.

65 Because of Randolph's father: TAT and *Bystander,* 11/22/39; Martin Gilbert, *Winston Churchill.* Vol. VI (1983), pp. 120–122, 154, 633; Gilbert One Volume, p. 631.

65 "drawn and pinched": *The Churchill War Papers,* p. 778.

65 at his London home and: A. J. P. Taylor, *Beaverbrook* (1972), p. 72.

65 Born in Canada: Ibid., pp. 1–99.

65 When he was given a peerage: Ibid., p. 127.

65 Beaverbrook audaciously used: Ibid., pp. 130, 337, 411.

65 "Max was a strange": Sarah Churchill, *A Thread in the Tapestry* (1967), p. 39.

65 Although he stood: Taylor, pp. xiv, 8.

65 "urchin's wink": W. J. Brown, unpublished manuscript, 10/11/40 (MB-HLRO).

65 "of puckish illusion": Taylor, p. 252.

66 His political opinions: Ibid., p. xiii.

66 "chose not to regard his": Anne Chisholm and Michael Davie, *Beaverbrook* (1992), p. 376.

66 "Max, the old horror": Interview with Sarah Norton Baring.

66 "the minister of midnight": Channon, p. 385.

66 "My darling—Try ridding": Pearson, pp. 324–325.

66 The source of Beaverbrook's: Taylor, pp. xv, 174; Lockhart, Vol. II, p. 62; Sarah Churchill, p. 39.

66 "Of course at heart": Randolph Churchill, p. 126.

66 Beaverbrook rarely dined: Taylor, pp. 234, 239, 339.

66 Night after night: Chisholm and Davie, p. 404.

66 From time to time she came: MB-DD, 1939: 10/25, 10/28; 1940: 2/26, 2/27, 3/21, 3/22, 3/24, 6/4, 8/1, 10/29, 11/2, 12/3, 12/28 (MB-HLRO).

66 The regular entourage: Colville, p. 733; Chisholm and Davie, p. 254.

66 There was a changing cast: MB-DD, 1939: 10/28–29 (MB-HLRO).

66 Beaverbrook occupied: Chisholm and Davie, pp. 370–374.

66 "Randolph was defending": Interview with Michael Foot.

67 Pamela held back: Ibid.

67 "Pamela had a very difficult": Interview with Loelia Westminster.

67 "Randolph's manners could be": Interview with Michael Foot.

67 In January 1940 she got: Abramson, p. 310; interview with Sarah Norton Baring.

67 "Nobody ever had the chance": NYT, 3/22/77.

67 Although Winston and Clementine: Pearson, p. 294.

67 "She told me in the early": Transcript of BBC interview with Pamela Harriman, interviewer 21/1, p. 7.

68 Churchill could be easily: Pearson, p. 249.

68 "he adored Pam": Interview with Mary Dunn.

68 Sometimes Pamela served: Pamela Churchill letter to Harry Hopkins, 5/2/43 (HH-GU).

68 "Winston was fascinating": Interview with Diana Mitford Mosley.

68 When she was given: Transcript of BBC interview with Pamela Harriman, interviewer 8/1, p. 9.

68 But Churchill was mesmerized: Michael Korda, *Charmed Lives* (1979), pp. 152–153.

68 "He just thought it": Transcript of BBC interview with Pamela Harriman, 21/1, p. 2.

68 "He would come in to meals": Transcript of BBC interview with Pamela Harriman, 8/1, pp. 8–9.

69 "lovely beyond even an": Goodwin, p. 691.

69 New plays and films: Cowles, p. 347; McTaggart, p. 76.

69 "I found something strangely": Cowles, p. 347.

69 That vaguely optimistic mood: Gilbert One Volume, pp. 635–636, 641–642; Nicolson, p. 67; Channon, p. 250.

69 Randolph hastened: Roberts, p. 192; Cooper, p. 530.

69 "I have nothing to offer": Gilbert, Vol. VI, p. 333.

69   "Beaverbrook is like the town": Channon, p. 257.

69   "his power to inspire": Chisholm and Davie, p. 374.

69   In late May, one grim: Nicolson, p. 67; Gilbert, Vol. VI, p. 456; Goodwin, p. 693.

69   "at this grim moment": Gilbert, Vol. VI, p. 454.

70   The Churchills finally moved: Churchill, p. 13; Lockhart, Vol. II, p. 62; Goodwin, p. 694; McTaggart, p. 80; Cooper, p. 533.

70   "What can we do without": Transcript of BBC interview with Pamela Harriman, 8/7: transcript of John Pearson interview with Pamela Harriman; Churchill, p. 13.

70   She tried to keep fit: Colville, p. 232.

70   "complacency in high places": Ibid., p. 177.

70   "I wouldn't be able to": Gilbert, Vol. VI, p. 758.

70   By the last days of August: Nicolson, p. 106; Goodwin, p. 705; Gilbert, Vol. VI, pp. 757–758.

70   The air-raid sirens sounded: Cecil Beaton, *The Years Between* (1965), p. 38 (cited hereafter as Beaton 1); Cowles, p. 434; Gilbert One Volume, pp. 675, 680–681, 696.

70   Underneath 10 Downing: Gilbert, Vol. VI, p. 757; Gilbert One Volume, p. 677.

71   In her reminiscences: Churchill, pp. 14–15.

71   "She had a joke": Transcript of Marie Brenner interview with William Walton.

71   "He is known to have": Gilbert One Volume, p. 677

71   "One thing that worries": Gilbert, Vol. VI, p. 782.

71   Each morning: Beaton 1, p. 37; Cowles, pp. 439, 442, 446; Goodwin, p. 705.

71   "The shops were full": Cowles, p. 439.

71   "Thank God that did not": Lockhart, Vol. II, p. 80.

71   On the day the Blitz: Pearson, p. 295.

71   "There was champagne": Cooper, p. 548; also Gilbert, Vol. VI, p. 758.

71   "But how do you know": Transcript of John Pearson interview with Pamela Harriman.

72   Winston and Clementine Churchill moved: Gilbert, Vol. VI, p. 783.

72   Because of a wartime truce: Leslie, p. 48; Pearson, p. 283; Roberts, p. 193.

72   Randolph took his seat: Leslie, p. 48; Roberts, p. 194.

72   Sitting in the gallery: Abramson, p. 311.

72   When the family was still: Ogden, p. 101.

72   Upon hearing that she had: Abramson, p. 311.

72   Yet according to Pamela: Ogden, p. 106.

72   After Pamela gave birth at: Churchill, p. 1.

72   "I've told you five": Transcript of John Pearson interview with Pamela Harriman.

72   "What sort of a world": Beaton 1, p. 54.

72   The following weekend: Colville, pp. 262, 264.

72   "Pam looked exceedingly pretty": Interview with Alastair Forbes.

72   He held forth: Colville, p. 264.

73   That month, Pamela leased: Churchill, p. 20; interview with Winston Churchill.

73   "Oh! Randy": Churchill, p. 20.

73   Standing at White's: Leslie, p. 49; Roberts, p. 196.

73   "Randolph, who had thought": Leslie, p. 49.

73   In early November, Randolph: Churchill, pp. 21–22, 25; Roberts, p. 197; Beaton 1, p. 53.

73   "radiant and triumphant": Beaton 1, p. 53.

73   "For two days we photographed": Cecil Beaton Diary for November 1940, from The Library, St. John's College, Cambridge, copyright © the literary executors of the late Cecil Beaton.

73   "smug, substantial": Waugh Diaries, p. 488 (11/13/40).

73   "smart set": Ibid.

73   Randolph didn't stint: *The Letters of Evelyn Waugh,* ed. Mark Amory (1980), pp. 147–148 (11/40).

74   "Mrs. Randolph has freckles": Ibid., p. 147 (11/40).

74   "If you are ever in any": Ibid., p. 149 (2/18/41).

74   "perhaps to arouse": Leslie, p. 50.

74   Fortunately, Colonel Laycock: Waugh Letters, p. 147 (11/40); Waugh Diaries, p. 488 (11/40); Roberts, p. 198;

74   "They gave up the water": Churchill, p. 23.

74   Back in Hitchin: Ibid., p. 25.

74   Randolph kept up his: Waugh Diaries, p. 488 (11/40); Roberts, p. 197.

74   When Randolph made his maiden: Churchill, p. 21.

74   Winston was on the front: Roberts, p. 195; Pearson, p. 293.

74   A week later, baby: Churchill, p. 19.

74   "I had always heard": Cowles, *Winston Churchill: The Great Man,* quoted in Churchill p. 19.

74   The entire Churchill: Gilbert, Vol. VI, p. 962.

74   "one of the happiest": Pearson, pp. 297, 299.

74   Randolph had been in: Waugh Diaries, p. 491 (12/40).

75   The January 27, 1941: Life, 1/27/41.

75   An even more suggestive: *The Sketch,* 12/4/40.

75   Inside *Life* magazine: Life, 1/27/41.

75   "showed me with obvious pride": Gilbert, Vol. VI, p. 981.

75   Before Randolph left: Waugh Diaries, p. 493 (1/41).

75   "It's going to be terrible": Churchill, p. 25.

75   But from the moment Randolph: Ibid.

75   "little poker game with": Waugh Letters, p. 149 (2/18/41).

75   "Poor Pamela will have to": Waugh Letters, p. 150 (2/23/41).

75   "in the best way possible": Churchill, p. 26.

75   Nor could she go: Abramson, p. 311.

75   "a very tart letter": Roberts, p. 201.

75   She asked for an advance: Churchill, p. 26.

76   Her stated reason was: Ogden, p. 113.

76   Other authoritative sources: Chisholm and Davie, p. 444.

76   "It was a lesson": Churchill, p. 26.

76   "The bombshell which was": Ibid.

76   "I'd have liked to have been able": Transcript of John Pearson interview with Pamela Harriman.

76   "She met a lot of people": Interview with Alan Hare.

CHAPTER EIGHT

77   Eager to abandon: Pearson, p. 300; Abramson, p. 312.

77   "so that my Churchill": Churchill, p 26.

77   By early March 1941: Colville, p. 362; Nicolson, p. 152; Channon, p. 294; Lambert, p. 210; McTaggart, p. 87; Barrow, p. 109.

77   "The capital looks like": Channon, pp. 302, 304.

77   At the Ritz: Cowles, pp. 441–442.

77   The Dorchester was thought: Ann Fleming Letters, p. 38; Ziegler, p. 201.

77   "What a mixed brew": Beaton 1, p. 52

78   "modern wartime Babylon": Channon, p. 272.

78   But even the wailing: Cowles, p. 441; Cooper, p. 549; Channon, p. 265.

78   The room cost six pounds: Interview with Sarah Norton Baring; Lambert, pp. 208, 212; Barrow, p. 117; McTaggart, p. 85.

78   At the Dorchester, there were: Channon, p. 332.

78   On weekends Pamela continued: Colville, p. 362.

78   "It was the most exciting": Susan Watters and Patrick McCarthy, "Pamela Harriman: Queen of the Democrats," W, 11/30–12/7/87.

78   "My sister has never been": VF, 7/88.

78   His father was the famous: Abramson, p. 21.

78   "malefactors of great wealth": Myra MacPherson, "Averell Harriman Knows the Right People," WP, 12/7/75.

79   "enemy of the republic," Jacob Heilbrunn, "The Playboy of the Western World," TNR, 7/27/92.

79   As a trader he proved: Abramson, p. 33.

79   "one of the best speculators": Rush Loving, Jr., "W. Averell Harriman Remembers Life with Father," Fortune, 5/8/78.

79   After his firstborn: Abramson, pp. 39, 70; Fortune, 5/8/78.

79   In less than a decade: Abramson, pp. 22, 52, 91.

79   "little giant": Abramson, p. 42.

79   "He was secretive": Abramson, p. 21.

79   "lacked the pangs": WP, 12/7/75.

79   E.H.'s wife: Abramson, pp. 33, 92, 106.

79   Averell grew up in: Ibid., pp. 43, 80; Smith, p. 111.

79   "In everything he did": Fortune, 5/8/78.

79   "never-ending lesson": Abramson, p. 65.

79   He even hired: Ibid., p. 79.

79   "Averell's tougher than": WP, 12/7/75.

79   A diary he kept: Interview with Nancy Whitney Lutz.

79   "He had the dreariest life": Ibid.

79   Both E.H. and Mary: Abramson, pp. 64–65.

80   The Harrimans were never: WP, 12/7/75.

80   The couple clearly: Abramson, p. 65.

80   "be something and somebody": Ibid., p. 73.

80   Averell also endured: TNR, 7/27/92; Abramson, pp. 83–87.

80   Just before Averell entered: Fortune, 5/8/78; Abramson, p. 91; TNR, 7/27/92.

80   "men should use their capital": Fortune, 5/8/78.

80   Yet as a young: Abramson, pp. 124–138, 144, 186–194, 205.

80   After bailing out: Ibid., pp. 214, 217.

80   "consuming personal mission": Ibid., p. 221.

80   Eager to exploit: Ibid., pp. 222–230.

80   By the time he returned: Ibid., p. 223; WP, 12/7/75.

81   In polo, as in his other: Interview with Edward Morgan.

81   But by the age of thirty-seven: Abramson, pp. 109–110; interview with Nancy Lutz.

81   Although they came: Abramson, pp. 115, 122.

81   "notoriously promiscuous": Dodie Kazanjian and Calvin Tomkins, *Alex: The Life of Alexander Liberman* (1993), p. 73.

81   Harriman's most famous lover: Abramson, pp. 170–176.

81   By 1929, Harriman: Ibid., pp. 183–184.

81   In 1928 Harriman had fallen for: Ibid., pp. 175–176; June Bingham, "Her Witty Asides Put Washington Solemnity Down," WP, 8/6/67; *Long Island Sunday Press,* 8/10/58.

81   "It came from her upbringing": Interview with Nancy Lutz.

81   "she felt she ought to get": Ibid.

82   He was all business: Abramson, pp. 9, 17, 110.

82   He was impatient: Interview with Charles Maechling.

82   Notoriously tightfisted: WP, 12/7/75; Abramson, p. 271.

82   "always went to the best": *Fortune,* 5/8/78; Chalmers M. Roberts, "Averell Harriman at 90," WP, 11/8/81.

82   Harriman and Marie Norton Whitney: Abramson, p. 184; interview with Peter Duchin.

82   The Harrimans hosted: Smith, pp. 111–112; WP, 12/7/75.

82   "Mummy told me he never": Interview with Nancy Lutz.

82   Marie Harriman further broadened: Abramson, pp. 183, 220; WP, 8/6/67.

82   "She didn't like that world": Interview with Nancy Lutz.

82   By the early 1930s: Abramson, pp. 241, 245, 195–200; TNR, 7/27/92.

83   Harriman could see: TNR, 7/27/92; Stewart Alsop, "Battle of the Million-aires," *Saturday Evening Post,* 10/25/58.

83   There was also an element: WP, 12/7/75.

83   Although FDR and Harriman: Abramson, pp. 237–238, 267.

83   Determined to find: Ibid., pp. 269–271.

83   "expediter" (his official title): Ibid., p. 277.

83   Not only would Harriman: Ibid., pp. 279–280; TT-L, 4/12/41.

83   "He was responsible for all": Abramson, p. 279.

83   Hopkins saw Harriman: Ibid., p. 277.

83   When Averell Harriman arrived: WAH-DD for 3/15/45: WAH arrived in Bristol, went to Chequers (WAH-LC); W. Averell Harriman and Elie Abel, *Special Envoy to Churchill and Stalin* (1975), pp. 21–22; Gilbert, Vol. VI, p. 1033; TT-L, 3/17/41.

83   Pamela, only days away: CVB: 3/17/41 Pamela C. Churchill (MB-HLRO); Sarah Norton Diary, 3/16/41: "Pam appeared" [at the cottage].

84   By Pamela's account: Ogden, pp. 115–116, 124–129; Abramson, pp. 305, 313.

84   "the most beautiful man": WP, 6/12/83.

84   "peel off her dinner dress": Ogden, pp. 128–129.

84   In March 1941 Emerald: Chips Channon, an intimate friend of Emerald Cunard, noted in his diary on 5/19/40 (p. 254) that she was "now in New York." She didn't reappear in his daily chronicle until 11/16/42 (p. 342),

when he "dined with Lady Cunard . . . my favorite woman . . . her heart is broken over Thomas Beecham's desertion." Diana Cooper, who was also close to Cunard, noted in her memoir that in 8/41 (p. 584), Cunard was living in New York. In December, Cooper wrote (p. 646), "So ended 1942. Emerald Cunard had arrived back before the new year and had installed herself on the seventh floor of the Dorchester. She had been desperately unhappy in America." Andrew Barrow also wrote that in 11/42 (p. 119), "Lady Cunard had returned to England after a long spell in America." Finally, Anne Chisholm, the biographer of Emerald Cunard's daughter Nancy, said Emerald "was definitely in the United States in 1941."

84 On the Wednesday evening: WAH-DD for 3/19/41 Wed: "WAH dinner PM at 10 Downing Street" (WAH-LC).

84 "watch the fun": Gilbert, Vol. VI, p. 1038.

84 Harriman had already dined: WAH-DD for 3/17/41: WAH dinner with Max B (WAH-LC).

84 Harriman's calendar during: WAH-DD for March and April (WAH-LC).

84 "I am with the PM": Averell letter to Marie Harriman, 5/6/41 (WAH-LC).

84 The one weekend: WAH-DD for 3/22/41: WAH dinner Rodman Wanamaker (WAH-LC).

84 the following night with: Averell letter to Marie Harriman, 3/30/41 (WAH-LC).

84 Otherwise, he was a guest: Harriman and Abel, p. 23; Averell letter to Marie Harriman, 3/30/41.

84 It was at Chequers: WAH-DD for 3/29/41: WAH to country PM (WAH-LC); WP, 6/12/83; Colville, pp. 368–369.

84 "I first met Pam at Chequers": TT-L, 10/31/82.

85 the night of Wednesday, April 16: Averell letter to Marie Harriman, 4/17/41 (WAH-LC).

85 That night, 450 bombers: Gilbert, Vol. VI, p. 1062; Colville, p. 374; Nicolson, p. 163.

85 "extraordinary sight": Averell letter to Marie Harriman, 4/17/41 (WAH-LC).

85 Then a bomb exploded: Ibid.

85 "Needless to say": Ibid.

85 The following morning: Colville, p. 375.

85 Just before leaving for England: Interview with Brigitta Lieberson (formerly Vera Zorina).

85 "absolutely marvelous": WP, 6/12/83.

85 Clearly middle-aged: WP, 11/8/81.

85 gaunt aspect of an undertaker: WP, 12/7/75.

85 "When he's working": Kennan quoted in ibid.

85 "that curious contempt": WP, 11/8/81.

85 Yet his wide smile: Interviews with Nancy Lutz, Peter Duchin.

86 Harriman's multi-million: Abramson, p. 110.

86 "He was debonair": Interview with Brigitta Lieberson.

86 "He seemed a little shy": Interview with Nancy Lutz.

86 "his sad, brown eyes": Abramson, p. 110.

86 "All his life, Averell needed": Galbraith quoted in Ibid., p. 16.

86 "the New York financier": TT-L, 2/19/41.

86 "was the most important American": Abramson, p. 312.

CHAPTER NINE

87 They maintained separate: Abramson, p. 313.

87 Stornoway House: Chisholm and Davie, pp. 377, 431.

87 Only the most attentive: MB-DD, 4/22/41 (MB-HLRO); WAH-DD 4/30/41 (WAH-LC); Averell letter to Marie Harriman, 5/6/41.

87 Still, aside from: Abramson, p. 313.

87 "intercepted glances and felt": Ibid., pp. 313–314.

87 The arrival of Harriman's: WAH-DD, 5/16/41 Fri 8:30 Kathleen arrives London (WAH-LC).

87 A graduate of: Averell Harriman memo 5/8/41 (WAH-LC); Colville, p. 415; interview with Peter Duchin.

87 Since her college graduation: Abramson, p. 225.

87 "desperate" to see action: Kathleen telegram to Averell Harriman, 4/12/41 (WAH-LC); also Abramson, p. 305.

87 Laden with scarce items: Averell Harriman telegrams to Kathleen, 4/15/41, 5/7/41 (WAH-LC).

88 Kathleen headed for England: Abramson, p. 305.

88 Less than a week earlier: Gilbert, Vol. VI, p. 1086; Joseph E. Persico, *Edward R. Murrow* (1988), p. 187; Abramson, p. 300; Colville, p. 386.

88 "A spring sun bathed": Quentin Reynolds, *Only the Stars Are Neutral* (1942), p. 39.

88 Two days after her arrival: Sarah Norton Diary, 5/18/41: "Pam gave a party for Kathleen Harriman at the Dorchester."

88 "one of the wisest": Kathleen letter to Mary Fisk, 5/30/41 (WAH-LC); Abramson, p. 306.

88 Kathleen opened the door: Abramson, p. 313.

88 "Pamela was ravishing": Steven M. L. Aronson, "The Quiet Man," T&C, 2/94.

88 when they moved to a spacious: Averell letter to Marie Harriman, 6/11/41 (WAH-LC).

88 At about that time: Abramson, p. 306.

88 "She knows and I know": Interview with Rudy Abramson.

89 She and her sister Mary: Abramson, pp. 184, 301.

89 As a consequence, Kathleen: Ibid., pp. 312–313.

89 "I don't think she pictured": Interview with Nancy Lutz.

89 In 1939, she was seen: Alice Leone Moats letter, 1/9/39.

89 And as the war: Abramson, pp. 227, 305, 317, 414.

89 "She loved Eddy": Interview with Nancy Lutz.

89 Averell "knew about Marie": Interview with Dorothy Hirshon.

89 Many American friends felt: Interview with Edward Morgan; Abramson, p. 305.

89 Her vision had been: Interview with Edmund Goodman.

90 "We're all dying to know": Marie letter to Averell Harriman, 5/7/41 (WAH-LC).

90 "Thinking . . . of you": Averell telegram to Marie Harriman, 6/8/41 (WAH-LC).

90 "I miss being with": Averell letter to Marie Harriman, 11/22/41 (WAH-LC).

90 "Kathleen has teamed up": Averell letter to Marie Harriman, 6/9/41 (WAH-LC).

90 At one point he even took: Averell letter to Marie Harriman, 11/22/41 (WAH-LC).

90 events in the spring: Gilbert, Vol. VI, p. 1054; Harriman and Abel, pp. 29, 56; WP, 6/12/83; *Illustrated London News,* 6/7/41; Averell letter to Marie Harriman, 4/4/41 (WAH-LC).

90 Each morning he plowed: WAH-DD; Kathleen letter to Marie Harriman, 5/17/41 (WAH-LC).

90 "Ave never knows": Kathleen letter to Mary Fisk, 7/16/41 (WAH-LC).

90 Kathleen was busy herself: Kathleen letters to Mary Fisk, 5/30/41 and 6/7/41 (WAH-LC); *TAT,* 2/26/41; Pamela Churchill letter to Harry Hopkins, 10/13/41 (HH-GU).

90 From June 1941: WAH-DD 6/41 through 1/42 (WAH-LC).

91 "I saw them together": Interview with Mary Dunn.

91 "Ave liked women": Interview with Peter Duchin.

91 By Pamela's own account: Ogden, p. 132.

91 After Beaverbrook resigned: Chisholm and Davie, pp. 309, 403; Colville, p. 732.

91 "Beaverbrook was using": Interview with Tex McCrary.

91 Quite apart from Pamela: TT-L, 4/12/41, notes that Harriman was given the rank of minister in the British government.

92 "never believed [their affair]": Ogden, p. 156.

92 They took their time: Interview with Charles Maechling.

92 Both collected people: WP, 12/7/75; WP 11/8/81; TNR, 7/27/92.

92 Petersfield Farm: Pamela letter to Harry Hopkins, 10/13/41 (HH-GU); Averell letter to Marie Harriman, 6/9/41; Kathleen letter to Marie Harriman, 6/9/41; Kathleen letter to Mary Fisk, 6/27/41 (WAH-LC).

92 Pamela readily took: Abramson, p. 314; Kathleen letter to Mary Fisk, 7/7/41 (WAH-LC).

92 Pamela and Kathleen spent: Kathleen letter to Mary Fisk, 6/27/41 (WAH-LC).

92 Kathleen often assembled: Kathleen letter to Mary Fisk, 6/11/42; Kathleen letter to Marie Harriman, 6/28/42 (WAH-LC).

92 "the armour of carefree gaiety": Beaton 1, p. 88.

92 Cherkley during wartime: Channon, p. 62; Taylor, p. 72; Chisholm and Davie, p. 405.

92 "an amazing mixture": Ann Fleming Letters, p. 40.

92 "one of the finest": Lockhart, Vol. I, p. 374.

93 Even though the staff: Ibid., Vol. II, p. 218; Colville, p. 488; Taylor, p. 251.

93 For background music: Kathleen letter to Mary Fisk, 2/10/42 (WAH-LC).

93 "cool, chic and ultracharming": Channon, p. 62.

93 Amicably separated: Chisholm and Davie, pp. 254, 451; interview with Sarah Norton Baring.

93 Beaverbrook collected journalists: Channon, p. 33.

93 "Come and eat": Lockhart, Vol. I, p. 374.

93 "Sit there, and you there": Chisholm and Davie, p. 405.

93 "his attitude toward women": Ann Fleming Letters, p. 40.

93 he included everyone: Taylor, p. 239.

93 "The Beaver," as everyone: Ibid., p. 637; Chisholm and Davie, p. 313; Reynolds, p. 89.

93 "He has the faculty of": Taylor, p. 234.

93 Sitting in the middle: Ibid., p. 239.

93 "he conducted like the leader": Davie and Chisholm, p. 367.

93 "I don't remember her": Interview with Jean Campbell.

93 "even more annoying": Sarah Norton Diary, 3/16/41.

93 "She irritates me so much": Ibid., 4/28/41.

94 "Needless to say": Ibid., 5/9/41.

94 "Michael Tree was very": Ibid., 5/18/41.

94 "The result," wrote Sarah: Ibid., 9/8/41.

94 "Poor Randolph has had": Waugh Letters, p. 151 (5/7/41).

94 Winston continued to send: Gilbert, Vol. VI, p. 1107; Churchill, p. 30 (letter from Randolph to his father, 7/5/41).

94 "to the bottom of which": Gilbert, Vol. VI, p. 1178.

94 In Cairo, he chased: Pearson, pp. 301–302; Roberts, p. 210; Channon, p. 280; Waugh Letters, p. 152 (6/2/41).

94 "They were not platonic": Roberts, p. 210.

94 Randolph even had an official: Ibid., p. 211.

94 "the problem child": Alastair Forbes, "Keeping Mum on Mum," *The Spectator*, 5/6/89.

94 In June 1941: Abramson, p. 284.

94 "I hope you will try": Gilbert, Vol. VI, p. 1106.

95 They spent ten days: Pearson, p. 304; Churchill, pp. 29–30; Abramson, p. 284.

95 "absolutely charming": Churchill, p. 29 (Randolph letter to Pamela Churchill, 7/5/41).

95 "extraordinary maturity": Gilbert, Vol. VI, p. 1127.

95 "Beginning to understand": Averell Harriman telegram to Pamela Churchill, 7/41 (WAH-LC).

95 "I had no idea": Churchill, p. 350.

CHAPTER TEN

96 As the war neared: Pamela Churchill letter to Harry Hopkins, 10/13/41 (HH-GU); Nicolson, p. 173; Abramson, p. 288.

96 Harriman was increasingly: Abramson, p. 289.

96 "I thought I'd scream": Kathleen letter to Mary Fisk, 9/16/41 (WAH-LC).

96 The Moscow mission: Abramson, p. 294.

96 "doing propaganda": Pamela Churchill letter to Harry Hopkins, 10/13/41 (HH-GU).

96 "We all wanted to fly": Interview with Sarah Norton Baring.

96 Pamela kept her intentions: Abramson, p. 315.

96 "Have exhausted my": Kathleen telegram to Averell Harriman, 10/23/41 (WAH-LC).

97 "Have taken it": Pamela Churchill telegram to Averell Harriman, 10/23/41 (WAH-LC).

97 "Averell is a sick": Pamela Churchill letter to Harry Hopkins, 10/13/41 (HH-GU).

97   Already worn down: Abramson, p. 295; interview with Edmund Goodman.

97   "Eating meals": Averell telegram to Marie Harriman, 12/3/41 (WAH-LC).

97   But on Saturday: Gilbert, Vol. VI, pp. 1264, 1266.

97   During dinner the next: Harriman and Abel, pp. 111–112.

97   "One might have thought": Gilbert, Vol. VI, p. 1267; Harriman and Abel, p. 112.

97   "kitten eyes": Waugh Letters, p. 155 (9/26/41).

97   "It seems frightful": Churchill, p. 31 (Randolph Churchill letter to Pamela, 9/21/41).

97   In early January 1942: TAT, 1/21/42.

98   "a happy trio": Pamela Churchill telegram to Averell Harriman, 1/8/42 (WAH-LC).

98   "Randolph in good form": Lockhart, Vol. II, p. 136.

98   "half a husband": Kathleen to Marie Harriman and Mary Fisk, 2/3/42 (WAH-LC).

98   "Hoping I will arrive": Averell Harriman telegram to Randolph Churchill, 1/24/42 (WAH-LC).

98   "Bitterly disappointed": Averell Harriman telegram to Randolph Churchill, 1/42 (WAH-LC).

98   One reason was Churchill's: Nicolson, p. 207; Channon, pp. 314, 318; Beaton I, p. 126.

98   On the second day: Pearson, p. 308, Nicolson, pp. 208–209.

98   "his little wife squirming": Nicolson, p. 208.

98   "brilliant, spontaneous": Kathleen letter to Marie Harriman and Mary Fisk, 2/3/42 (WAH-LC).

98   his bags overflowing: Ibid.

98   "most beautiful gal": Ibid.

98   For the remainder of his: Kathleen letter to Marie Harriman and Mary Fisk, 2/10/42 (WAH-LC).

98   Harriman and Randolph dined: WAH-DD, 2/9/42: WAH dinner, Randolph Churchill, Beaverbrook; 2/16/42 Mon: Maj. Churchill for lunch; 3/3/42 Tues: 7:45 WAH dinner with Major and Mrs. Randolph Churchill (WAH-LC).

99   "It was a bad evening": Lockhart, Vol. II, pp. 142–143 (Sunday, 2/22/42).

99   "We both realized": Roberts, p. 228.

99   "greatly resented Pamela's": Ibid.

99   Pamela let Randolph: Transcript of John Pearson interview with Pamela Harriman.

99   At other times: Pearson, pp. 310–311.

99   "I want you to be": Lockhart, Vol. II p. 159 (4/6/42).

99   Clementine tried: William Manchester, *The Last Lion*. Vol. II (1988), p. 256; Pearson, p. 312.

99   "Pamela had no intention": Roberts, p. 229, quoting from James Lees-Milne diary of 3/18/42.

99   "She closed up": Interview with Mary Dunn.

99   Pamela continued to spend: CVB: 2/25/42: Averell Harriman, Pamela S. Churchill; 2/28/42: Mr. and Miss Harriman, Mrs. Randolph Churchill; MB-DD 2/27/42: dinner Mr. and Miss Harriman, Mrs Randolph Churchill (MB-HLRO); WAH-DD: 3/26/42 WAH dinner with Mr. Alexander Korda, KLH, Mrs. R. Churchill: Claridges (WAH-LC).

99   When Randolph finally left: Roberts 215; TT-L, 5/1/42.

99   "Throughout Randolph's brief": Roberts, p. 229.

99   The Harrimans moved out: Averell letter to Marie Harriman, 4/11/42; Kathleen Harriman letter to C. E. Peczenick, 3 Grosvenor Square, 3/2/42, regarding the third-floor flat.

100 The first two floors: Goodwin, p. 594.

100 The Harrimans had a spacious: Kathleen letter to Marie Harriman, 4/16/42 (WAH-LC).

100 "service flat": Averell letter to Marie Harriman, 4/11/42 (WAH-LC).

100 While on a trip: Abramson, p. 315; Harriman and Abel, p. 134.

100 Whatever he needed: Kathleen letter to Marie Harriman, 5/2/42 (WAH-LC); Abramson, p. 316.

100 brought in three American: Kathleen telegram to Mary Fisk, 4/28/42 (WAH-LC).

100 Harriman was bedridden: WAH-DD, May 1942; Kathleen telegram to Marie Harriman, 5/1/42 (WAH-LC).

100 a new house he rented: Pamela Churchill letter to Harry Hopkins, 4/42 (HH-GU).

100 "the other nurse": Averell Harriman note to Kathleen, 5/28/43.

100 Pamela did her best to: Pamela Churchill letter to Harry Hopkins, 12/16/41 (HH-GU).

100 "They were caught out": Interview with Sarah Norton Baring.

100 One person who braced: Averell letter to Marie Harriman, 4/17/41 (WAH-LC); Cecil Beaton, *Memoirs of the Forties* (1972), p. 95 (cited hereafter as Beaton 2).

100 "funny, lewd": Averell letter to Marie Harriman, 4/17/41 (WAH-LC).

101 She used so many: Interview with Tex McCrary.

101 "I'd like to bring a girl": Interview with Anita Colby.

101 America's entry into the war: Barrow, p. 116; Kathleen letter to Mary Fisk, 7/30/42 (WAH-LC); McTaggart, p. 133.

101 "Life is such fun": Kathleen letter to Marie Harriman, 2/3/42 (WAH-LC).

101 Kathleen and Pamela entertained: Kathleen letter to Mary Fisk, 6/15/42 (WAH-LC).

101 "all night binge": Kathleen letter to Mary Fisk, 6/11/42 (WAH-LC); also Pamela Churchill letter to Harry Hopkins, 7/1/42 (HH-GU).

101 Pamela had left her job: ES, 7/22/42; Pamela Churchill letter to Harry Hopkins, 7/10/42 (HH-GU).

101 Wearing a green: *TAT* and *Bystander,* 11/19/41.

101 She served as a guide: Abramson, pp. 314–315.

101 "She was the girl": Transcript of Marie Brenner interview with William Walton.

101 "helluva harouche": Kathleen letter to Marie Harriman, 7/14/42; Kathleen letter to Mary Fisk, 7/30/42 (WAH-LC).

101 The Red Cross started: Kathleen letters to Marie Harriman, 6/28/42, 7/6/42 (WAH-LC).

101 Under orders from: Robert H. Bremner, et al., *History of the American National Red Cross.* Vol. XIII: *American Red Cross Services in the War Against the Europe Axis, Pearl Harbor to 1947* (1950), pp. 58, 61, 63, 77–79.

102 She wrote him a long: Pamela Churchill letter to Harry Hopkins, 7/10/42 (HH-GU).

102   Pamela failed to win: Kathleen letter to Mary Fisk, 7/30/42 (WAH-LC); Bremner, et al., p. 77.

102   "He was a dear": WP, 6/12/87.

102   "the first light from": *Washington Star*, 10/21/76.

102   "a pinup": WP, 6/12/87.

102   "man of steel": *Washington Star*, 10/21/76.

102   "nobility of expression": 1/22/41 report on Hopkins meeting with newspaper editors (MB-HLRO); Colville, pp. 331, 750.

102   After stomach cancer: Doris Kearns Goodwin, *No Ordinary Time* (1994), p. 31 (cited hereafter as Goodwin 2); also Lockhart, Vol. II, pp. 657–658.

103   "Hurry Up Hopkins": Reynolds, p. 7.

103   Hopkins had a keen appetite: Abramson, p. 269.

103   "detached, cynical charm": Ann Fleming Letters, p. 40.

103   "aware that Harry Hopkins": Ogden, p. 135.

103   he remained a close friend: Marie letter to Averell Harriman, 4/29/42 (WAH-LC).

103   Hopkins and Pamela began: Pamela Churchill and Harry Hopkins correspondence, 1941–1944 (HH-GU).

103   "I remember thinking": WP, 6/12/83.

103   Mostly, she offered tidbits: Pamela Churchill letter to Harry Hopkins, 11/30/42 (HH-GU).

103   "You'd better come": Pamela Churchill letter to Harry Hopkins, 10/13/41 (HH-GU)

103   "Averell is getting": Pamela Churchill letter to Harry Hopkins, 4/42 (HH-GU).

103   Manhattan hostess to whom: Marie letter to Averell Harriman, 4/29/42: "I've whipped up a fine romance for him" (WAH-LC).

103   "What is all this I hear": Pamela Churchill letter to Harry Hopkins, 7/1/42 (HH-GU).

103   She rarely missed: Pamela Churchill letters to Harry Hopkins, 10/31/41, 4/42 (HH-GU).

103   While Pamela was busy: Martin Gilbert, *Winston S. Churchill* Vol. VII (1986), p. 136.

104   "everything went wrong": Leslie, pp. 64–68.

104   In considerable pain: Roberts, p. 225.

104   "severe bruises": Pamela Churchill letter to Harry Hopkins, 5/31/42 (HH-GU).

104   Friends who visited: Beaton 1, p. 183 (6/25/42).

104   "Bless you darling": Churchill, p. 32 (letter from "Randy" to "Pamela," 7/1/42).

104   Pamela named Eisenhower: Ibid., p. 33.

104   It was during his: Abramson, p. 316.

104   "He was not jealous": Interview with John Pearson.

104   Randolph was due to go: Leslie, p. 66; Roberts, p. 226.

104   "a rapid shift around": Kathleen letter to Mary Fisk, 7/30/42 (WAH-LC).

104   "can no longer bear the sight": Lockhart, Vol. II, p. 227.

104   "Mr. Pam": Leslie, p. 71.

104   burst into the open: Roberts, p. 230.

104   "She hates him so much": Waugh Diaries, p. 525 (8/42).

105   Pamela and Randolph still: Roberts, p. 231.

105   The bombing raids: Kathleen letters to Mary Fisk, 7/30/42, 8/10/42 (WAH-LC).

105   When CBS Chairman: Smith, pp. 204–205.

105   On another weekend: Leslie, p. 70, Roberts, p. 231.

105   Even so, the two men: WAH-DD 7/31/42: 1:30 lunch Maj. Randolph Churchill; 8/28/42, Fri WAH with Randolph Churchill; 9/16/42, lunch with Capt. Randolph Churchill (WAH-LC).

105   Although many people eagerly: Pearson, pp. 312, 322.

105   "a great treasure and blessing": Gilbert, Vol. VII, p. 101 (Sir Winston to Randolph 5/2/42).

105   "accused Randolph of": Interview with John Pearson.

105   "was impressed by the efforts": Ibid.

105   he even gave him the rank: TT-L, 4/12/41.

105   Harriman went out of his way: Abramson, p. 301.

105   "no more than a kindly": Ibid., p. 340.

106   "never had a sense that": Ogden, p. 135.

106   "had condoned adultery": Abramson, p. 316.

106   "He used terrible language": Interview with Alastair Forbes.

106   Randolph burst into tears: Pearson, p. 324.

106   "I cannot understand": Lockhart, Vol. II, p. 227.

106   When Harriman was home for two: Abramson, pp. 317–318.

106   "She hated Pam": Interview with Nancy Lutz.

106   Harriman backed off: Interview with Rudy Abramson.

107   "She was very fond": Interview with Nancy Lutz.

107   "It will be fun": Averell letter to Marie Harriman, 9/14/42 (WAH-LC).

107   "Have a lovely Christmas": Marie letter to Averell Harriman, 12/19/42 (WAH-LC).

107   Despite her severely: WP, 8/6/67; Kathleen letter to Marie Harriman, 7/6/42 (WAH-LC); Abramson, p. 317.

107   "I don't care a rap": WP, 8/6/67.

107   But Harriman knew she: Kathleen letter to Marie Harriman, 4/16/42 (WAH-LC).

107   "terribly proud": Kathleen letter to Marie Harriman, 7/6/42 (WAH-LC).

107   "I will gladly finance": Averell letter to Marie Harriman, 4/11/42 (WAH-LC).

107   He urged Marie to fly: Averell letter to Marie Harriman, 10/8/42 (WAH-LC).

107   "a risk to disturb": Alvan Barach letter to Averell Harriman, 10/14/42 (WAH-LC).

107   "There was always coolness": Interview with Nancy Lutz.

107   "the loot suitcase": Kathleen letter to Marie Harriman, 12/7/42 (WAH-LC).

107   the "envy of all": Pamela Churchill letter to Marie Harriman, 12/26/42 (WAH-LC).

107   Beaverbrook, who entwined: Interview with Sarah Norton Baring.

107   And he would do anything: Taylor, p. 501; Chisholm and Davie, pp. 427, 430.

108   "In his view divorce": Taylor, p. 643.

108   With Pamela's marriage: MB-DD 9/42 and 10/42 (MB-HLRO); WAH-DD 9/42 and 10/42 (WAH-LC).

108   At the end of October: Roberts, p. 231.

108   "he had been rude": *Time*, 12/31/45.

108 "He was very upset": Transcript of BBC interview with Pamela Harriman, 20/1, pp. 13–14.

108 By early November 1942: Pamela Churchill letters to Harry Hopkins, 11/42; 11/30/42 (HH-GU); Harriman and Abel, p. 176; WAH-DD 11/4/42: WAH arrives in U.S. (WAH-LC); TT-L, 11/5/42; Churchill, p. 33 (Sir Winston Churchill letter to Randolph 11/19/42: "Winston & his mother are completely installed in their flat").

108 "The Attic": CVB 11/15/42 (MB-HLRO).

108 The entire tab: The arrangement between Beaverbrook and Harriman played out in a series of letters and memos written from April 1944 to April 1950—communiqués between Beaverbrook and his financial secretary, George Millar, as well as letters between Millar and Harriman. After two years as the conduit for Harriman's subsidy of Pamela's apartment, Beaverbrook asked Millar on 4/20/44 for an accounting. Harriman had told Beaverbrook on 4/5/44 that he had asked his brother Roland to transfer £1,000 to the Beaverbrook account at the Royal Bank of Canada. Millar replied on 4/20, "Since November 1942 you have paid out in rental of Mrs. Randolph Churchill's flat 1,028 pounds. Toward this you received in July 1943 550 pounds. You are therefore out of pocket 478 pounds, and this is being increased by 162 pounds each quarter. There is no word of this 1,000 pounds and Royal Bank of Canada here." On 5/5/44 Millar told his boss that the Harriman funds had been paid to Beaverbrook's account at Westminster Bank, and that £1,000 had been paid for the apartment. A year later, after a complaint from Beaverbrook that Harriman was always behind in his payments, Millar wrote Harriman in Moscow on 6/26/45 that he owed Beaverbrook £592. In subsequent letters—always marked "private" and "personal" (6/26/46, 9/16/46, 9/18/46, 11/25/47, 12/20/47, 3/25/48, 6/7/48, 9/30/48, 12/22/48, 3/29/49)—Millar tracked Harriman from Moscow to New York to Paris to remind him of his delinquencies, and Harriman ultimately made his payments. On 4/13/49, with £817 due him, Beaverbrook advised Harriman that the lease would soon be up for renewal and "should be allowed to expire." Harriman kept the arrangement in place for another year, making his final payment on 4/14/50 (MB-HLRO).

108 "should keep us in funds": Max Beaverbrook to George Millar, 5/31/45 (MB-HLRO).

109 "on our own": Churchill, p. 26.

Chapter Eleven

110 Pamela's new aerie: author observations; P. Recanati, tenant of 49 Grosvenor Square, flat 11, letter to author, 4/6/93, describing the layout of the apartment; Churchill, pp. 36, 48.

110 "He is the most": Channon, p. 345.

110 Pamela pointed to a: Pamela Churchill letter to Franklin D. Roosevelt, 7/1/42 (HH-GU).

110 "It shocked me": Churchill, p. 39 (Beaverbrook letter to Pamela Churchill, 12/13/43).

110 "piercing, spine-chilling": Ibid., p. 36.

111 "raced me downstairs": Ibid., pp. 37–38.

111   "It's nice, isn't it?": Interview with Tom Parr.

111   England's wartime deprivations: McTaggart, p. 131; *Illustrated London News,* 6/7/41.

111   Few private citizens: Capt. N. T. Bartlett, AAF, letter to Pamela Churchill, 8/9/43, transfer of a Ford FYL 392 from Harriman to her (WAH-LC).

111   Although gasoline was: Morgan, p. 314; Cooper, p. 653.

111   Those duties fell: Churchill, p. 47; TT-L, 10/31/82.

111   Clothes had been rationed: *Illustrated London News,* 6/7/41; Kathleen letter to Marie Harriman, 7/16/43 (WAH-LC); Morgan, p. 314; Channon, p. 307; McTaggart, p. 132; interview with Sarah Norton Baring.

111   "old clothes": Kathleen letter to Marie Harriman, 7/16/43 (WAH-LC).

111   Like Lady Baillie: Lockhart, Vol. 2, p. 282; Abramson, p. 316.

111   "We were really sort": Abramson, p. 316.

111   Generals George Marshall: NYT, 3/2/77; *Baltimore Sun,* 7/4/82; TT-L, 10/31/82; Kathleen letter to Averell Harriman, 5/43 (WAH-LC).

112   "Pamela ignored me": Interview with Janet Murrow.

112   the American heiress who: Cooper, p. 646; Barrow, p. 119; Channon, p. 342.

112   "She pressed my hand": Channon, p. 314.

112   "eloquent listener": *Time,* 7/5/93.

112   "immense half-knowledge": Interview with Alastair Forbes.

112   "Her politics were": Interview with William Shirer.

113   "These relationships were solid": Transcript of Marie Brenner interview with William Walton.

113   What is most revealing: Ogden, p. 133.

113   "We would be sitting": Transcript of Marie Brenner interview with William Walton.

113   "Every now and again": Transcript of BBC interview with Pamela Harriman, 11/1, p. 4; *Baltimore Sun,* 4/4/82; transcript of John Pearson interview with Pamela Harriman.

113   "She was close to": Transcript of Marie Brenner interview with William Walton.

113   "Her horizons were": *The Spectator,* 5/6/89.

113   In the summer of 1942: E. J. Kahn, *Jock* (1981), pp. 147, 149.

113   She soon became a regular: David Grafton, *The Sisters* (1992), p. 107.

113   That winter Whitney took: Transcript of Marie Brenner interview with William Walton.

114   Whitney had an even bigger: Grafton, p. 90; Kahn, pp. 38–39, 65, 72, 81.

114   Before marrying Betsey: Grafton, pp. 93–96; Kahn, p. 81.

114   "Jock did sleep": Interview with Tex McCrary.

114   "would have loved": Ogden, p. 168.

114   The two men had: WAH-DD 12/24/42 dinner with Capt. Whitney at his flat (WAH-LC).

114   even shared Christmas: WAH-DD 12/25/42: 5–7 WAH cocktail party at the flat; Averell telegram to Marie Harriman, 12/30/42 (WAH-LC).

114   Pamela did not attend: Gilbert, Vol. VII, p. 283.

114   Harriman praised Jock: Averell letter to Marie Harriman, 12/19/42 (WAH-LC).

114   "Jock knew he shared": Interview with Tex McCrary.

114   when Whitney left London: Kahn, p. 151.

114   He was a soft touch: Ibid., p. 111.

114 "One marvelous": Ibid., p. 70.
115 Back home he went his: Abramson, p. 431.
115 returned from the United States: McTaggart, p. 66.
115 "In that society": Interview with Peter Glenville.
116 In 1943, Sheila Digby: Averell letter to Marie Harriman, 2/17/43 (WAH-LC).
116 "Although her family": Averell Harriman letter to Dr. Alvan Barach, 2/17/43 (WAH-LC).
116 He had moved into a position: Abramson, pp. 302–304, 345.
116 The relationship with the Churchills: Pearson, pp. 337–338. In 1947, after returning to New Hampshire from London, Winant committed suicide (Pearson, p. 356).
116 Harriman thoroughly enjoyed: Abramson, p. 344.
116 Only six months later: Averell letter to Marie Harriman, 4/18/42 (WAH-LC).
116 The matter assumed: Harriman and Abel, pp. 213, 219–229; Abramson, pp. 347–351.
117 When she wrote to him: Pamela Churchill letter to Averell Harriman, 9/24/43 (WAH-LC).
117 "I have put a rug to lie on": Ibid.
117 Roosevelt announced: Harriman and Abel, p. 230; TT-L, 10/2/43, 10/5/43; Abramson, p. 351.
117 Although Kathleen had heard: Kathleen letter to Averell Harriman, 9/24/43 (WAH-LC).
117 Pamela threw herself into: Averell Harriman telegram to Pamela Churchill, 12/8/43 (WAH-LC).
117 Pamela and Harriman dined: MB-DD 10/10/43 (MB-HLRO).
117 three days later: Harriman and Abel, p. 231.
117 By December, Pamela: Abramson, pp. 316, 682.

CHAPTER TWELVE

118 look like a "gangster": C. L. Sulzberger, p. 579.
118 To the British: Persico, p. 147.
118 "seemed to come from": Smith, p. 176.
118 Murrow was born in 1908: Persico, pp. 15–18, 24–26.
118 "Hey-o": Interview with Howard K. Smith.
118 In lean times: Persico, pp. 21–26.
118 Somber, moody: Ibid., pp. 22, 24, 29, 31, 39.
118 "subtle, guarded": A. M. Sperber *Murrow* (1986), p. 74.
118 In London: Persico, p. 149.
118 "Even at the peak": Smith, p. 176.
119 Murrow was married to: Persico, pp. 75, 80, 179, 184–187; interviews with Howard K. Smith, Janet Murrow; Sperber, p. 243.
119 "He was indifferent": Interview with Howard K. Smith.
119 Returning from a trip: Persico, p. 191.
119 Janet Murrow only grew: Sperber, p. 212.
119 "Ed said if he took": Interview with Janet Murrow.
119 During a trip to New York: Persico, p. 106.

119 Late that month: CVB 12/29/43 E. R. Murrow, 49 Halkin Street, Pamela S. Churchill (MB-HLRO).

119 "It was when Averell": Interview with Janet Murrow.

119 "I know they used to": Ibid.

120 "Ed never talked to me": Ibid.

120 Instead, she retreated: Sperber, p. 243.

120 As winter ended: Colville, p. 475.

120 At the suggestion of: Gilbert, Vol. VII, pp. 709–726 (Sir Winston Churchill letter to Randolph, 4/1/44); Pamela Churchill letter to Harry Hopkins, 4/21/44 (HH-GU).

120 "seemed rather happy with": Interview with William Shirer.

120 "She would be there": Ibid.

120 "Having a romance": Interview with Mary Warburg.

120 "Ed was knocked off": Persico, p. 217.

120 "She didn't have that": Interview with William Shirer.

120 forced lightheartedness: Persico, p. 218.

120 "a romantic figure": Interview with Clay Felker.

121 "I did feel a strain": Interview with Janet Murrow.

121 "quiet impressive manner": Lockhart, Vol. II, p. 280.

121 Beaverbrook invited them: CVB: 2/26/44, 6/24/44 (MB-HLRO).

121 "the bomb fell at 4:30 AM": CVB: 7/17/44 (MB-HLRO).

121 Pamela was also linked: Interview with Slim Keith.

121 "I have no doubt": Interview with Dorothy Hirshon.

121 "very proprietary": Interview with Mary Dunn; Smith, p. 218.

121 "a radical departure": Sperber, p. 244.

121 Pamela sometimes went: Abramson, p. 683.

122 "I didn't dare ring up": Diane Sawyer interview with Pamela Harriman on CBS Morning News 3/2/83 (reading from letter to Kathleen Harriman, 6/44).

122 A week later the Germans: Gilbert, Vol. VII, pp. 864, 867; Nicolson, p. 371; Goodwin, p. 792; Persico, p. 224.

122 "I had just gotten to sleep": Diane Sawyer interview with Pamela Harriman on CBS Morning News, 3/1/83 (reading from letter to Averell Harriman, 6/44).

122 "escape from the noisy": Kenneth Clark, *The Other Half* (1977), p. 56.

122 England was filled; Lockhart, Vol. II, p. 749; McTaggart, p. 124; Barrow, p. 122.

122 But there was nothing: Charles C.P.M. eleventh Earl of Drogheda, *Double Harness* (1978), p. 105; *Washington Star*, 10/21/76; Abramson, p. 315.

122 Although Pamela was often: Clark, p. 56; Pamela Churchill letter to Harry Hopkins, 8/14/43 (HH-GU).

122 Ashburnham House: Leapman, pp. 90, 157–158; Abramson, p. 315; Colville, p. 472.

122 When the club opened: Abramson, p. 315; Pamela Churchill letter to Averell Harriman, 2/23/44 (WAH-LC); Lees-Milne 2, p. 27.

123 On one memorable occasion: Clark, p. 58.

123 "was jammed all day long": Transcript of Marie Brenner interview with William Walton.

123 Pamela was nearly always: NYT, 3/2/77; WP, 6/12/83; TT-L, 10/31/82.

123 But it was the top brass: Pamela Churchill letter to Averell Harriman, 9/24/43 (WAH-LC).

123 She kept the club: Pamela Churchill note to Gil Winant, 9/20/45.

123 During the latter years: Roberts, p. 248; Pearson, pp. 321, 339; Lockhart, Vol. II, p. 352.

123 two bottles of gin: Ziegler, p. 221.

123 Before he and Pamela had: Randolph Churchill letters to Laura Long, 10/24/42, 1/9/43, 1/20/43, 1/28/43; Channon, p. 352.

123 In January 1944, Randolph: Colville, pp. 463–464; Roberts, p. 254; Pearson, p. 339.

123 After Randolph's trip: Gilbert, Vol. VII, p. 854; Roberts, p. 269.

123 By then the war: Gilbert One Volume, pp. 777–795; Vol. VII, pp. 873, 903–904, 911, 913.

123 "those familiar, well fed": Alexander Kendrick, *Prime Time* (1969), p. 273.

124 After forty-eight hours: Sperber, p. 242.

124 They introduced her to: WP, 3/1/81; Churchill, p. 92.

124 "I can see her there": Transcript of Marie Brenner interview with William Walton.

124 "mental and physical exhaustion": Interview with Janet Murrow.

124 During her absence: Abramson, p. 682.

124 "At that point, Bill sat": Interview with Frank Stanton.

124 Murrow continued to see: Sperber, p. 246.

124 "wonder what you are making": Ed letter to Janet Murrow, 9/26/44 (Sperber, p. 244).

124 "missed too much": Ed letter to Janet Murrow, 9/29/44 (Sperber, pp. 245–246).

124 "Let's renew": Ed letter to Janet Murrow, 10/26/44 (Sperber, p. 246).

125 "brother Paley": Ed letter to Janet Murrow, 9/29/44 (Sperber, p. 245).

125 "little P": Ed letter to Janet Murrow, 10/26/44 (Sperber, p. 246).

125 "didn't go down so well": Ibid.

125 Although he was powerful: Channon, p. 277; Cooper, p. 558, called him "king of the air force."

125 Portal was very homely: Kathleen letter to Marie Harriman, 3/19/43, described him as "cadaverous looking" (WAH-LC); transcript of Marie Brenner interview with William Walton. Walton called Portal's letters to Pamela "touching."

125 By mid-December: Persico, pp. 225–226; Sperber, p. 246.

125 "We didn't talk about": Interview with Janet Murrow.

125 "We had always tried": Ibid.

125 Murrow declared that: Sperber, pp. 246, 254; Persico, p. 226.

125 "I've never been so": Interview with Mary Warburg.

125 "I think Ed was seeing Pamela": Interview with Janet Murrow.

125 "Then, like everybody": Face the Nation, 5/7/95, broadcast transcript, p. 5.

125 Murrow spent the day: Sperber, p. 254; Persico, p. 230.

125 "Ed had always wanted": Interview with Janet Murrow.

125 Pamela's divorce: Decree Nisi in the High Court of Justice: Probate, Divorce and Admiralty Division (Divorce) Und. 4566 "deserted the petitioner without cause for a period of at least three years" 12/18/45; Roberts, p. 290.

125 "I want to sue": Interview with Stuart Scheftel.

126 "I scarcely knew": Churchill, p. 54.

126 Only days later: Pamela Churchill telegram to Kathleen, 12/20/45 (WAH-LC); Ogden, p. 191.

126 "The Hon. Mrs. Pamela": Cholly Knickerbocker, "The Smart Set," NYJA, 12/28/45.

126 "Ed was in America": Interview with Janet Murrow.

126 After spending Christmas: Ogden, p. 193.

126 "Everyone is influenced": TT-L, 10/31/82.

126 by her account: Ogden, p. 192.

126 "throwing her arms": Ibid.

126 Murrow supposedly left: Ibid., pp. 193–194.

126 "full of apologies": Ibid., p. 195.

126 Even then, Murrow: Ibid., p. 196.

127 "I never saw Pam": Interview with Mary Warburg.

127 he wrote to Janet nearly: Ed letters to Janet Murrow (pp. 521–522 Persico appendix), 12/8/45, 12/10/45, 12/11/45, 12/12/45, 12/13/45, 12/21/45, 12/22/45, 12/24/45, 1/4/46, 1/9/46, 1/13/46, 1/25/46.

127 "pouring out his love": Persico, p. 235; interview with Joseph Persico.

127 Murrow also agonized: Persico, pp. 235–236.

127 He took the job on December 21: Ibid., p. 236: "Have taken executive job" (Ed cable to Janet Murrow, 12/21/45).

127 "He missed her": Ibid. (letter, 12/22/45).

127 Pamela's version: Ogden, p. 193.

127 William Walton, for one: Transcript of Marie Brenner interview with William Walton.

127 "Brother Seward is beating": Persico, 236.

127 Every few days: Ibid., pp. 236–237 (appendix, pp. 521–522).

127 At the end of the month: Ibid., p. 237.

127 he too was in London: TT-L, 1/12/46, announced Harriman's arrival in Britain; MB-DD 1/13/46 lunch: Mr. A Harriman and Miss K Harriman (MB-HLRO).

127 Murrow returned to New York: Sperber, p. 262.

127 "the myth of Murrow": Interview with Lauren Bacall.

CHAPTER THIRTEEN

128 "There is a great shortage": Pamela Churchill letter to Kathleen Harriman, as read by Pamela on CBS Morning News, 3/2/83.

128 Following a courtship: McTaggart, pp. 155, 160, 190, 194, 203–204, 206; Goodwin, pp. 778, 804.

128 In the evenings: *Chicago Tribune*, 2/2/48.

128 Recognizing that Kick's house: Transcript of interview with Pamela Harriman by "The American Experience," p. 3 (cited hereafter as PBS interview).

128 The Kennedys had been: Goodwin, pp. 453, 494.

128 "Bastard-Spanish": WP, 3/30/95.

128 Years later Pamela recalled: Transcript of PBS interview with Pamela Harriman, p. 4.

129 "Best Sundressed": NYJA, 3/6/46.

129 Rose Kennedy drew: Transcript of PBS interview with Pamela Harriman, pp. 4–7.

129 Returning to New York: NYJA, 3/6/46.
129 Pamela found a city: Jan Morris, *Manhattan '45* (1987), pp. 9, 46–47.
129 "luxuriating in her": NYJA, 12/28/45.
129 "Whatever her motives": Interview with Clayton Fritchey.
130 Among the men she met: Interviews with Henry Mortimer, Linda Mortimer.
130 Babe's marital difficulties: Ogden, pp. 194–195.
130 "Pamela Churchill and Stanley": NYJA, 4/1/46.
130 One evening Pamela and Henry: Interview with Henry Mortimer.
130 In early March: Harriman and Abel, p. 506; MB-DD 9/21/45: with Mr. Harriman and Mrs. Churchill at Cherkley to dine and stay the night; CVB 9/21–22/45, signed by Kathleen, Averell and Pamela (MB-HLRO).
130 She had been a faithful: Abramson, p. 682.
130 "Except for one": Averell Harriman letter to Max Beaverbrook, 4/10/44 (WAH-LC).
130 Pamela and Harriman reunited: MB-DD 3/6/46: New York (Friday) Max B with Mrs. Randolph Churchill, Mr. Harriman, Sir James and Lady Dunn, Mrs. Alan Aitken, Mr. B. Smith, James W. Gerard (then Beaverbrook to Vanderpool cottage, Bermuda)(MB-HLRO).
130 had been a "widower": Chisholm and Davie, p. 452.
130 Pamela obligingly served: MB-DD: 3/22/46 Bermuda: 7:00 P.M. Mrs. Randolph Churchill to stay; 3/26/46 Bermuda lunch with the governor and Lieut. Lichfield . . . Mrs. Randolph Churchill, dine with Mrs. Randolph Churchill; also 3/24/46, 3/25/46, 3/26/46, 3/27/46; 3/28/46: Mrs. Randolph Churchill leaves (MB-HLRO).
130 On March 24, 1946: TT-L 3/25/46; Max Beaverbrook letter to Averell Harriman at 4 East 66th Street, congratulating him (MB-HLRO); Harriman and Abel, pp. 531, 546, 548; Abramson, p. 408.
131 "I want to have time": Averell letter to Marie Harriman, 1/16/46 (WAH-LC).
131 But Truman appealed: Harriman and Abel, p. 548.
131 Smiling pleasantly: TT-L, 4/23/46.
131 Pamela came home from: Ogden, p. 196: "On April 7, 1946 . . . a desolate Pamela [sailed home] . . . her puffy face and the dark circles under eyes which were bloodshot from tears."
131 "bruised many a manly": NYJA, 4/7/46.
131 a three-room suite: Averell letters to Marie Harriman, 4/25/46, 5/4/46; memo in WAH files: April 21–July 2, Room 212 at Claridges—3 furnished rooms, rental of $17,700 for the year (WAH-LC).
131 spent weekends at Great Enton: Averell letters to Marie Harriman, 5/18/46, 5/29/46, 6/18/46 (WAH-LC).
131 Pamela also kept in close: Kathleen letter to Averell Harriman, 5/2/46, 5/4/46, 6/30/46; Kathleen letter to Pamela Churchill, 5/11/46 (WAH-LC).
131 even as she was telling: Kathleen letter to Averell Harriman, 6/7/46 (WAH-LC).
131 It appeared that Marie: Abramson, p. 409.
131 Throughout the summer: Averell letters to Marie Harriman, 5/4/46, 6/18/46; TAT letter to Marie Harriman, 7/30/46, about cover photo (WAH-LC).
131 At the same time: George Millar letter to Averell Harriman, 6/24/46, ". . . balance now due 641 pounds" (MB-HLRO).
131 Harriman was unhappy: Abramson, p. 409.

132 Marie's five trunks: Averell telegram to Marie Harriman, 8/18/46 re arrival of clothes (WAH-LC).

132 He paid her £ 15: TT-L, 10/31/82.

132 Beaverbrook offered to underwrite: Abramson, p. 681.

132 The offices of the *Evening:* Roberts, p. 166; Taylor, p. 216.

132 "No fine writing": Interview with Angus McGill.

132 The *Evening Standard* was his house: Taylor, p. 216.

132 "on the assumption that": Malcolm Muggeridge, *The Infernal Grove:* (1974), p. 54.

132 "He believed in having": Interview with Angus McGill.

133 "I knew a lot of Americans": TT-L, 10/31/82.

133 Late in his life: Interview with Sylvia Morris, biographer of Clare Boothe Luce.

133 "She put in a very short": Interview with Charles Wintour.

133 Her first story was: Pamela Churchill, "The Giant of Cerne Abbas: Aperitif for a Country Weekend," ES, 6/15/46.

133 in later years she: NYT, 3/2/77; *Washington Star,* 10/21/76.

133 "She wasn't there very long": Interview with Charles Wintour.

133 The stories and column items: "The Londoner's Diary," ES, 9/2/46; Pamela Churchill, "On the Riviera Now—Millionaires Must Count Their Francs Before They Eat," ES, 9/12/46.

133 "is back again to pre-war": Pamela Churchill, "The Great Hostess is Herself Again," ES, 7/5/46.

133 "everyone's favorite golddigger": Vreeland, p. 74.

133 "alimoniously rich": ES, 5/31/56.

133 Joyce inspired Anita: *Daily Telegraph,* 6/14/57.

133 "It is better to be mercenary": *Evening News,* 10/1/30.

134 "a beautiful blonde American": Pamela Churchill, "A Woman Built a House and She Called It The Little Blue Dog," ES, 9/3/46.

134 Harriman was preparing: Abramson, p. 410; Harriman and Abel, p. 553.

134 "quiet weekend": "The Londoner's Diary," ES, 9/23/46.

134 George Millar, Beaverbrook's: George Millar note to Averell Harriman, 4/14/50; George Millar note to Max Beaverbrook, 4/18/50 (MB-HLRO).

134 "Many have put the annual": Khoi Nguyen, "Wham, Bam, Pam," TAT, 6/93.

134 Indeed, according to members: Interviews with Peter Duchin, Cheray Duchin Hodges.

134 "Mr. Harriman plans": "The Londoner's Diary," ES, 9/27/46.

134 Then, on October 1: TT-L, 10/1/46; WAH-DD 10/3/46 arrive New York (WAH-LC).

134 At the end of the month: MB-DD: 10/31/46 Max B in NYC Mrs. Churchill to dinner and theater; 11/5/46 Tues. 5 PM appointment with Mrs. Churchill; 11/6/46 Max B 4 PM appointment with Mrs. Churchill (MB-HLRO).

135 With the help of: "The Londoner's Diary," ES, 11/5/46, 11/9/46.

135 "the man who looks": Pamela Churchill, "Who Is This Man? Everyone Says, 'Why, He Looks Like Winston Churchill,' " ES, 11/20/46.

135 "important English Press Lords": Pamela Churchill, "The British Set Makes News in New York," ES, 11/12/46.

135 "British Beauties": NYJA, 11/10/46.

135 "quietly seeing the town": Ibid., 11/11/46.

135 "innocent in the party": Abramson, p. 676.

135 Recognizing the volatility: Ibid., p. 681; MB-DD 11/18/46 Mrs. Churchill
and Miss Ernst leave half an hour after midnight for Miami; 11/19/46 Tues
8:30 AM Mrs. Churchill and Miss Ernst arrive in Miami, Mrs. Churchill and
Miss Ernst to lunch and dinner; 11/20/46 Max B lunch with Mrs. Churchill
and Miss Ernst; 11/21/46 Mrs. Churchill and Miss Ernst leave for Jamaica.

135 Pamela was incensed: Abramson, p. 681.

136 turned out two features: Pamela Churchill, "Stranger Than Fiction is this
Moving, Poignant Story of Passion, Cruelty, and Revenge, Centered Around
a Lovely Old House over which a Cloud of Evil Hung: The Witch of Rose
Hall," ES, 12/11/46.

136 "as puppies do": Pamela Churchill, "Were They Set Free From Slavery For
This?: Dramatic, Moving and Significant is this Document—an Exclusive
Report from a British Colonial Hospital," ES, 1/14/47.

136 "I realised I'd never": TT-L, 10/31/82.

136 "a passage into another": interview with Jean Campbell.

CHAPTER FOURTEEN

137 Postwar London was a bleak: James Lees-Milne, *Caves of Ice* (1983), p. 134
(cited hereafter as Lees-Milne 3); Barrow, p. 142.

137 The House of Commons: Crawley, p. 213.

137 "It was galling": Colville, p. 618.

137 Shortly after the Allied: Gilbert One Volume, pp. 845–857; Martin Gilbert,
Winston S. Churchill. Vol. VIII (1988) pp. 107, 113.

137 "Everybody in dinner": Nicolson, p. 311 (5/28/46).

137 "There were so many": TT-L, 10/31/82.

137 "because I'd run": Susan Watters, "Pamela Harriman: A Man's Woman," W,
10/24–31/80; TT-L, 10/31/82.

138 "airy country house": Cooper, p. 706.

138 "I used to see quite": Interview with Loelia Westminster.

138 The British Embassy was a grand: Ziegler, p. 230; Mary Beal and John Cornforth, *The British Embassy, Paris* (1992), pp. 1–8.

138 "an Ambassadress of": Harold Acton, *More Memoirs of an Aesthete* (1970),
p. 151 (cited hereafter as Acton 2).

138 The men dressed in: Beaton 2, p. 15, Ziegler, pp. 232–233; Beal and Cornforth,
p. 8.

138 Like Olive Baillie, Diana: *The Letters of Evelyn Waugh and Diana Cooper*, ed.
Artemis Cooper (1992), pp. 6–9; Ziegler, pp. 3, 20, 23.

138 "love in the mist": Beaton 2, p. 12.

138 "torrential flow": Ibid., pp. 13, 17.

139 "short and stocky": Acton 2, p. 150; Ziegler p. 35; Waugh-Cooper Letters,
p. 7; Nancy Mitford Letters, p. 230.

139 The strongest connection: Ziegler, pp. 94–96, 121, 163–164, 188.

139 While Diana was kind: Interview with Loelia Westminster.

139 "I would not have listed": Interview with Philip Ziegler.

139 Diana was much more: Cooper, p. 404.

139 "Diana Cooper viewed": Interview with Anthony Marreco.

139 "the notoriously promiscuous": Ziegler, p. 238.

139 Acknowledging that Pamela: Interview with Ziegler.

139 men and women who could ease: Nancy Mitford Letters, pp. 134, 163–165, 178, 182, 227, 279, 287; interview with Frédéric and Daisy de Cabrol.

139 "insolent luxury": Harold Acton, *Memoirs of an Aesthete* (1948), p. 172; Nancy Mitford Letters, pp. 144, 149; Beaton 2, pp. 45–46; Janet Flanner (Genet), *Paris Journal 1944–1965* (1965), p. 48.

140 "an astonishing revival": Flanner, p. 57.

140 Pamela dined: ES, 7/5/46.

140 The more uncomfortable: Waugh Diaries, p. 645 (3/30/46); *The Diaries and Letters of Marie Belloc Lowndes 1911–1947,* ed. Susan Lowndes (1971), p. 280 (8/4/47).

140 "Never have the English": Nicolson, p. 403.

140 the magic of the Churchill: Gilbert One Volume, p. 804.

140 "Churcheel": Pearson, p. 332.

140 "In Paris, Winston's": Cooper, p. 707.

140 "She was very very healthy": Interview with François Valéry.

140 "She took the light": Interview with Daisy de Cabrol.

140 "Nothing enchants the French": Colville, p. 624.

140 "She had very good poise": Interview with Alexandre (Sandy) Bertrand.

140 "It was easier for Pam": Interview with Aliki Russell.

140 "I hadn't played": TT-L, 10/31/82.

140 Her self-pity was: W, 10/24–31/80.

140 "Suddenly," she remarked: WP, 6/12/83.

140 She said she disliked . . . "insipid": Transcript of John Pearson interview with Pamela Harriman.

141 "a boisterous boy": Waugh Diaries, p. 632 (8/16/45).

141 "Of all those who": Churchill, pp. 47–48, 53.

141 With his grandparents: Ibid., pp. 43, 53–55.

141 "If I lost something": Interview with Winston Churchill.

141 "Everything must be centered": Churchill, p. 53: Sir Winston Churchill letter to Lady Digby, 1/6/46.

141 For his fifth birthday: Churchill, p. 52.

141 "She was living her own": Angela Levin, "Mummy, I Hardly Knew You," *You* magazine, 11/21/93.

141 she often turned up: Transcript of PBS interview with Pamela Harriman: "Kick and I went to Paris quite often for racing weekends together," p. 10.

141 Kick was having an affair: McTaggart, pp. 207–209, 218; Goodwin, p. 847.

142 Thirty-six-year-old Prince: Leonard Slater, *Aly* (1964), pp. 15, 68, 78, 132, 190; NYJA, 11/10/57.

142 As they danced together: Ogden, p. 210.

142 At five foot six: *Time,* 5/23/60; Slater, p. 213; *Sunday News,* 11/7/48.

142 the "husky strangled": *Time,* 5/23/60.

142 "exactly the color of a gardenia": Vreeland, p. 83; *Sunday News,* 11/7/48: "creamy skin and soulful eyes."

142 Aly Khan wasn't remotely like: Slater, pp. 25, 45–47, 124; *Current Biography, 1960;* Elsa Maxwell, *R.S.V.P.* (1954), p. 286.

142 Masking his feelings: Slater, p. 26.

142 "They called me a bloody": Ibid., p. 50.

142 His more prominent conquests: Ibid., pp. 56–59, 87, 91–94, 124; Barrow, pp. 51, 140; Maxwell, pp. 287, 289.

143 "I only think of the": Slater, p. 4.

143 Compulsively on the move: Ibid., pp. 132, 135, 238; NYJA, 11/10/54.

143 "I've never seen him sit": Maxwell, p. 286.

143 Most nights he just skipped: Slater, pp. 114, 131.

143 He was intelligent: *Time*, 5/23/60; Michael Wishart, *High Diver* (1977), p. 105; Slater, pp. 46, 103, 117, 119–120, 124–125.

143 Yet his conversation: Ibid., pp. 6, 8; NYJA, 11/12/54.

143 He could overwhelm: Slater, pp. 99, 132–136, 240.

143 "resplendent as a basking": Wishart, p. 105.

143 "madly and deeply": Slater, p. 6.

143 his almost ritualistic approach: Ibid., pp. 240–241.

143 "His mood and manner never": Maxwell, p. 285.

143 Most women found: Slater, p. 202.

144 The centerpiece: Ibid., pp. 29, 138–139, 241, 266.

144 One friend said Aly: Wishart, p. 106: "He told me that he suffered so badly from premature ejaculation that he had consulted a specialist, who had advised him to keep one hand dipped in a tumbler of water beside the bed during erections. I sympathised with his distressing problem."

144 Pamela's figure was: Slater, pp. 6–7.

144 Aly was not known: Ibid., pp. 5, 117, 127, 133.

144 "Every girl was entitled": Interview with Leonora Hornblow.

144 The relationship was conducted: Slater, p. 131.

144 "Furious with frustration": Ibid., p. 127.

144 In September 1947, she and Kick: Goodwin, pp. 843, 845–846; McTaggart, p. 212.

145 There Kennedy located: Goodwin, p. 846.

145 "in a flow of nostalgia": James Magregor Burns, *John Kennedy* (1959), p. 4.

145 "That was just like": Ibid.

145 "I felt like kicking her": Richard Reeves, *President Kennedy* (1993), p. 537.

145 Davis immediately sent: Goodwin, p. 849.

145 "very impressed": Ibid., p. 846.

145 "They never could figure": Ibid.

145 'Well, did they have': Ibid.

145 Weiller had been married: Ziegler, p. 268.

145 "the coat of shame": Ann Fleming Letters, p. 135.

146 "was impressed by the magic": Interview with Aliki Russell.

146 The son of cultivated: Hugo Vickers, "La Reine Jeanne," *The Tatler*, 4/89; Robert Lenzner, *Getty* (1985), pp. 110–111; interviews with Anthony Marreco, John Galliher.

146 "At the end of the evening": Interview with Peter Viertel.

146 Pamela was back: McTaggart, pp. 228, 232; Goodwin, pp. 851–854; *Boston Globe*, 5/14/48.

146 "put them on the plane": Transcript of PBS interview with Pamela Harriman, p. 11.

146 Hundreds of Kick's: Goodwin, p. 856; McTaggart, p. 240.

146 Their meeting at the funeral: Leslie, pp. 114–115.

146 "Dear Randolph": *The Noel Coward Diaries*, eds. Graham Payn and Sheridan Morley (1983), p. 38.

146 "a huge belly": Lees-Milne 3, p. 81.

146 Randolph lived beyond: Lockhart, Vol. II, p. 563; Leslie, p. 114.

146 "He was still looking for": Leslie, p. 115.
147 "It was a brief": Interview with Alastair Forbes.
147 "swiftly brought her to": *The Spectator*, 5/6/89.
147 By her account: Ogden, p. 218.
147 After Aly returned: Slater, pp. 152–153.
147 Elsa Maxwell brought: Maxwell, p. 287.
147 When he lost interest in one: Slater, pp. 9, 136.

CHAPTER FIFTEEN

148 "Gianni was very young": Interview with Lydia Redmond.
148 "motivation, excitement": Sally Bedell Smith, "Gianni Agnelli: Still Master of the Game?" VF, 7/91.
148 "She was appetizing": Interview with Lydia Redmond.
148 The *Tomahawk,* his 21-meter: Interview with Gualberto Ranieri.
148 Little Winston, aged: Interview with Winston Churchill.
148 According to Pamela's account: Ogden, pp. 221–224.
149 "For Gianni, the woman means": Marie-France Pochna, *Agnelli* (1989), p. 240.
149 "I don't like people": VF, 7/91.
149 His father's family: Ibid.
149 "He was very mean": Interview with Lydia Redmond.
149 Edoardo made an unconventional: VF 7/91.
149 Virginia was a delicate: Susanna Agnelli, *We Always Wore Sailor Suits* (1975), pp. 29–44.
149 She and Edoardo had: Pochna, pp. 131–133; Agnelli, pp. 4–5, 18.
150 Surrounded by servants: Pochna, p. 133; Agnelli, pp. 5, 32.
150 Edoardo Agnelli died. Agnelli, p. 26; VF, 7/91.
150 As a thirty-five-year-old widow: Agnelli, p. 44.
150 "esthetic morality": Pochna, p. 139.
150 "I like beautiful things": VF, 7/91.
150 The Senator provided: Ibid.
150 "taking chances": Ibid.
150 Driving south with his sister: Agnelli, p. 140.
150 In November 1945: Pochna, p. 183.
151 "he had become a grown-up": Agnelli, p. 92.
151 "Have a fling for a few": VF, 7/91.
151 "rough playtime": Ibid.
151 "he had known only": Interview with Lydia Redmond.
151 Agnelli had heard: Pochna, p. 235.
151 he had also encountered: Pearson, pp. 347–348.
151 "She appealed to his": Interview with Igor "Ghighi" Cassini.
151 "Aly Khan turned her over": Interview with Lydia Redmond.
151 "Averell was the first one": Interview with Sandy Bertrand.
152 Château de la Garoupe was: Churchill, p. 100; interviews with Carlo di Robilant, Lydia Redmond, Consuelo Crespi, John Galliher.
152 "If you smoked": Interview with Lydia Redmond.
152 "The secret of her": Interview with Anita Colby.
152 "the Hollywood birds": Interview with Gianni Agnelli.

152   "She was good for Gianni": Interview with Lydia Redmond.

152   On the social side: Pochna, pp. 31–34.

152   Pamela organized a lunch: MB-DD 6/17/49, 7/3/49, 7/30/49 (MB-HLRO).

152   "Agnelli was always very": Interview with Jean Campbell.

153   After his party had: Gilbert One Volume, pp. 896–900, 904–909, 911–926, 931–939.

153   "What's this I hear": Pearson, p. 439.

153   Little Winston stayed: Churchill, p. 100.

153   "My father took umbrage": Interview with Winston Churchill.

153   the Fiat distributorship: James Roosevelt, with Bill Libby, *My Parents* (1976), pp. 316–317.

153   "got Gianni in with": Interview with Lydia Redmond.

153   "She was good for any man": Interview with Tex McCrary.

153   "When I heard about": Interview with Mary Dunn.

153   "He was very generous": Interview with Lydia Redmond.

153   "She dressed abominably": Ibid.

154   Her new home was on: Author's observations; interviews with Winston Churchill, Sandy Bertrand, Tom Parr.

154   "a great deal of beautiful": Billy Baldwin, with Michael Gardine, *Billy Baldwin* (1985), p. 327.

154   The rooms were quite formal: Interviews with Winston Churchill, Susan Mary Alsop, Sandy Bertrand.

154   exotic miniature ostriches: Baldwin, p. 328.

154   a cost of $10,000 a year: Brooke Hayward, *Haywire* (1977), p. 274.

154   At night the apartment: Ibid., p. 20.

154   her "second home": Ogden, p. 234.

154   Winston recalled visiting: Interview with Winston Churchill.

154   Pamela and Agnelli also made: Interview with Ghighi Cassini.

154   Her address at 11 Hyde: Letter to author from Z. Ziv, tenant of flat 10, 11 Hyde Park Gardens, 4/20/93; Churchill, p. 63; interview with Jeanne Murray Vanderbilt.

155   "It was very simple": Interview with Leonora Hornblow.

155   Pamela's public manner: Interview with Jean Campbell.

155   "more indifferent than": Interview with Anita Colby.

155   Since he regarded open displays: Interview with Marie-France Pochna.

155   "the leading foreign catch": NYJA, 12/8/48.

155   "monkey curiosity": VF, 7/91.

156   "When Pamela met a man": Interview with Leonora Hornblow.

156   "Pronto!": Interview with John Galliher.

156   "Pam used to swan over": Interview with Linda Mortimer.

156   "They would dine": Interview with Rosemarie Kanzler.

156   "It seemed like he went": Interview with Taki Theodoracopulos (cited hereafter as Taki).

156   "a full night out": VF, 7/91.

156   "Gianni took cocaine": Interview with Ghighi Cassini.

157   Pamela once confided to: Interview with Clay Felker.

157   Pamela's moderate habits: Interview with Taki.

157   In the sophisticated circles: Interviews with Ghighi Cassini, John Galliher.

157 It was leading nowhere: Transcript of Marie Brenner interview with William Walton: "Publicly she disliked her role versus Agnelli."

157 At his insistence, she had: Ogden, pp. 243–244.

157 "Being Italian": Taki, "A Hostess with the Mostest," *Interview,* 10/86.

157 "In that she didn't": Interview with Carlo di Robilant.

157 In March 1950: Interview with Father Geoffrey Holt, archivist, the Church of the Immaculate Conception Farm Street: "Father Joseph Christie received her into the church March 1950 at Farm Street. . . . There was a conditional baptism just in case she had baptism in another place. Then she was received into the church"; letter from Father Holt to author, 1/6/93: "The Register does not give the names of any witnesses."

157 Since the end of 1948 she had: Ogden, p. 241; interview with Winston Churchill.

157 Despite the presence: *The Spectator,* 5/6/89; interview with Alastair Forbes; Ogden, p. 245.

158 "When she was received": Interview with Father Geoffrey Holt.

158 "Pam Churchill thought": Interview with Peter Davis.

158 "I don't know what that": Interview with Winston Churchill.

158 Instead, Agnelli bought: Hampton, p. 178.

158 "one vast drawing room": Interview with Taki.

158 "Boudin really did": Interview with Paul Manno.

158 "I felt that Gianni was just": Interview with Anita Colby.

158 "She ran La Leopolda": Interview with Aimee de Heeren.

158 His younger brother Giorgio: Interview with Gianni Agnelli: "He was not well. He was in a clinic. He was neurotic, had nervous derangement. Somebody once said or wrote he tried to kill me. It is not true. He died in a clinic of illness and neurosis."

158 "Pam wanted a jewel case": Interview with Lydia Redmond.

159 "I wasn't thinking of": Interview with Gianni Agnelli.

159 "Gianni was ready to blow": Interview with Anita Colby.

159 "Pamela never doubted": Interview with Lydia Redmond.

159 "the first woman to sleep": Interview with Peter Duchin.

159 In 1951, Pamela took up: Interviews with Ghighi Cassini, Aimee de Heeren, Alexis de Rede; Doris Lilly, *Those Fabulous Greeks* (1970), p. 357; NYJA, 12/31/45.

160 Pamela's affair with Agnelli drifted: VF, 7/91.

160 "She came in and threw": Interview with Anne-Marie d'Estainville.

160 "For heaven's sake": Ibid.

160 "not especially been drinking": VF, 7/91.

160 As Agnelli pressed: Ibid.; interview with Anne-Marie d'Estainville; Pochna, pp. 1–14.

160 By Pamela's account, she single-handedly: Ogden, p. 241.

161 In her version of events: Ibid., p. 249.

161 According to Pamela: Ibid., pp. 245–247.

161 The trigger for the: Ibid., p. 245.

161 She "didn't fool": Ibid., p. 246.

161 "stood in the road": Ibid.

161 During his convalescence: VF, 7/91.

161 "magnificent": Ibid.

161 "Marella was from": Interview with Carlo di Robilant.
162 "from the Italian-American group": VF, 7/91.
162 "It changed my life": *The Observer*, 9/88.
162 "I would have married": VF, 7/91.
162 "an element of order": Ibid.
162 "I think my mother had": Interview with Winston Churchill.
162 "Instead of crying": Interview with Aliki Russell.
162 "international flotsam": Ann Fleming Letters, p. 131.
162 she danced with her son: *Picture Post*, 2/21/53.
162 to the South of France: MB-DD 8/11/53 [Capponcina] Dinner: Mrs. Randolph Churchill, Mr. John Gallia [sic: Galliher], Mme. Escarra, Sir Patrick Hennessy, Mr. Stanley Morrison.
162 her friend Arturo: Nancy Mitford Letters, p. 254; interview with Alexandre, the Paris coiffeur.
163 "a small Versailles": Channon, p. 459.

Chapter Sixteen

164 "Everyone knew it was": Interview with John Galliher.
164 The progenitor of: Virginia Cowles, *The Rothschilds* (1973), p. 9 (cited hereafter as Cowles 2); Frederic Morton, *The Rothschilds* (1962), p. 14.
164 "Europe's friendly finance": Sanche de Gramont, "Does 'R.F.' Mean République Française Or Rothschild Frères?", *NYT Magazine*, 6/25/67.
164 The Emperor of Austria: Cowles 2, pp. 92, 94; Morton, p. 57.
164 Mayer's youngest: Morton, pp. 70–73; Cowles 2, pp. 96–99.
164 "The House of Rothschild plays": Cowles 2, p. 96.
165 By the twentieth century: Morton, pp. 5, 73, 275; Cowles 2, p. 138; *NYT Magazine*, 6/25/67.
165 "Kings couldn't afford": Cowles, p. 143.
165 In the tradition of: "New Elan in an Old Clan," *Time*, 12/20/63; *NYT Magazine*, 6/25/67; Cowles 2, pp. 137, 210, 247; Morton, p. 241.
165 Leading the revival: *Time*, 12/20/63; *NYT Magazine*, 6/25/67; Cowles 2, p. 253; Morton, p. 279.
165 Known more as a sportsman: *NYT Magazine*, 6/25/67; Cowles 2, pp. 248, 271; Morton, p. 284.
165 His father Baron Robert: Cowles 2, pp. 210, 227, 271.
166 "like Pancho Villa": Marcel Schneider, *L'Eternité Fragile: Le Palais des Mirages: Mémoires* (1992), p. 117.
166 After German forces: Cowles 2, pp. 234, 243; Morton, p. 265.
166 Elie tried to escape: Schneider, pp. 116–117.
166 "We were sixteen": Ibid., p. 116.
166 "the way kings used to": Schneider, p. 117.
166 Half French: Cowles 2, p. 235; Mitford Letters, pp. 144–145.
166 Although she was not: Cowles 2, p. 293.
166 Elie took his vows: Cowles 2, p. 235.
166 Elie de Rothschild was twenty-seven: Cowles 2, pp, 241, 271, 291; Morton, pp. 268, 290; *New York Times Magazine*, 6/25/67.
167 "perfect Sèvres": Acton 2, p. 37.
167 Their only concession: Cowles 2, p. 253.

167 "Most of us have a filter": Interview with Alan Pryce-Jones.

167 she excelled as the: Morton, p. 290; Cowles 2, p. 292; Schneider, pp. 122–123.

167 She had begun to circulate: Interview with Alan Pryce-Jones.

167 "Pamela thought she looked": Ogden, p. 252.

167 "targeted and chose": Ibid., pp. 249, 280.

168 "the bed part is less": Interview with Peter Viertel.

168 "My life has given me": Eugenia Sheppard, "A Shopper's Shop," NYHT, 9/8/63.

168 experts like Gerald: Flanner, p. 287; Susan Mary Alsop, *To Marietta from Paris 1945–1960* (1975), p. 274; Ogden, p. 259.

169 "He only cares for": Mitford Letters, p. 319.

169 Known as the best interior: Beal and Cornforth, p. 68; interviews with Jimmy Douglas, Roderick Coupe, Hervé Mille.

169 "Georges was more than": Wishart, p. 48.

169 He was bald: Interviews with Jimmy Douglas, Roderick Coupe, Yves Vidal.

169 "entourage of gigolos": Wishart, p. 48.

169 her "guiding light": AD, 6/84.

169 "Geoffroy had a lot": Interview with André Ostier.

169 Liliane, who favored: Schneider, p. 123.

169 "I spent days and days": AD, 6/84.

169 "like a squirrel storing": T&C, 9/67.

169 called himself Pamela's "gigolo": Interview with Pierre de Ségur.

170 "It was a time when": Interview with André Ostier.

170 his oak-paneled office: *NYT Magazine,* 6/25/67.

170 "It was a question of": Interview with Alan Pryce-Jones.

170 Parisian society knew at once: Interviews with Frédéric and Daisy de Cabrol, Sandy Bertrand.

171 "The women of Paris": Interview with Lydia Redmond.

171 "It was a very very tough": Interview with Evangeline Bruce.

171 Knowing that Pamela wanted: Interviews with Sandy Bertrand, Hervé Mille.

171 "Liliane used to pursue": Interview with Alan Pryce-Jones.

171 "Pam told me about": Interview with Sandy Bertrand.

171 "Her view was that": Ibid.

171 "moral coward": Interview with Alan Pryce-Jones.

172 One evening in 1954: *The Diaries of Cynthia Gladwyn,* ed. Miles Jebb (1995), p. 164 (letter dated 7/18/54); interviews with Luke Burnap, James Lord.

CHAPTER SEVENTEEN

173 "I remember the first": Interview with Jimmy Douglas.

173 Pamela perfected the art: Interview with Alexandre; W, 3/14–21/80.

173 "Pam was not a woman": Interview with Alexandre.

173 "She would offer me coffee": Interview with Eliane Martin; letter to author from Eliane Martin, 1/10/93.

174 From Dior, Pamela generally: Interview with Eliane Martin.

174 "She was well dressed": Interview with John Galliher.

174 "I had on my best black": Interview with Mary Dunn.

174 "brittle but very bright": TT-L, 10/31/82.

175 "She was very seldom": Interview with Sandy Bertrand.

175 "She and I would walk": Interview with Peter Viertel.

175 Many evenings Pamela: Interview with Sandy Bertrand.

175 "Everyone would go": Interview with John Galliher.

175 Two orchestras played: Flanner, p. 279.

175 At an extravaganza: Acton 2, pp. 340–343, Alsop, p. 282; interview with Sandy Bertrand.

175 "She would have converted": Acton 2, p. 342.

175 At a dinner beforehand: Alsop, p. 282; interview with Sandy Bertrand.

175 "It was like a rehearsal": Ann Fleming Letters, p. 176.

175 Three hundred guests: Acton 2, p. 341; Alsop, p. 284; Ann Fleming Letters, p. 176.

175 Beistegui lived outside: Nancy Mitford Letters, p. 176; Beaton 2, p. 43; Alsop, p. 183; interview with Alexandre.

175 "an elaborate pastiche": Beaton 2, p. 44.

175 "She would go to Groussay: Interview with Anthony Marreco.

176 Pamela joined the seasonal: Interview with Eliane Martin.

176 "her own maid, her silk": Grafton, p. 205.

176 Her "first move": AD, 6/84.

176 "a boat that crossed": VF, 7/91.

176 "in a dreadful dilemma": Coward, p. 398.

176 weekend retreat in Versailles: Interview with Aliki Russell.

176 "A major feat for her": Interview with Alexandre.

176 With the help of her staff: Hayward, p. 273.

176 a formal dinner party: Interview with Sandy Bertrand.

176 The famous salonières: Acton 2, p. 176; Beaton 2, p. 16; Nancy Mitford Letters, p. 164; interviews with Evangeline Bruce, François Valéry.

177 "the most eloquent": Ziegler, p. 237.

177 "an egocentric maniac": Quoted in ibid., p. 236.

177 An essential part of: Ogden, p. 270; VF, 7/88.

177 Pamela encountered them: Interviews with François Valéry, Evangeline Bruce.

177 It didn't matter if she: Interviews with Alexis de Rede, Anthony Marreco.

177 "gilded cage": Waugh Diaries, p. 759 (4/10–18/56).

177 "Boy was I glad": *Marina*, ed. C.L. Sulzberger (1978), p. 121 (3/55).

177 "would spoil and attract": Interview with Alexander Liberman.

177 "She invited people": Interview with Sandy Bertrand.

177 She tried to keep: Interview with Susan Mary Alsop.

177 "Pam was surrounded by": Interview with Sandy Bertrand.

178 "She listened carefully": Ibid.

178 "the witness box": Nancy Mitford, *The Blessing* (1957 ed.), pp. 67, 151.

178 "She was lots of fun": Baldwin, p. 328.

178 A beautiful, slender: Alsop, p. 73; Jean Bothorel, *Louise* (1993), p. 24; Ziegler, p. 236; interviews with Anthony Marreco, Jimmy Douglas.

178 She had been married: Bothorel, pp. 111, 115, 136; interview with Anthony Marreco.

179 "Louise had the star": Interview with Anthony Marreco.

179 Pam understood that she: Ibid.

179 "Louise de Vilmorin posed": Sulzberger, pp. 288–289.

179 Whenever she could: Interview with Anthony Marreco.

179 "My mother loved": Interview with Helena Leigh-Hunt.

179 "Louise occasionally disparaged": Interview with Anthony Marreco.

179 "Once when Louise was": Interview with Hervé Mille.

179 Twice divorced: Francesca Stanfill, "Living Well Is Still the Best Revenge," *NYT Magazine*, 12/21/80.

179 "She and Pam mingled": Interview with John Galliher.

179 "It was almost as though": Interview with Sandy Bertrand.

180 Tired of wandering: Nicolson, p. 323; Suzy Menkes, *The Windsor Style* (1987), pp. 12, 16, 25, 30, 48, 52, 30.

180 her elegantly simple: Lowndes, p. 143.

180 "elevated sobriety": Menkes, p. 95.

180 the extravagant detail: Ralph G. Martin, *The Woman He Loved* (1973), p. 448.

180 her meticulous tidiness: Menkes, pp. 13, 17; Lowndes, p. 142.

180 most notably the famous: Interview with Cheray Duchin Hodges.

180 "slim and svelte": Ziegler, p. 242

180 "to dress better than": Maxwell, p. 291.

180 Confronted with withering: Channon, p. 51.

180 "I'd rather shop": Menkes, p. 132.

180 "inseparable chums": ES, 12/15/57.

180 She sent her Bentley: Interview with Alastair Forbes; Grafton, p. 238.

180 a "tasty morsel": Waugh Letters, p. 349.

180 "I hated to be such": Baldwin, p. 328.

181 "Pamela was looked at": Interview with Alexander Liberman.

181 "Irene was impressed": Interview with Peter Glenville.

181 "rather sanctimoniously": Abramson, p. 681.

181 "dispensed so much": *The Spectator*, 5/6/89.

181 "the gratin would have been": Gladwyn Diaries, p. 167.

181 The following year: Ibid., p. 176.

181 "I could tell you some": Nancy Mitford Letters, p. 431.

181 "l'Embrassadeur": Ibid., p. 367.

181 "better very private": Ibid., p. 335.

182 "She was very much": Interview with Lydia Redmond.

182 "years of laughter and fun": VF, 7/88.

182 her time in Paris was neither: Transcript of Marie Brenner interview with William Walton, who called Pamela "rather an outcast" in Paris.

182 "Pamela never gave": Interview with Sandy Bertrand.

183 Perhaps the most intriguing: Interviews with Alan Pryce-Jones, Irene Selznick, Kenneth Jay Lane.

183 "leg man": Interview with Irene Selznick.

183 "With Mathias she used": Interview with Alan Pryce-Jones.

183 "useful but a menace": Interview with Irene Selznick.

183 "The men didn't really": Interview with Sandy Bertrand.

183 "on, not in": Ogden, p. 259.

183 "All those times": Interview with Linda Mortimer.

183 "Maybe I was the pause": Interview with Sandy Bertrand.

184 "There were no real rules": Ibid.

184 "She also loved a poor": Michael Gross, "Queen Mother of the Clinton Court: How Pamela Harriman Became Washington's Power Broker of the Nineties," NY, 1/18/93.

184 She proudly showed him: Ogden, pp. 269–270.

184 At forty-six, Niarchos was: Sally Bedell Smith, "The Twilight of Midas: Stavros Niarchos's Greek Tragedy," VF, 8/92.
185 "as sensuous and as dangerous": Lilly, p. 191.
185 Partially deaf: VF, 8/92.
185 To win the favor: Ibid.; Ziegler, p. 284.
185 "curiously remote": Coward, p. 414.
185 Niarchos personified: VF, 8/92.
185 "the biggest private-owned": Winston Churchill letter to Max Beaverbrook, summer, 1954 (MB-HLRO).
186 "they saw each other": Interview with Rosemarie Kanzler.
186 "Niarchos embarrassed": Interview with Anita Colby.
186 "shouted at him": Ann Fleming letter to Max Beaverbrook, 5/27/55 (MB-HLRO).
186 "was a very rough person": Interview with Sandy Bertrand.

Chapter Eighteen

187 "In those days": Churchill, p. 118.
187 By her account: Ogden, pp. 261–263.
187 "a serious operation": ES, 12/5/55.
187 "seriously ill": Churchill, p. 118.
187 "felt particularly lonely": Ogden, p. 263.
187 After leaving the hospital: Churchill, pp. 119–122.
187 in the following months: Alsop, pp. 282–284 (Marie-Laure de Noailles ball, 1/56); MB-DD, 3/19/56, 10 PM Lord Margesson, Mrs. P Churchill, Mr. Rothschild; 3/24/56, Mrs. Pamela Churchill to dine; 4/6/56, Mrs. Pamela Churchill arrives at Capponcina; 4/9/56, Mrs. Churchill leaves (MB-HLRO); Sulzberger, p. 274 (4/11/56), Pamela Churchill has just been down visiting her ex-father-in-law on the Riviera; Evelyn Waugh Diaries, p. 758 (4/18/56, cocktails with Pam Churchill); Coward, p. 322 (6/3/56, Edward Molyneux and I dined with Pam Churchill); Sulzberger, p. 288 (6/9/56, last night . . . extraordinary dinner party at Pamela Churchill's).
187 She even paid $1,500: Pamela Churchill letter to Max Beaverbrook, 7/3/56 (MB-HLRO); Churchill, p. 124 (Winston Churchill letter to his grandfather, 6/9/56).
188 In June, Pamela: Pamela Churchill letter to Max Beaverbrook, 7/3/56 (MB-HLRO).
188 "I feel reborn": Ibid.
188 "My mother is very strong": Interview with Jan Cushing Amory.
188 "Most of her friends checked": Ogden, p. 264.
188 asked him to convey: Pamela Churchill letter to Max Beaverbrook, 7/3/56 (MB-HLRO).
188 Situated amid six hundred acres: Author's observations; Kahn, pp. 30, 35, 173–174, 323–324.
189 "their own flesh": Pamela Churchill letter to Max Beaverbrook, 7/3/56 (MB-HLRO).
189 "See no one": Pamela Churchill letter to Max Beaverbrook, 7/20/56 (MB-HLRO).
189 "Bill and Babe took": Interview with Anita Colby.

189 She asked Beaverbrook: Pamela Churchill letter to Max Beaverbrook, 7/3/56 (MB-HLRO).
189 "she chartered a yacht": ES, 7/13/56.
189 "humourless table talk": *The Spectator*, 5/6/89.
189 After each of her: *Daily Mail*, 12/21/55.
189 she had packed him off: ES, 1/11/49.
189 his mother felt the mountain: Churchill, p. 90.
190 "wonderfully well": Ibid., p. 91.
190 young Winston learned: Ibid., p. 96.
190 "terrible invasion": Transcript of BBC interview with Pamela Harriman, 16/1, p. 8; transcript of John Pearson interview with Pamela Harriman.
190 She installed Winston: Churchill, pp. 97–98.
190 "I always seemed to draw": Ibid., p. 98.
190 When he reached thirteen: Ibid, p. 112.
190 "I had a strange": Interview with Winston Churchill.
190 "I spent more time": Churchill, p. 63.
190 Randolph had married: Ibid, pp. 58–60, 117; Roberts, p. 297; Pearson, p. 357; Leslie, p. 115.
190 But life for anyone: Churchill, pp. 55–56.
190 He and June quarreled: Pearson, p. 358.
190 "her smiles faded": Roberts, p. 316.
190 "a paltry little middle-class": Leslie, pp. 133–134.
191 "ill-concealed distaste": Churchill, p. 137.
191 "Gianni was always open": Interview with Winston Churchill.
191 "Little Winston's mother": *The Spectator*, 5/6/89.
191 "My mother couldn't come": Interview with Winston Churchill.
191 "heads would turn": Churchill, p. 132.
191 "We waited in the rain": Interview with Nicholas Haslam.
191 "Why shouldn't she": Interview with Sandy Bertrand.
191 "I was on board": Interview with Winston Churchill.
191 "grow up very quickly": Sarah Sands, "Bullies, My Mother, and The Brick-layer," ES, 6/3/93.
192 "Winston was a sweet": Interview with Susan Mary Alsop.
192 "I was very rapidly sucked": Interview with Winston Churchill.
192 "Le Petit Winston": Interview with Rod Coupe.
192 Many nights he sat: *You* magazine, 11/21/93.
192 "not every mother who is": Interview with Winston Churchill.
192 at Oxford he devoted: Churchill, pp. 143–144, 147.
192 "never struck me as": Interview with Winston Churchill.
192 "She was one of the best": Interview with Leonora Hornblow.

Chapter Nineteen

193 "In the dreaming hours": AD, 6/84.
193 "She was telling herself": Interview with Sandy Bertrand.
193 He and Liliane had moved: Schneider, p. 121; Cowles 2, p. 271; Morton, p. 91.
193 "an enthusiastic": Alsop, p. 274.
193 "Don't you think": VF, 7/88.
193 "We had lunch": Interview with Jean Howard.

193   Pamela paid more: NY, 1/18/93; *The Spectator,* 5/6/89.

194   "She was hell-bent": Interview with Irene Selznick.

194   In 1957, Pamela took: Interviews with Myles Lowell, Nancy Holmes.

195   The following year, in July: NYT, 7/19/59.

195   Pamela said she met: TT-L, 10/31/82; Slim Keith, with Annette Tapert, *Slim:* (1990), p. 221.

195   a "notorious egomaniac": Stephen Farber and Marc Green, *Hollywood on the Couch* (1993), p. 43.

195   "a look of tense": Keith Munroe, "Leland Hayward," *Life,* 9/20/48.

195   riveting blue eyes: Keith, pp. 115, 119.

195   "radiant effervescent: Hayward, p. 133.

195   "the aspect of an elderly": *Life,* 9/20/48.

195   He was tall: Allene Talmey, "Leland Hayward: Notes on a Remarkable Producer, Idea Man, Financier, and Photographer, Whose Cable Address Is 'Haywire New York,' " *Vogue,* 5/15/53; *Current Biography, 1949;* interview with Brooke Hayward.

195   He spoke in a rasping: *San Francisco Examiner,* 7/10/61; Keith, pp. 152–153.

195   "He slanted backward": Ben Hecht, *Charlie* (1957), p. 183.

195   "Leland was blasphemous": Keith, p. 152.

195   Leland Hayward was born: *Current Biography, 1949;* Hayward, pp. 99, 101–103; interview with Brooke Hayward.

195   Hayward attended: Interview with Bill Hayward.

195   "He would have been": Ibid.

196   "The boys picked": Interview with Jones Harris.

196   While still a college: *Current Biography, 1949; Life,* 9/20/48; Hayward, p. 78; Sonia Berman, *The Crossing* (1980), p. 78.

196   He negotiated: *Current Biography, 1949;* Hayward, pp. 22, 78–79; *Life,* 9/20/48; interview with Jeanne Murray Vanderbilt.

196   Hayward had a passion: NYHT, 12/24/44; *Life,* 9/20/48; Keith, p. 154; Hayward, p. 272; Margaret Case Harriman, *Take Them Up Tenderly* (1944), p. 215.

196   "firecracker femmes": NYHT, 12/29/48.

196   Women were captivated: Keith, pp. 119–120.

196   "How can you like": Barbara Leaming, *Katharine Hepburn* (1995), p. 293.

196   "nothing was a problem": Katharine Hepburn, *Me* (1992 ed.), p. 191.

196   During the thirties: Hayward, pp. 68, 178; Keith, p. 123; *Life,* 9/20/48.

197   "I was thunderstruck": Hepburn, p. 192.

197   Margaret Sullavan was petite: Ibid., pp. 182, 189–190; Joshua Logan, *Josh* (1976), p. 238.

197   "elusive, gallant": Pauline Kael, *5001 Nights at the Movies* (1991), pp. 764–765.

197   Offscreen, Sullavan: Hayward, p. 193.

197   The three children: Ibid., p. 272.

197   "This family was characterized": Interview with Michael Thomas.

197   There was a dark side: Hayward, pp. 151, 166, 196, 215–216; Keith, p. 124.

197   Sullavan hated: Hayward, p. 104.

197   "Flesh peddler!": Ibid., p. 78.

197   sold his agency: Berman, p. 105.

197   "a highly organized": Ibid., p. 221 (letter from Alex Federoff, 11/15/51).

197   After spotting: John Leggett, *Ross and Tom* (1974), p. 343; Logan, pp. 261–262.

197 "I would put Leland": Interview with Alexander Cohen.

198 "I think you have to": Leland Hayward letter to Sam Zolotow, 1/28/63 (LH-NYPL).

198 He was the first producer: Interview with Anna Crouse.

198 "Leland was a great": Interview with Alexander Cohen.

198 "When there were": Interview with Bill Hammerstein.

198 As Hayward enjoyed: Hayward, pp. 151, 229; Keith, pp. 57–58, 92–99.

198 The daughter of a prosperous: Keith, pp. 19, 29, 32, 34, 42, 55, 57–58.

198 "Handsome, charming": Ibid., p. 60.

198 She had to wait: Ibid., p. 63.

198 Slim, who got her nickname: Patrick McCarthy, "Slim: An Original," W, 5/19–26/86.

198 "straight like a dagger": Ibid.

198 "spare and sensual": Hayward, p. 228.

198 But Leland Hayward fell: Keith, p. 115.

198 "It was an essential arrogance": Hayward, p. 167.

198 "Basically I'm absolutely": Ibid, p. 166.

198 "Leland broke": Interview with Jean Howard.

198 Leland Hayward married: Keith, pp. 146–147, 162, 165.

199 Slim was a popular: Interview with Jeanne Murray Vanderbilt.

199 "He adored having": Interview with Kitty Hawks.

199 Slim also took great: Keith, p. 94.

199 Once a week: Interview with Leonora Hornblow.

199 Sutton Place apartment: Letter dated 5/3/55 re Hayward apartment at 60 Sutton Place South saying owners will renew two-year lease at $499/month (LH-NYPL).

199 much of the emotional focus: Keith, p. 157.

199 "In Mom's household": Interview with Kitty Hawks.

199 It was Slim who coaxed: Viertel, p. 183; Keith, p. 176; Leland Hayward letter to Ernest Hemingway, 12/3/52 (LH-NYPL).

199 "Slim and Leland talked": Interview with Jeanne Murray Vanderbilt.

199 Hayward had three quick: *Rat Race* (12/22/49): Wolcott Gibbs of *The New Yorker* called it a "remarkably foolish and vulgar play" (Berman, p. 176); *The Wisteria Trees* (3/29/50): Josh Logan's Americanized version of *The Cherry Orchard* that Noël Coward called "a month in the wrong country," evidently confusing Chekhov with Turgenev; according to *Variety*, 9/20/50, the play lost $40,000 (Berman, p. 180); *Daphne Laureola* (9/18/50): A hit comedy in England that fell flat on Broadway (Berman, pp. 185–187).

199 regained his footing: *Call Me Madam* opened 10/12/50: Berman, p. 195; Laurence Bergreen, *As Thousands Cheer* (1990), p. 506.

199 But then came another: *Remains to Be Seen* (10/3/51): "just missed" (Leland Hayward letter to Sam Zolotow, 2/1/63), although Slim called it "a dog" (Keith, p. 154); *The Prescott Proposals* (12/16/53): "took a terrible licking," Hayward later said (Leland Hayward letter to Sam Zolotow, 1/28/63) and sustained a significant loss (Berman, p. 243); *Point of No Return* (12/13/51) and *Wish You Were Here* (6/25/52): both had rocky beginnings but eventually made money (Leland Hayward letters to Sam Zolotow, 1/30/63 and 1/31/63) (LH-NYPL) (Berman, pp. 217–218, 222).

199 "Please forgive me": Logan, p. 348.

200 The Haywards moved: Lauren Bacall, *Now* (1994), p. 179.

200 His final effort: Keith, p. 204.

200 "Hollywood was the Waterloo": Interview with Michael Thomas.

200 Hayward achieved his: WP, 12/31/93; NYT, 3/19/71; interview with Slim Aarons.

200 A year later, Hayward: *Peter Pan* opened on Broadway on 10/20/54 and closed on 2/26/55. Hayward's TV production was several weeks after the Broadway closing (interview with Frank Rich).

200 Hayward had become: *Mister Roberts* opened 2/18/48 and closed 1/6/51 after 1,157 performances; *South Pacific* opened 4/7/49 and closed 1/16/54 after 1,925 performances. According to *Vogue*, 5/15/53, *Mister Roberts* made $1.3 million onstage, and *South Pacific* made nearly $4 million on Broadway, excluding the road companies.

200 poured hundreds of: 1959 statements from Bankers Trust.

200 "He would walk past": Interview with Leonora Hornblow.

200 "a strange character who": Interview with Bill Hayward.

200 weekends at the Ritz: Keith, p. 131.

200 "we go at the drop": Slim Hayward letter to Mary Martin, 3/9/53 (LH-NYPL).

200 Hayward owned upward: Hayward, pp. 74, 148; Leland Hayward letter to Spencer Tracy, 2/13/53; Leland Hayward letter to Leo Freedman, 9/29/52 (LH-NYPL).

200 "better than giving": Interview with Slim Aarons.

201 "He was cozy": Interview with Leonora Hornblow.

201 "he was also capable": Hayward, p. 275.

201 He signed his letters: Leland Hayward letter to Lauren Bacall, 6/16/59; Leland Hayward letter to Harry Kurnitz, 7/2/59 (LH-NYPL).

201 "Early in his life": Interview with Michael Thomas.

201 "He seemed so sure": Interview with Lauren Bacall.

201 "a mosquito the way": Hayward, p. 108.

201 "I have a complete": Leland Hayward letter to Hubbell Robinson, 7/15/53 (LH-NYPL).

201 Once a work binge: Keith, pp. 128, 154, 182–186; Hayward, pp. 63, 150, 228.

201 Hayward was eccentric: Hayward, pp. 28, 114; *Life*, 9/20/48;

201 He also used an array: Leland Hayward letter to Saul Fox, 12/31/58 (LH-NYPL).

201 "If you take one": Interview with Leonora Hornblow.

201 "perch it while": Hayward, p. 115.

201 "He had tremendous": Interview with Mary Hunter Wolfe.

201 "There's no question": Farber and Green, pp. 43–44.

202 "Leland was having": Keith, p. 224.

202 In the summer of 1955: Hayward, p. 244.

202 "Maggie announced": Leland Hayward letter to Arthur Hornblow, 9/21/55 (LH-NYPL).

202 "Leland had a difficult": Keith, pp. 187, 188–193.

202 "He didn't like the dirty": Interview with Kitty Hawks.

202 "I would be the first": Interview with Brooke Hayward.

202 "mild-mannered, slightly": Hayward, p. 213.

202 and in late 1956: Hayward, p. 253; NYJA, 1/2/60.

202 When she was found: Hayward, p. 256.

202 "Our family was so": Interview with Brooke Hayward.

202   Both Bridget and Bill: Hayward, p. 264; Keith, pp. 210–216.
202   "He can still see": Interview with Leonora Hornblow.
202   "I've been in states": Hayward, p. 293.
202   His father had him removed: Hayward, p. 260; Farber and Green, pp. 75–80;
       Keith, p. 210.
202   "If his father": Keith, p. 210.
202   As it turned out: Hayward, p. 298.
202   In the early 1950s: Keith, p. 159.
203   "Slim was a restless": Interview with Lauren Bacall.
203   "used to drive Leland": Keith, p. 156.
203   fortified by an inheritance: Interviews with Peter Viertel, Kitty Hawks.
203   "wanderlust tendencies": Keith, p. 222.
203   She had a one-night stand: Interviews with Leonora Hornblow, Peter Viertel.
203   "had become a companionate": Viertel, p. 270.
203   "I begged her": Interview with Leonora Hornblow.
203   "She thought he would": Interview with Lauren Bacall.
203   "Slim was lovable": Interview with Leonora Hornblow.
203   "She was so mean": Interview with Jeanne Murray Vanderbilt.
203   the most furiously productive: Leland Hayward letter to Arthur Hornblow,
       8/4/58 (LH-NYPL); *Who Was That Lady I Saw You With?* opened 3/3/58
       and closed 8/30/58; *The Old Man and the Sea* opened 10/14/58.
203   "one of the most difficult": Leland Hayward letter to Sam Zolotow, 2/5/63
       (LH-NYPL).
203   Around the same time: Leland Hayward letter to Sam Zolotow, 1/28/63
       (LH-NYPL).
204   His mood seemed: Keith, p. 240; Leland Hayward letter to Bobbie and
       Alan Geismer, 10/8/58; Peter Viertel letter to Leland Hayward, 9/16/58
       (LH-NYPL); interview with Slim Keith.
204   "Leland was a fooler": Interview with Peter Viertel.

Chapter Twenty

205   Betsey Whitney had called: Keith, pp. 241–245; interview with Slim Keith.
205   "We were sitting": Interview with Jeanne Murray Vanderbilt.
205   "Pam said, 'Guess' ": Interview with Brooke Hayward.
205   A week or so later: Keith, p. 243.
206   "I remember Pamela": Interview with Lauren Bacall.
206   Pamela organized: Ibid; Keith, p. 244.
206   "like a brilliant": Keith, p. 253.
206   "I can't help": W, 11/30–12/7/87.
206   His mother came: Leland Hayward letter to Jerome Robbins, 11/26/58 (LH-
       NYPL).
206   maintained her busy social: Coward, p. 398; ES, 1/4/59.
206   "Pamela became solicitous": Interview with Lauren Bacall.
206   "He was planning": Interview with Marshall Jamison.
207   The following February: Keith, p. 245; Hayward, p. 273.
207   "She has been so": Interview with Leonora Hornblow.
207   in a musical comedy: *Redhead* opened 2/5/59, NYJA, 2/6/59.
207   "The first thing": Keith, p. 245.

207 "The talk of the international": NYJA, 2/24/59.
207 "It was just the three": Interview with Lauren Bacall.
207 By Pamela's account: Ogden, p. 288.
207 "He wasn't in great": Interview with Leonora Hornblow.
207 "he wanted to marry": Interview with Peter Viertel.
207 "Leland was always": Interview with Marshall Jamison.
208 Murrow in particular: Ibid.
208 "ripe and round": Interview with Slim Aarons.
208 "She was someone": Ibid.
208 he needed a "nanny": Hayward, p. 274.
208 "Leland didn't need": Interview with Leonora Hornblow.
208 "Leland really loved": Interview with Lauren Bacall.
208 "the eternal problems": Leland Hayward letter to Charles Miller at MCA, 9/9/59 (LH-NYPL).
208 "women's continuing": Leland Hayward cable to Richard Avedon, 9/30/59.
209 "Françoise didn't have too": Interview with Sandy Bertrand. Pamela tried to protect her interests by asking Françoise to keep an eye on Elie; several months later, Elie invited Françoise to join him at his cousin Guy's country home for a weekend. In the middle of the night he made his way to her room and they became lovers.
209 Besides slipping away: Ritz Hotel bill, 4/18–20/59; Leland Hayward letter to Richard Halliday, 5/13/59 (LH-NYPL).
209 Slim busied herself: Keith, p. 246.
209 "two weeks rest": Leland Hayward letter to Richard Halliday, 4/30/59 (LH-NYPL).
209 The *Gypsy* opening: List of invitees dated 5/4/59 (LH-NYPL).
209 "Start shopping": Slim wire to Harry Kurnitz, 5/22/59.
209 Because the *Gypsy:* Leland Hayward letter to Richard Halliday, 4/30/59 (LH-NYPL).
209 "I want to leave": Interview with Leonora Hornblow.
209 Toward the end of May: *A Raisin in the Sun* opened 3/11/59.
209 looked "ravishing": Interview with Leonora Hornblow.
209 Afterward he dashed: Ibid.
209 The Hornblows were outraged: Ibid.
209 "arrived here secretly": NYJA, 6/1/59.
210 In early June: Keith, pp. 248–250.
210 "That should have been": Ibid., p. 251.
210 Just to deepen: Ibid.
210 Sam Spiegel told her: Ibid., p. 253.
210 "Slim was in such": Interview with Lauren Bacall.
210 Slim sailed off: Keith, pp. 259–260, 263; interview with Peter Viertel.
210 "She wasn't used to losing": Interview with Kitty Hawks.
210 When Kitty Hawks was leaving: Keith, p. 264.
210 "The note was romantic": Interview with Kitty Hawks.
210 "a garden . . . full": Marina Sulzberger, p. 222.
210 Pamela sold the: Ogden, p. 289.
211 She left her dog: Interview with Alexis de Rede; Hayward, p. 273: "She was giving up . . . the bulk of her priceless Louis XV furniture"; NYJA, 9/18/59: "She is importing some of her furniture and . . . bibelots and will auction off the rest."

211 "To the general amazement": Nancy Mitford Letters, p. 431.
211 "on a glide path": Interview with Peter Viertel.

CHAPTER TWENTY-ONE

212 "Tout New York": Clarke, p. 316 (FN 8/24/59 Capote letter to Cecil Beaton).
212 "rich and powerful": NYJA, 6/30/59.
212 "beautiful Pamela": Ibid., 7/17/59.
212 "the elegant Slim": Ibid., 7/28/59.
212 "the very famous": Ibid., 8/11/59.
212 "the battle of Britain": Ibid., 9/18/59.
212 Her sister Sheila: Interview with Ghighi Cassini.
213 That was certainly the case: Interview with Leonora Hornblow.
213 "always felt responsible": Interview with Slim Keith.
213 "Pamela will never darken": Interview with Lauren Bacall.
213 Even Capote, the devoted: Truman Capote letters to Leland Hayward, 7/1/61, 3/23/63.
213 "They could see": Interview with Leonora Hornblow.
213 both still institutionalized: Keith, p. 246.
213 "he and Slim were having": Interview with Bill Hayward.
213 In the summer of 1959; Hayward, pp. 8, 278; interviews with Brooke Hayward, Michael Thomas.
213 pretty profile had graced: *Life*, 6/1/53.
213 In her mannerisms: Interview with Michael Thomas.
213 "moody and mercurial": Hayward, p. 242.
213 "adored her father": Interview with Michael Thomas.
213 "was critical of Leland": Interview with Marshall Jamison.
213 Hayward favored Bridget: Interviews with Michael Thomas, Leonora Hornblow; Hayward, p. 76.
213 "had no anchor anywhere": Interview with Michael Thomas.
213 As Brooke described: Hayward, pp. 272–274; interview with Brooke Hayward.
214 "one of the most": Interview with Brooke Hayward.
214 "She sounded like a mixture": Hayward, p. 273.
214 "I talked to Leland": Interview with Leonora Hornblow.
214 "He never referred": Interview with Bill Hayward.
214 managed by the fashionable: NYJA, 7/16/59.
214 Pamela quickly personalized: Interview with Brooke Hayward.
214 "Pamela's first words": Ibid.
214 "the 'in' jewelry": Ibid.
214 "in rows and rows": Vreeland, p. 72.
214 was "vulgar": Interview with Brooke Hayward.
214 "Pamela revealed the first": Ibid.
214 "My father's sales": Ibid.
215 "Pamela arrived in": Interview with Michael Thomas.
215 "She was no longer flat": Interview with Brooke Hayward.
215 "I had never been exposed": W, 10/24–31/80.
215 "Pamela spent a lot": Interview with Bill Hayward.

215 She doted on: Hayward, pp. 11–12.
215 "I didn't like her": Interview with Brooke Hayward.
215 "For Brooke, Pam would": Interview with Michael Thomas.
215 Bridget Hayward moved: Hayward, pp. 7, 9.
215 "Bridget was very devoted": Interview with Leonora Hornblow.
215 "My feeling was that": Interview with Bill Francisco.
216 In the months after: Leland Hayward letter to Jerome Robbins, 8/25/59 (LH-NYPL).
216 "It was a harrowing": Interview with George Axelrod.
216 "I remember long": Leland Hayward letter to Sam Zolotow, 2/1/63 (LH-NYPL).
216 "It is utterly": Leland Hayward letter to Lauren Bacall, 7/24/59 (LH-NYPL).
216 "I'm spinning": Leland Hayward letter to Lauren Bacall, 9/4/59 (LH-NYPL).
216 "This show is": Leland Hayward letter to Dick Lewine, 9/4/59 (LH-NYPL).
216 While she stayed: Leland Hayward letters and telegrams to Harry Kurnitz, 6/15/59, 6/23/59, 7/2/59 (LH-NYPL).
216 By September, Pamela had: In his book, Christopher Ogden reported (p. 301) that the Carlyle apartment was a "sweetheart lease" arranged by Walter Thayer, Jock Whitney's aide, for $2,000 a month ($10,500 in current dollars), a seemingly extravagant price at a time when six-room apartments on Fifth and Park Avenues went for $800 a month (memo from Leland Hayward Papers, 9/19/57).
216 "redecorating the apartment": NYJA, 8/11/59.
216 "given to her back": NYJA, 9/18/59.
216 she enlisted Paul Manno: Interview with Paul Manno.
216 "You must not": Interview with Anna Crouse.
216 Pamela remained so: Russel Crouse diary, 10/12/59.
216 a black-tie party: 11/16/59 invitation from Hayward, Halliday, Rodgers, and Hammerstein (LH-NYPL)
216 "It was a rare": NYJA, 11/17/59.
217 "eclipsed the entire": 12/59 letter from Colin Romoff to Leland Hayward (LH-NYPL).
217 The most influential: NYT, 11/7/59.
217 "Rodgers and Hammerstein's": TNY, 11/28/59.
217 "Make no mistake": Russel Crouse diary, 11/17/59.
217 Hayward was not so: Leland Hayward letter to Sam Zolotow, 2/1/63 (LH-NYPL).
217 On December 16: Ibid; *Goodbye Charlie* opened 12/16/59 and closed 3/19/60.
217 "I want to come and rest": Pamela Hayward letter to Harold Christie, 12/17/59 (LH-NYPL).
217 "Give Nan my love": Leland Hayward letter to Lauren Bacall, 8/3/59 (LH-NYPL).
217 "Slim Hayward's close": NYJA, 8/16/59.
217 "rooting interest": Herman Bernstein letter to Slim Hayward, 10/14/59 (LH-NYPL).
217 As producer of the show: *Sound of Music* memo of understanding, 4/9/58 (LH-NYPL).

218 "I had the right": Leland Hayward letter to Sam Spiegel, 8/31/59 (LH-NYPL).

218 "I went to our": Keith, p. 254; NYJA, 11/12/59: "What gives with the Leland Haywards? Now that Slim is back from Europe everyone expected some definite divorce announcement, but so far all's quiet"; NYJA, 11/19/59: "The international femme fatale and her famous producer are busy making marriage plans. Slim . . . will be off for Mexico to give him . . . a South of the Border divorce"; NYJA, 11/23/59: "Slim's friends say she has no definite plans, and . . . hasn't made up her mind yet what she'll do."

218 "She told us this": Interview with Brooke Hayward.

218 On New Year's Day: NYJA, 1/2/60, 1/3/60.

218 "her face a phantasmagoria": Hayward, p. 17.

218 The "indescribably sweet": Ibid., pp. 21–22.

218 "some sort of macabre": Ibid., p. 22.

218 "Leland and Pamela kept": Interview with Bill Francisco.

218 "Leland darling": Hayward, p. 24.

219 "Life was so easy": Interview with Brooke Hayward.

219 "Mrs. Pamela Churchill": ES, 1/9/60.

219 Television fascinated: Leland Hayward letters to William Paley, 8/18/53, and Henry Jaffe, 7/53 (LH-NYPL); United Press International dispatch, 5/21/54.

219 "tremendous guilt": Leland Hayward letter to Wickliffe Crider at Kenyon & Eckhardt, 9/13/54 (LH-NYPL).

219 "roller coaster ride": Leland Hayward proposal, 7/1/59 (LH-NYPL).

219 "Leland always had": Interview with Marshall Jamison.

219 "give the audience": Leland Hayward letter to Winston Churchill at Oxford, 1/12/60 (LH-NYPL).

219 "neither the time nor": Raoul Levy letter to Leland Hayward, 1/18/60 (LH-NYPL).

219 "three or four weeks rest": Leland Hayward letter to Richard Avedon, 2/15/69; Jim Aubrey letter to Leland Hayward, 3/14/60, and Leland Hayward letters to Arthur Laurents, 2/23/60, and Jim Aubrey, 3/5/60 (LH-NYPL); interview with Leonora Hornblow.

219 "Leland had the balls": Keith, p. 254; NYJA, 4/13/60, on Slim's refusal to file, figuring "if she made Leland go through with it he might change his mind."

220 Hayward and Pamela played: Ogden, pp. 306–307; Leland Hayward letter to Arthur Laurents, 2/23/60 (LH-NYPL).

220 According to an affidavit: 4/13/71 affidavit of Ralph B. Kelley, attorney with Gilbert, Segall & Young.

220 Her new boyfriend: Keith, pp. 266–267; Ogden, p. 307.

220 The banking records: Leland Hayward's Bankers Trust records for 1959 (LH-NYPL).

220 Slim got the house: Interview with Brooke Hayward.

220 Eventually the animosity: Keith, pp. 274, 277–278.

220 "Ten years, that was": Annette Tapert and Diana Edkins, *The Power of Style* (1994), p. 173.

220 "you have no right": Leland Hayward letter to Slim Keith, 7/22/68 (LH-NYPL).

220 "My number isn't": Slim Keith letter to Leland Hayward, 7/24/68 (LH-NYPL).

220 "Can I come up": Keith, p. 255.

220 Pamela and Leland were married: NYT, 5/5/60.
220 "It happened all": Interview with Winston Churchill.
220 "was a problem": W, 10/24–31/80.
221 "So now Pamela": NYJA, 5/6/60.
221 On paper she styled: Morgan Guaranty Trust letter to Pamela Hayward, 9/24/62, re account no. 2 in the name of The Honorable Mrs. Pamela Churchill Hayward (LH-NYPL).
221 As if Las Vegas: Hayward, p. 39; interview with Bill Hayward.
221 by "some lady": Interview with Bill Hayward; Hayward, pp. 300–301.
221 "She just made me feel": Interview with Bill Hayward.
221 "Father took everyone": Hayward, p. 44.
221 After a brief stop: ES, 5/20/60; Leland Hayward letters to Binkie Beaumont, 5/13/60, Alec Guinness, 5/25/60, Harold Freedman, 5/25/60; Kathleen Malley letter to Leland Hayward at Ritz Hotel in Paris, 5/27/60 (LH-NYPL).
222 "From the beginning of lunch": NYJA, 6/11/60.
222 "Once Pam appeared": Interview with Brooke Hayward.
222 "I saw happy people": Interview with Leonora Hornblow.

CHAPTER TWENTY-TWO

223 a fifteen-room apartment: T&C, 9/67.
223 "the equivalent of $1 million": Interview with Paul Manno; Ogden, p. 309, said the price for the apartment was $220,000.
223 the bill for redecorating: Interview with Paul Manno.
223 The effect Boudin: Interviews with Paul Manno, Leonora Hornblow, Anita Colby.
223 "clocks like lions": T&C, 9/67.
223 The only notable: Leland Hayward memos to Miss Labelle, 4/27/44, 5/22/44, 8/18/44 (LH-NYPL).
223 On one side of the foyer: Interviews with Leonora Hornblow, Paul Manno, Anita Colby, Brooke Hayward.
224 After Pamela's new chef: Leland Hayward letter to Paul Wassmansdorf at General Electric, 7/12/60 (LH-NYPL).
224 "It was too grand": Interview with Anita Colby.
224 Besides decorating: NYT, 5/26/93.
224 On weekends they: Hayward, p. 35; interviews with Irene Selznick, Brooke Hayward.
224 "I enjoyed his open": Churchill, p. 137.
224 "got word that there was": Interview with Winston Churchill.
224 When Winston came back: Churchill, p. 135.
224 " 'I don't think' ": Ibid., p. 148.
224 "Winston seemed a nice": Interview with Brooke Hayward.
224 "I had not seen": Churchill, p. 142.
224 The radiance dimmed: Hayward, pp. 7–15, 24; NYT 10/19/60 (Wednesday) said Bridget had been found on Monday at 4:30 P.M. after Bill Francisco and Leland Hayward had tried repeatedly to reach her by telephone.
224 "I am convinced": Interview with Bill Francisco.
224 In her memoir: Hayward, pp. 14, 44.
225 "The doctor she saw": Interview with Bill Francisco; Hayward, pp. 45–46.

225 which, like her father: Interview with Bill Francisco.
225 "the only thing": Leland Hayward letter to Dr. Saul Fox, 10/5/60 (LH-NYPL).
225 "Sure, I was horrified": Interview with Brooke Hayward.
225 "I gazed at her": Hayward, p. 12.
225 "disturbing": Ibid, p. 13.
225 "brisk businesslike tone": Ibid, p. 15.
225 "It was a helluva": Interview with Brooke Hayward.
225 "automatically": Hayward, pp. 25–26.
225 "Come Leland darling": Ibid. p. 28.
225 "The night of the": Interview with Bill Francisco.
225 With her customary: Hayward, pp. 29, 56, 59.
225 Brooke and Pamela went: Ibid, pp. 56–57.
226 The safe extended: Ibid, p. 57; interview with Brooke Hayward.
226 "What jewels?": WP, 6/12/83.
226 "certainly will come in": Hayward, pp. 57–58.
226 A French agent: Achard and Hayward memo of agreement, 2/13/60; Leland Hayward letters to André Bernheim, 10/31/60 and 11/9/60; to Bill Fitelson, 11/17/60; to Sam Zolotow, 2/5/63 (LH-NYPL); Berman, pp. 268–269; interview with Frank Rich.
226 The Haywards, writers: Russel Crouse diary, 2/23/61.
227 "I remember Leland and Pam": Interview with Marshall Jamison.
227 Many members of: Pamela Hayward note to Jerry Whyte, 3/15/61 (LH-NYPL).
227 "Tonight royalty": Interview with Anna Crouse; Russel Crouse diary, 5/17/61.
227 laid down precise: 8/22/61 note re reservation at Warwick Hotel; 10/6/61 and 4/30/62 re Huntington Hotel suite; 8/10/62 rearrangements for Mayflower Hotel suite (LH-NYPL); WP, 6/12/83.
227 "I would cook them": Diane Sawyer interview with Pamela Harriman, CBS Morning News, 3/2/83; Lynn Rosellini, "Pamela Harriman, the Power Broker," NYT, 10/1/82.
227 "The theater and politics": T&C, 9/67; NYT, 6/28/65, 3/2/77, and 10/1/82.
227 Following the success: Leland Hayward letter to Sam Zolotow, 2/5/63 (LH-NYPL); Bergreen, pp. 498–499, 533–534.
228 The show would cost: Bergreen, p. 535; letter from Anna Crouse to author, 11/29/94.
228 Having succeeded by: Bergreen, p. 534.
228 In the postwar years: Leland Hayward letters to Thomas Bell, 1/9/52, and Tex McCrary, 1/18/52 and 1/21/51; Leland Hayward letters from Irving Berlin, 1/12/52, Fleur Cowles, 1/14/52; 10/7/52 list of committee members (LH-NYPL).
228 "strong support": Dwight Eisenhower letter to Leland Hayward, 6/20/52 (LH-NYPL).
228 In November 1960: Leland Hayward letter to Joseph P. Kennedy, 11/21/60 (LH-NYPL).
228 Pamela told a television interviewer: PBS interview with Pamela Harriman, pp. 12–13.
228 In fact, Pamela and Leland: Leland Hayward letter to Harry Kurnitz, 1/19/61: "I am leading a hard life at the Loel Guinness house" (LH-NYPL).

228 Yet the Haywards were on equally: Leland Hayward letters to Jacob Javits, 9/11/64, and John Lindsay, 10/19/64 (LH-NYPL).

228 "politically involved": *Washington Star*, 10/21/76.

229 activism was limited: 10/20/64: $100 contribution to LBJ; 10/12/64: $200 contribution to Bobby Kennedy (LH-NYPL).

229 The Kennedys were flattered: Bergreen, pp. 538, 542–544.

229 "they wanted someone": Interview with Anna Crouse.

229 "Ronald Reagan is very": Leland Hayward memo to Crouse, Berlin, Lindsay, Logan, and Whitfield, 4/24/62.

229 *Variety* touted: Bergreen, p. 545.

229 Ryan was miscast: Ibid., p. 540; interview with Frank Rich.

229 "I begged Leland": Interview with Anna Crouse; Bergreen, pp. 540–541.

229 The Washington premiere: Bergreen, pp. 542–544.

229 "the biggest party": Ibid., p. 542.

230 He had been watching: Ibid.

230 "Don't you come": Interview with Anna Crouse.

230 "Anyone with any sense": Russel Crouse diary, 9/27/62.

230 "I could have killed her": Interview with Anna Crouse.

230 The show opened a month: Bergreen, p. 545 (opening 10/20/62).

230 When the Cuban missile: Bergreen, p. 546; A week after Kennedy learned about the Soviet missiles in Cuba, the news broke on 10/22/62 (Reeves, pp. 368, 370, 390).

230 "Leland never got": Interview with Anna Crouse.

230 "the day I reach": Leland Hayward letter to Harry Kurnitz, 9/7/62 (LH-NYPL).

230 He tried in vain: Transcript of Leland Hayward phone conversation with Hedda Hopper, 11/13/63; Leland Hayward letters to Harry Kurnitz, 10/2/65, and Andrew Bernheim, 10/18/65, 11/24/65, 12/2/65 (LH-NYPL); Berman, pp. 279–281.

230 In 1965 Hayward seemed: Berman, pp. 282–283.

230 accompanied as usual: Warren O'Hara, general manager for *Hot September*, note to Ritz Hotel, 9/1/65 (LH-NYPL).

230 The show ran barely: Leland Hayward letter to the company, 10/9/65 (LH-NYPL).

230 "Bad luck plagues": Leland Hayward letter to Harry Kurnitz, 10/11/65 (LH-NYPL).

230 Hayward's relentlessly: Interviews with Frank Rich, Flora Roberts.

231 "The money was easy": Interview with Alexander Cohen.

231 "genuinely frightened": Berman, p. 273.

231 "a stubbornness": Leland Hayward letter to Helen Harvey at William Morris, 4/22/66 (LH-NYPL).

231 In 1964, his longtime: Jo Forrestal letter to Leland Hayward, 6/1/64 (LH-NYPL); interviews with Alexander Cohen, Marshall Jamison.

231 "He would have a couple": Interview with Marshall Jamison.

231 "Pam rolled with it": Ibid.

231 "After I made my exit": Keith, p. 152.

232 "Pam never had the same": Interview with Marshall Jamison.

232 "She would come out with": Interview with Bill Hayward; Virginia Lee Warren, "Baron's Daughter Finds Shopkeeping to Her Taste," NYT, 6/28/65, quoting Pamela: "I was told that as a producer's wife I must never

offer an opinion, not even if I were asked for one. I am permitted to read scripts, but that is really rough because if I don't like one I'm told I know nothing about the theater."

232 "Pamela said, 'You know' ": Interview with Anita Colby.

<h2>CHAPTER TWENTY-THREE</h2>

233 "There was a sense that": Interview with Kitty Hawks.
233 Pamela enticed him home: Interview with Brooke Hayward.
233 Friends who called: Interview with Clay Felker.
233 Visitors to their: Interview with Jack Valenti.
233 "He was looking rather": Interview with Mary Dunn.
233 She started watching: Interview with Nicholas Haslam.
233 "In her conversation": Interview with Tom Parr.
233 "She paid total": Interview with Jeanne Thayer.
234 "I had the feeling": Interview with Clay Felker.
234 Hayward allowed Pamela: Interview with Marshall Jamison.
234 At her urging: Valentine Lawford, "The Leland Haywards of Haywire House," *Vogue*, 2/14/64; Deed, 6/1/62, between Walter S. and Edna Mae Baumann and Pamela Hayward.
234 Hayward paid the $90,000: Ogden, p. 312.
234 Pamela was able to: Interviews with Bill Hayward, Clayton Fritchey.
234 "a hideous modern house": Baldwin, p. 332.
234 But the house sat: *Vogue*, 2/15/64.
234 Pamela and Hayward settled: Hayward, p. 287.
234 Once again Pamela: Interview with Paul Manno.
234 Like the Duchess: Interview with Brooke Hayward.
234 Even in a crowd: Interviews with Jeanne Thayer, Jean Howard.
234 "She never stopped": Interview with Kenneth Jay Lane.
234 "Leland was more subdued": Interview with George Plimpton.
235 "Weekends at Haywire": Interview with Nicholas Haslam.
235 While the Haywards continued: Interviews with Kitty Hawks, Bill Hayward, Jeanne Murray Vanderbilt.
235 "I would call Father": Interview with Brooke Hayward.
235 "There was no question": Interview with Kitty Hawks.
235 Hayward, for his part: Ibid.
235 "Pam told me that": Interview with Cheray Duchin Hodges.
235 In 1961, Brooke met: Hayward, p. 284; interview with Brooke Hayward.
235 Hopper had come: Microsoft Cinemania '94 CD, profile from *The Motion Picture Guide Annual 1993*, BASELINE II.
236 two breaches of propriety: Interview with Bill Hayward.
236 John Frankenheimer: Cinemania '94 profile.
236 "I didn't like the idea": Interview with Brooke Hayward.
236 "Pamela was trying": Interview with Bill Hayward.
236 "I was way below": Interview with Dennis Hopper.
236 "Don't marry him": Interview with Brooke Hayward.
236 "It's not too late": Ibid.
236 "The wedding bouquet": Josie Mankiewicz Davis letter to her mother, 8/15/61.

236 "I would stay": Interview with Bill Hayward.

236 That spring his father: Ibid.

236 According to Bill: Ibid.

237 By the 1960s: NYJA, 4/7/60.

237 "Apparently Kay Summersby": Interview with Bill Hayward.

237 "I have a vague recollection": Interview with Winston Churchill.

237 "traveling across": Interview with Bill Hayward.

237 "Everything changed": Ibid.

237 "worked herself into a": Interview with Brooke Hayward.

237 "I smoked a joint": Interview with Dennis Hopper.

237 In an effort to appear: Interview with Brooke Hayward

237 "Pamela said to Leland": Interview with Dennis Hopper; Hayward, p. 284.

238 "the rest of the": Interview with Brooke Hayward.

238 "Pamela did everything": Interview with Dennis Hopper.

238 When Bill was discharged: Interview with Bill Hayward.

238 their marriage fell apart: Interview with Brooke Hayward; Hayward, p. 284.

238 "Brooke had the ability": Interview with Bill Hayward.

238 "to say nothing of": Leland Hayward letter to Mary Martin and Richard Halliday, 11/22/62 (LH-NYPL).

238 "Leland never saw": Interview with Dennis Hopper.

239 "I hardly knew her": *Baltimore Sun*, 7/4/82.

239 "dedicated shopper": NYHT, 9/8/63.

239 approached Paul Manno: Interview with Paul Manno.

239 "When we make money": Ibid.

239 On October 1, 1963: NYHT, 9/8/63.

239 She got free legal: Interview with Jeanne Thayer.

239 "These women were not": Interview with Paul Manno.

239 Pamela stocked her shop: Ibid.; *Vogue*, 2/15/64; NYHT, 9/8/63; NYT, 6/28/65.

240 "In a very very short": Interview with Paul Manno.

240 Pamela hired a: Ibid.

240 "She was a real working": Interview with Anita Colby.

240 "I hated to see her": Ibid.

240 "She had tremendous business": Interview with Paul Manno.

240 Several times a year: Interviews with Paul Manno, Marcia Meehan Schaeffer, Mary Dunn.

240 "At first she gave": Interview with Paul Manno.

240 She supervised her staff: Interview with Marcia Meehan Schaeffer.

240 The shop made a modest: Interview with Paul Manno.

240 Both the *New York*: NYHT, 9/8/63, and NYT, 6/28/65.

240 Leland Hayward was intrigued: Interviews with Marcia Meehan Schaeffer, Marshall Jamison, Bill Hayward.

241 "There was a woman": Interview with Anita Colby.

241 "His attitude was": Interview with Leonora Hornblow.

241 When he bought Pamela: *Vogue*, 2/15/64.

241 Haywire House became: Baldwin, p. 332; Lesley Blanch, *The Wilder Shores of Love* (1983 ed.), p. 191.

241 "the most luxurious": Baldwin, p. 332.

241 To this, Pamela added: Interview with Bill Hayward.

241 With Pamela's encouragement: *Vogue*, 2/15/64.

241 To help run: Leland Hayward letter to Winston Churchill, 11/22/62 (LH-NYPL).
241 Between the apartment: Interviews with Bill Hayward, Brooke Hayward.
241 For a time, Hayward's: Interview with Marshall Jamison.
241 In addition to the 10 percent: Interview with Burl Stiff.
241 "Halliday got": Ibid.
241 "You don't know how painful": Ibid.
241 He had signed a: Interview with Perry Woolf; Leland Hayward letters to Mike Dann, 12/3/65 and 12/29/65; Tom Ryan letter to Leland Hayward, 11/18/65, on CBS program with "magazine format" (LH-NYPL).
242 *That Was the Week:* Tim Brooks and Earle Marsh, *The Complete Directory of Prime Time Network TV Shows 1946-Present* (1992), p. 885.
242 Hayward was taking: Interview with Marshall Jamison; *TW3* estimated budget for 1964–65 season . . . services of LH $5,000, 1/10/64 (LH-NYPL).
242 long memos filled with: Leland Hayward to Marshall Jamison, 3/13/64, 3/25/64, 3/27/64, 4/7/64, 4/15/64, (LH-NYPL).
242 "The writing is mushy": Leland Hayward memo to Jamison, 3/27/64 (LH-NYPL).
242 *TW3* did move: Interview with Marshall Jamison: "We were making a profit of $7,000-$10,000 a week and he was making $5,000 a week before turning a profit."
242 But because of: Leland Hayward memo to Freeman Keyes, 1/23/64 (LH-NYPL).
242 "Kintner said, 'No more' ": Interview with Marshall Jamison.
242 Jamison quit: Ibid.
242 The following fall: Tom Ryan memo to Leland Hayward, 1/15/65 (LH-NYPL).
243 "The problem of TW3": Leland Hayward to Robert Kintner, 1/29/65 (LH-NYPL).
243 "Leland was not making": Interview with Marshall Jamison.
243 "At least we all": Interview with Clay Felker.
243 "an excruciating attack": Hayward, p. 284.
243 Not long afterward: Interview with Paul Manno.
243 Lord Digby had died: TT-L, 1/30/64; TT-L, 3/26/64 listing unsettled estate; Edward Kenelm Baron Digby last Will, 11/3/61.
243 The Haywards' troubles: NYT, 11/22/68 and 3/19/71.
243 "To have two establishments": Interview with Clay Felker.
244 They kept a cook, maid: Interview with Brooke Hayward.
244 "This was a real pied": Baldwin, p. 332.
244 After a four-year drought: Berman, pp. 284-287, 376-377.
244 "He had a lot": Interview with Marshall Jamison.
244 "cruel, disgusting": Berman, pp. 284-285.
244 It closed before: Ibid, p. 375.
244 That summer at age: Hayward, p. 314.
244 "left him irritable": Ibid.
244 "Leland would get": Interview with Cheray Duchin Hodges.
245 "One of the big": Interview with Marshall Jamison.
245 As Hayward became more: Interview with Brigitta Lieberson.
245 "Leland is not well": Interview with Stuart Scheftel.
245 " 'Congratulations' ": Hayward, p. 284.

245   Bill had restored: Interview with Bill Hayward.
245   "For Pam, it was a disaster": Ibid.
245   "One day Pam": Interview with Brooke Hayward.
245   "Leland had debts": Interview with Jeanne Thayer.
246   *The Trial of:* Berman, pp. 288–295.
246   "I want to buy it": Interview with Flora Roberts.
246   "It was an interesting": Interview with Bill Hayward.
246   When Daniel Berrigan: Hayward, p. 285; WWD, 1/25/71.
246   Back in New York: Berman, pp. 295, 378.
246   "I hate to talk": WWD, 1/25/71.
246   Barely a week later: Hayward, pp. 284–285, 307.
246   "An unqualified success": Hayward, p. 284.
246   Coming out of his: Ibid., p. 286.
246   Pamela went to the opening: William Cahan, *No Stranger to Tears* (1992), p. 211.
247   "Leland and I talked": Interview with Ashton Hawkins.
247   Although praised: Berman, pp. 298, 378.
247   Hayward left the: Hayward, pp. 287, 307, 310, 315.
247   but it was Pamela: Interview with Leonora Hornblow.
247   During one visit: Hayward, p. 317; interview with Bill Hayward.
247   Although Hayward could still: Hayward, pp. 310–314.
247   "He didn't want to go back": Leland Hayward letter to Maisie Hayward, 9/25/46 (LH-NYPL).
247   At Haywire, Pamela hired: Hayward, p. 323.
247   "Leland is dying": Hepburn, p. 192.
247   "He woke up": Interview with Marshall Jamison.
247   The next day: NYT, 3/19/71.
247   A line of limousines: Interviews with Brooke Hayward, Leonora Hornblow, Marshall Jamison.
248   "It was almost like": Interview with Anna Crouse.
248   she had impressed: Marina Sulzberger, p. 398.
248   "With Pamela, a deal": Interview with Leonora Hornblow.
248   "cheerful and nice": Interview with Brooke Astor.

CHAPTER TWENTY-FOUR

249   "Pamela was trying to tell": VF, 7/88.
249   "an enormous temper": Interview with Brooke Hayward.
249   "Before Leland": Interview with Winston Churchill, recounting a statement from his mother.
249   "Leland told everyone": Interview with Leonora Hornblow.
249   Hayward's attorney: 8/28/62 Leland Hayward Last Will and Testament.
250   none of them sworn: Interview with Marshall Jamison.
250   On February 17, 1971: Kathleen Malley Kavanagh affidavit, 3/17/71.
250   in signed documents: Bill Hayward waiver and consent, 3/23/71; Brooke Hopper waiver and consent, 3/23/71.
250   "Pamela was terribly": Interview with Bill Hayward.

250 By Bill and Brooke's: Interviews with Bill Hayward, Brooke Hayward.
250 The total value: Petition for Letters of Administration, 3/23/71, from Pamela Hayward.
250 "Pamela had spent too much": Interview with Bill Hayward.
250 Bill was to get: Ibid.
250 "Probably thirty to forty": Ibid.
250 "Our policy has": Interviews with Kalman Fox, Emile Carlisi.
251 "changed the ground rules": Interview with Bill Hayward.
251 By Brooke's account: Interview with Brooke Hayward.
251 Bill said the matter: Interview with Bill Hayward.
251 "What about the pearls?" Interview with Brooke Hayward.
251 "I don't remember a thing": Interview with Leonora Hornblow.
251 Pamela's friends: Interviews with Leonora Hornblow, Cheray Duchin Hodges.
251 "this absolute mad dog": Interview with Bill Hayward.
252 "The Pearls!": Evan Thomas, *The Man to See* (1991), p. 383.
252 "I was pissed": Interview with Bill Hayward.
252 "She didn't go out": Interview with Kenneth Jay Lane.
252 "He was irritated": Interview with Jeanne Thayer.
252 Instead, she got: Mortgage agreement with Bankers Trust Company signed by Pamela Hayward in the presence of Winfield Jones, 6/24/71.
252 "I was standing": Interview with Leonora Hornblow.
252 Then fifty-six: Kitty Kelley, *His Way* (1986), pp. 227, 333, 346–347, 391, 402–404.
252 "the older crowd": Ibid., p. 346.
253 Sinatra even designated: Interview with Leonora Hornblow.
253 "hung around our house": Keith, p. 214.
253 Even after Slim: Leland Hayward letter to Frank Sinatra, 1/20/60, signed "love and kisses" (LH-NYPL).
253 After the *Hot September:* Leland and Pamela Hayward letter to Frank Sinatra, 10/5/65; Leland Hayward letter to Harry Kurnitz, 10/11/65 (LH-NYPL).
253 Two months later: Leland Hayward wire to Frank Sinatra, 12/30/65 (LH-NYPL).
253 "would have married": Kelley, p. 431.
253 Christopher Ogden, on the: Ogden, pp. 347, 350–351.
253 Annenberg, who was serving: Walter Annenberg letter to the author, 12/5/94.
253 "The singer found her": Ogden, p. 351.
254 "Pamela was a guest": Interview with Leonora Hornblow.
254 "I wouldn't bet against": Ibid.
254 English gossip columnists: *Sunday Express,* 5/6/71; ES 6/6/71; *Daily Mirror,* 8/28/71.
254 "I remember going": Interview with Tom Parr.
254 "became another bone": Cahan, p. 211.
254 Instead of staying: Interview with Winston Churchill.
254 "That was the only time": W, 10/24–31/80.
254 having converted half: *Country Life,* 2/28/80.
255 Young Winston was a: " 'No Chicken—Some Neck,' The Terry Coleman Interview with Winston," *The Guardian,* 8/25/73; Churchill, pp. 235–237, 247, 262.

255 "she was more American": Interview with Brooke Astor.

255 "I'd headed home": W, 10/24–31/80.

255 Shortly after her arrival: Interview with Katharine Graham.

255 "Do you mind if I fink": Ibid.

255 On the official guest: Informal dinner for Mr. and Mrs. Arthur Schlesinger on Thursday, August 5, 1971, eight o'clock, 2920 R Street, NW: accepted 45.

255 "had no inkling": Abramson, p. 682.

255 "It was just as if ": NY, 1/18/93.

255 They were seated at different: Katharine Graham seating chart for 8/5/71.

255 There was a story that: Ogden, p. 354; interview with Nancy Lutz.

255 "The idea that she": Interview with Katharine Graham.

255 "I didn't know who": Interview with Liz Stevens.

256 After leaving Pamela: Abramson, pp. 102, 421, 425–429, 433–435; interview with Charles Maechling.

256 contributed only $500: Walter Isaacson and Evan Thomas, *The Wise Men* (1986), p. 510.

256 Harriman's next assignment: Ibid., pp. 510, 540; Abramson, pp. 421, 435, 472, 482, 485, 498, 503.

256 Two years later: Abramson, p. 515.

256 "Attaboy, Ave": Ibid., p. 510.

256 Harriman overcame: *Saturday Evening Post,* 10/25/58; Abramson, p. 513.

256 "a pedestrian performance": Abramson, p. 567.

256 He had neither: Ibid., pp. 515–517.

257 "He talked a good": Ibid., p. 518.

257 Midway through: Ibid., pp. 535–539, 555, 562, 575.

257 "tool of the machine": Ibid., pp. 564–565.

257 Schiff later confided: Interview with Clay Felker.

257 Resilient as ever: Abramson, pp. 572, 577, 603.

257 When Communist forces: Ibid., pp. 582–587, 590–593; Reeves, p. 308.

257 "Averell artfully set": Interview with Charles Maechling.

257 In 1963, Harriman stumbled: Abramson, pp. 606, 620, 624; Reeves, pp. 558, 561–563, 566.

258 "a largely unsuccessful": Abramson, p. 630.

258 Johnson eventually named: Ibid., pp. 632, 635.

258 Johnson acknowledged: Ibid., pp. 658–659, 668, 671–673.

258 Harriman felt he had: Ibid., p. 672.

258 "a tribute to sticking": Interview with Katharine Graham.

258 When he was Secretary: Abramson, p. 431.

258 "Ol' Averell likes": Joseph A. Califano, Jr., *The Triumph and Tragedy of Lyndon Johnson* (1991), p. 102.

258 Marie became a successful: WP, 8/6/67; *Long Island Sunday Press,* 8/10/58.

258 "Oh Ave, come off it": Interview with Edward Morgan.

258 They were a capable: Abramson, pp. 431, 522; interview with Nancy Lutz.

259 "he decided to use her": Interview with Nancy Lutz.

259 It was Marie who pushed: Abramson, p. 577.

259 "She had an instinctive": Interview with Nancy Lutz.

259 He never seemed to mind: Interviews with Nancy Lutz, Peter Duchin.

259 "Marie was a wonderful": Interview with Edward Morgan.

259 She grew stout: Interviews with Nancy Lutz, Charles Maechling.

259 Whether it was changing: Abramson, p. 413; interview with Nancy Lutz.

259   "Cheap old bastard": Abramson, p. 676.
259   What he craved: Ibid., p. 677; interviews with Peter Duchin, Michael Kuruc.
259   "Marie was a Washington": Interview with Alice Acheson.
259   In the last several: Interview with Edward Morgan; Abramson, p. 675.
259   "I don't want to be": Interview with Nancy Lutz.
259   In September 1970: Ibid.; Abramson, p. 677.
260   "Mary Russell wasn't": Interview with Nancy Lutz.
260   Marie came down with: Abramson, pp. 675, 677.
260   "Ave took it off": Interview with Nancy Lutz.
260   In an even more peculiar: Interview with Cheray Duchin Hodges.
260   Marie's funeral was held: Abramson, p. 677; interview with Nancy Lutz.
260   "walking from room": Interview with Nancy Lutz.
260   Knowing that Harriman: Interview with Alida Morgan.
260   "in that melancholy autumn": Abramson, p. 678.
260   He spent the winter: Interviews with Peter Duchin, Cheray Duchin Hodges, Nancy Lutz.
260   In the spring of 1971: Abramson, p. 679; interviews with Peter Duchin, Edward Morgan.
261   "It had been a memorable": Abramson, p. 681.
261   In the following years: Averell Harriman letters to Winston Churchill, 11/3/67, 12/19/67; Winston Churchill letter to Averell Harriman, 12/8/67 (WAH-LC).
261   When Winston came: Interview with Winston Churchill; Winston Churchill letter to Averell Harriman from Haywire House, 2/10/68 (WAH-LC).
261   "I would see": Interview with Clayton Fritchey.
261   "I had no idea Leland": Interview with Cheray Duchin Hodges.
261   he "had been thinking": Abramson, pp. 682–683.
261   "Averell said, 'Do you' ": Transcript of Marie Brenner interview with William Walton.
261   "It didn't show in his": Interview with Alida Morgan.
261   "his whole world had turned": Interview with Nancy Lutz.

CHAPTER TWENTY-FIVE

263   "Mais on ne peut pas": Interview with Florence Van der Kemp. Literally translated, the expression means "one cannot rekindle the central heating system."
263   After the Graham dinner party: Interview with Peter Duchin.
263   "I don't know if Ave": Interview with Cheray Duchin Hodges.
263   "She leapt out": Interview with Peter Duchin.
263   "Averell's top was open": Ibid.
263   "It was like catching": Interview with Cheray Duchin Hodges.
263   "Fine," she said: Interview with Peter Duchin.
264   "She told me how": Interview with Cheray Duchin Hodges.
264   "Pam was very cheerful": Ibid.
264   "he went into her house": Ibid.
264   "She told him she would": Ibid.
264   "very firm friends": NYT, 9/18/71.
264   "He was determined": Interview with Winston Churchill.

264 They married even sooner: NYT, 9/28/71; WWD, 9/28/71.
265 "Don't publish": WWD, 9/28/71.
265 Afterward, they went: WWD, 9/29/71.
265 "We did it!": WWD, 9/28/71.
265 "He never looked happier": WWD, 9/29/71.
265 "This reminds me": WWD, 9/29/71.
265 Pamela decorated: WWD, 9/28/71, 9/29/71.
265 For a wedding present: Ibid.; memo 5/4/53 from R. W. Hart to W. A. Harriman with inventory of the Marie Harriman Gallery. *Lady Hamilton as the Vestal Virgin* listed at $20,000 (WAH-LC).
265 Pamela's gift: NYT, 12/14/71.
265 "There were columnists": WWD, 10/12/71.
265 It was a vanity deal: Thomas H. Guinzburg, President, The Viking Press, letter to Averell Harriman, 12/3/71 confirming the contract terms (WAH-LC).
265 "Harriman was wildly": Interviews with William Wright, Thomas Guinzburg.
266 "dark nights and foggy": Winston Churchill letter to Averell Harriman, 10/15/71 (WAH-LC).
266 "She had some money": Interview with Winston Churchill.
266 "what you plan to do for us": Winston Churchill letter to Averell Harriman, 10/15/71 (WAH-LC).
266 Even with an inheritance: Ibid.
266 a three-story red-brick: Sotheby's International Realty fact sheet for "The Harriman House," 5/94.
266 "This is not a beautiful": Baldwin, p. 333.
266 "I must say": Ibid, p. 334.
267 She replaced Marie's: *Baltimore Sun,* 7/4/82; VF, 7/88; Lucy Moorhead, *Entertaining in Washington* (1978), p. 38.
267 "fresh garden hues": AD, 6/84.
267 For the dining room: Ibid.
267 "quite a big bedroom": Baldwin, p. 334.
267 Pamela made sure: Ibid., p. 333.
267 In 1970, Harriman had talked: Abramson, p. 680.
267 "Every space in the": Baldwin, p. 334.
267 Under the revised: National Gallery of Art Donor History for Harriman 1/26/72; AD, 6/84.
267 The paintings were valued: W. Averell Harriman Foundation Form 990 PF 1972: market value of works of art.
267 They took their winter: Interview with Michael Kuruc.
268 The house had been Marie's: Abramson, p. 413.
268 Pamela replaced Marie's: Interview with Nancy Lutz.
268 "Under Pamela, Hobe": Interview with Alida Morgan.
268 It wasn't until 1979: Interview with Guy Waltman.
268 Harriman rented it: Interviews with Guy Waltman, Alida Morgan.
268 in 1973 sought permission: NYT, 7/18/93.
268 During the early years: Interview with Michael Kuruc; AD, 6/84.
268 in 1977 Harriman bought her: Deed, 11/21/77, between Pamela C. Harriman and Millicent MacKenzie for house and 41 acres; deed, 9/18/79, between Pamela Harriman and Millicent W. West (formerly MacKenzie) for 1.7 acres;

deed, 5/26/82, between Pamela Harriman and Millicent West for 17.9 acres (total acreage: 60).

268 for $740,000: *Washingtonian*, 8/94.

268 It was called: Kate Tyndall, "A Knack for Winners," *Spur: The Magazine of Thoroughbred and Country Life*, 1–2/92.

268 Willow Oaks became: Adrian Higgins, "Hunt Country Hideaway," *Garden Design*, 9/91; Elaine B. Steiner, "Gardens: At Willow Oaks: The W. Averell Harrimans' Estate in Virginia," AD, 10/82.

268 In addition to redecorating: Prudence Squier, "Roots of an English Country Garden," WP, 6/18/67; AD, 10/82; author observations.

269 "A lot of people used to": Interview with Guy Waltman.

269 As she had done: interview with Michael Kuruc; W, 11/30–12/7/87; WP, 5/5/77.

269 "pout and stick out": Interview with Rudy Abramson.

269 "She wouldn't walk in": Interview with Guy Waltman.

269 When Harriman balked: Ibid.

269 Finally, in March 1983: Bill of sale 3/4/83 between Canberra Jet Charter and Minterne Corp, one "used" Westwind I Model 1124 Aircraft.

269 It was less elaborate: Paul Mellon, with John Baskett, *Reflections in a Silver Spoon* (1992), pp. 380–381; VF, 11/93; interviews with Michael Kuruc, Dave Hurley of The Flight Service Group.

269 "Pamela's energies": Interview with Guy Waltman.

270 "We had to discuss": Ibid.

270 "I know Pamela spends": Ibid.

270 Over time, Pamela: Interviews with Nancy Lutz, Edward Morgan, Cheray Duchin Hodges; Alida Morgan.

270 She assumed Marie's place: Annual reports for APHF and MWHF (FCL).

270 "Perhaps this is a": VF, 7/88.

270 "If you are a decent": Interview with Nancy Lutz.

270 Marie's granddaughter: Ibid.

271 "Ave knew them better": Interview with Edward Morgan.

271 "A butler I didn't": Interview with Alida Morgan.

271 "If you got him on": Ibid.

271 "How do you like": Interview with Nancy Lutz.

271 "Ma and Ave": Peter Duchin letter to Averell and Marie Harriman, 12/11/68 (WAH-LC).

271 "Peter is a member": Averell Harriman letter to The Hon. Henry R. Labouisse, 6/21/63 (WAH-LC).

271 The Harrimans had overseen: Averell Harriman letter to the Council on Foreign Relations, 9/7/67, proposing Peter Duchin for membership (WAH-LC).

271 "Peter fit in": Interview with Cheray Duchin Hodges.

271 Marie had planned: Ibid.; Interview with Peter Duchin.

272 to help fulfill an: Abramson, p. 694; APHF annual reports for 1990, 1991, 1992, 1993 show total gifts of $4.7 million to the W. Averell Harriman Institute (FCL).

272 "every single picture": Interview with Cheray Duchin Hodges.

272 No longer could Duchin: Interview with Peter Duchin.

272 "a little acre on the ocean": Ibid.

272 Harriman had deeded: Interview with Edmund Goodman.
272 The Duchins had hired: Interviews with Peter Duchin, Cheray Duchin Hodges.
272 "What about the acre": Interview with Peter Duchin.
272 "I wrote him a note": Interview with Nancy Lutz.
272 "I am not aware of any": Interview with Guy Waltman.
272 "Pam knew I wouldn't say": Interview with Peter Duchin.
273 in 1985 married Brooke: *Who's Who in America* (wedding date: 12/24/85).
273 Bill dropped his lawsuit: Interview with Bill Hayward.
273 "a nice side": Ibid.
273 Both his daughters approved: Interview with Mary Fisk.
273 Kathleen and Mary knew: Ibid.
273 Rather, in the manner: Abramson, p. 96; interview with Amanda Mortimer Burden.
273 Mary Fisk hewed: Interviews with Mary Fisk, Robert Fisk.
274 But after marrying: NYT, 10/12/47.
274 "Kath was more of a mother": Interview with Amanda Mortimer Burden.
274 Arden, the vast estate: Abramson, pp. 43, 63, 79–80, 89–90.
274 Averell Harriman had given: Ibid., pp. 261–265.
274 With its stables: Interview with Robert Fisk.
274 Mortimer worked for: Interviews with Amanda Mortimer Burden, Linda Mortimer.
274 The Mortimer fortune: Interview with Linda Mortimer.
275 Both Kathleen and Mary: USNY Complaint, 9/13/94, pp. 18–19.
275 worth more than $1 million: Interview with Guy Waltman.
275 In 1960, Harriman: USNY complaint, 9/13/94, pp. 19–20.
275 A fund originally: MWHF Annual Report 1986 and 1987 grant recipients include Bennington College ($30,000); Arden Hill Hospital ($15,000); Cornell Medical College, Dept of Neurology—Dr. Fred Plum—($2,000); The Deafness Research Foundation ($7,500); Sun Valley Ski Education Foundation Inc. ($2,500); Tuxedo Volunteer Ambulance Corp. Inc. ($2,000) (FCL).
275 After Yale: Interview with Robert Fisk.
275 She also served: MWHF Annual Reports 1986–1992, grants to Concord Academy totaled $185,000 (FCL).
275 Ames blended easily: Averell Harriman letter to Averell Mortimer, 11/14/77 (WAH-LC).
275 After graduating from: Interview with Mary Fisk.
276 manufacturing T-shirts: Interview with Robert Fisk.
276 high-risk commodities: Averell Fisk letter to Averell Harriman, 2/3/81, describes the $120,000 he made in commodities trading in the previous year.
276 "quick money": Interview with Guy Waltman.
276 subsidized by $50,000: MWHF Annual Reports 1986–1992, grants to the American Assembly totaled $350,000 (FCL).
276 "Averell was not a Norman": Interview with Robert Fisk.
276 such as the note he wrote: Averell Harriman letter to Dean Boris Yavitz, 8/8/80 (WAH-LC).
276 "try to advance": David Mortimer letter to Averell Harriman, 5/9/77 (WAH-LC).
276 "sleeping on bunks": David Mortimer letter to Averell Harriman, 1/10/75 (WAH-LC).

276 "if you are given": Averell Mortimer letter to Averell Harriman, 1/31/80 (WAH-LC).

276 "it *would* be taken": Averell Harriman letter to Averell Mortimer, 2/11/80 (WAH-LC).

276 Even Averell Fisk: Averell Fisk letter to Averell Harriman, 2/3/81 (WAH-LC).

277 Harriman saw his daughters: Interviews with Guy Waltman, Robert Fisk.

277 "Don't you get it?": Interview with Alida Morgan.

277 "After a while she will": Interview with Brooke Hayward.

CHAPTER TWENTY-SIX

278 she was honored: NYT, 12/16/71.

278 "I have a vision of the older": Interview with Esme Cromer.

278 "She cut a quick": Interview with Barbara Howar.

278 "accepted Pam with": Ibid.

278 "adored my grandmother": Interview with Alida Morgan.

278 "publicly bore no": Interview with Piers Dixon.

278 "She was lonely": Interview with Cheray Duchin Hodges.

279 "The desirable guests": Quoted in Cleveland Amory, *Who Killed Society?* (1960), p. 152.

279 "It seems an insult": Susan Watters, "Inside Georgetown," W, 12/4–11/81.

279 The postwar Georgetown: Martha Sherrill, "Georgetown on My Mind," T& C, 5/92.

279 "always act as if": Henry Allen, "Dan Quayle's Gray Matter," WP, 10/21/92.

280 "all come and go": Quoted in Stephen Birmingham, *The Right People* (1958), p. 223.

280 "Right now I'm interested": NYT, 12/16/71.

280 "or at least I had": Averell Harriman letter to Pam Morgan, 3/26/73 (WAH-LC).

280 He gave $6,000: Federal Election Campaign Act of 1971: Alphabetical Listing of 1972 Presidential Campaign Receipts.

280 He had given nothing: Herbert E. Alexander and Caroline D. Jones, *Political Contributors of $500 or More in 1968,* Citizens' Research Foundation (1969): zero contributions from Averell Harriman; 1969 (zero); 1970 ($1,000); 1971 ($1,864).

280 Harriman's brother Roland: Alexander and Jones, 1968 ($17,000), 1969 ($11,000), 1970 ($26,500), 1971 ($23,000).

280 and in 1972 gave: *Political Contributors and Lenders of $10,000 or More in 1972,* Barbara O. Paul, Mary Jo Long, Elizabeth C. Burns, and Herbert Alexander, Citizens' Research Foundation (1973).

280 When Muskie faltered: Abramson, pp. 686–687.

281 "would take Averell's": Interview with Winston Churchill.

281 When she was named: Interview with Michael Kuruc.

281 "walk-in for coats": WWD, 4/30–5/7/76.

281 "Bob, I can do many": Interview with Robert Strauss.

281 Pamela was delighted: Margaret McManus, "Washington's Other First Lady," *Baltimore Sun,* 6/26/77.

281 "She used to do her homework": Interview with Guy Waltman.

282   "She was a real star": Interview with Perry Bass.

282   In 1980 alone, the airline: NYT, 2/24/81.

282   "There was no way": Interview with Perry Bass.

282   "As every close student": Moorhead, p. 16.

282   "that glow that comes": Ibid., p. 49.

282   "the ideal British tradition": Ibid., p. 39.

283   "now circulating among": NYT, 10/1/82.

283   "She isn't the number": *Baltimore Sun*, 6/26/77.

283   "Pamela spent those early": Interview with Barbara Howar.

283   "Now the ladies": Interview with Sally Quinn.

283   "There was not a word": Ibid.

283   "when the ladies": Nicholas Henderson, *Mandarin* (1994), p. 280.

283   "I wish the phrase": Moorhead, p. 50.

284   The Democrats were set: NYT, 7/10/76; 8/3/76.

284   "give Bella the chance": NYT, 7/22/76.

284   an "early and fervent": NYT, 3/2/77.

284   "Jimmy Carter?": Christopher Matthews, *Hardball* (1989 ed.), p. 155.

284   On April 1, Pamela: FEC Selected List of Receipts and Expenditures: Individuals 1976, W. A. and Pamela C. Harriman, p. 196.

284   a reception so: NYT, 10/22/76; WWD, 10/22/76.

284   THE AMERICANIZATION: *Washington Star*, 10/21/76.

284   PAMELA HARRIMAN'S ROLE: NYT, 3/2/77.

284   WASHINGTON'S OTHER: *Baltimore Sun*, 6/26/77.

285   "socialists . . . I knew": Ibid.

285   "low necked flowered": NYT, 5/16/74.

285   "She shuns": NYT, 3/2/77.

285   "Backstage people": NYT, 3/2/77.

285   On the eve: Moorhead, pp. 40, 49; WWD, 1/24/77.

285   Pamela was on the phone: Interview with Zbigniew Brzezinski.

285   "Harriman was anxious not": Abramson, p. 690.

285   "What would you expect": Interview with Zbigniew Brzezinski.

285   "to put in strong": Abramson, p. 690.

286   "was very protective": Interview with Zbigniew Brzezinski.

286   "I was never pressed": Ibid.

286   After Brzezinski moved: Ibid.

286   Harriman continued to seek: Abramson, pp. 658–659, 691.

286   Holbrooke had been in: Marjorie Williams, "Mr. Holbrooke Builds His Dream Job," VF, 10/94.

286   When Holbrooke needed: VCLC, Estate of William Averell Harriman, deceased. In account with Pamela C. Harriman, Executor, first settlement of accounts 7/26/86–12/31/87, schedule B, p. 2 (cited hereafter as WAH Estate-First Accounting).

287   "He's a Washington fanatic": VF, 10/94.

287   Holbrooke was an unabashed: Abramson, p. 691.

287   "Holbrooke was a great": Interview with Barbara Howar.

287   "When she started": Transcript of Marie Brenner interview with William Walton.

287   In 1979 and 1980 they gave: CRP, Contributions from Harriman to Party Committees (1979–1992), Presidential Candidates (1979–1992), Congressional Candidates (1979–1992).

287 So it came as: W, 10/24–31/80.
288 "Quite frankly": Interview with Carol Williams.
288 A crowd of 250: *Washington Star*, 5/23/80.
288 "wasn't a people's person": NY, 1/18/93.
288 in 1983 their foundation: APHF, annual report for 1983 (FCL).
288 Late in the summer of: Interviews with Janet Howard, John Bowles.
288 She had been intrigued: Interview with Janet Howard.
288 Howard caught the eye: Interviews with Janet Howard, John Bowles.
289 "She was such a strong": Interview with Clement Conger.
289 Howard spent much: Interview with Janet Howard: The fundraiser, she said, "was not a big thing in my life . . . I don't remember that there was any trouble. I don't remember a press thing. I have never been in fund-raising to do quid pro quo."
289 "Pamela called me": Interview with John Bowles.
289 Within months, Howard moved: Interviews with Janet Howard, Peter Fenn.
290 On election night 1980: NY, 1/18/93.
290 "I loved him in": WWD, 6/12/80.
290 "dismal event": WP, 6/10/81.
290 "The Democratic Party was": Interview with Stuart Eizenstat.
290 "a tremendous performance": NY, 1/18/93.
290 Such committees had been: Brooks Jackson, *Honest Graft* (1990), pp. 71–72; Edward Zuckerman, *Almanac of Federal PACS 1992–1993* (1992).
290 "Ave didn't have": Interview with Rudy Abramson.
290 "Pam was the first to say": TT-L, 10/31/92.
291 "put into her head": NY, 1/18/93.
291 At eighty-nine, Harriman: Interviews with Peter Fenn, John Bowles.
291 "might work but": Interview with Robert Strauss.
291 "didn't think she": Interview with Stuart Eizenstat.
291 "Pamela kept saying": Interview with John Bowles.
291 "After she did": Interview with Jesse Calhoon.
291 Its stated goals: WP, 2/11/81.
291 "The idea of the PAC": Interview with John Bowles.
292 "We said, 'We will raise' ": Ibid.
292 "I know how it feels": WP, 6/10/81.
292 In December 1980: Democrats for the 80's, G Index, Selected List of Receipts and Expenditures (79–80), Individuals and Parties and PACs, (FEC) (cited hereafter as G Index-All); Democrats for the 80's, RRD 12/18/80–1/31/81 (FEC).
292 "it was like buying": Interview with John Bowles.
292 "I had great respect": Interview with Jesse Calhoon.
292 "Normally to have fifteen": Interview with John Bowles.
292 PAMELA HARRIMAN'S PLAN: WP, 2/11/81.
292 "She doesn't seem to have": Interview with Clay Felker.
293 "If ever there was a place": Interview with Barbara Howar.

CHAPTER TWENTY-SEVEN

294 Custom-made suits by: W, 10/24–31/80; WP, 6/12/83.
294 "She has a strength": Interview with Stuart Eizenstat.

294   "The three of us selected": Ibid.
294   "He was the first": Julia Reed, "Party Girl," *Vogue*, 6/92.
295   Clinton was actually: Interviews with Peter Fenn, Stuart Eizenstat, John Bowles.
295   "It was clear someone": Interview with John Bowles.
295   By early 1982: Democrats for the 80's, March 1982, Report from the Chairman Pamela C. Harriman.
295   Some board members: Interviews with Stuart Eizenstat, Peter Fenn, John Bowles.
295   Strauss's instincts for: Interview with Robert Strauss.
296   When a *Washington Post:* Interview with Elisabeth Bumiller.
296   "At the beginning she was": Interview with Harry McPherson.
296   "I hated shaking down": interview with Peter Fenn.
296   A turning point came: NYT, 5/27/81.
296   Fenn had firsthand: Interview with Peter Fenn.
296   "liked the idea": Ibid.
296   Pam nevertheless held her: *Miami Herald*, 6/17/81.
296   "she was concerned": Interview with Peter Fenn.
297   The CBS Evening News: NYT, 5/1/81; *Baltimore Sun*, 5/1/81.
297   "the most vitriolic": *Newsweek*, 6/1/81.
297   "She thought it was": Interview with Peter Fenn.
297   "That made her feel": Ibid.
297   During PamPAC's initial: Democrats for the 80's, RRD 1/1/81–7/1/81 (FEC).
297   In the first two years: Democrats for the 80's, RRD 1/1/81–12/31/90 (FEC).
297   In the same period: Zuckerman, p. 556.
297   the maximum permitted: Ibid., p. III.
297   Pamela's list included: Democrats for the 80's, G Index, Selected List of Receipts and Expenditures, Individual Contributions (79–80, 81–82, 83–84, 85–86, 87–88, 89–90) (FEC) (cited hereafter as G Index-Individuals).
298   During the 1980s, Pamela held: *Vogue*, 8/92; WP, 6/10/81.
298   Stuart Eizenstat developed: Interviews with Stuart Eizenstat, John Bowles.
298   "She often told me why": Interview with Joan Challinor.
298   "She tried to make sure": Interview with Peter Fenn.
298   "juices flowing": WSJ, 10/8/81.
298   "I was dazzled": Interview with Barbara Howar.
299   "Psychologically, it made": Interview with Joan Challinor.
299   In the autumn of 1981: James M. Perry, "For the Democrats, Pam's Is the Place for the Elite to Meet," WSJ, 10/8/81.
299   Pamela customarily taped: *Newsweek* file from Smardz, Washington, 11/5/81.
299   "affluence and influence": WSJ, 10/8/81.
299   an "amiable dunce": WSJ, 10/8/81.
299   "gems of the genre": NYT, 10/21/81.
299   "It's better to be": *Newsweek* file, 11/5/81.
299   "She has thousands": Interview with Mary Sethness.
299   who contributed $19,000: G Index-Individuals (79–90) (FEC).
299   "You go in there and": Interview with John Bowles.
300   she coaxed $15,000: G Index-Individuals (81–84) (FEC).
300   "It was nice and quiet": Interview with John J. Cafaro.
300   Illinois attorney Kenneth: G Index-Individuals (79–90) (FEC).

300 "would end in the wastebasket": Interview with Harle Montgomery.
300 found fund-raising "frightening": NYT, 10/1/82.
300 "It's terrible to be so concerned": Ibid.
300 "Janet and Pamela were the": Interview with John Bowles.
301 the "exciting event": Interview with Mary Sethness.
301 "I'm a man": Interview with Jay P. Altmayer.
301 who gave PamPAC $12,475: G Index-Individuals (79–90) (FEC).
301 Under federal law: Zuckerman, pp. iii–iv.
301 In the 1981–82 election cycle: Democrats for the 80's, D Index, Committee Index of Candidates Supported (81–82) (FEC) (cited hereafter as D Index).
301 Pamela's first round: Interview with Peter Fenn.
301 Pamela not only gave: D Index (81–82) (FEC).
301 "She is not interested": Interview with Peter Fenn.
302 "soul of the Democratic party": WP, 11/4/88.
302 Beginning in 1983: D Index (83–84, 85–86, 87–88) (FEC).
302 "Senators are more prestigious": Interview with John Bowles.
302 "never less than $100,000": Donnie Radcliffe, "Pamela Harriman, Life of the Party," WP, 11/6/92.
302 Though candidates appreciated: Interview with John Bowles.
302 Alan Cranston, for instance: Zuckerman, p. 581.
302 A nearly 400-page: Democrats for the 80's press release, 6/25/82; WP, 6/20/82; Maxwell Glen, "A Formidable Fundraiser: Neither a Lobbyist Nor a Public Official, Pamela Harriman May Help Raise More Democratic Money Than Anyone Else. But Could Her PAC Survive Without Her?", *National Journal*, 4/29/86; interview with Peter Fenn.
303 Like the issues evenings: Interviews with Stuart Eizenstat, Peter Fenn.
303 "For Pam it was a": Interview with John Bowles.
303 In various news accounts: *National Journal*, 4/29/86; *Newsweek*, 6/5/87.
303 In fact, aside from: G Index-Individuals (79–86) (FEC).
303 Averell Harriman gave a mere: CRP, Averell W. Harriman Individual Contributions, 1979–1986.
303 He contributed no money: Ibid.
303 As for Pamela, she gave: CRP, Pamela Harriman Individual Contributions, 1979–1986.
303 Curiously, Pamela didn't: G Index-Individuals (85–86) (87–88).
303 In 1983, for example: Democrats for the 80's, RRD, 1/1–12/31/83.
303 Pamela fell short: Jackson, p. 143.
303 Soft money—also known: WP, 7/19/88, NYT, 9/12/92; Larry Makinson, *Open Secrets* (1992), p. 16.
304 In 1982, Coelho hatched: Jackson, p. 143.
304 "She was initially very": Interview with Peter Fenn.
304 "Clifford thought it was": Ibid.
304 When the Democratic National: Jackson, pp. 12, 151, 153; interview with Peter Fenn.
304 Pamela publicly associated: Democrats for the 80's, Winter 1986 newsletter.
304 The new studio opened: Jackson, pp. 151, 165.

CHAPTER TWENTY-EIGHT

305 "If anybody can bring": NYT, 10/21/81.
305 "helped keep Ave alive": Interview with Stuart Eizenstat.
305 "It was clearly her deal": Interview with Peter Fenn.
305 "I never saw anybody": WP, 6/12/83.
305 the ninetieth birthday party: WWD, 11/13/81.
305 With contributions ranging: Democrats for the 80's, RRD, 8/11–12/31/81, schedule A: $200,000 deposited 12/9/81 and $832 deposited 11/2/81; 37 pages of itemized receipts (FEC).
305 "My wife and I have": WWD, 11/13/81.
305 "there was an audible boo": Interview with Marie Ridder.
306 When he went for walks: Interview with Michael Kuruc.
306 "She never let down": Ibid.
306 Although they had separate: Ibid.
306 "Pam was very warm": Interview with Edmund Goodman.
306 "That was the bible": Interview with Michael Kuruc.
306 "Marie was a much more": Interview with Mary Warburg.
306 "Grandmère's style humanized": Interview with Alida Morgan.
307 To Harriman, Pamela was: Interview with Rudy Abramson; WP, 6/12/83.
307 This time Harriman brought her: WP, 6/12/83.
307 "I am grateful": VF, 7/88.
307 "lyrically and at length": WWD, 8/29/83.
307 Later that year, during: Interview with Michael Kuruc.
307 for $1.2 million: VCLC, 8/8/86 Inventory of the Estate of William Averell Harriman: Barbados Real Estate (Mango Bay Corporation) $1.2 million (signed by Pamela C. Harriman, fiduciary/executrix, 2/10/87)(cited hereafter as WAH-inventory).
307 "Constructed of pale coral": William Walton, "Mango Bay: Pamela Harriman's Residence on Barbados," AD, 1/87.
308 It was evident to everyone: Interview with Rudy Abramson.
308 Pamela took steps: Interview with Michael Kuruc; Abramson, p. 694.
308 They needed no special: Interview with George Albright, former chairman of the Virginia State Bar's Trusts and Estates Board of Governors.
308 On January 8, 1984: Deed dated 1/8/84 between W. Averell Harriman and Highlands, L.P., a Delaware limited partnership, notarized in Barbados, W.I., signed by James A. Budeit, Consul General, 1/10/84.
308 Pamela, who had previously: Deed of Gift 6/15/84, signed by Pamela C. Harriman and W. Averell Harriman.
308 To ensure that her: Interviews with Charles Maechling, Alice Acheson.
308 "I know why you came": Interview with Clayton Fritchey.
308 Harriman's most frequent: Interview with Michael Kuruc.
308 "When she arrived": Ibid.
308 "He was totally compos": Interview with Charles Maechling.
309 "I would go down to": Transcript of Marie Brenner interview with William Walton.
309 Sometimes she lost: Interviews with Cheray Duchin Hodges, Derry Moore.
309 "Please, I'm being": Interview with Rudy Abramson.
309 "She told me he could": Interview with Carol Williams.

309   "She looked after him the way": Interview with Michael Kuruc.

309   "The many days on": *National Journal,* 4/29/86.

309   Pamela had to spend 183: Interview with Mark Salzman, CPA.

310   "Averell viewed taxes": Interview with Guy Waltman.

310   For decades the Harriman fortune: Ibid.

310   Daniel Cook served: Interview with Peter Duchin.

310   "They were very involved": Interview with Guy Waltman.

310   In the late 1970s Harriman's: Ibid.

310   Once an expanse of 40,000: Ibid.; Abramson, p. 693.

310   When Roland Harriman died: Abramson, p. 693.

310   Under the law at the time: Interview with Guy Waltman.

311   "they were adequately": Ibid.

311   When Waltman left: Interview with Shannon White.

311   Not long after Rich's: Interview with Guy Waltman.

311   "Pam never really liked": Ibid.

311   Under the new provisions: Interviews with Guy Waltman, George Albright.

311   Harriman acted fast: Abramson, p. 695.

311   In 1979, the van Gogh: Interview with Guy Waltman.

311   Harriman's original plan: Ibid.

311   "Averell trusted her": Ibid.

311   A year later, Pamela established: USNY Complaint, 9/13/94, p. 62. The yearly annuity was estimated at $179,000, an amount that lawyers for the Harriman family subsequently learned was actually $350,000.

311   In April 1984: USNY Complaint, 9/13/94, p. 10.

312   According to Harriman's plan: Ibid., pp. 10–13.

312   Three investment firms: Ibid., p. 24.

312   named Clifford and Warnke: Ibid., p. 19.

312   "you don't have to see": Interview with Clark Clifford.

312   "The puzzling thing": Interview with Guy Waltman.

312   persuaded him to release her trust: USNY Complaint, 9/13/94, p. 13.

312   The nine trusts put under: Ibid.

312   Averell Harriman signed: William Averell Harriman Last Will and Testament 9/12/84, Part I—32, pages, Part II—15 pages (VCLC) (cited hereafter as WAH-Will).

312   A ten-page codicil: William Averell Harriman Codicil, 8/7/85 (VCLC).

312   Harriman made Pamela his: WAH-Will, Part I, p. 1.

312   "not from any lack": Ibid., p. 32.

312   For his six grandchildren: Ibid., p. 6.

312   through three new trusts: Ibid., pp. 10–13, 15–19.

312   Pamela . . . along with Clifford and Waruke: Ibid., pp. 26–27.

313   "She'll take care of herself": WP, 6/12/83.

313   "Ave had a strong financial": Interview with Guy Waltman.

313   Harriman never explained to her: Ibid.

313   He had been diagnosed: Interview with Edmund Goodman.

313   "He had no real side": Ibid.

313   "If he was in pain": Abramson, p. 695.

314   Forced to use a walker: Ibid., pp. 695–696.

314   to whom the Harrimans gave: Interview with Peter Duchin.

314   "She was extremely cordial": Ibid.

314   "Some sort of peace": Interview with Bill Hayward.

314 "One of Brooke's problems": W, 11/30–12/7/87.
314 "I have never heard Brooke": Interview with Bill Hayward.
314 By 1986, Janet Howard: Democrats for the 80's, RRD 1985 (FEC).
314 From April through July: Ibid., 1986: 4/1–30, 5/1–31, 6/1–30, 7/1–31; *National Journal,* 4/29/86; Democrats for the 80's, Winter 1986 Newsletter.
315 Within days, Averell and Pamela: Abramson, p. 697.
315 "Kathleen sat by his": Ibid.
315 "just decided that enough": Ibid.
315 Three days later: Ibid.; WP, 9/19/86.
315 Led by New York State: Abramson, p. 698; WP, 9/19/86.
316 The memorial service: Interview with Charles Maechling.
316 When the final bill for the funeral: VCLC, WAH Estate-First Accounting, schedule C. By way of comparison, when Richard Nixon died eight years later, his funeral cost $311,039. At 1994 values, Averell Harriman's funeral would have cost $237,891.
316 Two months later: Interviews with Katharine Graham, Ben Bradlee.
316 "Well, where *is* he?": Interview with Ben Bradlee.
316 "Oh, for God's sake": Interview with Katharine Graham.
316 That evening, Graham: Interview with Ben Bradlee.
316 "You can't publish that": Ibid.
316 Pamela then called Graham: Interview with Katharine Graham.
316 "appeared startled": WP, 9/19/86.
316 "Averell Harriman had decided": Ibid.
316 "the family also decided": Ibid.
317 a plot within view of: Abramson, p. 699.
317 "She was in the wrong": Transcript of Marie Brenner interview with William Walton.
317 "PATRIOT, PUBLIC SERVANT": Abramson, p. 699.

CHAPTER TWENTY-NINE

318 Harriman's estate was valued: USNY Complaint, 9/13/94, p. 28.
318 Pamela received nearly $37 million: Ibid. The complaint states that Pamela received $33 million, which excludes an additional amount revealed in WAH Estate-First Accounting: On 10/20/86, she received $3.7 million as a "loan repayment" from the estate (schedule D, p. 4) (VCLC).
318 A total of $13.2 million: VCLC, WAH-Inventory.
318 The "residuary estate": VCLC, WAH Estate-First Accounting, Summary Statement.
318 One of the more: Ibid., schedule D, p. 4.
318 Just as Averell Harriman had planned: Ibid., schedule C shows federal tax paid of $850,000. In WAH Estate-Second Accounting (1/1/88–12/31/88), schedule C, $324,043 in federal taxes had been refunded, leaving a net payment of $525,957. The total of $714,428 includes state taxes paid.
318 Among these holdings: VCLC WAH-Inventory, plus WAH-Amended Inventory signed on 4/4/88; also USNY affidavit of Charles C. Ames 9/13/94, p. 13.
318 As for Birchgrove: Deeds dated 12/4/86 and 12/15/86 between Pamela Har-

riman and S&M Partnership, general partnership c/o Philip Friedman; *The Village Voice,* 3/23/93.

318 a political consultant: Democrats for the 80's RRD 1984 shows payments of $7,150 to Friedman's Campaign Strategies, Inc.

318 The other half of: USNY Complaint 9/13/94, p. 28.

319 In addition, Harriman had created: Ibid.

319 First, she had the right to name: WAH-Will, Part I, pp. 17–18.

319 Second, Harriman also stipulated: WAH-Will, Part II, pp. 13–14.

319 Kathleen, who had been closer: Interviews with Amanda Mortimer Burden, Rudy Abramson.

319 "My father was furious": Interview with Amanda Mortimer Burden.

319 "You will be committing slow": Bryan Burrough, "The Perils of Pamela," VF, 1/95.

320 By the late 1980s there were twenty-four: Interview with Douglas Winthrop at Wilmer, Cutler and Pickering.

320 "I get the feeling": Interview with Amanda Mortimer Burden.

320 When Kathleen wanted an "eyelift": Ibid.

320 Kathleen was a loyal: G Index-individuals (79–90) (FEC).

321 Pamela reciprocated: APHF Annual Reports 1986–1993 (FCL).

321 His wife, a book editor: Walter Wanger, who had been a friend of Leland Hayward, "was thought to be an intellectual because he had once gone to Dartmouth," wrote journalist and popular historian Otto Friedrich in *City of Nets* (1987) (p. 53). Wanger also served a short jail term after being convicted of shooting Bennett's agent in the groin during a jealous rage.

321 "Winston . . . seems to have": W, 11/30–12/7/87.

321 "so the whole family": Interview with Winston Churchill.

322 After Harriman's death: *You Magazine,* 11/21/93; TT-L, 6/4/93.

322 The financing, he said: Interview with Winston Churchill.

322 "generously gave us": Interview with Winston Churchill.

322 "a lot of Harriman money": Ibid.

322 She gave Winston, Minnie: Interview with Jan Cushing Amory.

322 "young" Winston—as he was: *Sunday Telegraph,* 10/18/92.

322 His goal, he once: *You Magazine,* 11/21/93.

322 "His single greatest": *Guardian,* 8/25/73.

322 in November 1976: *Daily Express,* 12/21/79.

322 "I was over the": *Guardian,* 10/20/92.

322 Although he wasn't: *Daily Mail,* 5/9/93.

322 He lashed out: *Daily Express Now!* 12/21/79; *Sunday Telegraph,* 5/30/93.

322 "cast into the outer": TT-L, 6/4/93; Pearson, p. 426.

322 He seemed to share: *Daily Express Now!* 12/21/79.

322 Winston still expected: *Daily Telegraph,* 12/15/79; *Sunday Telegraph,* 10/18/92.

323 Her unwillingness to do so: Pearson, p. 426; *Daily Telegraph,* 12/15/79; Sunday Mirror, 12/16/79.

323 "It was not, after all": *Daily Express,* 12/21/79.

323 "He is a bit of a robot": Interview with Peregrine Worsthorne.

323 "melancholy destiny": *Sunday Telegraph,* 10/18/92.

323 "have always struck me": *Spectator,* 5/6/89.

323 "swanky": *Sunday Telegraph,* 5/30/93.

323 "I go on a lecture tour": *You Magazine*, 11/21/93.
323 Pamela had shared: *Baltimore Sun*, 6/26/77.
324 "I like that": WP, 11/6/92.
324 Winston talked to his mother: Interview with Winston Churchill.
324 Yet Pamela's relationship with Winston: Interviews with Jan Cushing Amory, Michael Kuruc.
324 "chameleon." "Had she": Interview with Winston Churchill.
324 "Winston it seemed": Interview with Cheray Duchin Hodges.
324 "Winston is resentful": Interview with Jan Cushing Amory.

CHAPTER THIRTY

325 Aside from occasional episodes: Interview with Michael Kuruc.
325 For snacks during: NYT, 10/1/82; WP, 6/12/83.
325 Although personal trainers: Interview with Michael Kuruc.
325 Most weekends in the fall: *Spur*, 1–2/92.
325 She was usually accompanied: Interview with Marion Becker, who rode with the Middleburg Hunt.
325 "I like to hunt up front": *Spur*, 1–2/92.
325 One avid hunter: Interview with Linda Mortimer.
325 Away from the hunting: *Spur*, 1–2/92.
326 "a miracle worker": Aimee Lee Ball, "Smooth Operators," T&C, 4/95.
326 He taught at: *Aesthetic Plastic Surgery*, Second Ed., edited by Thomas D. Rees and Gregory S. LaTrenta (1994), p. V. (cited hereafter as APS).
326 "freshen up": T&C, 4/95.
326 "Some consider it to be": Melissa Paleologos, Joseph Steuer, and Stephanie Tuck, "The Rage for Plastic Surgery," W, 5/14–21/90.
326 Aston considered himself: Interview with Sherrell Aston.
326 major surgery of two to three hours: APS, "Selection of Patients," Rees, p. 6.
326 First she was sedated: APS, "Anesthesia for Cosmetic Surgery," J. Thomas Herbert, M.D., pp. 678–687.
326 her hair was tied: APS, "Preoperative Preparation and Evaluation," Sherell J. Aston, M.D., Charles H. Thorne, M.D., and Rees, pp. 676–677.
326 "skin skribe": T&C, 4/95.
326 The classic Aston: APS, "Contemporary Rhytidectomy," Aston and Thorne, pp. 708–721.
326 "deep tissue dissection": Ibid., p. 708. Also known as the "deep facelift" (APS, "History," by Aston, Thorne and Rees, p. 661), this procedure was introduced in 1976 (APS, "The Classic Operation," Rees, p. 683), and Aston was one of its early and most skilled practitioners.
326 Aston would remove: APS, Aston and Thorne, pp. 708–721.
326 Face-lifts are not usually: APS, "Postoperative Considerations and Complications," Rees, Aston, and Thorne, pp. 742, 745, and 751.
327 "That's not the bandage": Interview with Mary Warburg.
327 "as though time and magic": Interview with Irene Selznick.
327 "Looking great": Margit Mayer, "King Karl," W, 12/9–16/91.
327 In Washington, Pamela would simply: Interview with Cheray Duchin Hodges.

328 "Pam has a way with her": Interview with Lauren Bacall.
328 When Diane Sawyer: CBS Morning News, 3/1/83 and 3/2/83.
328 assumed equal footing: Susan Watters, "Saint Teresa," W, 1/95.
328 "Young man, you are": Interview with Jan Cushing Amory.
329 The reward for befriending: Interview with Kitty Hart.
329 "She has great followthrough": Interview with Ann Jordan.
329 The two women were: Kitty Carlisle Hart, *Kitty* (1988), p. 149.
329 "Leonora and Kitty are not": Interview with Nancy Holmes.
329 "We were all very disciplined": Marie Brenner, "The Art of Mrs. Hart," TNY, 7/5/93.
330 Hornblow was born Leonora: Interview with Leonora Hornblow; Steven A. L. Aronson, "Memory and Desire," T&C, 7/93.
330 "The two man-pleasers": Interview with Leonora Hornblow.
330 They had met in 1951: Hart, p. 159.
330 "She was fascinated by": Interview with Kitty Hart.
330 "I have no idea if she": Ibid.
330 "the most incurious woman": TNY, 7/5/93.
330 She transformed herself: Ibid.
330 She grew up: Hart, pp. 3–45.
330 "the worst room in": Hart, p. 12.
330 Kitty went to finishing: Ibid., pp. 112, 116.
331 "the prince of Broadway": TNY, 7/5/93.
331 Hart, who used to rehearse: Ibid.
331 "continuous drawing room": Hart, p. 152.
331 Hart was homosexual: Farber and Green, pp. 57–58.
331 "I believe in denial": TNY, 7/5/93.
331 When Moss Hart died: Hart, p. 205; TNY, 7/5/93.
331 the popular television quiz show: Brooks and Marsh, pp. 441, 902–903.
331 "We weren't encouraged": Interview with Kitty Hart.
331 "she puts herself out": Ibid.
331 "Kitty is thrilled": Interview with Lauren Bacall.
332 "No, absolutely not": *Savvy*, 6/88.
332 The Browns arrived: Calvin Tomkins, "For the Nation," TNY, 9/3/90.
332 "extraordinary household": Ibid.
332 With a master's: Ibid.
332 The Browns dined: Larry Van Dyne, "Art & Money," *The Washingtonian*, 4/88.
332 lived in three luxurious: TNY, 9/3/90.
332 "slightly ignored": Ibid.
332 he was fascinated by: *Washington Times*, 3/9/93.
332 Several years later: TNY, 9/3/90.
332 "a sense of the practicalities": *The Washingtonian*, 4/88.
333 "Ever since he was a young": *Washington Times*, 3/9/93.
333 "aggressive aplomb": TNY, 9/3/90.
333 "Carter has snowed": Ibid.
333 Brown transformed: Ibid.
333 When he was thirty-six: *The Washingtonian*, 4/88.
333 "quite mad but": Interview with Alan Pryce-Jones.
333 "was embezzled twice": Interview with Nicholas Brown.
333 "She kept breaking": Ibid.

334 "Carter felt ill-used": Ibid.

334 With that much mutual: TNY, 9/3/90.

334 "It was her way": Interview with J. Carter Brown.

334 In 1976 when Carter: TNY, 9/30/90.

334 Carter Brown was forty-three: Elizabeth Kastor, "Carter Brown, Personally Speaking: The Very Private National Gallery Director on Retirement, Rumors and Real Life," WP 4/2/92.

334 His wife found: Interview with J. Carter Brown.

334 "My poor brother": Interview with Nicholas Brown.

335 "It is one thing to be": Ibid.

335 "I didn't know him": TNY, 9/3/90.

335 In the summer of 1987: WP, 4/2/92.

335 Carter and Pam contrived: Ibid.

335 "Averell and Marie were great: Interview with J. Carter Brown.

335 "to see such corroboration": J. Carter Brown letter to Averell Harriman, 9/24/71 (WAH-LC).

335 Only months later: National Gallery of Art Harriman donor history, 1/26/72; TNY, 9/3/90.

335 In 1982 he named her: Executive Branch Financial Disclosure Report 3/19/93 Schedule D: National Gallery of Art, Trustees Council, 1982–1993. (cited hereafter as Financial Disclosure Report-1993).

335 Four years later Pamela: APHF annual reports: 1986 and 1987 (FCL).

335 After Brown and his wife: WP, 4/2/92.

336 "She was a very good friend": Interview with J. Carter Brown.

336 "I have never understood": Ibid.

336 "jealousy, and the stereotype": Interview with Nicholas Brown.

336 "Being in a common world": Ibid.

336 Although not a scholar: TNY, 9/3/90.

336 "black box who has": Interview with Nicholas Brown.

336 Following a consultation: Interview with J. Carter Brown.

337 At that time, Pamela had promised: WP, 6/21/89.

337 Pamela promised to: Richard Walker, "A $60 Million van Gogh," Art News, 9/89.

337 By 1989, at the peak of: Ibid.

377 In October 1990 the Senate: BG, 11/21/90.

377 In January 1991: Interview with Philip Jessup, Secretary and General Counsel of the National Gallery.

338 which by then had dropped: Interview with David Rust.

338 In 1993, Congress: WP, 3/31/93.

338 "magnificent act": Press Release, National Gallery of Art, 6/20/89.

338 "I've been so very upset": WP, 6/21/89.

338 Missing from the announcement: Abramson, p. 184.

338 The divorce of Carter: Custody agreement signed 12/19/91, according to WP, 4/2/92.

338 "The irony is, she": Interview with J. Carter Brown.

338 there was never any suggestion: Interview with Winston Churchill.

338 The previous January he had: WP, 2/2/92.

338 "more time and energy": WP, 1/25/92.

339 He also seemed to want: WP, 3/3/93.

339 he organized an ambitious: WP, 12/12/95.

339 "He hasn't retired": Interview with Nicholas Brown.
339 Harriman Foundation had donated $12,000: APHF Annual Reports 1989–1992 (FCL).
339 "It was pretty one-sided": Interview with Winston Churchill.
339 "I don't know what one": Interview with J. Carter Brown.

CHAPTER THIRTY-ONE

340 "upper reaches": VF, 7/88.
340 "seek her political advice": BG, 6/20/90.
340 "politician": The Century Association: The New Members, 11/89–10/90.
340 "among people who matter": NY, 1/18/93.
340 "She has made herself": Interview with Cynthia Sainsbury.
340 When Joan Kroc: Jackson, p. 149.
340 As the newly appointed: APHF annual reports, 1986–1993; MWHF annual reports, 1986–1993 (FCL).
340 In 1987, for example: APHF and MWHF annual reports 1987 (FCL).
340 in 1988 she was: Financial Disclosure Report-1993.
340 From 1989 through 1993: APHF and MWHF annual reports 1989–1993 (FCL); VCLC *Robert C. Fisk et al. v. Pamela C. Harriman et al.*: Motion of APHF to intervene as a plaintiff against certain defendants, 8/25/95, p. 5 (cited hereafter as Motion of APHF to intervene).
341 In 1985 Pamela signed: Financial Disclosure Report-1993
341 The following year: MWHF and APHF annual reports 1986 (FCL).
341 Pamela was elected vice: Financial Disclosure Report-1993.
341 after she donated: APHF annual report 1988 (FCL).
341 She gave an additional: APHF annual reports 1990–1993 (FCL).
341 Proof that Pamela: Financial Disclosure Report-1993.
341 Averell Harriman had joined: W. Averell Harriman: A Register of His Papers in the Library of Congress (1991), p. 22.
341 Pamela and Averell had: APHF annual reports 1983, 1989–1993; MWHF annual reports 1986–1993 (FCL).
341 The "delegation" included: VF, 7/88.
341 Pamela undertook: *Savvy*, 6/88.
341 On each visit to Moscow she represented: Interview with Robert Legvold.
341 "I think there is": Ibid.
342 The two women had met: WP, 12/11/87; VF, 7/88; *Savvy*, 6/88.
342 "She had cultivated": Transcript of Marie Brenner interview with William Walton.
342 "how seriously the Kremlin": VF, 7/88.
342 on the Chinese view: Pamela C. Harriman, "In China, Kremlin Watching," NYT op-ed, 8/19/87; Pamela Harriman, "Turkey Deserves Priority Attention," NYT op-ed, 2/20/88.
342 written as she was maneuvering: Pamela C. Harriman, "Have the Democrats Lost Their Soul?," NYT op-ed, 10/12/89.
342 Alfred Friendly, Jr.: Interview with Alfred Friendly, Jr.
342 "She wanted to pay me": Interview with Peter Fenn.
342 "She didn't pay me": Interview with Robert Shrum.
343 "I am an American by choice": Ibid.

343 Both Robert Shrum and: Interview with Robert Shrum.
343 Sandy Berger, Pamela's principal: Interviews with Stuart Eizenstat, Peter Fenn.
343 "diplomatic coming out": WP, 4/28/88.
343 "to be seen as something": Ibid.
343 For several weeks: Interviews with Alfred Friendly, Robert Shrum, Stuart Eizenstat.
344 "We can, and I believe": Henry Fairlie, "Shamela," TNR, 8/2/88. Fairlie's title was taken from Henry Fielding's parody of Samuel Richardson's virtuous heroine in *Pamela*.
344 "scores of stifled yawns": WP, 4/28/88.
344 "Let me be the first": Ibid.
344 "regaled the table": *Vogue*, 8/92.
344 "the only Washington hostess with her own": WP, 4/28/88.
344 "high standards": WP, 5/7/88.
344 a consultant who had received: Democrats for the 80's: RRD 1985 ($5,733) and 1988 ($4,493) (FEC).
344 Tom Harkin, had benefited: D Index 1983–84.
344 as well as fund-raising help: *National Journal*, 4/29/86.
344 "memorial to Pamela": TNR, 8/2/88.
344 In 1988, she made: APHF annual report 1988 (FCL).
344 Averell had previously: Ogden, p. 450.
344 "graduated from Downham College": Pamela Harriman's Address to the School, 2/21/89.
344 "How wonderful it is": Ibid.
344 "I cannot help": Winston Churchill, *Blood, Toil, Tears and Sweat* (1989), p. 226.
345 A fixture in Washington: NYT, 11/18/91; Newsweek, 8/26/91; WSJ, 5/31/91.
345 "in awe": Transcript of Marjorie Williams interview with Pamela Harriman.
345 "Pamela would line up": Interview with Robert Legvold.
346 When Sandy Berger or Robert Shrum: Ogden, p. 461.

CHAPTER THIRTY-TWO

347 "Now she has the image": Transcript of Marie Brenner interview with William Walton.
347 She kept five separate: WP, 6/12/83.
347 along with computer printouts: Ogden, p. 485.
347 She was so heavily: *Savvy*, 6/88.
347 The upstairs maid: Interview with Michael Kuruc.
347 "Her maid scurries": WP, 6/12/83.
347 Pamela's chefs: WP, 5/5/77; Interview with Peter Fenn.
348 Following Harriman's death: Interview with Michael Kuruc.
348 "I modeled myself after": Ibid.
348 "I didn't use the word": Ibid.
348 "Janet and Pam have a chemistry": Interview with John Bowles.
348 Pamela stayed by her side: Interview with Janet Howard.
349 Only a portion came from: Democrats for the 80's and Democrats for the 90's, RRD (85–90)(FEC).

349   including $50,000 worth: Ogden, p. 459.

349   Janet Howard became omnipresent: Interview with Peter Fenn.

349   "almost an extension": Interview with Stuart Eizenstat.

349   "Janet is a human Rolodex": Interview with Bill Carrick.

349   "a great chief of staff": Interview with Robert Shrum.

350   Yet the public record: Democrats for the 80's and Democrats for the 90's RRD (80–90) (FEC).

350   In the 1983–84: Democrats for the 80's RRD, 1983 and 1984 (FEC).

350   but by 1989–90: Democrats for the 90's RRD, 1989 and 1990 (FEC).

350   In 1983–84: Democrats for the 80's RRD, 1983 and 1984 (FEC).

350   By 1989–90 they had: Democrats for the 90's RRD, 1989 and 1990 (FEC).

350   "national polling operation": Pamela Harriman address to the Groton School, 2/21/89.

351   Regular federal fund-raising peaked: Democrats for the 80's and Democrats for the 90's RRD, 1979–1990 (FEC).

351   "it was felt that it was": Interview with Stuart Eizenstat.

351   Pamela announced the transformation: WP, 2/28/89.

351   "Like many prominent": W, 9/4–11/89.

351   "floating salon": WWD, 9/5/89.

352   "We expect the dinner": Democrats for the 90's Press Release, 5/10/89.

352   Federal records indicate: Democrats for the 90's RRD, 1/1/89–6/30/89 (FEC).

352   The public record did show: Democrats for the 90's RRD, 1/1/89–6/30/89 and 7/1/89–12/31/89, Schedule B (FEC).

352   "I have a background": *Newsweek*, 6/25/90.

352   The aim, she said: Democratic Decade Press Release, 6/20/90.

352   "party of the decade": WP, 4/17/90.

352   "defiant in defeat": BG, 6/20/90.

353   "wearing a black Givenchy": WWD, 6/27/90.

353   "Party regulars fretted": *Newsweek*, 12/24/90.

353   Records filed with the FEC: Democratic Decade RRD, 4/1/90–6/30/90 and 7/1/90–9/30/90 (FEC).

353   FEC reports showed only: Democrats for the 90's RRD, 7/1/90–12/31/90, Schedule B (FEC).

353   "I think I've paid": WP, 12/11/90.

353   "It's as if someone": *Newsweek*, 12/24/90.

353   "told friends she felt": Ibid.

353   Stuart Eizenstat urged: Interview with Stuart Eizenstat.

353   She repeatedly claimed: NY, 1/18/93; Ogden, p. 6.

354   "doling out some $14 million": *Newsweek*, 12/24/90.

354   Pamela actually raised: Democrats for the 80's and Democrats for the 90's RRD 1979–1990.

354   "masterminded": VF, 7/88.

354   "saved the seat": *The Independent* (London), 1/16/93.

354   Sarbanes in 1982: Congressional Quarterly Online: Paul S. Sarbanes Campaign Finance Records 1982–1994.

354   neither PamPAC nor Pamela: D Index 81–82 (FEC); CRP Contributions from Harriman to Congressional Candidates 1979–1992.

354   PamPAC did pay: Democrats for the 80's RRD 1/1/81–7/1/81 (FEC).

354   Pamela assigned herself: VF, 7/88.

354   In the 1985–86 election: D Index 85–86 (FEC).
354   Pamela personally gave: CRP Contributions from Harriman 1985–86.
354   "She was right in the middle": Interview with Bill Carrick.
354   "It gave more visibility": Interview with Jesse Calhoon.
355   "clubhouse cum think tank": NY, 1/18/93.
355   "did become a very unique": Interview with John Bowles.
355   "People liked going": Interview with Bill Carrick.
355   "She ran the inn": Interview with Gordon Stewart.
355   "If I had ever gotten": WP, 6/12/83.
355   "enormous success": Savvy, 6/88.
355   "I lunch only at": Vogue, 8/92.
356   "unnecessarily antagonistic": Interview with Felicity Barringer.
356   "rarely gives interviews": People, 4/26/93; Savvy, 6/88: "repeatedly turns down interview requests."
356   "Their five years simply": NY, 1/18/93.
357   "She kept them in": Interview with Michael Kuruc.
357   "At this point in her": Transcript of Marie Brenner interview with William Walton.
357   When Rudy Abramson's: Interview with Rudy Abramson.
357   "between lovers": Interview with Marie-France Pochna.
357   Among her champions: TNR, 9/12/88.
357   "wrote a single word": Interview with Brooke Hayward.
357   When award-winning: Interview with Doris Kearns Goodwin.
357   "Arthur Schlesinger was always": Washington Star, 10/21/76.
358   In the spring of 1991: Interview with Morton Janklow; Pamela "wanted her story told," according to the Washington Post (4/27/94), "in response to" the biography being prepared by this author, an assertion confirmed by several of Pamela's friends.
358   Ogden was the sort of man: WP, 4/27/94.
358   Richard Holbrooke, who introduced: Interview with Christopher Ogden.
358   Investigators had discovered: Time, 7/29/91.
358   "a strange defense": WSJ, 5/31/91.
358   "They did it against": Interview with Morton Janklow.
358   "It was in the context": Interview with Christopher Ogden.
358   "She was like a girl": Interview with Barbara Howar.
359   "a full and frank": Interview with Christopher Ogden.
359   Connected to the Random: Interview with Morton Janklow.
359   Pamela signed the: Interview with Christopher Ogden.
359   Ogden gave the collaboration: Ibid.
359   "panicked": Ibid.
359   "lay herself open": Interview with Winston Churchill.
360   Pamela returned the Random: Interview with Christopher Ogden.
360   "America is not ready": Interview with Peter Duchin.
360   Sharing the news: Interview with Brooke Hayward.
360   "will be handsomely paid": Interview with Lynn Nesbit.
360   "making it an unauthorized": Interview with Christopher Ogden.
360   "peculiarly tense": Khoi Nguyen interview with Christopher Ogden.
360   He asked for a payment: Interview with Christopher Ogden.
360   exclaimed, "We had no": Khoi Nguyen interview with Christopher Ogden.
360   "She had signed the": Interview with Christopher Ogden.

360 "All I was looking for": Ibid.
361 "I felt I was being": Ibid.
361 When Sorenson finally: Ibid.
361 "those interviews are": Khoi Nguyen interview with Christopher Ogden.
361 ° "At first Sorenson was": Interview with Christopher Ogden.
361 "hefty six figure": WP, 6/9/92.
361 Under the terms: Interview with Christopher Ogden.
361 "I find it extraordinarily": Interview with Morton Janklow.
361 "It has so much to do": Interview with Brooke Hayward.
362 "The information she gave": Ibid.

CHAPTER THIRTY-THREE

363 She was still involved: WP, 2/3/91.
363 During the primaries: CRP, Contributions from Harriman to Presidential Candidates 1979–1992.
363 Once when he was scheduled: WP, 6/12/83.
363 a political payoff: Interview with Bill Carrick.
363 the brunch she hosted: WP, 7/16/84.
364 "Her circle of advisers": Interview with Bill Carrick.
364 Throughout 1987: CRP, Contributions from Harriman to Presidential Candidates 1979–1992.
364 His father, Albert Gore: Bill Turque, "The Three Faces of Al Gore," *Newsweek*, 7/20/92; Walter Shapiro, "Gore: A Hard-Won Sense of Ease," *Time*, 7/29/92; Michael Kelly, "A Life of Advantage, Enhanced by the Will to Excel," NYT, 7/17/92; Celia Dugger, "The Prime Time of Tipper Gore," NYT, 7/19/92.
364 Pamela contributed $1,000: CRP, Contributions from Harriman to Congressional Candidates 1979–1992.
364 PamPAC donated: D Index 1984 (FEC).
364 "around quite a bit": Interview with Peter Fenn.
365 Michael Dukakis and Jesse: NYT, 4/21/88.
365 "Hymietown": Eileen Shields-West, *The World Almanac of Presidential Campaigns* (1992), p. 236.
365 Koch said that Jews: BG, 4/13/88.
365 "We're not choosing a preacher": BG, 4/15/88.
365 Gore finished a poor: NYT, 4/20/88.
365 "She's a pragmatist": BG, 7/15/88.
365 She did help Gore retire: *Cleveland Plain Dealer*, 10/6/92.
365 "former power crowd": BG, 7/15/88.
365 "There's a lot of advice": Ibid.
365 "He never called": NY, 1/18/93.
365 According to Democratic: WP, 7/19/88.
366 In the autumn, Pamela convened: WP, 11/4/88.
366 "Mrs. Harriman, in fact": Ibid.
366 "Why should there be": WP, 6/12/83.
366 "That would be a fun": *Daily Mail*, 4/13/84.
366 "Now she tells people that": Transcript of Marie Brenner interview with William Walton.

366 Massachusetts Senator: BG, 5/1/91.

366 Part of that public: G Index-Individuals, 1979–1990; D Index 1979–1990 (FEC).

366 Rockefeller, who stood: *Congressional Quarterly* online profile, updated March 1995; *Congressional Quarterly* online: Jay Rockefeller campaign finance profile.

367 "leadership quality": *People*, 5/20/89.

367 In mid-June 1991, Pamela hosted: "The Best Campaign Money Can Buy," PBS 10/27/92: transcript.

367 She wrote no checks of: CRP, Soft Money from Pamela Harriman 1991 and 1992; 1991 and 1992 contributions from Harriman to party committees, contributions from Harriman to congressional candidates.

367 At the meeting's conclusion: PBS, 10/27/92.

367 "frantic Democrats": Michael Kinsley, "Noblesse Oblige," WP, 8/15/91.

367 "comical": Ibid.

367 He had been received: *Philadelphia Inquirer*, 8/8/91; WP, 8/15/91.

368 "I'm helping all": WP, 9/27/91.

368 "It was the minimum you": Interview with Louis Auchincloss.

368 "we don't have many Marios": *New York Newsday*, 11/18/91.

368 The new front-runner: *Philadelphia Inquirer*, 12/21/91.

368 After Clinton had been nearly: Interview with Robert Shrum.

369 "always subject to further": Michael Kelly, "The President's Past," NYT Magazine, 7/31/94.

369 "resilience and inner": *The Spectator*, 2/13/93.

369 Even as Pamela had: CRP, Contributions from Harriman to Presidential Candidates.

369 Fearful of another: *Newsweek*, 11/12/92.

369 In April, she invited: Peter Bradshaw, "Is Power-Broker Pamela Set to Return and Conquer?" ES, 10/23/92; *Vogue*, 8/92.

370 She had financed: APHF and MWHF annual reports, 1991 and 1992.

370 An uncomfortable moment: Interview with Rudy Abramson.

370 To Pamela's relief: NYT, 11/14/91; WP, 11/15/91.

370 In March 1992, Pamela traveled: W, 3/2–9/92.

370 "slightly overemphatic": Meredith Etherington-Smith, "Star Spangled Pamela," *Sunday Express Magazine*, 5/17/92.

370 her home at Torosay: Rory Knight Bruce, "The Hidden Sisters of Scandalous Pam," ES, 5/12/94.

370 TONGUES WAG OVER: *Daily Mail*, 4/16/92.

370 They had met: Interviews with Jan Amory, Peter Duchin.

371 "We had automatic physical": Interview with Jan Amory.

371 The romance played out: Interview with Jan Amory.

371 "He would call his aides": Ibid.

371 "Hand me these in two": Ibid.

371 Amory had been an early: Democrats for the 80's RRD: Averell Harriman 90th Birthday Celebration, Joint Fundraiser with the DNC, 8/11/81–12/31/81.

371 "I don't know whether": Interview with Jan Amory.

371 "Winston, darling": Ibid.

371 "When he told his mother": Ibid.

371 "Winston told me it was the first": Ibid.

371   "She told Arthur she didn't": Ibid.

372   Pamela played the financial: W, 11/9–16/92.

372   As an investor in: Interview with Winston Churchill.

372   For the next several weeks: Interview with Jan Amory.

372   "a pleasing sight": *Daily Mail,* 5/25/92.

372   "She's almost too quick": WP, 11/6/92.

372   He was one of: *Newsweek* Special Election Issue, 12/92, p. 56.

372   Pamela was among many: Interview with Robert Shrum.

372   Pamela arrived at: *Vogue,* 8/92.

372   She started the social: WP, 7/13/92.

373   "I haven't felt this": Ibid.

374   The biggest donors: "In Honor of Governor Bill Clinton and Senator Al Gore," Willow Oaks, Middleburg, Va., September 12, 1992: invitation and reply card.

374   By September, the Democrats: BG, 9/17/92.

374   they might exceed the $53 million: NYT, 9/13/92.

374   Four days following: *Los Angeles Times,* 9/16/92; WP, 9/17/92.

374   Howard collapsed from the strain: Interview with Janet Brown.

374   Between them they had: Democratic National Committee computer printouts: "checks as of 3:45 AM 9/12/92" and "pledges as of 9/12/92 4:39 AM."

374   the $100,00 in soft money he had hurriedly: WSJ, 11/9/92.

375   At that moment, more than a thousand: Author observation.

375   "Now this is one plantation": Ibid.

375   "through the fire": Ibid.

375   "the first lady of": Ibid.

376   "It's a great thing in life": *Vogue,* 8/92.

376   "We raised $3.2 million": WP, 11/6/92.

376   By the evening of the 12th: DNC computer printouts, 9/12/92.

376   Little Rock, where Pamela: WP, 11/6/92.

376   The resulting article: Ibid.

CHAPTER THIRTY-FOUR

378   "What's in it": WP, 11/6/92.

378   Although there was speculation: ES, 10/23/92; *New York Observer,* 10/5/92.

378   Pamela told friends: Interview with Clayton Fritchey.

378   "I told her I thought": Interview with Robert Shrum.

378   "It would be such a revenge": Interview with Sandy Bertrand.

379   "She will have impact": NY, 1/18/93.

379   "leading host": *Newsweek,* 11/16/92, 12/28/92; NYT 12/29/92.

379   Pamela threw a highly publicized: Donnie Radcliffe, "The In Crowd at Pam Harriman's," WP, 11/20/92.

379   "warm and private": "The Reliable Source," WP, 11/20/92.

379   "scores of VIPs": Radcliffe, WP, 11/20/92.

380   "clasping his hand": NYT, 11/21/92.

380   "the night of the": WP, 11/20/92.

380   "I knew there was a": Joseph Fitchett, "Pamela Takes on Paris," T&C, 2/94.

380   Publicly she continued: NY, 1/18/93.

380 "an accomplished political": NYT, 3/24/93.

380 "winning hearts": WP, 3/27/93.

380 "no one in this country": Elizabeth Gleick, "Life of the Party," *People,* 4/26/93.

380 "She has no diplomatic": WSJ, 3/11/93.

380 "what's wrong with the system": *New York Post,* 3/24/93.

380 "Mrs. Harriman's most obvious": Ibid, 3/19/93.

381 "powerful king maker": WP, 3/27/93.

381 "a cross between": *L'Express,* 4/22/93.

381 "one of the most subtle": *Paris Match,* 7/22/93.

381 which had been built by Elie's: Morton, p. 275.

381 To supplement her schoolwork: Associated Press, 5/27/93.

382 "She has this inborn intuition": Charles Bremner, "The Eagle Has Landed," TT-L (Magazine), 8/28/93.

382 Pamela took the unusual: Interview with Lela Margiou, American Embassy press attaché.

382 On May 4 at 2:15 P.M.: Author observation.

282 "Madame Ambassador, how are ya?": Ibid.

382 Pamela had greased: D Index, 1979–1991 (FEC).

382 From her own pocket: CRP, Contributions from Harriman to Congressional Candidates 1979–1992.

382 She also claimed to have: WP, 3/7/89.

383 "Where's Biden?": Author observation.

383 "My own firsthand knowledge": Statement of Ambassador Designate Pamela Harriman, 5/4/93.

383 The senators were fawning: Author observation.

383 "I think he's dug his own": WP, 10/17/91.

383 "extraordinary": Author observation.

383 what "only the French could call . . . cohabitation?": Ibid.

383 "I think the . . . uh . . .": Ibid.

384 "a very handsome and dashing": Ibid.

384 *"Ohhhwwww,* it's Claude": Ibid.

384 "Are you prepared to supplement": Ibid.

384 "phenomenal job": Ibid.

384 "Pam seemed rather emotional": Interview with Ina Ginsburg.

384 Investment banker: *W,* 5/24–31/93.

385 "The French are difficult": Interview with Jack Valenti.

385 The setting was: "The Diplomatic Reception Rooms," United States Department of State 1993, p. 7.

385 She appeared confident: Videotape: "Swearing In Ceremony Pamela Harriman, U.S. Ambassador to France," 5/17/93, State Department, Washington, D.C. Harriman Communications Center.

385 holding the Bible: TT-L, 6/4/93.

CHAPTER THIRTY-FIVE

387 In the American and: Associated Press, 5/27/93; TT-L, 5/28/93; W, 7/5–12/93.

387 "When the adrenaline": Rosamond Bernier, "The First Lady of Paris," *Vogue*, 2/94.

387 "working": *Time*, 7/5/93.

387 "One of the things": Alan Riding, "In the City of Light, Her Accent Seems Just Right," NYT, 1/18/94.

387 "I'm happy to say": *Vogue*, 2/94.

387 "The one thing the President": T&C, 2/94.

388 "fluent": Ibid.

388 "elegant": TT-L, 8/28/93.

388 "major collection": *Time*, 7/5/93.

388 "something like a hundred": Martin Walker, "That's Why the Lady Is a Champ," *The Guardian*, 6/14/93.

388 "fabulous paintings": Kevin Doyle, "Pammi Does Paris," *W*, 1/94.

389 Instead, she agreed to: *20/20*, 11/26/93.

389 reminisced about World War II: *Face the Nation*, 5/7/95; *This Week with David Brinkley*, 6/5/94.

389 She told *Washington Post* correspondent: Interview with William Drozdiak.

390 "fly straight to Washington": Gully Wells, "The Last Empress," VF, 2/95.

390 Each day she tucked: T&C, 2/94.

390 "The French cannot always be": Ibid.

391 she took pride in: NYT, 1/8/94; T&C, 2/94.

392 But she did give Kantor: Interview with Mickey Kantor.

392 "After that," recalled: Ibid.

392 "Pamela and I were talking": Ibid.

392 Culture Minister Jacques: WSJ, 12/6/93.

392 "I wish she would have done": Interview with Jack Valenti.

392 "You can shove only": Interview with Mickey Kantor.

393 After Jacques Chirac was elected: WP, 9/11/95.

393 She selected a group: *W*, 8/94.

393 she gathered twenty-eight: WP, 6/8/94; *Washington Times*, 6/8/94.

393 When Bill Clinton wanted: WP, 6/8/94.

394 On January 26, 1995: WP, 2/23/95; NYT, 2/24/95, WSJ, 2/24/95.

394 "the most serious trans-Atlantic": WSJ, 2/24/95.

394 "rare public humiliation": WP, 2/23/95.

394 "spectacular public sparks": NYT, 2/24/95.

394 "unwarranted", "unnecessary": Ibid., WP, 2/23/95.

394 "inaccurate and incomplete": BG, 2/25/95.

395 Economic espionage between allies: NYT, 2/24/95.

395 "President Clinton made gathering": NYT, 10/15/95.

395 Pamela had been so concerned: Gregory L. Vistica and Evan Thomas, "The Man Who Spied Too Long," *Newsweek*, 4/29/96.

395 It turned out that the Interior Minister: NYT, 2/24/95.

395 "I'm available the whole time": *Vogue*, 2/94.

396 "She has the same French friends": *W*, 1/94.

396 "looking like the world's": Ibid., 7/5–12/93.

396 "christen" their "fabulous": Ibid., 10/93.

396 "Her past?": TAT, 6/93.

396 "When Gianni was": Interview with Paul Manno.

396 "Pamela said, 'If you' ": Interview with Jeanne Thayer.

397 Pamela had been in Paris only: *W*, 1/94.
397 By the fall, Pamela had a new: T&C, 2/94.
397 "indispensable ally": *Vogue*, 2/94.
398 Pamela spent $10,000: USNY, *Charles C. Ames et al. v. Clark Clifford et al.,* Declaration of Michael S. Helfer . . . in support of Defendant Pamela C. Harriman, 9/19/94 (cited hereafter as Helfer declaration); interview with William Perlstein.
398 The work, which took five: Interview with Mark Hampton.
398 The asking prices were: Pardoe Real Estate computer printout 80220 and 80219, 5/4/94.

Chapter Thirty-six

400 The sale price was: Interview with Elaine Storey at Allene, Aguiler and Altman (Barbados realtors).
400 On March 5 she took: Financial Disclosure Report-1993; Charles Ames letter to Lloyd Cutler, 3/6/95.
400 Three days before: interview with Gary Conklin, Great Planes Sales: Sales agreement 5/14/93.
400 Of the $115 million: VCLC, WAH-Inventory; WAH-Estate-First and Second Accountings; WAH-Marital Trust, First and Second Accountings.
401 In the year before: The estimate of Pamela Harriman's expenses in 1992 was based largely on interviews with confidential sources knowledgeable about her finances, as well as information on property taxes from offices in Middleburg, Sun Valley, and Barbados, along with WAH-Estate First Accounting, which lists Sands Point taxes, and the tax information on the 5/4/94 Pardoe listing for the two Georgetown homes. The cost of her private jet was based on an interview with Dave Hurley, The Flight Services Group, and a report from Conklin and de Decker Associates, Inc.: Israeli Aircraft Westwind I Annual Fixed Costs, Annual Budget and Indicated Direct Costs. Her 1992 political contribution came from CRP—Harriman 1992 contributions.
401 Her private jet cost: Interview with Dave Hurley.
401 He earned $250,000: VF, 1/95.
401 In somewhat Dickensian: Ibid.
401 "lack of judgment": Ibid.
402 a $3 million loan from: USNY Complaint, 9/13/94, pp. 67–68.
402 Clifford and Warnke became: USNY Complaint, 9/13/94, p. 6.
403 indicted in July 1992: Douglas Frantz and David McKean, *Friends in High Places* (1995), p. 379.
403 Due to his poor health: Ibid., pp. 383, 388.
403 seeking more than $100 million: USNY Charles Ames affidavit, 9/13/94, p. 9.
403 At one point she even: WP, 5/23/91.
403 He withdrew as her: Interview with Clark Clifford.
403 $21 million from the: USNY Complaint, 9/13/94, p. 14.
403 $4.2 million from: Ibid., p. 53.
403 Pamela, it turned out: Ibid., p. 75.
403 The grim sequence: Ibid., pp. 13, 24, 60.
403 "were pressing Bill Rich": Interview with Clark Clifford.

404 "They had no patience": VF, 1/95.

404 Harriman had hired him: USNY Complaint, 9/13/94, p. 25.

404 In 1987, he had spent: Interview with Sara Moss.

404 Out of the $3.1 million: VCLC, Cross bill of Defendant Pamela C. Harriman re: claims asserted in the amended complaint, 10/18/95, p. 15. (cited hereafter as PCH Cross Claim-1).

404 One of the dealmakers: USNY Complaint, 9/13/94, pp. 34–37.

404 Mulvihill took him: NYT, 10/16/94; WP, 10/15/94; VF, 1/95.

404 "great potential": WP, 10/15/94.

404 "greatly taken": Interview with Clark Clifford.

405 But Clifford, Warnke, and: USNY Complaint, 9/13/94, pp. 36–37.

405 "I had never crossed": Interview with Clark Clifford.

405 Rich invested a quick: USNY Complaint, 9/13/94, pp. 35, 44–46.

405 "never knew about the loan": Interview with Clark Clifford.

405 By the spring of 1991: USNY Complaint, 9/13/94, pp. 46–47, 72–75.

405 An investment in Polymer: Ibid., pp. 51–53; VCLC, PCH Cross Claim-1, p. 6.

406 Kathleen Mortimer and: USNY Complaint, 9/13/94, p. 61; 2/25/95 memo re: settlement impact on Mary A. Fisk.

407 "You have acted in disregard": Letter from Kathleen Mortimer, Mary Fisk, and grandchildren to Bill Rich, 12/22/93.

407 In April 1994, the heirs: USNY Complaint, 9/13/94, p. 61.

408 Nevertheless, Kathleen: USNY Ames affidavit, 9/13/94, p. 15.

408 On Cutler's advice: Ibid.; USNY Helfer declaration, 9/19/94, p. 4; Executive Branch Financial Disclosure Report, 7/26/95; Schedule B Transactions; Schedule C Liabilities (cited hereafter as Financial Disclosure Report-95).

408 That left her with only: USNY Helfer declaration, 9/19/94, pp. 2, 4; USNY Ames affidavit, 9/13/94, pp. 12–15.

408 "precarious financial state": USNY Ames affidavit, 9/13/94, p. 16.

408 Pamela's lawyers told: Ibid, p. 14.

408 Unfortunately for them: USNY, Ames et al. v. Pamela Harriman, Affidavit of Charles Ames, 6/5/95, p. 33 (cited hereafter as Ames affidavit 6/5/95).

409 In May 1994, the Harriman heirs: USNY, supplemental affidavit: Kaye, Scholer, Fierman, Hays and Handler, dated 8/14/94, p. 3.

410 The heirs put the Seasons: Ibid.

410 "an extraordinary number of inaccuracies": NYT, 5/4/94.

411 "faithless fiduciary": USNY Complaint, 9/13/94, p. 2.

CHAPTER THIRTY-SEVEN

412 "conspiracy to breach": USNY Complaint, 9/13/94, p. 79.

412 "It was with real pleasure": Interview with Brooke Hayward.

412 "outraged": *New York Newsday*, 11/1/94.

412 Lloyd Cutler let it be: Kim Masters, "The Harriman Bunch," WP, 10/11/94.

412 "I cannot be more strong": Interview with Peter Duchin.

412 "The grandchildren naturally": Interview with Clark Clifford.

413 "remittance children," VF, 1/95.

413 "There are very few people": WP, 10/11/94.

413 "Our woman in France": W, 12/94.

413 "The family very seriously": Interview with Winston Churchill.

413 "accusations of insolvency": USNY Pamela Harriman Memorandum of Law in Opposition to Motion for Extraordinary Order of Attachment, 9/19/94, p. 3 (cited hereafter as PCH Memo of Law 9/19/94).

413 Acknowledging her low: USNY, Helfer declaration 9/19/94, p. 5.

413 paintings valued: USNY, Ames affidavit 9/13/94, pp. 12–15; 2/25/95 memo re: settlement impact on Pamela Harriman.

413 "to meet her living": USNY, Helfer declaration 9/19/94, p. 4.

414 Shortly after filing: VCLC re: trust of William Averell Harriman article eighth, objections of decedent's grandchildren and great-grandchildren to the trustees' sixth settlement of accounts 9/30/94, p. 5 (cited hereafter as Objections-Article Eighth).

414 All told, the heirs: VCLC, *Robert Fisk et al. v. Pamela Harriman et al.*, Amended Bill of Complaint, 7/7/95, pp.3, 36, 45–58.

414 "negligence, lack of prudence": VCLC, Objections-Article Eighth, p. 8.

414 "the individual most responsible: VCLC, Amended Complaint, 7/7/95, p. 58.

414 The $12 million marital: VCLC, Amended Complaint, 7/7/95, pp. 57–58.

414 "imprudent investments": Ibid, p. 42.

414 variety of loans: Ibid., p. 36.

414 "for her personal use": Ibid., p. 49.

414 The marital trust's portfolio: Ibid, pp. 29–30.

414 The building, worth roughly: Ibid., pp. 44–49.

414 The two "charitable": USNY Complaint, p. 70; VCLC Amended Complaint, pp. 68, 70, 75.

414 only part of the trusts' 1994: VCLC, *Robert C. Fisk et al. and APHF v. Pamela C. Harriman*. Answer of Pamela Harriman to the intervening petition of the APHF 10/3/95, p. 7 (cited hereafter as PCH answer to petition of APHF).

414 As a result, the foundation: Letter from William E. Hibberd of APHF to B. K. MacLaury of Brookings, 12/21/94.

415 "We acted like middlemen": Interview with James Grossman.

415 The heart of her defense: Interview with Kitty Hart.

415 "I don't really think I": VF, 1/95.

415 "She was signing": Interview with Winston Churchill.

416 "personal commitment": Surrogate's Court, New York County, 10/25/95 Petition to Compel Trust Accountings, pp. 8–9 (cited hereafter as SCNY-Petition to Compel).

416 Pamela was well aware: VF, 1/95.

417 But with legal bills already: Financial Disclosure Report-95, Schedule C; 2/25/95 memo re: settlement impact on Pamela Harriman.

417 "to build up some": NYT, 2/24/95.

417 Starting with a lofty: WP, 5/11/95.

417 Matisse's *Woman:* Abramson, pp. 431–432.

417 "private collectors whose": WP, 6/21/89.

417 The Christie's pitch: Interview with Laurie Dodge, Christie's; T&C 5/95.

418 Once Pamela signed: Consignment agreement 1/18/95 between Pamela C. Harriman and Christie, Manson and Woods International, Inc.

418 Christie's transferred: WP, 2/23/95.

418 "It was a hard": Interview with Winston Churchill.

418 one of her favorite routines: T&C, 2/94.

418   During a conference: USNY Declaration of Lloyd Cutler in opposition to plaintiffs' motion for preliminary injunction, 6/16/95, p. 5 (cited hereafter as Cutler declaration 6/16/95).

418   Nevertheless, the following: VCLC, *Robert Fisk et al. v. Pamela Harriman et al.* Bill of Complaint, 1/25/95.

418   A week later, Pamela fired: VCLC PCH Cross Claim-1, 10/18/95, pp. 6–7.

418   Using Cutler's $15 million: U.S. Court of Appeals for Second Circuit, *Ames et al. v. Pamela Harriman,* Brief of Plaintiff-Appellants 9/29/95, pp. 9–10 (cited hereafter as Appeals Court Brief 9/29/95).

418   The "central issue": USNY Ames affidavit 6/5/95, pp. 7–8.

418   "most contentious issues": USNY Declaration of William J. Perlstein in opposition to plaintiffs' motion for preliminary injunction, 6/16/95, pp. 2–3 (cited hereafter as Perlstein declaration 6/16/95).

418   By March 6, 1995: Charles C. Ames letter to Lloyd Cutler 3/6/95, signed by Cutler 3/7/95.

418   Cutler, who had received: USNY Cutler declaration 6/16/95.

419   later negotiated down: 5/11/95 agreement between Pamela C. Harriman and Oldfields and Southfields.

419   The settlement was structured: USNY Ames affidavit 6/5/95, p. 7; 2/25/95 memo re: settlement impact on Pamela Harriman.

419   "regular contact with": USNY Ames affidavit 6/5/95, pp. 10–11.

420   Barely a month later: NYT, 4/28/95.

420   Winston; his sons Randolph and Jack": Interview with Winston Churchill.

420   "While Sir Winston won": *Daily Mail,* 4/27/95.

420   "cashing in": Ibid., 4/28/95.

421   "I like to be well": Ibid., "So Richly Deserved, a Legacy from the Grand Old Moneymaker," Paul Johnson commentary.

421   "100 per cent discretion": TT-L, 5/1/95.

421   the trustees chose, at least: Interview with Winston Churchill.

421   a prospect that inspired: Ibid.

421   In mid-April, an unexpected: USNY Cutler declaration 6/16/95, pp. 18–19, 21–22; Ames affidavit 6/5/95, pp. 18–19, 34.

422   According to Ames: Ames affidavit 6/5/95, p. 22.

422   On Sunday night, May 7: Author observation.

422   "to present the": USNY, Ames affidavit 6/5/95, p. 22.

422   "She probably knows I don't": Interview with Kitty Hart.

422   "replay of boom times": WP, 5/9/95.

422   Perlstein spent: USNY Perlstein declaration 6/16/95, p. 9.

422   THE BIDDING FLATTENS: NYT, 5/10/95.

423   She returned to: USNY, Ames affidavit 6/5/95, p. 24.

423   Pamela's escape hatch: Appeals Court brief, 9/29/95, p. 15.

423   In the weeks: USNY Cutler declaration 6/16/95, p. 17.

423   In fact, the "contribution": USNY Ames affidavit 6/5/95, pp. 26–28.

423   "penniless": Ibid., p. 24.

423   "give up the bulk": USNY Cutler declaration 6/16/95, p. 22.

423   "The true reason": USNY *Ames et al. v. Pamela Harriman,* Complaint re: enforcement of settlement agreement, 6/6/95, p. 33 (cited hereafter as Complaint 6/6/95).

424   "hard sell": USNY Cutler declaration 6/16/95, p. 24.

424   "persuasive powers": USNY Perlstein declaration 6/16/95, p. 8.

424 Yet all the information: USNY Ames affidavit 6/5/95, p. 20.
424 "while we were": Lloyd Cutler letter to Charles Ames, 5/11/95.

CHAPTER THIRTY-EIGHT

425 "You wouldn't want": Interview with Fred Davis.
425 The two women had struck: Interview with Linda Wachner.
425 "It's very wearing": Sandra McElwaine, "Cosmo Talks to Linda Wachner, Fashion Industry Tycoon," *Cosmopolitan*, 6/90.
425 Wachner came to: Ibid., Warnaco bio of Linda Wachner; *Who's Who in America*, 1995.
426 By 1994 her annual: *W*, 7/95.
426 "Linda, you've finally": Louise J. Esterhazy, "Louise at Sea," *W*, 9/95.
426 Wachner put her jet: Maureen Orth, "Jet Compulsion," VF, 12/95.
426 in the spring of: Interview with Linda Wachner.
426 "I helped her focus": Ibid.
426 "We are both women": Ibid.
427 Wachner gave $146,000: FEC, Selected List of Receipts and Expenditures, Linda Wachner, 1983–1995.
427 Early that morning: Interview with Kitty Hart.
427 They were using: USNY Kaye, Scholer affidavit 8/14/94, p. 3.
427 Lloyd Cutler was there: Author observation.
427 "Tell Pamela Harriman": Interview with Carl Icahn.
427 Pamela told Burge: Christopher Burge press conference, 5/11/95.
427 her lawyers later said: USNY Complaint 6/6/95, pp. 34–35.
428 If Pamela had settled: USNY Ames affidavit 6/5/95, pp. 31–36.
428 The new action brought out: Ibid.
428 documents her lawyers sought: WP, 6/28/95.
428 A New York judge dismissed: USNY Memorandum Order, John S. Martin, Jr., District Judge, 6/27/95.
428 "mutual objects": *New York Post*, 6/14/95.
429 "For heaven's sake": WP, 7/1/95.
429 "I laughed like hell": Interview with Kitty Hart.
429 From an image: VCLC Amended Complaint 7/7/95, p. 76.
429 If she restored: Ibid, pp. 74–75; WP, 6/28/95.
429 A financial consulting: PCH Answer to Petition of APHF, 10/3/95, pp. 17–23.
429 "intentionally derailing": Ibid., p. 22.
429 A month later: VCLC, Motion of APHF to intervene 8/25/95, pp. 4–5.
429 As of August: VCLC, memo of APHF 9/3/95, p. 1.
430 Early in 1995: 1191 North Lake Way listing with Martha Gottfried Realty, Palm Beach.
430 "to preserve the": USNY, Cutler declaration 6/16/95, p. 4.
430 She had sold: USNY, Ames affidavit 6/5/95, pp. 31–32.
431 the $850 nightly tab: Rates from The Sun Valley Corporation.
431 With an assessed: D.C. Tax Assessor's Office 1994 assessment: $638,181 land, $1,221,418 improvements.
431 most realtors considered: Interview with Ann Brower of Pardoe Real Estate, Inc.

431 "Without her glamour": Ibid.
431 Pamela had briefly dropped: Ibid.
432 "It's not the accolades": *Vogue,* 2/94.
432 "She's not thinking beyond": Interview with Robert Shrum.
432 "I don't think she's": Interview with Winston Churchill.
432 "She very much loves": Ibid.
432 "She would be a great addition": Interview with Linda Wachner.
433 "legal malpractice": VCLC, Third Party Cross Bill of Pamela C. Harriman with respect to the claims asserted in the intervening petition, 10/3/95, p. 19.
433 "negligence": Ibid., p. 15.
433 "unclean hands": VCLC PCH Answer to Petition of APHF 10/3/95, p. 17.
433 And she went after: VCLC PCH Cross Claim-1, 10/18/95, pp. 2–22.
433 "nasty new phase": WP, 10/5/95.
433 The family war chest grew: VCLC Pamela Harriman answer to petition of APHF 10/3/95, p. 7.
434 "as a friend": Interview with Linda Wachner.
435 a security agreement: Deed of Trust, 12/29/95, between Pamela C. Harriman and C. L. Dimos, Trustee.
435 Pamela renounced the power: Irrevocable Release of Appointment Power Under Article 8 Trust, signed by Pamela Harriman, 12/29/95.
436 "It won't be a case": Interview with Winston Churchill.
436 eight days after: NYT, 1/10/96.

Bibliography

Abramson, Rudy. *Spanning the Century. The Life of W. Averell Harriman, 1891–1986.* New York: William Morrow, 1992.

Acton, Harold. *Memoirs of an Aesthete.* London: Methuen & Co., 1948.

———. *More Memoirs of an Aesthete.* London: Methuen & Co., 1970.

Agnelli, Susanna. *We Always Wore Sailor Suits.* New York: Viking Press, 1975.

Aldis, Janet. *Madame Geoffrin: Her Salon and Her Times, 1750–1777.* London: Methuen & Co, 1905.

Alsop, Susan Mary. *To Marietta from Paris, 1945–1960.* New York: Doubleday, 1975.

Amory, Cleveland. *Who Killed Society?* New York: Harper & Brothers, 1960.

Aslet, Clive. *The Last Country Houses.* New Haven: Yale University Press, 1982.

Bacall, Lauren. *Now.* New York: Alfred A. Knopf, 1994.

Baldwin, Billy, with Michael Gardine. *Billy Baldwin: An Autobiography.* Boston: Little, Brown, 1985.

Balzac, Honoré de. *The Lily of the Valley,* translated by Lucienne Hall. New York: Carroll & Graf, 1989.

Barrow, Andrew. *Gossip: A History of High Society from 1920 to 1970.* New York: Coward, McCann & Geoghegan, 1979.

Beal, Mary, and John Cornforth. *The British Embassy, Paris: The House and Its Works of Art.* London: Christie's, 1992.

Beaton, Cecil. *The Years Between: Diaries 1939–1944.* London: C. Timling & Co., 1965.

———. *Memoirs of the Forties.* New York: McGraw-Hill, 1972.

———. *The Restless Years: Diaries 1955–63.* London: Weidenfeld & Nicolson, 1976.

Bergreen, Laurence. *As Thousands Cheer: The Life of Irving Berlin.* New York: Viking Penguin, 1990.

Berman, Sonia. *The Crossing: Adano to Catonsville: Leland Hayward's Producing Career.* New York: Columbia University, Ph.D. 1980.

Birmingham, Stephen. *The Right People: A Portrait of the American Social Establishment.* Boston: Little, Brown, 1958.

Blanch, Lesley. *The Wilder Shores of Love.* New York: Carroll & Graf, 1983.

Bothorel, Jean. *Louise: Ou La Vie de Louise de Vilmorin.* Paris: Bernard Grasset, 1993.

Braudy, Susan. *This Crazy Thing Called Love: The Golden World and Fatal Marriage of Ann and Billy Woodward.* New York: Alfred A. Knopf, 1992.

Bremner, Robert H., Minna Adams Hutcheson, and Lucille Stein Greenberg. *History of the American National Red Cross.* Vol. XIII: *American Red Cross Services in the War Against the Europe Axis, Pearl Harbor to 1947.* Washington, DC: American National Red Cross, 1950.

Brooks, Tim, and Earle Marsh. *The Complete Directory of Prime Time Network TV Shows, 1946–Present.* New York: Ballantine Books, 1992.

Brown, Marjorie W. *Arden House.* New York: The American Assembly, Columbia University, 1981.

Brydges, Sir Egerton. *Collins's Peerage of England: Genealogical, Biographical, and Historical.* Vol. V. London: 1812.

Burns, James MacGregor. *John Kennedy: A Political Profile.* New York: Harcourt Brace, 1959.

Cahan, M.D., William G. *No Stranger to Tears: A Surgeon's Story.* New York: Random House, 1992.

Califano, Jr., Joseph A. *The Triumph and Tragedy of Lyndon Johnson: The White House Years.* New York: Simon & Schuster, 1991.

Cannadine, David. *The Decline and Fall of the British Aristocracy.* New York: Anchor Books, Doubleday, 1992.

Channon, Henry. *Chips: The Diaries of Sir Henry Channon,* edited by Robert Rhodes James. London: Weidenfeld & Nicolson, 1967.

Chisholm, Anne, and Michael Davie. *Beaverbrook: A Life.* London: Hutchinson, 1992.

Churchill, Randolph. *Twenty-One Years.* London: Weidenfeld & Nicolson, 1964.

Churchill, Sarah. *A Thread in the Tapestry.* London: Andre Deutsch, 1967.

Churchill, Winston S. *Memories and Adventures.* London: Coronet Books, 1990.

Churchill, Winston, Sir. *Blood, Toil, Tears and Sweat: The Speeches of Winston Churchill,* edited by David Cannadine. Boston: Houghton Mifflin, 1989.

Clark, Kenneth. *The Other Half: A Self-Portrait.* New York: Harper & Row, 1977.

Clarke, Gerald. *Capote: A Biography.* New York: Simon & Schuster, 1988.

Clifford, Clark, with Richard Holbrooke. *Counsel to the President: A Memoir.* New York: Random House, 1991.

Cohen, Edgar H. *Mademoiselle Libertine: A Portrait of Ninon de Lanclos.* Boston: Houghton Mifflin, 1970.

Colby, Reginald. *Mayfair: A Town Within London.* London: Country Life Ltd., 1966.

Colville, John. *The Fringes of Power: 10 Downing Street Diaries 1939–1955.* New York: W. W. Norton, 1986.

Cooper, Diana. *Autobiography: The Rainbow Comes and Goes; The Lights of Common Day; Trumpets from the Steep.* New York: Carroll & Graf, 1988.

Coward, Noël. *The Noel Coward Diaries,* edited by Graham Payn and Sheridan Morley. London: PAPERMAC, 1983.

Cowles, Virginia. *Looking for Trouble.* London: Hamish Hamilton, 1941.

———. *The Rothschilds: A Family of Fortune.* New York: Alfred A. Knopf, 1973.

Crawley, Aiden. *Leap Before You Look.* London: Collins, 1988.

Debrett's Illustrated Peerage. London: Debretts Ltd., 1960.

Drogheda, Charles C.P.M., eleventh Earl of. *Double Harness.* London: Weidenfeld & Nicolson, 1978.

Druon, Maurice. *The Film of Memory: A Novel.* New York: Charles Scribner's Sons, 1955.

Farber, Stephen, and Marc Green. *Hollywood on the Couch: A Candid Look at the Overheated Love Affair Between Psychiatrists and Moviemakers.* New York: William Morrow, 1993.

Faucigny-Lucinge, Prince Jean-Louis de. *Legendary Parties 1922–1972.* New York: The Vendome Press, 1987.

Flanner, Janet (Genet). *Paris Journal 1944–1965,* edited by William Shawn. New York: Atheneum, 1965.

Fleming, Ann. *The Letters of Ann Fleming,* edited by Mark Amory. London: Collins Harvill, 1985.

Frantz, Douglas, and David McKean. *Friends in High Places: The Rise and Fall of Clark Clifford.* Boston: Little, Brown, 1995.

Friedman, Alan. *Agnelli and the Network of Italian Power.* London: Harrap Ltd., 1988.

Friedrich, Otto. *City of Nets: A Portrait of Hollywood in the 1940's.* New York: Perennial Library, Harper & Row, 1987.

Gentleman, David. *David Gentleman's London.* London: Weidenfeld & Nicolson, 1985.

Gibbs, the Hon. Vicary, G.E.C. *The Complete Peerage of England, Scotland, Ireland, Great Britain and the United Kingdom, Extant, Extinct or Dormant by G.E.C.,* rev. ed. Vol. 1. London, 1910.

Gilbert, Martin. *Churchill: A Life.* New York: Henry Holt, 1991.

———. *The Churchill War Papers: At the Admiralty, September 1939–May 1940.* Vol. I. New York: W. W. Norton, 1993.

———. *Winston Churchill: Finest Hour, 1939–1941.* Vol. VI. Boston: Houghton Mifflin, 1983.

———. *Winston S. Churchill: Road to Victory, 1941–1945.* Vol. VII. Boston: Houghton Mifflin, 1986.

———. *Winston S. Churchill: Never Despair, 1945–1965.* Vol. VIII. Boston: Houghton Mifflin, 1988.

Gladwyn, Cynthia. *The Diaries of Cynthia Gladwyn,* edited by Miles Jebb. London: Constable, 1995.

Goodwin, Doris Kearns. *The Fitzgeralds and the Kennedys.* New York: St. Martin's Press (paperback), 1987.

———. *No Ordinary Time: Franklin and Eleanor Roosevelt: The Home Front in World War II.* New York: Simon & Schuster, 1994.

Grafton, David. *The Sisters: The Lives and Times of the Fabulous Cushing Sisters.* New York: Villard Books, 1992.

Hampton, Mark. *Legendary Decorators of the Twentieth Century.* New York: Doubleday, 1992.

Harriman, Margaret Case. *Take Them Up Tenderly: A Collection of Profiles.* New York: Alfred A. Knopf, 1944.

Harriman, W. Averell, and Elie Abel. *Special Envoy to Churchill and Stalin: 1941–1946.* New York: Random House, 1975.

Hart, Kitty Carlisle. *Kitty: An Autobiography.* New York: Doubleday, 1988.

Hastings, Selina. *Nancy Mitford: A Biography.* London: PAPERMAC, 1986.

Hayward, Brooke. *Haywire.* New York: Alfred A. Knopf, 1977.

Hecht, Ben. *Charlie: The Improbable Life and Times of Charles MacArthur.* New York: Harper & Brothers, 1957.

Henderson, Nicholas. *Mandarin: The Diaries of an Ambassador 1969–1982.* London: Weidenfeld & Nicolson, 1994.

Hepburn, Katharine. *Me: Stories of My Life.* New York: Ballantine Books, 1992.

Horne, Alistair. *Harold Macmillan.* Vol. 1. *1894–1956.* New York: Viking Press, 1989.

Isaacson, Walter, and Evan Thomas. *The Wise Men: Six Friends and the World They Made.* New York: Simon & Schuster, 1986.

Jackson, Brooks. *Honest Graft: How Special Interests Buy Influence in Washington.* Washington, DC: Farragut Publishing, 1990.

Kael, Pauline. *5001 Nights at the Movies.* New York: Henry Holt, 1991.

Kahn, Jr., E. J. *Jock: The Life and Times of John Hay Whitney.* New York: Doubleday, 1981.

Kazanjian, Dodie, and Calvin Tomkins. *Alex. The Life of Alexander Liberman.* New York: Alfred A. Knopf, 1993.

Keith, Slim, with Annette Tapert. *Slim: Memories of a Rich and Imperfect Life.* New York: Simon & Schuster, 1990.

Kelley, Kitty. *His Way: The Unauthorized Biography of Frank Sinatra.* New York: Bantam Books, 1986.

Kendrick, Alexander. *Prime Time: The Life of Edward R. Murrow.* Boston: Little, Brown, 1969.

Korda, Michael. *Charmed Lives: A Family Romance.* New York: Random House, 1979.

Lambert, Angela. *1939: The Last Season of Peace.* London: Weidenfeld & Nicolson, 1989.

Leaming, Barbara. *Katharine Hepburn.* New York: Crown, 1995.

Leapman, Michael. *The Book of London: The Evolution of a Great City.* New York: Weidenfeld & Nicolson, 1989.

Leeds Castle Foundation. *Leeds Castle.* Maidstone, Kent: Philip Watson Publishers Ltd., 1989.

Lees-Milne, James. *Ancestral Voices.* New York: Charles Scribner's Sons, 1975.

———. *Prophesying Peace.* London: Chatto & Windus, 1977.

———. *Caves of Ice: Diaries: 1946 and 1947.* London: Chatto & Windus, 1983.

Legg, Rodney. *Cerne's Giant and Village Guide.* Wincanton, Somerset: Dorset Publishing Co., 1990.

Leggett, John. *Ross and Tom: Two American Tragedies.* New York: Simon & Schuster, 1974.

Lenzner, Robert. *Getty: The Richest Man in the World.* London: Hutchinson, 1985.

Leonard, William Torbert. *Broadway Bound: A Guide to Shows That Died Aborning.* Metuchen, NJ, and London: Scarecrow Press, 1983.

Leslie, Anita. *Cousin Randolph: The Life of Randolph Churchill.* London: Hutchinson, 1985.

Lilly, Doris. *Those Fabulous Greeks: Onassis, Niarchos, and Livanos.* New York: Cowles Book Co., 1970.

Lockhart, Sir Robert Bruce. *The Diaries of Sir Robert Bruce Lockhart,* edited by Kenneth Young. London: Macmillan, 1973.

Logan, Joshua. *Josh: My Up and Down, In and Out Life.* New York: Delacorte Press, 1976.

Longrigg, Roger. *The History of Foxhunting.* London: Macmillan, 1975.

Lowndes, Marie Belloc. *The Diaries and Letters of Marie Belloc Lowndes 1911–1947,* edited by Susan Lowndes. London: Chatto & Windus, 1971.

MacColl, Gail, and Carol McD. Wallace. *To Marry an English Lord: Or, How Anglomania Really Got Started.* New York: Workman, 1989.

Makinson, Larry. *Open Secrets: The Encyclopedia of Congressional Money and Politics.* Washington, DC: Congressional Quarterly, 1992.

Manchester, William. *The Last Lion: Winston Spencer Churchill: Visions of Glory 1874–1932.* Vol. I. Boston: Little, Brown. 1983.

————. *The Last Lion: Winston Spencer Churchill: Alone 1932–1940*. Vol. II. Boston: Little, Brown, 1988.

Martin, Ralph G. *Henry & Clare: An Intimate Portrait of the Luces*. New York: Putnam, 1991.

————. *The Woman He Loved*. New York: Simon & Schuster, 1973.

Matthews, Christopher. *Hardball: How Politics Is Played—Told by One Who Knows the Game*. New York: Harper & Row, 1989.

Maxwell, Elsa. *R.S.V.P: Elsa Maxwell's Own Story*. Boston: Little, Brown. 1954.

————. *The Celebrity Circus*. New York: Appleton-Century, 1963.

McCrary, Captain John R., and David Scherman. *First of the Many: A Journal of Action with the Men of the Eighth Air Force*. London: Robson Books, 1981.

McTaggart, Lynne. *Kathleen Kennedy: Her Life and Times*. New York: Dial Press, 1983.

Mellon, Paul, with John Baskett. *Reflections in a Silver Spoon: A Memoir*. New York: William Morrow, 1992.

Menkes, Suzy. *The Windsor Style*. Topsfield, MA: Salem House, 1987.

Mitford, Nancy. *The Pursuit of Love*. London: Penguin Books, 1949.

————. *The Blessing*. London: Penguin Books, 1957.

————. *Don't Tell Alfred*. London: Penguin Books, 1963.

————. *The Letters of Nancy Mitford: Love from Nancy*, edited by Charlotte Mosley. Boston: Houghton Mifflin, 1993.

Moorhead, Lucy. *Entertaining in Washington*. New York: Putnam, 1978.

Morgan, Janet. *Edwina Mountbatten: A Life of Her Own*. London: HarperCollins, 1991.

Morris, Jan. *Manhattan '45*. New York: Oxford University Press, 1987.

Morton, Frederic. *The Rothschilds: A Family Portrait*. New York: Atheneum, 1962.

Muggeridge, Malcolm. *The Infernal Grove: Chronicles of Wasted Time: Number 2*. New York: William Morrow, 1974.

Nicholson, Louise. *London: Louise Nicholson's Definitive Guide*. London: The Bodley Head, 1988.

Nicolson, Harold. *Harold Nicolson: Diaries and Letters 1939–1945*, edited by Nigel Nicolson. London: Collins, 1967.

Obolensky, Serge. *One Man in His Time: The Memoirs of Serge Obolensky*. New York: McDowell, Obolensky, 1958.

Oddie, E. M. *The Odyssey of a Loving Woman: Being a Study of Jane Digby Lady Ellenborough*. New York and London: Harper & Brothers, 1936.

Ogden, Christopher. *Life of the Party: The Biography of Pamela Digby Churchill Hayward Harriman*. New York: Warner Books, 1995.

Pearson, John. *The Private Lives of Winston Churchill*. New York: Simon & Schuster, 1991.

Persico, Joseph E. *Edward R. Murrow: An American Original*. New York: McGraw-Hill, 1988.

Pochna, Marie-France. *Agnelli: L'Irresistible*. Paris: L'Expansion Hachette, 1989.

Pryce-Jones, David. *Unity Mitford: A Quest*. London: Weidenfeld & Nicolson, 1976.

Rees, Thomas D., and Gregory S. LaTrenta, eds. *Aesthetic Plastic Surgery*. 2nd ed. Philadelphia: Saunders, 1994.

Reeves, Richard. *President Kennedy: Profile of Power*. New York: Simon & Schuster, 1993.

Reynolds, Quentin. *Only the Stars Are Neutral*. New York: Random House, 1942.

Richardson, Joanna. *The Courtesans: The Demi-Monde in Nineteenth Century France*. Cleveland and New York: World Publishing, 1967.

Roberts, Brian. *Randolph: A Study of Churchill's Son*. London: Hamish Hamilton, 1984.

Roosevelt, James, with Bill Libby. *My Parents: A Differing View*. Chicago: Playboy Press, 1976.

Russell, John. *Paris*. New York: Harry Abrams, 1983.

Sassoon, Siegfried. *Memoirs of a Fox-Hunting Man*. London: Faber & Faber, 1989.

Schmidt, Margaret Fox. *Passion's Child: The Extraordinary Life of Jane Digby*. London: Hamish Hamilton, 1977.

Schneider, Marcel. *L'Eternité Fragile: Le Palais des Mirages: Mémoires*. Paris: Bernard Grasset, 1992.

Selznick, Irene Mayer. *A Private View*. New York: Alfred A. Knopf, 1983.

Shields-West, Eileen. *The World Almanac of Presidential Campaigns*. New York: Pharos Books, 1992.

Slater, Leonard. *Aly: A Biography*. New York: Random House, 1964.

Smith, Sally Bedell. *In All His Glory: The Life and Times of William S. Paley and the Birth of Modern Broadcasting*. New York: Touchstone, 1991.

Soames, Mary. *Clementine Churchill: The Biography of a Marriage*. Boston: Houghton Mifflin, 1979.

————. *Winston Churchill: His Life as a Painter*. Boston: Houghton Mifflin, 1990.

Sperber, A. M. *Murrow: His Life and Times*. New York: Freundlich Books, 1986.

Sulzberger, C. L. *The Last of the Giants*. New York: Macmillan, 1970.

Sulzberger, Marina. *Letters and Diaries of Marina Sulzberger*, edited by C. L. Sulzberger. New York: Crown, 1978.

Tapert, Annette, and Diana Edkins. *The Power of Style*. New York: Crown, 1994.

Taylor, A. J. P. *Beaverbrook*. New York: Simon & Schuster, 1972.

Thomas, Evan. *The Man to See: Edward Bennett Williams: Ultimate Insider, Legendary Trial Lawyer*. New York: Simon & Schuster, 1991.

Viertel, Peter. *Dangerous Friends: At Large with Huston and Hemingway in the Fifties*. New York: Nan A. Talese-Doubleday, 1992.

Vilmorin, Louise de. *Madame de*, translated by Duff Cooper. London: Collins, 1952.

Vreeland, Diana. *D.V.* New York: Vintage Books, 1985.

Waugh, Evelyn. *The Diaries of Evelyn Waugh*, edited by Michael Davie. Boston: Little, Brown, 1976.

————. *The Letters of Evelyn Waugh*, edited by Mark Amory. London: Weidenfeld & Nicolson, 1980.

Waugh, Evelyn, and Diana Cooper. *The Letters of Evelyn Waugh and Diana Cooper*, edited by Artemis Cooper. New York: Ticknor & Fields, 1992.

White, Geoffrey H., ed. *The Complete Peerage or a History of the House of Lords*. Vol. II. London: 1949.

Wishart, Michael. *High Diver*. London: Blond & Briggs, 1977.

Ziegler, Philip. *Diana Cooper*. London: Hamish Hamilton, 1981.

Zuckerman, Edward. *Almanac of Federal PACS 1992–1993*. Washington, DC: Amward Publications, 1992.

Index

Case, Margaret, 235
Cassini, Igor (Ghighi; Cholly
    Knickerbocker), 126, 129, 130, 131, 135,
    159, 182, 207, 221
  Agnelli and, 151, 155, 156–57
  Pamela's affair with Leland and, 212,
    216
Castlerosse, Doris, 57
Castlerosse, Valentine, 57, 66, 84
Castro, Nash, 310
Cavendish, Adele Astaire, 85, 100–101, 196
Cavendish, Charles, 85
Cazalet, Zara, 36
CBS, 125, 126, 127, 216, 219, 252
CBS Evening News, 297
CBS Morning News, 32, 227, 328
CBS Radio, 118, 119, 120, 122
Centennial Film Foundation, 376
Century Association, 340
Cerf, Bennett, 208, 235, 252–53, 254, 368
Cerf, Phyllis, *see* Wagner, Phyllis Cerf
Cerne Giant, 27, 133
Challinor, Joan, 298, 299, 374, 375
Chamberlain, Neville, 41, 47, 52, 53, 54,
    59, 69
Chambers, Anne Cox, 365, 379, 431
Channon, Chips, 52–53, 78, 110, 112,
    163
Charles, Oatsie, 382
Charles, Prince, 277
Charles, Ray, 376
Charles-Roux, Edmonde, 184
Charteris, Ann, *see* Rothermere, Ann
Charteris, Laura, 57–58, 123, 146
Chartwell, 60, 190, 370
Château de la Garoupe, 149, 152–53, 156,
    191
Château de l'Horizon, 143, 144, 147, 148,
    152
Chequers, 70, 72, 78, 90, 93, 112
  Averell's visits to, 83, 84, 87, 97, 98
  young Winston at, 74, 120
Cherkley, 83–84, 87, 91, 92–93, 98, 99, 112,
    130, 131
  baby Winston at, 77, 78, 92
  guest book at, 108, 119, 121
Chernomyrdin, Viktor, 434
China, People's Republic of, 321, 341
Chirac, Jacques, 391, 393–94, 395, 434
Chisholm, Anne, 66, 69, 93
Christie, Father Joseph, 157, 158, 264
Christie, Harold, 217
Christie's, 417–18, 422, 423, 427
Christopher, Warren, 386
Chrysler, Walter P., 194
Church, Frank, 283, 294, 296
Churchill, Arabella, 190, 370
Churchill, Clarissa, 99

Churchill, Clementine Hozier, 61–62, 66,
    67–68, 385
  in Blitz, 70–71
  House of Commons visited by, 74, 76
  Janet Murrow and, 117, 119
  Pamela's correspondence with, 189–90
  Pamela's relationship with, 60, 67, 72,
    99, 105–6, 224
  Randolph's relationship with, 55, 56, 99,
    105, 146
Churchill, Diana, *see* Sandys, Diana
    Churchill
Churchill, Jack, 420
Churchill, Jennie, 322
Churchill, John Averell, 266
Churchill, June Osborne, 190
Churchill, Lord Randolph, 51, 55, 105, 138
Churchill, Marina, 322
Churchill, Mary, *see* Soames, Mary
    Churchill
Churchill, Minnie d'Erlanger, 255, 265,
    266, 322, 324, 370, 371, 372, 385, 420,
    421
Churchill, Peregrine, 421
Churchill, Randolph (grandson), 255, 266,
    322, 370, 421
Churchill, Randolph Frederick Edward
    Spencer, 54–76, 120, 139, 278, 420
  appearance of, 55, 57, 58, 64, 97–98, 104,
    146
  Averell and, 94–95, 97, 98, 104, 105, 106
  background and personality of, 55–57
  Beaverbrook and, 65, 66–67
  in Cairo, 94–95, 97, 104, 105, 108
  Colville's view of, 72–73
  death of, 255
  dissolute life style of, 15, 56–57, 58, 64,
    73–76, 94, 99, 123, 146, 190, 231
  education of, 56
  father's relationship with, 55, 56, 57, 70,
    94, 105, 123, 190
  in Fourth Hussars, 58, 61, 63, 64, 73
  health problems of, 104, 123
  in House of Commons, 72, 74, 90, 98
  as journalist, 56–57, 63, 132
  as male chauvinist, 58, 63, 67, 99
  mother's relationship with, 55, 56, 99,
    105, 146
  Pamela's annulment of marriage to,
    157–58, 161, 221
  Pamela's correspondence with, 73, 75,
    76, 94, 95, 97, 99, 104
  Pamela's divorce from, 15, 108, 125–26,
    140, 171
  Pamela's engagement and wedding to,
    15, 58–61
  Pamela's first meeting with, 54–55, 58–
    60

Photo Credits